ROUTLEDGE HANDBOOK OF HUMAN RESOURCE MANAGEMENT IN ASIA

Human Resource Management (HRM) is fundamentally shaped by institutional and cultural factors, such as the different political environments and social philosophies of particular countries and regions. By examining the various organizational aspects of business life and systems of people management in Asia, the study of HRM across the continent can, therefore, give us a greater understanding of Asian societies, as well as the contemporary world of work more generally.

This handbook provides an up-to-date and intellectually engaging overview of HRM in the Asian context. Distinctive in its comprehensive coverage of traditional as well as emerging topics of HRM, it analyzes important themes, such as the regulatory framework for work and employment, religiosity, family business, and gender. Using a comparative approach, it also effectively highlights the unique features of each country's attitudes toward HRM. Covering a range of themes and case studies, sections include:

- Institutional and cultural contexts,
- Labor regulation and industrial relations,
- Thematic and functional HRM,
- HRM in selected Asian countries, such as China, Japan, Vietnam, India, and Singapore.

Written in a highly accessible style, this book will be useful to students and scholars of Human Resource Management, Asian Business, Economics, and Sociology.

Fang Lee Cooke is Distinguished Professor of HRM and Asia Studies at Monash University, Australia.

Sunghoon Kim is Senior Lecturer in the School of Management at the University of New South Wales, Australia.

ROUTLEDGE HANDBOOK OF HUMAN RESOURCE MANAGEMENT IN ASIA

Edited by Fang Lee Cooke and Sunghoon Kim

Routledge
Taylor & Francis Group

LONDON AND NEW YORK

First published 2018
by Routledge
2 Park Square, Milton Park, Abingdon, Oxon OX14 4RN

and by Routledge
52 Vanderbilt Avenue, New York, NY 10017

Routledge is an imprint of the Taylor & Francis Group, an informa business

British Library Cataloguing in Publication Data
A catalogue record for this book is available from the British Library

Library of Congress Cataloging in Publication Data
Names: Cooke, Fang Lee, editor. | Kim, Sunghoon, 1973– editor.
Title: Routledge handbook of human resource management in Asia /
[edited by] Fang Lee Cooke and Sunghoon Kim.
Description: Abingdon, Oxon ; New York, NY : Routledge, 2018. |
Includes bibliographical references and index.
Identifiers: LCCN 2017014684| ISBN 9781138917477 (hardback) |
ISBN 9781315689005 (ebook)
Subjects: LCSH: Personnel management–Asia.
Classification: LCC HF5549.2.A75 R68 2018 | DDC 658.30095–dc23
LC record available at https://lccn.loc.gov/2017014684

ISBN 13: 978-0-367-58113-8 (pbk)
ISBN 13: 978-1-138-91747-7 (hbk)

Typeset in Bembo
by Wearset Ltd, Boldon, Tyne and Wear

CONTENTS

List of figures	viii
List of tables	ix
Notes on contributors	x

Introduction   **1**

1   Human Resource Management in Asia in the global context   3
Fang Lee Cooke and Sunghoon Kim

PART I
Institutional and cultural contexts   **21**

2   State and HRM in Asia   23
Kyoung-Hee Yu and Sung Chul Noh

3   Confucianism and Human Resource Management in East Asia   46
Sunghoon Kim, Pingping Fu, and Jiali Duan

4   Religiosity, ethics, and the spirit of capitalism in HRM   66
Mohamed Branine

PART II
Labor regulation and industrial relations   **85**

5   Employment regulation and industrial relations systems in East Asia: China,
Japan, and South Korea   87
Fang Lee Cooke, Katsuyuki Kubo, and Byoung-Hoon Lee

Contents

6 Employment regulation and industrial relations in Indonesia, Malaysia, the Philippines, Thailand, and Vietnam   109
   Ingrid Landau and Fang Lee Cooke

7 Employment regulation and industrial relations in South Asia   128
   Michael Gillan

PART III
Thematic and functional HRM   **147**

8 Performance management practices in Asia   149
   Arup Varma, Pawan S. Budhwar, and Peter Norlander

9 Innovation and Human Resource Management in Asia   166
   Jyotsna Bhatnagar and Shweta Jaiswal Thakur

10 Leadership and leadership development in Asia   183
    Alexander Newman, Nathan Eva, and Kendall Herbert

11 Compensation systems and pay practices in Asia   201
    Tae-Youn Park and Jason D. Shaw

12 Human capital flows and talent management in Asia   222
    Anthony McDonnell and Ying Guo

13 Managing multinational companies in Asia   240
    Yu Zheng and Chris Smith

14 Equal opportunity and workforce diversity in Asia   256
    Ahu Tatli, Mustafa Bilgehan Ozturk, and Maryam Aldossari

PART IV
HRM in selected Asian countries   **273**

15 Human Resource Management in Japan and South Korea   275
    Fabian Jintae Froese, Tomoki Sekiguchi, and Mohan Pyari Maharjan

16 Human Resource Management in China and Vietnam   295
    Jie Shen and Anne Cox

17 Human Resource Management in Hong Kong, Macau, and Taiwan   314
    Shu-Yuan Chen and David Ahlstrom

18 Human Resource Management in Indonesia, Malaysia, and Thailand   333
    Chaturong Napathorn and Sarosh Kuruvilla

19 Human Resource Management in city states: Dubai and Singapore   355
    Julia Connell, John Burgess, and Peter Waring

20 Human Resource Management in India and the Philippines   373
    Jennifer Ann L. Lajom, Simon Lloyd D. Restubog, Mendiola Teng-Calleja,
    Raymund Habaradas, and Ma Cristina Esquivel-Saldivar

21 Human Resource Management in Bangladesh and Sri Lanka   392
    Vathsala Wickramasinghe and Monowar H. Mahmood

Conclusions   **413**

22 The future of Human Resource Management in Asia in a world of change   415
    Sunghoon Kim and Fang Lee Cooke

Index   431

FIGURES

2.1 Model of state and HRM   24
2.2 State influence on HRM   28
5.1 Proportion of non-regular employees, 1984–2015   92
5.2 Trends of non-regular employment in Korea, 1995–2014   93
5.3 Wage-age profile in 1981, 2000, and 2014 for male and female workers in Japan 103
5.4 Monthly wage curve by age and firm size in Korea   104
6.1 Average monthly wages with broadly comparable data, 2013 or latest
     available year   117
17.1 Historical trend of GDP 1950–2008, Hong Kong, Taiwan, and China   316

TABLES

2.1	Typologies of Asian states	25
2.2	External dependence of the national business system	31
2.3	Outcomes of state influence	33
5.1	Number of regular and non-regular employees in Japan	91
5.2	List of major labor laws and regulations in China, Japan, and Korea	94
5.3	Annual average wage for all employees in urban sector in China	101
6.1	List of major labor laws and regulations in selected Southeast Asian states	114
6.2	Summary of IR characteristics in selected Southeast Asian countries	120
7.1	Selected list of labor laws and regulations in South Asia	134
9.1	Classification of innovation	168
11.1	The effects of national culture on compensation practices	205
12.1	Selection of countries ranking on the Global Talent Competitiveness Index 2014	224
12.2	Labor market conditions in ASEAN	225
12.3	Summary of articles focused on talent management with an Asian empirical component	227
14.1	Salary ranges for engineers	264
15.1	Comparison of HR systems	276
16.1	Similarities in HRM between China and Vietnam	308
18.1	Indonesia, Malaysia, and Thailand's economies at a glance	334
19.1	Percentage distribution of employed fifteen years and over by nationality, gender, and occupation: Emirate of Dubai, 2015	359
19.2	Singapore's occupational categories (2015)	363
19.3	Pass types, workforce numbers, and types of employment in Singapore	363
20.1	GDP growth rate and GDP per capita (current US$) of India and the Philippines, 2010–2014	374
20.2	Summary of key issues and challenges	382
21.1	Labor force—Sri Lanka and Bangladesh	393

CONTRIBUTORS

David Ahlstrom is a professor at The Chinese University of Hong Kong. He obtained his PhD in Management and International Business after working in the IT industry. His research interests include managing in Asia, entrepreneurship, and organizational history. He has published over 100 peer-reviewed articles in journals such as the *Strategic Management Journal*, *Academy of Management Review*, *Journal of International Business Studies*, *Journal of Management Studies*, *Journal of Business Venturing*, *Entrepreneurship: Theory and Practice*, and the *Brown Journal of World Affairs*. His work has also appeared multiple times in *The Wall Street Journal*. He is former chief editor of *Asia Pacific Journal of Management*, and is currently senior editor of *Journal of World Business*.

Maryam Aldossari is Lecturer in International Human Resource Management at the University of Edinburgh Business School. Her research interests span several fields including human resource management, organizational behavior/theory, and cultural studies. To date her research has focused on the effect of national and organizational culture on the repatriation process and human resource management (HRM) practices in general. Her research has demonstrated the influence of strong national/organizational culture on the way in which psychological contract are constituted, and how they may change following international assignment and repatriation. Maryam Aldossari has also conducted a further research project exploring the issues that professional Saudi Arabian women face institutionally and organizationally when working in Saudi Arabia.

Jyotsna Bhatnagar is Professor of Human Resource Management at the Management Development Institute Gurugram. Professor Bhatnagar is a Harvard Business School Executive alumnus and has over twenty years of corporate and academic experience. She received Best Research Paper for Practical Implications, 2009-Emerald Literati, UK at AOM Conference, Montreal, Canada, 2010. She recently published a well-received case study in *Harvard Business Review* (2016) titled "Should you hire a defector?". Professor Bhatnagar has received Excellence in research and teaching at the Management Development Institute Gurgaon. She has over eighty publications in high impact journals including the *Journal of Labor Research*.

Mohamed Branine is Professor of International HRM and Director of Research Degrees in the Dundee Business School (DBS), University of Abertay. He is also academic Fellow of the

Chartered Institute of Personnel and Development (CIPD). He teaches Human Resource Management courses at undergraduate and postgraduate levels. His research interests include the practical challenges of managing across cultures, the impact of religion on managing resources, talent management and organizational change, leadership and culture, and employee response to change in times of crisis. He is the author of *Managing Across Cultures: Concepts, Policies and Practices* (2011), and has written more than seventy refereed journal articles and book chapters.

Pawan S. Budhwar is a Professor of International HRM at Aston Business School, Birmingham, UK. He is also the Joint-Director of Aston India Foundation for Applied Research and the Co-Editor-in-Chief of *British Journal of Management* and an Associate Editor of *Human Resource Management*. Budhwar's research interests are in the areas of International HRM, Emerging Markets, Expatriate Management and Work processes in firms operating in India. He has published over 100 articles in leading journals and has also written and/or co-edited seventeen books. Pawan Budhwar is a Fellow of the Higher Education Academy, British Academy of Management, the Academy of Social Sciences and the Indian Academy of Management. He is also a Chartered Member of the Chartered Institute of Personnel and Development.

John Burgess is Professor of Management, School of Management, RMIT University, Australia. His research interests include: graduate employability; workforce attraction and retention strategies in the aged care sector; HRM strategies of multinational enterprises; working hours and health; and knowledge sharing in wine tourism clusters. He is Associate Editor of *Personnel Review* and area editor of *The Economic & Labour Relations Review*.

Shu-Yuan Chen is an associate professor in management at the National United University in Taiwan. Her research interests include HR roles and influence, HR strategic participation, HR power, strategic talent management, and recruitment issues. She has published several peer-reviewed articles in management journals such as the *Asia Pacific Journal of Management*, *Human Resource Management*, *Asia Pacific Journal of Human Resource*, *Asia Pacific Management Review* in Taiwan, and *Personnel Review*.

Julia Connell is currently Visiting Professor, Graduate School of Research at the University of Technology, Sydney (UTS) and an adjunct Professor of Management, at Curtin Business School, Curtin University, Perth. Julia Connell has published numerous journal articles and book chapters on employment, change and employee effectiveness. She has also co-edited six books—the most recent *Flexible Work Organizations: The Challenges of Capacity Building in Asia* (Springer, 2016).

Fang Lee Cooke is Professor of Human Resource Management (HRM) and Asia Studies at Monash Business School, Monash University. She is also a Fellow of the Academy of the Social Sciences in Australia. Previously, she was a full professor (since 2005) at Manchester Business School, University of Manchester, UK. Her research interests are in the area of employment relations, gender studies, diversity management, strategic HRM, knowledge management and innovation, outsourcing, Chinese outward FDI and HRM, employment of Chinese migrants, and HRM in the care sector. Fang is the author of *HRM, Work and Employment in China* (Routledge, 2005) and *Human Resource Management in China: New Trends and Practices* (Routledge, 2012).

Anne Cox is a Senior Lecturer at the University of Wollongong, Australia. She researches and publishes in three main areas, namely, the transfer of multinational companies' IR/HRM policies and practices across borders, the transformation of HR/IR systems in developing countries, and gender equity. Her book *The Transformation of HRM and Industrial Relations in Vietnam* was published in 2009. Her current research addresses the implications of multinational companies' management practices on the social and economic fabric of Australia.

Jiali Duan is a PhD candidate in management at the Business School, University of New South Wales (UNSW). She received her Master in labor economics from Renmin University of China. Her research primarily focuses on strategic human resource management, collective human capital, and job mobility. She is also interested in institutional theory, social capital, and cross culture.

Ma Cristina Esquivel-Saldivar is Professor of Psychology and Head of the Office of Institutional Testing at De La Salle-College of Saint Benilde, Manila, Philippines. She completed her PhD in Counseling Psychology at De La Salle University. Her research interests include training and development, work–life balance, and integrative wellness. Her work has been published in the *Philippine Journal of Counseling Psychology*. She is a consultant at In Touch Community Services and is a Registered Psychologist (RPsy) and Guidance Counselor (RGC). Currently, she is the President of the Association of Psychological and Educational Counselors of Asia-Pacific (APECA).

Nathan Eva is a lecturer in the Department of Management at Monash Business School. His research has focused on the antecedents and outcomes of servant, ethical, and entrepreneurial leadership across multiple countries, having published in the *Human Resource Management Review*, the *Journal of Small Business Management*, *Public Administration Review*, and *Education + Training*. He is a multi-award-winning lecturer in leadership, and was named a Greenleaf Scholar by the Greenleaf Centre for Servant Leadership in 2016.

Fabian Jintae Froese is a Professor and chair of human resource management and Asian business at the University of Göttingen. Prior to this, he taught at the Korea University, Seoul, and the Kobe University, Japan. He obtained a doctorate in international management from the University of St. Gallen and another doctorate in sociology from Waseda University, Tokyo. His research interests lie in international human resource management and cross-cultural management.

Pingping Fu, Professor of Organizational Behavior, is now teaching at the Nottingham University Business School China (NUBS China). She obtained her PhD in Organizational Studies at the State University at Albany, New York. Professor Fu has been a member of the Global Leadership and Organizational Behavior Effectiveness (GLOBE) research project team since 1997, and has been a member of the GLOBE board. She has led a dozen research projects supported by grants from the Hong Kong government. Her works have been published in various journals, including the *Administrative Science Quarterly*, *Journal of International Business Studies*, *Journal of Organizational Behavior*, *Leadership Quarterly*, *Management International Review*, and *Organizational Dynamics*. In recent years, she and her team have been studying the influence of traditional culture on Chinese firms, including Fotile, the case in Chapter 3.

Michael Gillan teaches and researches employment relations and is based at the University of Western Australia. He has published in a wide range of national and international journals including *Economic Geography*, *Journal of Contemporary Asia*, *Asian Studies Review*, *South Asia*,

Contemporary South Asia, and the *Journal of Industrial Relations*. His current research interests include: global union federations; transnational labor regulation; the political economy of liberalization and labor movements in India; and employment relations in Myanmar.

Ying Guo is a Lecturer and Program Director of BA Human Resource Management at IBSS, Xi'an Jiaotong-Liverpool University, China. She received her PhD from the UniSA Business School, University of South Australia. Her research interests include expatriate management, talent management and staffing, cross-cultural management, knowledge transfer, and leadership. She teaches the subjects of Introduction to Human Resource Management and Training, and Learning & Development. She is also an active member of the Academy of International Business (AIB), and the Australia and New Zealand International Business Academy (ANZIBA). In 2016, she co-edited *Global Talent Management and Staffing in MNEs* (Multinational Enterprises).

Raymund Habaradas is an Associate Professor in the Management and Organization Department at De La Salle University (DLSU) and Director of the DLSU Center for Business Research and Development (CBRD). He received his Doctor of Business Administration (DBA) degree from DLSU, Manila, Philippines. His research areas include: corporate social initiatives, social enterprise management, national innovation systems, city innovations, innovation of firms, upgrading in global value chains, and SME development. His research has been published in the *Asian Journal of Technology Innovation*, *International Journal of Business and Social Sciences*, the *Journal of International Business Research*, *Journal of Legal, Ethical and Regulatory Issues*, and the *DLSU Business and Economics Review*.

Kendall Herbert is a lecturer at RMIT University in the Graduate School of Business and Law, Melbourne. Her key research interests surround global teams, cross-cultural management, leadership, and team innovation. She has published in *Asian Business & Management* and *International Business Review*. Kendall Herbert was a team finalist for the 2014 "Annual HRM Researcher/Research Group of the Year Award" in Sweden—an award for research in HRM, organization, or leadership.

Sunghoon Kim is a Senior Lecturer at the University of New South Wales (UNSW) Sydney, Australia. He received his PhD from Cornell University, and his MBA and BA from the Seoul National University. Sunghoon Kim's research interests include: HRM and labor relations in Asian emerging economies, international HRM, strategic HRM, and migrant professionals. His work has appeared in various journals including *Organization Studies*, *Industrial and Labor Relations Review*, *Human Resource Management*, *The International Journal of Human Resource Management*, and the *Management and Organization Review*. Sunghoon Kim is a co-editor of *China's Changing Workplace: Dynamism, Diversity and Disparity* (Routledge, 2011)

Katsuyuki Kubo is Professor of Business Economics at Waseda University, Tokyo. Dr. Kubo received his BA and MA both in economics from Keio University, and a PhD in industrial relations from the London School of Economics. He teaches and undertakes research in the areas of compensation and incentives, corporate governance, and industrial relations. He has published articles in journals such as *Corporate Governance: An International Review*, *Japanese Economic Review*, and the *Journal of the Japanese and International Economies*.

Sarosh Kuruvilla is the Andrew J. Nathanson Family Professor in Industrial and Labor Relations at the School of Industrial and Labor Relations at Cornell University and visiting Professor at the London School of Economics. His research interests focus on the intersection between economic development and national labor and human resource policies, and comparative industrial relations more generally. He is currently working on labor standards in global garment chains.

Jennifer Ann L. Lajom is a Lecturer of Management in the School of Business and Law at Edith Cowan University, Western Australia. She received her PhD in Organizational Behavior at the Australian National University. Her research interests include workplace passion and motivation, career persistence, and supports and barriers in career development. Her work has been published in the *Journal of Vocational Behavior* and the *Journal of Career Assessment*. Prior to obtaining her PhD, she worked as HR staff of the Bank of Tokyo-Mitsubishi, UFJ (Manila Branch).

Ingrid Landau is a Research Fellow in the Centre for Employment and Labor Relations Law (CELRL) and a doctoral candidate within the CELRL and the Centre for International Law and the Humanities at Melbourne Law School. She holds Bachelor Degrees in Asian Studies and Law from the Australian National University, and has worked at Melbourne Law School, the Faculty of Business Law and Taxation at Monash University and at the Australian Council of Trade Unions. She has published in Australian and international journals, and has worked as principal researcher on major research projects commissioned by the Fair Work Commission and the International Labour Organization. Ingrid Landau's research interests include Australian labor law, international and comparative labor law (with a focus on the Asia-Pacific), and corporate accountability and labor rights.

Byoung-Hoon Lee is a professor of the Sociology Department and the dean of Social Science College at Chung-Ang University, Seoul, South Korea. His research interests are in job quality polarization and labor market segmentation, non-regular labor movements, labor solidarity, and union's power and strategic capacity. His recent publications include: *Worker Militancy at the Margins* (2016), *Changing Cross-Movement Coalitions between Labor Unions and Civil Society Organizations in South Korea* (2015), *Temporary Agency Work and Globalization* (co-authored, 2015), and *After-Development Dynamics: South Korea's Contemporary Engagement with Asia* (co-authored, 2015).

Anthony McDonnell is Professor of Management at the Cork University Business School, University College Cork, Ireland. Prior to joining UCC, Anthony McDonnell was Head of the Management Department and Reader in Management at Queen's University, Belfast. He is currently the Co-Editor-in-Chief of *Human Resource Management Journal*. His primary research interests lie is in the areas of talent management and international HRM, and more specifically—on better understanding the HRM approaches of MNCs across countries.

Mohan Pyari Maharjan is a Postdoctoral Researcher at the Chair of Human Resources Management and Asian Business, University of Göttingen, Germany. Her research interests include international human resource management and cross-cultural studies.

Monowar H. Mahmood is a Professor of Management, Bang College of Business, KIMEP University, Almaty, Kazakhstan. He obtained an MBA from Saint Mary's University, Canada; an MA from the University of Leeds, UK, and a PhD from University of Manchester, UK. Dr. Mahmood's research focused on HRM practices in MNCs, corporate governance and corporate social responsibility, and gender and equal employment policies in emerging economies.

Chaturong Napathorn is a lecturer in the Department of Organization, Entrepreneurship, and Human Resource Management at Thammasat Business School at Thammasat University in Thailand. He graduated with a PhD from the ILR School at Cornell University, New York. His research interests include strategic human resource management, international human resource management, and international and comparative employment relations.

Alexander Newman is Professor of Management at Deakin Business School, Deakin University in Australia. He has published widely in the areas of entrepreneurship and organizational behavior in such journals as the *Journal of Applied Psychology*, *Entrepreneurship: Theory and Practice*, the *Leadership Quarterly*, *Human Resource Management*, and the *Journal of Organizational Behavior*.

Sung Chul Noh is an assistant professor in the Graduate School of Humanities and Social Sciences at Saitama University. His current research interest is in Non-Union Employee Representation and non-standard work arrangement. Sung-Chul Noh's work has appeared in the *Journal of Management Studies* and the *Human Resource Management Journal*. He earned his doctorate from the Desautels Faculty of Management at McGill University.

Peter Norlander is an Assistant Professor of Management at the Quinlan School of Business, Loyola University Chicago. He completed his doctorate in management at University of California, Los Angeles in 2014, and is a graduate of the Cornell School of Industrial and Labor Relations. His research interests include globalization and employment relations.

Mustafa Bilgehan Ozturk is Lecturer in Management at Queen Mary University of London. His research interests are mainly centered on workplace diversity. Dr. Ozturk has conducted research that involves a variety of country contexts such as China, Turkey, the UK and the USA in such issue areas as gender, sexual orientation, and gender identity equality. His work has appeared in *British Journal of Management*, *Human Relations*, *Human Resource Management*, and *The International Journal of Human Resource Management*, as well as in distinguished edited volumes by Routledge, amongst others.

Tae-Youn Park is an assistant professor in Organization Studies at the Owen Graduate School of Management, Vanderbilt University, Nashville, Tennessee. He received his PhD from the University of Minnesota. His research interests include employment relationships, employee turnover, and compensation.

Simon Lloyd D. Restubog is the Lab Director of the Work Effectiveness & Leadership Lab (www.wellab.org) and Professor of Management and Organizational Behavior at the Australian National University. He earned his PhD in Industrial/Organizational Psychology (2005) from the University of Queensland. His research interests include the dark side of human behavior in organizations, psychological contracts, and career development. To date, he has produced seventy-four journal articles, five best paper proceedings, and three book chapters. His work has been published in leading journals such as the *Journal of Applied Psychology*, the *Journal of Management*, the *Journal of Management Studies*, the *Journal of Organizational Behavior*, *Organization Studies*, the *Academy of Management Journal*, the *Leadership Quarterly*, and the *Journal of Vocational Behavior*. He has a consistent track record of receiving nationally competitive external funding (Discovery and Linkage schemes) from both Australia and overseas. Currently, he serves on the editorial boards of the *Journal of Management*, the *Journal of Management Studies*, the *Journal of Vocational*

Behavior, the *Journal of Business Ethics*, the *Journal of Business and Psychology*, the *Journal of Management & Organization*, and *The Asia-Pacific Education Researcher*.

Tomoki Sekiguchi is Professor at the Graduate School of Management, Kyoto University, Japan. His research interests center on employee behaviors, organizational justice person-environment fit, hiring decision-making, cross-cultural organizational behavior, and international human resource management. His work has been published in such journals as *Personnel Psychology*, *Organizational Behavior and Human Decision Processes*, the *Journal of World Business*, the *Asia Pacific Journal of Management*, *Applied Psychology: An International Review*, and *The International Journal of Human Resource Management*. He currently serves as the associate editor for *Applied Psychology: An International Review* and is a member of the editorial boards of several other international journals.

Jason D. Shaw is Chair Professor, Head of Department, and Director of the Centre for Leadership and Innovation in the Faculty of Business at The Hong Kong Polytechnic University. He received his PhD from the University of Arkansas. He is Editor-in-Chief of the *Academy of Management Journal*. His research interests include employment relationships, turnover, and financial incentives.

Jie Shen is a Professor of HRM in Shenzhen Audencia Business School, Shenzhen University, Shenzhen, Guangdong, China. His research interests including HRM, organizational behavior, and cross-cultural management. He has published seven research books and over sixty refereed journal articles in journals such as the *Journal of Management* and the *Human Resource Management Journal*.

Chris Smith is Professor of Organisation Studies and Comparative Management, School of Management, Royal Holloway, University of London. He has research interests in labor process theory, knowledge transfer through the transnational firm, comparative analysis of work and employment, and professional labor. He is currently researching the organization of the labor process in Chinese factories and the Chinese Business Model abroad. He has been active in the International Labour Process Conference for many years. Recent book publications include: *China at Work* with Mingwei Liu (2016); *Working Life Renewing Labour Process Analysis* with Paul Thompson (2010); and *Creative Labour—Working in the Creative Industries* with Alan McKinlay (2009).

Ahu Tatli is Professor of International Human Resource Management and the Director of the Centre for Research in Equality and Diversity in the School of Business and Management at Queen Mary University of London. Her research explores the intersectionality of disadvantage and privilege at work; inequality and discrimination in recruitment and employment; and diversity management, agency, and change in organizations. She has widely published in edited collections, practitioner and policy outlets, and academic journals such as the *Academy of Management Review*, the *British Journal of Management*, *Human Relations*, and the *Human Resource Management Journal*. Her recent books include *Global Diversity Management: An Evidence-Based Approach* (2015) and *Pierre Bourdieu, Organisation and Management* (2015, Routledge).

Mendiola Teng-Calleja is the Director for Research of the Ateneo Center for Organization Research and Development (Ateneo CORD) and an Associate Professor in the Department of Psychology at the Ateneo de Manila University (ADMU). She obtained her PhD in

Social-Organizational Psychology from the ADMU. Her research interests include humanitarian work psychology, labor relations and issues, strategic human resources management, and organization behavior. Her work has been published in *Negotiation and Conflict Management Research*, the *Journal of Pacific Rim Psychology*, *Local Government Studies*, the *Asia Pacific Journal of Human Resources*, and the *Philippine Journal of Psychology*. She has undertaken consulting work with SGV-DDI, Oracle Systems Corp., and Bristol-Myers Squibb Philippines (Mead Johnson), amongst others.

Shweta Jaiswal Thakur is a doctoral student at the Management Development Institute Gurugram. She is a double postgraduate with degrees in Management and Labor Laws and Labor Welfare. Her research interests include HR analytics, strategic HRM, psychological testing and scale development, performance management systems, and talent management. She has close to seven years of corporate experience in the Human Resources field and has worked with various industries including The India Today Group and Aon Hewitt. She has published cases, book reviews, and research papers in various outlets including Ivey Publishing, Employee Relations, and Personnel Psychology.

Arup Varma is Professor of Management at the Quinlan School of Business, Loyola University Chicago. He has published over fifty articles in leading refereed journals such as the *Academy of Management Journal*, *Personnel Psychology*, and the *Journal of Applied Psychology*. He has also presented over ninety refereed research papers at leading international conferences, and authored thirty-five book chapters. His current research focuses on performance management, and expatriate categorization and adjustment issues. He has been recognized by his colleagues and students with multiple awards for teaching, research, and service.

Peter Waring is Murdoch's Singapore Dean and is based in Singapore. He is responsible for advancing the University's academic and strategic interests in Singapore. A qualified lawyer, Peter Waring also holds degrees in Commerce and Management. He is the co-author of four books on employment relations. His research and teaching interests span the business and law fields of employment relations, human resource management, corporate governance, and labor law. He has lived in Southeast Asia for the last sixteen years.

Vathsala Wickramasinghe is a Professor based at the Department of Management of Technology, Faculty of Engineering in the University of Moratuwa, Sri Lanka. Her research experience includes work in the areas of strategic human resource management, the human side of technology management, and labor market issues. She holds a PhD from the University of Manchester, United Kingdom and research fellowships from the Lancaster University Management School, United Kingdom, and the College of Business, University of Colorado, Colorado Springs, USA.

Kyoung-Hee Yu is a Senior Lecturer at the UNSW Business School, Sydney. Her research has focused on institutional and organizational change processes affecting work and employment. Kyoung-Hee's recent work has examined the generative potential of organizational politics, mobility of workers across borders and issues of inclusion, and comparative employment relations in Asia. Her work has been published in *Organization Studies*, the *British Journal of Industrial Relations*, *Human Relations*, and *Work, Employment and Society*. She earned her doctorate from MIT's Sloan School of Management, Cambridge, Massachusetts.

Yu Zheng is a Senior Lecturer in Asian Business and International Human Resource Management at Royal Holloway, University of London. She has published a research monograph *Managing Human Resources in China: The View from Inside MNCs* with the Cambridge University Press. She has also published papers in academic journals such as *Work, Employment and Society*, the *International Journal of Human Resource Management*, the *Asia Pacific Journal of Management*, *Asian Business & Management*, and the *International Journal of Entrepreneurial Behavior & Research*. Yu Zheng's research interests are in work and employment in multinational firms. She is a committee member of the Euro-Asia Management Studies Association. Her research has been funded by the Sanwa Foundation, the Japan Foundation, and the European Trade Union Institute.

Introduction

1

HUMAN RESOURCE MANAGEMENT IN ASIA IN THE GLOBAL CONTEXT

Fang Lee Cooke and Sunghoon Kim

Objectives of the Handbook

This Handbook of Human Resource Management (HRM) in Asia (hereafter Handbook) is motivated by two observations. First, existing books on HRM in Asia have not given sufficient attention to several important aspects of organizational life in Asian societies. For instance, in many Asian countries religion plays a significant role in people management. Family-oriented culture and gender inequality exert significant influences on Asian employees' everyday organizational life. However, such themes have been insufficiently covered, if at all, in existing handbooks in this area. In addition, there is a continuing under-representation of employment/industrial relations (IR) issues in existing scholarly books on HRM in Asia. Yet, a proper understanding of Asian firms' HRM necessitates in-depth knowledge about the changes of labor regulations and IR both at the national and local level that are taking place under the context of rapid marketization and globalization. HR practices observed in Asian emerging economies (e.g., China,[1] India, and Vietnam) are often the results of the dynamics between organizations, regulators, and employee relations institutions.

Second, existing books on HRM in Asia include multiple chapters on country-specific HRM practices, with those chapters typically focusing on one country per chapter. The limitation of this approach is the difficulty of knowing which aspects of the national HR model are unique to the country and which aspects are not. For instance, when a national model of Chinese HRM is explained, prior books tend to address only Chinese contexts in their relevant chapters. As a consequence, they fail to differentiate truly unique aspects of HRM in China from the HR aspects shared by other Asian transitional economies such as Vietnam.

Addressing these gaps, this Handbook aims to provide an intellectually engaging and comprehensive overview of HRM in the Asian context that is well informed with empirical research. First, the handbook not only provides an up-to-date review of the current stock of knowledge on traditional HRM in Asian nations, but also covers important, yet less examined, themes and issues in existing books on HRM in Asia, such as the regulatory framework for work and employment, religiosity and diversity. Second, we aim to provide engaging comparative analyses on HRM in Asian contexts by juxtaposing particular Asian countries, for instance, by comparing China with Vietnam, India with Philippines, Indonesia with Malaysia and Thailand, and

Dubai with Singapore. Written by authors who have track records in the areas of research, and many are leading scholars in their field, this Handbook offers fresh insights for education and future research related to HRM in Asia.

Why is HRM in Asia important?

Asia holds strategic significance in geopolitics regarding the counterbalancing of political forces in both Europe and North America. The political dynamics between these forces may affect the level of the foreign direct investment (FDI) price and consequent economic and employment growth. Economic globalization and geopolitics have deeply influenced many Asian countries' domestic development and internationalization. In short, Asia is an indispensable and integral part of the global political economy. Developing a deeper understanding of HRM in Asia is therefore important for both practical and intellectual reasons.

From a practical perspective, examining HRM in Asia has political, economic, and cultural significance for several reasons. First, Asia is the largest and most populous continent, with forty-eight countries and nearly 60 percent of the total global population. The number of wage earners in China alone is more than three times larger than that of the entire European Union. Therefore, without a proper understanding of Asian HRM, it is impossible to draw a complete picture of today's world of work.

Second, Asia is a region of dynamic economic development. It showcases several of the world's largest and fastest growing economies (e.g., China, India, Japan, and Korea), rapidly emerging economies (e.g., Vietnam and Malaysia), and inspiring global cities (e.g., Singapore, Hong Kong, and Dubai), each of which plays an important yet different role in economic globalization. Asia receives the largest amount of FDI and is the global center of high-technology products manufacturing and professional services offshoring. Therefore, without sufficient understanding of how Asian companies manage their people, economic globalization cannot be fully understood.

Third, today's Asia is where a growing number of multinational companies (MNCs) originated. While Japanese and Korean MNCs have been a familiar feature in the global economy since the 1980s (for Japan) and 1990s (for Korea), the global footprints of both Indian and Chinese MNCs have emerged in more recent decades, especially in the global South, with critical implications for host country development (e.g., Cooke, Wood, & Horwitz, 2015; French, 2014; Jackson, 2014). Therefore, it is important to understand the context of how and where these Asian MNCs formulated their HRM.

HRM in Asia has been shaped by its own distinctive institutional and cultural environments, which require special managerial attention. The political arrangement in Asia is complex and diverse, including the governing structures of a constitutional monarchy, autocratic monarchy, one-party system, federalism, liberal democracy, and military dictatorship. Strong governmental control has become common in developing states in recent decades, which makes rapid economic development a reality, as seen in Singapore and China (e.g., Huang, 2008; Witt & Redding, 2013). However, strong state power carries its own problems and tends to affect the relationships between the state and other institutional actors, such as through corruption, when law enforcement lacks stringency. In addition, Asian societies are heavily influenced by their own cultural values, traditions, and philosophies (Barkema, Chen, George, Luo, & Tsui, 2015). For example, Confucianism has a deep influence in China, Japan, Korea, Singapore, and Taiwan; Buddhism influences China, Hong Kong, Japan, Myanmar, Sri Lanka, Taiwan, and Thailand; Christianity influences the Philippines; and Islamism influences Indonesia, Malaysia, and the Middle East. Thus, business leaders must forge good relationships with government authorities on the one hand, and demonstrate a strong understanding of the historical traditions and societal values in their decisions on the other.

From an intellectual point of view, examining HRM in Asia could lead to novel insights on the impact of institutional and cultural environments on a firm's HR practices. Existing theories of HRM have been derived primarily by observing HRM practices in developed economies. HRM literature tends to underplay the role of institutions and societal culture, in view of the growing trend of positivist studies (e.g., Jackson, Schuler, & Jiang, 2014; Kaufman, 2015). This is unfortunate because HRM practices are heavily influenced by contexts. Institutions, political regimes, and societal cultures affect national business systems (e.g., Hall & Soskice, 2001; Witt & Redding, 2013), and labor market and employment systems (e.g., Bosch, Rubery, & Lehndorff, 2009), within which HRM practices at the firm level are formulated and implemented. This broad context includes not only political, economic, social, and cultural factors but also how key stakeholders (or institutional actors) are portrayed in the public and how they are perceived by each other, as these perceptions shape opportunities for/constraints to actions and interactions amongst stakeholders. Moreover, intra-national diversity of business environments should not be ignored. Although HRM and IR environments and practices are primarily shaped at the national level, local diversity and dynamism may play a more important role in shaping the bargaining power of key actors and HR outcomes (e.g., Almond, 2011). Therefore, HRM scholarship requires context-sensitive research that explicitly considers various aspects of institutional and cultural environments like those of Asia.

There are several ways that researchers can immediately benefit from studying Asian HRM. First, it enables us to locate indigenous practices in a global context. For instance, *guanxi*—an indigenous Chinese notion of social relationship—is known to be highly influential in the Chinese workplace (Chen, Chen, & Huang, 2013). Although *guanxi* is certainly a Chinese phenomenon, an intensive study of Asian HRM could reveal that it has common features with other indigenous concepts in Asian countries, such as *tinh cam* in Vietnam, *yon-go* in Korea, and *wa* in Japan (cf. Chapter 3). It is therefore a rewarding exercise to be engaged in an in-depth and focused comparative institutional and cultural analysis of HRM across Asian countries. It is with this intention that the Handbook adopts a comparative approach in some of its thematic and country-specific chapters.

Second, examining HRM in Asia may enrich the theories developed in Western contexts. Indigenous firms in Asia may rely on significantly different means to influence employee behavior from those frequently used in Western companies. Such divergences may generate situations where an HR practice that is considered of marginal importance in Western-based HRM literature is shown to be highly influential in Asia (or vice versa). For example, workplace-based employee benefits are heavily used in developing Asian countries, such as China, India, Vietnam, and Malaysia, which carry both symbolic and substantive values and are important lubricants for smoothening workplace relationships (e.g., Cooke, 2014; Saini, 2006). Such a phenomenon may be rare in developed economies, in part due to income tax regulations.

Third, studying Asian experiences with HRM and IR systems would enable us to revisit certain taken-for-granted assumptions in the field. For instance, existing Western-based scholarship tends to clearly distinguish the domains of HRM from those of IR. Such distinctions may not be relevant in Asia, especially in the case of developing Asian countries, where: (a) social regulations, which often stem from religiosity, a caste system, and Confucian values rather than hard regulations, may be more influential in governing workplace relationships; and (b) the powers of the state, employee organizations, and employers are unevenly spread but are also often intertwined. Exploring the nuances of both the historical and political economic contexts of Asian countries will help conceptualize the long tradition of employment and HRM practices in Asia as well as define emerging issues and new trends as they integrate into the global system.

The history of HRM scholarship testifies that Asia could provide major inspirations for intellectual advancement. Notably, while many HRM theories have stemmed from Western-based research, the concept of HRM that originated in the USA in the early 1980s drew empirical insights from Japanese employment practices (Appelbaum & Batt, 1993; Warner, 1994; Womack, Jones, & Roos, 1991). In the 1980s, when "Japanese firms came to prominence," their management practices were hailed as the "best practices" for Western firms to model (Endo, Delbridge, & Morris, 2015: 101). Although the prominence of Japanese firms and their management practices have declined since the "bubble economy" burst in the early 1990s, research on Japanese firms' management practices still matters, albeit with distinctively different foci that reflect the current socio-economic changes, the new regional economic context in which Japanese firms operate, and emerging business concerns (Endo et al., 2015).

Many developed economies have suffered from the global financial crisis in 2008, and Western firms have continued to search for new ideas to revive their businesses. Conversely, Asian countries, such as China, have weathered the crisis reasonably well and have been depended upon as an engine for growth. As Chen and Miller (2010) argued, there is a shift from the "West leads the East" to the "West meets the East," about which they stated the following:

> A thriving Chinese business culture represents not only a source of economic partnership but a potential fount of managerial wisdom that can help renew Western economies. Unfortunately, the cultural distance between East and West makes Chinese examples too different, and at times inappropriate, for Western firms to emulate.
>
> *(2010: 17)*

Indeed, it is often difficult for Western researchers to understand, much less accept, what occurs either in Asia or other regions outside their knowledge base/comfort zone. A natural response from some would be to question the validity or reliability of the data and theory presented rather than to adopt an open mind to learn and understand what is happening in other parts of the world. Such a presumed superiority, if only subconscious and implicit, prevents cross-fertilization, experience sharing, and theory building, which are founded on equitable grounds and mutual respect. The aim of this Handbook is to help bridge the gap between the West and the East. As Popper remarked, "I may be wrong and you may be right, and by an effort, we may get nearer to the truth" (1996: 225).

Issues confronting HRM in Asia

HRM in Asia, like other parts of the world, is confronted by a number of issues and labor market trends that are triggered by institutional changes at the national and industry level, as well as employer strategy at the firm level in response to the globalization of the economy. Four important and related issues are worth noting in this section.

Informalization of employment

One is the growing use of non-standard employment and subcontracting in order to reduce cost, to increase staffing flexibility, and to bypass legal constraints (e.g., Cooke & Brown, 2015). As Wang, Cooke, and Lin (2016) observed in the Chinese context, the growth of non-standard employment is taking place not just in the low-skilled work area, but also in university graduate employment in part as a result of the rapid expansion of the higher education sector since the early 2000s. As a result, a growing proportion of university graduates are taking non-graduate jobs. Non-standard employment, while creating HR advantages for employers and increasing their competitiveness in some ways, brings forth another set of pressures at different levels. These include: declined workers well-being due to poor terms and conditions and job security; reduced investment in human capital as user firms are less likely to invest in training and development for workers in non-standard employment; and in some cases, reduced commitment from the workers due to the transactional nature of the employment. Employers' aggressive use of various forms of non-standard employment also creates pressure for the state to regulate the non-standard labor market to provide protection to the workers to ensure decent work. However, regulative efforts are often lagging behind management practices and the remedial effect may be less than adequate, as has been commonly observed in less developed Asia (cf. Chapters 6 and 7).

Talent shortages

A second issue relates to talent management. In many developing Asian countries, the impact of globalization is not just economic, but cultural. The young generation of the workforce, which is characteristic of the labor market in most developing Asian countries, is becoming more highly educated, more individualistic, more eager to succeed, and more ready to change jobs to progress than their counterparts of the older generation. They also demand for more autonomy, control of the work process, participation in decisions fairness, more development/career opportunities, and a greater share of the reward in exchange for their performance and commitment to the firm (e.g., Cooke & Saini, 2010). The psychological change of individuals in demanding more as the society becomes more individualized and the economy develops suggests that the driving force for HRM changes comes from workers who are not shy, and who are in a position to bargain for their employment outcomes. For instance, an Australia-based HR regional team leader of a US-owned IT MNC observed: "highly educated young workers in China are very ambitious and eager to succeed. They have a very sophisticated understanding of the power to damage a corporate brand and use it subtly as a bargaining chip."[2]

As the majority of Asian countries are facing skill shortages, this requires employers to design and adopt a set of HRM practices that are capable of attracting, motivating, and retaining talented employees (cf. Chapter 12). Given the different characteristics of the workforce and the local labor market conditions, (prescribed) Western HRM practices may not be directly applicable to this workforce. For example, Ulrich and Allen's (2014: 1) study examined the talent trend and how investment in talent is linked to business results in top Asian companies—based on the data from over 570 separate businesses in Singapore, China, and India, about thirteen talent management processes. The study found that: "investments in managing current talent have more impact on business performance than hiring new talent or retaining existing talent [with job quit intent]" (Ulrich & Allen, 2014: 1). At the same time, heightened competition forces businesses to improve their performance continuously and requires their employees to be broad-minded, innovative, flexible both in skills and attitude, responsive, and adaptive (cf. Chapter 9). This indicates that employers may need to re-evaluate their relationships with their employees and design a performance management system that is capable of meeting the needs of, and motivating, different groups of employees (cf. Chapter 8). A key challenge for many Asian firms is to develop a HR capability that is: enabled by modern technology; underpinned by an HR philosophy that is shared across the organization; informed by an HR strategy that is well aligned with the business strategy; and delivered by HR practices that are accepted by the workforce.

However, it is important to cast our focus on the broader institutional and cultural causes of talent shortage of a given nation, instead of adopting a narrow firm-level view of this problem, or by simply attributing the problem to the failure of the country's education system to produce the right kind and quantity of skills. As noted earlier, individual aspirations and expectations of life are changing—young Chinese now want to change jobs every few years, no matter how good a firm's HR policy is, and individuals are gaming to advance their career faster. In addition, in many ways, the talent retention problem may be an IR problem, often taking place on an individual basis in a disguised manner, but with a collective impact.

Increased labor mobility

A third related issue is the growing labor mobility, not in job hopping as mentioned above, but in the form of migration internally and cross-border. Internal migration typically occurs from rural to urban area such as that found in China and India (Elias & Gunawardana, 2013), whereas cross-border migration mainly takes place from less developed states to relatively more developed economies that suffer from labor/skill shortages (e.g., Dubai and Singapore, cf. Chapter 19) or population aging (e.g., Japan). These migrants form the majority of the workforce in non-standard employment with limited prospects of permanent migration (e.g., in Japan and Dubai), or becoming an urban citizen in the real sense by enjoying the same citizen's rights and social treatment, as is the case in China, despite continuing state regulatory efforts to improve the situation. The coexistence of various groups of workers with different demographic background, employment terms and conditions, and expectations of labor market outcomes not only creates challenges to diversity management, but also engenders tensions between groups of workers carrying similar work alongside each other and create industrial relations (IR) problems that undermine firm performance as well as workers' well-being (e.g., Cooke, 2015; Lee & Frenkel, 2004).

Rising level of labor disputes

A fourth issue is the rising level of labor disputes, some of which are highly destructive, across many Asian economies, notably, but not restricted to, Japan, Korea, China, India, and Vietnam. For example, the rising level of labor disputes, some with radical actions and disastrous consequences in the Indian manufacturing sector, was in part caused by the growing sense of inequality of social class and pent-up grievance on the caste system. Caste issues and labor surpluses incline some poorly trained Indian managers to marginalize grievances—with potentially explosive consequences, as we have found in the violent Maruti Suzuki dispute in which an HR manager lost his life in the line of fire, literally (cf. Saini, 2016). Neither HRM nor pluralist IR seems close to their heart. In many ways, labor disputes are not only a reflection of the failure of HRM, but are also a sign of the growing confidence and demands of workers, in the light of labor/skill shortages, as noted earlier. For example, Chinese workers now have the economic and political opportunities to take radical actions—strikes in China by the younger generation of workers are made possible because of the social and family support they receive in the decision and process of strikes, and if the actions fail. In the case of young rural migrant workers, they have less to lose than urban workers with family and are much less mobile in the labor market (Cooke, 2013).

A common feature in the labor disputes in developing Asian countries, whose labor regime was shaped by an autocratic political system and a paternalistic culture (e.g., Cooke, 2013; Ford,

2012), is that grass-roots workers, mostly unorganized and with limited bargaining power, tend to endure management malpractices until their grievance reaches a boiling point and then explodes with a seemingly small incident as the fuse. In these countries, there are two forms of bargaining. One is top-down—official—led by the trade unions. The other is self-organized negotiation/bargaining, a bottom-up approach led by the grass-roots worker leaders. The former is by and large absent in a real sense or ineffective due to the weak presence of unionism, and the latter may be short-lived due to the suppression of labor activism by the state in favor of economic development. A broader implication of the rising level of labor disputes for the state is the need for institutional reform and commitment to offer greater protection to workers as nation states advance their economy.

The above issues highlight three important aspects of HRM, that is, human resource supply, human resource flow, and human resource strategy. A crucial indication of the effectiveness of these aspects would be the quality of industrial relations and workers' well-being. As such, the HR problems that have emerged involve both classic IR and modern HRM. For the former, organizations should be developed to represent workers to ensure that firms treat workers fairly and manage IR and labor disputes effectively. For the latter, more employee-oriented HR strategy and practices will go a long way to prevent HR problems and incentivize workers to work productively to enhance organizational performance. It will also require firms to formulate HR strategy and practices that are culturally sensitive at the societal and organizational level. That said, are HR interventions at the workplace level capable of addressing some of the workplace tensions that reflect wider social inequalities, for example, the caste system of India and similar social hierarchy systems found in other societies? Should employers bear the sole responsibility for failures in HRM and IR?

Thematic coverage and structure of the book

This volume consists of twenty-two chapters including this Introduction and a Conclusions chapter. The twenty subject-matter-specific chapters are contained in four parts that cover: institutional and cultural contexts (Chapters 2–4); labor regulation and IR environment in East, Southeast, and South Asia (Chapters 5–7); thematic and functional HRM, including for example, innovation and HRM, leadership compensation, performance management, and equal opportunity and diversity management (Chapter 8–14); and comparison of HRM in fifteen selected countries (Chapter 15–21). This Handbook, therefore, covers a comprehensive range of thematic topics as well as geographic areas of Asia, including nation states that have been much less well examined. We outline these sections and chapters in more detail below.

Part I: institutional and cultural contexts

In understanding how HRM policies and practices are formed and implemented, institutional and cultural perspectives remain the dominant theoretical lens in the international context (for a comprehensive review, cf. Cooke, Veen, & Wood, 2017). With this in mind, Part I includes three chapters that provide an overview about the role of the state and the role of societal culture and religious values, as macro-level contexts against which the HRM system of Asian countries is developed and functions. While the role of the state as a regulator and major institutional actor may be evident and formalized, the role of societal culture as manifested in customs and practice may permeate organizational practices and day-to-day workplace relationships in a more subtle and taken-for-granted way. However, ignorance and violation of these cultural norms, which may be more likely to occur in foreign MNCs than in domestic firms operating in developing Asian countries, may cause serious damage to management–worker relationships.

Chapter 2, State and HRM in Asia, contributed by Kyoung-Hee Yu and Sung Chul Noh, reviews models of the state in Asia in conjunction with the pressures on the nation state from an increasingly integrated world economy. It examines the role of the state in influencing HRM as a result of interactions between models of the nation state and global pressures. Empirical evidence was drawn from selected countries for illustration, with a focus on how state influence might affect HRM styles, as well as inequality and worker voice. Yu and Noh's theoretical framework advances a model of state influence on HRM that is dynamic yet reflects historic legacies. They also argue that the constraints placed on the nation state with the introduction of global pressures paradoxically allows it more discretion for policy experimentation.

Chapter 3, Confucianism and Human Resource Management in East Asia, contributed by Sunghoon Kim, Pingping Fu, and Jiali Duan examines how the tradition of Confucianism in East Asia is reflected in contemporary HR practices in the region. The authors argue that, Confucianism, a defining element of East Asian culture, has had a profound influence on politics, education, religion, family, and business practices in greater China, as well as in such neighboring countries as Korea, Japan, Singapore, and Vietnam. Despite several waves of Westernization, Confucian tradition has continued to inspire East Asian organizations to develop their own distinctive HR practices. The authors provide a revealing overview on how Confucianism underpins East Asian HR practices in the area of selection, managerial succession, compensation, training, retention, and international assignments in a unique manner. They also shed light on how Confucianism influences gender discrimination, IR, and the practice of corporate ceremonies in East Asia.

Chapter 4, Religiosity, Ethics, and the Spirit of Capitalism in HRM, authored by Mohamed Branine, contributes to the debate on the extent to which religion and religiosity have had any effects on the management of people and employee relations in Asian countries and in particular in East Asia, where there has been a revival of religious beliefs after many years of suppression of religious practices. As Branine observed, studies on the relationship between religious beliefs, organizational behavior, managerial practices, and organizational outcomes are very limited and much of the debate over the rise of religiosity and spirituality as a form of personal identity has focused on the effects of religion at the national rather than the organizational and workplace level, and has been concerned with the negative aspects of religious extremism rather than on the positive implications of religious enlightenment on work and employee relations. This chapter addresses this imbalance and argues that the gap is still wider between the theory or what religious teachings promote and the reality, or how people are managed in the workplace. Branine provides emerging evidence that suggests that Asian ethical work behavior inspired by non-religious beliefs has had a significant impact on HRM, despite the spread of capitalism and the rise of religiosity, and calls for more empirical research on the topic to deepen our understanding.

Part II: labor regulation and industrial relations

HRM systems operate within the broader regulatory environment that is primarily shaped by national, sub-national, and industry-related regulations. In the globalized economy, international regulations, many of which voluntary and non-binding, may also impact the employment and HR practices of firms in the global value chain. In some countries, national governments may be under pressure to relax their regulatory environment to create labor flexibility to aid economic revival and increase business competitiveness. For example, both Japan and Korea were under international pressure to deregulate the labor market in the late 1980s and 1990s, resulting in the rapid casualization of the Japanese and Korean labor market (Cooke & Brown, 2015). To contain labor cost, some employers in Japan and Korea replaced regular workers with non-regular workers and hire non-regular workers for most new positions. As a result, only 30 percent of Korean workers had a regular job in 1999 (OECD, 2000), and the "absolute number of precarious workers has continuously increased from about 3.8 million in 2002 to about 6 million in 2011" (Shin, 2013: 336). The Chinese governments, by contrast, have been under pressure to increase labor protection and have enacted a series of legislations since the 2008, in the light of growing labor discontent and the widening economic disparity across the society (Cooke, 2016). Contrary to China, India's complex labor regulation system has been widely regarded as a severe constraint for business competitiveness. Unable to pressurize the government to change the laws, employers have opted for ways to casualize their staffing arrangements. As a result, some 90 percent of the workforce is engaged in informal employment (Venkata Ratnam, 2009).

As Frenkel and Yu observed, there are a number of similar IR features and pressures for convergence across many Asian countries, but at the same time, distinct differences persist across the nations studied, in part as a result of the strategic actions and interactions "between elites and interest groups" (2013: 407). It seems that despite very different political regimes across Asian countries—for instance, China is a one-party led country and India is the largest democratic country in the world—these countries share similar outcomes of political, economic, and social inequality of the grass-roots workers, with some being more disadvantaged and disempowered than others. This part examines in depth the evolution of the regulatory environment and IR systems in East Asia, Southeast Asia, and South Asia.

Chapter 5, Employment Regulation and Industrial Relations Systems in East Asia: China, Japan, and South Korea, is contributed by Fang Lee Cooke, Katsuyuki Kubo, and Byoung-Hoom Lee. The authors provide an overview of how the economy and the labor market have evolved in these three major Asian economies since the 1980s. The chapter highlights how the labor market in the three countries was de-regulated and re-regulated simultaneously in the 1990s. In particular, the re-regulation reflects the governments' attempt to combat employers' opportunistic behavior and to offer a greater level of protection to workers. The chapter also compares and contrasts the role of the trade unions in these economies, suggesting that while union strength has been in decline in Japan and Korea, they are in general, much more powerful, particularly the Korean unions, than their counterparts in China. However, the unions in all three countries have yet to develop their real presence to organize those in informal employment. The chapter finally examines the evolution and patterns of the wage system in these three countries in the presence or absence of a collective bargaining mechanism.

In Chapter 6, Ingrid Landau and Fang Lee Cooke examine employment regulation and IR in five major Southeast Asian countries: Indonesia, Malaysia, the Philippines, Thailand, and Vietnam. Southeast Asia is one of the fastest growing, dynamic and diverse regions in the world, with high and sustained levels of foreign investment. This level of economic achievement, however, is to a large extent facilitated by the relaxed enforcement of labor regulation or the growing use of informal employment by the employers to bypass legal responsibilities. Landau and Cooke reveal that state intervention in the development of the IR system in these five Southeast Asian countries has largely been repressive, with the nation's economic interest being the priority. Union strength has been weak and in many cases weakening, whereas international non-government organizations (NGOs) are only partially active to fill a small part of the representational gap, mainly in sectors in the global value chain.

Chapter 7, contributed by Michael Gillan, examines employment regulation and IR in South Asia. As a general survey, the chapter provides a brief assessment of how and why an understanding of historical and political context and the composition of employment are necessary for understanding contemporary IR and employment regulation in the region. It considers the major parties to IR and the formal framework of employment regulation in South Asia. It highlights the limited reach and effectiveness of many of the parties and IR institutions and the evident gap between formal regulation and practice. This chapter also provides an assessment of the interaction between the practice of contemporary HRM, IR, and the weakening collective bargaining power of workers by the increased utilization of contract and agency employment.

It is within this broader context of regulatory environment, IR climate, and the relative power base and power of each key institutional actor that the HRM system is shaped and understood in specific countries. Although this section has not covered all Asian countries included in the discussion in this Handbook, it nevertheless provides a broad institutional backdrop for the next two parts that examine HRM in specific themes and functions across a number of Asian countries.

Part III: thematic and functional HRM

This part includes seven chapters (Chapters 8–14), each dealing with one thematic or functional area of HRM, drawing on research on, and practices from, various Asian countries.

Chapter 8, Performance Management Practices in Asia, contributed by Arup Varma, Pawan Budhwar and Peter Norlander, examines how Asian organizations organize their Performance Management Systems (PMS) and thereby manage their employees' individual performances. The chapter first summarizes key components of PMS and delineates the major determinants of effective PMS such as distal factors (e.g., social norms), proximal factors (e.g., organizational norms), judgment factors (e.g., availability of performance standard), intervening factors (e.g., supervisor–subordinate relationships), and distortion factors (e.g., forced ranking systems). The authors discuss how the core elements of PMS interact with prevailing Asian cultures, such as collectivism, and Asia-specific institutional arrangements, such as family-oriented corporate governance. The chapter recognizes the importance of well-implemented PMS in Asian companies. It also highlights the need to develop a more nuanced understanding of Asia-specific ways in order to manage employee performance.

Chapter 9, Innovation and HRM in Asia, authored by Jyotsna Bhatnagar and Shweta Jaiswal Thakur, examines a topic that remains under-studied, despite having gained growing research attention in recent years. Given the critical role of innovation to sustain business competitiveness, innovation and HRM should be seen from two related dimensions. One is the role of the HR function and HR practices in fostering employee creativity, because human resources are considered to be the most valuable asset of an organization, as they have become an important source of innovation and competitive advantage. The other is innovation in HR practices and the delivery of the HR function in improving HRM, that will in turn contribute to improving organizational performance. Globalization has changed the allocation of employment opportunities toward rapidly growing emerging markets, and in particular, India and China have become important locations of innovation. In this chapter, Bhatnagar and Thakur provide an overview of studies of innovation and HRM in Asian countries, drawing on evidence from China and India quite heavily as examples for illustration. The chapter highlights the significance of innovation for sustainable competitive advantage and how HR practices may contribute to achieving this organizational objective. It also exemplifies innovations in HR practices with case studies from India.

A key challenge to national development and organizational competitiveness in the global economy in developing Asian countries is the deficiency of management talent and leaders capable of managing international operations (Nankervis, Cooke, Chatterjee, & Warner, 2013). Chapter 10, Leadership and Leadership Development in Asia, authored by Alex Newman, Nathan Eva, and Kendall Herbert, offers a succinct review of literature on leadership in Asia. The authors examine how the cultural and institutional environment influences the leadership styles adopted by Asian managers and what constitutes effective leadership in Asia. Specifically, they suggest that paternalistic and authoritative leadership is commonly found across Asian countries, although some Asian employees do not prefer to be under such leadership style. While Western styles of leadership are increasingly popular in Asia, their effectiveness is not always guaranteed. The authors also discuss the implications of these findings for leadership development in Asia, and the role played by leadership development programs in fostering female managers and nurturing young talent. The chapter sets out an agenda for future research on leadership in Asia.

Chapter 11, Compensation System and Pay Practices in Asia, contributed by Tae-Youn Park and Jason Shaw, reviews the international compensation literature, with specific focus on the cultural differences across countries. Building on the literature review, the authors suggest that research should focus less on the differences in compensation practice preferences across different countries, and instead focus more on how the cultures interplay with a given form of compensation practice (e.g., individual performance-based pay) and thereby influence people's attitudinal and behavioral outcomes. The authors put forward several research questions to illustrate their points in the hope of advancing the debate on the effectiveness of (Western-style) performance-based compensation practices in Asian organizations.

As noted earlier, skill shortage has been a major bottleneck for many Asian countries in the era of economic globalization. Chapter 12, Human Capital Flows and Talent Management in Asia, contributed by Anthony McDonnell and Ying Guo, provides an up-to-date evaluation of the state of play on talent management and human capital flows in Asia. The authors discuss the challenges regarding talent attraction and retention faced by local firms and multinational companies, as well as managing foreign talent working in Asian countries. McDonnell and Guo note that effective management of human capital is often considered as a comparative advantage of organizations in extant research. They also note that not enough research in this field has paid proper attention to the context in which talent management is being implemented. Culturally and institutionally appropriate HR practices play an important role in relation to talent recruitment and retention in Asia. Therefore, much more research efforts are needed in this arena to address the vast research gap.

Asian countries offer rich and diverse contexts to examine how multinational companies (MNCs) manage the workforce and engage amid institutional transitions. In Chapter 13, Managing MNCs in Asia, Yu Zheng and Chris Smith identify three key areas where institutions in Asian countries have informed our understanding of managing MNCs. The first area is the exploration of employment regimes, paradigms, and practices as the result of the intersection between comparative political economy and organizational strategy. The second area is the interplay between different employment systems at workplaces, which have envisaged novelty in organizing work and managing the workforce. The third area is the emergence of MNCs from less-developed countries, which have presented significant challenges and, at the same time, brought unique opportunities to managing people across countries. Contrary to the wisdom that is often seen in strategic HRM, the authors urge researchers to move away from being tempted to draw out integration or coherence in the management of MNCs in Asia. Instead, they suggest that the appropriation of complexity in Asian countries is more promising for building theory from context-rich empirical work on managing MNCs in and from Asia.

In Chapter 14, Equal Opportunity and Workforce Diversity in Asia, Ahu Tatli, Mustafa Bilgehan Ozturk, and Maryam Aldossari present an overview of equal opportunities and workforce diversity in Asia. Given the vast geography the chapter sets out to explore, they start by scoping key equality and diversity issues in three regions: the Middle East, South Asia, and East Asia. Their review of extant research evidence shows that there is both divergence and convergence across Asia in the area of equality and diversity at work. In other words, the continent faces several common challenges in achieving equality of opportunity, but there are also equality issues that are more pressing in some countries and regions than in others. The chapter pays particular attention to three strands of equality issues: sexual orientation; nationality and tribal affiliations; and gender in three different country contexts—Turkey, Saudi Arabia, and China respectively—in order to provide a more in-depth depiction of the unique manifestation of inequality challenges in Asia. The authors also provide a set of policy recommendations to promote equal opportunities and diversity at work, and identify areas for future research.

Part IV: HRM in selected Asian countries

We sequence the seven country-specific chapters (Chapters 15–21) roughly following the lines of geographic locations, starting from Northeast Asia (Japan and Korea), followed by East Asia, Southeast Asia, and South Asia. Where countries from different regions are paired for comparison/discussion, we position the chapter based on the first country listed in the chapter title. It should be noted that countries are listed in the chapter title in alphabetical order. This pragmatic arrangement may, inevitably, seem odd at times, but is deemed plausible to avoid the complicated working out of logics to place one country before another. Each chapter adopts a broadly similar structure by providing an overview of the institutional and cultural background, from a historical lens, of the countries studied. This is followed by the examination of specific HRM practices in the state and private sector, and a discussion of key challenges to HRM and the emergence of strategic HRM.

Several key findings are shared to various degree across the countries examined. First, HR practices still carry strong traditional elements that are society specific, resulting in persisting inequalities along the lines of gender, ethnicity, class, and immigration status. Second, most Asian countries still have a long way to go in developing their strategic HRM capability and capacity. In particular, the state-owned sector continues to operate largely in a traditional personnel management mode, whereas the majority of small domestic private firms operate in a paternalistic style with decision power centralized to the senior management level. Foreign-funded MNCs, by contrast, are seen as the leaders of systematic HRM and are better able to attract, motivate, and retain talent than the state-owned and domestic private firms.

Chapter 15 examines HRM in Japan and South Korea. The two neighboring nations situated in Northeast Asia have mixed feelings toward each other for historical reasons, despite traditionally sharing much in their HRM systems. Since the early 1980s, Japan and South Korea have been two high performing economies in Asia that have developed many successful MNCs. Both countries experience similar labor markets changes such as growing unskilled immigrants from other Asian countries (e.g., Cooke & Brown, 2015; Ford & Kawashima, 2013) and rapid casualization of labor (Song, 2014). In this chapter, Fabian Jintae Froese, Tomoki Sekiguchi, and Mohan Pyari Maharjan provide a comparative overview of the unique HR systems of the large enterprises of these two countries. While the respective Japanese and Korean HR systems have resembled each other in the past, economic recessions and globalization have led Korean enterprises to modify their HR systems more aggressively, mostly in line with Anglo-Saxon practices, in contrast to Japanese enterprises which have been more reluctant to implement changes. The authors argue that in today's increasingly globalized and knowledge-intensive environment, global integration of HRM has become one of the key HR challenges to Japanese and Korean MNCs. For instance, Japanese and Korean MNCs need to overcome the tradition of homogeneous and ethnocentric organizational culture that undermines the integration of foreign nationals into the core functions of the company. The authors suggest that more research should examine the "internal internationalization" at headquarters and "external internationalization" at subsidiaries of Japanese and Korean MNCs.

We pair (mainland) China and Vietnam for analysis in Chapter 16 because both countries are highly successful transitional economies. Both states are, interestingly, still governed by the Communist Party, but the trade unions of each country function rather differently. MNCs are often comparing these two countries when seeking their next manufacturing base. In this chapter, Jie Shen and Anne Cox observe that China and Vietnam have undertaken a process of a gradual liberalization of their Socialist economies—a process which has been marked by an initial experimental phase in the late 1970s giving rise to more extensive reforms in the mid-1980s and accelerating since the 1990s. The authors examine whether the reforms in these two (post-)Socialist economies have produced a convergence in employment practices in enterprises by observing trends in labor recruitment and selection, training and development, and appraisal and reward practices. They find that transforming employee management from personnel management to modern HRM has been an integral part of the economic reform in both nations. In the last four decades, Shen and Cox observe that both China and Vietnam have shifted the responsibility for managing the workforce from the government to enterprises, and have transformed people management from a centrally planned to a market-oriented system. While modern HRM approaches have been gradually adopted, the current HRM systems have a range of issues in both countries. For example, *guanxi* or nepotism plays an important role in HRM and little attention has been paid to employee development. Overall, the authors argue that China and Vietnam present a convergent HRM model, despite significant differences in the two nations' HRM systems.

In Chapter 17, Shu-Yuan Chen and David Ahlstrom take stock of HRM in the newly developed ethnic Chinese economies of Hong Kong, Macau, and Taiwan. The shared cultural lineage and other selected characteristics of these three economies facilitate comparison. Family business has been a major type of enterprise in these economies and their traditional HRM has been rather unsystematic and family focused. With economic growth, globalization, and institutional reform in the East Asian region, HRM has undergone considerable development and change. Firms in these ethnic Chinese societies have adopted a number of practices from Anglo-American HRM, while at the same time adapting them to the cultural and institutional conditions in their respective environments. MNCs have similarly made necessary adjustments in doing business in Hong Kong, Macau, and Taiwan. Drawing on the existing literature of research in this area, the authors provide an interesting comparison and analysis of the three ethnic Chinese societies that are markedly different from that in Mainland China.

Chapter 18 juxtaposes Indonesia, Malaysia, and Thailand. These three—the largest economies in ASEAN—are actively collaborating as well as competing with one another, pursuing largely similar models of economic growth. Despite the lack of systematic studies of HR practices in all of the three countries, Chaturong Napathorn and Sarosh Kuruvilla provide an overview of the evolution of the HRM systems in Indonesia, Malaysia, and Thailand. Specifically, this chapter provides a brief history and basic data about the three countries. It then outlines employment relations and cultural factors (primarily according to Hofstede's dimensions) as a context within which to discuss the evolution of HRM systems in each country. The authors examine a number of firm-level HR practices, including recruitment and selection, training and development, and pay and reward practices in the three countries. Moreover, they assess changes in the role of the HR function and discuss trends in strategic HRM as well as emerging new HRM practices. Finally, the authors highlight some potential future challenges in HRM and their implications for the three countries.

Chapter 19 compares HRM practices and challenges in two major city states: Dubai and Singapore. Both city states have a strong record of economic growth that is underpinned by impressive economic development strategies. In addition, both states have been a driving force for regional development. In this chapter, Julia Connell, John Burgess, and Peter Waring investigate HRM in relation to the two rapidly globalizing city states. Both city states have diverse workforces that are dependent on expatriate professionals and migrant labor to meet the skill needs associated with economic growth. While both city states attract foreign investment and emphasize free trade and market-led growth, there are extensive government regulations and controls evident across all aspects of commerce. The strong presence of MNCs in Dubai and Singapore has supported the best practice HRM programs and practices adapted for local conditions, although such practices have been largely directed to professional and expatriate workers. Both city states have also introduced policies and practices focused on developing human capital as a means to support future economic growth, however, they also face challenges concerning the development and employment of local talent alongside expatriate workers. The authors evaluate the labor market conditions and HRM in each city state and compare the challenges confronting the two city states in regard to diversity management, protecting unskilled and low-paid immigrant workers, talent management, and providing opportunities for nationals (Emiratization), particularly within the private sector.

Chapter 20 examines HRM in India and the Philippines. These two countries are paired together because they share a history of colonialism with considerable traces of a Western cultural legacy. Both are English-speaking countries with a young and increasingly well-educated workforce. These important factors have given the two nations considerable advantages in offshore business process outsourcing that has contributed to their rapid economic growth, technological catch-up and integration into the global economy. Recently, the two countries have emerged as global rivals in outsourcing industry (call centers). Jennifer Ann Lajom, Simon Lloyd Restubog, Mendiola Teng-Calleja, Raymund Habaradas, and Mª Cristina Esquivel-Saldivar compare the contextual backgrounds of the two countries. They then review a number of HR practices, with a focus on recruitment and selection, performance management, and training and development. They identify key challenges to people management in these two fast-growing countries and examine the role and development of strategic HRM in business organizations. The authors argue that historical, political, and cultural factors shape the development of HR practices in both countries. By comparison, HRM in India has been more influenced by Western HRM and is relatively more strategic, whereas the Philippines retains more societal characteristics and is more traditional in its HR practices. However, both countries face severe challenges in HR strategic capability building as well as in the effectiveness of HR practices in order to foster long-term productivity.

Chapter 21 is devoted to HRM in two important nation states in South Asia: Bangladesh and Sri Lanka. In spite of the significantly different religious beliefs held by the majority of the population of the two nations (Buddhism being the main religion in Sri Lanka and Islamism in Bangladesh), they share similar historical and cultural roots due to their colonial past. Both countries are heavily dependent upon foreign direct investment (FDI) for economic development, but have adopted a somewhat different development strategy. For example, Sri Lanka focuses more on tourism, whereas Bangladesh focuses more on manufacturing. Both countries have been forging close links, more consistently so for Bangladesh than Sri Lanka, with the Chinese government and rely on Chinese investment for infrastructure building. Broadly speaking, both countries have benefited from offshore business process outsourcing and are becoming more integrated into the global value chain, especially in garment manufacturing. In this chapter, Vathsala Wickramasinghe and Monowar Mahmood analyze the socio-economic and cultural context that influences the development of HRM in the two countries. They examine distinctive features of HRM in the state sector and the private sector, including MNCs and small- and medium-sized enterprises. They discuss reform initiatives taken by the governments to modernize the HRM and identify the barriers to the effective implementation of HRM in the state sector. The authors argue that the accomplishment of HRM in the private sector of the two countries implies the effects of globalization of business operations and intense competition in the free market economy. The authors also assess recent changes, strategic focus, and the challenges faced by the HRM function of the two countries.

To conclude, we present this Handbook, contributed by a mixed team of Western and Asian scholars, as a valuable source of intellectual thoughts and empirical insights to readers who are interested in HRM and IR in Asia. As far as possible, we include leading scholars on the subject matter as well as scholars from specific regions and countries to contribute to the relevant chapters in order to maximize local expertise and indigenous views. This Handbook will help a scholarly audience to identify what we know about HRM in Asia, and what areas are in need of further research. The Handbook will also help HRM practitioners to enhance their confidence in managing employees under the Asian context. This book can be a useful resource for graduate and upper level undergraduate courses of HRM, international HRM, industrial relations, and international business.

As with all edited volumes of this size and spread of coverage, some degree of over-simplification and generalization is inevitable. While all the chapter authors have done their best to produce their respective chapters, some chapters have more opportunities than others in terms of the level of expertise and literature available, as some countries have been more studied than others, so have some thematic topics. An ultimate goal of this Handbook is to advance knowledge within various constraints and entice further research interest in HRM (broadly defined) in Asia. For that purpose, we welcome more dedicated research efforts in this area to deepen our understanding and to better inform management practices.

Notes

1 For the purpose of this Handbook, we refer China as the People's Republic of China (mainland China); Hong Kong and Taiwan as Chinese societies.
2 Interview by the lead author of this chapter, Fang Lee Cooke, in 2013.

References

Appelbaum, E. & Batt, R. (1993). *The new American workplace: Transforming work systems in the United States.* Ithaca, NY: Cornell University Press.
Almond, P. (2011). The sub-national embeddedness of international HRM. *Human Relations, 64*(4), 531–551.
Barkema, H. G., Chen, X. P., George, G., Luo, Y., & Tsui, A. S. (2015). West meets East: New concepts and theories. *Academy of Management Journal, 58*(2), 460–479.
Bosch, G., Rubery, J., & Lehndorff, S. (Eds.). (2009). *European employment models in flux: A comparison of institutional change in nine European countries.* Basingstoke: Palgrave Macmillan.
Chen, C. C., Chen, X. P., & Huang, S. (2013). Chinese Guanxi: An integrative review and new directions for future research. *Management and Organization Review, 9*(1), 167–207.

Chen, M. J. & Miller, D. (2010). West meets East: Toward an ambicultural approach to management. *Academy of Management Perspectives, 24*(4), 17–24.

Cooke, F. L. (2013). New dynamics of industrial conflicts in China: Causes, expressions and resolution alternatives. In G. Gall (Ed.), *New forms and expressions of conflict at work* (pp. 108–129). Basingstoke: Palgrave Macmillan.

Cooke, F. L. (2014). Chinese industrial relations research: In search of a broader analytical framework and representation. *Asia Pacific Journal of Management, 31*(3), 875–898.

Cooke, F. L. (2015). Corporate social responsibility and sustainability through ethical HRM practices. In A. Harzing & A. Pinnington (Eds.), *International human resource management* (4th ed.) (pp. 498–529). London: Sage.

Cooke, F. L. (2016). Employment relations in China. In G. Bamber, R. Lansbury, N. Wailes, & C. Wright (Eds.), *International and comparative employment relations* (6th ed.) (pp. 291–315). London: Sage and Sydney: Allen & Unwin.

Cooke, F. L. & Brown, R. (2015). *The regulation of non-standard forms of employment in China, Japan and the Republic of Korea*. International Labour Organization Working papers.

Cooke, F. L. & Saini, D. S. (2010). (How) does the HR strategy support an innovation-oriented business strategy?: An investigation of institutional context and organizational practices in Indian firm. *Human Resource Management, 49*(3), 377–400.

Cooke, F. L., Veen, A., & Wood, G. (2017). What do we know about cross-country comparative studies in HRM?: A critical review of literature in the period of 2000–2014. *The International Journal of Human Resource Management, 28*(1), 196–233.

Cooke, F. L., Wood, G., & Horwitz, F. (2015). Multinational firms from emerging economies in Africa: Implications for research and practice in human resource management. *The International Journal of Human Resource Management, 26*(21), 2653–2675.

Elias, J. & Gunawardana, S. (Eds.). (2013). *The global political economy of the household in Asia*. Basingstoke: Palgrave Macmillan.

Endo, T., Delbridge, R., & Morris, J. (2015). Does Japan still matter?: Past tendencies and future opportunities in the study of Japanese firms. *International Journal of Management Reviews, 17*(1), 101–123.

Ford, M. (2012, February 17). Violent industrial protest in Indonesia. *New dynamics of industrial conflicts in Asia: Causes, expressions and resolution alternatives*. One-day symposium, Monash University, Melbourne, Australia.

Ford, M. & Kawashima, K. (2013). Temporary labor migration and care work: The Japanese experience. *Journal of Industrial Relations, 55*(3), 430–444.

French, H. (2014). *China's second continent: How a million migrants are building a new empire in Africa*. New York: Alfred A. Knopf Doubleday.

Frenkel, S. & Yu, K. H. (2013). Explaining patterns of employment relations in Asian societies. In M. Witt & G. Redding (Eds.), *Oxford handbook of Asian capitalism* (pp. 383–418). Oxford: Oxford University Press.

Hall, A. & Soskice, D. (Eds.). (2001). *Varieties of capitalism: The institutional foundations of comparative advantage*. Oxford: Oxford University Press.

Huang, Y. S. (2008). *Capitalism with Chinese characteristics: Entrepreneurship and the state*. Cambridge: Cambridge University Press.

Jackson, S., Schuler, R., & Jiang, K. (2014). An aspirational framework for strategic human resource management. *Academy of Management Annals, 8*(1), 1–56.

Jackson, T. (2014). Employment in Chinese MNEs: Appraising the dragon's gift to sub-Saharan Africa. *Human Resource Management, 53*(6), 897–919.

Kaufman, B. (2015). Evolution of strategic HRM as seen through two founding books: A 30th anniversary perspective on development of the field. *Human Resource Management, 54*(3), 389–407.

Lee, B. & Frenkel, S. (2004). Divided workers: Social relations between contract and regular workers in a Korean auto company. *Work, Employment and Society, 18*(3), 507–530.

Nankervis, A., Cooke, F. L., Chatterjee, S., & Warner, M. (2013). *New models of human resource management in China and India*. London: Routledge.

OECD. (2000). *Pushing ahead with reform in Korea: Labor market and social safety-net Policies*. OECD Publishing. Retrieved from www.oecd.org/korea/36868635.pdf.

Popper, K. (1996). *The open society and its enemies, volume II, the high tide of prophecy: Hegel, Marx and the aftermath* (5th ed. revised). Princeton, NJ: Princeton University Press.

Saini, D. S. (2006). Managing employee relations through strategic human resource management: Evidence from two Tata companies. *Indian Journal of Industrial Relations, 42*(2), 170–189.

Saini, D. (2016). A popular HR chief burned to death: People–management dynamics at the Indian subsidiary of Suzuki Ltd. Hong Kong: Asia Case Research Centre, University of Hong Kong (Ref. 15/566C).

Shin, K. (2013). Economic crisis, neoliberal reforms, and the rise of precarious work in South Korea. *American Behavioral Scientist, 57*(3), 335–353.

Song, J. (2014). *Inequality in the workplace: Labor market reform in Japan and Korea.* Ithaca, NY: Cornell University Press.

Ulrich, D. & Allen, J. (2014). Talent accelerator: Understanding how talent delivers performance for Asian firms. *South Asian Journal of Human Resources Management, 1*(1), 1–23.

Venkata Ratnam, C. S. (2009). Employment relations in India. In P. Budhwar & J. Bhatnagar (Eds.), *The changing face of people management in India* (pp. 23–59). London: Routledge.

Wang, J., Cooke, F. L., & Lin, Z. (2016). Informal employment in China: Recent development and human resource implications. *Asia Pacific Journal of Human Resources, 54*(3), 292–311.

Warner, M. (1994). Japanese culture, Western management: Taylorism and human resources in Japan. *Organization Studies, 15*(4), 509–533.

Witt, M. & Redding, G. (Eds.). (2013). *Oxford handbook of Asian capitalism.* Oxford: Oxford University Press.

Womack, J. P., Jones, D. T., & Roos, D. (1991). *The machine that changed the world: The story of lean production.* New York: HarperCollins.

PART I

Institutional and cultural contexts

2

STATE AND HRM IN ASIA

Kyoung-Hee Yu and Sung Chul Noh

Introduction

The diversity in the institutional histories and political trajectories of Asian states make it a daunting exercise to theorize the relationship between the state and HRM in Asia. Our objective in this chapter is to review the existing models of the state in Asia critically, to elaborate the existing typologies based on an appreciation for exposure to global forces, and to apply the resulting understanding of state influence to societal outcomes of HRM. Extant classifications of the state have theorized the state with respect to interest organization in society and have neglected the state's embeddedness in a global environment. Our review embraces recent calls for theorizing the state and the employment relationship in the midst of global financial, organizational, and economic pressures (Crouch, 2011; Lakhani, Kuruvilla, & Avgar, 2013). This chapter is organized in two sections. In the first section, a theoretical framework is developed in which models of the state in Asia are reviewed in conjunction with pressures on the nation state from an increasingly integrated world economy. We conceptualize the latter in terms of influences from supranational institutions, as well as pressures from global value chains and global financial interests acting as constrains on state autonomy. State influence on HRM is then theorized as resulting from an interaction between models of the nation state and global pressures. With respect to outcomes of state influence, our framework examines societal outcomes such as inequality and voice in addition to the extent to which HRM styles provide flexibility in the employment relationship. The theoretical framework thus advanced is summarized in Figure 2.1. In the second section of the chapter, the theoretical framework developed in the first section is applied to Asian countries through a review of empirical works and relevant indexes for selected countries.

Beyond embedded autonomy: models of the state in Asia

Theories of the state have sought to distinguish it analytically from society, presenting the state as both a political system and an organization defined as an "autonomous entity whose actions are not reducible to or determined by forces in society" (Mitchell, 1991: 82). Two models of the state that have emerged from post-war governance in European countries are the regulatory and the welfare states. A regulatory state sets and maintains standards of behavior through

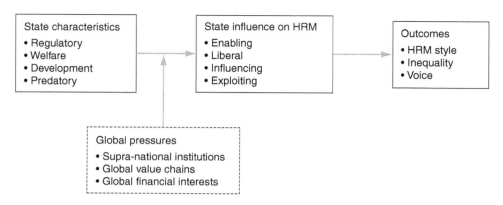

Figure 2.1 Model of state and HRM

Source: compiled by the authors.

regulatory agencies. It adopts a generally laissez-faire attitude to economic activity, not inter-vening except in instances of market failure, such as regulation of monopolistic behavior and the provision of collective goods (Levi-Faur, 2005). Economies governed by regulatory states are characterized by strong and open financial markets, shareholder governance, and high levels of institutionalized trust. The welfare state's primary objective is to ensure the social and economic well-being of citizens through various redistributive mechanisms. Economic governance under the welfare state strives for cooperative relationships amongst stakeholders such as owners, man-agers, employees, and interested social actors, as well as for employment stability and social protection for workers throughout and beyond the employment relationship. The financial system under the welfare state relies more on bank financing than on stock markets (Van Kers-bergen, 2003). Societies under the welfare state are characterized by enduring forms of interper-sonal trust. Asian states prompted political scientists to theorize about a third model of the state in which the state plays a strong and often interventionist role in economic development by leading, or selectively providing targets and incentives to key businesses (Hancké, Rhodes, & Thatcher, 2007). This understanding of the Asian state as the "developmental state" has charac-terized Japan since the 1960s and the newly industrialized countries of East Asia since the 1970s (Amsden, 1989, 2001; Wade, 1990). It has also provided a template to which several Southeast Asian countries, most prominently Malaysia, aspired in the 1980s (Carney & Witt, 2014). His-torically, developmental states were repressive of labor on the one hand, and on the other hand, they fostered state- and enterprise-based welfare through provision of lifetime employment. The state also acted as a major employer and provided training and education institutions which ensured that the human capital supply for economic development was highly qualified.

Although some classifications of Asian states have characterized them as one type—variously termed "Asian capitalism," "étatism," or "state-led capitalism"—based on the influence of the developmental state (Amable, 2003; Boyer, 2005; Whitley, 2006), we argue that a unitary treat-ment of Asian capitalism overlooks the diversity of state models in Asia. It also fails to account for dynamic trajectories as Asian countries are integrated into the global economy through trade, foreign direct investment, and migration. Our own classification recognizes that countries that previously followed the developmental state model as well as its negative counterpart, the preda-tory state model (Evans, 1995), have each undergone institutional change, resulting in dynamic trajectories. Predatory states are dominated by oligarchic groups that seek to appropriate rent through privileged access to exclusive economic and political resources. Instead of pursuing the national interest and generalized economic advancement, predatory states exploit resources to advance the vested interests of the oligarchy. We include three out of the four typologies of the state—the regulatory, developmental, and predatory states—in type-casting states in Asia. We list these classifications in Table 2.1, with the caveat that in reality many individual countries will fit the mold only partially. Thus, for example, whilst we classify Hong Kong, Singapore, and South Korea as regulatory states, Singapore and South Korea arguably retain developmental state characteristics (Carney & Witt, 2014). We find that no Asian state quite fulfills the typology of the welfare state. Although Japan has adopted some characteristics of the welfare state, particularly when it comes to dealing with an aging population, we argue that it is overall a regulatory state with decentralized industrial relations and a low level of state intervention onto the growing inequality and dualism in the labor market (Song, 2014). Thus, we selectively apply Carney and Witt's (2014: 546–550) classification of Asian countries, in which they characterized Asian countries into four state typologies of regulatory, welfare, developmental, and predatory. We have further added South Asian and Middle Eastern countries in our three-state typology.

Most theorizations of the role of the state in understanding typologies of economic governance directly apply models of the state to models of capitalism (Hancké et al., 2007; Schmidt, 2009), or to business systems (Carney & Witt, 2014; Walter & Zhang, 2011; Whitley, 1998) to explain variations in the latter. As mentioned above, we believe that doing so omits a crucial context in which states today operate—that of the global institutional and economic environment—which acts to variously enable, constrain, and modify state influence on economic practice. Empirical examination of states in Southeast Asia, for example, has questioned the ability of states in this region to exert control over internal and sectarian conflict, as well as retain independence in the face of pressures from supranational institutions, global financial markets, and trade and foreign investment (Beeson, 2003; Fritzen, 2007). We turn to a discussion of global pressures constraining and enabling nation states next.

Table 2.1 Typologies of Asian states

Model of state	External dependence	State influence	Relevant countries	HRM outcomes		
				Flexibility	Voice	Inequality
Regulatory	High external dependence	Liberalizing	Hong Kong, Singapore, Taiwan, Korea	Low	High	Low to medium
	Low external dependence	Enabling	Japan			
Developmental	High external dependence	Influencing	Malaysia, Thailand	Medium	Low to medium	Medium to high
	Low external dependence	Enabling	China			
Predatory	High external dependence	Influencing	Indonesia, Bangladesh, Qatar, UAE	Low	Low	High
	Medium external dependence	Exploiting	Vietnam, Philippines, Laos, Pakistan, Sri Lanka, Myanmar			

Source: compiled by the authors based on Carney and Witt's classification (2014: 546–550).

Global institutional and organizational pressures

The global context that conditions state influence on HRM includes pressures from supra-national institutions, norms and standards governing global value chains, and pressures from global financial interests.

Supranational institutions

International organizations such as the International Labour Organization (ILO) seek to directly influence national regulatory frameworks governing issues ranging from hours worked to freedom of association. While developed countries such as the USA often exempt themselves from ratifying international conventions, developing countries in Asia are more susceptible to international norms, especially if they are linked to aid or financing as in the case of loans from the World Bank or the International Monetary Fund. Bilateral and multilateral trade agreements increasingly embody provisions for protecting the wages and bargaining rights of workers in the least developed countries, often triggered through political pressure from organized labor in developed countries that are signatory to the agreements (Abrami, 2003). Trade with members of the European Union entails similar provisions for social responsibility and labor protection (Compa, 1993). Another form of supranational institutional pressure arises from international framework agreements—labor agreements covering more than one national jurisdiction and involving one or more national and/or international trade unions (Hammer, 2005). Increasingly, international framework agreements target the length of the global supply chain. Where government capacity or willingness to monitor and enforce labor standards on corporations is lacking, these supranational institutions can act as incentives for governments and social actors to modify existing practice (Gereffi, Humphrey, & Sturgeon, 2005).

Pressures from global value chains

The vertical disintegration of transnational enterprises has led to the creation of international production networks (Gereffi et al., 2005). The global value chain perspective to economic governance has argued that inter-firm relationships between buyers and suppliers and the quality of jobs are determined by the amount of value added by each firm participating in the global supply network (Gereffi, Humphrey, & Kaplinsky, 2001). The literature on dependent development has pointed out that countries such as Bangladesh, Cambodia, and Vietnam lack the ability to invest in human capital and develop into high-wage welfare economies due to their dependence on foreign investment and their lack of technological capacity. On the other hand, many other Asian countries today have given rise to their own multinational corporations and are large investors in Asia and elsewhere, at the same time as being recipients of FDI themselves. China, for example, is Africa's second largest trading partner since 2007 after the USA, and the fourth largest investor (Romei, 2015) in the continent.

An emergent stream of research in employment relations (Lakhani et al., 2013) and HRM (Edwards, Tregaskis, Levesque, McDonnell, & Quintanilla, 2013) seeks to re-frame the employment relationship as a relationship that is not only embedded in national institutions and organizations but also in global production systems and organizational relationships. Although no one way of measuring global value chains can predict outcomes for HRM, a significant distinction can be made between buyer-driven and supplier-driven global value chains (Gereffi et al., 2005). In the former, typically found in the garment and agricultural supply chains, buyers control design, pricing, and access to markets; hence, job quality in supplier firms, typically engaged in labor-intensive and low value-added work, is relatively low. In the latter, character-istic of supply chains in electronics and auto industries, brand owners transfer parts manufac-turing technologies to developing country suppliers, resulting in relatively high training and development of workers in these firms. A further distinction can be made based on the nature of inter-firm relationships, distinguishing between relational, networked, and hierarchical value chains (e.g., Lakhani et al., 2013). Amongst these, hierarchical value chains arguably offer the least discretion for "upstream" suppliers. The extent to which lead firms can influence suppliers' HRM practices is an important question. In a typical buyer-driven production chain such as garments, global buyers hold the power to ensure higher levels of protection for workers and professional and merit-based HR practices, but may not always act on this power to do good (Locke, Amengual, & Mangla, 2009).

Global financial interests

The privatization and liberalization of assets that ensued after the Asian financial crisis of 1997 demonstrates that global financial interests can affect state policy toward labor, entrepreneurship, and investments in skills development (Crouch, 2011; Kim & Kim, 2003). In large Asian coun-tries such as China and India, provincial governments have sought to attract foreign capital in key development projects or export processing zones by reducing or exempting taxes and/or exempt-ing firms from abiding by national labor codes (Xu, 2011). Again, it is important to note that the presence of global financial interests in a country does not result in a uniform influence on HRM, whether positive or negative. In South Korea (hereafter Korea for brevity), for example, foreign ownership eventually led to foreign management of key companies in the financial and manufac-turing sectors, and the HRM policies in these companies were received favorably by professional women who saw these policies as more equitable and family friendly (Lee & Rowley, 2008; Rowley & Bae, 2002). As pointed out in the case of Chinese and Indian provincial governments, it is often the response from local governments and policy makers to global financial interests that can have an enduring impact on firm level HRM (Zhu, Warner, & Rowley, 2007).

State influence on HRM

We draw from extant work that has theorized state influence on economic governance from the varieties of capitalism and comparative business systems tradition to arrive at typologies of state influence on HRM. While the comparative capitalism literature has not explicitly addressed HRM, we believe the typologies of state roles developed by this literature provide a theoretical foundation for explaining state action affecting HRM specified by Martínez-Lucio and Stuart (2011): supporting networks, establishing standards, and using targets and objectives.

The original varieties of capitalism framework focused on the firm as the central actor in economic coordination and governance, conspicuously leaving out the state (Hall & Gingerich, 2009; Hall & Soskice, 2001; Hall & Thelen, 2009). Key developments in this vein of scholarship in later years have sought to amend this by expositing the role of the state in economic govern-ance (Hancké et al., 2007; Martin & Thelen, 2007; Schmidt, 2009; Walter & Zhang, 2011). Amongst these, we draw on Schmidt's (2009) typology of *enabling, liberal,* and *influencing* to describe state influences on HRM in Asia for two reasons. First, Schmidt's typology refers directly to modes of state action as opposed to other typologies that refer to models of economic governance resulting from the types of relationships that are formed between the state and eco-nomic actors, such as Hancké et al. (2007) and Walter and Zhang's (2011). A further advantage of Schmidt's (2009) typology is that because it describes what states *do* instead of providing static models, it adds dynamism to the analysis. Schmidt (2009) typologized state action based on whether states took unilateral action (ranging from *state action* to *market action*) or whether they employed strategies to influence market actors. She distinguished between two styles of state influence on market actors: action *with* market actors (*faire avec*) and having market actors act (*faire faire*). Using these criteria, Schmidt (2009) proposed three ideal typical state roles with respect to market actors, the *enabling state*, which collaborates with market actors, the *liberal state*, which provides minimum standards through regulation but otherwise leaves market actors to coordinate action through markets, and the *influencing state*, which alternates between guiding market actors and, at times, intervening directly. We add a fourth type to Schmidt's (2009) typology of state action. In economies where the state extracts resources from market actors and selects winners based on preferential ties and personalized exchange, we classify the influence type as *exploiting*. While *predatory* states are more likely to engage in *exploiting* behavior, we do not advocate a one-to-one correspondence between models of the state and state influence on HRM. We note, for example, the possibility that developmental states can at times engage in *enabling* as well as *exploiting* behaviors depending on political currents and influence from the global environment. Our model of state influence on HRM is depicted in Figure 2.2. A description of each of the roles that states can take in HRM is provided below.

Enabling. Enabling refers to state influences in constructing and supporting new and existing relational networks amongst employers and unions within the country in question, as well as between domestic and external actors such as investors and trading partners. The state may define the "supply" of HRM by influencing organizational membership via citizenship and

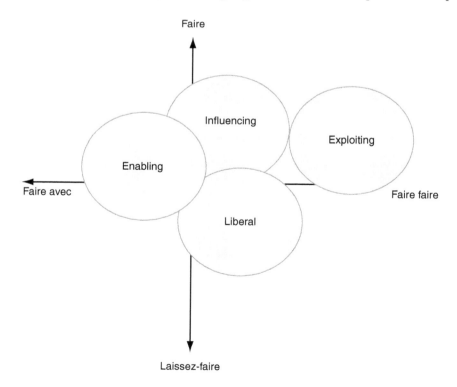

Figure 2.2 State influence on HRM

Source: adapted from Schmidt (2009: 526), Figure 1.

migration programs, setting minimum labor and wage standards, regulating the treatment of workers in the workplace via anti-discrimination and harassment laws, and setting limits to firms' exercise of flexibility through legal boundaries set on firing and downsizing. Targets and objectives set by the enabling state emphasize social protection and societal equity rather than firm performance targets; for example, the enabling state may set affirmative action quotas aimed at the integration of minority groups.

Liberal. The *liberal* state adopts a relatively laissez-faire disposition to economic actors and their networks, deferring to the market as the primary coordination mechanism. The state is likely to set minimum standards of compliance rather than extensive guidelines; however, the logic of job creation is likely to overshadow and problematize these standards. Minimum wage laws thus are likely to be controversial. Regulation is seen as an impediment to flexible HRM rather than an enabler; for erstwhile developmental states enacting the liberal mode, deregulation—of investment, corporate restructuring, and hiring and firing—is the preferred norm. The liberal state is likely to use targets and objectives in liberalizing the economy and HRM in order to integrate itself into the global economy via increased FDI.

Influencing. The *influencing* state is active across all spheres of activity that affect HRM. It is likely to take an active stance in charting the course of economic development, especially in times of economic downturn or crisis. The state is likely to host and require the presence of market actors in tripartite committees, as well as to use both regulatory methods and incentives in order to achieve objectives. Influencing states are likely to identify and seek to bridge gaps in skills development by providing direct training or guiding curricula development in educational institutions. They are likely to require sacrifices from the workforce in voice and remuneration in exchange for paternalistic welfare provision by large corporations.

Exploiting. Exploiting refers to state action toward HRM that regards it primarily as a means of resource extraction rather than of resource development. These states privilege economic actors that reinforce their regime's power base; hence, they are likely to overlook or even participate in the appropriation of human resources by their corporate partners. States in transitional economies are likely to adopt such an influencing mode to take advantage of and control weak relational ties amongst market actors and compensate for losses in state ownership. States that heavily depend on a particular sector for revenue—such as oil producing states in the Middle East—are likely to exploit human resources in other sectors to afford preferential treatment of workers in the revenue-generating sector. Exploiting states rarely seek to establish common standards or guide behavior through targets and objectives; instead, they seek compliance by directly rewarding or sanctioning individual behaviors.

Outcomes

The strategic HRM literature has maintained a relatively narrow focus in outcomes of interest, such as the existence of indicators of high performance work systems (Marler, 2012), or meritocratic systems of pay (Bartlett & Ghoshal, 1989; Kaufman, 2010). Similarly, comparative IR literatures focusing on Asia have been concerned with firm-level outcomes, such as the pursuit of numerical or functional flexibility (Kuruvilla & Erickson, 2002). But firm-level outcomes focusing on specific HR practices are inadequate in understanding the long-term outcomes resulting from formal and informal state policy, politics, and polity (Schmidt, 2009). In addition to whether state action toward HRM is likely to produce HRM styles favoring workers or employers, we focus on two mid-level outcomes: equality and voice.

HRM style. Whether HRM systems are employee-centered or centered on managerial prerogatives is not only important for firms and their employees, but from the perspective of

29

outcomes of state influence on HRM, it is a societally relevant outcome. It is widely acknow-ledged that employee-centered HRM, all else being equal, provides longevity in employment thereby curtailing the need for public welfare provision, whereas HRM centered on managerial prerogatives affords flexibility, which is essential for growth and economic adjustment (Boxall & Purcell, 2000). Therefore, assessing whether HRM in a particular country is employee or management centered is an outcome of significant interest.

Inequality. State influence on HRM—via policies on income distribution, taxation, skills development, as well as via legislation that may ban or, on the contrary, exacerbate discrimina-tion—can affect whether people management works to equalize or enlarge inequality. We are interested in both economic inequality as measured by, for example, wage disparities, as well as social inequality—that is, whether significant differences can be found across gender, race, and ethnicity in terms of opportunities.

Voice. In the HRM literature, there has been a tension between conceptualizing "voice" as a right versus understanding it as a management imperative based on the utility of workers' participation in improving managerial decisions and processes (Wilkinson, Donaghey, Dundon, & Freeman, 2014). We agree with numerous employment relations scholars, who have pointed to the shortcoming of a business case for voice (e.g., Budd, 2004). We therefore focus on workers' rights to freedom of association and collective bargaining.

Measurements

We draw on existing categorizations and measures to classify Asian states, to determine the extent to which a country is impacted by globalization, and to assess the outcomes of state influ-ence on HRM.

Models of the state

As discussed earlier, we modified Carney and Witt's (2014) classification of East Asian and Southeast Asian states into four typologies in two ways. First, we removed the "welfare state" as a typology as we did not find enough empirical evidence for the existence of welfare states in Asia. Second, we added select South Asian and Middle Eastern countries to Carney and Witt's (2014) classification to be consistent with the geographic coverage of this handbook (see Table 2.1).

External dependence

We measured external dependence using three indicators from the World Economic Forum (WEF)'s Global Competitive Index (GCI) (Schwab, 2014–2015), as well as a measure of the share of FDI in total GDP (see Table 2.2). Amongst GCI indicators, we chose the "prevalence of foreign ownership," which measures the salience of foreign-owned enterprises in the national business system (1 = extremely rare; 7 = highly prevalent). The indicator "FDI and technology transfer" measures the extent to which FDI contributes to transferring new technology to the host country. "Control of international distribution" assesses the extent to which domestic companies control international distribution and marketing of goods in the host country. Thus, the higher score on this indicator reflects a lower level of external dependence of the national business system on foreign capital. FDI share in GDP was cited from each country's central bank or bureau of statistics.

Table 2.2 External dependence of the national business system

	Foreign ownership[1]	FDI & technology transfer[2]	Control of international[1] distribution[3]	FDI share in GDP (%)
East Asia				
China	4.532	4.469	4.489	16
Japan	5.307	4.733	5.579	3.50
Korea	4.166	4.581	4.538	10.80
Taiwan	5.219	4.824	4.541	13.00
Southeast Asia				
Bangladesh	3.740	3.940	3.553	5.00
Indonesia	4.570	4.911	4.407	N/A
Malaysia	5.261	5.519	5.179	53.80
Philippines	4.910	5.071	4.361	11.90
Singapore	6.129	5.944	4.133	22.00
Thailand	4.546	5.180	4.381	55.00
Vietnam	4.094	4.235	3.701	N/A
South Asia				
Cambodia	4.699	4.773	3.424	0.38
India	4.241	4.223	4.249	1.30
Pakistan	3.824	4.283	3.845	0.10
Nepal	3.329	3.730	3.266	0.005
Sri Lanka	4.809	4.763	4.637	1.00
Middle East				
Iran	2.194	3.763	4.354	N/A
Jordan	4.648	5.010	4.463	N/A
Lebanon	3.876	3.360	4.672	6.40
Oman	4.459	4.767	4.640	2.04
Qatar	4.781	5.598	3.845	N/A
Saudi Arabia	4.050	5.372	4.857	1.50
UAE	5.658	5.840	5.345	N/A

Source: Global Competitive Index 2014–2015, published by World Economic Forum.

Notes
1 1 = extremely rare; 7 = highly prevalent
2 1 = not at all; 7 = to a great extent—FDI is a key source of new technology
3 1 = not at all—they take place through foreign companies; 7 = to a great extent—they are primarily owned and controlled by domestic companies

Outcome measures

HRM style. In order to measure HRM styles in terms of flexibility, we used several measures of the GCI. The GCI estimates a factor of the country's labor market efficiency (pillar 7) by means of ten indicators. Amongst them, we chose the following three indicators:

1   Flexibility of wage determination (In your country, how are wages generally set? 1 = by a centralized bargaining process; 7 = by each individual company).
2   Hiring and firing practices (How would you characterize the hiring and firing of workers? 1 = heavily impeded by regulations; 7 = extremely flexible).

3   Pay and productivity (In your country, to what extent is pay related to worker productivity?)

Social inequality. In order to measure social inequality of each country, we focused on gender inequality using the Global Gender Gap Index 2014 (Schwab, 2014). We focused on the remuneration gap among other measures included in the sub-index of Economic Participation and Opportunity. The remuneration gap is captured by combining a subjective indicator gathered through the World Economic Forum's Executive Opinion Survey and an objective indicator of the ratio of female-to-male earned income.

Economic inequality. The Gini coefficient is a widely used measure of economic inequality that captures the extent to which the distribution of income amongst individuals or households within an economy deviates from a perfectly equal distribution (coefficient = zero).[1]

Voice. The Freedom in the World survey measures freedom according to two broad categories: political rights and civil liberties. Amongst four subcategories to evaluate civil liberties, we used "associational and organizational rights" to measure voice. Countries were rated on a zero to four scale on each of the following questions, with zero representing the smallest degree and four the greatest degree of freedom.

1   Is there freedom of assembly, demonstration, and open public discussion?
2   Is there freedom for non-governmental organizations?
3   Are there free trade unions and peasant organizations or the equivalent, and is there effective collective bargaining? Are there free professional and other private organizations?

Table 2.3 displays all three of outcomes of state influence on HRM, along with the sources of data.

Developmental states in Asia

The developmental state is characterized by a commitment to growth, productivity, competitiveness, and privatization of property and market at the expense of social equality and welfare (Yeung, 2014). Government effectiveness is often used as a measure to distinguish development states from the predatory state model. Taiwan, Korea, and Japan until the 1980s were governed by developmental states; contemporary Malaysia, Indonesia, and Chinese states fall under this category.

1 Developmental states with relatively high external dependence: influencing

Malaysia and Thailand have adopted low-wage manufacturing and coercive legislation suppressing labor in an effort to boost export-oriented industrialization and become attractive destinations for FDI (Nolan, 2002). However, in recent years economic growth has increased average wage levels, labor unrest, and the pressure to adhere to global labor standards. Thus, the state seeks to move the economy up the value chain by promoting investment in higher value-added manufacturing and service sectors, and channeling FDI into economic activities that can provide high-skilled employment opportunities. For example, The Malaysian Investment Development Authority (MIDA) reviews all the foreign and domestic investment projects in terms of the extent to which they align with the state's Third Industrial Master Plan (2006–2020).

States have increased investments in occupational education and training for skilled workers, the shortage of which is often cited as an impediment to economic growth (Debrah, McGovern,

Table 2.3 Outcomes of state influence

	Inequality		HRM style			Voice
	Gender equality (survey[1]/ratio[2]/ rank)	Economic inequality (year)	Hiring/firing practices[3]	Wage determination[4]	Performance-based pay[5]	Associational right[6]
East Asia						
China	4.42/0.63/77	37(2011)	4.065	4.840	4.751	3
Japan	4.77/0.68/53	32.1(2008)	2.972	5.859	4.809	11
Korea	3.56/0.51/125	31.1(2011)	3.193	5.718	4.392	11
Taiwan	N/A	34.2(2011)	4.595	5.496	5.081	10
Southeast Asia						
Bangladesh	3.97/0.57/105	32.1(2010)	4.654	4.835	3.524	6
Indonesia	4.80/0.69/51	38.1(2011)	4.382	4.404	4.489	8
Malaysia	5.67/0.81/5	46.2(2009)	2.212	5.479	5.420	6
Philippines	5.50/0.79/9	44.8(2009)	3.173	4.827	4.506	8
Singapore	5.50/0.79/10	46.3(2013)	5.921	5.968	5.340	4
Thailand	5.67/0.81/4	39.4(2010)	4.486	4.278	4.195	4
Vietnam	4.41/0.63/79	35.6(2012)	4.466	5.142	4.561	1
South Asia						
Cambodia	4.88/0.7/44	41.9(2008)	4.243	4.762	4.341	3
India	3.90/0.56/109	36.8(2004)	3.694	4.430	3.957	11
Pakistan	3.87/0.55/111	29.6(2011)	4.211	4.620	3.802	7
Nepal	4.34/0.62/84	32.8(2010)	3.452	4.364	3.128	6
Sri Lanka	5.49/0.78/11	49.0(2010)	3.500	5.384	4.380	6
Middle East						
Iran	4.13/0.59/98	44.5(2006)	3.615	3.760	3.905	1
Jordan	4.44/0.63/66	39.7(2007)	3.524	4.993	4.279	4
Lebanon	4.03/0.58/104	N/A	4.189	5.302	4.009	7
Oman	5.18/0.74/21	N/A	4.369	5.602	3.948	3
Qatar	5.67/0.81/3	N/A	4.852	6.006	5.370	2
Saudi Arabia	3.92/0.56/108	N/A	4.603	5.772	4.545	0
UAE	5.51/0.79/7	N/A	4.703	6.140	5.223	2

Source: combined from Executive Opinion Survey 2014, Global Gender Gap Report 2014, and Global Competitiveness Index 2014–2015 (published by World Economic forum), and Freedom in the World 2013 Survey (published by Freedom House).

Notes

1 Wage equality between women and men for similar work from World Economic Forum, Executive Opinion Survey (EOS), 2014 (1 = not at all—significantly below those of men; 7 = fully—equal to those of men) from the Global Gender Gap Report, World Economic Forum.

2 Ratio of estimated female-to-male earned income from the Global Gender Gap Report, World Economic Forum.

3 Ease of hiring/firing practices: 1 = impeded by regulations, 7 = flexibly determined by employer from the Global Competiveness Index, World Economic Forum.

4 Centrality of wage determination: 1 = by a centralized bargaining process; 7 = by each individual company from the Global Competiveness Index, World Economic Forum.

5 The extent to which pay is related to worker productivity: 1~7(best) from the Global Competiveness Index, World Economic Forum.

6 The Freedom in the World survey, 0 = the smallest degree, 12 = the greatest degree of freedom.

& Budhwar, 2000). For instance, the Thai government enacted the 'Skill Development Promotion Act' in 2002 to upgrade skills for its own workforce and to reserve certain occupations for the Thai labor force in response to multinational firms' hiring of expatriates (Lauridsen, 2004). However, governments are indifferent to the use of irregular migrant workers that reduces labor costs in low-skilled jobs. Both Thailand and Malaysia engage in active coordination with neighboring countries such as Burma, Laos, and Cambodia to facilitate the migration process. According to the United Nations (UN) estimation in 2013, Thailand (3.7 million), and Malaysia (2.4 million) had the highest number of international migrant residents in Southeast Asia (UNDESA, 2013).

2 Developmental states with low external dependence: enabling

China maintains the characteristics of an authoritarian developmental state which has kept unions and industrial conflict under strict control. However, as Chinese firms expand into overseas markets and integrate into global supply chains, the role of the state is changing from controlling or directing home-grown MNEs to enabling and leveraging their growth in global markets. The Chinese state today promotes "Go Global" initiatives to encourage Chinese companies to invest overseas and mobilizes state-owned banks to support the construction of regional production networks by acquiring foreign firms. Replicating Japan's overseas development aid that facilitated Japanese MNEs to engage in cross-border cooperations in Southeast Asia (Chun et al., 2010; Wade, 1996; Furuoka, 2002), China focuses its foreign investment on extractive industries in Africa. As a result, since 2014, China's outward FDI, which rose 14.1 percent from the previous year to $102.9 billion, has overtaken its inward FDI, which increased by 1.7 percent to $119.6 billion (UNCTAD, 2015).

HRM outcomes in developmental states

HRM style. The HRM style of Malaysia and Thailand shows high variability along the three sub-dimensions studied here, and is distinct from that of earlier developmental states, which were characterized by long-term employment guarantees and seniority-based wages. This mixed, inconsistent picture appears to reflect the ongoing tensions and conflicting interests amongst the state, MNEs, and the growing civil society (Bhopal & Rowley, 2002). It can also be attributed to an ambiguity in the state's development strategy which on the one hand pursues industrial upgrading based on functional flexibility, while still relying on labor-intensive manufacturing and immigrant workers from neighboring predatory states (Crinis & Parasuraman, 2016; Wad, 2012).

Voice. Compared to HRM under predatory states, countries with developmental states rate higher on the Freedom House associational and organizational rights index (Freedom House, 2015), indicating weak-to-moderate levels of associational rights (e.g., Malaysia: 6, Thailand: 4). Countries with relatively high reliance on developmental aid, trade, and FDI are under pressure to improve their labor conditions. Thus, Thailand adopted the Labor Protection Act in 1998 to comply with International Labour Organization (ILO) standards and amended it in 2008 to strengthen protection and benefits for contract laborers. However, these countries have had a poor enforcement record of labor rights. Government controls strongly discourage strikes and an independent labor movement, promoting managerial unilateralism. These constraints on collective voice are officially justified in terms of attracting new foreign investments and creating employment opportunities (Bhopal & Rowley, 2002; Kumar, Martínez Lucio & Rose, 2013). Hence, developmental states with high external dependence combine predatory elements in their policies toward labor.

Inequality. While HRM policies prevalent in earlier developmental states contributed significantly to societal equity, late developmental states preside over growing income inequality. Commentators attribute the income inequality to the increased use of contract and migrant labor in low-skilled jobs, which still make up three-quarters of all jobs in Malaysia (Gil Sander, Blancas Mendivil, & Westra, 2015). Likewise, China is experiencing a rapid rise in income inequality due to economic growth favoring urban, coastal areas over rural, inland regions. According to a recent study, China's Gini coefficient for family income is around 0.55, far surpassing that of regulatory states in this study (Xie & Zhou, 2014). Massive internal migration has created a large group of rural migrants, who suffer from low wages and discrimination and abuse. The sub-standard living conditions of migrant workers were brought into sharp focus as migrant workers have engaged in collective action, posing a threat to social and political stability. Despite limited freedom of association, contract migrant workers staged most of the labor protests in Malaysia over the past ten years (Crinis & Parasuraman, 2016). Similarly, large strikes by internal migrant workers have become increasingly common in the industrialized areas of China such as Guangdong, Shanxi, and Zhejiang. In order to tackle inequality, these states continuously amend labor laws and guidelines, introduce redistributive tax reforms, and increase the national minimum wage, often generating tensions with their strategies for economic growth.

Regulatory states in Asia

Unlike the regulatory states of liberal market economies, regulatory states in Asia emerged from the developmental state model. The once-admired role of the state bureaucracy in national development is now often cited in these same countries as a liability for domestic MNEs to operate in a globalized market (O'Riain, 2004). As local firms once nurtured by developmental states grew into MNEs, their interests often align more closely with those of international partners than with the state (Wong, 2004). Pressure from domestic MNEs, international capital, and globalized labor impels regulatory states to adapt their role, liberalizing in order to attract international investment or enabling a knowledge-based economy. Asian regulatory states are still likely to play a more active role in promoting economic growth and restructuring to benefit national agendas than are Anglo-Saxon regulatory states. Japan, Taiwan, Singapore, and Korea exhibit characteristics of this model.

1 Regulatory states with high external dependence: liberalizing

Such states as Korea and Taiwan have at least formally departed from developmental state policies, fostering a business-friendly environment by liberalizing the labor market, while setting minimum standards for labor protection (Fields, 2012). While these countries are relatively more independent of FDI, as is manifest in the lower level of total inbound stock of FDI as a percentage of GDP (10.8 percent for Korea and 13 percent Taiwan respectively) compared to those of developmental states (e.g., 53.8 percent and 55 percent for Malaysia and Thailand, respectively) (Schwab, 2014–2015), their national economies remain heavily reliant on export-oriented industries. Domestic MNEs have subsumed the role, previously played by the state, of facilitating industrial restructuring by retraining employees in declining industries.

2 Regulatory state with low external dependence: enabling

Compared to other regulatory states in Asia, the Japanese economy has been more resilient to external shocks owing to its relatively low external dependence (Kawai & Takagi, 2011). Japan's stock of FDI as a percentage of gross domestic product (GDP) stood at 3.5 percent at the end of 2013, compared with 32.1 percent on average for all OECD member countries (OECD, 2015a). The Japanese state has taken on a more active role as an enabler by adopting monetary easing and flexible fiscal policies, as well as growth strategies focused on structural reform. A key example of the state's enabling influence on HRM is manifest in its approach to alleviating labor shortage. A new legislation was passed in 2013 extending the retirement age from sixty to sixty-five. The government has repeatedly sought to broaden employment options for women, announcing it as a policy priority in 2013. Moreover, regulatory reform was undertaken to attract more skilled labor from abroad under fixed-term labor contracts. Originally intended as a skills-transfer program for workers from developing countries, the foreign Technical Intern and Trainee Program (TITP) is being used to address immediate labor shortages in specific sectors such as construction. Additionally, there is a new trend in Japanese foreign aid policy, which puts more emphasis on developing human capital—education and health care—rather than on physical capital, such as infrastructure construction.

HRM outcomes in regulatory states

HRM style. Regulatory states in East Asia still share such elements of HRM styles as a relatively egalitarian pay system, seniority-based rewards, and long-term job security (Zhu, Zhang, & Shen, 2012). But these mutually constitutive elements of HRM style developed in the era of the developmental state were blamed for producing inflexibility in the labor market, and reforms have sought to increase flexibility. In particular, the 1997 financial crisis questioned the effectiveness of legacy HRM systems and justified the call for a more meritocratic HRM (Bae, Chen, & Rowley, 2011; Yang & Rowley, 2008). In Japan, the state sorted out a complex web of labor regulations to enable companies to easily deploy non-standard workers. As a result, the proportion of non-standard employees including temporary, part-time, and contract workers has significantly increased from 15 percent of the labor force in 1984 to 37 percent in 2015 (Statistics Japan, 2016). In Korea, the post-crisis bailout program resulted in legal changes that did away with lifetime employment and enabled firms to adopt flexible dismissal practices. "New" HRM practices promoted by employers' federations in Korea rapidly expanded performance-based remuneration and promoted worker mobility and outsourcing across firms (Rowley & Bae, 2004).

Nevertheless, institutional inertia combined with vested political interests act as barriers to reform. Reforms, especially in Japan, focused on non-regular workers, who lack representation in the industrial relations system, while regular workers still maintain a high level of employment protection (Song, 2014). Most corporations still represent hierarchies with redundant functions and excessive staffing. This difficulty in transforming traditional HRM practices explains why these countries' labor-market flexibility index remains low amongst OECD countries. Japan and Korea score 2.972 and 3.193 respectively on the ease of hiring and firing on a scale from 1 to 7 (where 1 = impeded by regulations, 7 = flexibly determined by employer) (Schwab, 2014–2015).

Voice. Regulatory states seek to enlist labor's cooperation rather than exclude them from key institutional processes. Especially after the economic crisis of 1997, the states have attempted to establish peak-level consultative bodies in order to ensure the smooth implementation of reforms, as seen in South Korea's efforts to establish a tripartite economic planning and wage policy body. These bodies were thought to enable wage restraint and ensure industrial peace. As a result, countries with regulatory states score higher on associational rights in the Freedom in the World 2015 index (e.g., South Korea: 11 and Taiwan: 10) compared to developmental states (Freedom House, 2015).

However, declining union density and the individualization of employment relations is continuously eroding collective channels for the voice of workers in these countries, and states have tended to reinforce such trends in their efforts to promote a business-friendly environment. For instance, in Korea, the 2010 revision of the Trade Union and Labor Relations Act restricted the number of full-time labor union officials and made it possible for employers to exclude them from the payroll. Although labor unions still play a role in the annual determination of wage scales, their social and political influence is rapidly diminishing and other avenues for employee voice remain rare (Barnes, 2007).

Inequality. While the former "Newly Industrialized Countries" have been renowned for relatively egalitarian societies, inequality has grown over recent decades. The favoring of export-oriented conglomerates during the developmental era engendered a twofold labor market. While in previous years sustained economic growth offset the growing polarization of the labor market, economic recession and labor market reforms have exacerbated the disparity between regular and irregular workers (Song, 2014). Widening gaps in wages and opportunities for skills development became evident amongst non-standard and standard employees, amongst adult men, women, and youth, as well as between local and foreign migrant workers. In Korea, there were approximately 6.59 million non-regular workers, comprising approximately 25.3 percent of the total workforce as of March 2014 (Statistics Korea, 2011). Non-regular workers performing comparable work to regular workers received approximately 57 percent of their wages (Statistics Korea, 2011).

Predatory states in Asia

Predatory states are characterized by the hijacking of the government apparatus by a political and economic oligarchy, a lack of democratic checks and balances, and underdeveloped market competition that allows crony networks to appropriate rents at the expense of society at large (Robinson, 1999; Hutchison, 2016). Several South and Southeast Asian counties such as India, Indonesia, the Philippines, Laos, and Vietnam, and most Middle Eastern countries fall into this category. Nevertheless, there is considerable variation in terms of political regimes and corporate governance structure (Carney & Witt, 2014). In states under Community Party control, such as China, Vietnam, and Laos, state ownership is prevalent, whereas patrimonial oligarchy is more salient in Indonesia and the Philippines (Hutchison, 2012). In India, there is regional variation: state governments such as Gujarat can be categorized as developmental in nature, whereas Kerala exhibits traits of a welfare state (Sinha, 2005).

Under predatory states, lack of institutionalized trust prompts economic actors to secede from the formal economy, turning to informal exchange. Corruption is prevalent as a result of "crony capitalism" (Roberts, 2010). Predatory states' influence on HRM can be typologized as a mix of *Influencing* and *Exploiting*, depending on the extent to which they are exposed to global pressures.

1 Predatory states under medium-level external dependence: exploiting

Predatory states that have relatively low external dependence are characterized by rent seeking in state-owned sectors as well as reliance on out-migration of the workforce. State-owned enterprises (SOEs) function as pillars of the economy in countries like Vietnam, Laos, and Pakistan. For instance, SOEs in Vietnam account for approximately 40 percent of the country's total GDP. In Pakistan, SOEs represent one-third of the total stock market capitalization and retain a monopoly in key sectors like manufacturing, energy, and public services. The state provides

SOEs with favorable operating conditions including preferred access to credit, land use, licenses, and market access. Predatory states exert direct influence on HRM in SOEs by dictating personnel appointments and wage scales (Clarke et al., 2007). In Vietnam, the Communist Party's "Organizational Department/Committee" controls a wide range of official posts in state enterprises, from the strategic down to the operational (Warner, 2013). The state also maintains its influence on employment relations in the private sector by monitoring pay rates and industrial conflict.

Over-reliance on the inflow of remittances discourages states from investing in new industries and infrastructure. In Sri Lanka and the Philippines, remittances amount to over 50 percent and 38 percent of export revenues, respectively. In India, the flow of remittances is larger than earnings from software services exports. Remittances in Bangladesh were equivalent to 84 percent of the country's garment exports. For Southeast Asia as a whole, remittance inflows increased from $17 billion in 2000 to approximately $80 billion in 2010. Remittances are mainly used to fund things like education and health care, which the state fails to provide. Although remittances fuel domestic consumption, they arguably dampen public spending and lead to currency appreciation. The Philippine government's spending on infrastructure and equipment, for example, has consistently declined since the 1970s, and remains well below that of other Southeast Asian countries (Ablaza et al., 2014).

2 Predatory states under high external dependence: influencing

Predatory states with relatively high external dependence place more emphasis on attracting FDI as a means of economic growth than on skills development. These include Malaysia, Thailand, Qatar, the United Arab Emirates (UAE), and Bangladesh. Accordingly, government policies and legislative aim to attract and retain corporations by ensuring labor is abundant at low cost.

The reliance in oil producing countries of the Gulf on inexpensive foreign labor has created an enduring dual labor market in these countries (Doeringer & Piore, 1973; Dickens & Lang, 1985). Over time, private sector employers, where up to 99 percent of the workforce comprises of foreign workers (Al-Waqfi & Forstenlechner, 2013), and where ownership is often foreign, have developed staffing and management practices that reinforce dependence on foreign workers. The low wages, insecurity, and competitive working conditions in the private sector discourages locals from seeking employment there; many indicate preferring to be unemployed rather than seek work in these sectors (Al-Waqfi & Forstenlechner, 2013; Shaban, Assaad, & Al Qudsi, 1995).

HRM outcomes in predatory states

HRM style. Familistic hierarchical control, based on the reciprocal exchange of obligations, dominates HRM in countries with predatory states. This kind of personalized, informal HRM style often spawns low productivity and inflexibility, confirmed by the relatively low scores for such countries as the Philippines (3.4) and Vietnam (3.9) on the Flexibility in Hiring and Firing Practice index (Schwab, 2014–2015). In countries controlled by the Communist Party, remnants of hierarchical and personalized relationships have transferred over to private companies from the Party and SOEs. For instance, in Vietnam, "Mentor–Protégé" relationships are common in the Communist Party and this relationship also influences governance in SOEs. The lack of institutionalized trust leads to high levels of centralization and low delegation in the workplace (Truong & Quang, 2007).

Failed industrialization has led to excessive reliance on out-migration of citizens and their remittances in lieu of proper investment in skills development. States in the Philippines and Sri Lanka have traditionally placed emphasis on sending workers overseas for human resource development (Tyner, 2009; Kaye, 2010). In 2009, in Sri Lanka, which has the highest literacy in South Asia, 30 percent of people with a tertiary education emigrated abroad (Wahab, Ahmed, & Mahmood, 2013). Skilled female workers, who are often denied equal opportunities for high-skill jobs, have additional reasons for seeking work abroad (Alam, 2009). Due to the stable inflow of remittances, these states can afford to undermine pressure from international bodies or MNEs on their domestic economic and labor policies. Thus, enforcement of labor rights becomes secondary to the registration and licensing of activities for which a fee can be extracted.

Voice. Few predatory states provide workers with channels for voice. They score significantly low on "associational and organizational rights" (e.g., Vietnam: 1; and Cambodia: 3) compared to regulatory states (e.g., Japan: 11; Korea: 11; and Taiwan: 10). Although those states under the control of the Communist Party boast high levels of union density, actual opportunities for voice is limited in a union that is under party-state control (Clark & Pringle, 2009). Increasingly, workers may stage wildcat strikes without the involvement of formal trade unions. Unofficial strikes have become the central issue of Vietnamese employment relations over the past decade (Anner & Liu, 2015; Cox, 2015), steadily rising since 2005 and peaking in 2011 at a record 978 (Chi & van den Broek, 2013). Similarly, a large number of wildcat strikes take place in China every year (Chan, 2011). Many countries in the Middle East, and most notably the member countries of the Gulf Cooperation Council (GCC: Bahrain, Kuwait, Oman, Qatar, Saudi Arabia, and the United Arab Emirates), outlaw trade unions and the right to strike. The UAE has not ratified core ILO conventions including that on the freedom of association (Davis, 2006). The provision of permanent jobs with extensive benefits to their own citizens through the public sector in these countries serves to pacify potential dissent. On the other hand, migrant workers in the Middle East have practically no rights. While the law stipulates the content of labor contracts administered through recruitment agencies, many migrants are forced to sign new contracts once they start employment (Zachariah, Prakash, & Rajan, 2002).

Inequality. Most predatory states preside over highly unequal societies. Economic inequality typically translates into social inequality because labor market policy is often designed to favor the state's political constituency. For instance, race-based preferences in hiring and promotion are widespread in the public sector in Malaysia. Employment policy, corporate ownership, access to educational institutions, and corporate financing in Malaysia have promoted affirmative action in favor of ethnic Malays. Employment policy in GCC countries has been focused for decades on localization, otherwise known as Emiratization (Afiouni, Karm, & El-Hajj, 2013; Rees, Mamman, & Braik, 2007). In none of these cases has localization policy rendered much success (Afiouni et al., 2013). Partly as a result of failed localization efforts, long-term unemployment in the Middle East ranged between 10–25 percent (O'Sullivan, Rey, & Mendez, 2011). Exploitation of vulnerable groups of workers, especially migrant workers, is prevalent. The Khafala system of short-term migrant labor contracts ties legal status in the UAE to the sponsoring employer, leaving migrant workers vulnerable to exploitation and deportation should they seek to organize or improve their conditions (Fernandez, 2010). Likewise, there are reports of significant abuses of the rights of migrant workers in the seafood and agricultural supply chains in Thailand.

Conclusions

This chapter aimed to elaborate on existing models of the state in Asia and build a theory on state influence on HRM that incorporates pressures from supranational institutions and global value chains. If earlier state theories focused on defining the state as separate from society, the objective of this chapter has been to re-embed the state conceptually in new and changing global institutions, as well as amidst capital and production networks spanning national boundaries. Thus, our analysis has sought to recognize that contemporary nation states face powerful lobbies to provide a business environment that not only works for national corporations but also for MNEs and global buyers. Consistent with our theoretical framework, our empirical examination demonstrates clear differences in approaches to HRM between countries whose states share similar models of government yet have relatively high and low levels of external dependence. Hence, regulatory states' influence on HRM vary between liberalizing and enabling, developmental states' effects on HRM vary between influencing and enabling, and predatory states' vary between influencing and exploiting.

This chapter also contributes to understanding the state as a dynamic yet somewhat path-dependent entity, whose present actions reflect new and changing contexts, yet whose outcomes reflect past legacies. Historic legacies, for example, explain the differences seen in this chapter between Asian regulatory states and theoretical depictions of the regulatory state, which of course were based on Western (specifically, Anglo-Saxon) states. Asian regulatory states, then, are somewhere on the trajectory from developing to regulatory states. The dynamic nature of their trajectory also affects outcomes, so that the relatively low levels of inequality found in Asian regulatory states (e.g., Korea, Taiwan, Hong Kong), many of whom are liberalizing the economy, can only be explained in terms of the legacy HRM they followed as developmental states where wage distribution was relatively compressed. Likewise, the relatively high levels of inequality in Asian developmental states today (e.g., Malaysia, Thailand, and China) reflect the legacy of their past as predatory states.

Last, our examination shows that far from being deterministic, the tools that national states in Asia are using to ensure human capital development contributes to prosperity are truly varied. Hence, we would argue that the constraints placed on the nation state with the introduction of global pressures paradoxically allow it more discretion for policy experimentation. This is especially true at the level of local governments, an issue we touch upon in the next paragraph. States demonstrate creative measures that may deviate from their general policy framework in order to tackle a key social problem, such as can be seen in Japan's response to an aging population. On the other hand, pockets of purposeful neglect can linger in countries where interests align to maintain a status quo of exploitation, such as in industries heavily dependent on cheap migrant labor.

This chapter has relied on existing indicators rather than on a full-fledged empirical investigation to sketch out a theoretical model expressed in Figure 2.1. More research is needed to test the relationships proposed here between state influence and HRM outcomes. Moreover, an aspect that was not part of the scope of this chapter but merits further study is the role of subnational governments. In particular, governments at different levels may be exposed to global pressures to varying degrees. Hence, while national governments may seek sovereignty and autonomy from global players, local governments are often interested in pursuing economic growth and encouraging HR practices that favor foreign investment (Cooke, 2011; Xu, 2011). Future research may wish to examine the variation in state influence on HRM across state levels.

Note

1 The dataset on the Gini index (World Bank estimate) of countries is available at the World Bank's web page. Retrieved from http://data.worldbank.org/indicator/SI.POV.GINI.

References

Ablaza, C. M., et al. (2014). Philippine economic update: Investing in the future—sharing growth and job opportunities for all. Washington, DC: World Bank Group. Retrieved from http://documents.world bank.org/curated/en/713661468297549646/Philippine-economic-update-investing-in-the-future-sharing-growth-and-job-opportunities-for-all.

Abrami, R. (2003, March). Worker rights and global trade: The U.S.–Cambodia bilateral textile trade agreement. *Harvard Business School Case, 703–734*.

Afiouni, F., Karam, C. M., & El-Hajj, H. (2013). The HR value proposition model in the Arab Middle East: Identifying the contours of an Arab Middle Eastern HR model. *The International Journal of Human Resource Management, 24*(10), 1895–1932. doi:10.1080/09585192.2012.722559.

Alam, M. F. (2009). Learning organization and development of women managers in Pakistan, *Human Resource Development International, 12*(1), 105–114.

Al-Waqfi, M. A. & Forstenlechner, I. (2013). Barriers to Emiratization: The role of policy design and institutional environment in determining the effectiveness of Emiratization. *The International Journal of Human Resource Management, 25*(2), 167–189. doi:10.1080/09585192.2013.826913.

Amable, B. (2003). *The diversity of modern capitalism.* Oxford: Oxford University Press.

Amsden, A. H. (1989). *Asia's next giant: South Korea and late industrialization.* New York: Oxford University Press.

Amsden, A. H. (2001). *The rise of "the rest": Challenges to the West from late-industrializing economies.* Oxford and New York: Oxford University Press.

Anner, M. & Liu, X. (2015). Harmonious unions and rebellious workers a study of wildcat strikes in Vietnam. *ILR Review, 69*(1), 3–28.

Bae, J., Chen, S. J., & Rowley, C. (2011). From a paternalistic model towards what?: HRM trends in Korea and Taiwan. *Personnel Review, 40*(6), 700–722.

Barnes, B. E. (2007). *Culture, conflict, and mediation in the Asian Pacific.* Lanham, MD: University Press of America.

Bartlett, C. A. & Ghoshal, S. (1989). *Managing across boundaries: The transnational solution.* Boston: Harvard Business School.

Beeson, M. (2003). Sovereignty under siege: Globalisation and the state in Southeast Asia. *Third World Quarterly, 24*(2), 357–374.

Bhopal, M. & Rowley, C. (2002). The state in employment: The case of Malaysian electronics. *The International Journal of Human Resource Management, 13*(8), 1166–1185.

Boxall, P. & Purcell, J. (2000). Strategic human resource management: Where have we come from and where should we be going?. *International Journal of Management Reviews, 2*(2), 183–203.

Boyer, R. (2005). How and why capitalisms differ. *Economy and Society, 34*(4), 509–557.

Budd, J. W. (2004). Ethics of the employment relationship. In *Employment with a human face: Balancing efficiency, equity, and voice* (pp. xiv, 263). Ithaca, NY: ILR Press.

Carney, M. & Witt, M. A. (2014). The role of the state in Asian business systems. In M. A. Witt & S. G. Redding (Eds.), *The Oxford handbook of Asian business systems* (1st ed.) (pp. 538–560). Oxford: Oxford University Press.

Chan, A. (2011). Strikes in China's export industries in comparative perspective. *The China Journal, 65*(1), 27–51.

Chi, D. Q. & van den Broek, D. (2013). Wildcat strikes: A catalyst for union reform in Vietnam?. *Journal of Industrial Relations, 55*(5), 783–799.

Chun, H. M., Munyi, E. N., & Lee, H. (2010). South Korea as an emerging donor: Challenges and changes on its entering OECD/DAC. *Journal of International Development, 22*(6), 788–802.

Clarke, S. & Lee, C. H. (2007). From rights to interests: The challenge of industrial relations in Vietnam. *Journal of Industrial Relations, 49*(4), 545–568.

Clarke, S. & Pringle, T. (2009). Can party-led trade unions represent their members? *Post-Communist Economies, 21*(1), 85–101.

Compa, L. (1993). Labor rights and labor standards in international trade. *Law and Policy in International Business, 25*(1), 165–191.

Cooke, F. L. (2011). The role of the state and emergent actors in the development of human resource management in China. *The International Journal of Human Resource Management, 22*(18), 3830–3848.

Cox, A. (2015). The pressure of wildcat strikes on the transformation of industrial relations in a developing country: The case of the garment and textile industry in Vietnam. *Journal of Industrial Relations, 57*(2), 271–290.

Crinis, V. & Parasuraman, B. (2016). Employment relations and the state in Malaysia. *Journal of Industrial Relations, 58*(2), 215–228.

Crouch, C. (2011). *The strange non-death of neoliberalism.* Cambridge and Malden, MA: Polity Press.

Davis, M. (2006, September–October). Fear and money in Dubai. *New Left Review, 46,* 47–69.

Debrah, A. Y., McGovern, I. & Budhwar, P. (2000). Complementarity or competition: The development of human resources in a South-East Asian growth triangle: Indonesia, Malaysia and Singapore. *International Journal of Human Resource Management, 11*(2), 314–335.

Dickens, W. T. & Lang, K. (1985). A test of dual labor market theory. *The American Economic Review, 75*(4), 792–805.

Doeringer, P. B. & Piore, M. J. (1971). *Internal labor markets and manpower analysis.* Lexington, MA: Heath.

Edwards, P. K., Tregaskis, O., Levesque, C., McDonnell, A., & Quintanilla, J. (2013). Human resource management practices in the multinational company: A test of system, societal, and dominance effects. *Industrial and Labor Relations Review, 66*(3), 588–617.

Evans, P. (1995). *Embedded autonomy: States and industrial transformation.* Princeton, NJ: Princeton University Press.

Fernandez, B. (2010). Cheap and disposable? The impact of the global economic crisis on the migration of Ethiopian women domestic workers to the Gulf. *Gender and Development, 18*(2), 249–262.

Fields, K. J. (2012). Not of a piece: Developmental states, industrial policy, and evolving patterns of capitalism. In A. Walter & X. Zhang (Eds.). *Japan, Korea, and Taiwan. East Asian capitalism: Diversity, continuity, and change* (pp. 46–67). Oxford: Oxford University Press.

Freedom House. (2015). Discarding democracy: Return to the iron fist. Freedom in the World 2015. Retrieved from https://freedomhouse.org/report/freedom-world/freedom-world-2015.

Fritzen, S. A. (2007). Discipline and democratize: Patterns of bureaucratic accountability in Southeast Asia. *Intl Journal of Public Administration, 30*(12–14), 1435–1457.

Furuoka, F. (2002). Challenges for Japanese diplomacy after the end of the Cold War. *Contemporary Southeast Asia, 24*(1), 68–81.

Gereffi, G., Humphrey, J., & Kaplinsky, R. (2001). Introduction: Globalisation, value chains and development. *IDS Bulletin, 32*(3), 1–8.

Gereffi, G., Humphrey, J., & Sturgeon, T. (2005). The governance of global value chains. *International Economy Review of Political, 12*(1), 78–104.

Gil Sander, F., Blancas Mendivil, L. C., & Westra, R. (2015).Malaysia economic monitor: Transforming urban transport. Washington, DC: World Bank Group. Retrieved from http://documents.worldbank.org/curated/en/509991467998814353/Malaysia-economic-monitor-transforming-urban-transport.

Hall, P. A. & Gingerich, D. W. (2009). Varieties of capitalism and institutional complementarities in the political economy: An empirical analysis. *British Journal of Political Science, 39*(03), 449–482.

Hall, P. A. & Soskice, D. (2001). An introduction to varieties of capitalism. In P. A. Hall & D. Soskice (Eds.), *Varieties of capitalism: The institutional foundations of comparative advantage.* Oxford: Oxford University Press, 50–51.

Hall, P. A. & Thelen, K. (2009). Institutional change in varieties of capitalism. *Socio-Economic Review, 7*(1), 7–34.

Hammer, N. (2005). International framework agreements: Global industrial relations between rights and bargaining. *Transfer: European Review of Labour and Research, 11*(4), 511–530.

Hancké, B., Rhodes, M., & Thatcher, M. (2007). Introduction: Beyond varieties of capitalism. In B. Hancké, M. Rhodes & M. Thatcher (Eds.), *Beyond varieties of capitalism: Conflict, contradiction, and complementarities in the European economy.* Oxford; New York: Oxford University Press.

Hutchison, J. (2012). Labour politics in Southeast Asia: The Philippines in comparative perspective. In R. Robison (Ed.), *Routledge handbook of Southeast Asian politics* (pp. 40–52). London and New York: Routledge.

Hutchison, J. (2016). The state and employment relations in the Philippines. *Journal of Industrial Relations, 58*(2), 183–198.

Kaufman, B. E. (2010). SHRM theory in the post-Huselid era: Why it is fundamentally misspecified. *Industrial Relations: A Journal of Economy and Society, 49*(2), 286–313.

Kawai, M. & Takagi, S. (2011). Why was Japan hit so hard by the global financial crisis?. In Daigee Shaw & Bih Jane Liu (Eds.), *The impact of the economic crisis on East Asia: Policy responses from four economies* (pp. 131–48). Cheltenham: Edward Elgar.

Kaye, J. (2010). *Moving millions: How coyote capitalism fuels global immigration.* Hoboken, NJ: Wiley.

Kim, D. O. & Kim, S. (2003). Globalization, financial crisis, and industrial relations: The case of South Korea. *Industrial Relations: A Journal of Economy and Society, 42*(3), 341–367.

Kumar, N., Martínez Lucio, M., & Rose, R. C. (2013). Workplace industrial relations in a developing environment: Barriers to renewal within unions in Malaysia. *Asia Pacific Journal of Human Resources, 51*(1), 22–44.

Kuruvilla, S. & Erickson, C. L. (2002). Change and transformation in Asian industrial relations. *Industrial Relations, 41*(2), 171–227.

Lakhani, T., Kuruvilla, S., & Avgar, A. (2013). From the firm to the network: Global value chains and employment relations theory. *British Journal of Industrial Relations, 51*(3), 440–472.

Lauridsen, L. S. (2004). Foreign direct investment, linkage formation and supplier development in Thailand during the 1990s: The role of state governance. *The European Journal of Development Research, 16*(3), 561–586.

Lee, J. & Rowley, C. (2008). The changing face of women managers in South Korea. In C. Rowley & V. Yukongdi (Eds.), *The changing face of women in Asian management* (pp. 148–170). London: Routledge.

Levi-Faur, D. (2005). The global diffusion of regulatory capitalism. *The Annals of the American Academy of Political and Social Science, 598*(1), 12–32.

Locke, R., Amengual, M., & Mangla, A. (2009). Virtue out of necessity?: Compliance, commitment, and the improvement of labor conditions in global supply chains. *Politics & Society, 37*(3), 319–351.

Marler, J. H. (2012). Strategic human resource management in context: A historical and global perspective. *The Academy of Management Perspectives, 26*(2), 6–11.

Martin, C. J. & Thelen, K. (2007). The state and coordinated capitalism: Contributions of the public sector to social solidarity in postindustrial societies. *World Politics, 60*(1), 1–36.

Martínez Lucio, M. & Stuart, M. (2011). The state, public policy and the renewal of HRM. *The International Journal of Human Resource Management, 22*(18), 3661–3671.

MIDA (n.d.). Malaysian Investment Development Authority: About. Retrieved from www.mida.gov.my/home/about-mida/posts/.

Mitchell, T. (1991). The limits of the state: Beyond statist approaches and their critics. *American Political Science Review, 85*(1), 77–96.

Nolan, P. (2002). China and the global business revolution. *Cambridge Journal of Economics, 26*(1), 119–137.

OECD (2013). Southeast Asian economic outlook 2013: Structural policy country notes—Philippines. Retrieved from www.oecd.org/dev/asia-pacific/Philippines.pdf.

OECD (2015a). Foreign direct investment (FDI) statistics: OECD data, analysis and forecasts. Retrieved from www.oecd.org/investment/statistics.htm.

OECD (2015b). *OECD economic surveys Japan 2015.* Retrieved from www.oecd-ilibrary.org/economics/oecd-economic-surveys-japan-2015_eco_surveys-jpn-2015-en;jsessionid=1kpyfxyetxpap.x-oecd-live-01.

O'Riain, S. (2004). *The politics of high tech growth: Developmental network states in the global economy* (No. 23). Cambridge: Cambridge University Press.

O'Sullivan, A., Rey, M.-E., & Mendez, J. G. (2011). Opportunities and challenges in the MENA region. Arab World competitive report 2011–2012. Retrieved from www.oecd.org/mena/49036903.pdf.

Rees, C. J., Mamman, A., & Braik, A. B. (2007). Emiratization as a strategic HRM change initiative: Case study evidence from a UAE petroleum company. *The International Journal of Human Resource Management, 18*(1), 33–53.

Roberts, J. M. (2010, August 9). Cronyism: Undermining economic freedom and prosperity around the world. *Backgrounder, 2447.* Washington DC: Heritage Foundation.

Robinson, J. A. (1999). When is a state predatory? *CESifo Working Paper Series No. 178.* Munich: CESifo.

Romei, V. (2015, December 3). China and Africa: Trade relationship evolves. The *Financial Times.*

Rowley, C. & Bae, J. (2002). Globalization and transformation of Human Resource Management in South Korea. *The International Journal of Human Resource Management, 13*(3), 522–549.

Rowley, C. & Bae, J. (2004). Human resource management in South Korea after the Asian financial crisis: Emerging patterns from the labyrinth. *International Studies of Management & Organization, 34*(1), 52–82.

Song, J. (2014). *Inequality in the workplace: Labor market reform in Japan and Korea.* Ithaca, NY: Cornell University Press.

Schmidt, V. A. (2009). Putting the political back into political economy by bringing the state back in yet again. *World Politics, 61*(3), 516–546.

Schwab, K. (Ed.) (2014). The global gender gap index 2014. World Economic Forum. Retrieved May 15, 2017, from http://reports.weforum.org/global-gender-gap-report-2014/

Schwab, K. (Ed.) (2014–2015). The global competitiveness report 2014–2015. World Economic Forum. Retrieved May 15, 2017, from www3.weforum.org/docs/WEF_GlobalCompetitivenessReport_2014-15.pdf

Shaban, R. A., Assaad, R., & Al Qudsi, S. S. (1995). The challenge of unemployment in the Arab region. *International Labour Review, 134*(1), 65–81.

Sinha, A. (2005). *The regional roots of developmental politics in India: A divided leviathan.* Bloomington, IN: Indiana University Press.

Statistics Japan (2016). Labour force survey. Retrieved from www.stat.go.jp/english/data/roudou/lng index.htm.

Statistics Korea (2011). Economically active population survey.

Truong, D. X. & Quang, T. (2007). The psychological contract in employment in Vietnam: Preliminary empirical evidence from an economy in transition. *Asia Pacific Business Review, 13*(1), 113–131.

Tyner, J. A. (2009). *The Philippines: Mobilities, identities, globalization.* New York: Routledge.

UNCTAD. (2015). World investment report 2015: Reforming international investment governance. United Nations conference on trade and department. Retrieved from http://unctad.org/en/pages/PublicationWebflyer.aspx?publicationid=1245.

UNDESA. (2013). International migrant stock: The 2013 revision. United Nations Department of Economic and Social Affairs. Retrieved from www.un.org/en/development/desa/population/migration/data/estimates2/index.shtml.

Van Kersbergen, K. (2003). *Social capitalism: A study of Christian democracy and the welfare state.* London: Routledge.

Wad, P. (2012). Revitalizing the Malaysian trade union movement: The case of the electronics industry. *Journal of Industrial Relations, 54*(4), 494–509.

Wade, R. (1990). *Governing the market: Economic theory and the role of government in East Asian industrialization.* Princeton, NJ: Princeton University Press.

Wade, R. (1996). Japan, the World Bank, and the art of paradigm maintenance: "The East Asian Miracle" in political perspective. *New Left Review, 1*(217), 3–37.

Wahab, M. A., Ahmed, V., & Mahmood, H. (2013). Human resource development (HRD) and foreign remittances. *World Economics, 14*(4), 29–56.

Walter, A. & Zhang, X. (2011). Debating East Asian capitalism: Issues and themes. In A. Walter & X. Zhang (Eds.), *East Asian capitalism: Diversity, change, and continuity.* Oxford: Oxford University Press.

Warner, M. (2013). Comparing human resource management in China and Vietnam: An overview. *Human Systems Management, 32*(4), 217–229.

Wilkinson, A., Donaghey, J., Dundon, T., & Freeman, R. B. (Eds.). (2014). *Handbook of research on employee voice.* Cheltenham: Edward Elgar Publishing.

Wong, J. (2004). The adaptive developmental state in East Asia. *Journal of East Asian Studies, 4*(3), 345–362.

Whitley, R. (1998). *Business systems in East Asia: Firms, markets and societies.* London: Sage.

Whitley, R. (2006). How national are business systems?: The role of states and complementary institutions in standardizing systems of economic coordination and control at the national level. In G. Morgan, R. Whitley, & E. Moen, (Eds.), *Changing capitalisms?: Internationalization, institutional change, and systems of economic organization.* Oxford: Oxford University Press.

Witt, M. A. & Redding, G. (Eds.). (2014). *The Oxford handbook of Asian business systems.* Oxford: Oxford University Press.

Xie, Y. & Zhou, X. (2014). Income inequality in today's China. *Proceedings of the National Academy of Sciences, 111*(19), 6928–6933.

Xu, C. (2011). The fundamental institutions of China's reforms and development. *Journal of Economic Literature, 49*(4), 1076–1151.

Yang, H. & Rowley, C. (2008). Performance management in South Korea. In A. Varma, P. S. Budhwar, & A. S. DeNisi (Eds.), *Performance management systems: A global perspective.* London: Routledge.

Yeung, H. W. C. (2014). Governing the market in a globalizing era: Developmental states, global production networks and inter-firm dynamics in East Asia. *Review of International Political Economy, 21*(1), 70–101.

Zachariah, K. C., Prakash, B. A., & Rajan, S. I. (2002). Gulf migration study: Employment, wages and working conditions of Kerala emigrants in the United Arab Emirates. Retrieved from www.cds.edu/download_files/326.pdf.

Zhu, Y., Warner, M., & Rowley, C. (2007). Human resource management with "Asian" characteristics: A hybrid people-management system in East Asia. *The International Journal of Human Resource Management, 18*(5), 745–768.

Zhu, C. J., Zhang, M., & Shen, J. (2012). Paternalistic and transactional HRM: The nature and transformation of HRM in contemporary China. *The International Journal of Human Resource Management, 23*(19), 3964–3982.

3

CONFUCIANISM AND HUMAN RESOURCE MANAGEMENT IN EAST ASIA

Sunghoon Kim, Pingping Fu, and Jiali Duan

Introduction

Confucianism is a defining element of East Asian culture. Named after the Chinese scholar Confucius (551–479 BC), Confucianism represents a collection of philosophical ideas that has had a profound influence on politics, education, religion, and family life in greater China, as well as in neighboring countries such as Korea, Japan, Singapore, and Vietnam. During the period of modernization in the early twentieth century, Confucianism lost its traditional influence in the region and was criticized as a regressive mental framework that had delayed economic and political advances (Fetzer & Soper, 2014; Shin, 2011). However, Confucianism survived and has regained its influence in lockstep with the growth in its host nations' economic and political power (Bell, 2010; Paramore, 2016). In recent years, Confucianism's global visibility has grown rapidly as the Chinese government has sought to elevate it as a national brand of Chinese cultural heritage (Sun, 2013).

This chapter examines how the tradition of Confucianism in East Asia is reflected in contemporary human resource management (HRM) practices in the region. Although people in those countries no longer identify themselves explicitly as Confucians, this long-held tradition has undeniably had a strong influence on all sectors of East Asian society, including the business community. Consciously or subconsciously, many business leaders in the region have relied on Confucianism for ethical guidance and managerial ideas (Bhappu, 2000; Du, 2015; Fu & Tsui, 2003; Fu, Tsui, & Liu, 2010; Lee, 2012). As Confucianism is primarily concerned with appropriate human social behavior, it is no surprise that its influence on business practices is strongest in the domain of HR management.

With this in mind, in this chapter we outline East Asian HR practices in their relation to Confucian tradition. The first part summarizes the tradition of Confucianism, briefly discussing its historical development and its geographical expansion in East Asia. The second part discusses how Confucian tradition informs contemporary HR practices in the region. In assessing the influence of this historically dominant ideology in HR functions in the East Asian countries, we acknowledge the possible influence of other ideologies such as Western liberalism and Marxism, and the unique trajectory of political, cultural, and economic development in each country. In this regard, citing a Confucian influence on any of HR practices should be understood as a matter of degree rather than a clear-cut categorization. That acknowledged, we will review a selected set of HR practices, for which the rationale could be strongly connected to the influence of Confucianism traditions in East Asia.

Confucianism in East Asia: an overview

Although Confucianism originated in China, the term *Confucianism* has no direct equivalent in the Chinese language. In fact, the term was coined by sixteenth-century Jesuit missionaries, who recognized the centrality of Confucius in this intellectual tradition (Goldin, 2014; Yao, 2000). In East Asia, this tradition is commonly referred to as "*Ru Jiao*" (儒教: *Yu-kyo* in Korean; *Jukyo* in Japanese; *Nho Giáo* in Vietnamese), which translates roughly as *the doctrine* or *tradition of scholars* (Yao, 2000). Although the primacy of Confucius is indisputable, the tradition was formulated, advanced, and constantly reinterpreted by many scholars and politicians over the centuries. Prominent contributors to early Confucianism include *Mengzi* (孟子), who believed in the inherent goodness of human beings, and *Xunzi* (荀子), who warned against inherent human vices.

In China, Confucianism emerged as a national doctrine around the second century BC, during the Han dynasty. Although Daoism and Buddhism also enjoyed wide popularity amongst the Chinese people, Confucianism largely maintained its prestige as national orthodoxy until the early twentieth century. However, it was found to be helpless in sustaining the Chinese empire against industrialized foreign powers, and proponents of the May Fourth Movement (1919) explicitly condemned Confucianism as a regressive mental framework that had failed China. With subsequent modernization and the rise of communism, Confucianism attracted heavy criticism in Mainland China. Up to the 1970s, the Communist Party attacked Confucianism as neglecting the value of physical labor and blinding people to economic realities (Goldman, 1975; Gregor & Chang, 1979). In school textbooks, the precepts of Confucius were described as negative examples of old ways. However, despite decades of persecution and repression, Confucianism has remained influential amongst today's business and political leaders (Li & Liang, 2015). Since the late 1980s, Confucian tradition was publicly reassessed and once more came to be valued in Mainland China. More recently, the Communist government has made conscious efforts to revive Confucianism, promoting it as a remedy for the social problems of an increasingly capitalist China (Bell, 2010).

Once established in China, Confucianism began to spread to neighboring countries. Arriving in Korea in 108 BC, it began to influence national politics during the Three Kingdoms period (57 BC–AD 668) and continued to overtake competing ideologies such as Buddhism and Daoism (Shin, 2011). Confucianism's popularity in Korea reached its peak during the Joseon Dynasty (1392–1910), whose founding elites envisioned an idealistic Confucian state. During the Joseon period, Koreans' adherence to Confucianism was so fervent that people could be executed for not following the orthodox version of Confucianism (Shin, 2011). The version of Confucianism authorized by the Joseon Dynasty was *Seong-li-hak* or "neo-Confucianism" that placed a high value on cosmology and individual self-cultivation. While Confucianism is no longer the national orthodoxy, contemporary Koreans remain heavily exposed to its everyday influence in family interactions, formal education, and popular entertainment material. The Munmyo Confucian Shrine in Seoul (established in 1398) is still operating, with regular ritual worship of Confucius.

To Japan, Confucianism transferred via Korea as early as the third century AD. Although it never acquired the status of national orthodoxy, Confucianism did influence Japanese intellectual and cultural traditions, especially during the early modern period (Paramore, 2016). During the Tokugawa regime of the seventeenth and eighteenth centuries, Confucianism became a popular subject of study amongst the Samurai class, but in the subsequent Meiji restoration period, it came to be despised as an obsolete Chinese tradition that contradicted advances in Western science. Nevertheless, Confucianism later emerged as a nationally endorsed ideology, justifying Japanese imperialism when Japan engaged in aggressive military advances into Korean and Chinese territories. Around that time, Confucianism was also portrayed as an indigenous Japanese tradition that would complement the limitations of Western capitalism. Shibusawa Eiichi, often referred to as the father of Japanese capitalism, argued publicly that Confucianism should form the basis of a sustainable capitalist social order. Today, Confucianism is not openly discussed in Japan, in part because of the stigma it bears as a facilitator of pre-1945 fascism (Paramore, 2016). For all that, Confucianism's long-standing influence on Japanese society and business culture is undeniable (Boardman & Kato, 2003).

In Vietnam, Confucianism was introduced during the period of Chinese domination that began in 118 BC (Shin, 2011). After the country became independent from China in AD 939, the Vietnamese ruling class promoted Confucian ideas as the basis of a harmonious and hierarchical social order. National support for Confucianism was expressed in the construction in 1070 of the Temple of Learning (*Van Mieu*), which still stands in Hanoi, and in the introduction of a civil service examination, which focused on Confucian literature. Confucianism maintained its primacy in Vietnamese political, social, and moral philosophy until the introduction of Western educational systems in the nineteenth century. Although the influence of Confucianism remains strong in everyday Vietnamese life (as in other Confucian countries), the evolution of Vietnamese Confucianism differs somewhat from China or Korea. For instance, the Vietnamese understand the Confucian idea of loyalty as a love of country rather than of the country's ruler. This conception of loyalty empowered many Vietnamese to sacrifice themselves in wars against foreign invaders from France and the USA (Sheehan, 1988; Shin, 2011).

In Taiwan, Confucianism was introduced in the seventeenth century by immigrants from the mainland. Although it has never been proclaimed as a national ideology, it has enjoyed explicit support from Taiwan's governing elites (Kim, S., 2014). Chiang Kai-shek, the founder of modern Taiwan, was a strong advocate of Confucian traditions. His ambitious New Life Movement (1934–1949) explicitly promoted Confucian values such as *Li* (propriety), *Yi* (righteousness), *Lian* (honest), and *Chi* (shamefulness). When Confucian temples in Mainland China were attacked by young cultural revolutionaries, Taiwan's nationalist government ensured that young students were exposed to classic Confucian texts. Although government support has dwindled since political democratization in the 1990s, Confucianism remains influential in the daily lives of the Taiwanese (Lin & Ho, 2009).

As in Taiwan, Confucianism came to Singapore with the ethnic Chinese, who became the majority population. Although never officially endorsed as the national orthodoxy, Singapore's government has made conscious efforts to promote Confucianism under the rubric of "Asian values" (Shin, 2011). These efforts were well received in Singapore, where many ethnic Chinese are eager to maintain their cultural heritage, and send their children to private schools with the curriculum of Confucian classics. The persisting and pervasive influence of Confucianism in Singapore is further exemplified in the filial piety law, which obliges Singaporeans to support their parents (Kim, S., 2014). The Singaporean government offers special favorable terms on housing to young couples who are willing to live with their parents.

Although Confucianism has been differently interpreted across different peoples and contexts, it is commonly understood to promote five core virtues: *Ren* (humaneness or benevolence), *Yi* (justice or righteousness), *Li* (propriety or ritual), *Zhi* (wisdom or knowledge), and *Xin* (integrity or faithfulness). Confucian literature also stresses harmonious social relationships through five fundamental principles of relational ethics: filial piety (between father and son), loyalty (between ruler and subject), gendered roles (between husband and wife), seniority-based order (between old and young), and faithfulness (between friends). These virtues and ethics are considered characteristics of *Junzi* (usually translated as a noble man or gentleman). Confucianism encourages individuals to train themselves in these virtues to become *Junzi*—one who knows how to behave properly under all circumstances and is a role model for others. It also prescribes that communities and nation states should ensure that their leadership positions be occupied by individuals possessing such virtues.

Over thousands of years, East Asians were taught to cultivate Confucian virtues and moral codes, and they also expect their leaders to embody these virtues, including those in settings such as government offices and kinship communities. In respect of government officials, Confucian virtues were the prime criteria for selecting and promoting talents in these societies (especially in China and Korea) for more than 1,000 years. Although Confucianism is no longer the dominant national orthodoxy in East Asia, it continues to govern many aspects of everyday life in this region. It is not surprising, then, to find traces of Confucianism in the contemporary HRM practices of East Asian companies.

Confucianism and HRM

In discussing a selected set of HR practices in East Asia associated with Confucian traditions in the region, we must acknowledge that tracing the philosophical or cultural origins of a given HR practice is inherently challenging. Labeling an organizational practice as Confucian is especially difficult, as Confucianism is a diverse set of ideas formulated long before the emergence of the modern industrial organization. However, like other managerial functions, a firm's HR practices are always significantly influenced by the surrounding socio-cultural environment (Jackson & Schuler, 1995; Kim & Wright, 2011). Therefore, it should be possible to identify signs of Confucian influence in the HR practices of East Asian companies. Indeed, scholars have noted many unique features of East Asian HRM that indicate the major formative influence of Confucian heritage (e.g., Bae & Lawler, 2000; Bae, Chen, & Rowley, 2011; Warner, 2010). Building on such literature, we aim to present an overview of Confucian influence on modern HRM in East Asia, and to encourage future researchers and practitioners to further explore how HR practices could be shaped by local cultural traditions.

Recruitment and selection

Under the influence of Confucianism, East Asian companies have developed some distinctive recruiting and selection practices. In this regard, three features are worthy of special attention: (1) hiring on the basis of personal relationships; (2) the extensive use of formal examinations; and (3) the emphasis on moral character as a selection criterion.

Hiring on the basis of personal relationships. One distinct feature of East Asian culture is its emphasis on harmonious social relations. This cultural tradition is expressed in various indigenous concepts such as *Guanxi* and *Renqing* in China, *Yon-go* and *In-hwa* in Korea, *Wa* in Japan, and *Tinh Cam* and *Quan He* in Vietnam. Reflecting this cultural emphasis on social relations, East Asian companies tend to place a high value on relationship-based recruiting. Studies found that personal relations indeed make substantial differences in recruitment of East Asian companies. For instance, Han and Han (2009) reported that network-based recruiting is quite prevalent in China, especially amongst large firms. Kim (2010) found that over 60 percent of job placements in South Korea relate to candidates' social networks. This tendency can be ascribed to the Confucian emphasis on social harmony and interpersonal relationships (Horak, 2014).

East Asia is not the only region where the hiring process is subject to such influences. Western companies are also known to utilize network-based recruiting practices such as employee referrals (Galenianos, 2014; Pieper, 2015). However, the nature of social networks and the degree of reliance on such methods differs. In Western countries, "weak" rather than strong social networks are known to be effective as channels for sharing and exchanging job-related information (Granovetter, 1974). In East Asian countries, however, job market outcomes depend on strong or closed social networks, involving not only the exchange of information but also the reciprocation of favors. Therefore, whether a job seeker has parents, relatives, or friends with good social networks does make a difference in job market outcomes in China and South Korea (Kim, 2010; Horak, 2017; Liu, 2016).

The prevalence of hiring through kinship networks is a matter of concern for many East Asians, who feel that this kind of relationship-based recruiting may undermine the spirit of meritocracy and perpetuate social inequality (Liu, 2016). However, recruiting through personal ties does not always lead to negative workplace outcomes. From a company's point of view, information about candidates may be more trustworthy when it is acquired in this way. Additionally, kinship networks may serve to motivate recruits by obliging them not to disappoint those who recommended them.

Selection based on formal examination. An interesting feature of recruitment and selection in many East Asian companies is their extensive reliance on formal examinations. In South Korea, many large corporations require graduate job applicants to sit a company entrance exam of several hours duration. For instance, Samsung requires candidates to complete the Samsung Aptitude Test, and Hyundai Motor Group has a similar requirement for all graduate applicants. Written examinations are especially prevalent in the South Korean public sector, and the results almost entirely determine selection outcomes (Lee, 2016). In China, written exams are also widely used in the public sector recruiting process and, increasingly, in the private sector. Company entrance exams in China usually comprise two parts: an essay (*Lunwen*) and an administrative aptitude test (*xingzheng nengli ceshi*). In addition, recruitment exams typically include tests of relevant professional knowledge.

Clearly, East Asia is not alone in using written tests for selection. In the USA, psychometric tests assessing personality and cognitive abilities are widely used for personnel selection, particularly in military organizations. However, the written selection tests in East Asian companies often extend beyond the candidate's personality or cognitive abilities. In South Korean and Chinese companies, such tests often encompass knowledge domains beyond those of direct relevance to the specific job. For instance, Hyundai Motor Group's 2016 selection test included a 700-word history essay, in which applicants were asked to demonstrate their knowledge and perspective of the European Renaissance (Lee, 2016).

The distinctive use of formal selection examinations in East Asia appears related to the tradition of imperial examinations. In China, a written examination for imperial government officials was introduced in around the sixth century, which is the first known use of such method for the selection of talents. Until 1905, the rigorous and highly competitive imperial examination (*keju* in Chinese) was a regular nationwide event in China for more than 1,000 years. In Korea, a similar imperial examination (*Gwageo*) was introduced in 788 and conducted periodically until 1894. In Vietnam, an imperial examination was implemented between 1075 and 1913. Japan also had an imperial examination, although its influence was limited. In this rigorous and highly competitive exam, participants were expected to demonstrate their mastery of Confucian literature and, more importantly, their maturity in Confucian virtues (Elman, 2013; Liu, 2007). The influence of this emphasis on classic literature and moral virtues remains visible in today's company entrance examinations in South Korea and China.

Historically, the imperial examination was an institutional device to realize the ideal of Confucian meritocracy (Xiao & Li, 2013). Where properly implemented, the imperial examination allowed gifted young men to enhance their economic and social status by virtue of hard work, regardless of their family background. In China and South Korea, where kinship relations are known to influence selection, it is a matter of serious practical concern to ensure a sense of fairness and legitimacy in the selection process (Wang, 2011), and a properly implemented written examination serves to ensure this perceived fairness (Zhang, Xu, & Zhang, 2015). Some companies make explicit reference to the utility of written examinations—for instance, KPMG China places a huge weight on written tests in its recruiting decisions, claiming that such tests "ensure that all candidates are treated EQUALLY" (KPMG, 2015, emphasis in the original text).

Selection on the basis of Confucian moral character. According to Confucian tradition, the efficacy of human beings is determined by the degree to which individuals embody Confucian moral virtues. According to the Confucian canon *Da Xue* (Great Learning), virtue is the root and wealth is the result, suggesting that moral virtue is a driver or predictor of economic performance. Following this line of reasoning, organizations in East Asia have come to consider moral character as an important recruitment criterion.

In Chinese culture, Confucian moral standards are an essential component in the evaluation of people at any level, making it natural to include these amongst hiring criteria, especially in large companies. Hempel and Chang (2002) found that Taiwanese companies prioritize job applicants who appear to have moral character and social skills to work harmoniously with colleagues. Moral character is a particularly important component of the paternalistic style of leadership commonly found in greater China. Paternalistic leaders with a low moral character score tend to have difficulty in gaining credibility and respect from their followers (Cheng et al., 2014).

In South Korea, it is customary for companies to select individuals based on *In-seong* (meaning an individual's moral quality)—a concept closely associated with Confucian moral virtues such as filial piety, loyalty, trustworthiness, and propriety. To measure candidates' *In-seong*, South Korean companies require them to answer various questions about their personal and social lives, which Western counterparts might find illegitimate or a breach of privacy. In Singapore, too, an applicant's moral character is deemed critical in recruitment and selection. According to Khim (2002), Singaporean managers prioritize the virtuous characteristics of honesty and integrity in selecting job applicants.

Managerial succession

In Confucian societies, family-controlled businesses are the norm rather than the exception (Sharma & Chua, 2013). Although family businesses also play a critical role in Western societies, their pervasiveness and persistence are much stronger in Confucian East Asian economies. Therefore, in greater China, family capitalism constitutes an integral part of the economy. In Taiwan, the economy has been dominated by small- and medium-sized enterprises that are usually controlled by members of the founding family. In Hong Kong, entrepreneurs commonly aspire to bequeath their business to their children (Au, Chiang, Birch, & Ding, 2013). In Mainland China, where no private businesses were allowed for several decades, private companies are now playing significant roles in the national economy, accounting for almost all employment growth and most of increase in manufacturing output (Lardy, 2014). This rapid growth in private entrepreneurship is primarily driven by family businesses, which account for more than 80 percent of all private enterprises (Liang, Wang, & Cui, 2014). Chinese family capitalism is also strong in countries such as Malaysia, Indonesia, Thailand, and Philippines, where the Chinese are ethnic minorities (Bruton, Ahlstrom, & Wan, 2003; Tsui-Auch, 2004).

In Korea, almost all major private enterprises can be categorized as family firms. For instance, Samsung is owned and managed by descendants of its founder Lee Byong-chul, who was born into a family of Confucian scholars. In like fashion, LG is owned and controlled by the Gu family and Hyundai by the Jung family. The Japanese economy is also known for its strong tradition of family inheritance. In addition to large global firms such as Toyota, many small- and medium-sized Japanese enterprises are run by members of founding families. In Vietnam, more than one-third of the top 500 enterprises follow the family business model (Viet, 2015).

A core HR concern for family businesses is managerial succession (Lee, Lim, & Lim, 2003; Sharma & Chua, 2013). Traditionally, East Asian family firms have been very keen to ensure that immediate family members inherit managerial positions. Yan and Sorenson (2006) suggested that this commitment to family succession in East Asia reflects the high value that Confucian tradition places on family. Inheritance of managerial positions is primarily from father to sons, although extended family members may also be involved. In Korea, family firms prepare descendants of the founder for future corporate leadership by exposing them to various functional areas of management and giving them responsibility for small-scale business initiatives (Park & Lee, 2011). In Japan, when the owner family cannot find appropriate managerial talent within their own family, adult adoption has been used to preserve the tradition of family business (Mehrotra, Morck, Shim, & Wiwattanakantang, 2013).

This family oriented managerial succession has, however, become a matter of debate and critical concern. As East Asian countries integrate into the global economy, family business succession is increasingly viewed as a sign of nepotism and a potential source of economic inefficiency. In response, a growing number of East Asian family firms have enlisted non-family members as professional managers. However, hiring non-family members in this way does not necessarily eliminate the influence of the founding family. Through majority ownership or board membership, the founding family often maintains its controlling power long after physical withdrawal.

Scholars have debated on questions of whether and how non-family professional managers may benefit East Asian family firms. Some argue that, in today's global market, the performance of family businesses can be improved by reducing the founding family's influence. For instance, studies found that family-owned companies can improve performance by handing over the managerial control to qualified non-family professional managers in Taiwan (Chung & Luo, 2013) and Japan (Chang & Shim, 2015). In contrast, others highlight the benefits of intergenerational succession, reporting that family businesses can perform better under inherited leadership in China (Cai, Luo, & Wan, 2012; Liang, Yang, Lin, & Zheng, 2013). Others argue that, rather than whether a family member inherits a managerial position, what matters is how that family successor is selected (Dou & Li, 2013; Yoo, Schenkel, & Kim, 2014).

Compensation

The English words *compensation* and *remuneration* imply that employees are to be compensated or paid back for service to their employer. In industrialized East Asia, compensation also refers to something given to an employee in recognition of that service. However, under the Confucian tradition, compensation extends beyond paying individuals for their services, as a quintessential mechanism for building social relationships amongst members of the organization.

Reward based on group performance and seniority. The traditional emphasis in East Asian companies on a collectivist workplace culture is well documented in the literature. Gomez-Mejia and Welbourne (1991) suggested that countries such as Singapore, South Korea, Japan, and Taiwan are characterized by a low level of individualism, and that this cultural tendency is reflected in compensation systems that strongly emphasize group performance criteria. Although some East Asians (e.g., those in Singapore and Hong Kong) are known to be more individualistic than others (e.g., those in Japan), the overall preference for group-based reward in East Asia is apparently stronger than that in Western countries (White & Goodman, 1998). In Mainland China and Vietnam, where the Communist Party has been in power, group-based pay arrangements are often seen as a legacy of the planned economy, and therefore its affinity to collectivist cultural values is less apparent. However, even in these transitional economies, there is evidence that employees—especially those with traditional cultural values—tend to react negatively to high pay dispersion, suggesting an influence in the workplace of the long-standing Confucian cultural emphasis on community and social harmony (He, Long, & Kuvaas, 2016).

Another compensation practice informed by Confucian virtues is the seniority-based wage increase (*Nenko* in Japanese; *Nyun-gong* in Korean) prevalent in Japan, South Korea, and to a lesser extent in Taiwan. Although it is possible to explain the emergence of seniority-based pay in terms of other factors (Conrad, 2014), the Confucian tradition of respecting elders is seen to be a major driver of this approach in East Asia (Khanna, Song, & Lee, 2011; Zhu, Chen, & Warner, 2000). Under the seniority system, individuals receive an automatic yearly increase in pay for longer service. In Japan and South Korea, seniority-based pay is often combined with tenure-based promotion, where pay is determined largely by organizational status, with mandatory age-related retirement. From a company perspective, seniority-based pay is a way of rewarding an individual's loyalty and promoting social harmony within the firm.

However, the traditional dominance in the region of group and seniority-based pay arrangements is increasingly being challenged by the rapid spread of individual performance-based pay. In Mainland China and Vietnam, economic reform toward marketization enabled firms to introduce individualized pay arrangements. The Asian economic crisis in 1997 was a strong shock to many East Asian countries, such as South Korea, and consequently companies in those countries have aggressively embraced the idea of an individualized pay system. In Japan, the economic slowdown in the 1990s prompted companies to adopt this individualized system.

Nevertheless, the culture of rewarding seniority and loyalty to the group has not yet disappeared in East Asia. Even in companies that have explicitly adopted individualized pay systems, workers often find ways of maintaining group-based HR practices informed by traditional cultural values. For instance, in South Korea, employees and middle managers often get around the individual performance pay system by manipulating performance ratings to reflect seniority- and group-based norms, or by informally redistributing the performance-based portion of pay amongst group members. In Japan, individual performance-based pay is often applied only to those in managerial positions (Conrad, 2010).

Seasonal bonuses and livelihood support. An interesting feature of pay practice in many East Asian companies is the emphasis on employee seasonal bonuses. In Japan, South Korea, and China, companies regularly pay a substantial seasonal bonus—usually more than one month's salary. Unless a company is in serious financial difficulty, employees can expect to receive seasonal bonuses, just as they receive a salary at the end of each month. Apparently, East Asia is not the only region where companies pay seasonal bonuses. In Western societies, some companies also offer bonuses in a seasonal way to recognize employee's exceptional contributions. However, such bonus schemes differ from seasonal bonuses of East Asian companies in which the amount of bonus is not closely linked to individual workers' performance. Seasonal bonuses in East Asian countries are also different from legally mandated year-end holiday allowance practice (or "thirteenth month salary") in several countries such as Netherland, Argentina, and Brazil. Unlike in these countries, seasonal bonuses in East Asia are largely enforced by informal cultural norms rather than formal regulations.

In Japan, companies customarily award two seasonal bonuses, for summer and winter holidays. Each bonus commonly represents about three to four months of salary, so accounting for a substantial proportion of total annual payment. Because the seasonal bonus is so large and so common, Japanese domestic consumption patterns are visibly linked to the cycle of seasonal bonuses. Amounts are normally determined by a company's overall performance and are not generally linked to individual performance. South Korean companies follow the example of Japanese companies with seasonal bonuses called *Sang-yeo-gum*, commonly amounting to a multiple of monthly base pay. Originally, *Sang-yeo-gum* was intended express an employer's gratitude for employees' collective contribution to the success of the firm. However, the practice has become so common in Korea that it is now considered a normal part of predetermined pay. Many companies award this bonus around major traditional family holidays such as *Choo-suck* (Korean Thanksgiving Day) or *Seollal* (the first day of the Korean lunar calendar).

In China, it is customary for companies to award a cash bonus around the Chinese New Year holiday as a form of year-end bonus. Although not a legal requirement, more than 80 percent of Chinese companies pay a substantial year-end bonus, normally equivalent to one month's salary.

Seasonal bonuses in East Asian companies can be attributed to Confucian tradition. Its association with firm (rather than individual) performance encourages employees to develop loyalty to the company. In addition, the connection to traditional seasonal holidays (usually related to ritual gatherings of the extended family) means that companies play the role of financial supporter of family events. In other words, the seasonal bonus is a mechanism that fosters a sense of "family" in the workplace.

Livelihood support is another important and prevalent East Asian pay practice. In Japan, a family allowance (*kazokukyu*) is a normal part of employee pay. The family allowance is given to employees as head of their household, varying in amount according to the number of dependents. Although it has decreased in popularity over the last decade, the family allowance traditionally represents about 5 percent of total annual compensation given to Japanese employees (Conrad, 2010). In South Korea, a similar family allowance (*Ga-jok-su-dang*) has become a tradition. Again, its importance has diminished significantly in recent years, but most public sector employees in South Korea still receive this allowance in various forms.

Training and development

The essential component of Confucianism is a heavy emphasis on continuous learning and education. While other philosophical traditions (such as Socratic philosophy) also place a high value on education, Confucian ideas of learning are distinctive in several respects. First, under Confucian tradition, education is considered to be an almost sacred duty. This cultural belief is enacted by parents who happily make personal sacrifices in the interests of their children's education (Lam, Ho, & Wong, 2002). This aspect of Confucian tradition has led to the development in East Asian countries of a distinctive Confucian model of education, characterized by the nation state's strong governance of the educational system, family prioritization of children's education, highly competitive national examinations, and the accelerated development of tertiary education (Marginson, 2011). Confucian tradition also emphasizes learning that values the faithful acquisition of established knowledge rather than critical questioning of existing authorities. For that reason, learning is often equated with laborious reading, reflection, and memorizing of the words of respected teachers.

This Confucian emphasis on education has had many benefits for East Asian companies, including a public education system that provides companies with an ample supply of highly educated labor. And because highly educated people are quick learners, companies find it relatively easy to train their employees (Bae & Lawler, 2000), affording East Asian companies a high level of absorptive capacity (Tung, 1994). This may explain these companies' superior performance in catching up with their Western counterparts. However, there are mixed views about the Confucian tradition of learning; for example, Sloman (2007) criticized Confucian tradition for its tendency to produce passive learners rather than active innovators.

The Confucian tradition of learning has inspired East Asian companies to develop some distinctive training and development practices. One interesting example is the Korean practice of Reading Management (*Dok-suh-kyoung-young*), which requires employees to read recommended books and to submit book reports. The required books cover a range of topics that include self-help skills, business knowledge, social science, and classical literature. For instance, a South Korean conglomerate named E-Land asks employees to master books in the company's mandatory reading list, which currently includes more than 400 books. As the list is constantly updated, E-Land employees are always under pressure to read new books. This practice aligns with the company's declared goal of making the company a "school," where learning and personal growth are primary daily activities in the workplace.

In addition to the method of training, Confucianism substantially determines the content of corporate training. In South Korea, most large companies include *Ye-jeol* (禮節, manner or propriety) as required training for newcomers. Confucian virtues also influence corporate training programs in China. For instance, a Chinese technology company named Good-Ark requires all employees to bow toward Confucius' statue, and participate in weekly learning sessions on Confucian classics. Wu Nianbo, the founder and Chairman of the company, believes that by educating employees in Confucian values (such as filial piety and self-cultivation), they will become better and happier human beings, who will naturally be productive employees (Qu, Fu, & Huang, 2016).

Retention

The Confucian emphasis on quasi-family relationship is reflected in relatively high job security and long-term or even lifelong employment. Japan is widely known for its traditional lifelong approach to employment, and large Korean firms have also developed this tradition. In Mainland China, the employment system used to be described as the "iron-rice bowl" because of its unbreakable stability. However, the long-term employment relationship has diminished in recent times, and labor mobility is increasing rapidly across East Asian countries. Therefore, employee retention is increasingly a critical concern for East Asian companies.

While many of the retention strategies known to be effective in Western contexts—meritocratic compensation arrangement, extensive training and development, and positive organizational climate—have also proved effective in East Asia, a number of other scholars have found that several practices have been found particularly useful in the East Asian context, one of which is relationship-based retention.

East Asian employees are believed to make important career changes in close consultation with family members and significant others. Hom and Xiao (2011) found that employees' social networks beyond work colleagues play an important role in Chinese employees' intention to stay. For that reason, practitioner-oriented literature often recommends managers in China pay attention to employees' relationships to their family and friends (Howard, Williams, Wellins, & Liu, 2014). In Korea, many companies offer strong family support to their employees. For instance, it is customary for Korean firms to offer university tuition support for employees' children. This is an effective retention mechanism, as employees are likely to remain at least until their children finish tertiary education. Some Korean companies offer a "filial piety allowance" (*Hyo-do-su-dang*), sending cash to employees' parents on a regular basis. This filial piety program creates family pressure for employees to remain longer in their current employment. A similar allowance is also becoming increasingly popular in Mainland China.

Organizational prestige also plays an important role in employee turnover intention in East Asia. Although there is as yet no systematic evidence concerning the stronger influence of a firm's reputation in East Asia than other parts of the world, people in Confucian-influenced regions seem to care more about their family and friends' perceptions of their firm. In this regard, Reiche (2009) found that turnover intention amongst Singaporean employees is influenced by their current firm's reputation. For instance, Ng (2016) found that Chinese workers' turnover intention is significantly influenced by their firm's external prestige, suggesting that enhanced employer branding may be important for employee retention in East Asia.

Gender discrimination

Confucianism has often been criticized for its endorsement of a patriarchal social order and male dominance. In his only known reference to females, Confucius seemed to equate women with "*xiaoren*" (petty men—the opposite of "*junzi*" or noble men): "Only women and petty men are difficult to handle. Be close to them and they are not humble, keep them at arm's length and they complain" (*Lunyu*, Chapter 17, *Yanghuo;* 论语 阳货篇). One might argue that gender inequality has been an enduring social concern in other cultural traditions such as Christianity and Islam (Seguino, 2011). However, at least in East Asia, Confucianism seems to be an important contributory factor in sustaining male dominance (Cooke, 2010). For instance, until the early twentieth century, East Asian women were openly discriminated against in education and employment. They were not allowed to take imperial examinations or to participate in formal education. Although gender equality has made significant advances in the region over recent decades, that tradition of male dominance still lingers in the region.

Gender discrimination can still be seen in many aspects of HR practice in East Asian firms. For example, recruitment and selection processes often discriminate against female candidates. Woodhams, Lupton, and Xian (2009) found that 40 percent of job advertisements were overtly discriminatory in specifying the required gender of applicants. Similarly, Leong, Tan, and Loh (2004) found that 41 percent of job advertisements in Singapore contained discriminatory remarks. In her study of the Taiwanese labor market, Bowen (2003) found that about 40 percent of job advertisements in a major newspaper included explicit instances of gender discrimination. The situation is much worse in Mainland China, with explicit gender discrimination in almost every job advertisement.

Female employees also find it difficult to have their performance properly recognized, often seeing themselves as disadvantaged in terms of payment and promotion opportunities as compared to their male counterparts. Kang and Rowley (2005) observed that Confucian-influenced Asian men found it difficult to see female workers as equal or competent colleagues. Korabik concluded that such stereotypes "hinder women's preparation for managerial roles as well as their opportunities for promotion" (Korabik 1993: 53). As a consequence, females are significantly under-represented in executive positions and high-paying jobs.

Furthermore, female workers are often forced to retire earlier than their male counterparts. In Mainland China, women are legally mandated to retire almost ten years earlier than men (i.e., blue collar female workers retire at fifty while men retire at sixty; white-collar females retire at fifty-five, while men retire at sixty-five). Even in the absence of any mandatory arrangement, East Asian women are often encouraged to resign voluntarily when they get married or have babies. In the Confucian tradition, women were usually expected to stay at home, taking care of the children and the household chores while men were the breadwinners. Although women have joined the workforce in increasing numbers, they are still expected to prioritize household tasks and childcare rather than their career. For instance, Korean married women are obliged to look after their children as well as their aging parents and parents-in-law, regardless of how busy they are in their own job (Sung, 2003). Such social arrangements unfairly disadvantage married women in developing their professional career (Kim, 2015). As a result, female employment rates in Confucian Asian countries begin to decline beyond the age of thirty (Chow, 2013).

Company ceremonies

Ceremonies or rituals are recognized as an important component of company culture (Schein, 1990). Company rituals could serve as a mechanism for maintaining existing social arrangements within a firm (Dacin, Munir, & Tracey, 2010), controlling employees (Golding, 1991), and moderating social conflict and improving social relations (Anand & Watson, 2004). Confucianism has strong views on rituals and propriety. According to Confucius, ritual is not just a "ritual" activity but a crucial means by which individuals build moral character and societies affirm a social order in its most desirable form. On that basis, rituals have remained an important aspect of life in Confucian-influenced East Asia.

Influenced by this view, East Asian companies observe various social rites and ceremonies, conducted in a pseudo-religious atmosphere. The highest-level leaders (CEO or top executives) host many of these ceremonies in the manner of a head of family. In Mainland China, Confucian-style ceremonies were forbidden during the Cultural Revolution but are now regaining its traditional popularity.

Ceremonials for newcomers and retirees. Along with its emphasis on the notion of family, Confucianism's tendency to distinguish between in-group and out-group members reinforces the idea of membership in East Asian societies. Any significant changes to the boundaries of membership tend to be perceived as important events, and numerous ceremonials are devoted to these changes for such actors as newcomers and retirees.

The welcome ceremony serves as a marker that indicates the beginning of pseudo-family corporate membership. In many East Asian companies, this is more than an introductory social event. For example, in South Korea and Japan, the welcome ceremony normally includes a highly scripted ritual, in which new recruits dressed in uniform stand in militaristic formation to offer their solemn pledge as faithful corporate "soldiers."

In many East Asian companies, retirement is another important event that is to be solemnly celebrated. The retirement ceremony is somewhat like the commencement ceremony. Here, retiring employees are awarded new membership status as a former employee. Careful observance of the retirement ceremony is also intended as a signal to incumbent employees that their dedication and commitment to the organization will be appreciated.

In some companies (especially those that are family owned), deceased founders and former employees are regularly commemorated as company "ancestors." Such ceremonies are often conducted at the company founder's burial site, following a public ritual that resembles Confucian ceremonies of ancestor worship. In South Korea, for example, Samsung observes annual memorial ceremonies in November at Yong-In, where the founder Lee Byung-chul is buried. AmorePacific, a leading South Korean cosmetic company, organizes annual events each January to celebrate its founder, Seo Seong-hwan. The company arranges group tours of executives and senior managers to his burial site to participate in commemoration ceremonies. On the founder's commemoration day, all employees of the company receive messages that encourage them to reflect on the founding father and his entrepreneurial spirit. In Hong Kong, for more than forty years, a food company Lee Kum Kee (established in 1888) has organized a Founder's Day ritual each year in April. In this event, thousands employees and business partners around the world gather at the burial ground of the company founder to commemorate their company ancestors.

Ritualistic group meals. Group meals with work colleagues offer an interesting opportunity to observe East Asian ritualism. In China, South Korea, and Japan, companies (or unit leaders) regularly organize group dinners, sometimes incorporating Karaoke parties. In Singapore, managers of small- and medium-sized firms are expected to dine regularly with their subordinates (Low, 2012). Although these activities have the appearance of a voluntary social gathering, they are seen as an extension of the working day, and employees are essentially required to join them. At these gatherings, participants must closely follow a set of ritual rules, even when engaged in entertainment activities (Bell, 2010). For instance, each participant is expected to occupy a seat appropriate to their social position in the workplace. In this sense, such company dinners are rituals, in which employees' organizational status is acknowledged and reinforced.

Labor relations

In East Asia, the Confucian emphasis on hierarchy and social harmony has frequently been mobilized to advance the agenda of industrial peace and to pacify aggressive labor unions. In the process of industrialization, governments in East Asia have sought to tame and control trade unions. In this endeavor, Confucian tradition has proved a useful ideological resource for authoritarian leaders.

In Taiwan, prior to the lifting of martial law in 1987, the Kuomintang government brought labor unions under their strict control (Ho, 2012). During that period, trade unions were not allowed to organize strikes but were instead expected to build a harmonious and family-like workplace. Although democratization and the change of regime to Democratic Progressive Party in the late 1980s loosened national government's control of industrial relations, Taiwanese trade unions are still not free of the culture of state control. Scholars pointed out that Confucian cultural heritage enabled the Taiwanese government to install and sustain such a hierarchical and conflict-avoiding style of industrial relations (Chen, 2007).

In Mainland China, where the Communist Party has a monopoly of power, there is very strong state control of trade unions. Although China's centralized system of industrial relations has its roots in the Socialist state-planned economy, it is arguably also influenced by Confucianism. When the Chinese government launched a strong unionization campaign in the mid-2000s, the political slogan was "harmonious society"—a clear indication that the Chinese leadership saw Confucianism as an effective ideology in combination with Marxism. The mobilization of Confucianism to regulate workplace relationship can be seen as an attempt to use a socially accepted value to suppress and de-legitimize capital–labor conflicts.

In South Korea, rapid industrialization was orchestrated by the authoritarian leaders Park Chung-hee (1961–1979) and Chun Doo-hwan (1980–1988). During that period, the independent labor movement was systematically oppressed. In cases of large-scale labor disputes, the government often played the role of authoritative mediator between management and workers. The aim of the authoritative governments was to maintain a peace and "harmony" between management and labor (Nam, 1995). Although democratization in 1987 rendered South Korean labor relations highly antagonistic, the rhetoric of "harmonious labor relations" remains influential in conservative-minded public discourse.

During the early period of industrialization in Japan, Confucianists contributed to the development of a tradition of peaceful labor–management relations. Historians have suggested that the establishment of Kyochokai (the Conciliation Association) in 1919 was a significant element in building harmonious labor relations (Paramore, 2016). Shibusawa Eiichi, the founder of this pseudo-government agency, was an overt advocate of Confucianism in his time. He argued that industrial conflicts would be unnecessary if labor and management followed the ideal of Confucian virtues in their dealings with each other (Paramore, 2016).

In addition to national industrial relations systems, Confucian influence can also be observed in corporate-level employment relations. Chew and Lim (1995) found that Confucian tradition contributed to Chinese managers' preference for non-confrontational conflict resolution strategies. In South Korea, Choi (2004) suggested that a company is likely to experience friendlier labor–management relations when there is a stronger Confucian organizational culture. In Taiwan, Chen (2007) indicated that Confucian tradition enabled Taiwanese companies to build paternalistic employment relations.

International assignments

The recent global expansion of East Asian companies has led to a rapid increase in the number of expatriates originating from Confucian cultures. Accordingly, there is growing scholarly interest in the behavioral patterns of international assignees from this cultural background. Studies found that Confucian values significantly influence East Asians' decisions to take on expatriate assignments. For instance, Kim and Slocum (2008) reported that many Korean expatriates accept challenging international assignments to express their loyalty to the company. They also suggest that the same motivation prevents Korean expatriates from returning prematurely. Cho, Hutchings, and Marchant (2013) also suggested that Korean expatriates make major decisions about expatriation and repatriation on the basis of Confucian values. They found that Koreans expatriates feel obliged to make such decisions in accordance with the will of their superior (out of loyalty) or for the sake of their children's education (family value). A similar phenomenon was observed amongst Chinese expatriates; Yao, Arrowsmith, and Thorn (2015) found that Chinese expatriates' acceptance of international assignments was motivated by their Confucian values of respect for authority and social harmony.

Confucian values also seem to influence expatriates' adjustment experiences during international assignments. Kim and Tung (2013) suggested that because of their home-grown Confucian values, Korean expatriates encounter unique challenges during international assignments. For instance, Korean expatriates whose organizational status is abruptly elevated by an international assignment find their job less satisfying because of the disruption of their hierarchical relations within the firm. In a recent study, Yu (2016) found that Chinese expatriates working in the USA tend to bring their Confucian values with them, and that their value system is vulnerable to cultural misunderstanding amongst host country nationals.

Confucianism as a managerial strategy: the case of FOTILE

In some East Asian companies, Confucianism is referred as their overarching business strategy that drives all aspects of managerial operations. Although Confucianism itself is rarely recognized as a concept of business strategy, scholars have argued for its potential as a guiding principle that enables business operations to be successful in a virtuous way (e.g., Chai & Rhee, 2010; Romar, 2002; Li & Liang, 2015). Some managers, especially those in Mainland China, have embraced such ideas with a degree of enthusiasm, and try to run their companies according to the Confucian principles they believe in. An illustrative case in point is FOTILE (McFarlan, Warren, Fang, & Zhang, 2013).

FOTILE is a Chinese company that occupies over 40 percent of domestic market for high-end kitchen hoods. The company is well known for its explicit reference to Confucianism as the primary foundation of its organizational culture and business strategy. In early 2000, Mao Zhongqun, the founding CEO, realized that Confucian tradition could be a valuable managerial resource for Chinese organizations as Japanese culture was for Japanese companies. Mr. Mao came to believe that Confucianism makes better employees, better leaders, and better organizations. Therefore, Mr. Mao declares that Confucian virtues (such as benevolence, righteousness, propriety, wisdom, and credibility) are the central values of the company. He set out to build an organization whose organizational culture is defined by Confucian virtues.

One notable initiative in this regard is to increase employees' exposure to Confucian teachings. In the corporate headquarters, Mr. Mao set up a classroom named Confucius Hall (*Kongzi Tang*). This 200-square-meter room in a prime location is decorated like an ancient Confucian school with a big statue of Confucius standing beside the podium. In this room, employees in leadership positions are required to take monthly classes on Confucianism. Furthermore, all employees of the company are encouraged to begin their daily work by reading aloud fifteen minutes Confucian teaching every morning.

In addition, Mr. Mao tried to ensure that his company treats employees according to the teachings of Confucius. For example, he found that penalty-based approach to workplace mis-behaviors goes against Confucian ideas of virtue-based leadership. Therefore, in 2009, he stopped charging penalties for minor misbehavior such as coming late to work or leaving early. Instead, he required immediate supervisors of misbehaving employees to talk to the employee in person to find out the reason behind it and to offer help if needed. Such a humane approach is believed to significantly reduce the occurrence of minor misbehaviors and enhance company effectiveness. Driven by the spirit of benevolence, Mr. Mao also tries to give generous benefits to his employees. Unlike most other companies in the region, FOTILE provides employees with extra days of paid holiday, profit-sharing schemes, and a substantial amount of interest-free loans.

Mr. Mao has made conscious efforts to set Confucianism as the defining feature of FOTILE's business strategy. The company specifies its primary mission as being to enable people to feel better about their *Jia* (家, home or family). This mission statement expresses the company's ambition to be a leading home appliances provider as well as its commitment to family-like organizational climate. He urges all employees to embody these virtues and to exhibit a sincere love for the customers, for the products, and for each other. When asked if learning Confucian ideologies have negatively affected the company's innovation, Mr. Mao said it has produced just the opposite because the love for the customers has enabled them to come up with the best rather than meet a particular standard. The company's total number of patents has exceeded the sum of those by the next nine competitors for the past ten years. The introduction of Confucian management is believed to make significant contributions to FOTILE's competitiveness and its market performance.

It is not yet clear whether the anecdotal stories such as FOTILE case is widely generalizable, and whether Confucian management could be established as a viable, coherent, and rigorous managerial concept. However, it seems to be clear that Confucianism inspires a growing number of East Asian managers to rediscover the potential managerial values of their indigenous cultural traditions.

Conclusions

Confucianism has had an indelible influence on East Asian society. For over 2,000 years, Confucian ideals have shaped the political arrangements, educational systems, and everyday lives of people in greater China and in the neighboring countries of Korea, Japan, Vietnam, and Singapore. Confucianism has taught East Asians to respect hierarchy, prioritize family, pursue self-development, and build harmonious social relations. During the period of modernization, Confucianism was criticized as a regressive legacy of pre-industrialized generations. It has survived to inspire developmental governments in the region and is now the subject of growing attention as an alternative ideological resource for sustainable East Asian capitalism.

Confucianism has been a formative influence on HRM in East Asia. Despite several waves of Westernization, Confucian tradition has continued to inspire East Asian organizations to develop their own unique HR practices, and the examples discussed here confirm this influence on selection, compensation, training, and retention practices. Confucianism has also contributed to sustained gender bias in East Asian workplaces, diluting or suppressing some collective labor activities. The unique corporate rituals of East Asian companies are also inspired in many cases by Confucianism.

We encourage HR researchers to pay serious attention to the implications of Confucianism for East Asian HR practices in future studies. In various areas of social sciences, Confucianism is an active scholarly concern, prompting debate about whether and how it may contribute to sustainable economic development in the region (Franke, Hofstede & Bond, 1991; Hofstede & Bond, 1988; Warner, 2010). Political scientists ask whether and how Confucian tradition can facilitate the advancement of democracy and the rule of law (Fukuyama, 1995; Shin, 2011), and management scholars have recognized the utility of Confucianism as an explanatory framework for Asia-specific phenomena (e.g., Chuang & Shim, 2015; Li & Liang, 2015; Kim & Strudler, 2012; Zhu, 2015). Business ethicists suggest that Confucianism may be a valuable moral resource for managers in greater China and beyond (Cheung & King, 2004; Boardman & Kato, 2003; Kim, 2014a, 2014b; Kim & Strudler, 2012). This exciting growth of scholarly interest in Confucianism offers great opportunities for researchers of HRM in Asia. Many previous studies of HRM in East Asia have addressed Confucianism in a rather superficial way, often reducing it to a contextual background overshadowed by Hofstede's cultural dimensions. By explicitly taking into account the long-standing influence of Confucianism as a cultural tradition, future research can enhance understanding of the determinants and outcomes of East Asian HR.

References

Au, K., Chiang, F. F., Birtch, T. A., & Ding, Z. (2013). Incubating the next generation to venture: The case of a family business in Hong Kong. *Asia Pacific Journal of Management, 30*(3), 749–767.

Anand, N. & Watson, M. (2004). Tournament rituals in the evolution of fields: The case of the Grammy awards. *Academy of Management Journal, 47*(1), 59–80.

Bae, J., Chen, S. J., & Rowley, C. (2011). From a paternalistic model towards what? HRM trends in Korea and Taiwan. *Personnel Review, 40*(6), 700–722.

Bae, J. & Lawler, J. J. (2000). Organizational and HRM strategies in Korea: Impact on firm performance in an emerging economy. *Academy of Management Journal, 43*(3), 502–517.

Bell, Daniel A. (2010). *China's new Confucianism: Politics and everyday life in a changing society.* Princeton, NJ: Princeton University Press.

Bhappu, A. D. (2000). The Japanese family: An institutional logic for Japanese corporate networks and Japanese management. *Academy of Management Review, 25*(2), 409–415.

Boardman, C. M. & Kato, H. K. (2003). The Confucian roots of business Kyosei. *Journal of Business Ethics, 48*(4), 317–333.

Bowen, C. C. (2003). Sex discrimination in selection and compensation in Taiwan. *International Journal of Human Resource Management, 14*(2), 297–315.

Bruton, G. D., Ahlstrom, D., & Wan, J. C. (2003). Turnaround in East Asian firms: Evidence from ethnic overseas Chinese communities. *Strategic Management Journal, 24*(6), 519–540.

Cai, D., Luo, J. H., & Wan, D. F. (2012). Family CEOs: Do they benefit firm performance in China?. *Asia Pacific Journal of Management, 29*(4), 923–947.

Chai, S. K. & Rhee, M. (2010). Confucian capitalism and the paradox of closure and structural holes in East Asian firms. *Management and Organization Review, 6*(1), 5–29.

Chang, S. J. & Shim, J. (2015). When does transitioning from family to professional management improve firm performance?. *Strategic Management Journal, 36*(9), 1297–1316.

Chen, S. J. (2007). Human resource strategy and unionization: Evidence from Taiwan. *The International Journal of Human Resource Management, 18*(6), 1116–1131.

Cheng, B., Boer, D., Chou, L., Huang, M., Yoneyama, S., Shim, D., Sun, J., Lin, T., Chou, W., & Tsai, C. (2014). Paternalistic leadership in four East Asian societies: Generalizability and cultural differences of the triad model. *Journal of Cross-Cultural Psychology, 45*(1), 82–90.

Cheung, T. & King, A. (2004). Righteousness and profitableness: The moral choices of contemporary Confucian entrepreneurs. *Journal of Business Ethics, 54*(3), 245–260.

Chew, I. & Lim, C. (1995). A Confucian perspective on conflict resolution. *The International Journal of Human Resource Management, 6*(1), 143–157.

Cho, T., Hutchings, K., & Marchant, T. (2013). Key factors influencing Korean expatriates' and spouses' perceptions of expatriation and repatriation. *The International Journal of Human Resource Management, 24*(5), 1051–1075.

Choi, J. (2004). Transformation of Korean HRM based on Confucian values. *Seoul Journal of Business, 10*(1), 1–26.

Chow, E. N. L. (2013). *Transforming gender and development in East Asia.* New York: Routledge.

Chung, C.-N. & Luo, X. R. (2013). Leadership succession and firm performance in an emerging economy: Successor origin, relational embeddedness, and legitimacy. *Strategic Management Journal, 34*(3), 338–357.

Conrad, H. (2010). From seniority to performance principle: The evolution of pay practices in Japanese firms since the 1990s. *Social Science Japan Journal, 13*(1), 115–135.

Conrad, H. (2014). Continuity and change in Asian employment systems: A comparison of Japan, South Korea, and Taiwan. In A. Wilkinson, G. Wood, & R. Deeg (Eds.), *The Oxford handbook of employment relations: Comparative employment systems* (pp. 334–358). Oxford: Oxford University Press.

Cooke, F. L. (2010). Women's participation in employment in Asia: A comparative analysis of China, India, Japan and South Korea. *The International Journal of Human Resource Management, 21*(12), 2249–2270.

Dacin, M., Munir. K., & Tracey. P. (2010). Formal dining at Cambridge Colleges: Linking ritual performance and institutional maintenance. *Academy of Management Journal, 53*(6), 1393–1418.

Dou, J. & Li, S. (2013). The succession process in Chinese family firms: A guanxi perspective. *Asia Pacific Journal of Management, 30*(3), 893–917.

Du, X. (2015). Does Confucianism reduce minority shareholder expropriation?: Evidence from China. *Journal of Business Ethics, 132*(4), 661–716.

Elman, B. A. (2013) *Civil examinations and meritocracy in late Imperial China.* Cambridge, MA: Harvard University Press.

Fetzer, J. & Soper, J. C. (2014). *Confucianism, democratization, and human rights in Taiwan.* Lanham, MD: Lexington Books.

Franke, R. H., Hofstede, G., & Bond, M. H. (1991). Cultural roots of economic performance: A research note. *Strategic Management Journal, 12*(S1), 165–173.

Fu, P. P. & Tsui, A. S. (2003). Utilizing printed media to understand desired leadership attributes in the People's Republic of China. *Asia Pacific Journal of Management, 20*(4), 423–446.

Fu, P. P., Tsui, A. S., & Liu, J. (2010). Pursuit of whose happiness?: Executive leaders' transformational behaviors and personal values. *Administrative Science Quarterly, 55*(2), 222–254.

Fukuyama, F. (1995). Confucianism and democracy. *Journal of Democracy, 6*(2), 20–33.

Galenianos, M. (2014). Hiring through referrals. *Journal of Economic Theory, 152*, 304–323.

Golding, D. (1991). Some everyday rituals in management control. *Journal of Management Studies, 28*(6), 569–583.

Goldman, A. H. (1975). China's anti-Confucian campaign, 1973–74. *The China Quarterly, 63*, 435–462.

Gomez-Mejia, L.R., & Welbourne, T. (1991). Compensation strategies in a global context. *Human Resource Planning, 14*(1), 29–42.

Granovetter, M. S. (1974). *Getting a job: A study of contacts and careers.* Chicago: University of Chicago Press.

Gregor, A. J. & Chang, M. H. (1979). Anti-Confucianism: Mao's last campaign. *Asian Survey, 19*(11), 1073–1092.

Goldin, P. R. (2014). *Confucianism.* New York: Routledge.

Han, J. & Han, J. (2009). Network-based recruiting and applicant attraction in China: Insights from both organizational and individual perspectives. *The International Journal of Human Resource Management, 20*(11), 2228–2249.

He, W., Long, L., & Kuvaas, B. (2016). Workgroup salary dispersion and turnover intention in China: A contingent examination of individual differences and the dual deprivation path explanation. *Human Resource Management, 55*(2), 301–320.

Hempel, P. S. & Chang, C. Y. D. (2002). Reconciling traditional Chinese management with high-tech Taiwan. *Human Resource Management Journal, 12*(1), 77–95.

Ho, M. S. (2012). Beyond tokenism: The institutional conversion of party-controlled labour unions in Taiwan's state-owned enterprises (1951–86). *The China Quarterly, 212*, 1019–1039.

Hofstede, G. & Bond, M. H. (1988). The Confucius connection: From cultural roots to economic growth. *Organizational Dynamics, 16*(4), 5–21.

Hom, P. W. & Xiao, Z. (2011). Embedding social networks: How guanxi ties reinforce Chinese employees' retention. *Organizational Behavior and Human Decision Processes, 116*(2), 188–202.

Horak, S. (2014). Antecedents and characteristics of informal relation-based networks in Korea: Yongo, Yonjul and Inmaek. *Asia Pacific Business Review, 20*, 78–108.

Horak, S. (2017). The informal dimension of human resource management in Korea: Yongo, recruiting practices and career progression. *The International Journal of Human Resource Management, 28*(10), 1409–1432.

Howard, A., Williams, S., Wellins, R. S., & Liu, L. (2014). *Employee retention in China 2006/2007: The flight of human talent.* Pittsburgh, PA: Society for Human Resource Management.

Jackson, S. E. & Schuler, R. S. (1995). Understanding human resource management in the context of organizations and their environments. *Human Resource Management: Critical Perspectives on Business and Management, 2*, 45–74.

Kang, H. & Rowley, C. (2005). Women in management in South Korea: Advancement or retrenchment? *Asia Pacific Business Review, 11*(2), 213–231.

Khanna, T., Song, J., & Lee, K. (2011). The paradox of Samsung's rise. *Harvard Business Review, 89*(7–8), 142–147.

Khim, S. (2002). Influence of Confucian values on HRM practices in Singapore-based firms. Unpublished doctoral dissertation, Curtin University of Technology.

Kim, C. (2015, January 27). In South Korea, childcare burden derails women's careers. *Reuters.* Retrieved June 24, 2016, from www.reuters.com/article/us-southkorea-women-childcare-idUSKBN0L00B 220150127.

Kim, H. & Tung, R. (2013). Opportunities and challenges or expatriates in emerging markets: An exploratory study of Korean expatriates in India. *The International Journal of Human Resource Management, 24*(5), 1029–1050.

Kim, K. & Slocum, J. (2008). Individual differences and expatriate assignment effectiveness: The case of U.S.-based Korean expatriates. *Journal of World Business, 43*, 109–126.

Kim, S. (2014). *Confucian democracy in East Asia: Theory and practice.* New York: Cambridge University Press.

Kim, S. & Wright, P. M. (2011). Putting strategic human resource management in context: A contextualized model of high commitment work systems and its implications in China. *Management and Organization Review, 7*(1), 153–174.

Kim, T. W. (2014a). Confucian ethics and labor rights. *Business Ethics Quarterly, 24*(04), 565–594.

Kim, T. W. (2014b). Decent termination: A moral case for severance pay. *Business Ethics Quarterly, 24*(2), 203–227.

Kim, T. W. & Strudler, A. (2012). Workplace civility: A Confucian approach. *Business Ethics Quarterly, 22*(3), 557–577.

Kim, Y. C. (2010). *The effectiveness of social networks (individual social capital) in the labor market* (in Korean). Namsejong-ro: KDI Press.

Korabik, K. (1993). Managerial women in the People's Republic of China. *International Studies of Management & Organization, 23*(4), 47–64.

KPMG. (2015). FAQs aptitude test. Retrieved from www.kpmg.com/cn/en/careers/graduates/application/pages/faqsaptitudetest.aspx.

Lam, C., Ho, E., & Wong, N. (2002). Parents' beliefs and practices in education in Confucian heritage cultures: The Hong Kong case. *Journal of Southeast Asian Education, 3*(1), 99–114.

Lardy, N. R. (2014). *Markets over Mao: The rise of private business in China.* Washington, DC: Peterson Institute for International Economics.

Lee, C. Y. (2012). Korean culture and its influence on business practice in South Korea. *Journal of International Management Studies, 7*(2), 184–191.

Lee, J. (2016, April 10). "What the Renaissance would be in the 21st century?" … Hyundai asked their applicants. *Chosunilbo.* (in Korean). Retrieved from http://news.chosun.com/site/data/html_dir/2016/04/10/2016041000991.html

Lee, K. S., Lim, G. H., & Lim, W. S. (2003). Family business succession: Appropriation risk and choice of successor. *Academy of Management Review, 28*(4), 657–666.

Lee, Y. (2014). The development of human resource management in South Korea. In B. E. Kaufman (Ed.), *The development of human resource management across nations: Unity and diversity.* Cheltenham: Edward Elgar Publishing.

Leong, S. M., Tan, H. H., & Loh, M. S. Y. (2004). When the cat's away: A content analysis of MNC overseas recruitment print ads. *Journal of Business Ethics, 49*(2), 115–127.

Li, X. H. & Liang, X. (2015). A Confucian social model of political appointments among Chinese private-firm entrepreneurs. *Academy of Management Journal, 58*(2), 592–617.

Liang, Q., Li, X., Yang, X., Lin, D., & Zheng, D. (2013). How does family involvement affect innovation in China?. *Asia Pacific Journal of Management, 30*(3), 677–695.

Liang, X., Wang, L., & Cui, Z. (2014). Chinese private firms and internationalization effects of family involvement in management and family ownership. *Family Business Review, 27*(2), 126–141.

Lin, L. H. & Ho, Y. L. (2009). Confucian dynamism, culture and ethical changes in Chinese societies: A comparative study of China, Taiwan, and Hong Kong, *The International Journal of Human Resource Management, 20*(11), 2402–2417.

Liu, D. (2016). Parental involvement and university graduate employment in China. *Journal of Education and Work, 29*(1), 98–113.

Liu, H. (2007). Influence of China's imperial examinations on Japan, Korea and Vietnam. *Frontiers of History in China, 2*(4), 493–512.

Low, K. C. P. (2012). Applying rituals and ceremonies to strengthen one's leadership and management influence. *Business Journal for Entrepreneurs, 4*, 14–30.

McFarlan, F., Warren, X, Z., Fang, Y., & Zhang, H. (2013). *Ningbo FOTILE kitchen ware co., ltd.*, Tsinghua University Case.

Marginson, S. (2011). Higher education in East Asia and Singapore: Rise of the Confucian model. *Higher Education, 61*, 587–611.

Mehrotra, V., Morck, R., Shim, J., & Wiwattanakantang, Y. (2013). Adoptive expectations: Rising sons in Japanese family firms. *Journal of Financial Economics, 108*(3), 840–854.

Nam, C. (1995). South Korea's big business clientelism in democratic reform. *Asian Survey, 35*(4), 357–366.

Ng, M. (2016). Examining social exchange among Chinese service workers: The mediating effect of trust in organization. *Asia-Pacific Journal of Business Administration, 8*(2), 1757–4323.

Paramore, Kiri (2016). *Japanese Confucianism: A cultural history.* Cambridge: Cambridge University Press.

Park, K. J. & Lee, C. W. (2011). A case study on training and development of 2nd generation successor in six Korean small and medium sized family business. *Korean Small Business Review, 33*(2), 195–219.

Pieper, J. R. (2015). Uncovering the nuances of referral hiring: How referrer characteristics affect referral hires' performance and likelihood of voluntary turnover. *Personnel Psychology, 68*(4), 811–858.

Qu, Q., Fu, P. P., & Huang, X. (2016). *Changing employee mind-set by developing human spirituality: Case study of a company from China.* Paper to be presented at AOM, Anaheim, USA.

Reiche, B. S. (2009). To quit or not to quit: Organizational determinants of voluntary turnover in MNC subsidiaries in Singapore. *The International Journal of Human Resource Management, 20*(6), 1362–1380.

Romar, E. J. (2002). Virtue is good business: Confucianism as a practical business ethics. *Journal of Business Ethics, 38*(1–2), 119–131.

Schein, E. H. (1990). Organizational culture. *American Psychologist, 45*(2), 109–119.

Seguino, S. (2011). Help or hindrance?: Religion's impact on gender inequality in attitudes and outcomes. *World Development, 39*(8), 1308–1321.

Sharma, P. & Chua, J. (2013). Asian family enterprises and family business research. *Asia Pacific Journal of Management, 30*, 641–656.

Sheenhan, N. (1988). *A bright shining lie: John Paul Vann and America in Vietnam.* New York: Random House.

Shin, D. C. (2011). *Confucianism and democratization in East Asia.* Cambridge: Cambridge University Press.

Sloman, M. (2007). *The changing world of the trainer: Emerging good practice.* Oxford: Elsevier.

Sun, A. (2013). *Confucianism as a world religion: Contested histories and contemporary realities.* Princeton, NJ: Princeton University Press.

Sung, S. (2003). Women reconciling paid and unpaid work in a Confucian welfare state: The case of South Korea. *Social Policy & Administration, 37*(4), 342–360.

Tsui-Auch, L. S. (2004). The professionally managed family-ruled enterprise: Ethnic Chinese business in Singapore. *Journal of Management Studies, 41*, 693–723.

Tung, R. L. (1994). Human resource issues and technology transfer. *The International Journal of Human Resource Management, 5*(4), 807–825.

Viet, H. N. (2015). Succession decision in Vietnamese family companies. *International Journal of Business and Management, 10*(7), 208–214.

Wang, J. (2011, January 22). Records show fairness of civil service recruitment. *China Daily.* Retrieved from www.chinadaily.com.cn/china/2011-01/22/content_11899638.htm.

Warner, M. (2010). In search of Confucian HRM: Theory and practice in Greater China and beyond. *The International Journal of Human Resource Management, 21*(12), 2053–2078.

White, G., & Goodman, R. (1998). Welfare Orientalism and the search for an East Asian welfare model. In R. Goodman, G. White, & H.-J. Kwon (Eds.), *The East Asian welfare model: Welfare Orientalism and the state* (pp. 3–24). London: Routledge.

Woodhams, C., Lupton, B., & Xian, H. (2009). The persistence of gender discrimination in China—evidence from recruitment advertisements. *The International Journal of Human Resource Management, 20*(10), 2084–2109.

Xiao, H. & Li, C. (2013). China's meritocratic examinations and the ideal of virtuous talents. In D. Bell & C. Li, *The East Asian challenge for democracy: Political meritocracy in comparative perspective* (pp. 340–362). New York: Cambridge University Press.

Yan, J. & Sorenson, R. (2006). The effect of Confucian values on succession in family business. *Family Business Review, 19*(3), 235–250.

Yao, C., Arrowsmith, J., & Thorn, K. (2015). Exploring motivations in Chinese corporate expatriation through the lens of Confucianism. *Asia Pacific Journal of Human Resources, 54*(3), 312–331.

Yao, X. (2000). *An introduction to Confucianism.* Cambridge: Cambridge University Press.

Yoo, S. S., Schenkel, M. T., & Kim, J. (2014). Examining the impact of inherited succession identity on family firm performance. *Journal of Small Business Management, 52*(2), 246–265.

Yu, X. (2016). From East to West: A phenomenological study of Mainland Chinese expatriates' international adjustment experiences in the U.S. workplace. Retrieved from the University of Minnesota Digital Conservancy, http://hdl.handle.net/11299/180214.

Zhang, Y., Xu, B., & Zhang, J. (2015). Impact of procedural characteristics on justice perceptions of Chinese civil service candidates. *Public Personnel Management, 44*(4), 543–558.

Zhu, Y. (2015). The role of Qing (Positive Emotions) and Li 1 (Rationality) in Chinese entrepreneurial decision making: A Confucian Ren-Yi wisdom perspective. *Journal of Business Ethics, 126*(4), 613–630.

Zhu, Y., Chen, I., & Warner, M. (2000). HRM in Taiwan: An empirical case study. *Human Resource Management Journal, 10*(4), 32–44.

4

RELIGIOSITY, ETHICS, AND THE SPIRIT OF CAPITALISM IN HRM

Mohamed Branine

Introduction

The recent reawakening of religiosity in the world as whole and in Asia in particular has led to a significant increase in the number of people who claim to have a faith even in countries such as the People's Republic of China and Vietnam where the practice of religion was suppressed for many years. This phenomenon has attracted the attention of scholars from various disciplines and sparked a raft of macro level and politically oriented studies, but there is very little academic research on the impact of religion and religiosity on management practice. Studies on the relationship between religious beliefs, organizational behavior, managerial practices, and organizational outcomes are still scarce, as already pointed out by Tayeb (1997), Abuznaid (2006), Schwartz (2006), Mellahi and Budhwar (2010), and Razimi, Noor, and Daud (2014). Much of the debate over the rise of religiosity and spirituality as a form of personal identity has focused on the effects of religion at the national rather than the organizational and workplace levels, and has been concerned with the negative aspects of religious extremism rather than on the positive implications of religious enlightenment on work and employee relations.

This chapter aims to expand on the debate of the latter by exploring the role of religion, religiosity, and ethics in managing employees in East Asian countries for reasons discussed below. Very often, the literature on management and culture overlooks the importance of religious values in employee relations because many studies treat religion as part of cultural norms and values of secular societies (see, for example, Hofstede, 1991). As Mellahi and Budhwar (2010: 686) noted, there is an extensive amount of literature on the effects of rituals and ceremonies in Japanese organizations but there is very little reference to the impact of group prayers on organizational outcomes (cf. Abu Bakar, Cooke, & Muenjohn, 2016).

The focus of this chapter on East Asian countries is of particular importance because religion is hardly considered in the study of management and employee relations in this part of the world. Most of the recent studies of the effects of religion on management and organizational behavior have focused on the Middle Eastern countries (e.g., Ali, 1992; Yousef, 2001; Mellahi, 2007; Mellahi & Budhwar, 2010; Yamak, Ergur, Unsal, Uygur, & Özbilgin, 2015; Uygr, Spence, Simpson, & Karakas, 2016), Malaysia and Indonesia (Debrah, McGovern and Budhwar, 2000; Aziz & Shamsul, 2004; Mamman & Somantri, 2014), and India and Pakistan (Budhwar &

Bhatnagar, 2009; Cooke & Saini, 2012; Khilji, 2002; Rao, 2012, 2015) which are not intended to be within the confines of this discussion.

The other reason for focusing on East Asian countries is that the scale of information that is available on the complexity and diversity of beliefs in Asia makes it uneasy to describe with certainty what aspects of what particular religion have really influenced the making of a particular group. It is easy to generalize by saying that such countries have been influenced by Buddhism, Confucianism, Hinduism, Islam, and Taoism, but there is very little evidence of the extent or the specific outcomes of such influence in practice. This is mainly because of the lack of research in this area. This chapter attempts to re-emphasize the importance of empirical research for understanding the role of religion and religiosity in managing human resources in East Asian countries.

The reason why it is important to understand the role of religion and religiosity in managing human resources is that people in organizations tend to act and interact in response to established norms but according to their inner and outer perceptions of the world around them. Religion, when it exists, influences such perceptions because when people go to work they do not leave their religion at home. They take their whole self to work. In an uncertain economic climate where job security is something of the past and work-related stress is on the increase, many employees have "began to turn to their faith as a source of stability and comfort … often viewing the inclusion of spirituality at work as a panacea to their woes" (Mohamed, Hassan, & Wisnieski, 2001: 102 cited in Miler & Ewest, 2010: 52). Therefore, the aim of this chapter is not to compare religions, or to separate between religious beliefs and cultural values, or to claim that one faith is better or worse than the other. It attempts to describe and analyze the main beliefs, virtues, values, principles, and practices by which individuals conduct themselves in organizational contexts because they are influenced by a particular religion and/or philosophical doctrine. As far as East Asia is concerned, the most influential doctrine is that of Confucianism, followed by Buddhism and Taoism, and then Islam and Christianity. The common moral and ethical values of these belief systems are described and their influence on the main functions of human resource management is discussed, using evidence from the scriptures and published texts. Finally, a conclusion of the main issues is drawn after a discussion of religiosity and the spirit of capitalism in East Asia.

Religion, religiosity, and ethical behavior

Religion is a belief or a set of beliefs that form a common doctrine, ideology, faith, creed, and a system by which people conduct themselves, relate with each other and to God. This is a spiritual interpretation of the concept of religion and a general interpretation of the divine religions of Christianity, Judaism, and Islam that follow external revelations from God. However, there are definitions that see religion as a human thing with no relationship to God. For example, Smith defined religion as "a way of life woven around people's ultimate concerns" (1998: 183), while Nigosian postulated that religion is "the creative activity of the human mind that satisfies inherent spiritual needs and desires" (1990: 6). It can be argued that the later definitions apply to most of the Asian beliefs and in particular, to Hinduism, Buddhism, Taoism, and the like because they came from individuals' insights and consciousness, as a result of their concerns about human social order, justice, desires, sufferings, harmony, and so on (Barrett, 1993; McGreal, 1995; Hill, 2006). Different religions have had various effects on the attitudes, moral character, work ethics, and value systems of individuals in different societies (King, Bell, & Lawrence, 2009; Miler and Ewest, 2010; Pekerti & Sendjaya, 2010; Hage & Posner, 2015). Most of the world religions teach the virtues of piety, compassion, helping and giving, kindness, love, and sacrifice. They are supposed to help us to follow the right path to goodness and to reject what is bad for us. However, it can be argued that many ideologies, cultural values and norms have the same aims as those of great religions. This is because the relationship between religion and culture is in most cases a source of major confusions. It is generally assumed that religion is only one of the components of a broader cultural spectrum in a society but this differs from one society to another. In most countries, religion has some degree of influence on the cultural values of their people and their institutions (Hofstede, 1991; Tayeb, 1997). Such influence depends on the type of religion and the level of religiosity in a particular society. Although this analysis is beyond the scope of the chapter, it can be argued that religious beliefs make up only a small but growing element of the overall spiritual fabric and cultural norms and values of Asian societies.

Religiosity, which is also referred to as spirituality, is the extent to which religion is manifested in society in its different rituals, symbols, and forms of relationships (McCleary & Barro, 2006; Hage & Posner, 2015). It is also simply defined as the belief in a religion, a philosophy, or an ideology, and the devotion and commitment to follow its teachings, policies, and rules. According to McDaniel & Burnett (1990), religiosity can be measured behaviorally and cognitively. Behavioral measurements include attendance to the places of worship, involvement in religious activities, giving to religious charities, and supporting and promoting the causes of religious organizations. Cognitive measurements refer to the level of spiritual devotion a person holds toward his/her religion or the extent to which religion is important in the daily life of an individual. In other words, religiosity or spirituality can only exist when there is a belief system, which may or may not be a religion.

Ethical behaviors are influenced by a number of factors ranging from individual attributes to organizational and social factors. Individual attributes can be mental and physical, inherited or developed, and personally or group inspired. Religiosity plays a major role in the perception and expression of such attributes in an organizational context. While this cannot be denied, religion can only be one of the factors that may influence ethical behavior because the influence of other social, economic, political, and environmental factors cannot be underestimated. According to Magill (1992), the nature of ethical behavior depends on the person's level of personal religiosity. Moreover, according to Weaver and Agle, "religiosity is known to have an influence on human attitudes and behavior. This behavior is influenced by religious self-identity, which was formed as a result of the internalization of the role expectations offered by the religion" (Weaver & Agle, 2002, cited in Rashid & Ibrahim, 2008: 909).

Therefore, it can be concluded that religion is more of a social construct (Sengupta, 2010) that develops into socio-economic and political contexts, while religiosity is the spiritual aspect of that social construct which makes the difference between believing and implementing what is believed. One may believe in an idea or ideology to make it part of his/her religion without practicing that religion, making religion a prerequisite for religiosity (Hage & Posner, 2015). This is why there is a strong link between ethics and religion in the practice of management (see Sidani & Thornberry, 2010). Ethical values are good religious beliefs but being ethical does not always imply being religious and vice versa could be true. Moreover, many studies have linked religiosity to ethical behavior (Wiebe & Roland Fleck, 1980; Magill, 1992; Weaver & Agle, 2002; Vitell, Paolillo, & Singh, 2006). It has also been argued that ethical behavior may have no relationship to religiosity (Abratt, Nel, & Hays, 1992). A study by McDonald & Pak (1997) found that religious orientations had no influence on ethical behavior. Factors like ethnic origin, nationality, educational background, age, and status were also found to play a significant role in determining ethical behavior (Goodwin & Goodwin, 1999; Rashid & Ibrahim, 2008), rather than religion or religiosity.

People of different societies and communities have differing levels of religiosity (Goodwin & Goodwin, 1999; Ford, Nonis, & Hudson, 2005; Rashid & Ibrahim, 2008) because of their histories, cultures, political systems, and levels of economic development and industrialization. For example, the Chinese of Mainland China have less concern for religion than the Chinese of Malaysia, and the latter have less concern for religion than the Indians and Malays of the same country. Therefore, it can be deducted that although Buddhism, Confucianism, and Taoism are not divine religions, the ethical behaviors of their followers imply having a level of religiosity/spirituality. According to Lim, "Confucianism is not so much a religion as it is a code for social conduct and its influence is so pervasive that Chinese function unconsciously in a Confucian manner" (Lim 2015: 17). This implies the existence of religiosity without a religion amongst many Chinese people (for the influence of Confucianism in HRM in China, Japan, and South Korea, see Chapter 3).

The role of religion and religiosity/spirituality in East Asian societies

There are many religions and philosophies that have induced differing levels of religiosity amongst the various nations and societies of East Asia but the most influential ones are Confucianism and Taoism, Buddhism, Islam, and Christianity. Being mindful of the fact that the effects of each of these belief systems on the practice of management and employee relations are also covered in other parts of this book, the focus here will be on the role of these beliefs in managing people in selected East Asian countries.

Confucianism and Taoism

Confucianism and its effects on the practice of human resource management and employee relations in Asian societies are well and clearly discussed in other chapters of this book. This brief discussion here is to emphasize the point that both Confucianism and Taoism are not religions but philosophies that have characterized the cultures of Asian societies to the extent that they are often treated as religions in the absence of a dominant divine religion (Barrett, 1993; Oldstone-Moore, 1998, 2005).

Confucianism. Confucianism came from Confucius who was a teacher and a wise man in 551–479 BC. At a time when China was characterized by social anarchy, wars, elitism, and inequality, Confucius used his wisdom and strong character to teach the virtues of social relationships that led to the establishment of a harmonious society (Oldstone-Moore, 1998; Hill, 2006). Confucianism sees the existence of individuals through their relationships with others (Sungmoon, 2008; Lim, 2015), and is often summarized in this Confucius proverb:

> *If there is righteousness in the heart, there will be beauty in the character. If there is beauty in the character, there will be harmony in the home. If there is harmony in the home, there will be order in the nation. When there is order in the nation, there is peace in the world.*
> *(Smith, 1994: 10, cited in Steiner, Gilliland, & Skarlicki, 2002: 56)*

With the passing of time, Confucius' teachings became integrated with other beliefs and cultural values, initially of Buddhism and then Islam and Christianity. One of the aspects of following Confucianism is to be able to choose any religious belief, as a Buddhist, Christian, or Muslim, while adhering to the traditional Confucian principles of social relationships. Also, Confucianism fitted well with the strict enforcement of the law by the authoritarian and totalitarian governments that dominated Asian countries. This phenomenon is present to varying degrees in all Asian countries where for centuries the absolute authority resides with the head of state and it is natural for the individuals to be law obedient.

Taoism. Besides Confucianism, there was the emergence of Taoism (or Daoism), which was derived from *Tao Te Ching* and was introduced by Lao Zi in the sixth century BC. It is interpreted as the path to the right conduct or the way to achieving moral and physical order without having to strive in pain. It is believed that this kind of order can only be achieved through harmony with nature. Unlike Confucianism, which focuses on the moral behaviors of human beings, Taoism focuses on nature and its elements like darkness and light, day and night, moon and sun, *ying* and *yang*, as well as men and women. According to Taoism, these harmonious and complementary elements are continuously changing in their different formats but moving in one direction, which is "The Way." In this respect, natural rules—rather than societal rules of Confucianism—have to be followed with pure simplicity in the pursuit of eternal life or the way. Authority, seniority, family ties, and the virtues of decency, filial submission, and loyalty are seen as natural behaviors (Hill, 2006). Taoism came to complement the social rules of Confucianism and then it accepted the concept of spiritual guidance as it became in contact with Buddhism, which has been also influential in East Asia.

Buddhism

Buddhism came mainly from Hinduism because Buddha was a Hindu prince who denounced the practice of Hinduism in relation to caste, rituals, austerities, creation, and self, and accepted the belief in the existence through reincarnation and being guided by the laws of cause and effect (*karma*) (McNair, 2015). Hinduism is one of the oldest belief systems in Asia going back for more than 2,000 years BC. It started in India and then spread into Southeast Asia. There are many sects and different interpretations of the original Hindu ideas but it is based on the belief that the world has a source (*Brahman*), from where it began and it will return to that source after going through numerous reincarnations (rebirths). The process of life goes upwards toward *Brahman* and downwards toward material existence that is decided by the laws of *Karma*. According to Hinduism, a current life of a human being is determined by his/her actions in the previous life and the experiences of a future life are determined by the current life and so on (Knott, 2016). The practice of meditation is believed to free a person from his/her attachment to material existence to become a spiritual being. There are many and different gods in Hinduism and each god is a display of a particular superlative creature. Despite its influence on Buddhism, Hinduism is not widely practiced in East Asia, and therefore, its effects on people management and employee relations are not discussed in this chapter.

Siddhartha Gautama (around 563–483 BC), who is known as Gautama Buddha or the Buddha, was a sage and enlightened man who did not claim to be a prophet or a superhuman being but just someone who was able to identify and understand the sources of pain and suffering in people. He introduced a basic pattern of living that is meant to free human beings from suffering, sorrow, and despair to live a life of awakening and enlightenment through meditation and rejection of material existence. This basic way of life, which is known as *Theravada*, was preached in India and then spread into Southeast Asia until the first century AD, when *Mahayana* was introduced in Northern India as another version of Buddhism with more teachings and forms of meditation. The teachings of Buddha are called *Dharma*, which are based on four noble truths: (1) all life is suffering; (2) suffering is caused by desires; (3) suffering has an end; and (4) the end of suffering is achieved by reaching *Nirvana* through eight right paths of behavior which are: (1) understanding; (2) thought; (3) speech; (4) action; (5) livelihood; (6) effort; (7) mindfulness; and (8) concentration. In other words, the paths to the end of suffering involve good thinking, not harming others, not overindulging, not having malicious thoughts or intentions, awareness of what to do, and meditation (Rarick, 2007; McNair, 2015).

As Buddhism spread into East Asia, it integrated and developed with the belief systems of the societies it encountered. It shares with Confucianism the five core virtues as Buddha's five precepts and contributed to the emergence of Taoism in China (Ling, 2004). Today the majority of the Buddhist population is in China, mainly in the Tibet region, and East Asia with the highest percentage is in Thailand, Cambodia, Myanmar, and Japan. Together with legalism and other ideologies like Communism, these ancient philosophies (Buddhism, Confucianism, and Taoism) of social order, morality, and spirituality have contributed to the making of contemporary Chinese culture. However, one should not underestimate the increasing influences of other world religions such as Christianity and Islam as they are the fastest growing faiths in the People's Republic of China, and in all other East Asian countries.

Islam

Islam was first introduced to China in AD 650 with the arrival of a delegation led by the Companion of Prophet Mohammed, Sa'ad ibn Abi Waqqas. The delegation was sent by the Companion and the third Caliph of Islam, Uthman ibn Affan, eighteen years after the death of Prophet Mohammed, to invite the Chinese Emperor Gaozong during the Tang Dynasty (618–907) to accept the faith of Islam (Dillon, 1994; Lai & Mu, 2016; BBC, 2002). It was reported that the Emperor expressed his admiration and was pleased with the virtues and rules of the new religion, seeing that many of its aspects were compatible to the teachings of Confucius and granted the freedom to the Muslims to practice their religion in China (Ting, 1987; Cho, 2009; Gladney, 2004). Since then, Islam has been recognized as one of the religions of China even during the Cultural Revolution (1966–1976), when all religious practices were forbidden. As a recognized minority religion, it was officially declared by the new republican government after the fall of the Manchu dynasty in 1911 that the country belonged equally to the Han, Hui (Muslim), Tsang (Tibetan), and the Meng (Mongol) people (Gladney, 1996). Today's Muslims in China are likely to be born in China and they are likely to be nationalists, Confucians, and even Communists as there are very few Chinese converts and very few Muslim immigrants to China (Gladney, 2004), but they are still a minority in comparison to the overall population of China. Nevertheless, although a minority religion in East Asia (about 3 percent in China, 1 percent in Japan, and less than 1 percent in Korea), the number of Muslims is significantly large in comparison with those of other Muslim countries. For example, there are more Muslims in China today than they are in Malaysia, and more than every Arab country with the exception of Egypt.

Islam is a way of life that is guided by a set of rules and principles that are based on the revealed book, the holy *Quran*, the doings and sayings (*Sunnah* and *Hadith*) of the Prophet Mohammed, the consensus of the Muslim scholars (*Ijma'a*), and in some cases individual scholars' interpretations of the *Quran* and *Hadith* (*Ijtihad*). The *Quran*, which is also spelt *Koran*, contains the words of God that were revealed syllable by syllable to the Prophet Mohammed in Makkah and Medina (currently cities in Saudi Arabia) over a period of twenty-three years—starting on AD December 22, 609, when Prophet Mohammed was forty years old, and ending in AD 632, the year of his death. In Islam, there is no intermediary between humans and God as the person's relationship with the creator (God or *Allah* in Arabic) is direct through his/her deeds and acts of worship. To become a Muslim one has to believe in the existence and oneness of God, in the Angels, in the revealed books (*Torah* revealed to Moses, the Psalms [*Zabur*] revealed to David, the Gospel [*Injil*] revealed to Jesus, and the *Quran* revealed to Mohammed), in the Prophets, in the Day of Judgment, and in the Divine Order.

Unlike other religions, Islam is: "an all-encompassing creed, it governs every aspect of life, public and private, political and economic, and as such is relevant to business activities. In other words, there is no separation between worldly and religious aspects of life," (Tayeb, 1997: 355). In this context, there is a growing literature on Islamic economics, banking, finance, and management. As far as management is concerned, there are core values and principles of management that are derived from the holy *Quran*, and the Prophet's *Sunnah* and *Hadith* (see Kalantari, 2005; Branine & Pollard, 2010; Syed & Ali, 2010; Razimi et al. 2014), but the ways by which they are implemented are flexible and changeable depending on the interpretation of the text by different scholars. The core principles are intention, loyalty, truthfulness, obedience, discipline, patience, consultation, professionalism, fairness, dedication, respect for seniority, and moderate and accountable personality (Tayeb, 1997; Shah, Larbi, & Batley, 2007; Branine & Pollard, 2010). It can be seen that Islam has much in common with Buddhism and Confucianism in relation to the virtues of social order and interrelationships. The main difference, which is fundamental, is the belief in the oneness of God and the ways of worshiping and seeking the blessing and pleasure of the one God. In other words, while the social virtues and the principles of relationships in worldly matters are to some extent similar, the differences are in the more divine and spiritual aspects of the religion. Indonesia, Malaysia, and the Sultanate of Brunei are predominantly Muslim countries in Southeast Asia, but they are also homes to significant proportions of Christians and Buddhists. More than a third of their populations are from Chinese, Indian, and Western European origins, and so the traditions of Confucianism, Buddhism, and Christianity have had a major impact on management practices and social relations. This has resulted in the development of a distinctive mixture of Asian and Western management systems influenced by Islamic values and principles.

Christianity

The presence of Christianity in East Asia is relatively recent, comparatively small but potentially very influential because of the significant growth of Christian believers in the People's Republic of China over the last three decades. Historically, Christianity arrived to China in the late sixteenth century when the early waves of Christian missionaries led by the Italian Matteo Ricci started preaching in East Asia. By the nineteenth and twentieth centuries, Christianity had entered every part of Asia with the spread of Spanish, Dutch, Portuguese, British, and French empires into the East. However, by the 1960s, Christianity had declined significantly with the departure of Westerners, the rise of nationalism, and the introduction of communism in a number of East and Southeast Asian countries. After the opening up of China in 1979, the Chinese government officially recognized five religions: Buddhism, Catholicism, Daoism, Islam, and Protestantism. Currently, Christianity (Catholicism and Protestantism) is the fastest growing religion in China with some predictions that it will be the majority religion overtaking Buddhism within the next twenty years. It seems that the current economic prosperity has led to materialism and hence the creation of a spiritual vacuum. In search for happiness beyond the achievement of material desires, many Chinese are looking for spiritual enlightenment. Given the choice and the freedom to do so, more and more Chinese are choosing Christianity over other faiths, such as Tibetan Buddhism, Islam, or Falun Gong, because Christianity is seen perhaps politically a safer option especially for those who aspire to Western ways of life. Christianity has been present for many years and has been significantly influential in a number of East and Southeast Asian countries such as the Philippines, Vietnam, Singapore, and Thailand.

In Western societies, the classical book of Max Weber (1930 [1905]) on *The Protestant Ethics and the Spirit of Capitalism* is possibly the most serious work on the role of religion in management and organization. He argued that the moral values of Protestantism led to the rise of capitalism in Western industrialized societies. Weber (1930 [1905]) argued that a relationship exists between certain religions and economic activities of the countries where they are practiced, and that the Protestant theology in particular had the strongest link with economic growth and capitalism.

> In *The Protestant Ethic and the Spirit of Capitalism*, Weber argues that capitalism required a disciplined workforce and regularised investment of capital, driven by the motivation to increase wealth as a goal in itself, rather than to satisfy material needs.
>
> *(Shah et al., 2007: 3)*

Weber (1930 [1905]) observed that business success was seen as a sign of God's pleasure and a pointer to eternal reward. It was assumed that God blessed profitable work and the individuals who are bestowed this blessing through hard work, and economic use of resources and time are rewarded here and in the hereafter. However, he also stated that Hinduism and Confucianism were "unable to give rise to a capitalist ethic" (Shah et al., 2007: 11). It will be argued later in this chapter that Weber's assumptions have been proved to be wrong.

Effects of religion and religiosity on the practice of HRM in East Asia

After explaining the type of religions and the nature of religiosity in East Asia, this section is to attempt to analyze how each of the main people management functions might be influenced by these religions put together. It will discuss how the key common virtues of religiosity and spirituality might have contributed to the contemporary characteristics of human resource management in Asian countries. It can be inferred from the religions and philosophies described above that they all emphasize keeping harmony and order, providing justice, and empowering people. These fundamental goals are based on respect for seniority, acceptance of authority, long-term orientation, humility, self-restraint, and collectivism. In other words, they seem to promote a soft and gentle approach to human resource management where the workplace looks like a family unit. The organization as a social entity is based on a family-like structure and principles of behavior. It is not just in terms of family ownership of conglomerates as in Japan and South Korea but also in terms of management and employee relations even in state-owned companies and cooperatives in the People's Republic of China. "Familism" is characteristic of all of them regardless of type of ownership and plays a significant role in management–workers relations. Superiors as leaders and managers treat their subordinates like their children—with *ren* (benevolence)—and employees [subordinates] should exhibit *zhong* (loyalty) and *yi* (politeness or righteousness) to the organization [institution and its leaders] (see Xing, 1995; Laulusa, 2008; Sungmoon, 2008; Hashim, 2010; Razimi et al., 2014). The extent to which this type of "familism" or paternalism, and the spiritual virtues and principles associated with it, has influenced the theory and practice of HRM in East Asian countries will be discussed here.

Recruitment and selection

The importance of trust, fairness, equality, and competence in the recruitment and selection of employees is emphasized in all the religions described above. Trust seems to be the key to keeping the organization in harmony and free from deception and wrongdoings. Commenting on the importance of trust in Chinese society, Lim states that:

the extent to which one is willing to ascribe good intentions to and confidence in the words and actions of the other people should be strong enough to match favors and trusts of the givers so that they are giving "face" to those who receive their favors and trusts and that they gain "face" at the same time because they are thought of as being sincere.

(2015: 20)

Both Buddha and Confucius stressed the importance of trust for maintaining strong interpersonal relationships, while in Islam the concept of trust in recruitment is clearly related to strength and competence. The Quran reports what the wife to be of the Prophet Moses said to her father: "O my (dear) father! Engage him (Moses) on wages, truly the best of men for you to employ is the strong and trusty" (Al-Quran, 28:26). Accountability which implies having knowledge and skills to do the job is also emphasized in Islam. This can be found in the verse that reports the Prophet Yusuf saying to the King of Egypt: "set me over the store-houses of the land, I will indeed guard them, as one that knows" (Al-Quran, 12:55). Other important factors such as motivation, sincerity, knowledge, and responsibility are also mentioned in the Quran and in the *Hadith* (see Hashim, 2010; 2010; Branine & Pollard, 2010; Branine, 2011; Razimi et al., 2014).

Nevertheless, when you have an organization that is managed like a family unit, as explained earlier, the importance given to trust in recruitment and selection has often resulted in the inclination to recruit friends and relatives. These actions can be interpreted from a Western perspective as nepotism and favoritism. All actions that may promote inequality and discrimination are against the teachings of all religions and philosophies stated above but they are still widely carried out in many Asian countries. This is because the recruitment of friends and relatives is perceived as having positive rather than negative outcomes and reinforces the Confucian fundamental moral behavior, which is to honor the supervisor and to favor the friend and the relative in society (Hwang, 2001). The Chinese *guanxi* (reciprocal relationships), is used by the Buddhists and the Muslims as well as other religious and non-religious people all over East and Southeast Asia in the recruitment and selection of employees to gain employees' loyalty and to have their trust and commitment to the organization. It is believed that reliance on recommendations by friends and relatives and the use of *guanxi* based on kinship and political connections will result in trustworthy, loyal, and committed employees who will learn their job faster, work harder, and stay in the organization for longer (Tsang, 1998; Sheh, 2001; Hill, 2006). It can be concluded therefore that the HRM function of recruitment and selection in East Asian countries is influenced by a common tradition of social relationships (*guanxi*) rather than by religious beliefs because the over-reliance on trust alone in recruitment and selection is different from, if not contradictory to, the Buddhist and Islamic requirement of strength (ability) and accountability. Therefore, there is no evidence yet of religion and religiosity having any significant influence on the practice of recruitment and selection in Asian countries.

Training and development

The belief in the law of causality is embedded in all religions and philosophies that have influenced Asian people's perception of learning and development. It is believed that nothing exists in its own right because everything has been caused by something. The drive of oneself to enlightenment and perfection can only be through understanding that comes from learning, reasoning, and acting. For example, in the *Zen* doctrine of Buddhism, self-discipline, learning, self-determination, and control of one's path to mastery and perfection are the keys to personal development and the development of others. The Buddha is reported as saying: "Only a man himself can be the master of himself … then there is true help and self-possession." This can be also encapsulated in the Chinese proverb: "don't give me a fish today and I will starve tomorrow, teach me how to be a fisherman so I will never starve." Also the Buddha is reported as saying: "If a man should conquer in battle a thousand and thousand more, and another should conquer himself, his would be victory, because the greater of victories is the victory over oneself" (cited in Rarick, 2007: 4). Moreover, in Islam there are many verses of the Quran that emphasize the concepts of *Itqan* (perfection) and *Ikhlas* (sincerity) in all behaviors or deeds. Humans are expected to learn to do things with perfection and "to ensure that all activities in their daily life are planned and executed at the best level of performance" (Ahmad, 2008: 39). It can be inferred that self-improvement through continuous training and development while seeking perfection and goodness is a crucial element of all Asian societies. Human resource development in Asian countries is inspired by a tradition of learning and self-development.

Moreover, seeking knowledge through reading and learning is strongly advocated by all religions and moral philosophies in Asian countries. Both Buddha and Confucius were teachers. Confucius said: "there is both a great happiness and satisfaction in constant studies" (cited in Śleziak, 2013: 31–32). It is also reported that Confucius was "the first person in China to offer education to everyone who came to him, irrespective of that person's social status" (Liu & Stening, 2016: 5). His main aim was to educate as many people as possible to be the future leaders of a harmonious and prosperous Chinese society. The educated and the knowledgeable persons are highly valued and respected in Asian societies. Teachers are seen as masters and a source of knowledge and wisdom, and treated with high respect not only by their students but also by everyone in the community. Being obedient and respectful to the teacher or the "master" is seen as a character of a good learner in all Asian societies.

Challenging the authority of the teacher is seen to be a sign of disrespect, deviance, and unwillingness to excel in what is being learnt (Xue Cunningham & Rowley, 2007). In this context, Newell stated that:

> the teacher is the expert and the learner can simply learn by listening and following. Dialogue would be avoided in this situation because dialogue presupposes a process of joint knowledge production, which would undermine the belief in the expert teacher.
>
> *(1999: 291)*

This process of learning makes the learners passive receivers of information and dependent on their teachers. This passive, uncritical, and dependent approach to learning is common amongst most Asian societies where memorizing is a popular way of gaining knowledge. The religious scripts, the teachings of gurus and sage people, and even institutional rules, regulations, and policies are learnt by heart through learning by rote and memorizing.

Most Asian students have developed the ability to visualize and grasp the written text and accept it as knowledge not to be questioned. This passive process of learning does not stop after school or at university level but it transcends to the workplace, where employees learn instructions from their managers and the managers learn the rules and regulations by often memorizing policy documents produced by their superiors. This style of learning has been very often criticized for producing "a lot of 'vacuum cleaners'—students who sucked up a lot of information but participated little in the classroom" (Hutton, 2000: 22). However, Chan argues that what seems to be learning by rote and memorizing from a Western perspective is just a process of Chinese learning by repetition. "In this case, repetition is used to assist students in the accurate recall of information. Unlike rote learning, repetitive learning enabled the learner to attach meaning to the material learned" (Chan, 1999: 300).

It should be noted that the only way to memorize the Quran in Arabic, as many millions of Muslims do throughout the world, is through rote and repetitive learning. It is not a religious obligation but it is the easiest way to preserve the holy book in the minds and hearts of the believers and this is how it has been descended unchanged from one generation to another over fifteen centuries. Therefore, it can be concluded that the fact that most Asian students learn through rote and memorizing is traditionally an effective way of learning from texts written in a native language (Chinese, Japanese, or Arabic) and has nothing to do with any religious belief. It is a common way of learning that is influenced by tradition rather than religion.

Rewards and remuneration

All Asian religious teachings call for ethical considerations to take precedence over the financial ones. The ultimate reward for one's deeds and behavior is to be satisfied and to satisfy others, and God, for those who believe in God. Unethical earnings through deception, theft, corruption, laziness, and the like are not in the spirit of any belief system because they may satisfy one side but not the other. Therefore, the key factors in an ethical and spiritual reward system are justice, fairness, equality, and satisfaction. Those who believe in God and in the Day of Judgment will seek the eternal reward in the hereafter for all their work in this life.

For example, in Islam, the ultimate reward for any activity is God's pleasure. All deeds in whatever form or size are rewarded in this life and in the life after death. The Quran states: "Then shall everyone who has done an atom's weight of good, see it. And anyone who has done an atom's weight of evil, shall see it" *(*Al-Quran, 99:7–8). What does this mean at the organizational level? It means that workers should be treated equally and rewarded fairly for their work. It also implies that performance appraisal should be used at all levels. Work is considered as an act of worship that has to be done with perfection but employment contracts have to be honored and employees have to be rewarded in line with the terms and conditions of their contracts.

For example, in Islam, the Prophet Mohammed said: "Give the worker his wages before his sweats dries." And in another *Hadith*, the Prophet said that God will be against the person who employs a laborer and gets the full work done by him but does not pay him his wages. In reality, there is a big gap between what is expected, according to the belief systems, and what is actually practiced in the workplace. There are many cases of inequality in pay, discrimination in promotion, exploitation of low-wage employees, and so on. It seems that religion and religiosity have had no significant effects on the human resource management function of rewards and remuneration. Most of the current problems of inequality, discrimination, and exploitation have emanated from materialistic, non-religious, and unethical policies and practices.

Employee relations

The area where religion and religiosity should have had significant effects is employee relations because most of the religious teachings, as explained above, are about relationships in social and economic life. In a paper on the implications of Confucianism for employee relations in China, Laulusa (2008) confirms that the employee–employer relationships are still based on Confucian social rules and values rather than on the Western style of contract relationships. The employee–employer contractual relationship in Chinese organizations is very often described as a father–children relationship characterized by respect of authority, seniority and older age, obedience to the rules, and loyalty to individuals and institutions (Boisot & Liang, 1992; Chen, 1995; Xing, 1995). Also, according to Confucius, the best way to govern is by virtue or *ren*, which means through moral education with benevolence and leading by the example not by imposing legislation (Child & Warner, 2003). In this respect, Confucius is reported as saying:

> if you lead the people with political force and restrict them with law and punishment, they can just avoid law violation, but will have no honor and shame. If you lead them with morality and guide with *Li* [moral codes], they will develop a sense of honor and shame, and will do good of their own accord.
>
> *(McGreal, 1995: 7, cited in Child & Warner, 2003: 8)*

It can be concluded that those in position of power are requested to treat their subjects or subordinates with respect and kindness, and to consult them in the decisions that concern them. Both employees and employers are expected to have a positive relationship with a minimal level of conflict or aggression. Confucianism emphasizes the importance of group orientation and conflict avoidance. The existence of individuals is in the benefit of others and only within a harmonious relationship and therefore, "group pressure is applied to ensure conformity through eliciting shame (losing face), and conflict is generally handled through intra-group mediation rather than an external legal system" (Xing, 1995: 17).

In Islam, the Prophet Mohammed said: "Do not dispute with your bother, ridicule him, nor promise him and then break your promise." He also said: "A strong person is not the one who throws his adversaries to the ground. A strong person is the one who contains himself when he is angry." Also in Buddhism, emotions have to be controlled and anger is not encouraged as in the words of Buddha: "Never speak harsh words, for once spoken they may return to you. Angry words are painful and there may be blows for blows." This "familism" type of employee relations is a result of accumulated beliefs that promote the concept of "non-self" and reject the concept of "oneself." It is believed that individuals can only exist in harmony as groups and communities. For example, the role of trade unions is cooperative and non-adversary and has always been centered on "labor productivity, worker morale and welfare" (Henley & Nyaw, 1986: 648) in the workplace and at the national level (see also Child & Warner, 2003).

Moreover, stressing the importance of harmony, the Buddha said: "many do not know that we are here in this world to live in harmony. Those who know this do not fight against each other" (cited in Rarick, 2007: 5). He is also reported as saying: "all the great rivers on reaching the great ocean lose their former names and identities and are reckoned simply as the great ocean." Similarly, this notion of collectivism and "no-self" is found in Islam as the Prophet Mohammed said: "None of you truly believes until he loves for his brother that which he loves for himself." And he also said: "the wolf eats the sheep that wanders off alone." In other words, these religious teachings promote the right to association, to join trade unions, to collective bargaining, workers' participation, teamwork, and joint consultation. Analyzing the resurgence of Islam in Asian countries, Tayeb states that:

> self-discipline, trustfulness, honesty, resolve, loyalty, and abstinence, should encourage managers to trust their subordinates' judgement and integrity, which could in turn lead to a participative management style. Co-operation, patience, and family-like relationships among people, should encourage teamwork and mutual support within an organization and care for the community outside it.
>
> *(1997: 5)*

Participation in the decision-making process through consultation is clearly stated in the Quran. It is stated in the chapter of Consultation: "and their business is conducted through consultation among themselves" (Al-Quran, 42:38). The Prophet Mohammed also said: "He who consults is guarded against regret; one who mistreats those under him will not enter paradise."

Another argument for employees' right to representation and to be consulted and involved in the process of decision-making is that all religions came to free people from suffering including exploitation in the workplace. According to Syed and Ali,

> the existence of a union is treated as a virtuous endeavor and a necessary condition for the prevention of wickedness. This implies that the formation of trade union has a religious dimension and is a moral duty to counter possible abuse at the workplace.
>
> *(2010: 462)*

However, despite all these spiritual and religious teachings that promote workers' rights to organize and to join trade unions, many Asian countries have imposed tight controls on the activities of trade unions. Even when trade unions are recognized and employees are free to form and to join trade unions, genuine collective bargaining is very rare and industrial action is very often prohibited. Authoritarian regimes throughout Asian countries have controlled trade unions' movements and democratic freedoms under the disguise of national unity, national security, and economic growth. Asian employee relations are influenced by the state in power rather than by religion or philosophy because the state is the largest employer, the regulator, the policy-maker, and the decision-maker. Cultural values such as avoiding conflict, saving face, keeping harmonious relations, and respecting the lines of authority have contributed to preserving the domineering role of the state in employee relations. Therefore, it can be concluded that despite the emphasis of most Asian religions and philosophies on individuals' rights and freedoms, there is very little evidence of these at the organizational level in Asian countries.

Religiosity and the spirit of capitalism in East Asia

When talking about religiosity and the spirit of Capitalism, one cannot avoid the work of Max Weber (1930 [1905]) and the responses it has received over the years. Although Weber's theory has been widely reviewed and criticized, it still remains valid to a great extent in many Western countries. However, it is his evaluation of the effects of other religions such as Buddhism, Confucianism, and Islam that has not stood the test of time. His argument, that the core doctrines of Confucius were the main reasons for the failure of China to develop and industrialize as the Western countries, has been fiercely challenged. Many studies have concluded that Confucianism has had significant effects on the impressive economic growth and prosperity of Asian countries (Yu, 1987; Amsden, 2001). Yu (1987) provides a critical analysis of Weber's theory and has argued that the doctrines of Buddhism and Daoism were during the Tang dynasty (618–907) similar to the Protestant ethic and that these were strengthened by the neo-Confucianism during the Song dynasty (960–1279) and until the economic reforms of the 1980s. The slowness of Chinese economic and social development happened only when religious beliefs, including Confucianism and the spirit of capitalism, were deliberately suppressed, especially during the Cultural Revolution (1966–1976). The post-1979 reforms encouraged the spirit of consumerism, which has precipitated economic growth and social development. Japan, South Korea, and Singapore are industrialized and capitalist countries, while still maintaining their traditional values. For example, from a study of seventy-two Chinese entrepreneurs and executives, Redding concluded that: "Confucian core religious values such as paternalism, collectivism, feminism and social hierarchy have created a significant context from which new ventures are fostered" (Redding, 1995, cited in Miler & Ewest, 2010: 51). Woodrum (1985) also found that Buddhism had a similar effect in Japan to Protestantism in the West.

The economic dynamism of the region over the last three decades has often been attributed to the work ethics and the moral and spiritual values of their people. Economic and social success of Asian countries such as Singapore, Taiwan, Thailand, Malaysia, and South Korea can be attributed to "Confucian capitalism," but it can also be argued that Western influence or the globalization of capitalism is the major factor in bringing in such economic miracles. Yes, as stated above, the prevailing religious principles in Asian countries urge people to work hard, to produce, to earn, and to own but these are also the key drivers of capitalism. Most of the characteristics of current Western management practice such as commitment, loyalty, sharing, caring, continuous improvement, and harmony already exist in the management of employees in Asian countries such as Japan and South Korea. These characteristics are at the heart of every Asian culture and they condition employees' work ethics, employers' business, and consumers' ethical behavior. Studies of the economic miracles of Japan and the other Asian tigers in the 1980s agreed that the success of these countries is due to their ability to adopt Western technology and adapt them to their traditional cultural values and beliefs, especially the teachings of Confucius (Ouchi, 1980; Cheng, 1998, and many others).

Moreover, it is argued that the principles of management in Buddhism and Islam are consistent with much of Western management thinking (see Rarick, 2007; Branine & Pollard, 2010). However, it is also pointed out that the impact of socio-economic change and Western influence on the young population of Asians, who are attracted to Western values and ways of life, should not be underestimated. It is feared that the young generation of Asians will gradually move away from their traditional values because they have been constantly exposed to Western management education and lifestyle in the globalizing world of capitalism. For example, a study by Ralston, Egri, Stewart, Terpstra, and Yu found that in China:

> the emergent profile of the New Generation of Chinese managers and professionals who will be leading China into the 21st century is one of a generation whose values are clearly more individualistic, less collectivistic and less committed to Confucian philosophy than their previous generation counterparts.
>
> *(Ralston et al., 1999: 425)*

However, so far there is very little evidence that the young generation of Chinese managers and business people are abandoning their cultural norms and values. From a recent study on the role of Confucianism in South Korea, Śleziak concludes that:

> the younger generations, finding their own space within urban areas and being under influence of foreign value systems may depart from the economic and social interests of their parents and grandparents; nevertheless the respect for the elderly they were taught since childhood is not suppressed by the modernity. Similarly, the entire traditional Confucian aspect of Korean life is neither forgotten nor disregarded in the process of modernization.
>
> *(2013: 45)*

Another study by Lim in Singapore found that "the mentality of Chinese Singaporeans is still shaped largely by the teachings of Confucius" (2015: 17). Therefore, it can be concluded that religiosity in East Asian countries encourages the spirit of capitalism and there is no evidence of successful Chinese managers and entrepreneurs, old or young, moving away from their traditional values in the face of Western capitalism.

Conclusions

The recent renewed interest in religiosity in the world, and in Asia in particular, has attracted the attention of scholars from various disciplines but there is still very little academic research on the impact of religion and religiosity on management theory and practice. A contributing factor to this is that religion is seen as only one of the components of a broader cultural spectrum in a society. It can be confirmed that religious beliefs make only a small part of most of the East Asian countries' cultural norms and values. They are all secular countries and most of them are multi-religious and multicultural, while some of them are institutionally non-religious (atheists). Overall, the most influential doctrine is that of Confucianism but with the passing of time, Confucius teachings have become integrated with other beliefs and cultural values of the region, initially Buddhism and Taoism, and then Islam and Christianity. One of the aspects of following Confucius philosophy is to be able to choose any religious belief, as a Buddhist, Christian, or Muslim, while adhering to the traditional Confucian principles of social behavior. Also, Confucianism has fitted well with the strict enforcement of the law by the authoritarian and totalitarian governments that have dominated Asian countries. This integrated belief system that characterizes the cultures of East Asian societies emphasizes keeping harmony and order, providing justice, and empowering people. These fundamental goals are based on respect for seniority, acceptance of authority, long-term orientation, humility, self-restraint, and collectivism. In other words, they seem to promote a soft and gentle approach to human resource management where the workplace looks like a family unit. However, there is very little evidence of a significant influence of any religion on the practice of human resource management in East Asian countries because the gap between religious teachings and the policies and practices of managing people is very wide. Moreover, as far as the spirit of capitalism is concerned, religiosity in East Asian countries has no conflict with Western principles of management and there is no clear evidence of the claim that Chinese managers are moving away from their traditional values in the face of capitalism and modernity.

The above theoretical contribution to the debate on the role of religion and religiosity in the workplace and their effects on the management of human resources in Asian countries is in need of further empirical evidence. More research is needed on this subject. It should be noted that even those who can understand the different religions through learning their concepts, scriptures, guidance, practices, rituals, places, and leaders, may not be able to ascertain their effects on people management without empirical academic research. It is often easy to attribute the way people manage their resources to their culture rather than to their religion because of the confusing overlap between culture and religion. Hence, this chapter is a modest attempt to scheme through the vast array of norms, values, rituals, and practices that have characterized the cultures of the many Asian countries and conditioned, to various extents, HRM policies and practices in their organizations. Being aware of the sensitivity of the subject of religion, any possible unintentional generalizations should be treated in good faith with the understanding that in all religions, there are different interpretations.

References

Abratt, R., Nel, D., & Hays, N. S. (1992). An examination of the ethical beliefs of managers using selected scenarios in a cross-cultural environment. *Journal of Business Ethics, 11*(1), 29–35.

Abu Bakar, R., Cooke, F. L., & Muenjohn, N. (2016). Religiosity as a source of influence on job engagement: A study of the Malaysian finance industry. *The International Journal of Human Resource Management.*

Abuznaid, S. (2006). Islam and management: What can be learned?. *Thunderbird International Business Review, 48*(1), 125–140.

Ahmad, K. (2008). Challenges and practices in human resource management of the Muslim world. *The Journal of Human Resource and Adult Learning, 4*(2), 34–42.

Ali, A. J. (1992). The Islamic work ethics in Arabia. *The Journal of Psychology, 126*(5), 507–519.

Amsden, A. (2001). *The rise of the "rest": Challenges to the West from late-industrializing economies.* Oxford: Oxford University Press.

Aziz, A. & Shamsul, A. B. (2004). The religious, the plural, the secular and the modern: A brief critical survey on Islam in Malaysia. *Inter-Asia Cultural Studies, 5*(3), 341–356.

Barrett, T. H. (1993). China's religious traditions. In P. B. Clarke (Ed.), *The world's religions* (pp. 176–195). New York: Reader's Digest.

BBC (2002, October 2) Religion & Ethics—Islam in China (650–present): Origins. *BBC.* Retrieved January 5, 2016, from www.bbc.co.uk/religion/religions/islam/history/china_1.shtml.

Boisot, M. & Liang, G. (1992). The nature of managerial work in the Chinese enterprise reforms: A study of six directors. *Organization Studies, 13*(2), 161–184.

Branine, M. & Pollard, D. (2010). Human resource management with Islamic management principles: A dialect for a reverse management. *Personnel Review, 39*(6), 712–727.

Branine, M. (2011). *Managing across cultures: Concepts, policies and practices.* London: Sage.

Budhwar, P. & Bhatnagar, J. (2009). *The changing face of people management in India.* London: Routledge.

Chan, S. (1999). Chinese learner—a question of style. *Education and Training, 41*(6/7), 294–304.

Chen, M. (1995). *Asian management systems.* London: Routledge.

Cheng, T. (1998). Confucian ideology and business administration. In X. Pan, J. H. J. Qu, W. Jiang, X. Kong, & W. Xu (Eds.), *Chinese culture and industrial management* (pp. 187–192). River Edge, NJ: World Scientific Publishing.

Child, J. & Warner, M. (2003). Culture and management in China. *Research Papers in Management Studies* (pp. 1–36). Judge Institute of Management, Working Paper 3. Cambridge: University of Cambridge.

Cho, K. & Jung, Y. (2009). Islam in China. Muslim—Christian encounter. *Torch Trinity Center for Islamic Studies Journal, 2*(2), 7–18.

Cooke, F. L. & Saini, D. S. (2012). Managing diversity in Chinese and Indian organizations: A qualitative study. *Journal of Chinese Human Resource Management, 3*(1), 16–32.

Debrah, A. Y., McGovern, I. & Budhwar, P. (2000). Complementarity or competition: the development of human resources in a South-East Asian Growth Triangle: Indonesia, Malaysia and Singapore. *International Journal of Human Resource Management, 11*(2), 314–335.

Dillon, M. (1994). Muslim communities in contemporary China: The resurgence of Islam after the Cultural Revolution. *Journal of Islamic Studies, 5*(1), 70–101.

Ford, C. W., Nonis, S. A., & Hudson, G. I. (2005). A cross-cultural comparison of value systems and consumer ethics. *Cross-Cultural Management, 12*(4), 36–50.

Gladney, C. D. (1996). *Muslim Chinese: Ethnic nationalism in the People's Republic.* Cambridge, MA: Harvard University Press.

Gladney, C. D. (2004). Islam in China: Accommodation or separatism?. In R. M. Freener (Ed.), *Islam in world cultures: Comparative perspectives* (pp. 161–182). Oxford: IBC-CLIO.

Goodwin, J. & Goodwin, D. (1999). Ethical judgements across cultures: A comparison between business students from Malaysia and New Zealand. *Journal of Business Ethics, 18*(3), 267–281.

Hage, J. & Posner, B. Z. (2015). Religion, religiosity, and leadership practices: An examination in the Lebanese workplace. *Leadership & Organization Development Journal, 36*(4), 396–412.

Hashim, J. (2010). Human resource management practices on organizational commitment: The Islamic perspective. *Personnel Review, 39*(6), 785–799.

Henley, J. S. & Nyaw, M. K. (1986). Introducing market forces into managerial decision-making in Chinese industrial enterprises. *Journal of Management Studies, 23*(6), 635–656.

Hill, J. (2006). Confucianism and the art of Chinese management. *Journal of Asian Business Studies, 1*(1), 1–9.

Hofstede, G. (1991). *Cultures and organizations: Software of the mind.* London: McGraw-Hill.

Hutton, B. (2000). Working mothers with a yen for family life. *Financial Times* (pp. 22). Retrieved March 2, 2010.

Hwang, K. K. (2001). The deep structure of Confucianism: A social psychological approach. *Asian Philosophy, 11*(3), 179–204.

Kalantari, B. (2005). Middle Eastern public management: A cultural approach to development administration. *Public Organisation and Review: A Global Journal, 5*(2), 125–138.

Khilji, S. E. (2002). Modes of convergence and divergence: An integrative view of multinational practices in Pakistan. *The International Journal of Human Resource Management, 13*(2), 232–253.

King jr, J. E., Bell, M. P. & Lawrence, E. (2009). Religion as an aspect of workplace diversity: An examination of the US context and a call for international research. *Journal of Management, Spirituality and Religion, 6*(1), 43–57.

Knott, K. (2016). *Hinduism: A very short introduction* (2nd ed.). Oxford: Oxford University Press.

Lai, Q. & Mu, Z. (2016). Universal, yet local: The religious factor in Chinese Muslims' perception of world developmental hierarchy. *Chinese Journal of Sociology, 2*(4), 524–546.

Laulusa, L. (2008). Confucianism and its implications for industrial relations in China. *Journal of Management Spirituality and Religion, 5*(4), 385–403.

Lim, B. Y. (2015). Chinese cultural values as institutional forces in shaping board involvement. *Asian Journal of Social Sciences and Management Studies, 2*(1), 17–20.

Ling, H. (2004). *Buddhism in China.* Beijing: Chinese Intercontinental Press.

Liu, Q. T. & Stening, W. B. (2016). The contextualization and de-contextualization of Confucian morality: Making Confucianism relevant to China's contemporary challenges in business ethics. *Asia Pacific Journal of Management, 33*(3), 821–841. doi: 10.1007/s10490-015-9415-2.

Magill, G. (1992). Theology in business ethics: Appealing to the religious imagination, *Journal of Business Ethics, 11*(1), 129–135.

McCleary, R. M. & Barro, R. J. (2006). Religion and political economy in an international panel. *Journal for the Scientific Study of Religion, 45*(2), 149–175.

McDaniel, S. W. & Burnett, J. J. (1990). Consumer religiosity and retail store evaluative criteria. *Journal of the Academy of Marketing Science, 18*(2), 101–112.

McDonald, G. M. & Pak, C. K. (1997). Ethical perceptions of expatriate and local managers in Hong Kong. *Journal of Business Ethics, 16*(15), 1605–1623.

McGreal, I. (1995). *Great thinkers of the Eastern world.* New York: Harper Collins.

McNair, M. R. (2015). *Religions and nonviolence: The rise of effective advocacy for peace.* Santa Barbara, CA: ABC-CLIO, LIC

Mamman, A. & Somantri, Y. (2014). What role do HR practitioners play in developing countries: An exploratory study in an Indonesian organization undergoing major transformation. *The International Journal of Human Resource Management, 25*(11), 1567–1591.

Mellahi, K. (2007). The effects of regulations on HRM: Private sector firms in Saudi Arabia. *The International Journal of Human Resource Management, 18*(1), 85–99.

Mellahi, K. & Budhwar, P. (2010). Introduction: Islam and human resource management. *Personnel Review, 39*(6), 685–691.

Miler, D. & Ewest, T. (2010). Rethinking the impact of religion on business values: Understanding its reemergence and measuring its manifestations. *Journal of International Business Ethics, 3*(2), 49–57.

Mohamed, A. A., Hassan, A. M., & Wisnieski, J. M. (2001). Spirituality in the workplace: A literature review. *Global Competitiveness, 9*, 644–652.

Newell, S. (1999). The transfer of management to China: Building learning communities rather than translating Western textbooks?. *Education and Training, 41*(6/7), 286–293.

Nigosian, S. A. (1990). *World faiths.* New York: St. Martin's Press.

Oldstone-Moore, J. (1998). Chinese traditions. In M. D. Coogan (Ed.), *World religions* (pp. 200–235). New York: Oxford University Press.

Oldstone-Moore, J. (2005). Confucianism. In M. D. Coogan (Ed.), *Eastern religions* (pp. 314–415). New York: Oxford University Press.

Ouchi, W. G. (1980). Markets, bureaucracies, and clans. *Administrative Science Quarterly, 25*(1), 129–162.

Pekerti, A. A. & Sendjaya, S. (2010). Exploring servant leadership across cultures: Comparative study in Australia and Indonesia. *The International Journal of Human Resource Management, 21*(5), 754–780.

Ralston, D. A., Egri, C. P., Stewart, S., Terpstra, R., & Yu, K. (1999). Doing business in the 21st century with the new generation of Chinese managers: A study of generational shifts in work values in China. *Journal of International Business Studies, 30*(2), 415–428.

Rao, A. (2012). Managing diversity: Impact of religion in the Indian workplace. *Journal of World Business, 47*(2), 232–239.

Rao, P. (2015). The role of religion on human resource management (HRM) practices in India. In V. Pereira & A. Malik (Eds.), *Investigating cultural aspects in Indian organizations: Empirical evidence* (pp. 11–29). Cham: Springer International Publishing.

Rarick, A. C. (2007). Enlightened management: An analysis of Buddhist precepts applied to managerial activity. *Journal of Global Business Management, 3*(2), 1–7.

Rashid, M. Z. & Ibrahim, S. (2008). The effect of culture and religiosity on business ethics: A cross-cultural comparison. *Journal of Business Ethics, 82*(4), 907–917.

Razimi, M. S., Noor, M. M., & Daud, N. M. (2014). The concept of dimension in human resource management from Islamic management perspective. *Middle-East Journal of Scientific Research, 20*(9), 1175–1182.

Redding, G. (1995). *The spirit of Chinese capitalism.* New York: Walter de Gruyter.

Schwartz, M. (2006). God as a managerial stakeholder?. *Journal of Business Ethics, 66*(2), 291–306.

Sengupta, S. S. (2010). Correlates of spiritual orientation & managerial effectiveness. *Indian Journal of Industrial Relations, 45*(5), 45–60.

Shah, R., Larbi, G., & Batley, R. (2007). Religion and public management literature review. *Religions and Development Research Programme*, Working Paper I, University of Birmingham. Retrieved May 15, 2017, from https://core.ac.uk/download/pdf/1633013.pdf.

Sheh, S. W. (2001). Chinese cultural values and their implications for Chinese management. *Singapore Management Review, 23*(2), 75–84.

Sidani, Y. & Thornberry, J. (2010). The current Arab work ethic: Antecedents, implications, and potential remedies. *Journal of Business Ethics, 91*(1), 35–49.

Śleziak, T. (2013). The role of Confucianism in contemporary South Korean society. *Rocznik Orientalistyczn [Yearbook of Oriental Studies], 66*(1), 27–46.

Smith, H. (1998). *The world's religions.* San Francisco, CA: Harper.

Steiner, D. D., Gilliland, S., & Skarlicki, D. (2002). *Emerging perspectives on managing organizational justice.* Greenwich, CT: Information Age Publishing.

Sungmoon, K. (2008). Filiality, compassion and Confucian democracy. *Asian Philosophy, 18*(3), 279–298.

Syed, J. & Ali, A. J. (2010). Principles of employment relations in Islam: A normative view. *Employee Relations, 32*(5), 454–469.

Tayeb, M. (1997). Islamic revival in Asia and human resource management. *Employee Relations, 19*(4), 352–364.

Ting, Dawood C. M. (1987). Islamic culture in China. In K. W. Morgan (Ed.), *Islam—The straight path: Islam interpreted by Muslims.* New Delhi: Motilal Banarsidass publishers.

Tsang, E. W. K. (1998). Can guanxi be a source of competitive advantage for doing business in China?. *Academy of Management Executive, 12*(2), 64–72.

Uygur, S., Spence, L. J., Simpson, R., & Karakas, F. (2016). Work ethics, religion and moral energy: The case of Turkish SME owner-managers. *The International Journal of Human Resource Management.* Retrieved from http://dx.doi.org/10.1080/09585192.2016.1166790.

Vitell, S. J., Paolillo, G. P., & Singh, J. J. (2006). The role of money and religiosity in determining consumer ethical beliefs. *Journal of Business Ethics, 64*(2), 117–124.

Weaver, G. R. & Agle, B. R. (2002). Religiosity and ethical behavior in organizations: A symbolic inter-actionist perspective. *Academy of Management Review, 27*(1), 77–98.

Weber, M. (1930 [1905]). *The Protestant ethic and the spirit of capitalism.* New York: Penguin classics, Simon Shuster.

Wiebe, K. F. & Roland Fleck, J. (1980). Personality correlates of intrinsic, extrinsic, and nonreligious orientations. *Journal of Psychology, 105*(2), 181–187.

Woodrum, E. (1985). Religion and economics among Japanese Americans: A Weberian study. *Social Forces, 64*(1), 191–204.

Xing, F. (1995). The Chinese cultural system: Implications for cross-cultural management. *SAM Advanced Management Journal, 60*(1), 14–20.

Xue Cunningham, L. & Rowley, C. (2007). Human resource management in Chinese small and medium enterprises: A review and research agenda. *Personnel Review, 36*(3), 415–439.

Yamak, S. Ergur, A. Unsal, A. Uygur, S., & Özbilgin, M. (2015). Between a rock and a hard place: Corporate elites in the context of religion and secularism in Turkey. *The International Journal of Human Resource Management, 26*(11), 1474–1497.

Yu, Y. S. (1987). *Zhongguo jinshi zongjiao lunli yu shangren jingshen* [*The modern Chinese religious ethics and the spirit of merchants*]. Taipei: Lianjing chuban gongsi.

Yousef, D. A. (2001). Islamic work ethic: A moderator between organizational commitment and job satisfaction in a cross-cultural context. *Personnel Review, 30*(2), 152–169.

PART II

Labor regulation and industrial relations

5

EMPLOYMENT REGULATION AND INDUSTRIAL RELATIONS SYSTEMS IN EAST ASIA

China, Japan, and South Korea

Fang Lee Cooke, Katsuyuki Kubo, and Byoung-Hoon Lee

Introduction

The understanding of human resource management practices needs to be situated within the broader context of employment, labor market, and industrial relations (IR) systems at the national and sub-national level. In this chapter, we examine the transformation of these systems that has accompanied the growth of three major Asian economies: the People's Republic of China (hereafter China), Japan, and South Korea (hereafter Korea).[1] We grouped the three countries together not least because they share broadly similar cultural heritage, such as Confucianism, but also major economies in East Asia with close socio-economic ties. At the same time, their politico-economic systems vary, so are the respective roles and strengths of key institutional actors, such as the state, workers' unions, and employer associations in shaping the IR system (for more detailed discussion of each of the countries, see Bamber, Lansbury, Wailes, & Wright, 2016).

This chapter contains four main sections, in addition to this introduction and a conclusion. In the first main section, we provide an overview of how the economy and the labor market have evolved in the three countries since the 1980s. This is followed by the section that outlines the series of labor laws and regulations and their impact in the context of originally highly regulated labor markets, followed by labor market deregulation and re-regulation simultaneously in the 1990s. The third section examines the role of the trade unions and the key characteristics of industrial relations in order to understand how unions as key institutional actors may or may not act effectively in protecting workers in general, or workers in particular sectors or forms of employment. It is in the broader context of changes in the employment and labor market system and the role of the unions that the fourth main section discusses the evolution of, and main changes in, the wage system in China, Japan, and Korea.

Overview of economies and labor markets

In spite of significant differences in their contemporary political systems, China, Japan, and Korea share geographical and cultural proximities, relatively similar economic growth stages, and the profound historical influence they have on each other. In particular, Japan and Korea are developed countries, whereas China is an emerging economy with rising economic power globally. Compared to China, Japan and Korea are relatively small countries in terms of geographical and population size, and have different industrial structures. China is a socialist country that has been under the control of the Communist Party since 1949. It began its economic transformation in the late 1970s. Japan is a constitutional monarchy with Western influences, whereas the modern Republic of Korea, established in 1948, had been under the control of authoritarian governments until 1987. There has been a growing level of democracy since then, largely as a result of mass public demonstrations and the need for the government to respond to economic conditions (Cooke, 2010).

As of the end of 2014, China, Japan, and Korea had a workforce of 793.307 million, 65.54 million, and 26.07 million respectively (World Bank Group, 2015). Japan and Korea were two major driving forces of the Asian economy in the 1970s and 1980s, but were both heavily hit by the Asia financial crisis in 1997 and the global financial crisis in 2008 (e.g., Lee & Lee, 2003; Magoshi & Chang, 2009). Japan's economy was also hit by its 1992 asset bubble burst and the 2011 earthquake, tsunami, and nuclear disaster. Meanwhile, China has emerged as a major powerhouse in the development of Asian economy since the 1990s (Khanna, 2007; Witt & Redding, 2014). The governments of Japan, Korea, and China have all pursued an export-oriented economic growth path, one after another. These developments have been accompanied by a substantial fertility decline since the 1980s in all three countries. While the low birth rate in China is a result of the government's "one child" policy coercively enforced in the 1980s, the low birth rate in Japan and Korea is largely an outcome of women's choice (though the Korean government is providing incentives to encourage women to have more children). Declining fertility is affecting the labor market structure and women's role in it in both Japan and Korea (Cooke, 2010). After a period of labor market deregulation in response to economic pressure and global competition that has resulted in the rapid growth of non-standard employment with worsening workers' well-being in the 1980s and 1990s (e.g., Coe, Johns, & Ward, 2011; Kim & Park, 2006; Kuroki, 2012; Meng, 2012), the governments of these three countries have made attempts to introduce regulations to decrease inequality (Cooke & Brown, 2015, also for further discussion, see below). And the globalizing economy of the three countries adds further dynamics to the restructuring of their labor market since the 1980s, including the employment of foreign migrant labor (for Japan and Korea) and rural migrant labor en masse (for China), as we discuss below.

China

In China, state sector employment had made up 78 percent of the urban employment prior to its economic reform that commenced in 1978 (National Bureau of Statistics of China [NBSC], 2014). Major labor market reform started in the mid-1980s. The government began to lay off state-owned enterprise (SOE) workers and encourage the growth of the private sector. It also began the replacement of the "iron rice bowl" (i.e., job for life) with (fixed-term) labor contracts. The state and semi-state sector downsizing was most prevalent from 1998 to the early 2000s, when 30 million workers were laid off from the state-owned enterprises and collectively owned enterprises between 1998 and 2004 (cf. Hassard, Sheehan, Zhou, Terpstra-Tong, & Morris, 2007; Kuruvilla, Lee, & Gallagher, 2011; Yao & Zhong, 2013, for more detailed discussion). A significant proportion of them entered the external labor market for the first time, but their re-employment rate was only about 30 percent by 2003 (NBSC, 2006). According to the NBSC (2014), state-owned unit employment consisted of 59 percent of the total urban employment in 1995; this figure went down to 35 percent in 2000, and 16.6 percent in 2013.

The majority of the displaced workers have ended up in the peripheral labor market due to their lack of job market experience and skills needed for premium jobs in the growing private sector, and their relatively older age profile. This state sector reform practically dismantled the once solid internal labor market for urban workers and marked the end of a socialist commitment of protecting long-term employment.

In the meantime, over 160 million of rural migrant workers have been attracted to urban industrial employment, who make up the bulk of those in informal employment in China (Qiao, 2013). In the first two decades of its economic and social reform, the government adopted an efficiency-driven economic development policy at the expense of the welfare and well-being of millions of rural migrant workers, whose rural household registration status held them down firmly at the bottom of the urban labor market with little protection (Cooke, 2011b). On the one hand, the state has created employment opportunities for millions of surplus rural labor. On the other hand, these jobs are lowly paid and are the least protected by labor regulations.

In addition, 12–13 million young workers were entering the labor market each year between 2003 and 2011 (calculated from the World Bank Development Index and Chinese National Education Development Statistics Annual Reports). To release employment pressure, the Chinese government launched an expansion program for the higher and further education sector in 1999. Since then, the enrolment of new regular undergraduate students has grown rapidly by about 35.8 percent on average annually, increasing from 1.08 million in 1998 to 7.27 million in 2014 (China Education Online, 2014). This expansion strategy, while it helped to develop a more educated labor force, did not reduce unemployment pressure effectively. Instead, it raised employment expectations from well-educated job seekers due to their (family's) investment in education and enhanced education qualification attainment. For example, the number of university graduates had grown from 2.12 million in 2003 to 4.95 million in 2007, 6.31 million in 2010, 6.99 million in 2013, and by over seven million in 2014 (China Education Online, 2014). However, the prospect of gainful employment has not been optimistic for many, and the term "Ant Tribe" (蚁族) has been coined to describe the expanding force of underemployed or unemployed university graduates (Wang, Cooke, & Lin, 2016).

Japan

Long-term employment and seniority-based pay have been two key features in the traditional employment system for core employees in large firms in Japan. Workers enter the firm after they finish school. They continue working for the same company for a long time. They build up their careers by experiencing various positions within the firm and by being promoted to higher ranks. It is often the case that they stay in the same company until mandatory retirement. In 2008, there were thirty directors in Toyota. Amongst them, twenty-nine directors had joined the firm when they finished university.

It is not easy for firms to dismiss regular employees because of the "judicial principle of the abusive exercise of dismissal rights". This principle was developed as case law and is now incorporated into the Labor Contract Law, which was enacted in 2007. According to this principle, firms have the right to dismiss employees. However, dismissal is considered to be abusive use of the right, unless the firms show that it is absolutely necessary (for further discussion, see Kambayashi, 2010; and Hanami & Komiya, 2011).

One of the most important concepts behind the long-term employment and seniority pay practices is the "competence rank system" that all the employees belong to. There are usually twelve ranks (cf. Uehara, 2009), and these ranks are called competence ranks because they are considered to reflect employees' skills. In a competence rank system, young workers who have just entered the firm belong to one of the bottom ranks, whereas senior executives belong to the highest ranks. The competence rank system is designed to encourage workers and employers to invest in skill formation. It is argued that employees have an incentive to acquire firm-specific skills. They also have an incentive to work hard in order to be promoted even with the high correlation between age and pay. The Japan Productivity Centre conducts a questionnaire survey periodically on listed companies regarding how they determine salaries. According to the Japan Productivity Centre (2010), 80.9 percent of firms have a competence rank system for managers and 85.2 percent for non-managerial workers in 1999 (for further discussion on wage system, see below).

Two significant changes in the financial market during the late 1990s and 2000s impacted on firms' behavior. First, there was a change in ownership structure. The proportion of foreign shareholders increased significantly (Miyajima & Kuroki, 2007; Miyajima & Nitta, 2011). The proportion of shares owned by foreigners increased from 4.9 percent in 1970 to 28 percent in 2012, according to the Japan Exchange Group, which operates the Tokyo Stock Exchange and other exchanges. Investment by investment funds, such as private equity funds and activist hedge funds, increased. As ownership by foreigners and investment funds increased, top managers in large Japanese firms faced more pressure to improve performance, and in particular stock market performance.

A second important change in the financial market is that there have been many institutional changes that make it easier for firms to conduct reorganization through mergers, acquisitions, and divesture.[2] Because of these changes in financial markets, top managers are more likely to manage the firm to maximize shareholders' interests, for example by closing loss-making divisions of the firm. If this is the case, firms may not retain seniority-based pay and long-term employment practices, because they cannot keep employees when they close a division.

Several studies have examined whether Japan's economic changes have led to changes in long-term employment (e.g., Hamaaki, Hori, Maeda, & Murata, 2012; Shimizutani & Yokoyama, 2009; Ono, 2010; Kambayashi & Kato, 2012). These studies show that there is surprisingly little change in long-term employment practices for middle-aged regular workers who have spent many years in the firm, while there is a change for mid-career hires and young employees. For example, Kambayashi and Kato (2012) examine workers' retention rates using micro data from the Employment Status Survey from 1982 to 2007. They find that the ten-year job-retention rate was stable during this period in particular for core employees, who are aged thirty to forty-four years and have worked at their present firm for at least five years. At the same time, the ten-year job-retention rate has been declining for mid-career hires and young workers. Hamaaki et al.'s (2012) study, using micro data of the Basic Survey on Wage Structure from 1989 to 2008, reveals a similar pattern to the disadvantage of younger workers.

While long-term employment practices have been relatively stable for middle-aged to older core workers in large firms, the proportion of non-regular workers has been increasing as firms look for ways to contain labor cost and increase flexibility. Table 5.1 shows the composition of workers in 1985, 2002, and 2015. This table shows various types of non-regular workers. Part-time and temporary workers are typically hired directly by the firm they work for. Dispatched (agency) workers from temporary labor agencies are relatively new in Japan. According to the Employment Security Law of 1947, it is illegal for temporary staffing agencies to dispatch workers. However, this was changed in 1986 with the introduction of the Worker Dispatching Law (see Table 5.2). Although it was legalized only for a limited number of occupations, the amendment of the Worker Dispatching Law in 1999 legalized temporary staffing activity in most occupations. Notably, the amendment in 2004 made it possible for manufacturing firms to

Table 5.1 Number of regular and non-regular employees in Japan

Panel A: Male (10,000 workers)[1]

Year	Regular employees	Non-regular employees							
		Non-regular employee (total)	Part-time worker	Arbeit (temporary worker)	Dispatched worker from temporary labor agency	Contract employee	Contract employee	Entrusted employee	Other
1985	2,349	187	16	67	NA	NA		104	
2002	2,427	422	68	162	7		111		74
2015	2,251	636	111	204	48	159		73	41

Panel B: Female (10,000 workers)

Year	Regular employees	Non-regular employees							
		Non-regular employee (total)	Part-time worker	Arbeit (temporary worker)	Dispatched worker from temporary labor agency	Contract employee	Contract employee	Entrusted employee	Other
1985	994	470	344	73	NA	NA		53	
2002	1,059	983	632	160	32		107		51
2015	1,015	1,343	851	194	72	138		41	46

Source: adapted from the Labor Force Survey.

Note

1 In 1985, the combined total number of entrusted employee and other is shown. In 2002, the combined total number of contract employee and entrusted employee is shown.

use such workers (for further discussion on non-standard employment in Japan, see Cooke & Brown, 2015).

Table 5.1 and Figure 5.1 show that the proportion of non-regular workers has been increasing for both men and women, and for all types of non-regular workers. The number of non-regular workers increased from 1.87 million in 1985 to 6.36 million in 2015 for male workers, and from 4.7 million in 1985 to 13.43 million in 2015 for female workers. Notably, the proportion of non-regular workers amongst females exceeded 50 percent in the early 2000s (for further discussion, see Cooke, 2010). The proportion of non-regular workers is significant for male workers as well, at more than 20 percent in 2015. Table 5.1 also shows that the number of dispatched workers is increasing significantly. According to Asano, Ito, and Kawaguchi (2013), a significant proportion of non-regular workers are young male workers and are female workers of all ages. Their result is consistent with the idea that long-term employment is preserved for male core workers who are middle-aged or older.

Korea

Similarly, the rapid casualization of the Korean labor market took place in the late 1990s following the Asian financial crisis in 1997 (also see below). The dramatic increase in various forms of precarious employment (e.g., irregular employment and dependent self-employment in the

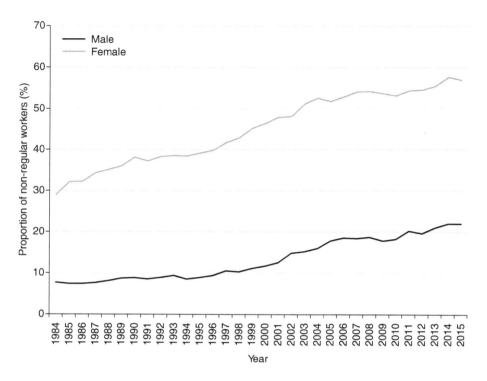

Figure 5.1 Proportion of non-regular employees, 1984–2015

Source: figures from Labour Force Survey published by the Statistics Bureau, Ministry of Internal Affairs and Communications, each year.

formal sector) was a direct consequence of the "neoliberal economic reform implemented by the new democratic government … under the guidance of the International Monetary Fund" (IMF) as a condition for the financial bailout program (Shin, 2013: 335). This reform program included: enhancement of flexibility in the labor market, restructuring of the financial market, and reforms of the public sector and corporate governance (Shin, 2013). When they recovered from the 1997 economic crisis (after late 1999), many employers, particularly large employers, replaced laid-off regular workers with non-regular workers.

As a consequence, non-regular employment sharply proliferated, as demonstrated in Figure 5.2. The share of contingent workforce, comprised of temporary and daily labor estimated by the Economically Active Population Survey, increased from 41.8 percent in 1995 to 52.1 percent in 2000. The size of non-regular employment rose from 26.8 percent in 2001 to 37.0 percent in 2004 and then dropped to 32.4 percent in 2009, according to official estimates of the Korean government, which started conducting the Economically Active Population Survey— Supplementary Section to capture the size and working conditions of non-regular employment from 2001, along with the growing social concern over the non-regular labor issue.[3]

In comparison, the Korean labor market reform may be politically more contentious than in Japan, but the outcomes are similar—while efforts were made, often through unions' militant actions in the case of Korea, to protect the employment terms and conditions of the core workers, employers have been increasingly relying on non-standard employment to reduce labor cost (Peng, 2012), before new laws sought to reign them in. As a result, both Japan and Korea have increased their labor market flexibility considerably since the late 1990s. For China,

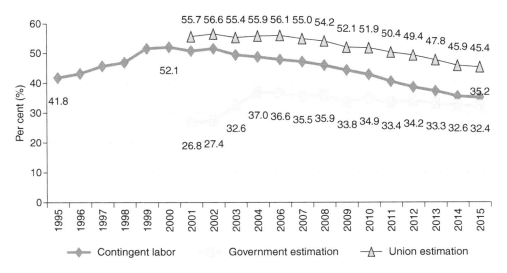

Figure 5.2 Trends of non-regular employment in Korea, 1995–2014 (unit: percent)

Source: Economically Active Population Survey—Supplementary Section in each year.

Note

Contingent labor is estimated as the averaged number each year; non-regular employment is estimated by the government and labor unions as of August each year.

the labor market duality emerged since the mid-1980s, mainly as a result of the migration of rural migrant workers. While many standard workers have experienced erosion in their employment terms and conditions, not least in Japan and Korea, a common labor market outcome for the majority of non-standard workers in all three countries has been the relatively poor employment terms and conditions for them. This is a direct result of their inadequate regulatory protection underpinned by the relative roles of key institutional actors, notably the ineffective role of the unions (Cooke & Brown, 2015).

Labor regulations and their impact

In China, Japan, and Korea, a series of labor laws and regulations have been promulgated since the late 1940s to provide a regulatory framework within which to govern the employment relationship (see Table 5.2). In China, the labor legislative system was developed relatively late and it was not until 1995 when the first main labor law was enacted (promulgated in 1994). This law, supplemented by a variety of administrative regulations at various governmental levels, was not sufficient to deal with radical changes in the labor market and the rising level of labor disputes, and resulted in the enactment of three major pieces of labor and employment legislation in 2008 (Cooke, 2011a).[4] In Japan, its first major piece of labor legislation, the Employment Security Law, was introduced in 1947, which has been amended several times especially since the 1990s in response to economic change and labor market reforms.[5] In the 1990s and 2000s, a number of laws were introduced or amended to reflect the more diverse labor market conditions. Similarly, Korea established its first set of labor laws in the early 1950s, followed by several major additions/revisions since the mid-1980s. The relatively quiet period on the legislative front during the period of 1960s and 1970s (and for China until the 1980s) reflected the dominance of internal labor markets in the urban sector in all three countries during that period.

Table 5.2 List of major labor laws and regulations in China, Japan, and Korea★

China
1950   Trade Union Law (replaced by the Trade Union Law of 2001)
1982   Opinions on Issues Concerning Labor Service Companies[1]
1990   Regulations on the Management of Labor Employment Service Enterprises[2]
1992   Trade Union Law (amended in 2001)
1995   Labor Law
1995   Employment Agency Regulation
2002   Law on Work Safety
2002   Law on Prevention and Control of Occupational Diseases
2004   Regulation on Enterprises Minimum Wage
2008   Labor Contract Law (amended in 2013)
2008   Labor Disputes Mediation and Arbitration Law
2008   Employment Promotion Law
2011   Social Security Law
2014   Provisional Regulations on Labor Dispatch
2015   Opinions on Building Harmonious Labor Relations

Japan
1947   Employment Security Law (amended in 1952, 1964, 1997, 1999, 2000, and 2004)
1947   Labor Standards Law (amended in 1998 and 2003)
1985   Equal Employment Opportunity Law (amended in 1997 and 2006)
1986   Worker Dispatching Law (also translated as Temporary Worker Law, amended in 1996, 1999, 2004, 2007, and 2015)
1991   Child Care Leave Law (amended and renamed as Child Care and Family Care Law in 1995)
1993   Act on Improvement, etc. of Employment Management for Part-Time Workers (amended in 1999, 2008, and 2015)
2000   Labor Contract Succession Law (amended in 2012 and 2013)
2001   Individual Dispute Resolution Law
2004   Whistleblowers Protection Law
2006   Labor Tribunal Law

Korea
1953   Trade Union Act
1953   Labor Dispute Adjustment Act
1953   Labor Standards Act (amended in 1997, 1998, 1999, 2001, 2003, 2005, 2006, 2008, 2009, 2010, 2011, and 2012)
1953   Labor Relations Commission Act
1986   Minimum Wage Act (applying to all firms with ten and more, and since 1999, five and more employees)
1987   Equal Employment Act (revised to Act on Equal Employment and Support for Work–Family Reconciliation in 2008)
1994   Employment Promotion for the Aged Act
1995   Framework Act on Employment Policy
1997   Trade Union and Labor Relations Adjustment Act (incorporating the 1953 Trade Union Act and Labor Dispute Adjustment Act and revised for allowing multiple unionization at the enterprise level and introducing time-off system for union officials' paid activities in 2010)
1998   Act on Protection for Dispatched Workers (amended in 2007)
1999   Act on the Establishment and Operation of Teachers Union
2000   National Basic Livelihood Security Law

Table 5.2 Continued

2004	Special Act on the Promotion of Youth Employment
2006	Act on the Establishment and Operation of Public Servants Union
2007	Act on Protection of Fixed-Term and Part-Time Workers

Notes

* Year refers to the year when the law was enacted and when the amended version was effective.
1 'Opinions on Issues Concerning Labor Service Companies' is an administrative regulation issued by the Ministry of Labor and Personnel on September 15, 1982; see *Chinese Law and Government, 34*(1), January/February 2001, 31–37.
2 'Regulations on the Management of Labor Employment Service Enterprises' was issued by the State Council on November 22, 1990; see *Chinese Law and Government, 34*(1), January/February 2001, 41–47.

While all three countries have regulations in place for non-standard employment, it is important to note that Japan is the only country amongst the three in this study that has ratified C181— Private Employment Agencies Convention, 1997 (No. 181) of ILO (for a more detailed analysis of labor laws and non-standard employment in the three countries, see Cooke & Brown, 2015).

China

The promulgation of the major labor laws in China since the 2008 has not led to a more harmonious and equitable employment relations as the government had hoped for. In particular, the introduction of the Labor Contract Law was highly controversial and resulted in its amendment in 2013, in part to prevent opportunistic behavior from employers. The primary objective of the Labor Contract Law was to provide a greater level of employment and social security protection to the workers. The implementational reality, however, has led to unintended consequences to the disadvantage of the workers. In order to evade employer's legal responsibility (e.g., paying social insurance premium for all employees and offering permanent employment to long-serving employees), many firms dismissed their employees and rehired them as agency workers (cf. Cooke, 2011a; Cooney, Biddulph, & Zhu, 2013 for a more detailed discussion). This has led to the substantial growth of agency employment in not just the manual and semi-skilled areas, but also in professional jobs and university graduate employment as noted earlier.

According to the research report produced by the All-China Federation of Trade Unions (ACFTU) Dispatched Employment Project Team (2012), there were over 60 million dispatched workers in the whole country in 2011, making up nearly 17 percent of the total workforce in urban employment (see NBSC, 2014). In particular, the same report shows that there were 37 million agency workers in enterprises, making up 13.1 percent of the total enterprise workers. Dispatched workers are more concentrated in some industries than others. For example, it was reported that 20 percent of the workers in the Bank of China, a major state-owned bank, were dispatched (Cairns, 2015). Many of these workers are young university graduates.

Since the enactment of the Amendment of the Labor Contract Law in 2013 and the Provisional Regulations on Labor Dispatch in 2014, labor strategy has displayed new characteristics, revealing employers' strategic responses to the new regulations (Qiao, 2014). More specifically, firms are adopting more diverse labor deployment practices, including turning informal positions into permanent positions, outsourcing, part-time work, intern placement, and volunteer work. In particular, business outsourcing has been a popular strategy for large state-owned enterprises and foreign firms to cope with the new labor regulations that are targeting at reducing agency employment (Wang et al., 2016; Qiao, 2014).

Japan

As shown in Table 5.2, there are several changes in labor laws in Japan. One of the important changes is on the regulation of non-regular workers. In general, these changes are intended to encourage firms to utilize non-regular workers. It was not possible for firms to use dispatched workers until the introduction of the Worker Dispatching Law in 1986. At first, the law designated certain occupations; only workers in these occupations, or on this "positive list," can work as dispatched workers. After several amendments, the list of occupations for these workers was enlarged. In 1999, it changed to the "negative list." Basically, workers of all types of occupation can work as dispatched workers unless they are on the "negative list." For example, medical doctors and nurses are on this "negative list."

In conjunction with the deregulation of the labor market for non-regular workers, there are some movements to strengthen the protection of non-regular workers. For example, the Part-Time Work Law was amended in 2008. Theoretically, non-regular workers are protected by labor laws, as are the regular workers. However, it is sometimes the case that the rights of non-regular workers are not well protected because they are not protected by enterprise unions. According to the Part-Time Work Law introduced in 1993 (amended in 2008), firms are banned from discriminating against part-time workers, if they satisfy certain conditions, such as that they are doing same job and that they have same responsibility as full-time workers.

Korea

In Korea, two major laws—the Labor Standards Act and The Trade Union and Labor Relations Adjustment Act—set out the primary legal framework to regulate employment and industrial relations. The former offers basic legal standards concerning such employment conditions as employment contracting, wages, working hours, paid vacation, dismissal, and industrial safety, while the latter stipulates the principal processes of IR, comprising union organizing, collective bargaining, and labor disputes. The labor regulations, including these two laws, have been revised several times over the past thirty years in pursuit of dual policy goals to expand the flexibility of labor markets and enhance labor rights. Employers claim that the flexibilization of the labor market and employment relations have been the main reasons for improving their business competitiveness, whereas unions and civil NGOs have been demanding the enhancement of labor rights to strengthen the collective voice of workers since the democratization of 1987 (Lee & Eun, 2009; Lee, 2015).

The flexibilization of the labor market and employment relations made substantial progress by the revision of the Labor Standards Act and the legislation of the Dispatched Labor Act[6] under the context of in 1998 economic crisis.[7] The revised Labor Standards Act stipulated a new clause (Article 24) to allow employers to conduct massive lay offs for business reasons. The Dispatched Labor Act was enacted to legalize employers' use of informal employment such as agency workers for temporary help. Such legislation on labor market flexibilization had a profound impact on enterprise-level employment relations, by enabling many companies to launch massive downsizing and corporate restructuring under the context of the 1998 economic crisis. According to a survey conducted by the Korea Labor Institute in 2000, 66 percent of enterprises downsized after the economic crisis, illustrating the huge extent of corporate restructuring then (Park & Roh, 2001). The survey also showed that 74 percent of respondents spun off their business units and 58 percent outsourced some part of their business. Those companies recruited non-regular workers to fill what previously had been regular jobs after the economy recovered in 1999. A net consequence of this employers' labor strategy has been the informalization of employment as noted earlier.

Non-regular workers, who had a growing presence in the post-crisis labor markets, suffered from discriminatory compensation and inferior working conditions. Given the sharp increase and discriminatory treatment of non-regular labor, the government, confronted with the growing public concern over this vulnerable workforce, legislated the Act on the Protection of Fixed-Term and Part-Time Workers in 2006, which enforces the two-year limit on the use of fixed-term and dispatched labor and prohibits employers' discrimination against those non-regular workers. With the implementation of legal regulation over the use of non-regular labor, the total share of the non-regular workforce has slightly declined from 35.9 percent in 2007 to 32.4 percent in 2014. At the same time, many companies replaced the fixed-term workers, protected by the new legislative regulations, with contracted workers, who are given no legal protection.

According to OECD (2013), the institutional protection (score 2.17) of permanent workers against individual and collective dismissal in Korea is lower than OECD average (2.29). However, it should be noted that the share of Korean workers (35.5 percent) having job tenure shorter than one year is the highest amongst the OECD member countries (OECD average 16.5 percent), and that the share of Korean workers (18.1 percent) having job tenure longer than ten years is the lowest amongst the OECD countries (OECD average 36.4 percent).[8] This international comparison demonstrates that Korean workers' job stability has been remarkably weakened under the transforming labor market institutions, which is tilted toward employment flexibility, as derived from the companies' recurrent employment adjustments (including downsizing, outsourcing, and business restructuring) and the proliferation of non-regular employment.

Moreover, a large number of workers in the labor market are excluded from the legal protection of statutory welfare and labor standards. Although the protective coverage of social welfare and labor standards for workers has over the past ten years expanded to some extent, a majority of non-regular workers and a portion of regular workers, who are mainly employed in small firms, are still excluded from such legal protection. In addition, it is a problem that such informal employment practices are widespread in the Korean labor markets. This is also identified by the fact that 12.4 percent (i.e., 2.33 million) of total workforce is paid below the national minimum wage, as of March 2015 (Kim, 2015).

In short, the institutional framework of labor markets and industrial relations in all three countries have been transformed for promoting employment flexibility under the context of economic crisis in the 1990s for Japan and Korea, and as part of the marketization of the economy in China since the 1980s but with accelerated and more widespread changes since the late 1990s. A common result of this transformation has been the proliferation of non-regular employment as well as the weakening of job stability and legal protection for workers in general. In Japan and Korea, legislative changes have also weakened the union bargaining leverage and organizational power in some sectors but have increased that in other sectors, notably the public sector in Korea (see below).

The role of the trade unions and industrial relations

There are significant differences in the role of the trade unions in China, Japan, and Korea and their ability to represent the workers, with Korean unions being by far the most militant ones (Cooke & Brown, 2015). Only one trade union is recognized by the Chinese government—All-China Federation of Trade Unions (ACFTU) (Cooke, 2011c). Founded in 1925, the

ACFTU is one of the eight "mass organizations" (or known as "NGOs") in China that operate under the leadership of the Chinese Communist Party. Representing workers in collective negotiation, amongst other tasks, is one of the key responsibilities of the union, as stipulated in the labor laws (Cooke, 2011c). However, existing studies on the Chinese trade unions have mostly been critical of their institutionally incapacitated position and operational inefficacy (e.g., Clarke, 2005). In particular, they suffer from low legitimacy amongst workers for representation in wage negotiations and labor disputes. In spite of institutional and resource constraints, the ACFTU has played an active role, at the senior level, in lobbying for legislative changes to offer greater protection to the workers, for example, in the drafting of the Labor Contract Law and in its intervention into the agency employment (also known as dispatched labor) debate (Cairns, 2015).

At the grass-roots level, ACFTU organizations are seeking new ways to organize and represent workers who have traditionally fallen outside their catchment, such as rural migrant workers, to improve their labor rights protection (Taylor & Li, 2010). Nevertheless, the ACFTU does not have the right to organize strikes in China, and without the right to organize strikes and other forms of industrial action, the power of the trade union is limited in representing workers on collective negotiation (Chang & Cooke, 2015). As such, ACFTU grass-roots organizations mainly play a welfare role in the state sector with a limited presence and strength in the private sector, and where they do exist, may be pseudo-unions controlled by the employer. In recent years, workers have tended to self-organize, often in the form of spontaneous industrial actions, to defend their rights and advance their interests (Duan & Li, 2014).

In Japan, unions are organized as enterprise unions. Typically, an enterprise union is composed of regular workers, though some try to include non-regular worker as well. Enterprise unions that belong to the same sector form industrial federation of unions, such as DENKI RENGO (the Japanese Electrical Electronic and Information Union). One important function of these industrial federations is to set basic strategy of wage bargaining. Although formal bargaining is at the enterprise level, the outcome of the bargaining in large firms is used as a reference for other firms. There are several centers at the national level. The largest organization is RENGO (the Japan Trade Union Confederation). The number of members in unions under RENGO is around 6.82 million in 2015. It is often the case that a representative of RENGO is involved in many policy-making processes.

One important characteristic of enterprise unions in Japan is that the relationship between the union and management is cooperative. From the viewpoint of union leaders, the growth of the firm is essential for the improvement of employment conditions. Therefore, employees have incentives to improve the firm's performance.

As in many countries, union density in Japan has been declining. The proportion of union members amongst workers declined from 34.8 percent in 1965 and 28.9 percent in 1985 to 17.9 percent in 2012. A certain proportion of the decline in union membership can be attributed to the increase of non-regular workers and the increase of workers in the service sector. In addition to formal wage bargaining, there are several mechanisms through which employees communicate with top managers. Most large firms have joint-labor management committees, in which top managers and the representatives of employees discuss various topics in management. It is often the case that top managers consult union leaders on important decisions, such as a merger, before they make public announcements.

Korean industrial relations can be characterized as an enterprise-based model. This means that the employer and the labor union at the enterprise level are the key IR actors. The unions have considerable autonomy in union administration and collective bargaining at the firm level. As of 2013, the unions are divided into four groups by their affiliation: The Federation of

Korean Trade Unions (FKTU); The Korean Confederation of Trade Unions (KCTU); The Korean Labor Union Confederation (KLUC); and independent unions, which are not affiliated with the three national centers. The membership of independent unions withdrawing their affiliation from the FKTU and the KCTU has almost doubled, from 176,700 in 2006 to 381,575 in 2013. The growing membership of independent unions might reflect their concern with the prohibition of employers paying wages to union officials, which is having a damaging impact on unions' finances.

Since the late 1990s, many unions have moved to transform their organizational structure from enterprise unionism to industrial unionism to strengthen their socio-political power. In 1998, the Korean Health and Medical Workers' Union (KHMWU) was the first one to revert to industrial unionism. Subsequently others followed suit, including the Korean Finance Industry Union (KFIU) and the Korea Metal Workers' Union (KMWU). As a consequence, membership in industrial unions grew from 10 percent of total union membership in 1996 to about 56 percent in 2011 (Lee & Kim 2013). In particular, the KCTU resolved to complete its return to industrial unionism by the end of 2007, and by 2012, nearly 84 percent of its members were affiliated with industrial unions.

In contrast, the FKTU has been less active at restructuring, and only 20 percent of its members are organized in industrial unions. Moreover, non-regular workers have made another attempt to organize community-based general unions to try to cope with the growing flexibility and mobility of labor markets since late 1990s. The Hope Solidarity Union, formed in 2009, is the exemplar case of community unionism, organizing around 3,200 non-regular workers in the Seoul Metropolitan area during the past seven years (2010–2016). In the recent years, moreover, new forms of union organizing have been attempted: a couple of age cohort groups, such as youth (Youth Union in 2009) and senior workers (Senior Hope Union in 2013), formed their own unions to represent each cohort's rights and interests by issue-fighting and policy consultation with the government.

In the Korean IR institutional framework, teachers and civil servants have been newly given the legal right to organize their unions, which is another part of the 1998 Social Pact.[9] In that their role and mission have public accountability and their working conditions are determined by the national budget planning process in the Congress, teachers and civil servants are entitled to exercise the right of union organizing and collective bargaining, but are precluded from collective action which other workers' unions can engage in. The unionization of teachers and civil servants (organizing around over 300,000 union members) helps the stagnant union movement regain new membership in 2000s.[10]

Another important change in the legal framework concerning the Korean IR was made in 2010, when the Trade Union and Labor Relations Adjustment Act was revised for allowing the organizing of multiple unions at the workplace level and constraining employer's wage payment for union officials. These institutional changes have the disadvantageous effect on unions, as faced with organizational divide-up and resource constraints. Some employers have attempted to promote the organizing company-friendly second unions to weaken and avoid the existing militant unions, taking advantage of the legal procedure of multiple-union organizing in recent years. In addition, employers and the government have often resorted to the claims for compensation to suppress the strike action launched by unions in the private and public sectors. The claims by employers, which have damaging effect on the striking unions by imposing a substantial amount of financial penalties, has been what the unions have demanded to be forbidden (Lee, 2015).

Changes in pay systems

Wage determination, is a core component of industrial relations, which has been a major cause of labor disputes that have been encountered in many economies in labor history and in current industrial relations. In this section, we examine how the wage system may have evolved as a result of changes in the employment system, or more precisely, the dismantling of a once strong internal labor market that favors seniority and lifelong employment, in China, Japan, and Korea.

China

The wage system in China has undergone significant change as its marketization process deepens. Until the 1980s, the wage system in urban employment, which was heavily dominated by the state sector, was characterized by its rigid and relatively flat wage structure that was insensitive to the occupational characteristics and the level of human capital required (cf. Cooke, 2005; Takahara, 1992). State sector reform and the growth of the private sector has led to a major shift from a predominantly egalitarian model of basic wage + workplace benefits to more variable pay systems, with the main components including: basic wage + performance related wage/bonuses + workplace benefits. In the private sector, performance-related pay is a key feature in which employers shift business risks to the workers. As such, the proportion of bonuses or performance-related pay may be as high as 80 percent of the total wage income in some businesses, such as sales and banking (e.g., Cooke, 2012; Gamble & Huang, 2009). While state-owned firms are under relatively more constraints than private firms in the level of income and types of benefits they can provide to their employees, private firms are adopting more varieties of workplace welfare benefits than hitherto in an attempt to attract and retain talent, bypass government wage-related tax, and retain reward flexibility without committing to a high basic wage level.

While wage growth for those at the upper end of the job ladder has experienced substantial growth in the last two decades, wage growth for the majority of (the grass-roots) workers has been moderate and increasingly disproportional to the GDP growth of the country. According to Zhang and Zhang (2010), wage income had been taking a declining proportion of the GDP from 43.82 percent in 1992 to 39.16 percent in 2007, compared to the nearly 60 percent share in developed economies such as Germany and the USA during the same period (Karabarbounis & Neiman, 2014). The rapid opening up of the economy to the private sector and foreign investment since the mid-1990s, and the government's prioritization of the interests of capital rather than that of labor in the interest of economic development, have led to widening income disparities across different social groupings and regions (e.g., Mukhopadhaya, 2013). While the Chinese national statistics are not sufficiently detailed to enable us to identify the low paying jobs and the likely gender and age patterns of wage rewards, Table 5.3 offers a snap shot of the average wage by sector. As we can see, the manufacturing sector is amongst the lowest pay sectors where labor unrest level is also the highest. Indeed, a large proportion of the labor disputes, particularly since 2010, are related to demands for increase in wage and benefits as well as fulfilling employers' responsibilities in social security premium contribution (e.g., Chan, 2010; Chan, 2011; Lyddon, Cao, Meng, & Lu, 2015).

Table 5.3 Annual average wage for all employees in urban sector in China (figures in yuan)

Sector	2005	2008	2011	2013
Total	18,200	28,898	41,799	51,483
Farming, Forestry, Animal Husbandry, & Fishery	8,207	12,560	19,469	25,820
Mining & Quarrying	20,449	34,233	52,230	60,138
Manufacturing	15,934	24,404	36,665	46,431
Electricity, Gas & Water Production & Supply	24,750	38,515	52,723	67,085
Construction	14,112	21,223	32,103	42,072
Transport, Storage, Post, & Telecommunication Services	20,911	32,041	47,078	57,993
Information Transmission, Computer Service, & Software	38,799	54,906	70,918	90,915
Wholesale & Retail Trade	15,256	25,818	40,654	50,308
Hotels & Catering	13,876	19,321	27,486	34,044
Finance & Insurance	29,229	53,897	81,109	99,653
Real Estate	20,253	30,118	42,837	51,048
Education	18,259	29,831	43,194	51,950
Health Care, Social Securities, & Social Welfare	20,808	32,185	46,206	57,979
Culture, Sports, & Entertainment	22,670	34,158	47,878	59,336
Public Management & Social Organization	20,234	32,296	42,062	49,259

Source: compiled from *China Statistical Yearbook 2014*, retrieved from www.stats.gov.cn/tjsj/ndsj/2014/indexeh.htm.

Japan

As noted earlier, seniority-based pay has been a key feature in the Japanese employment system. As employees' pay depends on their rank, this means that it takes many years for them to receive higher wages through the internal promotion ladder. Therefore, there is a strong correlation between length of service and wages. Employees have a strong incentive to work hard to be promoted to a higher position. Since the 1990s, many Japanese firms have attempted to introduce performance-related pay in an attempt to improve performance and competitiveness. One of the first companies that introduced performance-related pay was Fujitsu, an electronics company, which reformed its pay system in 1994. After Fujitsu, a significant number of firms introduced such pay systems. The General Survey on Working Conditions, which is compiled by the Ministry of Health, Labour and Welfare, shows how firms determine their pay. According to the survey in 2012, 60.4 percent of the firms with more than 1,000 employees responded that base pay reflects performance for managerial positions. Amongst those that responded that base pay is determined according to performance, 41.9 percent responded that short-term individual performance is most important, while 19.1 percent responded that long-term individual performance is important. In addition to performance, firms responded that skill and job are important factors that determine base pay. The survey also shows that larger firms are more likely to introduce performance-related pay.

Large firms have been introducing a performance-related element into the salaries they pay, and have also kept their competence rank system. According to the Japan Productivity Centre (2010), the proportion of listed firms that had competence rank-based salaries for managerial staff was 69.9 percent in 2009, down from 80.9 percent in 1999. The same study also shows that the proportion of firms that had introduced performance-related pay increased from 52.5 percent in 2003 to 73.3 percent in 2009.

Using micro data of individual employees for several companies, Tsuru, Abe, and Kubo (2005) examine the determinants of wages. In particular, they examine whether there is a change in the determinants of wages after the introduction of a new wage system. They find that the effect of length of service on wages decreases and that of performance assessment increases after the introduction of a new wage system. At the same time, it is shown that the effect of competence rank is significant. Tsuru et al.'s (2005) study also shows that the age–wage profile is changing in these firms. The profile becomes flatter after a wage reform. In particular, there is relatively little change in the age–wage profile for non-managerial workers, while there is a significant change for those in managerial positions. They suggest that large firms are reforming their wage structures for managerial positions while retaining the traditional system for relatively young workers.

There are criticisms of performance-related pay. In particular, employers find it difficult to make fair and consistent appraisals of workers. According to the General Survey of Working Conditions (Ministry of Health, Labour and Welfare, 2010), many firms think that revision is needed for their performance-related pay system. The proportion of firms that answer that major revision is needed for their performance-related pay is 23.6 percent. In particular, middle managers do not have enough skills to evaluate their subordinates. In response to these criticisms, some firms weaken the tie between individual performance and pay.

Existing wage statistics also reveals the decline of the significance of seniority (age and length of service) in wage. Specifically, Kubo and Saito (2012) use data from the Basic Survey on Wage Structure to examine whether there was a change in the age–wage profile for male and female workers in 1981, 2000, and 2014 (see Figure 5.3). These workers are university degree holders working in large firms with more than 1,000 employees. The wage data is standardized so that the wages of employees under twenty-four equal 100. The finding clearly shows that the wage profile is becoming flatter across different age groups. In 1981, workers aged fifty to fifty-four received wages that were more than three times higher than those paid to workers aged under twenty-four years; in 2014, however, the difference between the wages of workers aged under twenty-four and those aged fifty to fifty-four decreased. These results are consistent with Hamaaki et al.'s (2012) study.

Korea

In Korea, the ending of lifelong employment commitment for many companies has been accompanied by an attempt to replace the seniority-based model to a performance-based or job-based model in their wage system. According to Cho (2012), the share of companies which adopted the seniority-based pay scheme declined from 60.8 percent in 2005 to 50.2 percent in 2012. In the same period, the shares of performance-based pay and job-based pay rose from 13.2 percent to 26.4 percent and from 17.7 percent to 30.3 percent respectively.[11] As demonstrated in Figure 5.4, however, the seniority-based wage system remains intact in large firms, and those companies are faced with the sustained increase of wages for their aging workforce. Moreover, since the legal retirement age (sixty years old) was implemented in 2016, large firms have demanded the introduction of the wage-peak scheme, by which the wages of old employees whose retirement is extended by the law are cut to some extent, as well as to change the existing seniority-based pay model to the performance-based one to boost corporate productivity and competitiveness. As those large firms are mostly unionized and the unions are negative about the management's wage innovation proposal, it is not yet certain how the seniority-based wage system might be replaced by the performance-based, or job-based, scheme as management intended.

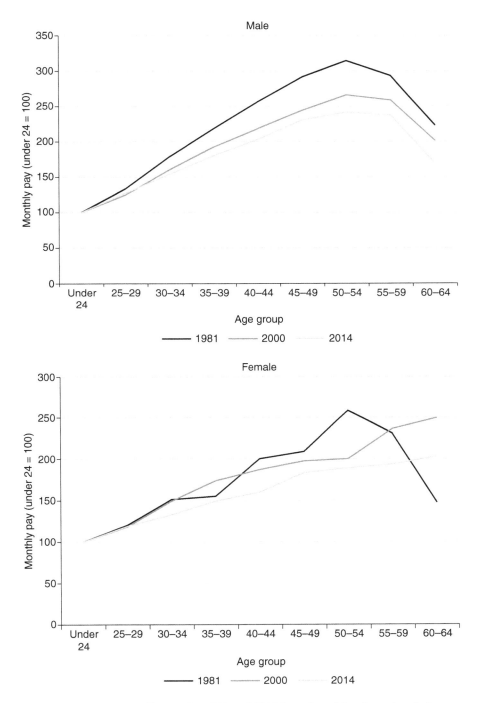

Figure 5.3 Wage-age profile in 1981, 2000, and 2014 for male and female workers in Japan
Source: Basic Survey on Wage Structure. Ministry of Employment and Labor, 2012.

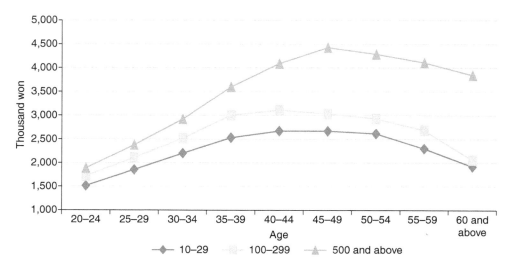

Figure 5.4 Monthly wage curve by age and firm Size in Korea (unit: thousand won)

Source: Basic Statistics of Wage Structure. Ministry of Employment and Labor, 2012.

Note
The wage data estimates the averaged monthly wages of workers employed in all the industries.

Conclusions

In this chapter, we examined how characteristics of industrial relations might have changed as a result of the transformation of the employment system in China, Japan, and Korea. We highlighted key changes in economic policies and the associated labor market reforms in all three countries since the 1980s against a context of economic globalization. Some of these changes were responses from the national government to international pressure, as was the case for Japan and Korea, whereas the pressure for change emerged internally for China in an attempt to revitalize the state sector and to speed up the economic development of the country. Either way, a major consequence of these changes has been the undermining of an established internal labor market system marked by long-term employment and pay rises through tenure and internal career progression in all three countries. As a result, the workforces have generally experienced a decline in job security, wage growth rate, and other employment terms and conditions. In particular, the younger generation of the workforces, despite their relatively high level of education, seems to be bearing the cost of such a downward trajectory of job quality when more and more employers have opted to replace the "make" model with the "buy" model through contingent employment or outsourcing of work.

In all three countries, the trade unions have proved less than effective, for many, in protecting job security, wage growth, and other rights and interests of the workers. While unions in Japan and Korea have been criticized for their lack of interest and ability to expand into the non-regular employment segment to represent those workers, the Chinese trade unions have been considered to be useless in defending workers and have largely failed to represent the workers in the private sector, many of whom are toiling under exploitative terms and conditions. While the impact of the trade unions is more effective at the workplace level for Japan and Korea, union impact in China is more likely to be created by union branches at the local government level beyond the workplaces because workplace unions, where they exist, are often controlled or represented by the management. Although the governments of all three countries have made attempts to re-regulate the employment relations after a period of labor market liberalization, these efforts have been undermined by the continuing ascendance of employer bargaining power in general and their strategic responses to overcoming new regulations through creative deployment of labor.

Notes

1 The listing of these three countries is in alphabetical order. For consistency purpose, this chapter will generally follow this order in its discussion.
2 These changes include the amendment of the Anti-Monopoly Law in 1997, the amendment of the Commercial Code in 1999, a major revision of the Financial Instruments and Exchange Law in 2006, and introduction of the Company Act in 2005.
3 By contrast, as shown in Figure 5.1, the union circle has presented different estimates, insisting that workers under the recurrent renewal of temporary employment contracts are categorized into non-regular employment. Those workers are treated as regular employment in the government estimates. Therefore, there has been a wide gap between the government's and the union's estimation of non-regular employment, ranging from 29.2 percent (2002) to 13.0 percent (2014).
4 See Neal (2011) for an overview of the development of the Chinese legislative system for labor regulation with a particular focus on the three major laws enacted in 2008; also see Brown (2010, 2012); Cooke (2011a); and Cooney et al. (2013).
5 See Yamakawa (2001) for an overview of labor law reform in the 1990s in response to the socioeconomic changes in Japan in the 1980s and 1990s.
6 The full title of the law is the Act on the Protection of Dispatched Workers, which was enacted in February, 1998.
7 The legislation of the massive lay-off clause and the Dispatched Labor Act was undertaken not only as the key part of the historic Social Pact, which was made for overcoming the economic crisis, but also as the precondition for obtaining the emergency loans from international financial organizations (i.e., IMF and World Bank) (Lee & Eun, 2009).
8 Moreover, OECD (2013) reports that it is easier for Korean employers to carry out regular employees than OECD counterparts, and that the conversion of non-regular labor into regular employee status after one year's employment in Korea (11.1 percent) is the lowest among OECD countries.
9 The Act on the Establishment and Operation of Trade Unions for Teachers and the Act on the Establishment and Operation of Public Official's Trade Unions was respectively enacted in 1999 and in 2005.
10 The size of union membership declined to 1.402 million in 1998 and has since rebounded to 1.848 million in 2013.
11 The total of three pay schemes in this survey is over 100 percent, since the combined pay scheme of the three wage-determination elements double counts such elements.

References

All-China Federation of Trade Unions Dispatched Employment Research Project Team. (2012). An investigation of the status quo of dispatched employment in China. *China Labor, 5*, 23–25.

Asano, H., Ito, T., & Kawaguchi, D. (2013). Why has the fraction of nonstandard workers increased?: A case study of Japan. *Scottish Journal of Political Economy, 60*(4), 360–389.

Bamber, G., Lansbury, R., Wailes, N., & Wright, C. F. (2016). *International and comparative employment relations* (6th ed.). London: Sage; Sydney: Allen & Unwin.

Brown, R. C. (2010). *Understanding labor and employment law in China*. New York: Cambridge University Press.

Brown, R. C. (2012). *East Asian labor and employment law international and comparative context*. New York: Cambridge University Press.

Cairns, D. (2015). New formalities for casual labor: Addressing unintended consequences of China's Labor Contract Law. *Washington International Law Journal, 24*(1), 1–34.

Chan, A. (2011). Strikes in China's export industries in comparative perspective. *The China Journal 65*(1), 27–51.

Chan, C. K. C. (2010). Strike and changing workplace relations in a Chinese global factory. *Industrial Relations Journal, 40*(1), 60–77.

Chang, K. & Cooke, F. L. (2015). Legislating the right to strike in China: Historical development and prospects. *Journal of Industrial Relations, 57*(3), 440–455.

China Education Online. (2014). Retrieved from www.eol.cn/html/c/2014xbys/index.shtml.

Cho, J. (2012). Policy study on the innovation of wage system. Project Report for the Korean Labor Economics Association.

Clarke, S. (2005). Post-socialist trade unions: China and Russia. *Industrial Relations Journal, 36*(1), 2–18.

Coe, N. M., Johns, J., & Ward, K. (2011). Transforming the Japanese labor market: Deregulation and the rise of temporary staffing. *Regional Studies, 45*(8), 1091–1106.

Cooke, F. L. (2005). *HRM, work and employment in China.* London: Routledge.

Cooke, F. L. (2010). Women's participation in employment in Asia: A comparative analysis of China, India, Japan and South Korea. *The International Journal of Human Resource Management, 21*(10–12), 2249–2270.

Cooke, F. L. (2011a). The enactment of three new labour laws in China: Unintended consequences and the emergence of "new" actors in employment relations. In S. Lee & D. McCann (Eds.), *Regulating for decent work: New directions in labour market regulation* (pp. 180–205). Basingstoke: Palgrave Macmillan; and Geneva: International Labour Organization.

Cooke, F. L. (2011b). Labour market regulations and informal employment in China: To what extent are workers protected?. *Journal of Chinese Human Resource Management, 2*(2), 100–116.

Cooke, F. L. (2011c). Unions in China in a period of marketization. In G. Gall, A. Wilkinson, & R. Hurd (Eds.), *International handbook on labour unions: Responses to neo-liberalism* (pp. 105–124). Cheltenham: Edward Elgar.

Cooke, F. L. (2012). *Human resource management in China: New trends and practices.* London: Routledge.

Cooke, F. L. & Brown, R. (2015). The regulation of non-standard forms of work in China, Japan and Republic of Korea. *Conditions of Work and Employment Series No. 64.* Geneva: International Labour Office. Retrieved from www.ilo.org/travail/whatwedo/publications/WCMS_414584/lang-en/index.htm.

Cooney, S., Biddulph, S., & Zhu, Y. (2013). *Law and fair work in China.* London and New York: Routledge.

Duan, Y. & Li., Q. (2014). Generation, development and maturity of collective labor relation in China—A bottom-up analytical perspective. *Human Resources Development of China, 23,* 94–104.

Gamble, J. & Huang, Q. H. (2009). One store, two employment systems: Core, periphery and flexibility in China's retail sector. *British Journal of Industrial Relations, 47*(1), 1–26.

Hamaaki, J., Hori, M., Maeda, S., & Murata, K. (2012). Changes in the Japanese employment system in the two lost decades. *Industrial and Labor Relations Review, 65*(4), 810–846.

Hanami, T. & Komiya, F. (2011). *Labour law in Japan.* Alphen aan den Rijn: Kluwer Law International.

Hassard, J., Sheehan, J., Zhou, M. X., Terpstra-Tong, J., & Morris, J. (2007). *China's state enterprise reform: From Marx to the market.* London: Routledge.

Japan Productivity Centre. (2010). *Nihonteki Koyo Zinzi No Henyoni Kansuru Chosa* [*Survey on Japanese employment and human resource management*]. Japan Productivity Centre.

Kambayashi, R. (2010). Dismissal regulation in Japan. *Global COE Hi-Stat Discussion Paper Series 119.* Hitotsubashi University, Tokyo.

Kambayashi, R. & Kato, T. (2012). Trends in long-term employment and job security in Japan and the United States: The last twenty-five years. *CJEB working paper No. 302.*

Karabarbounis, L. & Neiman, B. (2014). The global decline of the labor share. *The Quarterly Journal of Economics, 129*(1), 61–103.

Khanna, T. (2007). *Billions of entrepreneurs: How China and India are reshaping their futures and yours.* Boston, MA: Harvard Business School Press.

Kim, A. E. & Park, I. (2006). Changing trends of work in South Korea: The rapid growth of underemployment and job insecurity. *Asian Survey, 46*(3), 437–456.

Kim, Y. (2015). Size and situation of non–regular employment. *KLSI Issue Paper No. 7.* (In Korean).

Kubo, K. & Saito, T. (2012). The effect of mergers on employment and wages: Evidence from Japan. *Journal of the Japanese and International Economies, 26,* 263–284.

Kuroki, M. (2012). The deregulation of temporary employment and workers' perceptions of job insecurity. *Industrial and Labor Relations Review, 65*(3), 560–577.

Kuruvilla, S., Lee, C. K., & Gallagher, M. (Eds.). (2011). *From iron rice bowl to informalization.* Ithaca, NY and London: ILR Press.

Lee, B. H. (2015). Employment relations in South Korea. In G. Bamber, R. Lansbury, N. Weils, & C. F. Wright (Eds.), *International and comparative employment relations* (6th ed.). London: Sage Publications.

Lee, B. H. & Eun, S. (2009). Labor politics of employment protection legislation for non-regular workers in South Korea. *Korea Journal, 49*(4), 57–90.

Lee, B. H. & Kim, J. (2013). *Revitalizing strategies for industry union movement.* Seoul: KCTU (in Korean).

Lee, W. & Lee, B. (2003). Korean industrial relations in the era of globalization. *Journal of Industrial Relations, 45*(4), 505–520.

Lyddon, D, Cao, X. B., Meng, Q., & Lu, J. (2015). A strike of "unorganised" workers in a Chinese car factory: The Nanhai Honda events of 2010. *Industrial Relations Journal, 46*(2), 134–152.

Magoshi, E. & Chang, E. (2009). Diversity management and the effects on employees' organizational commitment: Evidence from Japan and Korea. *Journal of World Business, 44*(1), 31–40.

Meng, X. (2012). Labor market outcomes and reforms in China. *Journal of Economic Perspectives, 26*(4), 75–102.

Ministry of Health, Labour and Welfare. (2010). Summary Report of the General Survey on Working Conditions 2010. Ministry of Health, Labour and Welfare, Japan.

Miyajima, H. & Kuroki, F. (2007). The unwinding of cross-shareholding in Japan: Causes, effects, and implications. In M. Aoki, G. Jackson, & H. Miyajima (Eds.), *Corporate governance in Japan: Institutional change and organizational diversity.* Oxford: Oxford University Press.

Miyajima, H. & Nitta, K. (2011). Kabusiki syoyukozono tayokato sono kiketsu [Diversification of ownership structure and its effect on performance]. In H. Miyajima (Ed.) *Nihon no Kigyo Tochi [Corporate Governance in Japan]* (in Japanese). Tokyo: Toyokeizai Shimposha.

Mukhopadhaya, P. (2013). Trends in income inequality in China: The effects of various sources of income. *Journal of the Asia Pacific Economy, 18*(2), 304–317.

National Bureau of Statistics of China. (1996–2014). *China Statistical Yearbook 1995–2013.* Beijing: China Statistics Press.

Neal, A. C. (2011). Towards a functioning framework for individual labour law rights: Challenges for China in a changing world of work. *The International Journal of Comparative Labour Law and Industrial Relations, 27*(4), 365–385.

OECD. (2013). *Employment outlook.* Paris: OECD.

Ono, H. (2010). Lifetime employment in Japan: Concepts and measurements. *Journal of the Japanese and International Economies, 24,* 1–27.

Park, W. S. & Roh, Y. J. (2001). *Changes in human resource management and industrial relations in the period of post-crisis.* Seoul: KLI.

Peng, I. (2012). Dualization in Japan and South Korea. In P. Emmenegger, S. Hausermann, B. Palier, & M. Seeleib-Kaiser (Eds.), *The age of dualization: The changing face of inequality in deindustrializing societies economic* (pp. 1–24). Oxford University Press Scholarship Online.

Qiao, J. (2013). Towards higher quality employment: The situation of Chinese workers. In X. Y. Lu, G. Li, J. Chen, Y. Zhang, W. Li, & X. X. Xu (Eds.), *2014 Blue book of China's society: Society of China analysis and forecast* (pp. 273–292). Beijing: Social Science Academy Press.

Qiao, J. (2014). China labor relations in the economic structure adjustment. In P. L. Li, G. J. Chen, & Y. Zhang (Eds.), *2015 blue book of China's society: Society of China analysis and forecast* (pp. 252–271). Beijing: Social Science Academy Press.

Shimizutani, S. & Yokoyama, I. (2009). Has Japan's long-term employment practice survived? Developments since the 1990s. *Industrial and Labor Relations Review, 62,* 313–326.

Shin, K. (2013). Economic crisis, neoliberal reforms, and the rise of precarious work in South Korea. *American Behavioral Scientist, 57*(3), 335–353.

Takahara, A. (1992). *The politics of wage policy in post-revolutionary China.* London: Macmillan.

Taylor, B. & Li, Q. (2010). China's creative approach to "Union" organizing. *Labor History, 51*(3), 411–428.

Tsuru, T., Abe, M., & Kubo, K. (2005). *Nihon Kigyo No Zinzi Kaikaku: Zinzi Deta Ni Yoru Seika Shugi No Kensyo [Transforming incentives: Evaluating pay for performance in the Japanese firms].* Tokyo: Toyokeizai Shinposya.

Uehara, K. (2009). Early or late promotion/screening?: Empirical analysis of career ladders for Japanese white-collar workers using employees' list. *Japan Labour Review, 6,* 25–58.

Wang, J., Cooke, F. L., & Lin, Z. H. (2016). Informal employment in China: Recent development and human resource implications. *Asia Pacific Journal of Human Resources, 54*(3), 292–311.

World Bank Group. (2015). *World databank of world development indicators and gender statistics.* Washington, DC: The World Bank Group (accessed March 30, 2015).

Witt, M. A. & Redding, G. (2014). China: Authoritarian capitalism. In A. Witt & G. Redding (Eds.), *The Oxford handbook of Asian business systems* (pp. 11–32). Oxford: Oxford University Press.

Yamakawa, R. (2001). Labor law reform in Japan: A response to recent socio-economic changes. *The American Journal of Comparative Law, 49*, 627–652.

Yao, Y. & Zhong, N. H. (2013). Unions and workers' welfare in Chinese firms. *Journal of Labor Economics, 31*(3), 633–667.

Zhang, J. W. & Zhang. S. B. (2010). Changes in primary income distribution and resulting problems: A view of labor share in GDP. *Chinese Journal of Population Science, 5*(1), 25–35.

6

EMPLOYMENT REGULATION AND INDUSTRIAL RELATIONS IN INDONESIA, MALAYSIA, THE PHILIPPINES, THAILAND, AND VIETNAM

Ingrid Landau and Fang Lee Cooke

Introduction

The purpose of this chapter is to provide an overview of employment regulation and industrial relations (IR) systems in Southeast Asia. We focus primarily on the major economies of Indonesia, Malaysia, the Philippines, Thailand, and Vietnam. Southeast Asia is one of the most rapidly growing, dynamic, and diverse regions in the world. It is also one of the most economically integrated, with high and sustained levels of foreign investment. Growth and regional and global integration is only anticipated to accelerate in coming years, in light of intensified efforts by the Association of Southeast Asian Nations (ASEAN) member-states to establish a globally integrated and competitive single market and production base through the ASEAN Economic Community.

Presenting an overview of employment regulation and IR in the five Southeast Asia countries presents challenges not only in light of the number of countries included in the analysis, but also because of the diversity and complexity in their politico-economic structures, from constitutional monarchies in Thailand and Malaysia, to the constitutional democracy of Indonesia, and the Socialist Republic of Vietnam. Unsurprisingly, national IR systems also vary significantly, particularly between those states that have long-standing market economies and those like Vietnam that have only recently begun to build IR institutions suitable for a market-oriented economy. The countries each have diverse historical, cultural, religious, and social structures. Nonetheless, the countries share commonalities which go beyond mere geography. These include the pursuit of broadly similar economic development strategies based on export-oriented industrialization (EOI); extensive integration into the global economy; and relatively high and sustained rates of economic growth.

Two points are worth noting upfront. First, although we try our best to provide a comprehensive overview, extant literature on employment regulation and industrial relations in Southeast Asia continues to be limited when compared with the body of work on Western developed economies or on East Asian countries such as Japan and China. Over several recent decades, however, the growing economic success and influence of some Southeast Asian economies has led to heightened scholarly attention in the region. This is reflected in a growing number of national and comparative studies on IR in the more developed economies of Malaysia, Indonesia, Philippines, and Thailand. These studies have tended to focus on the impact of industrialization strategy and globalization on national employment relations systems (cf. Frenkel & Kuruvilla, 2002; Frenkel & Peetz, 1998; Kuruvilla, 1996; Kuruvilla & Erikson, 2002; Kuruvilla & Venkataratnam, 1996). There has also been important comparative work on trade unions in the region (e.g., Benson & Zhu, 2008). Few studies exist on IR systems in the smaller and less developed countries, however, although efforts are now being made to fill this gap (e.g., Ford & Gillan, 2016). Moreover, with some important exceptions (e.g., Cooney, Lindsey, Mitchell, & Zhu, 2002; Lee & Eyraud, 2008; Serrano, 2014), there remains a relative dearth of national and comparative studies on the nature and evolution of employment regulation in the region.

Second, as we have already noted, Southeast Asia is a region of great diversity and complexity. In providing this overview, we inevitably take a generalized approach and focus largely on institutions and actors at the national and supranational level. We recognize, however, that in doing so we are unable to do justice to the important and nuanced distinctions that exist not only between the different countries, but also between different industries and sectors, and different localities. To this end, we have attempted to refer the reader where relevant to extant studies and to other chapters in this edited volume.

This chapter contains six sections in addition to this introduction and a conclusion. Section 2 presents an overview of national economies in the selected Southeast Asian countries and identifies distinct features of labor markets in the region. In Section 3, we briefly review the evolution of employment regulation and IR, paying particular attention to developments in the latter half of the twentieth century. Section 4 describes key aspects of national regulatory frameworks, looking in turn at forms of employment; wages; trade unions and other forms of workers' representation; employer associations; collective bargaining; and dispute resolution. Section 5 briefly discusses the practical impact of legal regulation on workplaces in Southeast Asia, and identifies a number of factors that contribute to the persistent and significant gap between employment regulations and everyday life for many workers. Section 6 identifies other important sources of employment regulation that exist alongside, and interact with, formal state-based regulation in the region.

Economies and labor markets in Southeast Asia

In recent decades, Southeast Asia has experienced rapid growth, industrialization, and economic diversification. Countries in the region are often grouped according to the time they embarked on rapid economic development, with the economies of Malaysia and Thailand, and subsequently Philippines and Indonesia (sometimes collectively referred to as the "South Tigers") beginning to grow rapidly during the 1980s, followed by Vietnam in the 1990s (Kuruvilla & Venkataratnam, 1996). National economic development strategies in the region have been based on EOI, including increased foreign direct investment (FDI) and market liberalization. Malaysia embarked on a first-stage EOI strategy in 1970s which focused on the attraction of FDI to the electronics and electrical good sectors, but shifted in the late 1980s to a second-stage EOI strategy focusing on the attraction of more technology-intensive FDI in electronics and electrical goods and textiles, and on the adoption of more high-performance style human resource management (HRM) practices (Frenkel & Kuruvilla, 2002; Ramasamy & Rowley, 2008). The Philippines and Thailand also adopted EOI strategies in the early 1970s, seeking to capitalize on their comparative advantage of low labor costs. The Philippines, however, did not fully embrace EOI after the end of the Marcos era in the mid-1980s (Erikson, Kuruvilla, Ofreneo, & Asuncion

Ortiz, 2003). Unlike Malaysia, the Philippines has not transitioned beyond a focus on low-cost labor-intensive assembly operations, especially in the electronics and manufacturing industries (Erikson et al., 2003). As a result, in recent years, the country has faced intensified competition for FDI from other low-cost producers such as China, Cambodia, and Vietnam.

Those economies in the region most exposed to external markets (namely, Indonesia, Thailand, the Philippines, and Malaysia) were hit hard by the Asian Financial Crisis in 1997, leading to a substantial deceleration in growth rates. However economic indicators began to improve in the early mid-2000s, and the average annual GDP growth rates for the first decade of the twentieth century (2000–2011) ranged from around 4.7 percent in the Philippines, 5 percent in Indonesia and Malaysia, through to 7 percent in Vietnam (World Bank, 2014). Although the global economic crisis impacted economies in the region (cf. Green, 2010), most of the countries weathered the crisis relatively well and continue to growth faster than the global average (International Labour Organization [ILO] and Asian Development Bank [ADB] 2014; ILO, 2014). The region continues to attract high and steadily increasing flows of FDI, with significant implications for labor markets and employment relations. Since 2010, ASEAN received over US$400 billion in FDI, and the share of ASEAN FDI inflows relative to world inflows is now similar to that of China and higher than that of India (ILO & ADB, 2014). In 2011, for the first time, the region's main source of FDI flow shifted from the European Union to ASEAN (ILO & ADB, 2014).

While significant and sustained economic growth in the region has led to a rapid expansion in the proportion of the workforce with "middle-class" status (defined by the ILO as households with per capital income of US$4 or more per day) and a decline in the proportion of workers living in poverty, the numbers of people living in poverty has risen in absolute terms (ILO & ADB, 2014). There have also been rising rates of income inequality in a number of countries: increasing since the early 1990s in Indonesia, remaining relatively steady in the Philippines, Malaysia, and Vietnam, and declining in Thailand (ILO & ADB, 2014).

Numbering just over 300 million, ASEAN has the third-largest labor force in the world, behind China and India. The size of labor force varies widely between countries: from 118.2 million in Indonesia, 13.8 million in Malaysia, through to 53.2 million in Vietnam, 41 million in the Philippines, and 39.4 million in Thailand (ILO & ADB, 2014). While the overall rates of unemployment and underemployment remain low, there is significant variation between countries. In 2015, the highest rates of unemployment are found in the Philippines and Indonesia, where they exceed 5 percent. Youth unemployment is a significant issue in a number of countries, with a high percentage of young people in the labor market unemployed in the Philippines and Indonesia as well (ILO, 2015).

Labor markets in Southeast Asia have experienced significant structural transformation in recent decades, as labor moves away from agriculture toward labor-intensive manufacturing and service industries in urban areas. Looking at the ASEAN region as a whole, agriculture has now been surpassed by services as the most dominant form of employment (40.0 percent and 40.6 percent respectively), with the remaining 19.4 percent of workers engaged in industry (ILO & ADB, 2014). While some countries (such as Vietnam) have seen a significant increase in the proportion of workers engaged in industry, other countries such as Malaysia and Singapore have experienced a process of de-industrialization in recent decades (ILO & ADB, 2014). The proportion of workers engaged in the service sector has increased significantly in recent years in all countries in the region except Cambodia. Employment in services now accounts for 59.7 percent of employment in Malaysia, 53.4 percent in the Philippines, and 45.0 percent in Indonesia (ILO & ADB, 2014). These structural changes in the labor market, along with the development of new production patterns, has also led to the emergence of significant challenges of skills mismatch and skilled labor shortages in the region.

Southeast Asian labor markets continue to be characterized by very high rates of informality. The percentage of the labor force engaged outside wage or salaried employment is particularly prevalent in those countries with still largely agrarian-based economies (World Bank, 2014). This contrasts to Malaysia, where over 70 percent of workers are engaged in waged or salaried employment (World Bank, 2014). An estimated three in five workers in the region (179 million) are engaged in "vulnerable employment," defined as own-account and contributing family workers (ILO & ADB, 2014). Women are much more likely to be engaged in vulnerable employment than men (ILO & ADB, 2014).

Since the 1970s, structural changes have led to increasing rates of internal migration from rural areas to towns and cities. While it is difficult to compare data on internal migrants as a proportion of the population due to variance in national data collection, an estimated 2.3 percent of the Indonesian population are internal migrants, compared to 2 percent in Thailand, and 9.7 percent in Vietnam (World Bank, 2014). There are also high levels of cross-border migration in the region, with some states such as Malaysia, Singapore, and Thailand being destinations and hubs for large numbers of migrant workers. Other countries, such as Indonesia, the Philippines, and Vietnam are largely countries of emigration (Kaur, 2010). Between 1990 and 2013, migration within the ASEAN region increased from 1.5 million to 6.5 million and formal and informal migration is only expected to increase in the future (ILO and ADB, 2014).

The evolution of employment regulation and IR in Southeast Asia

Most Southeast Asian labor law systems are based on Western models, imposed through colonization and/or external occupation (Cooney et al., 2002; also see Table 6.1 for a list of major labor laws in selected Southeast Asian countries). The first employment regulations in Malaysia were passed under British rule, the Indonesian labor law system was inherited from the Dutch (cf. Lindsey & Masduki, 2002), and the Philippine system has been influenced by American occupation (Hutchison, 2016). The origins of the Thai and Vietnamese labor law systems are somewhat more complex. As Thailand was never colonized, it has a legal system with both common and civil law traits, and only began to develop a distinctive approach to IR in the early-mid 1970s (Brown, Thanachaisethavut, & Hewison, 2002; for a more comprehensive overview of the historical development, see also Brown 2016). In Vietnam, the period following independence in the North in 1954 saw the state administer and manage work according to Socialist precepts (cf. Collins, 2009; Nicholson, 2002).

With the exception of Vietnam, Lao PDR, and Cambodia, Southeast Asian countries retained aspects of the colonial labor laws following independence. However, they have engaged in "selective application" and adaptation of these laws (Cooney, Mahy, Mitchell, & Gahan, 2014: 144). The contention that employment and IR regulation in Southeast Asia have been used by governments to serve state-building objectives, namely, rapid industrialization, national unity, and regime stability, is well and widely advanced (cf. Cooney et al., 2002; Deyo, 1997; Hadiz, 1997). Regulations have been enacted that promote industrial stability through restricting trade unions and the right to strike; and through facilitating a degree of state intervention and control in IR (e.g., Brown, 2016; Kuruvilla & Erikson, 2002). In Malaysia, the years following independence in 1957 saw the replacement of a voluntarist system of collective bargaining and dispute settlement with legislation strictly regulating the formation and activities of unions, and prioritizing compulsory arbitration through an industrial tribunal system (for a detailed overview of the historical development of the IR and labor regulation system of Malaysia, see Crinis & Parasuraman, 2016).

In Indonesia, President Suharto's military-based authoritarian New Order regime (1966–1998) saw the violent repression of left-wing trade unions, followed by heavy restrictions on union activity and workers' rights, including the right to strike (Caraway, 2004; Ford & Sirait, 2016; Hadiz, 1997; Isaac & Sitalaksmi, 2008; Tjandra, 2008, 2010). Thailand also has a history of union suppression under the military-led regimes from 1957 until the mid-1970s (Yoshida, 2003). As Brown explains, the situation has not much improved since then with stagnated union membership in the last three decades:

> [t]hose private sector trade unions that do operate are—with some notable exceptions— small, largely single enterprise-based, poorly resourced and struggle to represent their members in processes of collective bargaining, let alone support any member attempting to seek redress through the machinery of employment relations and labor courts.
>
> *(2016: 209)*

The Philippines is somewhat of an outlier in this regard, as it has always had labor laws which are relatively liberal. This has been attributed to a legacy of American colonialism and geopolitical strategic objectives, in which relatively favorable labor laws were promoted as a means of staving off communist influences (Deyo, 1997; Hadiz, 2002). In 1953, following the country's ratification of the two core ILO conventions on freedom of association and collective bargaining, the Philippines legislature passed the Industrial Peace Act. This legislation, inspired by the US National Labor Relations Act, sought to put in place a system of bilateral collective bargaining as a means of promoting industrial peace and was shortly followed by a range of other labor legislation (Bitonio, 2012; Kuruvilla & Erikson, 2002). The declaration of martial law in 1972 led to significant changes in IR, including a greater focus on the suppression of industrial action and the introduction of compulsory arbitration to promote industrial peace. This period also saw the government assume greater control over the union movement, and the downward revision of minimum standards in labor laws (Kuruvilla & Erikson, 2002).

The late 1980s through to the early 2000s was a period of significant change in employment regulations and IR in Southeast Asia. Democratization in the Philippines, Indonesia, and Thailand saw the opening of greater political space for trade unions and civil society more broadly, and moves by governments to afford greater protection to workers and unions. In Indonesia, many of the more repressive aspects of the former regime in relation to labor relations were dismantled following the fall of the New Order regime, and government policy shifted toward a greater commitment to labor rights and standards (e.g., Rupidara and McGraw, 2010; Tjandra, 2010). A suite of new labor laws followed, including: the Trade Union Act (No. 21/2000); the Manpower Act (No. 13/2003); and the Settlement of Industrial Dispute Act (No. 2/2004). Certain labor rights were also given protection through amendments to the Constitution of 1945, and through the passage of the National Social Security Act (No. 40/2004) and The Protection of Indonesian Migrant Workers Act (No. 39/2004). In Thailand, the dramatic impact of the 1997 Asian Financial Crisis on what was widely regarded up to that time as a highly unregulated economy led the state to focus its efforts to achieving economic stability and balanced growth. The state's policy response included the introduction of a raft of active labor market policies, as well as a social safety net program that has since been progressively extended to unprotected groups of workers in the labor market, including those in the informal economy (see further Siengthai, 2008). In the Philippines, the end of the Marcos regime saw the removal of some of the more restrictive elements of the regulatory regime, though restrictions on the right to strike remain (Bitonio, 2012; Kuruvilla & Erikson, 2002; for more detailed discussion, see also Hutchison, 2016).

The late 1980s and 1990s also saw significant labor law reform in those countries which had adopted communist or socialist regimes following decolonization (Vietnam, Lao PDR, and

Table 6.1 List of major labor laws and regulations in selected Southeast Asian states

Indonesia

1970	Workplace Safety Act No. 1/1970
2000	Trade Union Act Law No. 21/2000
2002	Racial Discrimination Law No. 40/2002
2003	Manpower Act No. 13/2003
2004	Industrial Disputes Resolution Act No 2./2004
2004	Social Security Law No. 40/2004
2004	Minister for Labour Decision No. Kep100/Men/VI/2004 on the Implementation of Employment Agreement for a Definite Period
2012	Minister of Labour Regulation No. 19/2012 on Conditions for Outsourcing

Malaysia

1950	Labour Ordinance, Sabah
1952	Labour Ordinance, Sarawak
1952	Workmen's Compensation Act 1952
1955	Employment Act 1955
1959	Trade Unions Ordinance 1959
1967	Industrial Relations Act 1967
1967	Factories and Machinery Act 1967
1969	Employee's Social Security Act 1969
1975	Tripartite Code of Conduct for Industrial Harmony 1975
1981	Private Employment Act 1981
1994	Occupational Health and Safety Act 1994

The Philippines

1953	Industrial Peace Act
1987	Constitution of the Philippines
1974	Labor Code of the Philippines
1995	Anti-Sexual Harassment Act of 1995
1997	Social Security Law of 1997

Thailand

1975	Labor Relations Act
1979	Act on Establishment of Labor Courts and Labor Court Procedure, B.E. 2522
1990	Social Security Act No. 1 B.E. 2533
1994	Social Security Act No. 2
1994	Workmen's Compensation Act B.E. 2537
1998	Labour Protection Act B.E. 2541
1999	Social Security Act No. 3
2008	Civil and Commercial Code: Book 3, Title VI: Hire of Services, 1985, B.E. 2551, 2008
2008	Labour Protection Act (No. 2), B.E. 2551
2008	Labour Protection Act (No. 3), B.E. 2551

Vietnam

1994	Labour Code of Vietnam (amended in 2002 and 2006, replaced in 2012)
2006	Law on Social Insurance
2012	Labour Code of Vietnam
2012	Law on Trade Unions
2013	Decree No. 44-ND-CP Implementing the Labour Code on Labour Contracts
2015	Decree No. 55-ND-CP on Labour Outsourcing

Cambodia). In Vietnam, the transition from a centrally driven economy in which jobs and wages were administratively determined by the State to a "socialist-led market economy" has involved the development of a labor law system based on legally regulated individual and collective employment relationships (Collins, 2009; Nicholson, 2002). Following the formal adoption by the Communist Party of Vietnam of a series of economic reforms known as *Doi Moi* (renewal or renovation) in 1986, there were tentative moves by the government to reform employment relations in state-owned enterprises (SOEs), including through the introduction of employment contracts (Collins, 2009). The country adopted its first national Labor Code in 1994, which was subject to significant amendments in 2002 and 2006, and replaced by a new Labor Code in 2012, which came into effect on May 1, 2013.

In considering the evolution of employment regulation in Southeast Asia, it is important to recognize the role played by international organizations such as the International Labour Organization (ILO), the World Bank, and the International Monetary Fund (IMF). All the countries in Southeast Asia are members of the ILO, however, rates of ratification of ILO Conventions—including the eight fundamental conventions—are relatively low when compared to other regions. This is particularly the case with respect to the two fundamental conventions concerning freedom of association and the right to organize and bargain collectively (ILO, 2016). McCann (2008) identifies two broad ways in which the International Financial Institutions may influence approaches to employment regulation in the Asia Pacific: by way of regional and international comparisons (in which less restrictive approaches to labor markets are lauded); and by direct influence on labor law and policy issues at the national level. In Southeast Asia, the influence of the financial institutions has been particularly strong in some countries such as Indonesia (Hadiz, 2002; de Ruyter & Warnecke, 2008; Miles, 2015; Tjandraningsih, 2013) but less so in others such as Malaysia (Crinis & Parasuraman, 2016) and Vietnam (Collins, Nankervis, Sitalaksmi, & Warner, 2011).

A number of Southeast Asian states are also now party to bilateral and regional trade agreements, which include commitments to enforce national laws and respect certain international labor standards. In late 2015, the leaders of Australia, Brunei Darussalam, Canada, Chile, Japan, Malaysia, Mexico, New Zealand, Peru, Singapore, United States, and Vietnam reached agreement on the text of the Trans-Pacific Partnership (TPP). This agreement includes a comprehensive labor chapter. In addition, as part of the negotiation process, the USA has reached side agreements with Brunei, Malaysia, and Vietnam that have significant implications for their national labor law systems (see further Capling & Ravenhill, 2011; Vogt, 2015).

In contrast to other regions, there has been little by way of the establishment of a regional normative framework and/or harmonization of national labor laws within Southeast Asia. This relative neglect of the social dimension of integration is in contrast to the significant momentum surrounding economic integration—the ASEAN Community is formally comprised of three pillars: the ASEAN Economic Community (AEC), the ASEAN Political-Security Community, and the ASEAN Socio-Cultural Community. To date, ASEAN initiatives focusing on labor standards have included: the ASEAN Charter of 2007 (which includes commitments to the protection of human rights and fundamental freedoms); the ASEAN Human Rights Declaration of 2012; and work within ASEAN toward an ASEAN Socio-Cultural Community (ASCC), the blueprint for which includes a commitment to the promotion of decent work. There is also an ASEAN Labour Cooperation Structure, led by the biannual ASEAN Labour Ministers Meeting and a formal cooperation agreement between ASEAN and the ILO, ASEAN Guidelines on Good Industrial Relations Practices, and an ASEAN Declaration on the Protection and Promotion of the Rights of Migrant Workers (2007). To date, however, initiatives in this area have been largely limited to: comparative labor law analyses; the promotion and dissemination of good practices; and capacity building activities. This approach is consistent with, and reflects, ASEAN's emphasis on the norm of non-interference in the internal affairs of member-states (see further Kahler & MacIntyre, 2013; Poole 2015).

Employment regulation and industrial relations in Southeast Asia

Forms of employment

Recent decades have seen an increase in the proportion of workers engaged through non-standard forms of employment around the world, and Southeast Asia is no exception (cf. Landau, Mahy, & Mitchell, 2015; Serrano, 2014). Intensified competition and greater exposure to global managerial trends arising from increased international economic integration have led to intensified efforts by firms to reduce labor costs and maximize numerical flexibility through casualization, subcontracting, and labor outsourcing. In some countries such as the Philippines and Thailand, economic crises have only accelerated these trends (Erikson et al., 2003; Frenkel & Kuruvilla, 2002). These increases have occurred despite legislative restrictions on the use of these types of work.

While reliable statistics on the prevalence of non-standard work in Southeast Asia is difficult to come by, the available data suggests a high proportion of workers engaged through these types of arrangements. In Indonesia, approximately 40 percent of workers classified as "regular" have a job tenure of thirty-six months or less (ILO, 2015), and Indonesian unions report that up to 65 percent of workers engaged in the textile industry and 40 percent of workers in the metalworking industry are engaged through labor outsourcing arrangements (ITUC, 2014: 26; see also Marasigan & Serrano, 2014; Tjandraningsih, 2013). Since the 1990s, there have also been significant increases in the number of workers on short-term contracts and engaged through subcontracting and outsourcing arrangements in the Philippines, Thailand, and Vietnam (Brown, 2016; Erikson et al., 2003; Landau et al., 2015; McCann, 2008; Pupos, 2014; Siengthai, 2008).

Increasing concerns over the rise of non-standard work and its impact on workers has led trade unions and labor non-government organizations (NGOs) to campaign on the issue and further moves to regulate these types of arrangements. In the mid-2000s, Indonesian unions successfully opposed plans by the Indonesian state to remove restrictions on the use of fixed-term contracts, and in 2004 regulations requiring the licensing of labor supply agencies and the registration of labor supply contracts were introduced. In 2012, large-scale public demonstrations organized by three major Indonesian union federations helped to pressure the Indonesian state into imposing further restrictions on the use of labor outsourcing (Landau et al., 2015; Tjandraningsih, 2013). There are also some indications of Indonesian trade unions regulating non-standard work through collective agreements (Ebisui, 2012). In Vietnam, concerns over labor outsourcing led to the inclusion in 2012, for the first time, of a section of the Labor Code recognizing and regulating agency work. Based on ILO standards, this new regime includes licensing requirements, as well as restrictions on the types of jobs that labor outsourcing can be used for and the enumeration of rights and protections for agency workers (including the principle of equal treatment between agency workers and those directly engaged by an employer).

Wages

All of the countries in Southeast Asia have a statutory minimum wage, and these minima have assumed particular importance in public policy debates given the underdevelopment of institutions for collective bargaining and other wage policies in the region (ILO & ADB, 2014; Lee & Eyraud, 2008). National regulatory frameworks vary significantly in respect of the mechanism by which these minimum rates are set, as well as the goals or objectives that the wage rates are set to achieve. In Malaysia, Thailand, and Vietnam, minimum wage rates are set by the national government after consultation with tripartite bodies composed of representatives of workers, employers, and government. In Indonesia, minimum wage levels are set by regional governments following recommendations from provincial wage councils, and in the Philippines, minimum wages are determined by regional tripartite wage and productivity boards.

Minimum wages continue to feature prominently in policy debates in a number of Southeast Asian countries, including Indonesia, Thailand, Cambodia, Vietnam, and the Philippines. In these debates, concerns have been voiced that setting minimum wages too high would increase labor costs and undermine the region's comparative advantage (see further Lee & Eyraud 2008). A sharp rise in inflation in 2008 saw the real value of minimum wages fall for most countries in the region, placing significant pressure on workers and leading to protests in a number of countries including Cambodia and Thailand. Governments in Cambodia, Indonesia, Lao PDR, and Thailand subsequently significantly increased their minimum wage levels (World Bank, 2014).

Looking beyond legal minima, ILO data shows that real wages in Southeast Asia have grown by a little more than half between 1999 and 2013 (ILO, 2014). However, as Figure 6.1 demonstrates, there continues to be significant wage inequalities between countries in the region. Average monthly wages range from US$121 in Cambodia to US$651 in Malaysia. Moreover, while average GDP growth had returned to pre-global economic crisis levels in the major Southeast Asian economies by 2010, real wage growth during the same period remained subdued, resulting in wage growth falling behind productivity gains for the ASEAN region (see further ILO & ADB, 2014; ILO, 2014).

Trade unions and other forms of workers' representation

Employment regulations in Southeast Asia generally recognize the rights of workers to form and join unions, and participate in union activities. A number of countries also provide constitutional recognition of the right to organize (e.g., Indonesia, the Philippines, and Vietnam).

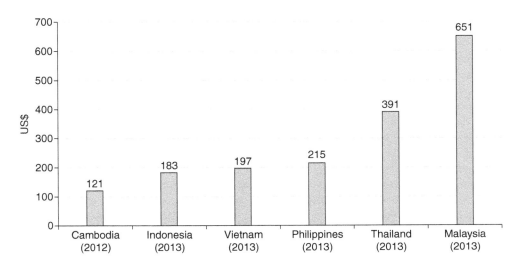

Figure 6.1 Average monthly wages with broadly comparable data, 2013 or latest available year (US$)

Source: compiled from ILO Global Wage Database 2014/15 (ILO, 2014: 2).

However, these rights are far from absolute, and tend to be restricted or non-existent for many workers, such as those in the public sector, migrant workers, or those engaged in certain industries or in enterprises below a certain size.

Trade union structures in the region are diverse. In Indonesia, trade unions are largely structured along occupational lines, although there are also a small number of industry-based unions (Isaac & Sitalaksmi, 2008: 245). In Malaysia, trade unions are largely structured on an enterprise basis (Ramasamy & Rowley, 2008), although industrial unions are permitted in some industries such as banking. In Thailand, unions may be organized at an enterprise or industrial level. Labor federations may be established by at least two unions and labor councils by at least fifteen unions or labor federations (Sakdina, 2015).

In Vietnam, all trade unions must be affiliated to the Vietnam General Confederation of Labour (VGCL), a mass organization that was formed and remains under the leadership of the Vietnamese Communist Party. The VGCL originally operated as a socialist-style trade union structure within the party-state apparatus, and performed functions such as providing social welfare and sporting, cultural and entertainment facilities in the workplace; participating in managing SOE assets and property; encouraging and motivating members so as to assist management to achieve production plans; maintaining labor discipline; and educating workers in socialist ideology and awareness (Clarke & Pringle, 2009; Collins, 2009; Collins, Sitalaksmi, & Lansbury, 2013). Since *Doi Moi*, the VGCL has responded to increased pressures from above and below to adopt a more active role in representing workers. Revisions to the Labour Code, the Law on Trade Unions, the Constitution of the VGCL, and subsidiary regulation reflects this shift in priorities toward a greater emphasis on worker representation. However, Vietnamese trade unions—particularly at the lower levels—have struggled to adapt to the realities of IR within a diversified economy, and have in many cases failed to perform the roles formally assigned to them (Clarke, Lee, & Do, 2007). There are clear political limits to union reform, with the VGCL remaining formally and in practice under the leadership of the Vietnamese Communist Party and unions at the enterprise level remaining largely subordinate to management (Do & van den Broek, 2013; for discussion of union roles in SOEs, also see Collins. et al., 2013). As noted above, Vietnam has—as part of the TPP negotiations—entered into a side agreement with the United States under which it undertakes to significantly reform its labor laws and institutional structures, including in relation to freedom of association. The practical implications of these undertakings remain to be seen.

Union density rates in the private sector in Southeast Asia are low and in decline (Table 6.2). Scholars have identified a number of factors that help to explain these low figures. These include factors internal to many trade unions in the region (e.g., a lack of organizational capacity and resources, and internal divisions), as well as low levels of relevant skills (e.g., bargaining and organizing) amongst union officials (Collins et al., 2011; Ford, 2009; Miles, 2015). A number of external factors are also said to contribute to low union membership numbers. These include the lack of adequate legal and political support for unionization in a number of countries (in Thailand, see e.g., Brown, 2016; Yoshida, 2003). Though obviously this is not a factor in Vietnam, where the law mandates the establishment of trade unions in enterprises, and provides for these unions to be funded by member dues and employer contributions of 2 percent of payroll. In Malaysia, the mobilization of workers, as Crinis and Parasuraman observe, "has been minimal because of the limited space available to the organized labor movement to exercise any collective power" (2016: 222) and the "capacity of the trade union movement to push for change is further weakened by a lack of international support" (Crinis & Parasuraman, 2016: 223). Features of labor markets may also impede unionization, such as significant and increasing percentages of workers employed informally or on a casual or subcontracting basis, high numbers of undocumented migrant workers, and high levels of unemployment (in Thailand, see Yukongdi, 2008).

Unionization is further impeded through the adoption by employers of tactics and strategies to discourage unionization and weaken union strength in bargaining, such as the dismissal of union leaders, shutting down factories where strong trade unions existed, subcontracting and casualization (see Tjandra & van Klaveren, 2015; Trinh, 2014). The failure of the state to adequately enforce laws protecting workers from employer retaliation for joining or forming unions and engaging in union-related activities also acts as a significant impediment to unionization. In Thailand, for example, Brown (2001) has argued that improvements in protections for freedom of association have proven largely illusory due to the poor enforcement of this right and active suppression of unionism by employers. Similarly, a lack of adequate enforcement of labor laws and persisting corruption in Indonesia has meant that workers are often unable to enforce their rights or organize collectively and are sometimes met with violence if they seek to do so (Connor & Haines, 2013). Finally, some scholars point to cultural factors as relevant to explaining low union membership rates in Southeast Asia: for example, Kelly et al. (2010) observe that many Thai workers are reluctant to upset traditional family relationships typically found within workplaces because of the protection these relationships afford.

Trade union movements in Indonesia, Malaysia, Thailand, and the Philippines are weakened by high levels of fragmentation (Brown, 2016; Erikson et al., 2003; Hadiz, 2002; Yukongdi, 2008). In Indonesia, the passage of the Trade Union Law of 2000 saw a sharp growth in the number of national federations, from one in 1998 to 100 by the late 2009, and the emergence of thousands of non-nationally registered plant-level unions (Isaac & Sitalaksmi 2008; Miles, 2015). Inter- and intra-union rivalry and a lack of coordination and cooperation amongst major union confederations further undermine union strength (Collins et al., 2011; Hadiz, 2001). In most cases, this fragmentation is facilitated, if not driven, by legal requirements relating to the establishment or membership of unions. This is exemplified by provisions within the Malaysian Trade Union Act 1959, which effectively limit union membership to one of three geographical regions (Peninsula Malaysia, Sabah, or Sarawak) and prohibit trade unions from operating across industries, trades, or occupations (see further Peetz & Todd, 2001; Ramasamy & Rowley, 2008).

Today, it is widely recognized that organized labor in Southeast Asia exerts less influence and power than in other regions. A number of explanations are offered for this relative weakness, including historical legacies associated with post-colonial political struggles (e.g., Hadiz, 1997, 2002), fragmentation and the timing and nature of rapid industrialization in the region (Deyo, 1997; Kuruvilla, 1996). The influence of workers and unions on policy-making in the region is argued to have been further weakened by globalization, which has favored highly mobile capital and led to states seeking to implement favorable investment climates, including the curbing of workers' rights and the extensive use of non-standard employment (Frenkel &, Kuruvilla 2002). In this climate, the already weakened labor organizing power to oppose state liberalization and privatization strategies has been further limited (Hadiz, 2002). Of course, there are differences in the strength of organized labor both between and within countries in the region, with organized labor in the Philippines and Thailand regarded as being more militant, despite both movements being subject to periodic persecution and suppression by the state. These traits continue to manifest themselves in the union movement's responses to significant issues such as economic crises (see Hadiz, 2002) and labor market issues such as the rise in non-standard work. It is important to recognize that civil society actors, such as domestic and international NGOs, also play an important role in representing and assisting workers in Southeast Asia. They perform a variety of roles, including representing workers in disputes against employers, meeting workers'

Table 6.2 Summary of IR characteristics in selected Southeast Asian countries

	Union density (%)★	Union structure	Bargaining structure	General characterization of IR system
Indonesia	11	Largely occupational based, some enterprise based	Very limited	State-employer dominated
Malaysia	10	Generally enterprise based, though some industrial unions (e.g., banking)	Generally enterprise based, though some industry-wide agreements (e.g., banking)	State-employer dominated
Philippines	12	Structured on enterprise, industrial, regional, and occupational lines. Highly fragmented	Limited enterprise-based collective bargaining in large firms and public sector	Pluralist decentralized and fragmented
Thailand	1.5	Largely enterprise based, some industrial unions	Very limited	Pluralist decentralized and fragmented
Vietnam	76 (public sector) 33 (private sector)	State-sponsored unionism. Unions structured on enterprise, regional and industrial lines. All unions must be affiliated to VGCL	Very limited enterprise based but capacity for industry-wide agreements	Transitional model

Note

★ As percentage of wage employment, except for Thailand, which is as percentage of labor force. Data on Indonesia and Philippines is from 2005, Malaysia from 2010, and Thailand and Vietnam from 2013 (Serrano, 2014; World Bank, 2015).

welfare and recreational needs, helping them form unions, and monitoring firm compliance with regulatory standards (Miles, 2015). In Indonesia, Ford (2006, 2009) describes how labor NGOs were able to function under Suharto's New Order government at a time that trade unions were effectively repressed. These NGOs played an influential role in opposition to the New Order's IR system in the 1980s and 1990s and continue to play an important role in Indonesia today. Their functions include some that would commonly be associated with trade unions such as grass-roots labor organizing and servicing (e.g., education, establishing community workers' groups, providing legal services, and encouraging strike actions) as well as research and policy advocacy (e.g., documenting the living and working conditions of factory labor, lobbying government and firms to increase the minimum wage, improving health and safety, and campaigning for changes to labor legislation). In many cases, NGOs work in coalitions with each other, with unions and with international organizations to advance worker rights and interests. Migrant labor associations and community legal associations also assist workers, and in Vietnam, the labor newspapers (affiliated to the VGCL) have emerged as important players in assisting workers and resolving labor disputes (Kerkvliet, 2010; Tran, 2007).

Employer associations

There is only limited literature on employer associations in Southeast Asia. This is despite the high number of these associations at national and lower levels, and evidence (at least from some of the countries) that these associations play a highly influential role in wage-setting and labor law reform processes (e.g., in Indonesia, see Hartono, 2011; Tjandra & van Klaveren, 2015). In Malaysia, employers are organized through sector- and state-based associations, as well as national employer federations (Crinis & Parasuraman, 2016). In Thailand, there were an estimated 344 employer associations, two employer federations and twelve employer councils active in 2012 (Brown, 2016). In Vietnam, as well as the two major government-established employer associations (the Vietnam Chamber of Commerce and Industry and the Vietnam Cooperative Alliance) that participate in tripartite consultations at the national level, there are over 200 business associations. These include a number of nationality-based associations formed by foreign investors and national chamber of commerces. According to Do (2012), while a number of the foreign chambers of commerce exercise significant influence over the wage and other labor policies of their members and politically, the local business community tends to be fragmented and uncoordinated.

Collective bargaining

Regulatory frameworks in Southeast Asia provide for the negotiation of terms and conditions of employment through collective agreements on an enterprise and/or multi-employer and industry-wide basis. With the exception of the Philippines, national regulatory frameworks do not appear to impose any statutory obligation on the parties to bargain in good faith. Laws also grant workers the right to industrial action in pursuit of collective bargaining claims, though in a number of jurisdictions, such as Malaysia, these rights are significantly more limited than international standards and may also (e.g., in the case of Vietnam) be contingent upon the following of lengthy and complicated pre-strike procedures. In general, and with the exception of Malaysia, there appears to be few statutory limits placed on the *content* of collective agreements.

In practice, collective bargaining in the region is very limited. While Malaysia has fairly high collective bargaining coverage in the banking industry by virtue of industry-wide bargaining, overall coverage of the workforce remains low at around 2.4 percent of private sector workers (Frenkel & Kuruvilla, 2002; Hayter & Stoevska, 2011). Laws on collective bargaining in the Philippines are described as "largely irrelevant" given low bargaining coverage, union fragmentation, and the limited enforcement of the law (Frenkel & Kuruvilla, 2002: 406). In Indonesia, collective agreements are limited in number and are described as largely being of poor quality in that they reproduce rather than build on legal minima or they are determined unilaterally by employers (Tjandra & van Klaveren, 2015; Palmer, 2009; Isaac & Sitalaksmi, 2008). In Thailand, despite the LRA requiring all private enterprises employing over twenty employees to register collective agreements, the number of such agreements is "miniscule" (Brown, 2016: 209; see also Sakdina, 2015). In Vietnam, while efforts have been made in recent years to improve collective bargaining (through reforms to the law and in practice), the regulation of terms and conditions of employment through collective agreements remains underdeveloped (Clarke & Pringle, 2009; see also Clarke, Lee, & Do, 2007).

In addition to collective bargaining, some countries in the region mandate worker–management consultation structures. The Philippines Labor Code provides for workers' participation in decisions that affect their "rights, benefits and welfare," including through the formation by workers of labor-management councils for this purpose (Article 255). In Thailand, employees may establish "Employees' Committees" in enterprises with fifty or more employees and where established, the employer must arrange to meet with this committee at least once every three months (LRA s. 45). In Vietnam, the Labor Code of 2012 provides for workers to be consulted by management in decision-making on a range of issues (e.g., redundancies and wages) and introduces a new requirement for regular "discussions at the workplace" (Labor Code, 2012, Articles 63–65).

The impact of legal regulation on employment and labor relations

Any discussion of employment regulation and labor relations in Southeast Asia would be incomplete without a discussion of the extensive gap between legal and policy frameworks and the realities of labor market practices. Most employers and workers in Southeast Asia continue to work either fully or partially beyond the realms of formal employment regulation. Writing on the Philippines, for example, Hutchison describes "the feeble enforcement of formal labor rights and protections" as "a defining feature of this country's employment relations" (Hutchison, 2016: 184). In Thailand, Brown observes that as well as failing to enforce laws requiring collective bargaining, "workers have consistently been unable to hold employers to account in relation to the payment of minimum wages, health and safety legislation, use of subcontracted labor, payment of a range of legally stipulated entitlements as well as union busting" (Brown, 2016: 209). In Vietnam, a 2012 study of manufacturing firms found that around one-third had violations related to wages and benefits (Del Carpio & Pabon, 2014). Non-compliance with basic standards is particularly acute in highly competitive low-wage industries such as garment and textiles, resulting in workers working long hours to supplement low base wages (ILO, 2014).

The limited impact of employment regulation is attributable to a number of factors. Many workers are not afforded protections because they are engaged in types of work or types of enterprises or industries that are excluded from the scope of a law (cf. Cooney et al., 2002; Casale, 2011; Teklè, 2010). Even where laws formally apply, they are often ignored in practice. This may be because of a lack of capacity and resources of state enforcement agencies and labor tribunals, and corruption (e.g., Ford & Gillan, 2016; Hutchison, 2016). Penalties for employer non-compliance are low and/or are rarely imposed, thus, further contributing to a culture of impunity (on Thailand, see Brown, 2016; and on Malaysia, see Crinis & Parasuraman, 2016). It has also been argued that the extensive law-practice gaps in Southeast Asia "reflect broader structures of political and economic power and a particular constellation of state objectives" (Ford & Gillan, 2016: 177; see also Hutchison 2016). Legal culture is often cited as another factor that explains the non-compliance phenomenon (see below).

Alternative forms of labor regulation

In Southeast Asia, traditional laws (customary or religious) and social norms play an important but often overlooked role in regulating employment relations, "with their distinct set of norms, sanctions and dispute resolution systems" (Teklè, 2010: 39–40). Scholars have emphasized the importance of cultural values such as hierarchy and fealty in Asian societies. For example, Yukongdi (2008) identifies Theravada Buddhism and a cultural deference to hierarchy as aspects of Thai culture that sit uncomfortably with IR concepts such as participative decision-making or trade unionism. These informal but powerful customary norms and practices may interact with, and condition, more formal modes of regulation in complex ways. They may, for example, have negative effects on gender equality at work (Teklè, 2010), or may contribute to workers' preference for more traditional forms of resolving disputes over state-based mechanisms.

Multinational companies (MNCs) constitute another important influence on, and source of, employment regulation in the region. Southeast Asia's extensive integration into the world economy, including high levels of foreign investment and an increasing role in global manufacturing and international trade, has been discussed above. Many enterprises in Southeast Asia are integrated into buyer-driven global industries, particularly in sectors such as labor-intensive textile, leather, and footwear industries (Vietnam and Cambodia), and the electronics and ICT equipment industries (Malaysia, Thailand, and the Philippines). In Malaysia, for example, production in the clothing industry is almost totally for export to developed countries (Crinis, 2012). MNCs from within the region and externally have brought with them international employment and HRM practices, which may be diffused to local firms. Furthermore, as a result of NGO and union activism targeting global brands that source from developing countries, increasing numbers of MNCs with supply chains in the region have adopted regulatory initiatives directed at improving labor standards within supplier factories (Connors & Haines 2013). Since their emergence in the early 1990s, these initiatives have evolved significantly, from basic codes of conduct through to much more sophisticated initiatives involving multiple stakeholders (public and/or private) in standard setting and compliance improvement (cf. Locke, Rissing, & Pal, 2013). The ILO's Better Work Programme, which now operates in Cambodia, Indonesia, and Vietnam, is a particularly notable initiative in this regard, and has received considerable attention from policy makers and scholars for its innovative approach to improving conditions for workers and enterprise productivity (Hall 2010; Dupper, Fenwick, & Hardy, 2016). To date, however, many of these types of private and hybrid regulatory initiatives have struggled to be effective in securing compliance amongst supplier factories, and have not been directed at, or achieved, significant empowerment of workers on a collective basis (e.g., Crinis & Parasuraman, 2016). Moreover, they are by their nature limited in scope to domestic enterprises integrated into global supply chains (see further Dao, 2008; Miles, 2015; Mohan & Morel, 2014; Tran, 2011).

Conclusions

The primary purpose of this chapter has been to provide an overview of the evolution and distinctive features of, and trends within, employment regulation and IR systems in Southeast Asia. As such, this chapter serves as an important context against which human resource management practices in these countries can be understood.

The chapter has outlined the main features of economies and labor markets in five major economies in Southeast Asia. It has traced the evolution of national employment regulation and IR systems, with a particular focus on developments in the latter half of the twentieth century. It has described key features of contemporary regulatory frameworks: focusing in turn on forms of employment, wages, trade unions and other forms of workers' representation, employer associations, collective bargaining, and dispute resolution. While this overview has revealed diverse legal, political, cultural and economic institutions and practices in the region, some common themes are also discernible. These include a shared history of strong and largely repressive state intervention in IR in Southeast Asian nations. Central to this problem is the role of the developmental states in the Southeast Asian economies. As Brown argues, "state power can be exercised in different and contradictory ways," often with the nation's economic interest as the priority (Brown, 2016: 211). Largely as a consequence, trade unions in Southeast Asia—as the traditional organizations through which workers are mobilized and represented—have generally been, and continue to be, comparatively weak and marginalized. This weakness is reflected in the limited capacity of unions to secure, defend, and promote workers' rights and interests in the workplace (including through collective bargaining) and in the political system more broadly.

Our review has revealed that while there are relatively long-standing legal frameworks in most of the selected countries, these legal frameworks continue to have only limited impact on employment practices. A significant law-practice gap is a common characteristic of developing countries in which enforcement capacity and resources and/or political will of state agencies are limited. Other factors such as "legal culture" also play a role.

Another theme throughout this chapter is the extensive and profound influences of intensifying regional and global economic integration on economies and labor markets in the region. While the forces and influences associated with these dynamics are felt acutely within each of the national economies, it is clear that they are shaped, mediated, and contested through domestic political processes and institutions (Frenkel & Peetz, 1998). It is also important to recognize that these forces and dynamics manifest themselves not only in the evolution of formal systems of employment regulation and IR but also in the way that these formal rules are enforced (or not enforced) in practice (Brown, 2016). Amongst other things, these dynamics have led to the emergence of new ways of managing workplaces, new actors, and new forms of organizing and representation. They have also led to the emergence of various private types of regulation, which, while increasingly influential, remain at best fragmented and narrow in scope, targeting limited groups of workers engaged in global supply chains. To date, there is little evidence of their capacity to transform into substantial power bases to advance workers' rights and interest at large.

References

Benson, J. & Zhu, Y. (Eds.) (2008). *Trade unions in Asia: An economic and sociological analysis*. Abingdon: Routledge.

Bitonio, B. E. R. (2012). *Industrial relations and collective bargaining in the Philippines*. Industrial and Employment Relations Department Report. Geneva: International Labour Office.

Brown, A. (2001). After the Kader fire: Labour organizing for health and safety standards in Thailand. In J. Hutchison & A. Brown (Eds.), *Organizing labor in globalizing Asia* (pp. 127–146). London: Routledge.

Brown, A. (2016). Political regimes and employment relations in Thailand. *Journal of Industrial Relations, 58*(2), 199–214.

Brown, A., Thanachaisethavut, B., & Hewison, K. (2002). *Labour relations and regulation in Thailand: Theory and practice*. Southeast Asia Research Centre Working Papers Series No. 27. Hong Kong: City University of Hong Kong.

Capling, A. & Ravenhill, J. (2011). Multilateralising regionalism: What role for the Trans-Pacific partnership agreement?. *The Pacific Review, 24*(5), 553–575.

Caraway, T. L. (2004). Protective repression, international pressure, and institutional design: Explaining labor reform in Indonesia. *Studies in Comparative International Development, 39*(3), 28–49.

Casale, G. (Ed.) (2011). *The employment relationship: A comparative overview*. Geneva: Hart Publishing.

Clarke, S., Lee, C., & Do Q. C. (2007). From rights to interests: the challenge of industrial relations in Vietnam. *Journal of Industrial Relations, 49*(4), 545–568.

Clarke, S. & Pringle, T. (2009). Can party-led trade unions represent their members?. *Post-Communist Economies, 21*(1), 85–101.

Collins, N. T. (2009). *Economic reform and employment relations in Vietnam*. London: Routledge.

Collins, N., Nankervis, A., Sitalaksmi, S., & Warner, M. (2011). Labor–management relationships in transitional economies: Convergence or divergence in Vietnam and Indonesia?. *Asia Pacific Business Review, 17*(3), 361–377.

Collins, N., Sitalaksmi, S., & Lansbury, R. (2013). Transforming employment relations in Vietnam and Indonesia: Case studies of state-owned enterprises. *Asia Pacific Journal of Human Resources, 52*(2), 131–151.

Connor, T. & Haines, F. (2013). Networked regulation as a solution to human rights abuse in global supply chains? The case of trade union rights violations by Indonesian sports shoe manufacturer. *Theoretical Criminology, 17*(2), 197–214.

Cooney, S., Lindsey, T., Mitchell, R., & Zhu, Y. (2002). Labour law and labour market regulation in East Asian states: Problems and issues for comparative inquiry. In S. Cooney, T. Lindsey, R. Mitchell, & Y. Zhu (Eds.), *Law and labour market regulation in East Asia* (pp. 1–26). London: Routledge.

Cooney, S., Mahy, P. Mitchell, R., & Gahan, P. (2014). The evolution of labor law in three Asian nations: An introductory comparative study. *Comparative Labor Law & Policy Journal, 36*(1), 23–68.

Crinis, V. (2012). Global commodity chains in crisis: The garment industry in Malaysia. *Institutions and Economies, 4*(3), 61–82.

Crinis, V. & Parasuraman, B. (2016). Employment relations and the state in Malaysia. *Journal of Industrial Relations, 58*(2), 215–228.

Dao V. Q. (2008). Viet Nam: Workers in transition. In S. Lee & F. Eyraud (Eds.), *Globalization, flexibilization and working conditions in Asia and the Pacific* (pp. 383–411). Geneva: International Labour Organization.

De Ruyter, A. & Warnecke, T. (2008). Gender, non-standard work and development regimes: A comparison of the USA and Indonesia. *Journal of Industrial Relations, 50*(5), 718–735.

Del Carpio, X. & Pabon, L. (2014). *Minimum wage policy: Lessons with a focus on the ASEAN region.* Washington, DC: World Bank Group.

Deyo, F. C. (1997). Labour and industrial restructuring in South-East Asia. In G. Rodan, K. Hewison, & R. Robison (Eds.), *The political economy of South-East Asia: An introduction* (pp. 205–224). Oxford: Oxford University Press.

Do, Q. C. (2012). *Employee participation in Vietnam.* Industrial and Employment Relations Department Working Paper No. 42. Geneva: International Labour Organization.

Do, Q. C. & van den Broek, D. (2013). Wildcat strikes: A catalyst for union reform in Vietnam. *Journal of Industrial Relations, 55*(5), 783–799.

Dupper, O., Fenwick, C., & Hardy, T. (2016). *The interaction of labour inspection and private compliance initiatives: A case study of Better Work Indonesia.* Better Work Discussion Paper series No. 21. Geneva: International Labour Organization and International Finance Corporation.

Ebisui, M. (2012). *Non-standard workers: Good practices of social dialogue and collective bargaining.* Working Paper No. 36, Industrial and Employment Relations Department, Geneva: International Labour Office.

Erikson, C. L, Kuruvilla, S., Ofreneo, R. E., & Asuncion Ortiz, M. (2003). From core to periphery?: Recent developments in employment relations in the Philippines. *Industrial Relations, 43*(3), 368–395.

Ford, M. (2006). Labor NGOs: An alternative form of labor organizing in Indonesia, 1991–1998. *Asia Pacific Business Review, 12*(2), 175–191.

Ford, M. (2009). *Workers and intellectuals: NGOs, trade unions and the Indonesian labour movement.* Singapore: National University of Singapore Press.

Ford, M. & Gillan, M. (2016). Employment relations and the state in Southeast Asia. *Journal of Industrial Relations, 58*(2), 167–182.

Ford, M. & Sirait, G. M. (2016). The state, democratic transition and employment relations in Indonesia. *Journal of Industrial Relations, 58*(2), 229–242.

Frenkel, S. & Kuruvilla, S. (2002). Logics of action, globalization, and changing employment relations in China, India, Malaysia and the Philippines. *Industrial and Labor Relations Review, 55*(3), 387–412.

Frenkel, S. & Peetz, D. (1998). Globalization and industrial relations in East Asia: A three-country comparison. *Industrial Relations, 37*(3), 282–310.

Green, D. J. (2010). Southeast Asia's policy response to the Global Economic Crisis. *ASEAN Economic Bulletin, 7*(1), 5–26.

Hadiz, V. R. (1997). *Workers and the state in new order Indonesia.* London: Routledge.

Hadiz, V. R. (2001). New organizing vehicles in Indonesia: Origins and prospects. In J. Hutchison & A. Brown (Eds.), *Organizing labour in globalising Asia* (pp. 111–130). London: Routledge.

Hadiz, V. R. (2002). Globalization, labor, and economic crisis: Insights from Southeast Asia. *Asian Business & Management, 1*(3), 249–266.

Hall, John A. (2010). The ILO's better factories Cambodia program: A viable blueprint for promoting international labor rights. *Stanford Law and Policy Review, 21*(3), 427–460.

Hartono, A. I. J. (2011). *State-business relations in post-1998 Indonesia: The role of Kadin.* Groningen: University of Groningen.

Hayter, S. & Stoevska, V. (2011). *Social dialogue indicators: International statistical inquiry 2008–09*. Technical Brief, Industrial and Employment Relations Department. Geneva: International Labour Office.

Hutchison, J. (2016). The state and employment relations in the Philippines. *Journal of Industrial Relations, 58*(2), 183–198.

ILO. (2012). *Building better industrial relations in an integrating ASEAN*. ASEAN-ILO/Japan Industrial Relations Project. Bangkok: ILO Regional Office for Asia and the Pacific.

ILO. (2014). *Wages in Asia and the Pacific: Dynamic but uneven progress*. Global Wage Report 2014/15, Asia and the Pacific Supplement. Bangkok: ILO Regional Office for Asia and the Pacific.

ILO. (2015). *Asia-Pacific labor market update*. Bangkok: ILO Regional Office for Asia and the Pacific.

ILO. (2016). Ratification of fundamental conventions. Retrieved from www.ilo.org/dyn/normlex/en/f?p=1000:10011:0::NO:10011:P10011_DISPLAY_BY,P10011_CONVENTION_TYPE_CODE:3,F#Asia.

ILO & ADB. (2014). *ASEAN Community 2015: managing integration for better jobs and shared prosperity*. Bangkok: ILO and ADB.

Isaac, J. & Sitalaksmi, S. (2008). Trade unions in Indonesia: From state incorporation to market orientation. In J. Benson & Y. Zhu (Eds.), *Trade unions in Asia: An economic and sociological analysis* (pp. 236–255). Abingdon: Routledge.

International Trade Union Confederation (ITUC). (2014). *Precarious work in the Asia-Pacific Region: A 10 country case study*. Brussels: ITUC.

Kahler, M. & MacIntyre, A. (Eds.) (2013). *Integrating regions: Asia in comparative context*. Stanford, CA: Stanford University Press.

Kaur, A. (2010). Labor migration in Southeast Asia: Migration policies, labor exploitation and regulation. *Journal of the Asia Pacific Economy, 15*(1), 6–19.

Kelly, M., Strazdins, L., Dellora, T., Khamman, S., Seubsman, S., & Sleigh, A. C. (2010). Thailand's work and health transition. *International Labor Review, 149*(3), 373–386.

Kerkvliet, B. (2010). Workers' protests in contemporary Vietnam (with some comparisons to those in the pre-1975 South). *Journal of Vietnamese studies, 5*(1), 162–204.

Kuruvilla, S. (1996). Linkages between industrialization strategies and industrial relations/human resource policies: Singapore, Malaysia, the Philippines and India. *Industrial and Labor Relations Review, 49*(4), 635–657.

Kuruvilla, S. & Erikson, C. L. (2002). Change and transformation in Asian industrial relations. *Industrial Relations, 41*(2), 171–228.

Kuruvilla, S. & Venkataratnam, C. S. (1996). Economic development and industrial relations: The case of South and Southeast Asia. *Industrial Relations, 27*(1), 9–23.

Landau, I., Mahy, P., & Mitchell, R. (2015). *The regulation of non-standard forms of employment in India, Indonesia and Viet Nam*. Conditions of Work and Employment Series No. 63. Geneva: International Labour Office.

Lee, S. & Eyraud, F. (2008). Globalization, institutional reforms and workers: Changes and outcomes. In S. Lee & F. Eyraud (Eds.), *Globalization, flexibilization and working conditions in Asia and the Pacific* (pp. 3–45). Geneva: International Labour Organization.

Lindsey, T. & Masduki, T. (2002). Labour law in Indonesia after Soeharto: *Reformasi* or replay? In S. Cooney, T. Lindsey, R. Mitchell, & Y. Zhu (Eds.), *Law and labour market regulation in East Asia* (pp. 246–274). London: Routledge.

Locke, R. M., Rissing, B. A., & Pal, T. (2013). Complements or substitutes?: Private codes, state regulation and the enforcement of labour standards in global supply chains. *British Journal of Industrial Relations, 51*(3) 519–552.

McCann, D. (2008). The regulation of working conditions in Asia and the Pacific: Flexibility, fragmentation and workers' rights. In S. Lee & F. Eyraud (Eds.), *Globalization, flexibilization and working conditions in Asia and the Pacific* (pp. 81–119). Geneva: International Labour Organization.

Marisagan, M. & Serrano, M. (2014). Indonesia. In M. Serrano (Ed.), *Between flexibility and security: The rise of non-standard employment in selected ASEAN countries* (pp. 29–53). Jakarta, Report prepared for the ASEAN Services Employees Trade Union Council.

Miles, L. (2015). The "integrative approach" and labor regulation and Indonesia: Prospects and challenges. *Economic and Industrial Democracy, 36*(1), 5–22.

Mohan, M. & Morel, C. (Eds.). (2014). *Business and human rights in Southeast Asia: Risk and the regulatory turn*. London and New York: Routledge.

Nicholson, P. (2002). Vietnam's labour market: Transition and the role of law. In S. Cooney, T. Lindsey, R. Mitchell, & Y. Zhu (Eds.), *Law and labour market regulation in East Asia* (pp. 122–155). London: Routledge.

Palmer, S. (2009). *Freedom of association and collective bargaining: Indonesian experience 2003–2008*. Working Paper. Geneva: International Labour Organization.

Polaski, S. (2006). Combining local and global forces: The case of labor rights in Cambodia. *World Development, 34*(5), 919–932.

Poole, A. (2015). "The world is outraged": Legitimacy in the making of the ASEAN human rights body. *Contemporary Southeast Asia, 37*(3), 355–380.

Pupos, V. (2014). Viet Nam. In M. R. Serrano (Ed.), *Between flexibility and security: The rise in nonstandard employment in selected ASEAN Countries* (pp. 139–166). ASEAN Services Employees Trades Union Council (ASETUC) and Friedrich-Ebert-Stiftung, Jakarta.

Ramasamy, N. & Rowley, C. (2008). Trade unions in Malaysia: Complexity of a state-employer system. In J. Benson & Y. Zhu (Eds.), *Trade unions in Asia: An economic and sociological analysis* (pp. 121–139). Abingdon: Routledge.

Rupidara, N. S. & McGraw, P. (2010). Institutional change, continuity and decoupling in the Indonesian industrial relations system. *Journal of Industrial Relations, 52*(5), 613–630.

Sakdina, C. N. A. (2015). Thailand. In D. Gregory, T. Schulten & M. van Klaveren (Eds.), *Minimum wages, collective bargaining and economic development in Asia and Europe* (pp. 156–172). Basingstoke: Palgrave Macmillan.

Serrano, M. (Ed.). (2014). *Between flexibility and security: The rise of non-standard employment in selected ASEAN countries.* Jakarta: Report prepared for the ASEAN Services Employees Trade Union Council.

Siengthai, S. (2008). Thailand: Globalization and unprotected workers. In S. Lee & F. Eyraud (Eds.), *Globalization, flexibilization and working conditions in Asia and the Pacific* (pp. 313–343). Geneva: International Labour Organization.

Teklè, T. (2010). Labour law and worker protection in the South: An evolving tension between models and reality. In T. Teklè (Ed.), *Labour law and worker protection in developing countries* (pp. 3–46). Geneva: International Labour Organization.

Tjandra, S. (2008). Understanding workers' law reform in Indonesia, 1998–2004. *Labor and Management in Development, 9.*

Tjandra, S. (2010). Disputing labor dispute settlement: Indonesia's workers' access to justice. *Law, Social Justice & Global Development Journal, 1.*

Tjandra, S. & van Klaveren, M. (2015). Indonesia. In D. Gregory, T. Schulten, & M. van Klaveren (Eds.), *Minimum wages, collective bargaining and economic development in Asia and Europe* (pp. 139–155). Basingstoke: Palgrave Macmillan.

Tjandraningsih, I. (2013). State sponsored precarious work in Indonesia. *American Behavioural Scientist, 57*(4), 403–419.

Todd, P. & Peetz, D. (2001). Malaysian industrial relations at century's turn: Vision 2020 or a spectre of the past? *The International Journal of Human Resource Management, 12*(8), 1365–1382.

Tran, A. N. (2007). The third sleeve: Emerging labor newspapers and the response of labor unions and the state to workers' resistance in Vietnam. *Labor Studies Journal, 32*(3), 257–279.

Tran, A. N. (2011). Corporate social responsibility in Socialist Vietnam: Implementation challenges, and local solutions. In A. Chan (Ed.), *Labour in Vietnam* (pp. 119–159). Singapore: ISEAS Publishing.

Trinh, L. K. (2014). Trade union organizing free from employers' interference: Evidence from Vietnam. *Southeast Asian Studies, 3*(3), 589–609.

Vogt, J. (2015). The evolution of labor rights and trade: A transatlantic comparison and lessons for the transatlantic trade and investment partnership. *Journal of International Economic Law, 18*(4), 827–860.

World Bank (2014). *East Asia Pacific at work: Employment, enterprise and well-being*. Washington, DC: World Bank.

World Bank (2015). *Taking stock: an update on Vietnam's recent economic developments*. Washington, DC: World Bank Group.

Yoshida, M. (2003). Fundamental characteristics of Thai labor law and the direction of reform. *International Journal of Comparative Labor Law and Industrial Relations, 19*(3), 347–362.

Yukongdi, V. (2008). Trade unions in Thailand: Declining strength and influence. In J. Benson & Y. Zhu (Eds.), *Trade unions in Asia: An economic and sociological analysis* (pp. 216–235). London, Routledge.

7

EMPLOYMENT REGULATION AND INDUSTRIAL RELATIONS IN SOUTH ASIA

Michael Gillan

Introduction

In the simplest definitional frame, South Asia can be represented and understood as a geographic subregion within Asia. It is also possible, however, to conceptualize the region by understanding commonalities and divergences that relate to historical development, especially with reference to the formation of its major nation states—India, Pakistan, Bangladesh, and Sri Lanka—processes that were closely linked to British imperialism, nationalist struggles, and subsequent modes of post-colonial governance. As a consequence, while these nations, and their sub-national regions, have underlying similarities, they also reflect an often bewildering diversity in the composition and character of politics and social, cultural, and economic differentiation. This differentiation is especially evident in various socio-economic structures and social identities such as class, caste, region, gender, religion, and ethno-nationalism.

This chapter will provide a broad and necessarily abbreviated understanding of employment regulation, industrial relations institutions and processes, and the dynamics of various organizations that are parties to these in South Asia.[1] Through the use of various examples, it will nonetheless show how and why the aforementioned historical legacies, political structures, social cleavages, and geographically differentiated patterns of economic development are important for understanding the form, implementation, and effect of labor regulation and industrial relations. Indeed, the basic terms "industrial relations" and "regulation" cannot be understood without reference to this enveloping context. Labor or employment regulation in South Asia has developed in the main with reference to, and concern for, a small pool of formal sector workers in the midst of a vast sea of informal employment. Industrial relations typically describes the institutional and legal apparatus of a so-called national industrial relations "system" but at the regional, local, or workplace level there is an uneven patchwork of the presence, effect and enforcement of these regulatory institutions. It is also possible to conceive of industrial relations with narrow reference to market-economic exchange (workers and employers determining contract) but the term can also draw attention to broader social and political dynamics, not least concerning the relationship between state intervention and the employment relationship. As this chapter will show, in South Asia the political context of industrial relations is unavoidable and central.

As a general survey, this chapter will provide a brief assessment of how and why historical and political context and the composition of employment is important for understanding contemporary industrial relations and employment regulation in South Asia. It will then consider the major parties to industrial relations in the region and the formal and informal dimensions of employment regulation. Finally, it will provide an assessment of the interaction between contemporary human resource management strategies and practices and industrial relations outcomes and the bargaining power of workers.

The historical and political context of employment regulation and industrial relations in South Asia

Despite the duration and intensity of nationalist movements in South Asia, the achievement of independence from British colonial rule was characterized by significant post-colonial continuities in politics, law, education, and the organization and functioning of the state bureaucracy, armed forces, and other institutional domains. This was, in part, because the elite classes that dominated the post-colonial nationalist leadership in the nations of the region were steeped educationally and, to a certain extent, ideologically in a tradition of British liberalism, law, and institutional design. For India and Pakistan (West and East—with the latter asserting itself as the new nation of Bangladesh in 1971) independent nationhood in 1947 was accompanied by partition—a traumatic event that led to the loss of millions of lives and deep structural economic damage.

In the context of the traumas of partition, economic underdevelopment, and the social and political mobilization—including workers—that surrounded the nationalist struggle, post-colonial South Asia was characterized by states that sought to solidify and consolidate institutions and political authority structures. It is not surprising therefore that newly formed states in the region retained many key pieces of labor law from the colonial period: and not least because these laws provided great scope for state intervention, direction, and control in industrial relations.

In India, for instance, colonial legislation was retained, including the Industrial Disputes Act 1947 and the Trade Unions Act 1926, which allowed extensive capacity for the state to regulate trade unions and intervene in industrial disputes amongst other powers (Mitchell, Mahy, & Gahan, 2014: 421–422). According to one line of argument, this legal framework, in conjunction with tripartite mechanisms for consultation and inclusion in labor policy development and trade union political fragmentation, led to the effective "incorporation" of labor interests within the state which demobilized labor movements and limited their political and regulatory effectiveness (Chibber, 2005). For others, however, this view understates the ongoing incidences of industrial conflict and political mobilization by unions in India that have continued to shape post-colonial state policy and industrial relations in profound ways (Teitelbaum, 2006).

In post-colonial Pakistan, state control over unions and industrial relations was direct and linked to oscillation between civilian and military authoritarian governments. According to Candland "military and civilian political regimes did not seek to incorporate organized labor, bureaucratically or politically" but rather intervened directly to "prohibit and limit labor organizing, to exclude organized labor from politics, and to decentralize labor organizationally" (2007: 36). Despite the success of state intervention in repressing unions, restricting collective bargaining, and confining industrial relations largely to the enterprise level, the union movement was thought nonetheless to have been "influential as a social movement at key phases in Pakistan's political development" (Candland, 2007: 73).

Bangladesh and Sri Lanka also have tumultuous political histories that have shaped industrial relations institutions and organizations in various ways. Bangladesh, born out of a bitter separation from Pakistan and the Indo-Pakistan war of 1971, has an economic history defined by its relative under-development and reliance on development assistance and a select group of export-oriented industries of which the ready-made garment sector is the most prominent for its contribution to employment and export earnings. Its political history has been such that both democratically elected and authoritarian governments have governed but for the most part have done so with weak institutional capacity and socio-economic effect. Politically, the nation has remained divided between two dominant political parties—the Awami League and the Bangladesh Nationalist Party. This has left its imprint on industrial relations because trade unions are weak and fragmented at all levels and often divided along political lines of affiliation. This weakness, compounded by the close nexus between business and political elites, has meant that industrial relations institutions and organizations have lacked meaningful presence or effect within the vast majority of workplaces even within the formal sector. Sri Lanka, as widely reported, has been most profoundly shaped by ethno-nationalist conflict between a Sinhalese Buddhist majority and a Tamil minority population, an extraordinarily violent conflict over more than three decades which continues in many ways to define politics, civil society, and even external relations.[2] In industrial relations, Sri Lanka had an early period of liberal constitutionalism and an active and independent labor movement that mobilized in the 1960s and 1970s for union recognition and progressive reforms to labor institutions. However, according to Biyanwila (2011: 5), a United National Party (UNP) Government (1977–1994) implemented "neo-liberal policies while asserting a Sinhala-Buddhist nationalist project" and in subsequent decades the state "drifted into authoritarian tendencies with the regular suspension of rule of law and democratic norms" (Biyanwila (2011: 6).

The relationship between democracy and the form and effect of industrial relations institutions and organizations has clearly been significant throughout the region. India, with the exception of the Emergency under Prime Minister Indira Gandhi (1975–1977), has the deepest and most embedded tradition of democratic governance. Nonetheless, this has not precluded certain instances where the judiciary and state-level administrations have intervened strongly to quell labor conflict and discipline workers. Alternately, however, the compulsions of electoral party-based competition remain important in shaping relative change or stasis in industrial relations policy and labor law. Indeed, this stands in contrast to the dynamics of labor policy and representation in non-democratic yet economically expanding China (Cooke, 2012)—a situation that has led some Indian policy makers and business lobbies to bemoan India's limited ability to impose change from "above." On the one hand, India's democratic governance is a cause of complexity: almost all national and regional political parties have trade union affiliates and these links shape union policy and strategy while electoral compulsions often direct government policy. On the other hand, given India's evident social complexity and variation, the ability for citizens and workers to exercise voice via democratic means both in the workplace and in society can also be seen as very significant for managing this complexity.

Economies and labor markets in South Asia

Formal industrial relations institutions and, perhaps more significantly, the actual practice of industrial relations, have been shaped by changes in state economic development strategies across the region. The dominant model of economic development in the post-colonial era, perhaps most notably in India under the so-called "Nehruvian" state, was state direction and regulation of production and investment, inclusive of direct state investment in publicly owned enterprises, economic planning and policies designed to protect nascent industries and promote "import substitution." Such policies were generally conducive to the accommodation of a labor voice via trade unions, albeit with the long-term effect of concentrating trade union membership in the public sector and public sector enterprises.

With a turn toward so-called "economic liberalization" across the region such policies were gradually displaced, first in Pakistan and Sri Lanka in the early 1980s and then at the beginning of the 1990s in India. Liberalization policies have sought to bring about greater integration with the global economy through facilitating export-oriented production and attracting foreign investment, while rolling back state economic control and direction by promoting privatization and financial sector reforms, ending industrial licenses, and, in general, bringing market-based competitive pressures to the fore. These have engendered very significant changes to industrial relations in each nation as the transformed development strategy of the state at various levels (national, regional) prioritized, over and above social regulation and protection, the promotion of business investment and growth. This agenda has then been linked directly to various labor law reform initiatives that are depicted as necessary for enhancing labor market "flexibility" and firm competitiveness.

Economic growth has been evident, with the World Bank noting that South Asia has averaged 6 percent annual growth for two decades and reporting a GDP of US$2.7 trillion and a total population of 1.74 billion people in 2015.[3] However, while aggregate economic growth has been observed across the region, amongst other effects, liberalization policies have also accelerated and intensified what has always been evident between and within each of these nations: significant geographic variation and socio-economic differentiation. In particular, these policies actively encourage intensified inter-regional and industry-based competition, which may encompass different labor regulatory regimes and industrial relations. This means that rather than conceiving of nations such as India as reflecting a homogenous and unified industrial relations landscape, it is in fact "operating under many different employment regimes" and with greater global economic integration, it makes it near "impossible to depict a cohesive and coherent Indian IR system" (Bhattacherjee & Ackers, 2010: 106). Arguably, this insight is relevant to South Asia as a whole because industrial relations, both in formal regulation and its organizational actors, intersects and interacts dynamically with different levels of governance, and social and economic variation.

Perhaps the most important feature of employment regulation and industrial relations across South Asia is, in fact, the limited reach of these institutions. The majority of workers in the region fall within the informal sector (in India referred to as "unorganized" and comprising an estimated 92 percent of all workers), which means that they lack employment protection in benefits, rights, and social security. Estimates of informality vary but according to the ILO "labor markets in South Asia continue to be dominated by informal and agricultural employment, where jobs are generally poorly paid and unprotected" and in 2013 only 22.5 percent of all workers across the region were employed via regular wage or salaried employment (International Labour Office, 2014). Defining informal work is not straightforward. Different categories of workers and sectors of the economy can be delineated by variables such as enterprise size and, especially, the exclusion of workers from access to formal employment relationships, employer provided benefits, and social security. In practice, the line between the formal and informal is blurred and overlapping and both categories of workers are often present within the same workplace and economic liberalization is thought also to have increased the number of informal workers in formal sector enterprises (Sankaran, 2007).

Despite the relative absence of formal regulation for these workers, their work and employment is, of course, socially "regulated" in various ways. Barbara Harriss-White, an eminent scholar of work and labor in India has noted that the "occupations of self-employed people and the 'markets' for labor are persistently embedded in social institutions such as the state, language, caste, ethnicity, religion, gender, life cycle, space/locality, and—even in the non-farm economy—the needs of the local agro-ecology" (Harriss-White, 2010: 172). Similarly, Hensman has argued that despite a "thin veneer of state-regulated industrial relations" most workers continue to be "exploited by capital while being regulated by traditional caste and gender relations" (2011: 181). These identities and associated political projects can "fracture labor as a category for collective action" (Harriss-White, 2010: 173), which is exacerbated by a "general failure of trade unions to be inclusive in their politics and representation of the intersecting identities and social situation of workers" (Hensman, 2011: 133).

Arguably, however, there is more attention on informal work than was the case in the past and this is evident in calls by various trade unions and NGOs for the state to improve social security, wages, representation, and rights for these workers (Agarwala, 2013). In India, these demands led to the introduction of new legislation such as The Unorganised Workers' Social Security Act 2008. The Government of Pakistan, in a new labor policy introduced in 2010, promised to extend the coverage of minimum wage protection and to protect informal workers in their health, safety, and social security. Such commitments to improving the rights and social security of informal workers demonstrate a degree of state responsiveness to campaigns in civil society and representation by unions and other organizations, but, in general, their actual implementation and effect remain weak across the region with laws and social protection schemes often limited in their coverage and inadequately resourced.

One of the changes in the composition of employment that has very significant implications for industrial relations, labor conflict, and the regulatory framework is the growth of contract and employment "agency" provided to workers in many industries and enterprises in the formal sector. This trend is especially significant as it erodes the bargaining power of regular and directly employed workers. Contract and agency workers are paid less than permanent or directly employed workers. According to one report, contract and agency workers in chemical, energy, and mining enterprises in India are paid one-third of the wages of the permanent and directly employed, and in the garment industry, "contract workers are paid less than half the amount paid to permanent workers, which is often below the legal minimum wage" (Holdcroft, 2012: 7). These workers have problems exercising collective voice—given their inherent vulnerability to dismissal or removal from the workplace—and in accessing workplace representation, and in some jurisdictions, they are legally incapable of joining the same union as permanent workers (Holdcroft, 2012). Clearly, therefore, the effective substitution of one (regular) worker with another indirectly employed worker weakens union capacity. In Pakistan, for instance, while there has always been a role for workers provided by employment agencies in seasonal and non-continuing tasks at workplace level, the recent "proliferation" of these arrangements is "potentially an attempt by employers to bypass statutory obligations concerning workers' statutory benefit entitlements and trade union rights" (Sheikh, 2008).

Such problems are even more evident for work outsourced from larger enterprises to small production units, including a substantial number of home-based workers in the major nations of South Asia. This takes place through various layers of subcontracting arrangements and, in some instances, can link informal home-based workers to global production networks and consumer brands. For example, one study that examined the manufacture of hand-stitched footballs in Pakistan and India found that outsourcing to small production units and homes "tends to reduce the incomes of football stitchers, resulting in income and occupational insecurity" and further noted that "institutionalization of subcontracting made it very difficult for trade unions to form and collective bargaining to emerge" (Lund-Thomsen, Nadvi, Chan, Khara, & Xue, 2012: 1231). Where international consumer brands are linked to these production networks, such strategies nonetheless open up the possibility of reputational damage and compliance risks, which is a new but relatively weak source of soft "regulation" of labor standards and employment practices.

Labor regulation in South Asia

As noted, labor laws and regulations across South Asia are linked to a colonial legacy that is evident in a shared common law tradition and the design and functioning of various institutions. The constitutions of the nations within the region have also been significant in establishing foundational principles for employment regulation including formally stated commitments to rights such as freedom of association and the relative powers of regional and national governments to make laws and regulations pertaining to industrial relations and employment law (for a list of major labor laws, see Table 7.1). From these shared institutional traditions, each nation has diverged at various times and in different ways in the form and characteristics of employment law and regulation. Many of these changes reflect broader transitions in government and politics in a region where democracy has sometimes given way to authoritarianism or, perhaps more pertinently, where these modes of governance interact in a relationship of dynamic tension. In each nation, there is ongoing discussion and debate about the need for reforms to labor law and industrial relations institutions, but there is no social consensus on the scope and form of required amendments and improvements to the formal legislative framework. These debates, in general, have only intensified in the context of economic liberalization and global integration but remain unresolved.

In India, the formal legislative framework of industrial relations is underpinned by various national Acts on trade unions, industrial employment, and industrial dispute mediation and resolution. Labor law and regulation are listed in the concurrent list of the Indian Constitution, which provides national as well as state (regional) legislatures with the power to enact employment regulation. This means that industrial relations and employment regulations are perhaps best understood at a regional level, although where there is a conflict between national and state level regulation the former should prevail unless presidential assent is granted for a state-specific variation from national labor law. Of the underpinning national legal framework, the Industrial Disputes Act, 1947 has perhaps been the most contentious as it sets out a requirement that enterprises above a threshold of employees must seek approval from government before retrenching permanent workers or closing an enterprise (Mitchell et al., 2014). Otherwise the Act sets out, amongst others, the procedures for taking industrial action and resolving disputes through conciliation, adjudication and arbitration. The requirements for establishing and registering unions and their functioning are set out by the Trade Unions Act 1926, which amongst other things, sets a low limit for the establishment of a workplace trade union. This, in conjunction with the absence of a national trade union recognition law, has been instrumental in fostering union fragmentation and weak collective bargaining coverage of unions, especially in the private sector. In the Trade Unions (Amendment) Act, 2001, some adjustments were made by introducing a requirement that unions applying for registration must have the support of at least 10 percent of all workers in the enterprise to be registered or 100 workers, whichever is lower (Mitchell et al., 2014). Other rules around employment are governed by the Industrial Employment (Standing Orders) Act, 1946.

The Contract Labour (Regulation and Abolition) Act of 1970 emerged in the context of the Left-populism that characterized the Indira Gandhi-led national Government of that period. This Act was intended to allow contract employment only for workers engaged in non-core tasks on an intermittent and non-perennial basis. It has provided some limited capacity for unions and workers to regulate and challenge the utilization of contract workers by the principal employers in various industries and workplaces. Nonetheless, as noted by a recent report on the growth of agency and contract work in India, the Act "does not provide for the absorption of contract workers into the permanent workforce, and is therefore not of much help in cases

Table 7.1 Selected list of labor laws and regulations in South Asia

India

1926	The Trade Unions Act
1936	The Payment of Wages Act
1946	The Industrial Employment (Standing Orders) Act
1947	The Industrial Disputes Act
1948	The Minimum Wages Act
1948	The Factories Act
1951	The Plantation Labour Act
1952	The Mines Act
1970	The Contract Labour (Regulation & Abolition) Act
1976	Bonded Labour System (Abolition) Act
1976	Equal Remuneration Act
1986	Child Labour (Prohibition and Regulation) Act
2001	The Trade Unions (Amendment) Act
2008	The Unorganised Workers' Social Security Act
2013	Sexual Harassment of Women at Workplace (Prevention, Prohibition, and Redressal) Act
2015	Labour Code on Industrial Relations Bill (draft legislation)

Pakistan

1934	The Factories Act
1936	Payment of Wages Act
1951	The Employment (Record of Services) Act
1952	The Pakistan Essential Services (Maintenance) Act
1959	Industrial Dispute Ordinance
1961	The Minimum Wages Ordinance
1962	Employees' Social Insurance Ordinance
1968	The West Pakistan Industrial and Commercial Employment (Standing Orders) Ordinance
1969	The Minimum Wages for Unskilled Workers Ordinance
1969	Industrial Relations Ordinance
1973	The Employees' Cost of Living (Relief) Act
1991	The Employment of Children Act
1992	Bonded Labour System (Abolition) Act
2002	Industrial Relations Ordinance
2008	Industrial Relations Act
2010	The Protection Against Harassment of Women at the Workplace Act
2011	Industrial Relations Ordinance
2012	Industrial Relations Act

Bangladesh

1923	The Boilers Act
1923	The Mines Act
1961	The Trade Organisations Ordinance
1962	The Tea Plantation Labour Ordinance
1965	The Control of Employment Ordinance
1980	The Foreign Private Investment (Promotion & Protection) Act
1980	The Bangladesh Export Processing Zones Authority Act
1984	The Agricultural Labour (Minimum Wages) Ordinance
1993	The State-Owned Manufacturing Industries Workers Ordinance
1996	The Bangladesh Private Export Processing Zones Act

Table 7.1 Continued

2004	The Export Processing Zones Workers Association and Industrial Relations Act
2006	The Bangladesh Labour Act (amended 2013)
2010	Export Processing Zones (EPZ) Workers Welfare Association and Industrial Relations Act

Sri Lanka

1934	Workmen's Compensation Ordinance
1935	Trade Unions Ordinance
1941	The Wages Boards Ordinance
1942	The Factories Ordinance
1950	The Industrial Disputes Act (amended 1968, 1983, 1990, 1999, 2003, and 2008)
1956	The Employment of Women, Young Persons & Children's Act
1958	Employees' Provident Fund Act
1971	The Termination of Employment (Special Provisions)
1979	Employees' Councils Act

Sources: Ghayur, 2009; Amerasinghe, 2009; Al Faruque, 2009; NATLEX Database of national labor, social security and related human rights legislation, and country profiles. Retrieved from www.ilo.org/dyn/natlex/country_profiles.byCountry?p_lang=en.

where the use of contract workers is proven to be 'sham and bogus'" (IndustriALL Global Union, 2012).[4]

Over several decades of "economic liberalization," various national governments in India have sought to launch major industrial relations and labor law "reforms" but have been largely frustrated in their ability to achieve these announced goals (Gillan, 2007). In 2014, a newly elected Bharatiya Janata Party (BJP) Government, led by Prime Minister Narendra Modi, announced a "Make in India" campaign and policy thrust with the stated intention of increasing investment and employment generation in labor-intensive manufacturing industries and this was linked directly to an agenda for labor law and industrial relations reform. While this reform agenda is still unfolding, it is apparent that the Modi Government will seek to concert and coordinate national changes to labor law—especially the aforementioned Acts pertaining to trade unions, industrial employment, and industrial disputes resolution—with equivalent changes in the states ruled by BJP governments. The Modi Government has also sought to make significant amendments to Acts pertaining to the employment of apprentices, regulation of factories, the labor inspection regime, and the reporting obligations for enterprises to comply with labor regulation (Secki, 2015).

In Pakistan, rights to engage in collective bargaining, industrial action, and to form and participate in trade unions were established by the colonial legal framework but weakened with the turn toward military authoritarianism (Ghayur, 2009). In 1959, an Industrial Disputes Ordinance removed the right to strike and "while the Ayub Khan era in the 1960s led to rapid industrialization and increased the industrial labor force considerably, it also witnessed retrogressive labor laws" (Ghayur, 2009: 9–10). Pakistan's union movement was a prominent and active participant in mass protests that led to the fall of General Ayub Khan in 1969. In that year, a reconstituted military regime introduced the Industrial Relations Ordinance 1969 which purported, amongst other things, to support the right to strike, bargain, and organize and which was preceded by tripartite policy consultation (Ghayur, 2009). However, according to Candland (2007), rather than supporting stronger and more cohesive industry based unionism, the technical design of the Ordinance actually encouraged enterprise unionism and union fragmentation—in part to curb the demonstrated political power of union federations. In particular, it "produced more unions, but with fewer members" (Candland, 2007: 50) with the ultimate effect of limiting labor mobilization and political and economic influence over subsequent decades.

A review of the Industrial Relations Ordinance led to the introduction of a new Industrial Relations Ordinance in 2002, which made adjustments that "greatly reduced penalties for labor law violations by employers and revoked the right of wrongfully terminated workers to rein-statement" (Munir, Naqvi, & Usmani, 2015: 178). This legislation was then succeeded by the Industrial Relations Act 2008, which was introduced without formal consultation with employer and union organizations and which, amongst other things, was thought to exclude workers employed by contractors from coverage under the law; to prevent public sector workers from taking industrial action; and to allow for non-union collective agreements with the potential for eroding the place of unions in collective bargaining (Ghayur, 2009). This Act, however, was interim legislation with a designated expiration in 2010 because of a Constitutional Amendment that decentralized legislative authority for most matters—including industrial relations—to pro-vincial level governments. As a consequence, a bridging Ordinance was necessary for 2011 before the promulgation of a new Industrial Relations Act, 2012. The latter applied to all "establishments and industries in the Islamabad Capital Territory or carrying out business in more than one province" and thereby allowed for the legal registration of national trade union federations and a reformed National Industrial Relations Commission to play a role in the res-olution of trans-provincial disputes. Nonetheless, the locus of industrial relations regulation has clearly shifted in Pakistan as most workers are outside the ambit of national labor law and the provinces have the "responsibilities of labor legislation, enforcement, policies and programmes" (LO/FTF Council, 2014b: 8).

The legislative framework for industrial relations in Bangladesh has also been shaped by that nation's political history and especially the authoritarian tendencies of various administrations. At the moment of its birth as an independent nation, Bangladesh had a double inheritance from both colonial and Pakistani labor law. Even within the first government of Bangladesh there were a series of regulatory amendments that had the effect of limiting or suspending the right to strike and to engage in collective bargaining and independent trade union worker representation (Al Faruque, 2009). Following the assassination of Prime Minister Sheikh Mujibur Rahman in 1975 and the replacement of his Awami League government by military rule, this repressive tradition continued with the Industrial Relations (Regulation) Ordinance, 1975 (Al Faruque, 2009).

Over subsequent decades, by means of various iterations of industrial relations ordinances and labor policies, there was oscillation between improvements to the freedom of association and worker rights and their near complete suspension. Only in the early 1990s, after the end of military rule and democratic elections, did the formal rights and regulatory regime stabilize (Al Faruque, 2009). The Labour Act of 2006 provides the current legal underpinning for industrial relations in Bangladesh. The Act was premised on the rationalization and consolidation of a plethora of Acts on health and safety at work, workers' compensation, inspection regimes, wage determination and core industrial relations functions such as dispute resolution, procedural rules for strikes and lockouts, and trade union registration (LO/FTF Council, 2014a). The Act was amended in 2013 in the context of national and international trade union demands that prob-lems with workers' rights for freedom of association and collective bargaining be addressed, although concerns remain with respect to the high (30 percent) threshold of worker support required at the enterprise level for union registration and the apparent exclusion from the scope of regulation of contract workers employed by agencies rather than directly by the enterprise (LO/FTF Council, 2014a).

In Sri Lanka, Biyanwila has described how a "liberal corporatist regime" prevailed between 1956 and 1977 with import substitution and an emphasis on "active state intervention in industrial production and distribution" as well as economic planning and regulation (2011: 44). Industrial relations during this period was also characterized by the relative accommodation and incorporation of unions with "enhanced tripartite mechanisms, labor legislation, labor tribunals" (Biyanwila, 2011: 44). From 1977 onwards the UNP Government initiated a sharp turn toward an export-oriented economic development strategy and neoliberal economic policies inclusive of privatization and deregulation of trade and investment, while, politically, the "implementation of neo-liberal policies was built on an authoritarian ethno-nationalist project" (Biyanwila, 2011: 56). This economic and political transition, therefore, not only weakened the labor movement and worker protection but it also increasingly drew trade unions within the ethno-nationalist conflict and to identity-based rather than class-based politics.

Aside from the lasting effect of this economic and political context in industrial relations, Sri Lanka is notable within South Asia for pioneering and relying on a strategy of exclusion of geographic zones and groups of workers from the ambit of existing labor legislation and regulation. This occurred through the establishment of export processing zones (EPZs), for which the existing labor law regime did not apply and with the regulation of the zones managed via a Board of Investment (BOI). This strategy, therefore, linked the attraction of foreign direct investment to a flexible and largely union-free labor regime and by the 1990s, the rapid growth of EPZs meant that the BOI regulated industrial relations for a significant share of the manufacturing sector. Although trade unions are not formally precluded from forming and functioning in the zones, in practice, organizing has been repressed and union substitution strategies deployed (Gunawardana, 2007). In the context of ongoing national and international union and civil society criticism of the labor governance of the zones, in 2003, the BOI issued a "Labour Standards & Employment Relations Manual," which purported to address the inadequate regulation of work and workers' rights and the commitment of relevant enterprises to respect core labor standards (Amerasinghe, 2009). Nonetheless, trade unions have made only limited gains in worker representation in the zones and an exclusionary labor regulatory regime continues. Bangladesh, Pakistan, and India have followed the Sri Lankan example by establishing EPZs (otherwise known as special economic zones or free trade zones) at various times and with different exclusions from the broader employment and industrial relations regulatory regime (Sankaran, 2007: 5).

Traditional and emerging institutional actors in industrial relations

Most of the organizational "actors" in industrial relations across South Asia—trade unions, employer and business organizations, industrial tribunals, tripartite bodies—have a long history and in this sense can be seen as well-established institutions. Alternately, however, there is also commonality across the region because these institutions have evident weaknesses and are limited in their reach and effect.

In worker representation, each nation can point to rich and complex histories of labor activism and trade unionism. For a variety of reasons—employer hostility and union avoidance, shifts in state policy, labor market structure, reorganization of employment and their own failure in organizational renewal, political, and strategic vision—trade unions are nonetheless limited in their presence in most workplaces and ability to represent effectively the interests of the vast majority of workers. They continue to be over-represented in the public sector, state-owned and large enterprises and lack presence in small to medium businesses and in informal employment. In general, trade unions in South Asia have a strong tradition of union-party political links, which when combined with the lack of favorable rules for union recognition, has led to fragmentation and a lack of effect as bargaining agents. These political affiliations, however, do provide a mechanism for at least partial influence over the state, often in the form of blocking or delaying neoliberal changes to the formal legislative framework of industrial relations and in India some capacity to prevent or limit privatizations (Candland, 2007; Teitelbaum, 2010).

In Pakistan, for instance, in 2012, there were only 1,209 registered unions with around one-quarter of a million in combined membership and coverage of less than 1 percent of all workers (Pakistan Institute of Labour Education & Research [PILER], 2015). The weakness of trade unions in Pakistan has been attributed to the design and implementation of the legislative and regulatory framework under various political regimes but, most of all, to a wave of privatization between 1991 and 2008 of public utilities and enterprises that led to widespread retrenchments, restructuring of employment (permanent to contractual) and the "disintegration of trade unions" (PILER, 2015: 23). This has been compounded by the internal failures of unions themselves which are "splintered along ethnic, sectarian, linguistic, and regional lines" (Ghayur, 2009: 2), characterized by weak leadership structures and gender inclusivity, and which have lacked the will or the capacity to organize, most especially amongst contract and informal workers (PILER, 2015: 23).

In general, Bangladesh also reflects a bleak scenario for trade unions and worker representation. As we have noted, the repressive nature of labor law and governance in Bangladesh has made union organizing and representation difficult. Even under democratic governments, unions have failed to flourish in growing areas of employment such as the export-oriented ready-made garment industry. The creation of EPZs as enclaves with a separate labor law regulatory regime, as well as the non-enforcement of existing labor legislation, has limited the unionization of garment manufacturing workers (Rahman & Langford, 2012). Trade unions in Bangladesh have strong affiliations with the main left and national political parties but are weak at the enterprise level and have made few inroads in organizing workers in the garment industry, with the emergence of independent union federations a partial exception to this trend (Rahman & Langford, 2012). In 2006 and 2010, there were a series of garment industry worker protests and mobilizations over inadequate workplace rights and employment conditions (Hossan, Sarker, & Afroze, 2012; Rahman & Langford, 2012). Nonetheless, it has been workers themselves rather than unions that have taken the lead in these agitations which, again, is indicative of the weakness of unions as a mechanism of collective voice.

In Sri Lanka, the effectiveness and role of unions are shaped by the political links between the traditional trade unions and the main political parties as well as the ethno-religious identities of these organizations (Gunawardana & Biyanwila, 2008). It has been estimated that some 15 percent of wage earners are unionized, and while the public sector and larger state-owned enterprises remain the core of the labor movement there is a notable shift in membership away from national federations toward smaller enterprise-based trade unions (Ranaraja, 2013). There have been organizing drives and a notable initiative to form an independent (non-politically aligned) trade union for EPZ/FTZ workers, although the effect of the latter has been limited by often intense employer opposition and the prevailing regulatory regime in the zones (Biyanwila, 2011).

Most of the external and internal factors discussed above that have limited union presence and effect in Sri Lanka, Bangladesh, and Pakistan have also been significant and evident in India. India has a strong tradition of unions affiliated or linked to national or regional political parties and this has led to union fragmentation and competition and a tendency toward political mobilization directed toward the state rather than grass-roots organizing (Ahn, 2010). In India, and indeed across South Asia, there is a clear need for the revitalization of trade unions to promote internal democracy, greater representativeness in the gender and social composition of leadership structures, and dynamism in their organizing and political strategies, including the organization and representation of informal sector workers (Gillan & Biyanwila, 2009). Nonetheless, there have been some positive developments in India such as greater union coordination across party political divides, growth in trade union membership, and some experiments in internationalizing local union struggles and organizing initiatives (Gillan & Lambert, 2013).

In South Asia, employer associations at the national and industry level have been weak in their coordination and representation of businesses. In many ways, this weakness is a sign of the sway of managerial prerogative and employer power at enterprise level and the limited reach of collective bargaining and industrial relations institutions. In each nation, the largest domestic business corporations can exercise strong voice over economic and public policy. In general, employers and business associations have pushed for reforms to the regulatory framework to reduce compliance costs and to allow for greater labor "flexibility." In India, these demands have been especially strong with regard to legal obligations relating to retrenchment, enterprise closures, and deployment of contract labor but firms have nonetheless achieved various forms of flexibility by regulatory non-compliance, the use of voluntary retirement schemes, outsourcing or the reorganization of employment.

Across the region, dispute resolution in industrial relations is linked to the role of the state whether through direct government intervention or the exercise of various powers, inclusive of the capacity to refer disputes to industrial tribunals and/or labor courts. This has had the general effect of discouraging the parties from resolving disputes through bipartite negotiations and voluntary settlements in the workplace and provided further incentives for trade unions to adopt a political model of unionism that seeks to influence the state above other goals. As Sankaran has noted the,

> early view of law as a "modern" force and the legal system as the superior normative order to settle disputes is also reflected in the ease with which compulsory adjudication as the method of settling industrial disputes came to have primacy in many countries in the region.
>
> *(2007: 7)*

and the strong and direct part played by "government and courts in labor disputes (often more frequent than settlement through collective bargaining) has led to the greater 'juridification' of all disputes and grievances" (Sankaran 2007: 7). From a practical point of view, the complex and legalistic nature of dispute resolution, especially in individual cases, means that these matters absorb a great deal of time and resources of trade unions, possibly to the detriment of other activities such as new organizing initiatives and industrial campaigns.

In formal institutional arrangements, tripartite bodies are a common feature of industrial relations across the region, which, in part, reflects the influence of the ILO in attempting to promote social dialogue and consultative mechanisms for policy and institutional development. Arguably, however, tripartite bodies and forums have been weakened over recent decades due to the unwillingness of relevant organizations to engage in genuine dialogue and political exchange on required reforms, a trend that seems to have intensified as liberalization policies have taken root in the various nations of the region. This means that the participants in tripartite bodies, perhaps most especially governments and employers, have a weak commitment to them and they have struggled to demonstrate their effect and relevance (Amerasinghe, 2009; Al Faruque, 2009; Ghayur, 2009).[5]

There are also issues across the region concerning the enforcement of industrial relations and employment regulation. There are various approaches to enforcement but most nations have monitoring, reporting, and inspection regimes backed by legal penalties (Sankaran, 2007: 14). Nonetheless, the scope of inspection is limited and penalties for breach of the law are often insufficient to deter evasion or avoidance, which has led to general concerns about the weakness of enforcement regimes. One of the major arguments of proponents of regulatory reform is that the complexity of labor regulations creates significant compliance costs in reporting employee data and that labor inspections can be used to harass employers or extract bribes (Sankaran, 2007: 14). This has led to calls for enterprises to self-certify their compliance with labor regulation, although, in the case of India, there is evidence that the labor inspection regimes have already been weakened over the last decade and now have very limited reach (Shyam Sundar, 2014). A recent study has also shown that a significant number of enterprises are non-compliant with the factories Act in India (Chatterjee & Kanbur, 2015), which again raises the question as to whether such reform agendas are simply formal acknowledgement that the state is presiding over the gradual dilution of the current regulatory and enforcement regime.

Indeed, the weak or limited nature of state regulation and enforcement has opened the space for non-state and voluntarist corporate, NGO and multi-stakeholder initiatives for the regulation of labor standards in South Asia and elsewhere. As Kuruvilla and Verma have noted in their discussion of the interaction between "hard" and "soft" regulation, "the current international pressure to improve labor standards stems from the fundamental failure of national governments to enforce their own labor laws" (2006: 43). Across South Asia, especially in industries characterized by their articulation to complex international supply and contract networks, these voluntary initiatives, supplier audits, and social responsibility reporting requirements are growing but, in general, their effect has been reported to be weak or lacking credibility. Nonetheless, in some instances, as shown by a study of Nike's sourcing arrangements for the production of branded footballs in Pakistan, supplier "non-compliance can result in exclusion from profitable markets" (Nadvi, 2008). In the aftermath of the horrific Rana Plaza garment factory collapse in 2013, two global union federations (UNI Global Union; IndustriALL Global Union) have worked in conjunction with partner NGOs to sign an "Accord on Fire and Building Safety in Bangladesh" with many major international brands. The Accord is co-signed with trade unions and has enforceable provisions, scope for worker participation, and independent monitoring, and this may be an indication of ongoing regulatory potential, especially in industries linked to international consumer brands. Nonetheless, in a context where unions remain weak and fragmented, and where support from the state is lacking, the sustainability of such initiatives is open to question.

HRM practices and employment relations in South Asia

The growth of human resource management (HRM) as a discourse and set of organizational practices in South Asia has implications for industrial relations, not least because the enterprise level management of employment regulation compliance and industrial relations functions are, typically, now encompassed within human resource management or human resource development sections or teams. This means that the discourse and collective framing of industrial relations is giving way in both private and public sector organizations to the more individualized and unitarist frames of human resource management and, while there are exceptions, in many instances HRM is associated with union-substitution or union-weakening strategies.

In India, for instance, this has led to different phases of development in HRM including the introduction of practices that clearly have industrial relations implications such as performance-related pay in private sector enterprises (Budhwar & Varma, 2011). The spread of these practices to other sectors has been such that in 2015, the Seventh Central Pay Commission, the body that determines wages and benefits for central government employees in India, has recommended the introduction of performance-related pay systems for all workers and linked salary increments to performance-based criterion (PTI, 2015). While trade unions in India have been successful in obstructing the privatization of many public sector enterprises, they have been far less capable of resisting such changes to workplace practices. There are also examples of productivity bargaining between unions and employers in collective bargaining agreements and, in some instances, this may have been achieved through cooperative employment relations at the enterprise level (Sodhi, 2013). A concessionary and accommodating approach to bargaining by unions and workers, however, may also reflect their weakness at the enterprise level and increased concern about declining employment security in the context of production outsourcing and/or increased utilization of contract and agency workers.

Bypassing regulatory restrictions and/or trade unions through the effective substitution of permanent core workers with contract or agency workers has profound implications for the integrity of industrial relations. In Pakistan, in an egregious example of cost avoidance, employment agencies can sometimes be phantom organizations whereby a firm or owner organizes or contracts an individual to form a nominally separate small business to process the payroll. This makes it difficult for state agencies to track and prove a legal employment relationship and allows some employers to remove themselves "from any legal obligation to offer statutorily required benefits to these workers" (Sheikh, 2008: 7). The general trend across the region toward contractualization, whether motivated by cost avoidance and/or the desire to limit or exclude trade union representation, has many implications for human resource management practitioners. As noted by one survey of the challenges that confront HRM in India, the inherent lack of equity that characterizes the widespread use of precarious contract-based employment generates "dissatisfaction and frustration for the contract labor, especially in situations where the two groups of employees work side-by-side" (Budhwar & Varma, 2011: 322).

The long-term implications of such strategies remain to be seen but it is notable that there have been several high-profile labor conflicts in India over recent years that have been related to union avoidance and the increased utilization of contract workers employed on lower terms and conditions than permanent workers. In some instances, these tensions have translated into a violent confrontation, which, in turn, have drawn a heavy-handed response from the state. The most high-profile conflict of this type occurred in a Maruti-Suzuki factory in Manesar in North India, and related to a campaign for the recognition of an independent trade union and the regularization and improvement of conditions of contract workers.[6]

In Bangladesh, in September and November 2013, there were sustained street protests by tens of thousands of garment workers to demand improved wages and safety standards in the industry. These protests disrupted or shut down production in many factories, resulted in police action against the workers, and secured a government promise of an increased standard wage (North, 2013). In Sri Lanka, labor practices within EPZs continue to be a point of contention, especially where workers seek to have independent union representation or to limit the use of contract labor. One example is a campaign by the Free Trade Zones and General Services Employees Union in Sri Lanka, in conjunction with international unions, to demand the reinstatement of 300 workers dismissed from a manufacturing unit of an Australian-based MNC (Ansell) for participating in strike action and union activities (IndustriALL, 2015). Across the region, strikes, protests, and worker mobilizations are generally under-reported both in the media and in official statistical data (Teitelbaum, 2010; Shyam Sundar, 2015).

Another contentious area of HRM practice in South Asia is the question of non-union mechanisms for worker consultation and dispute resolution in the workplace. Consultative committees and workplace-level dispute resolution mechanisms can be associated with more sophisticated approaches to HRM, but they also carry inherent risks in that a "shift from a legal-istic towards a strategic HRM approach means that the resolution of grievances may be increas-ingly dependent upon private mechanisms internal and specific to the organization instead of drawing on external systems and resources" (Cooke & Saini, 2015: 635) and, as such, may further marginalize trade unions and contribute to the individualization of employment rela-tions. In export processing and special economic zones, employer directed employee "voice" and "participation" initiatives are even more contentious as they reinforce other regulatory and management strategies to limit trade union representation. In Sri Lanka, for instance, worker councils established and promoted by the Board of Investment in the zones purport to facilitate direct communication between workers and managers to improve employment practices and resolve disputes (Amerasinghe, 2009), but have been criticized as institutional bulwarks for the continued exclusion of unions and genuine independent worker representation (Biyan-wila, 2011).

Conclusions

The regulation of employment and industrial relations in South Asia is complex—with labor laws and regulation interacting and overlapping across different jurisdictions and subject domains within the nations of the region. This "multiplicity and lack of uniformity in the law" is espe-cially evident in Pakistan and India where Constitutions created concurrent powers for both the center and regional governments to make laws on employment and industrial relations (Sanka-ran, 2007: 6). As shown in this chapter, the formal architecture of regulation must also be understood with reference to shifting patterns of politics and state governance over time, with the relationship between authoritarian and democratic modes especially significant.

Another crucial observation is the limited reach of this matrix of employment regulation, and even where formal regulation exists, the widening gap between legal rights and protections and the actual practices of industrial relations. There has always been an evident gap between employment regulation and industrial relations institutions and the working lives of most citizens in South Asia—the vast majority of whom are situated in informal and precarious employment with limited rights, market-based bargaining power, and social protections. There has been a slow growth of movements and organizations to represent the interests and demand improved working conditions for informal/unorganized workers, most notably in India. However, the social situation of such workers and their various identity markers remain most significant in "regulating" their employment and the extent to which they are vulnerable to exploitation or have the means to secure their livelihood. Across the whole region, patriarchy and gender bias is reflected in industrial relations institutions—including trade unions—a major challenge that must be overcome, if they are to become genuinely inclusive and representative.

For workers in formal sector employment, there are unresolved questions about the design of industrial relations and employment laws and their enforcement or lack thereof. These debates have intensified in the context of a general move by the governments of the region toward eco-nomic liberalization policies and neoliberal governance. This has led advocates for labor flex-ibility to propose radical restructuring of industrial relations and employment laws, privatization, and the application of private sector management principles to public sector workers.

The realization of these market-directed policy settings and institutional reforms across the region has varied because of the uneven strength of labor movements and their varying oppor-tunities, inclusive of political structures, to oppose and obstruct these agendas. For all of the weaknesses and strategic failings of trade unions in India, including an inability to articulate and advance a positive agenda for regulatory and social reform, they have succeeded over many years in obstructing sweeping changes to the existing legal architecture and privatization. In other nations within the region, most especially Bangladesh and Pakistan, unions have not had the same political opportunity structures to mediate institutional change, and, as noted in this chapter, remain divided between competing organizations, weak in membership and bargaining power, and politically ineffectual. In Sri Lanka, unions have demonstrated some capacity for effective political action and even some signs of strategic renewal but these have been overshadowed by their articulation with an enveloping ethno-nationalist politics and conflict. Moreover, they have also struggled to counter their effective exclusion or marginalization from many worksites. In particular, a state strategy to create export processing zones to facilitate foreign investment has, in effect, excluded these designated areas from prevailing labor regulation and, in some instances, limited or excluded trade union presence.

Another significant issue noted in this chapter is the gradual erosion of formal, regularized employment by means of the increasing use of contract and agency workers. This strategy can serve to both reduce costs and weaken or marginalize trade unions in the workplace. Some advocates of regulatory reform and labor flexibility point to what they consider to be undue protections and benefits afforded to regular workers for stimulating this restructuring of employment. However, where the restructuring of law and regulation to promote labor flexibility has taken place, there are few indicators that this has led to the creation of a larger share of regular and direct employment—indeed, such changes may only reinforce this trend away from regular to contingent employment.

The gap between formal regulation and weak practical effect and enforcement is also related to the limited or declining capacity of many industrial relations institutions and organizations across the region: trade unions, industrial tribunals, and tripartite bodies. This, in turn, raises the possibility of alternative institutions and regulatory initiatives. There has been an expansion of HRM mechanisms for dispute resolution and channeling employee "voice" but there is also the likelihood that this will further individualize the employment relationship and limit genuine independent collective representation. Codes of conduct and other voluntarist international social responsibility initiatives may be relevant for workplaces connected to global supply chains/ production networks—although the weight of evidence at present is that these are typically corporate directed rather than independent, and are weak in their "regulatory" effect. None of these developments or challenges to the relevance of industrial relations institutions is especially unique to South Asia, although, as discussed in this chapter, the way in which they will play out will certainly be shaped by the unique historical trajectory and the socio-political and economic context of each nation in the region.

Notes

1 I would like to thank the editors, an anonymous reviewer, and Janaka Biyanwila for their comments on this chapter. My thanks also to Alex Veen for providing research assistance.
2 Although, as Biyanwila has noted, the representation of the conflict as defined by monolithic and fixed majority and minority ethic identities is "simplistic" and "hides the complexity of these ethnic identities as well as tensions" (2011: 2).
3 See World Bank, South Asia region, retrieved from www.worldbank.org/en/region/sar.
4 Contract workers, according to a decision of the Supreme Court, can be employed in any operation, including core and perennial, unless this work is specifically prohibited by the concerned appropriate government in that process, operation, or industry. Contract workers, therefore, find it very difficult to legally enforce their rights of absorption into the permanent workforce, even in cases where the employment arrangement has been determined to be that of a sham contract. The author would like to thank an anonymous peer reviewer of this chapter for this observation.

5 In India, which has many national tripartite bodies, the term "atrophied tripartism" has been used to describe the decay and lack of effectiveness of national forums such as the annual Indian Labour Conference (ILC), which, in theory, should serve as a primary vehicle for policy development and consultation between unions, employers, and the state (Venkata Ratnam, 2009: 34).

6 In mid-2012, the company and state authorities accused protesting workers of murdering a senior HR manager after a fire broke out at the site and thereafter 500 permanent and 1,800 contract workers were dismissed (Nowak, 2014). Despite 147 workers who were arrested protesting their innocence, and in light of the fact that some of these workers had not been present at the site on the day of the alleged incident, they were detained without bail on an indefinite basis (Rangan, 2014).

References

Agarwala, R. (2013). *Informal labor, formal politics, and dignified discontent in India.* Cambridge: Cambridge University Press.

Ahn, P. S. (2010). *Growth and decline of political unionism in India: Need for a paradigm shift.* Bangkok: International Labour Organization.

Al Faruque, D. (2009). *Current status and evolution of industrial relations system in Bangladesh.* ILO Office for South Asia. New Delhi: International Labour Organization.

Amerasinghe, F. (2009). *The current status and evolution of industrial relations in Sri Lanka.* ILO Office for South Asia. New Delhi: International Labour Organization.

Bhattacherjee, D. & Ackers, P. (2010). Introduction: Employment relations in India—old narratives and new perspectives. *Industrial Relations Journal, 41*(2), 104–121.

Biyanwila, S. J. (2011). *The labour movement in the global south: Trade unions in Sri Lanka.* London: Routledge.

Budhwar, P. & Varma, A. (2011). Emerging HR management trends in India and the way forward. *Organizational Dynamics, 40,* 317–325.

Candland, C. (2007). *Labor, democratization and development in India and Pakistan.* London: Routledge.

Chatterjee, U. & Kanbur, R. (2015). Regulation and non-compliance: Magnitudes and patterns for India's factories act. *International Labor Review, 154*(3), 393–412.

Chibber, V. (2005). From class compromise to class accommodation: Labor's incorporation into the Indian political economy. In R. Ray & M. F. Katzenstein (Eds.), *Social movements in India: Poverty, power, and politics.* Lanham, MD: Rowman & Littlefield.

Cooke, F. L. (2012). Employment relations in China and India. In M. Barry & A. Wilkinson, (Eds.), *Handbook of comparative employment relations* (pp. 184–213). Cheltenham: Edward Elgar.

Cooke, F. L. & Saini, D. S. (2015). From legalism to strategic HRM in India?: Grievance management in transition. *Asia Pacific Journal of Management, 32*(3), 619–643.

Frenkel, S. J. & Yu, K. H. (2014). Employment relations and human resource management in Asia: Emerging patterns in Asian societies. In M. A. Witt & G. Redding (Eds.), *The Oxford handbook of Asian business systems.* Oxford: Oxford University Press.

Ghayur, S. (2009). *Evolution of the industrial relations system in Pakistan.* ILO Office for South Asia. New Delhi: International Labour Organization.

Gillan, M. (2007). Strange company?: Organised labour and the politics of liberalisation in India. In A. Gamble, S. Ludlam, A. Taylor, & S. J. Wood (Eds.), *Labour, the state, social movements and the challenge of neo-liberal globalisation* (pp. 110–128). Manchester: Manchester University Press.

Gillan, M. & Biyanwila, J. (2009). Revitalising trade unions as civil society actors in India. *South Asia: Journal of South Asian Studies, 32*(3), 425–447.

Gillan, M. & Lambert, R. (2013). Labour movements and the age of crisis: Scale, form and repertoires of action in India and beyond. *South Asia: Journal of South Asian Studies, 36*(2), 180–198.

Gunawardana, S. (2007). Struggle, perseverance and organization in Sri Lanka's export processing zones. In K. Bronfenbrenner (Ed.), *Global unions: Challenging transnational capital through cross-border campaigns* (pp. 78–98). New York: Cornell University Press.

Gunawardana, S. & Biyanwila, J. (2008). Trade unions in Sri Lanka. In J. Benson & Y. Zhu (Eds.), *Trade unions in Asia: An economic and sociological analysis.* London: Routledge.

Harriss-White, B. (2010). Work and wellbeing in informal economies: The regulative roles of institutions of identity and the state. *World Development, 38*(2), 170–183.

Hensman, R. (2011). *Workers, unions, and global capitalism: Lessons from India.* New York: Columbia University Press.

Holdcroft, J. (2012). *The triangular trap: Unions take action against agency labour*. Geneva: IndustriALL Global Union. Retrieved from www.industriall-union.org.

Hossan, C. G., Sarker, A. R., & Afroze, R. (2012). Recent unrest in the RMG sector of Bangladesh: Is this an outcome of poor labor practices? *International Journal of Business and Management, 7*(3), 206–218.

IndustriALL Global Union. (2012). *Precarious work in India*. Geneva: IndustriALL Global Union. Retrieved from www.industriall-union.org.

IndustriALL Global Union. (2015). Ansell faces Aussie protests against treatment of Sri Lankan workers. Retrieved August 25, from www.industriall-union.org/ansell-faces-aussie-protests-against-treatment-of-sri-lankan-workers.

International Labour Office. (2014). *Global employment trends 2014: Risk of a jobless recovery?* Geneva: International Labour Organization.

Kuruvilla, S., & Erikson, C. L. (2002). Change and transformation in Asian industrial relations. *Industrial Relations, 41*, 171–228.

Kuruvilla, S. & Verma, A. (2006). International labor standards, soft regulation, and national government roles. *Journal of Industrial Relations, 48*(1), 41–58.

LO/FTF Council [Danish Trade Union Council for International Development Cooperation] (2014a). *Bangladesh Labour Market Profile 2014*. Retrieved from www.ulandssekretariatet.dk/content/lande analyser.

LO/FTF Council [Danish Trade Union Council for International Development Cooperation] (2014b). *Pakistan Labour Market Profile 2014*. Retrieved from www.ulandssekretariatet.dk/content/lande analyser.

Lund-Thomsen, P., Nadvi, K., Chan, A., Khara, N., & Xue, H. (2012). Labour in global value chains: Work conditions in football manufacturing in China, India and Pakistan. *Development and Change, 43*(6), 1211–1237.

Mitchell, R., Mahy, P., & Gahan, P. (2014). The evolution of labor law in India: An overview and commentary on regulatory objectives and development. *Asian Journal of Law and Society, 1*(2), 413–453.

Munir, K. A., Naqvi, N., & Usmani, A. (2015). The abject condition of labor in Pakistan. *International Labor and Working-Class History, 87*, 174–183.

Nadvi, K. (2008). Global standards, global governance and the organization of global value chains. *Journal of Economic Geography, 8*(3), 323–343.

North, J. (2013, November 15). Bangladeshi garment workers fight back. *The Nation*. Retrieved from www.thenation.com/article/bangladeshi-garment-workers-fight-back/.

Nowak, J. (2014). March for justice: The protest of India's Maruti Suzuki auto workers against imprisonment and dismissals. *Working USA: The Journal of Labor and Society, 17*, 579–586.

Pakistan Institute of Labour Education & Research (PILER) (2015). *Status of labour rights in Pakistan: The Year 2014*. Karachi: Pakistan Institute of Labour Education& Research.

PTI (2015, November 22). No annual increment for nonperforming employees: 7th Pay panel. *The Economic Times*, Retrieved from http://economictimes.indiatimes.com/news/economy/policy/no%ADan nual%ADincrement%ADfor%ADnon%ADperforming%ADemployees%AD7th%ADpay%ADpanel/printarticle/49878985.cms.

Rahman, Z. & Langford, T. (2012). Why labour unions have failed Bangladesh's garment workers. In S. Mosoetsa & M. Williams (Eds.), *Labour in the global south: Challenges and alternatives for workers*. Geneva: International Labour Office.

Ranaraja, S. (2013). *Emerging trends in employee participation in Sri Lanka*. Geneva: International Labour Office.

Rangan, P.S. (2014, August 11). Those Men of Manesar. *Outlook Magazine*. Retrieved from www.outlook india.com/magazine/story/those-men-of-manesar/291560.

Sankaran, K. (2007). *Labour laws in South Asia: The need for an inclusive approach*. New Delhi: International Labour Organization for South Asia.

Secki, P. J. (2015). Seismic shifts in Indian labor laws. *Economic & Political Weekly, 50*(40), 19–22.

Sheikh, A. Z. (2008). Beyond "agency employment" in Pakistan: The outsourcing of employers' responsibilities to employment agencies. *New Zealand Journal of Employment Relations, 33*(2), 1–19.

Shyam Sundar, K. (2014). The myth of inspector-raj in India. *Economic & Political Weekly, 49*(42). Retrieved from www.epw.in/print/web-exclusives/myth-inspector-raj-india.html.

Shyam Sundar, K. (2015). Industrial conflict in India in the post-reform period. *Economic & Political Weekly, 50*(3), 43–53.

Sodhi, J. S. (2013). Trade unions in India: Changing role & perspective. *The Indian Journal of Industrial Relations, 49*(2), 169–184.

Teitelbaum, E. (2006). Was the Indian labor movement ever co-opted? *Critical Asian Studies, 38*(4), 389–417.

Teitelbaum, E. (2010). Mobilizing restraint: Economic reform and the politics of industrial protest in South Asia. *World Politics, 62*(04), 676–713.

Venkata Ratnam, C. S. (2009). Employment relations in India. In P. S. Budhwar & J. Bhatnagar (Eds.), *The changing face of people management in India*. London: Routledge.

PART III

Thematic and functional HRM

8

PERFORMANCE MANAGEMENT PRACTICES IN ASIA

Arup Varma, Pawan S. Budhwar, and Peter Norlander

Introduction

Performance management systems (PMS) are critical to any organization's ability to measure and monitor individual performance, to ensure that all employees are working at optimal levels in supporting organizational strategy (Varma, Budhwar, & DeNisi, 2008). It is through the effective implementation of PMS that organizations can assign tasks, set individual performance goals, and appraise and reward performance (Fletcher, 2001). As such, it is critical that both scholars and practitioners make efforts to understand the antecedents and consequences of performance through the lens of PMS. As Peretz and Fried have noted, "performance appraisal is a central human resource activity … critical in enhancing both employee and organizational performance" (2012). Given the contextual nature of individual human performance, it is essential that we recognize that the same systems and processes cannot work across the world, without necessary adaptation. Indeed, as DeNisi, Budhwar, and Varma noted, "these systems should not be adopted uncritically" (2008). Of course, multinational corporations often find it easy to implement the same systems in all their locations, for purposes of consistency and, where necessary, comparisons. However, what is needed is a careful consideration of the cultural context where the work is being performed by the individual.

In the context of Asian nations, the focus of this volume, the discussion of PMS becomes quite complex, as Asia is one of the biggest and most complex continents, thereby defying easy generalizations. As an example, Asia includes countries all the way from Saudi Arabia to Philippines, with China and India also in the mix. It should come as no surprise that China and India play major roles in determining and guiding HR practices in the region—between the two of them, these countries have a population of over 2.6 billion people, and these two nations also have two of the leading economies of the world. Not surprisingly, both China and India face numerous challenges—from lack of sufficient qualified talent to increasing levels of employee turnover, as well as the need to modify and/or update their HR systems and practices (Budhwar & Varma, 2013). While there are several similarities between these two nations as noted above (huge populations, leading economies), there are also several critical differences between the two, and these need to be taken into account when implementing and/or adapting systems. For example, China is governed by the one-party system, which allows the government to develop and implement policies and practices with relative ease. It is also a fairly homogeneous nation in terms of demographics, where almost everyone speaks the same language, which makes it relatively easier to understand and develop policies and practices that are culture-sensitive. India, on the other hand, is the world's largest democracy, and has a very diverse population, which makes it almost impossible to paint it in generalizations. Instead, one has to understand the nation with reference to the many diverse regions, religions, languages, and practices, etc. Another key difference between the two relates to the use of PMS. For example, when it comes to performance-related practices, while Indian organizations have utilized some form of appraisal system since the early 1900s (see, e.g., Sharma et al., 2008), the bulk of Chinese organizations did not use performance appraisals until the early 1990s (see Liu & Dong, 2012). While we have emphasized these two nations for discussion purposes, the same arguments hold true for all nations in the region. Furthermore, as several authors have noted (e.g., Froese, 2013), the traditional work values of many Asian nations are evolving in response to the demands of, and the need to be able to compete in, the new, global, business context. Clearly, Asia is a complex and dynamic region, and requires careful study and analysis of critical HR practices, such as PMS, the focus of this chapter.

In this chapter, we are interested in studying PMS in Asia, given the strategic importance of monitoring and managing individual performance. In order to understand PMS in the unique context of Asia, we begin by describing how performance management operates in a global context. Next, we outline the contextual factors that come into play in performance management with specific examples drawn from research on performance management in Asia. Some of the major national institutions and cultural dimensions that motivate the need for a regional- and country-specific approach are then described with reference to the Asian context. Throughout the chapter, we present relevant research on global and comparative performance management practices. Finally, we end the chapter with a discussion of the reasons why multinational organizations need to tailor performance management practices to each country and its cultural context (e.g., DeNisi et al., 2008), rather than simply adopt global "best practices."

The chapter contains seven sections. In Section 1, we introduce the topic, and explain why it is important to study PMS in Asia in detail. In Section 2, we present some key components of PMS. This is followed by a discussion of five key factors that influence PMS, with specific examples drawn from Asia. Next, in Sections 4 and 5 respectively, we address the impact of culture and institutions on PMS. In Section 6, we present some specific examples of PMS practices in Asia. Finally, in Section 7, we present our conclusions and discussion. To supplement our discussion and provide detailed information on the topics discussed, we also highlight certain countries in relation to certain topics.

Key components of performance management systems

In the broadest perspective, performance management involves: (i) assigning work; (ii) setting individual goals; (iii) monitoring outputs; (iv) providing feedback, as necessary; and (v) evaluating individual performance. Formal PMS serve both an administrative and a strategic function. The administrative function is to inform decisions such as promotions and rewards, while the strategic function is to provide employees with developmental coaching and feedback in order to improve future performance (Murphy & Cleveland, 1995) and link individual performance with organizational strategic objectives.

As we note above, performance management provides essential feedback to inform workers about their progress along the path toward achieving organizational and personal objectives (Murphy & Cleveland, 1995). In terms of evidence-backed practices, research strongly supports providing individuals with: (i) goals, (ii) feedback, and (iii) rewards. In this connection, goal-setting theory suggests that specific, difficult goals lead to higher performance than no goals, or easy or vague goals (Locke, 1968; Locke & Latham, 2002). Relatedly, the "SMART" criteria for goal-setting suggests that in order to be effective, goals should be: (i) specific, (ii) measurable, (iii) attainable, (iv) realistic, and (v) timely. Timely and specific feedback is also essential as it provides workers with information on their progress in achieving goals, which can effectively promote feelings of competence and positively reinforce individual effort (Hackman & Oldham 2008; Ryan & Deci, 2000; Amabile & Kramer, 2011). When performance is tied to rewards through compensation programs such as pay-for-performance and performance-based merit pay, such systems can be effective. For example, piece-rate pay (output-based pay) has been shown to lead to dramatic increase(s) in performance, by between 15–30 percent (Locke, Feren, McCaleb, Shaw, & Denny, 1980; Mitchell, Lewin, & Lawler, 1989).

In this connection, social or normative influences on individual behavior include individuals' deeply internalized goals of being liked and maintaining a positive self-concept, affiliating with others, and being accurate (Cialdini & Goldstein, 2004). Performance management practices that incorporate an understanding of these already embedded goals may be especially successful at inducing conformity to performance standards, and obtaining compliance with instructions. Given the emphasis on the group in Asian countries (Hofstede, 1980), it is clear that such considerations must be addressed in developing PMS.

As we note above, a key strategic purpose of PMS is to transmit organizational objectives to workers. Perhaps unsurprisingly, there is a strong correlation between the quality of PMS and both firm-level and national differences in productivity (Bloom, Genakos, Sadun, & van Reenen, 2012). In this connection, Bloom et al. (2012) designed a comparative survey of management practices across the globe with eighteen measures of the quality of management, including performance management practices. Amongst the global "best practices" that were measured in their survey, were factors such as whether: (i) performance is tracked; (ii) performance review is conducted frequently; (iii) performance dialogues take place; (iv) failure to achieve performance objectives carries negative consequences; (v) performance objectives for individuals are clear and comparable to referent others; and (vi) high performance levels are rewarded through incentives and promotions.

Up to this point in our description and discussion of PMS, it may appear that there are a simple set of standard best practices that can be readily adopted by any organization. The seemingly obvious "best practices" promulgated in Bloom et al. (2012) suggest that there are good and bad management practices and that the world should converge toward the good, as though if only good practices were adopted, all would be well. Of course, this is not the case. Instead, the key factors that influence PMS need to be investigated in detail.

Key factors that influence performance management

A number of reasons exist to explain why creating a culture of goal setting, performance monitoring, and feedback is easier said than done. In this connection, Murphy and DeNisi (2008) developed a comprehensive model that identified the following categories of factors as key components of performance management systems: (1) distal factors (e.g., national or cultural norms, technology); (2) proximal factors (e.g., purpose of appraisal and organizational norms); (3) judgment factors (e.g., time pressures and availability of standards); (4) intervening factors (supervisor–subordinate relationships and rater motivation); and (5) distortion factors (e.g., consequences of appraisal and reward systems). We elaborate here on the authors' model to emphasize the factors that need to be addressed by human resource departments working in an Asian context in order to design and execute successful performance management systems.

A. Varma et al.

1 Distal factors

A country's national institutions and cultural norms influence how well organizations can implement performance management. The successful execution of performance management practices rests upon the maturity, strategic importance, and power of HR within the firm, which varies substantially both within and between countries. Consider the centralization of the performance management function within HR, which can be viewed as indicative of the power HR holds. For example, in Japan, corporate HR largely retains the power to evaluate the performance of managers, whereas in the USA, an emphasis on decentralization has increased the power of line management (Jacoby, 2005). In a survey of 229 Japanese and 145 US firms, 38 percent of Japanese companies reported that the headquarters HR function has responsibility for performance management, in contrast to 15 percent of US companies. At the same time, the ability of HR to successfully track the implementation of performance management practices rests upon the capability and maturity of the HR professionals involved. In Japanese corporations, leaders who aspire to become board members often seek a rotation through HR, which may diminish the value of specialized training and career progression for HR professionals (Jacoby, 2005). In contrast, this job rotation of senior corporate leaders through HR may increase the influence HR has on corporate decision-making by giving senior executives a well-rounded view of the firm and knowledge of the importance of performance management practices. Interestingly, in their study of HR practices in different countries, Bowen, Galang, and Pillai (2002) reported that Australia afforded HR the highest status of any country in their study, significantly higher than the USA. As these comparative studies show, the ability of HR to require or influence managers to give feedback and the ability of HR to monitor performance management practices rests upon: (i) the power of HR within the organization; (ii) the capabilities of the HR department: and (iii) the broader position of HR as supported or undermined by national institutions and culture, which is discussed in more detail later in this chapter.

2 Proximal factors

Varying purposes for appraisal at the individual level and varying organizational norms can influence the success of performance management systems. In different countries and contexts, performance management can be viewed as a mere formality, or it can be viewed as a valuable opportunity for improvement and development. For example, managers might be motivated more by the need to "take care" of low-performing employees (Varma, Pichler, & Srinivas, 2005), rather than provide objective evaluations. In such cases, the fulfillment of the performance management process can be undermined by deviations from the original purpose, and the exercise becomes one of rote fulfillment of administrative mandate. Indeed, HR is often viewed as, and is also often actually engaged in, completing administrative functions of the organization in order to ensure compliance with external legal mandates and external pressures from accrediting bodies and social norms. Compelled to adopt "best practices," organizations within a culture may wind up looking alike from the perspective of stated practices in order to maintain credibility in the eyes of external parties (DiMaggio & Powell, 1983; Strang & Macy, 2001). As an example of legal mandates imposed from the outside, OECD (2015) indicators of employment protection legislation suggest that Asian countries have high levels of protections against individual and collective dismissals. Further, the promulgation of "best practices" cookbooks developed by attorneys and consultants within specific countries are often intended only to keep the organization out of trouble, and may lead organizations to implement or adapt performance management practices superficially aligned to local customs. However, with no internal mandate to actually implement true PMS, the effectiveness of "best practices" may suffer more in practice than in theory. Sociologists refer to this as a "decoupling" of action, where organizational routines are performed not as a rational activity, but as "myth and ceremony" for largely ornamental purposes (Meyer & Rowan, 1977). Thus, while the purpose and rational basis for performance management as described in the earlier section is obvious and apparent, the actual implementation through HR departments may lack true alignment with the stated rational goals. Consider for example, the oft-stated desire of HR to become a strategic partner to the business. Bhatnagar and Sharma (2005) studied 640 managers in India, and found that line managers rated the effectiveness of the HR business partners significantly lower than the HR business partners rated themselves. HR professionals in that study perhaps have an inflated view of their own influence and impact, with consequences for whether the purposes of performance management are actually implemented on the ground. In addition, Srimannarayana (2010) reported results from a study of 293 Indian managers, and concluded that HR in India is mainly engaged in Ulrich's (1997) administrative expert and employee champion roles. Thus, the administrative role of HR and the standard operating procedures of PMS can become administrative ends or purposes unto themselves, rather than integral elements of a process that ultimately intends to improve organizational performance. In such cases, managers can view performance management as either an administrative burden, or as a critical opportunity for offering developmental feedback. Given the somewhat pessimistic view offered here, it is important to acknowledge that the success of performance management ultimately relies heavily upon: (i) the internal organizational norms; and (ii) the revealed purposes of performance management as implemented on the ground, with special attention paid to the unique contextual realities of the country where the work is being performed. For example, it is well known that almost all the workers in Saudi Arabia are expatriates from countries around the world, though the top management comprises Saudi Arabian citizens. As such, top management would like to implement so-called Saudi Arabian values, because they often find Western practices conflict with their values. Interestingly, Harbi, Thursfield, and Bright (2016) found that workers in a Saudi Arabian corporation have begun to reject Saudi Arabian cultural norms, and are instead gravitating to Western values such as egalitarianism and justice.

3 Judgment factors

The availability of performance standards can significantly influence the success of PMS. However, in many Asian countries such as China and India, managers are reluctant to adopt sophisticated measurement and management systems (Cooke & Huang, 2011; Varma et al., 2008), as this may restrict their ability to favor certain employees over others, and adjust ratings as necessary. Of course, performance standards function best when they are set at the beginning of the performance period. Once set and discussed with the employee(s), evaluations can be measured against the established standards (see Bobko & Colella, 1994). This promotes fairness in performance evaluation, and also can motivate employees to proactively seek feedback on performance against standards previously agreed upon. In terms of patterns related to the variation in the availability of standards, the nature of the work being done often dictates how much performance can be specified in advance. In higher skill areas with greater uncertainty, performance benchmarks are notoriously difficult to create and are frequently subject to post-hoc rationalization of success and then a revision of original evaluation criteria. Of course, global variation in the availability of standards and HR practices may fluctuate according to the position of work in global value chains (Lakhani, Kuruvilla, & Avgar, 2013). In the ideal type of piece-rate work, where the output can be exactly specified in conformance with detailed standards,

PMS would be more capable of being clearly articulated a priori, and market-type management of performance is more likely to take place. In the ideal type of strong firm involvement with performance management, it is likely that tasks are more complex, less codifiable, and less subject to outsourcing. An additional concern related to variation in standards is the role of cultural expectations of standards for behaviors. For example, organizational leaders in collectivistic cultures are often responsible not only for their individual conduct, but also for the conduct of the group with which they are associated (Zemba, Young, & Morris, 2006). In contrast, American leaders of organizations are often held responsible only for their own conduct. Thus, it is important that performance management standards be developed with an awareness of: (i) the nature of the tasks; (ii) suitability of the standards to measure what is within the control of the individual as opposed to what is without (to avoid post-hoc rationalization and to adjust for varying expectations); (iii) the acceptability and agreement upon standards in advance with workers and managers to ensure fairness and adherence to the criteria; and (iv) an understanding of the cultural nuances of the country in question.

4 Intervening factors

As long as individuals work for, and report to, other individuals, the type of relationship they develop can significantly impact the success of PMS. According to leader–member exchange theory, managers create in-groups and out-groups amongst their subordinates (Graen & Cashman, 1975). Higher quality interactions with in-group members prevail, with greater support and attention following as a consequence, while out-group members are comparatively deprived. In the performance management context, those individuals in a manager's in-group are rated significantly higher than those who are in the manager's out-group, even when performance is held constant (Varma & Stroh, 2001). Although this theory originated in the USA, studies of LMX performed in other countries have found similar results (India—Varma, Srinivas, & Stroh, 2005; Japan—Wakabayashi, Graen, Graen, & Graen, 1988). In addition to the social influence of peer groups highlighted in LMX theory, PMS are challenging to implement because people are subject to universal cognitive limitations that restrict the ability of performance management to be effective. Biases such as the halo and recency error(s), as well as the heuristics of availability and representativeness, substantially limit the ability of raters to give objective assessments, especially in the absence of enabling structures such as pre-established criteria (Kahneman, 2011). HR professionals in mature organizations use research-supported practices to develop detailed rating forms and scales that identify specific job duties, set SMART goals, create ratings that more objectively assess those goals, and develop dispute resolution mechanisms to address performance management grievances. Further, HR departments in mature organizations can develop training programs that disseminate knowledge of research-backed practices that remediate the damaging impact of biases. Thus, it is critical that PMS are designed with an awareness of: (i) the tendency to create in-groups and out-groups; and (ii) the mechanisms that can help overcome the tendency to create such groups; (iii) the cognitive biases that can further hamper objective assessment; and (iv) the need for evidence-backed performance management practices to combat this tendency, rather than automatically relying on a belief that supervisor–subordinate relationships can achieve an objective assessment without additional support.

5 Distortion factors

Reward systems can influence how well performance management is implemented, and attaching rewards to the consequences of PMS can diminish the developmental aspect of the process and negatively impact the integrity of the data collection required to administer an honest appraisal. In this connection, Murphy & DeNisi (2008) argued that ratings are often inaccurate because managers are penalized for providing accurate ratings and rewarded for distorting ratings. Specifically, the forced distribution of ratings that requires managers to assign a fixed percentage of team members into certain rating categories is a notorious source of distortion effects. In a forced distribution system, a manager might be required to place no more than 10 percent of direct reports at "excellent." Even in an organization with a given overall distribution of performance of all of its employees, it is highly unlikely that the exact distribution mandated by the organization fits any given department. As an example, a particularly high performing team may have 20 percent of employees who performed outstandingly. However, giving these employees the highest rating would be rejected by the HR department, which would mandate that no more than 10 percent of employees can be rated "excellent," forcing each sub-unit of the organization to fit the required overall distribution. These processes can massively distort honest evaluation, and can undermine line support for HR and performance management systems. Despite their lingering popularity, forced ranking systems are highly suspect in terms of their effectiveness at delivering quality and performance (Pfeffer & Sutton, 2006). In a global context, there is always the possibility of distortion, especially in countries like China and India, where the supervisor–subordinate relationship may take precedence over objective performance and, thus, one must be aware of the possibility of these types of distortion effects in any environment.

The above discussion shows that while many organizations may adopt systems of performance management with the best intentions, the implementation and execution of performance management is ultimately a process overseen by people: individual supervisors, peers, employees, and HR professionals. Even an organization adopting a mantra of SMART goals can falter if the localized manner in which goals are set falls short. Achieving a successful implementation of even the best designed PMS is an enormous challenge in and of itself, requiring specialized expertise in technology, data analysis, job analysis, cognitive and behavioral psychology and more, as well as in-depth firm-specific knowledge. It is well known that managers and employees often find performance conversations difficult and avoid giving or receiving feedback in a developmental light. Individuals may resist feedback; managers may prefer not to alienate an employee or fear being disliked. To the extent that contextualized generalizations can be made in a region as vast as varied as Asia Pacific, we proceed in the following discussion to examine cultural and institutional features further in order to better inform our discussion.

The impact of culture on PMSs

The critical and undeniable impact of regional and national culture(s) on organizations is an important reason for taking a closer look at performance management in a local context. Hofstede (1980) largely began the academic study of this subject, and while his original data came from the multinational operations of a single organization (IBM), the general relevance of national culture for scholars and practitioners has led to further refinements and productive research in this line (House, Hanges, Javidan, Dorfman, & Gupta, 2004). Hofstede's (1980) analysis of national culture, focused attention upon measurable differences in the central tendency of a group of workers in terms of preferences and attitudes using psychological scales, and demonstrated that there are major differences in the way people around the world tend to think about power, individualism, masculinity, uncertainty, and time. A typical observation about culture in Asian nations, for example, is that it tends to be more collectivistic in contrast to the individualism of the USA and Western European nations. The utility of such high-level observations is somewhat debatable because cultural traits are expressed differently depending upon the context and situation, making predictions challenging (Gamble, 2000). Furthermore, variations exist even within supposedly monolithic cultures, and cultures are also shaped by the nature of work requirements and subject to change. For example, one hypothesis for why Chinese culture is collectivistic relates back to the nature of work in rice production, which required extensive cooperation between people, as opposed to the individual labor required in wheat production common in European regions. The legacy of different histories of production has startling consequences for culture: in a recent study comparing different wheat and rice farming regions within China, researchers found that people in rice farming regions are more interdependent and collectivistic, while wheat farming leads to greater independence (Talhelm et al., 2014). Thus, even today, the nature of work and its requirements of independence or interdependence can shape people's attitudes about individualism or collectivism. As this example shows, attempting to describe general characteristics of the enormously large and complex region such as Asia Pacific is full of challenges. Having said that, Hofstede's typology presents a useful framework for analyzing key differences. Indeed, tailoring HR systems, including performance management, to local conditions requires grappling with challenging trade-offs between global and local optimums, as well as addressing the individual norms of workers inside an organization. One way to start is to look closely at the dimensions of national culture that Hofstede's analysis identifies—we present brief analyses and summaries below:

i Power distance: the degree to which people accept status and authority differences between themselves and their supervisors;
ii Individualism versus collectivism: the degree to which people find their identity, or define themselves, as unique individuals, versus seeking group-identity;
iii Masculinity versus femininity: where masculine cultures are defined by assertiveness, competitiveness, success, etc., and feminine cultures are known for being relationship-oriented and valuing quality of life issues;
iv Uncertainty avoidance: the degree to which people seek structure versus their willingness to accept unstructured situations; and
v Long-term versus short-term orientation: which deals with whether the culture emphasizes long-term commitments and respect for tradition, while short-term orientation emphasizes the now and here, and change is more readily acceptable.

In developing universal dimensions for the analysis of culture, Hofstede created a highly accessible way to think through various implications of how typical patterns in local variation in preferences and attitudes can influence HR practices such as performance management. Several trends regarding Asia Pacific are possible to describe at a high level. First, people in the Asia Pacific region are on average more collectivistic than people in Western European or North American regions. Accordingly, the implementation of Western performance management and rewards systems may encounter challenges. As an example, culture and long-standing Confucian as well as religious beliefs have led to a certain pattern of hierarchy, gender relations, paternalism, and egalitarianism that lead people to view companies and corporate management very differently in East Asian societies than in the USA. The possibility of seemingly innocuous or taken-for-granted assumptions to offend and alienate people remains a possibility when operating in a foreign context. The use of bi-cultural interpreters who can help translate and intermediate practices into the appropriate context may help improve performance evaluation in multicultural scenarios. In this connection, Mok, Cheng, and Morris (2010) conducted an interesting study of bi-cultural Asian-Americans, and found that those who identified highly with both their Asian and American identities could accurately evaluate a performance dossier in both the Asian and American contexts, appropriately adjusting the assessment of external factors (as is the norm in Asia) and internal factors (as is the norm in the USA) depending upon the context.

So, for example, China and India both score highly on the dimension of power distance compared to global norms, suggesting that people in these countries are typically more accepting of large differences in status and hierarchy. Thus, on average, employees in these cultures may be more willing to accept feedback from a supervisor or authority figure without the resistance often seen in lower power distance cultures, and may be less willing to contribute ideas that are perceived to go against the management view. Accordingly, if feedback from rank-and-file employees is desirable in a workplace context, additional training may be necessary to coach employees and managers on giving and receiving feedback openly. Although we have seen above that there is substantial variation within countries, returning to the notions of stereotypically collectivistic cultures, people with collectivistic values may prefer team-based, rather than individually focused feedback (van de Vliert, Shi, Sanders, Wang, & Huang, 2004) as well as training (Earley, 1994).

Next, national cultures also have significant influence on the beliefs and values of people. In terms of performance management, these differences can impact how performance is managed and evaluated. For example, supervisory evaluations can also be influenced by cultural variation. Varma et al. (2005) found that Indian managers awarded significantly higher ratings to employees that they liked, above and beyond the level justified by performance. The cultural norms surrounding appraisal often motivate this behavior, as was reiterated in a study of Chinese managers, where it was found that managers are also likely to assist employees with whom their relationships are positive, possibly at the expense of an honest appraisal of performance (Law, Wong, Wang, & Wang, 2000).

Organizations that attempt to take culture into account would do well to consider the cultural dimensions identified in this line of research and consider the internalized norms of workers in their home environments. However, the use of the stereotypically accurate measures of national culture deserves a caveat. Cultures are influenced by a variety of factors, and are subject to change themselves, as well as to variation and differences amongst individuals within a group. Further, globalization of media and freer access to global markets has changed both the economic environment and the values that youth in Asia and other places hold in contrast to earlier periods of longer stability.

While cultural differences remain a significant force and obstacle to implementing global performance management platforms, multinational companies are not powerless in this respect and often promote and attempt to develop unique organizational cultures and, in some sense, indoctrinate workers around the globe to a common set of attitudes and beliefs about performance. In South Korea, for example, performance management systems that have emphasized individual performance and rewards have shifted a traditional culture of cooperation and collectivism. Similarly, in India, the paternalistic style in which companies looked after employees is also undergoing erosion, as the culture is becoming more individualistic, and a burgeoning population of younger workers is seeking greater autonomy. In contrast, while changes are occurring in Malaysia, an upper-class element of society continues to retain and promote traditional collectivistic values, seeing the rising middle class with more individualism as perhaps a threat to their traditional positions. These examples have shown that trying to understand, interpret, and incorporate an appreciation of the value of national cultural variation into HR systems is critical, yet complex. Competitive pressures and a need to adjust to workers' own cultures requires HR to constantly adapt and improve performance management systems to address the changing manifestations of the core issues identified in analysis of culture described above.

The impact of institutions on PMS

Institutions refer to the formal and informal set of rules that actors typically follow (North, 1990). Three aspects of institutional variation are described in this section: (i) the political economy, (ii) the legal environment, and (iii) the industrial organization. Unlike dimensions of culture measured by Hofstede (1980) and performance management measured by Bloom et al. (2012), which are subject to substantial variation within a country, institutions tend to be set for an entire nation. For example, there is typically only one set of institutions and employment laws governing the dismissal of employees within a nation, which thereby reduces the amount of variation within country, while heightening the differences between countries in terms of performance management practices.

In many Asian countries, the role of communist ideology, national industrialization strategies, and import barriers that had kept out multinational firms and capitalism have diminished, and mixed economies with heavy reliance on market structures have become more prevalent. The varieties of capitalistic approach to political economy, although originally centered on comparative analysis of OECD countries, provides an important distinction that rapidly summarizes major differences in legal and institutional environments between capitalistic countries. Hall and Soskice (2001) analyze the sphere of industrial relations with respect to the level of coordination of bargaining between workers and companies over wages and other working conditions, including performance management, and describe two ideal types: (i) coordinated market economies; and (ii) liberal market economies. In coordinated market economies, firms engage in relational contracting and networked forms of organization, with collaborative relationships playing a key role. In liberal market economies, firms are more engaged in competitive marketplaces with arms-length exchange, formal contracting, and price signals. In general, Asian countries are more often coordinated market economies than liberal market economies. Institutions of coordinated market economies frequently protect workers against arbitrary dismissal, and thereby provide job security to employees. The following description of legal restrictions illustrates the relationship between these institutional features and HR and performance management.

Legal restrictions on dismissal as well as institutional expectations of lifetime employment within a single firm (such as is classically seen in Japan) may create an imperative for managing performance within the context of longer-term employment relationships than is common in the USA. The OECD has constructed an Employment Protection Database that measures the strength of employment protection legislation, and covers items including: (i) protections of permanent workers against individual and collective dismissal; and (ii) regulations on temporary forms of employment. Here, Indonesia, India, China, and Thailand have relatively strong protections against individual dismissal compared to Australia and New Zealand. So, while Japan, Australia, and China offer the strongest protections against collective dismissal in Asia, the following four countries have the lowest possible requirements for collective dismissals: Indonesia, Thailand, Malaysia, and New Zealand. In terms of the regulation of temporary forms of employment, Thailand, Indonesia, and Korea have the strongest regulations, while Australia, New Zealand, and Malaysia have the least restrictions. Because workers and firms in Asia are often shielded from short-term market forces through longer-term employment relationships and coordinated markets, performance management may occur less frequently and with less harsh consequences than in liberal economies. This leads to the possibility of what political economists call "comparative institutional advantage"—a situation in which different sets of institutions provide different types of industries and businesses with unique advantages. For example, Asian countries with high levels of employment protection may enable managers and employees to place a greater emphasis upon development and continuous improvement, rather than short-term profit. The benefit of coordination and cooperation across individuals and firms may shield workers and companies from market forces and enable valuable companies to withstand short-term pressures in order to produce longer-term value. However, because national institutions may reduce the incentive to perform appraisal in order to discharge the least productive employees, performance management in Asia may be a less stressful, but also potentially less efficient (from a profit-maximizing firm perspective), process.

A final institutional consideration is the industrial organization of business within Asian countries, and the emphasis on network- and hierarchical-based rather than market-based structures. Given the emphasis on relational contracting described above in coordinated market economies, it is perhaps not surprising that vertically integrated global conglomerates, networks of interlocking firms, and systems of interpersonal influence have specific names in different countries. *Chaebols* are the sprawling business conglomerates of Korea, *keiretsus* are the interlocking networks of Japanese corporations, and the pattern of *guanxi* emphasizes the role of interpersonal influence relationships in Chinese family businesses. All are examples of different systems of organizing economic activity at an industrial level with an emphasis upon relationships in Asian societies, perhaps sometimes at the expense of narrowly defined productivity. These practices have deep roots in the core societal institutions of their respective societies, with a basis in both family structure and Confucianism (Whitley, 1991). Consequently, HRM systems are unique in each environment (see Begin, 1997; Rowley, 1998). Interestingly, competitive pressures and increased globalization have raised scrutiny regarding the ideal type of family business management (see Tsui-Auch & Lee, 2003; Tu, Kim, & Sullivan, 2002). These pressures have resulted in some corporate governance changes and tend to enhance the role of professional managers in Asian firms. In India, a trend has been emerging over the last decade or so, whereby professionals in HRM are emphasizing more formal rational procedures for performance management (Budhwar, 2003). Despite these indications of change, the patterns across Asia-Pacific countries are hard to neatly assess (White, 2002). Regardless, there are large differences between Asian countries themselves and between Asian countries and Western countries in terms of the role of relationships in both interpersonal and inter-firm conduct, and these patterns remain significant.

Performance management practices in Asia

The above section summarized performance management: it highlighted five factors that influence the implementation of performance management; it provided a special focus on national cultural norms and institutions; and it incorporated illustrative examples of how practices in Asia are in many ways different from in Western countries. This tour through the considerations required in the local implementation of performance management practices revealed the need for adapting performance management practices specifically in an Asian context. The following section provides specific details on the customization of PM practices in the Asia-Pacific region. First, in the emerging economies of Asia, rapid growth combined with a demographic bulge of young workers has sometimes led to an inexperienced workforce engaging for the first time with a formal PMS. Millions of new graduates emerge from universities each year in China and India (Budhwar & Varma, 2013), but many of these graduates lack the requisite soft skills, and are often unemployable without further training. Alongside this, talent shortages and the continuing growth of these economies have led to the rapid promotion of workers into positions for which they are unqualified (Cooke, 2011). Clearly, the basic assumptions about the readiness of managers and employees for difficult and candid conversations about performance need to be investigated in the Asian context, and additional training may be required. Furthermore, specialized training on assertiveness skills for younger employees in countries with high power distance may be essential to developing a level of comfort amongst individuals for conversing with management. In industries at the lower rung of global value chains where labor standards are often lacking in enforcement, many companies operate their HR performance practices as a drive system based upon piece rates that have barely been modified since Taylor (1911) first proposed the system of scientific management. In the developed economies of Asia Pacific and in industries that compete at the apex of global business, cultures remain fundamentally different in their outlook on many of the features that influence performance in line with theories of national differences in culture. The importance of collectivism and the group as a central concept in many Asian cultures gives primary importance to "saving face" in potentially embarrassing situations and developing positive and stable long-term relationships with peers and supervisors. The caution that leader–member relationships may lead to assessments that rely less on performance and more on relationships is an issue that can emerge in any context, but perhaps more so in those where relationships are given greater importance. Again, no matter what cultural or central tendencies exist in patterns of psychological preferences, each individual engaged in performance management is unique and thus HR practices requiring managers and employees to collaboratively establish performance standards, give and receive feedback, and measure and monitor performance still permit an almost infinitely vast possibility of arrangements. Despite the standard set of performance management criteria, the implementation and manifestation blossoms in an enormous variety of ways.

Given the emphasis on collectivism in Asia, a brief discussion of PMS for the team environment is appropriate here. Indeed, team-based production and performance management through norms and strong cultures have been the hallmarks of Asian management. For example, Japanese management and the concept of lean management, as well as the team-based production systems of Toyota have received substantial attention globally as a best practice (Ouchi, 1981; Sano, Morishima, & Seike, 1997). Thus, while much of the literature on the effectiveness of teams as motivation has been based on work done in the USA and other Western countries, much of the impetus for research was the perceived success of the Japanese model in the 1980s, along with the later rapid economic success of the Asian "Tigers" that became popular in the 1990s. Indeed, team-based management and lean management, in general, incorporate the use of teams as part of the imperative to "break down barriers" between people in different areas. As is well known, this was one of Deming's principles of lean management, which were molded and eagerly embraced in Japan in the second half of the twentieth century. During this period, US management remained more in line with the "principles of scientific management" with a focus on individual performance and production, and was perceived to fall behind Japanese and other Asian countries in terms of performance. Scientific management adopts the view that the more narrow the job, the better and easier it is to measure, reward, and punish performance. However, job rotation in the context of long-term employment relationships ("drive out fear" is another Deming principle) is seen as a way of improving engagement with the work through enhancing ownership over the final product, and the elimination of prescribed quotas ("eliminate arbitrary numerical targets"), which helps produce a group climate in which it is safe to offer productivity improvements that might otherwise result in the termination of an employee who was no longer needed. Thus, any approach in any country in the region would do well to consider the potential use of teams as the level at which to target both production goals and performance management processes. Given the amount of work required to accurately construct reliable performance measures, an aggregation to the level of the team may not only be more practical, but also more effective on the shop floor given the powerful influence of peer groups on individual performance.

A second consideration in terms of the use of teams in the Asia-Pacific context is the incorporation of peer feedback into evaluation. While techniques such as 360-degree feedback have been increasingly popular and easy to administer thanks to technological improvements, the cultural and local context of peer evaluation matters greatly since, for example, the use of peer evaluation for non-developmental purposes such as adjusting compensation can make the process highly political.

Conclusion and discussion

In this chapter, we provide an overview of PMS in Asia, as well as describe: (i) the general principles of performance management; (ii) the contextual factors that affect the implementation of performance management, with special reference to culture and institutions in Asia; and (iii) examples of some specific performance practices in Asia.

While Asian multinational firms typically have mature PMS, local and rapidly growing firms in Asia are likely to experience a deficit of talented HR personnel and a challenge in implementing stable procedures for performance management. In addition to a shortage of qualified HR personnel, this challenge of building a mature process is hampered further by the absence of support for the role of the HR function in many organizations. HR is rarely popular, but is even less popular when performance management is the subject. Situations where organizational leadership must choose between the integrity of the performance management process and pleasing important internal constituencies are true tests of that leadership, and the balancing between short-term needs and longer-term concerns like procedural fairness and equity can challenge any organization. Regardless, the status of the HR function in many Asian countries has improved substantially in recent decades. As an example, in India, the number of CEOs with a background in HR has steadily increased (Saini & Budhwar, 2008).

On the other hand, many multinational companies and mature organizations are experiencing a decentralization of performance management along with a demotion of HR's responsibilities to line management (Budhwar & Sparrow, 2002) as part of a worldwide trend toward liberalization of employment relations practices (Baccaro & Howell, 2011). The growing emphasis upon connecting performance management with strategy suggests one way that HR can counter this trend. Since strategy requires central coordination and planning, and since increasing emphasis is being placed upon the strategic importance of HR in many Indian organizations (see Agarwala, 2003; Singh, 2003), there is clear reason for hope. From the perspective of MNCs, global standardized practices are perhaps the easiest to administer, but adjusting to—and learning from—local circumstances may lead to further soft convergence. Multinational companies may have a difficult time implementing headquarters' HRM practices in an Asian context. Here, Kidd and Richter (2001) find that institutional and cultural differences impede the implementation of headquarters HR practices in the Chinese context.

Björkman and Lu (1999), in contrast, report the successful implementation of globally standardized HR systems in China, while Budhwar, Björkman, and Singh (2009) report similar findings for foreign firms doing business in India. Despite the findings that global practices have been successfully implemented in certain situations, most research suggests that some adaptation to the local context is necessary (Bae, Chen, & Lawler, 1998; DeNisi et al., 2008). Indeed, some research, such as that by Kao et al. (1999), emphasizes a need to indigenize the management practices of organizations in Asia to adjust better to the local cultural norms. For global HR executives at multinationals, sensitivity to the key factors highlighted above that influence the implementation of performance management is essential.

Perhaps the major question for PMS in the global context is whether to adjust practices to local circumstances. For Asian multinationals operating abroad, and for Western multinationals operating in Asia, the question of "convergence" toward a standard set of global best practices remains critical. This is true at the levels of culture and institutions as well, as the OECD measures of Employment Protection have also been used in some cases to rank the flexibility of labor markets in order to advise foreign investors on where to locate their investments. The role of finance and trade in globalization has increased the pressure on firms to increasingly resemble one another and to adopt standardized policies and practices (Rowley & Benson, 2002). This leads to the idea of "hard convergence" in which the financial direction of resources to the most efficient methods of practice would imply that someday, a global set of practices might exist under which all economies and firms will operate. The employment relations system of Asia-Pacific countries (cf. Verma, Kochan, & Lansbury, 1995) have experienced similar patterns to the rest of the world, such as a move toward neoliberalism found in Europe (Baccaro & Howell, 2011), a decline in unionization (Kuruvilla, Das, Kwon, & Kwon, 2002), and a push toward enhanced competitiveness and flexibility (Kuruvilla & Erickson, 2002). The Asian economic crisis of the late 1990s also affected the employment relations policies of Asian countries, including through changes in employment security legislation (for more details, see Hadiz, 2002). Despite these harbingers of convergence, research that has countered the convergence hypothesis suggests that managerial attitudes, values, behaviors, and efficacy remain substantially different across national cultures (cf. Mcgaughey & De Cieri, 1999). The very real differences in these factors suggest that simple efficiency criteria do not exist in a format that is universally accepted by people from diverse backgrounds. Furthermore, the large variations in both cultural norms and institutional arrangements in the Asia-Pacific region makes talk of "hard convergence" unrealistic (Hofstede, 2001; Warner, 2002). Rather, in Asia-Pacific, the notion of "soft convergence" has been recently highlighted as a consequence of increased globalization (Warner, 2000, 2002). The type and scope of data that have informed analyses of comparative capitalism in European countries are not yet available at the same level for Asian economies. As better data for cross-national analysis become available on the variety of institutions, cultures, and practices, more evidence on the role of HR practices will make it possible to better assess the convergence hypothesis (see Begin, 1997; Budhwar & Sparrow, 2002).

One note of caution—it is often assumed that improving individual level performance would lead to improvements in organizational level performance. However, as DeNisi and Smith noted, this link has not been proven empirically. Instead, the authors argue that: "certain bundles of HR practices, when aligned with the strategic goals of the organization, can be used to create a climate … needed to improve firm-level performance" (2014). The implication here is that in order to improve organizational performance, organizations must identify the appropriate HR activities, more so in concert with the relevant cultural context.

In conclusion, the general idea that performance management is universally good is not questioned in a local or national context; however, the actual implementation and structural environment which surrounds the performance management practices of firms, managers, teams, and individual employees in Asia are presented here as compelling examples of how simple global "best practices" are complicated by the circumstances on the ground. The general frameworks and analytical tools, as well as the descriptive examples of research findings, are hopefully helpful in identifying the features that are most important and what to look out for when doing business in a unique cultural, institutional, and local context.

References

Agarwala, T. (2003). Innovative human resource practices and organizational commitment: An empirical investigation. *The International Journal of Human Resource Management, 14*(2), 175–198.

Amabile, T. M. & Kramer, S. J. (2011). *The progress principle: Using small wins to ignite joy, engagement, and creativity at work.* Boston, MA: Harvard Business Press.

Baccaro, L. & Howell, C. (2011). A common neoliberal trajectory the transformation of industrial relations in advanced capitalism. *Politics & Society, 39*(4), 521–563.

Bae, J., Chen, S. J., & Lawler, J. J. (1998). Variations in human resource management in Asian countries: MNC home-country and host-country effects. *The International Journal of Human Resource Management, 9*(4), 653–670.

Begin, J. P. (1997). *Dynamic human resource systems: Cross-national comparisons.* Berlin: Walter de Gruyter.

Bhatnagar, J. & Sharma, A. (2005). The Indian perspective of strategic HR roles and organizational learning capability. *The International Journal of Human Resource Management, 16*, 1711–1739.

Björkman, I. & Lu, Y. (1999). A corporate perspective on the management of human resources in China. *Journal of World Business, 34*(1), 16–25.

Bloom, N., Genakos, C., Sadun, R., & Van Reenen, J. (2012). Management practices across firms and countries. *The Academy of Management Perspectives, 26*(1), 12–33.

Bobko, P. & Colella, A. (1994). Employee reactions to performance standards: A review and research propositions. *Personnel Psychology, 47*(1), 1–29.

Bowen, D. E., Galang, C., & Pillai, R. (2002). The role of human resource management: An exploratory study of cross-country variance. *Human Resource Management, 41*(1), 103–122.

Budhwar, P. (2003). Employment relations in India. *Employee Relations, 25*(2), 132–148.

Budhwar, P, Björkman, I, & Singh, V. (2009). Emerging HRM systems of foreign firms operating in India. In P. Budhwar & J. Bhatnagar (Eds.), *The changing face of people management in India.* Working in Asia. London: Routledge.

Budhwar, P. & Sparrow, P. (2002). Strategic HRM through the cultural looking glass: Mapping cognitions of British and Indian HRM managers. *Organization Studies, 23*(4), 599–638.

Budhwar, P. & Varma, A. (2013). Managing human resources in Asia-Pacific: An introduction. In A. Varma & P. S. Budhwar (Eds.), *Managing human resources in Asia-Pacific* (2nd ed.) (pp. 1–9). London: Routledge.

Cialdini, R. B. & Goldstein, N. J. (2004). Social influence: Compliance and conformity. *Annual Review of Psychology, 55*(1), 591–621.

Cooke, F. L. (2011). Gender organizing in China: A study of female workers' representation needs and their perceptions of union efficacy. *The International Journal of Human Resource Management, 22*(12), 2558–2574.

Cooke, F. L. & Huang, K. (2011). Post-acquisition evolution of the appraisal and reward systems: A study of Chinese IT firms acquired by US firms. *Human Resource Management, 50*(6), 839–858.

DeNisi, A. & Smith, C. E. (2014). Performance appraisal, performance management, and firm-level performance: A review, a proposed model, and new directions for future research. *The Academy of Management Annals, 8*(1), 127–179.

DeNisi, A. S., Varma, A., & Budhwar, P. (2008). Performance management around the globe: What have we learned? In A. Varma, P. S. Budhwar, & A. S. DeNisi (Eds.), *Performance management systems: A global perspective.* London: Routledge.

DiMaggio, P. J. & Powell, W. W. (1983). The iron cage revisited: Institutional isomorphism and collective rationality in organizational fields. *American Sociological Review, 48*(2), 147–160.

Earley, P. C. (1994). The individual and collective self: An assessment of self-efficacy and training across cultures. *Administrative Science Quarterly, 39*, 89–117.

Fletcher, C. (2001). Performance appraisal and management: The developing research agenda. *Journal of Occupational and Organizational Psychology, 74*(4), 473–487.

Froese, F. J. (2013). Work values of the new generation of business leaders in Shanghai, Tokyo and Seoul. *Asia Pacific Journal of Management, 30*(1), 297–315.

Gamble, J. (2000). Localizing management in foreign-invested enterprises in China: Practical, cultural, and strategic perspectives. *The International Journal of Human Resource Management, 11*(5), 883–903.

Graen, G. & Cashman, J. (1975). A role-making model of leadership in formal organizations: A developmental approach. In J. G. Hunt & L. L. Larson (Eds.), *Leadership frontiers* (pp. 143–165). Kent, OH: Kent State University Press.

Hackman, J. R. & Oldham, G. R. (1980). *Work redesign*. Englewood Cliffs, NJ: Prentice Hall.

Hadiz, V. R. (2002). Globalization, labor, and economic crisis: Insights from Southeast Asia. *Asian Business & Management, 1*(2), 249–266.

Hall, P. A. & Soskice, D. (2001). *Varieties of capitalism: The institutional foundations of comparative advantage*. Oxford: Oxford University Press.

Harbi, S. A., Thursfield, D., & Bright, D. (2016). Culture, *Wasta* and perceptions of performance appraisal in Saudi Arabia. *The International Journal of Human Resource Management*, 1–19.

Hofstede, G. H. (1980). *Culture's consequences: International differences in work-related values*. Beverly Hills, CA: Sage.

Hofstede, G. (2001). *Culture's consequences: Comparing values, behaviors, institutions and organizations across nations* (2nd ed. rev.). Thousand Oaks, CA: Sage.

House, R. J., Hanges, P. J., Javidan, M., Dorfman, P. W., & Gupta, V. (2004). *Culture, leadership, and organizations: The GLOBE study of 62 Societies*. Thousand Oaks, CA: SAGE Publications.

Jacoby, S. M. (2005). *The embedded corporation: Corporate governance and employment relations in Japan and the United States*. Princeton, NJ: Princeton University Press.

Kahneman, D. (2011). *Thinking, fast and slow*. London: Allen Lane.

Kao, H. S., Sinha, D., & Wilpert, B. (Eds.). (1999). *Management and cultural values: The indiginization of organizations in Asia*. Thousand Oaks, CA: Sage.

Kidd, J., Li, X., & Richter, F. (2001). Affirmation of the central role of human resource management in Asia. In J. B. Kidd, X. Li, & F. J. Richter (Eds.), *Advances in human resources management in Asia* (pp. 1–24). New York: Palgrave.

Kuruvilla, S., Das, S., Kwon, H., & Kwon, S. (2002). Trade union growth and decline in Asia. *British Journal of Industrial Relations, 40*(3), 431–461.

Kuruvilla, S. & Erickson, C. L. (2002). Change and transformation in Asian industrial relations. *Industrial Relations: A Journal of Economy and Society, 41*(2), 171–227.

Lakhani, T., Kuruvilla, S., & Avgar, A. (2013). From the firm to the network: Global value chains and employment relations theory. *British Journal of Industrial Relations, 51*(3), 440–472.

Law, K. S., Wong, C.-S., Wang, D., & Wang, L. (2000). Effect of supervisor–subordinate guanxi on supervisory decisions in China: An empirical investigation. *The International Journal of Human Resource Management, 11*(4), 751–765.

Liu, X. & Dong, K. (2012). Development of the civil servants performance appraisal system in China: Challenge and improvement. *Review of Public Personnel Administration, 32*(2), 149–168.

Locke, E. A. (1968). Toward a theory of task performance and incentives. *Organizational Behavior and Human Performance, 3*(2), 157–189.

Locke, E. A., Feren, D. B., McCaleb, V. M., Shaw, K. N., & Denny, A. T. (1980). The relative effectiveness of four methods of motivating employee performance. *Changes in Working Life, 363*(1), 388.

Locke, E. A. & Latham, G. P. (2002). Building a practically useful theory of goal setting and task motivation: A 35-year odyssey. *American Psychologist, 57*(9), 705–717.

Mcgaughey, S. L. & De Cieri, H. (1999). Reassessment of convergence and divergence dynamics: Implications for international HRM. *The International Journal of Human Resource Management, 10*(2), 235–250.

Meyer, J. W. & Rowan, B. (1977). Institutionalized organizations: Formal structure as myth and ceremony. *The American Journal of Sociology, 83*(2), 340–363.

Mok, A., Cheng, C.-Y., & Morris, M. W. (2010). Matching versus mismatching cultural norms in performance appraisal effects of the cultural setting and bicultural identity integration. *International Journal of Cross Cultural Management, 10*(1), 17–35.

Murphy, K. R. & Cleveland, J. N. (1995). *Understanding performance appraisal: Social, organizational, and goal-based perspectives*. Thousand Oaks, CA: Sage.

Murphy, K. R. & DeNisi, A. S. (2008). A model of the appraisal process. In A. Varma, P. S. Budhwar, & A. S. DeNisi, (Eds.), *Performance management systems: A global perspective*. London: Routledge.

North, D. C. (1990). *Institutions, institutional change and economic performance*. Cambridge: Cambridge University Press.

OECD. (2015). OECD Indicators of Employment Protection. Retrieved from www.oecd.org/els/emp/oecdindicatorsofemploymentprotection.htm.

Ouchi, W. G. (1981). *Theory Z: How American business can meet the Japanese challenge*. Reading, MA: Addison-Wesley.

Peretz, H. & Fried, Y. (2012). National cultures, performance appraisal practices, and organizational absenteeism and turnover: A study across 21 countries. *Journal of Applied Psychology, 97*(2), 448.

Pfeffer, J. & Sutton, R. I. (2006). *Hard facts, dangerous half-truths, and total nonsense: Profiting from evidence-based management*. Boston, MA: Harvard Business Press.

Rowley, C. (1998). *Human resource management in the Asia Pacific region: Convergence questioned*. London: Frank Cass.

Rowley, C. & Benson, J. (2002). Convergence and divergence in Asian human resource management. *California Management Review, 44*(2), 90–109.

Ryan, R. M. & Deci, E. L. (2000). Self-determination theory and the facilitation of intrinsic motivation, social development, and well-being. *American Psychologist, 55*(1), 68–78.

Saini, D. & Budhwar, P. (2008). Managing the human resource in Indian SMEs: The role of indigenous realities in organizational working. *Journal of World Business, 43*(3), 417–434.

Sano, Y., Morishima, M., & Seike, A. (1997). *Frontiers of Japanese human resource practices*. Tokyo: Japan Institute of Labor.

Sharma, T., Budhwar, P., & Varma, A. (2008). Performance management in India. In A. Varma, P. Budhwar, & A. S. DeNisi (Eds.), *Performance management systems: A global perspective*. London: Routledge.

Singh, S. (2003). Strategic orientation and firm performance in India. *The International Journal of Human Resource Management, 14*(4), 530–543.

Srimannarayana, M. (2010). Human resource roles in India. *Indian Journal of Industrial Relations, 46*(1), 88–99.

Strang, D. & Macy, M. W. (2001). In search of excellence: Fads, success stories, and adaptive emulation. *American Journal of Sociology, 107*(1), 147–182.

Talhelm, T., Zhang, X., Oishi, S., Shimin, C., Duan, D., Lan, X., & Kitayama, S. (2014). Large-scale psychological differences within China explained by rice versus wheat agriculture. *Science, 344*(6184), 603–608.

Taylor, F. W. (1911). *The principles of scientific management*. Düsseldorf: Verlag Wirtschaft und Finanzen.

Tsui-Auch, L. S. & Lee, Y. J. (2003). The state matters: Management models of Singaporean Chinese and Korean business groups. *Organization Studies, 24*(4), 507–534.

Tu, H. S., Kim, S. Y., & Sullivan, S. E. (2002). Global strategy lessons from Japanese and Korean business groups. *Business Horizons, 45*(2), 39–46.

Ulrich, D. (1997). *Human resource champions: The next agenda for adding value and delivering results*. Boston, MA: Harvard Business School Press.

Van de Vliert, E., Shi, K., Sanders, K., Wang, Y., & Huang, X. (2004). Chinese and Dutch interpretations of supervisory feedback. *Journal of Cross-Cultural Psychology, 35*(4), 417–435.

Varma, A., Budhwar, P., & DeNisi, A. 2008. Introduction: Performance management around the globe. In A. Varma, P. Budhwar, & A. S. DeNisi (Eds.), *Performance management systems: A global perspective*. London: Routledge.

Varma, A., Pichler, S., & Srinivas, E. S. (2005). The role of interpersonal affect in performance appraisal: Evidence from two samples—U.S. and India. *International Journal of Human Resource Management, 16*(11), 2029–2044.

Varma, A., Srinivas, E. S., & Stroh, L. K. (2005). A comparative study of the impact of leader member exchange relationships in U.S. and Indian samples. *Cross-Cultural Management: An International Journal, 12*(1), 84–95.

Varma, A. & Stroh, L. K. (2001). The impact of same-sex LMX dyads on performance evaluations. *Human Resource Management, 40*(4), 309–320.

Verma, A., Kochan, T. A., & Lansbury, R. D. (Eds.) (1995). Lessons from the Asian experience: A summary. *Employment relations in growing Asian economies* (pp. 336–367). London: Routledge.

Wakabaysahi, M., Graen, G., Graen, M., & Graen, M. (1988). Japanese management progress: Mobility into middle management. *Journal of Applied Psychology, 73*, 217–227.

Warner, M. (2000). Introduction: The Asia-Pacific HRM model revisited. *The International Journal of Human Resource Management, 11*(2), 171–182.

Warner, M. (2002). Globalization, labour markets and human resources in Asia-Pacific economies: An overview. *The International Journal of Human Resource Management, 13*(3), 384–398.

White, S. (2002). Rigor and relevance in Asian management research: Where are we and where can we go?. *Asia Pacific Journal of Management, 19*(2–3), 287–352.

Whitley, R. D. (1991). The social construction of business systems in East Asia. *Organization Studies, 12*(1), 1–28.

Zemba, Y., Young, M. J., & Morris, M. W. (2006). Blaming leaders for organizational accidents: Proxy logic in collective-versus individual-agency cultures. *Organizational Behavior and Human Decision Processes, 101*(1), 36–51.

9

INNOVATION AND HUMAN RESOURCE MANAGEMENT IN ASIA

Jyotsna Bhatnagar and Shweta Jaiswal Thakur

Introduction

Innovation has become a significant determinant of organizational continuity and attainment of sustainable competitive edge. Firms, which are not innovative, run the risk of becoming obsolete and extinct. Innovation plays an important role in organizational competitiveness (Shalley, Gilson, & Blum, 2009). Given the close link between the knowledge possessed by the employees and the services and products offered by the firm (Penrose, 1959), it is difficult to achieve innovation without the employees of the organization (Kozlowski & Klein, 2000). Innovation interventions are strongly dependent on employees' human capital and behavior at work as key inputs in the value creation process (Chen & Huang, 2009).

As per Bloomberg's 2015 ranking, Asia is leading the innovation race with South Korea ranked at the top followed by Japan. Also, China, Malaysia, Hong Kong, and Thailand are included in the list of the world's fifty most innovative countries on the basis of their overall ability to innovate. India and China have gained the reputation of being the most important locations for innovation. In these countries, the amount of investment in R&D has doubled in the last few years. India and China together contribute almost 20 percent of global Research and Development expenditure. Decomposition of GDP growth between 1981 and 2004 revealed that innovation capacity had contributed in the economic growth of India and China. This has been attributed largely to the increased investment in innovation system (Fan, 2011). These markets are known for reverse innovation, as they develop frugal products for use in their own country and gradually export them to Western countries.

In the light of above information, it is imperative to examine the studies on innovation and human resource management (HRM) in Asian countries (Roland Berger, 2012). Since the last twenty years or so, foreign direct investment (FDI) to the developing countries has increased significantly (Budhwar, Björkman, & Singh, 2009). China, Brazil, India, and Singapore have emerged as the most common new assignment locations (Brookfield Global Relocation Services, 2011; Sparrow, 2012). Rapid globalization, significant region specific growth, and development in the field of HRM have made investigation of the HR systems of Asian economies an imperative (Budhwar & Debrah, 2009). The movement of multinational firms and economic buoyancy in the region adds implications for the entire Asian market to respond to innovative and disruptive technology and jobs with synchronized innovative HR practices. It is essential for an organization to embrace supportive HRM practices that can motivate and support employees to be creative and innovative (Ling & Nasurdin, 2010).

Examining this context, this chapter contributes to the literature by providing research evidence from the emerging economy perspective. It examines the research on innovation and HRM in Asian countries with special emphasis on India. Kumar and Puranam (2012) highlighted India's rapid emergence as a global hub of innovation. It makes India "one of the most important places in the world to do knowledge work" (Venkatesan, 2013: 3). To highlight the complexity of the Indian business environment, Venkatesan (2013) drew an analogy between the military acronym VUCA, which stands for volatility, uncertainty, complexity, and ambiguity, and the business environment in India. India represents a huge and mounting talent pool which Western strategists have leveraged largely through the business process of offshoring (BPO) arrangements. Multinational company (MNC) CEOs, who perceived market leadership in China as a "no brainer," however, have realized the challenge when it comes to India, rising or failing to do so may be their most "defining" strategic legacy (cf. Leavy, 2014). Nasscom-McKinsey's study states that the industry has a potential to reach US$350 billion in revenue by 2025 (10–11 percent annual growth). According to the report, the next US$100 billion would add around 2 million jobs in the sector (Nasscom, 2015a). Additionally, India is currently witnessing a new wave of innovation and growth with the launch of the Start-up India campaign in early 2016. With the advent of start-up boom, the government is attempting to provide supporting ecosystems for promoting entrepreneurship and innovation in the country. As per the NASSCOM report (Nasscom, 2015b), India has truly become a start-up nation with the creation of innovative start-ups and has become world's fastest growing start-up ecosystem, and the third largest start-up ecosystem in the world after the USA and the UK. These developments make it imperative to examine the research on innovation and human resources in India.

The first section of this chapter provides an overview of innovation and innovative work behavior. The second section deals with HR practices and innovation. The third section provides an overview of studies in Asian countries; and the fourth section focuses on innovative human resource practices in India with case studies. The chapter concludes with the implications for future directions of research.

Innovation

The theory of strategic balance suggests that competing firms should be as different as possible (Deephouse, 1999: 147). One way to create this differentiation is through acts of innovation. Innovation has been defined as a new product, process or service (or portion thereof) and includes promoting its use (commercialization) (Schumpeter, 1950). Organizations frequently "adopt new ways" of managing their workforce but not all of it is perceived as innovative. This confusion exists due to lack of accord on what an innovation is (Nord & Tucker, 1987). Innovation and innovative practices have been viewed through two different lenses. The first is the objective newness, that is, something has never been done before or in the very early use of it stage (Becker & Whistler, 1967: 463), and the second is the subjective newness, which means that the innovation is new to a particular industry or organization regardless of how long it has existed in other industries or areas (Aiken & Hage, 1979). Innovation has been classified in a variety of ways (see Table 9.1).

Table 9.1 Classification of innovation

Author	Broad classification of innovation
Levitt (1962)	Marketing innovation
Daft (1978); Damanpour and Evan (1984)	Technological and administrative innovation
Doughartey (1992); Cohen and Klepper (1996); Utterback and Abernathy (1975) Davenport (1994)	Product innovation and process Innovation
Edvardsson and Olsson (1996); and Sundbo (1997)	Service innovation
Frambach and Barkema (1998)	Organizational innovation
Subramaniam and Youndt (2005)	Incremental and radical innovation

Innovative work behavior

Most of the research on innovation has pursued the efficiency-oriented perspective which suggests that organizations adopt innovation to maximize their efficiency gains (cf. Yuan & Woodman, 2010) and such a perspective is partly a source of pro-innovation bias (all adoption is good), which exists in the literature (Kimberly, 1981; Farr & Ford, 1990). Recently, the literature on innovation has moved from the efficiency-oriented perspective to socio-political perspective (Dean & Dean, 1987; Wolfe, 1994, Prieto & Pérez-Santana, 2014). It shifts the focus of the studies to explore how this phenomenon unfolds in the real world. Many studies have highlighted the significance of legitimacy in explaining the adoption of innovation (Tolber & Zucker, 1983; Westphal, Gulati, & Shortell, 1997). Consistent with this, there has been a burgeoning interest of management scholars in understanding what factors influence individuals' innovative behavior at work (Scott & Bruce, 1994; Woodman, Sawyer, & Griffin, 1993). Employees' innovative work behavior is a key to success in today's dynamic business environment. Employee innovativeness is a multifaceted phenomenon which is determined by individual as well contextual factors including HRM (Sanders, Moorkamp, Torka, Groeneveold, & Groeneveold, 2010; Hammond, Neff, Farr, Schwall, & Zhao, 2011). Abstein and Spieth (2014) found that four HRM meta-features, namely, individual orientation, discrete orientation, effort orientation, and expectancy orientation, were associated with innovative work behavior. HR practices can also be viewed as a communication mechanism, which may indicate that the organization values innovative work behavior (Guzzo & Noonan, 1994; Takeuchi, Chen, & Lepak, 2009).

Human Resource Management and innovation

Human resource practices and innovation

Employees are the main pillars of innovative organizations (Fu, 2012). Organizations endeavor to recruit the best talent to foster greater productivity and innovativeness in organizations. Mumford (2000) has suggested two ways in which HRM activities may help in organizational innovation: the first is related to hiring, developing, and motivating employees who help in idea generation; and the second is to help employees to implement these ideas. HR practices including induction, teamwork, training, performance appraisals, and exploratory learning focus are important predictors of innovation (Shipton, West, Dawson, Birdi, & Patterson, 2006). HR practices have also been found to enhance both organizational and individual level innovation performance (e.g., Shipton, West, Dawson, Birdi, & Patterson, 2006; Jiménez-Jiménez & Sanz-Valle, 2005; Dul, Ceylan, & Jaspers, 2011; Mumford, 2000). HR practices such as talent acquisition and rewards affect employees' creativity (Jian, Wang, & Zhao, 2012). Public recognition and monetary rewards have been found to be effective HR practice for stimulating innovation (Cano & Cano, 2006; Camelo-Ordaz, Fernández-Alles, & Valle-Cabrera, 2008). The literature also supports the view that rewards or motivation augment individual creativity (Mumford, 2000) and organizational innovation performance. It has been suggested that rewards and recognition should also be given for risk-taking and problem-solving to promote the diffusion of knowledge (Von Krogh, 1998). Training is also an important factor that contributes toward innovation. Employees' ability to gain new knowledge and insights can be enhanced by exposing them to varied training programs, which will equip them with innovative minds (Nonaka & Takeuchi, 1995). Laursen and Foss (2003) in their study found that seven out of a total of nine HR practices adopted by 1,900 Danish organizations, which include planned job rotation, performance-related pay, and the delegation of authority amongst a few others, led to a superior innovative performance. This finding was subsequently supported by the findings of Katou and Budhwar (2006). The use of task autonomy and flexible working hours was found to generate more radical innovations, whereas performance-based pay and training generated incremental innovation in a decentralized organization structure (Beugelsdijk, 2008). Individual involvement and organizational flexibility have also been found to positively influence innovation performance (Michie & Sheehan, 1999, 2003). Jackson, Schuler, and Rivero (1989) specifically focused on HR strategies and identified the promotion of a creative environment as being a key to innovation (cf. Bhatnagar, Puri, & Jha, 2004). Commitment-oriented HR practices help in developing the tacit knowledge, skills, and capabilities of their employees (Delery & Doty, 1996; Lepak & Snell, 1999) to contribute toward innovation activities. These practices comprise a bundle of strategic HR practices like recruitment and the selection of potential employees by evaluating the fitness with the firm. The role of knowledge in gaining a competitive edge has been deeply explored, however, there is sparse literature on the effect of internal organizational structure on innovation and its related outcome (Wiklund & Shepherd, 2003; Kang, Morris, & Snell, 2007).

Human resource practices, social/network dynamics, and innovation

Social Network is an important variable for innovative work behavior. There is vast research evidence which emphasizes the fact that social networking is critical for improving the innovative work behavior of employees (Cooke & Wills, 1999; Dhanraj & Parkhe, 2006; DeJong & Den Hartog, 2010; cf. Xerri & Brunetto, 2011). Commitment-oriented HR practices which focus on internal interconnectedness and collaboration-oriented HR practices, which focus on external connections, both have been found to influence innovation outcomes by managing employees' AMO (Ability, motivation, and opportunity) (Delery & Shaw, 2001; Lepak, Liao, Chung, & Harden, 2006), and by developing desirable social relationships (Evans & Davis, 2005; Gittell, Seidner, & Wimbush, 2010), which are favorable for innovation and subsequently affect the firms' bottom-line performance (Zhou, Hong, & Liu, 2013). Consistent with the above literature, Hope-Hailey (2001) found that organizational innovative capabilities rest in the organizing principles and social relationships that exist between people (Kogut & Zander, 1992). Diversity is also an important factor, which contributes toward innovation and creativity and is the base of competitive advantage in the global era. Bassett-Jones (2005) defined diversity management as the combined outcome of the HRM subsystem including recruitment, employee development, performance appraisal, reward, and the behavior of managers in delivering competitive advantage through teamwork and leadership. Diversity in the workforce has been accepted as an important condition for innovation, as it widens the extent of perspectives, knowledge, skills, and abilities (Kanter, 1988; Woodman et al., 1993; Ostergaard, Timmermans, & Kristinsson, 2011).

Learning environment and innovation

Intense competition in the global market has led to the realization of the significance of innovation issues. Learning has been found to be a significant absorptive process, which is driven by innovation (Cosier, 1981). Zhang, Lim, and Coa (2004) emphasized the importance of different forms of learning for incremental, radical, and institutional innovation in any organization. Learning organizations culture has found to make a direct and indirect impact on employees' innovative work behaviors. While investigating 326 responses from several Korean business organizations in different industrial settings, they found that HRD (human resource development) can develop effective innovations to enhance their employees innovative work behaviors by devoting efforts to create a workplace that promotes collaborative learning culture and work engagement (Yu, Song, Yoon, & Kim, 2014). This study bridges the concept of the learning organization, work engagement, and innovative work behavior by looking through the theoretical lens of absorptive capacity (Cohen & Levinthal, 1990), broaden-and-build theory (Fredrickson, 2004), and intrinsic motivation theory (Deci & Ryan, 1985). This makes mastery of knowledge imperative for innovation to happen in an organization (Žnidaršič & Jereb, 2011). Learning at all levels—the individual, group, and organization level—is critical for innovation and will affect an organization's performance by facilitating innovation (Jiménez-Jiménez & Sanz-Valle, 2011).

Innovation and Human Resource Management in Asia

Most of the existing studies on innovation and HRM have concentrated on developed economies and only a few studies have systematically investigated it in emerging economies like India in Asia. HRM in emerging markets may differ significantly from that in the developed nations (Cooke & Saini, 2010).

China

China and India are both considered as important locations for innovation, especially for reverse innovation and the related notion of "Jugaad." "Jugaad" has been referred to as a coping mechanism, a low-cost innovation, a quick fix, or make do approach (Singh, Gupta, & Mondal, 2012). Reverse Innovation involves developing new products in emerging markets, which are later modified for sale in developed nations (Agarwal & Brem, 2012). The differentiating factor is that China dominates the manufacturing segment whereas India dominates the service sector. India and China are also the world's biggest suppliers of talent for companies of all kinds and hence are important countries for this study. Strategic HRM has appeared as a critical factor for entrepreneurship and innovation in China. Wang and Zhang (2005) studied the effect of HRM and its main dimensions on organizational performance with respect to entrepreneurship and innovation. The study was conducted in two parts: the first was a field survey and the second part involved in-depth case analysis. The results showed that both the strategic and functional dimension of HRM had effects on organizational performance. Researchers are in accord that an employee's creativity and innovation contributes to organizational performance (Hirst, Knippenberg, & Zhou, 2009; Baron & Tang, 2011). HR practices such as talent acquisition, reward, teamwork, and job design have been found to be positively associated with employee creativity and organizational innovation in a sample of more than 100 firms in China (Jiang, Wang, & Zhao, 2012). In an attempt to explore the "black box" further, Lu, Zhu, and Bao (2015) found that innovation played a mediating role between high performance HR practices and firm performance. Li, Zhao, and Liu (2006) reflected upon the importance of HR practices such as employee recognition and training on technological innovation in Chinese high-tech firms—part of the Asian emerging markets economy. The role of HR practices (selection and training) in advancing radical and incremental innovation simultaneously was studied in the hospitality sector in China, where the findings of the study suggest that hiring multi-skilled core customer contact employees and training core customer contact employees for multiple skills result in enhanced radical and incremental innovation (Chang, Gong, & Shum, 2011). Taiwanese high-tech firms have become an important production source for a variety of high-tech products in the global market, meaning that the discovery of novel ways to enhance team innovation through HR practices is pertinent (Chang & Chi, 2007; Han, Chou, Chao, & Wright, 2006). Diversity in the workforce also plays an important role in team innovation. Organizational tenure diversity has been found to be associated with team innovation and is moderated by team-oriented HR practices (Chi, Huang, & Lin, 2009). According to the Boao Report (2015), Chinese innovation continues to expand.

Japan

The HR practices of Japanese corporations were in the limelight and of significant interest to academicians and practitioners during the 1980s and 1990s. The practices were found to be extremely influential (Ouchi, 1981; Schonberger, 1982; Womack, Jones, & Roos, 1990), and were referred to as the "Japanese model" and "best practice" (Aoki, Delbridge, & Endo, 2014). Lifetime employment, seniority-based pay and promotion, and enterprise-based trade unions were the three significant pillars of Japanese employment relations. However, since the 1990s (after the bubble burst), interest in Japanese HR practices has declined (Aoki, Delbridge, & Endo, 2014). Performance-based HR practices are defined as "HRM practices that assess and offer benefits based on relatively short term individual business results and performance" (cf. Sekiguchi, 2013). Pudelko and Harzing (2010) explored whether Japanese managers are willing to learn from the Western HRM (in this case, American and German HRM) and what they intend to adopt. Using Hofstede's framework, this study attempted to analyze the change in Japanese HR practices toward flexibility and individualization marked by an American culture. A change from traditional Japanese HRM was indicated, though there was no reference to innovative work behavior in the study.

Japanese corporations have increased their presence in China significantly over the last decade and China has become for Japanese companies much more than just a cheap place for production. Yu and Meyer-Ohle's (2008) qualitative study reported flexibility issues in Japanese corporations working in China. Local employees describe the management style of the Japanese as highly ethnocentric and local employees voice discontent over several points, ranging from seating arrangements to incentive issues. They stated that there are questions concerning the sequencing of innovation and change in HRM between home country and overseas operations and these can be developed for future studies (Yu & Meyer-Ohle, 2008). Scholars expect the management practices of Japan to become influential again, given the way the country and its corporate sector is coping with an increasingly aging working population and have identified it as an area where Japanese management practices will become increasingly influential again (Takahiro, Delbridge, & Morris, 2015).

Malaysia, Turkey, Nepal, Korea, Singapore, and Taiwan

The significance of the superior–subordinate relationship was highlighted in the study conducted by Ishak (2005), which reported that employee innovativeness led to organizational citizenship behavior through the superior–subordinate relationship in the Malaysian economy. The results of examining a conceptual framework, were reported above in a sample of 385 non-managerial employees of Malaysian commercial banks. The relationship of five HR practices (recruitment, performance appraisal, training, reward system, and career management) to three forms of organizational innovations (product, process, and administrative innovation) revealed that training alone had a positive and significant effect on three forms of organizational innovation and performance appraisals positively and significantly affected administrative innovation (Ling & Nasurdin, 2010).

Gautam (2012) conducted a survey of 204 organizations in Nepal and found that traditional HR practices were still prevalent: 20 percent of organizations represented the manufacturing sector, and 14 percent were from banking, finance, insurance, and business services. Educational institutes were also surveyed. The findings indicated that very few organizations were using human resource information systems and some reported special HR action programs for minority ethnic groups, older employees, and people with disabilities. Although there is a realization there for a movement toward HR as a people management function in a dynamic market, yet for it to be seen as a cost center in a traditional way and innovation was not reported from this region (Gautam, 2012).

Özbağ, Esen, and Esen (2013) examined the role of HRM in fostering the knowledge capability, which leads to more innovation in organizations based in Turkey. Kim and Choi (2014) studied the impact of HR practices on employees' innovative behavior through the mediating effect of organizational commitment in thirty-five organizations based in Korea. The results reflected that developmental appraisal, external or equitable reward, and comprehensive training increases developers' organizational commitment, which in turn positively affects their innovative behavior.

Chew and Horwitz (2004) found through case study data, how multinational firms in Singapore applied strategic approaches to HRM. The findings illustrate that adaptation to local context occurs, and that the diffusion of headquarters and centrally initiated but competitively differentiated strategies across cultural boundaries is significant. There is a need for closer attention to be paid to process dynamics in designing the implementation of strategic HRM, given the concept of reverse diffusion, where host country practices may influence that of the parent organization.

Innovative human resource practices in India

India has emerged as a powerhouse of innovation (Forum for the Future, 2013). India's ability to engage in low-cost unique innovation has already gained the gaze of publicity (Rai, 2014; Prabhu & Jain, 2015). The importance of innovation has been emphasized by the former prime minister declaring the decade 2010–2020 as India's Innovation decade. With the advent of the start-up boom, India is already on the path of innovation. Earlier research on innovative HRM has operationalized the construct in multiple ways. Some have stated it as high-performance work systems (e.g., Way 2002; Hartog & Verburg, 2004), while others have referred to it as high involvement work practices (Edwards & Wright 2001; Guthrie 2001), or progressive HR practices (Delaney & Huselid, 1996; Wright, Gardner, Moynihan, & Allen, 2005, Jain, Mathew, & Bedi, 2012). An early study on innovative HR practices was conducted by Schuster (1986), which suggested that the higher the number of innovative practices, the more people-focused the philosophy of management was, and the more effective the organization would be (cf. Agarwala, 2003). The majority of the studies on innovation have concentrated on developed nations, however, a few studies have thoroughly examined the extent to which HRM has been implemented strategically to facilitate an innovation oriented business strategy in emerging economies (for examples of exceptions, cf. Agrawal, 1999; Agrawal & Thite, 2003; Paul & Anantharaman, 2004). These studies have demonstrated a focus on the positive correlation between innovative HR practices, firm performance, and organizational commitment (Jain et al., 2012). Agarwala (2003) conducted one of the earliest studies on Innovative HR practices and found that the extent of introduction of innovative HR practices (IHRPs) in an organization was the most important predictor of organizational commitment in India. Other factors studied were its significance for the achievement of organizational goals and the satisfaction with the implementation of these practices with organizational commitment as an outcome variable. The definition of innovative HR practices was modified based on the feedback of industry experts and included modification of existing practices in the organization as innovative HR practice. Agarwala defined Innovative HR practices as:

> Innovative human resource practices refers to a modification in the existing or established human resource practices of the organization, which is new to the organization as well as improved, even if the modification is by way of adopting or adapting the human resource practices of other organizations.
>
> *(2003: 181)*

Agarwala (2003) conducted the study in two phases: the first phase included expert interviews of twenty-one HR professionals and in the second phase, a survey was conducted of 422 executives of seven different organizations. India was liberalized in 1991 and to confront rising competition post-liberalization Indian organizations adopted IHRPs to advance innovation and creativity in their employees (Som, 2006). To investigate the factors that influenced the adoption of these practices during post-liberalization, Som (2006) conducted in-depth case studies of eleven firms and found that multiple factors influenced the adoption of IHRPs in firms in India such as culture and incentive structure, national environment, unionization, the size of the organization, professionalization, involvement of consultants, the leadership style of top management, restructuring and the role of the HR department (Som, 2007). The author further clarified that not all changes are innovative because not everything that the organization adopts is perceived as new and HR practices which are perceived to be new in the current context and which create capabilities and competencies will be considered as innovative (Som, 2007). The role of innovative HR practices, such as recruitment, training, performance appraisals, in enhancing organizations performance during change process was studied by administering a multi-respondent survey to sixty-nine Indian firms. The results revealed that innovative recruitment and compensation practices had a positive and significant relationship with firm performance (Som, 2008). Jain et al. (2012) conducted a comparative study of three Indian and three foreign high-tech firms in India, which revealed that there was difference in the perception of innovation in HRM between foreign firms and their Indian counterparts. Foreign firms lay more emphasis on parent subsidiary alignment and Indian MNC's focused on managing performance from within and have put in place innovative culture-building practices (Jain et al., 2012).

Som and Bouchikhi (2003) state that the extensiveness of the typology of managerial innovation has centered on Western nations and has not diffused into many developing countries and their organizations. Cooke and Saini (2010: 377) reported that an increasing body of research had attempted to establish links between HRM and innovation, which eventually add to enhanced organizational performance (e.g., Jiménez-Jiménez & Sanz-Valle, 2008). Their study reported a range of HR interventions and initiatives adopted by fifty-four Indian firms, which support their innovation-oriented business strategy. In this qualitative study, of special mention are practices such as learning and development, employee involvement, and quality initiatives. Performance management, employee welfare, and employee engagement interventions were commonly reported. Their work supports innovative HR interventions in various sectors. Of the fifty-four companies, thirty-five were state-owned enterprises, twelve were privately owned enterprises, and seven were Indian-foreign joint ventures. A key finding from their study is that the majority of firms studied have yet to develop an HR system that supports an innovation-oriented business strategy.

While research findings vary slightly across studies, most of the above studies share a similar conclusion, that adopting an innovation-oriented strategy needs to be supported by a high commitment, and high performance approach to HRM. Indeed, innovation and entrepreneurship have played a crucial part in the success of leading Indian firms across different business sectors (Khanna, 2007; Prahalad & Krishnan, 2008).

A complex resource-based view of the firm (Colbert, 2004) is an underpinning theory in innovative HR practices and their implementation in an emerging economy context. It exemplifies the social network ties amongst the stakeholders and takes a path dependent view. Even if teams move together as a group from an organization to join a similar organization, they may not be able to be successful in their new organization. They may not be able to replicate their achievements to the same level as in the previous organization, as their success in that former organization may have been path dependent on the culture and the social network ties of the actors in that organization. It may be path dependent on the systems, processes, informal culture, and social network ties within an organization which may lead to a competitive advantage. HR practices aligned within a business strategy need to pay attention to the complex adoptive resource-based view. The socio-political context becomes imperative.

Innovative human resource practices—case studies from India

A recent article highlighted that funds are now easier to obtain for start-ups, however, building a culture and keeping the talent engaged is becoming tougher (Verma, 2015). These innovative firms are combating the issue by responding with innovative human resource practices. Juniper Networks, based in Bangalore in India, needed to reinvent its strategy to grow to one that is hinged on innovation. This required the HR department to design HR policies and practices that would create a talent pool that is empowered and motivated to innovate (Boudreau & Rice, 2015). Juniper Networks concentrated on: understanding the big picture, seizing on the most valuable ideas through open dialogue and discussions, applying them in the current context, and managing the impact. They worked through using collaboration, social and informal networks, as part of their culture to provide an emphasis on innovation in the workplace through proactive HR interventions (Boudreau & Rice, 2015). Colbert (2004) argues that honoring errors, one of the seven principles of Kelly's (1994, see Box below) seminal work, is a significant part of Asian HRM, which is undergoing change and innovation. Juniper Networks honored their errors and set the system right for making the grounds for innovative HR practices, so much so that they have a competitive advantage in the market place, such that an entrepreneurial firm, in an emerging economy like India has grown into a multinational firm, now headquartered in the USA (Boudreau & Rice, 2015).

Why InMobi may be India's most innovative company?

Inmobi (Freitas & Pradeep, 2015) is today the world's largest and most powerful independent mobile advertising platform. In four months—between April and July, 2012—the company's employee base surged from 200 to 900. It has the honor of being the most innovative company in the India by Fast Companies List, 2016. More recently, Inmobi, a start-up in India, found that there were errors in their system while scaling up the operations and headcount. They realized in 2012, that they had made a big mistake around managing their people, as per Teewari, CEO. They quickly went ahead with corrective actions and for the past few years, they have been experimenting with unique, refreshing, and counter-intuitive ideas for the recruitment, retention, engagement, and rewarding its employees. Taking a cue from John Sullivian's statement: "if you focus on measure and reward performance, you won't have attendance issues," employees at Inmobi are not required to seek permission from their bosses if they are going on leave for less than six days (Goyal, 2015). There are no international travel policies and employees are free to spend it as they please. At Inmobi, if an employee quits within a month, they are given three months' salary as a quitting bonus. Employees are offered $800 annually as a learning wallet, which they can use for learning anything including scuba diving, cooking classes, or any new technology (Goyal, 2015).

Now if we refer to the seven principles of a living system stated by Kelly (1994) and quoted in Colbert (2004: 353), these were: distribute being; control from the bottom up; cultivate increasing returns; grow by chunking; maximize the fringes; honor your errors; and pursue multiple goals. The application of this theoretical framework leads to a competitive advantage, especially in the small- and medium-enterprise (SME) sector, and in start-up firms. The organization honored its errors, maximized the fringes, and are cultivating increasing returns, thus making Kelly's Principles (1994) come true. These principles as specified above, when integrated with HR architecture, provide a competitive advantage in the domain of human capital and answer the question of how innovation HR processes can lead to competitive advantage in a fierce market and to talent retention. To reiterate the above theoretical underpinning, we have examples of start-ups like housing.com, which has worked on on-boarding new employees where they were part of film-making, which was their on-boarding experience. Urban Ladder, another start-up firm, stated that each new joinee spends at least two days attending to customer calls and spends two days in the field on customer delivery. This is part of the on-boarding process. Some start-ups state that employees continue to look for jobs even after joining and closing the position. Simplilearn has introduced a thirty-day "free look period" from the date of joining. This time allows employees to understand their role, team dynamics, work culture, and the possible impact all this will have on their career. The period is an opportunity to ensure that the new hire and the company are a perfect fit (Khosla & Dasgupta, 2015).

Critique and future research direction

Studies on innovation and HRM in Asia have considered both approaches to study the phenomena, that is, HRM as a system and individual or set of few HR practices. However, the majority of the studies have opted for a small set of HR practices. Studies of HR practices as a system are still sparse. Studies with the focus on HR architecture and its relationship with innovation are even more rare. The majority of studies in India have focused on innovation in

HRM rather than on innovation and HRM. Most of the studies of innovative HR practices in India have studied the adoption of these practices with an outcome variable (Agarwala, 2003; Som, 2006, 2007). The definition of Innovative HR practices mentioned that these practices should be new to the adopting organization, however, most of the studies do not delve deeply into objective or subjective newness of these practices (a noteworthy exception is Agarwala, 2003).

It is also difficult to comprehend the difference between the adoption of innovative practices and the imitation of these practices, as hardly any study has highlighted this difference. Most of the studies have ignored the concept of innovativeness which is a key identifier of how innovative the organization is. Innovativeness has been defined as the extent to which a person or any other unit of analysis is comparatively earlier to adopt things than others (Rogers, 1983). Diffusion of innovation research has divided it into innovators, early adopters, early majority, late majority, and laggards (Rogers, 1983). A few studies attempted to bridge this gap by asking experts to suggest the name of organizations which are innovative in their HR practices (Agarwala, 2003). However, none of the studies have clarified whether they studied the innovators, the early adopter, or the early majority. Distinguishing between these categories of adopters is important to study the phenomena, however, the majority of the studies have overlooked it. Often there could be a gap between the intended and perceived messages of these HR practices (Li, Frenkel, & Sanders, 2011) and hence it is imperative for organizations to communicate the information clearly (Delmotte, de Winne, & Sels, 2012). Additionally, while organizations report having adopted innovative practices, their effectiveness is often determined by the top management or HR professionals. We encourage researchers to consider multiple perspectives to evaluate such programs. Empirical research which explores mediating and moderating mechanisms between innovative HR practices and outcome variables is rare and hence opens up avenues for future research.

Additionally, considering the importance of innovative behavior for SMEs, there is limited empirical research which examines the innovative behavior of SME employees, particularly that of service-based SME employees (Scozzi, Carvelli, & Crowston, 2005). Future research could investigate innovative HR practices in the SME sector. Literature on open innovation is deep and extensive, however, HRM and open innovation is under-researched. One of the recent exceptions is the study by Clausen (2013), which suggests that training and educating employees has a positive influence on company's innovation cooperation with external agencies.

References

Abstein, A. & Spieth, P. (2014). Exploring HRM meta-features that foster employees' innovative work behavior in times of increasing work–life conflict. *Creativity and Innovation Management, 23*(2), 211–225.

Agarwala, T. (2003). Innovative human resource practices and organizational commitment: An empirical investigation. *The International Journal of Human Resource Management, 14*(2), 175–197.

Agrawal, N. M. (1999). Managing knowledge workers: Benchmarking Indian IT organizations. *Management Review, 11*(2), 81–92.

Agrawal, N. & Brem, A. (2012, June). Frugal and reverse innovation-literature overview and case study insights from a German MNC in India and China. In *Engineering, Technology and Innovation (ICE), 2012 18th International ICE Conference on IEEE*, 1–11.

Agrawal, N. M. & Thite, M. (2003). Human resource issues, challenges and strategies in the Indian software industry. *International Journal of Human Resources Development and Management, 3*(3), 249–264.

Aiken, M. & Hage, J. (1979). The organic organization and innovation. In M. Zey-Ferrell (Ed.), *Readings on the dimensions of organizations* (pp. 263–279). Santa Monica, CA: Goodyear.

Aoki, K., Delbridge, R., & Endo, T. (2014). "Japanese human resource management" in post-bubble Japan. *The International Journal of Human Resource Management, 25*(18), 2551–2572.

Baron, R. A. & Tang, J. (2011). The role of entrepreneurs in firm-level innovation: Joint effects of positive affect, creativity, and environmental dynamism. *Journal of Business Venturing, 26*(1), 49–60.

Bassett-Jones, N. (2005). The paradox of diversity management, creativity and innovation. *Creativity and Innovation Management, 14*(2), 169–175.

Becker, S. W. & Whisler, T. L. (1967). The innovative organization: A selective view of current theory and research. *Journal of Business, 40*(4), 462–469.

Beugelsdijk, S. (2008). Strategic human resource practices and product innovation. *Organization Studies, 29*(6), 821–847.

Bhatnagar, J., Puri, R., & Jha, H. M. (2004). Managing innovative strategic HRM: The balanced scorecard performance management system at ITC hotels. *South Asian Journal of Management, 11*(4), 92.

Boudreau, J. & Rice, S. (2015). Bright, shiny objects and the future of HR (cover story). *Harvard Business Review, 93*(7/8), 72–78.

Brookfield Global Relocation Services (2011, July). Retrieved from www.brookfieldgrs.com/.

Budhwar, P., Björkman, I., & Singh, V. (2009). Emerging HRM systems of foreign firms operating in India. In P. Budhwar & J. Bhatnagar (Eds.), *Changing face of people management in India*. London: Routledge.

Budhwar, P. & Debrah, Y. (2009). Future research on human resource management systems in Asia. *Asia Pacific Journal of Management, 26*(2), 197–218.

Cano, C. & Cano, P. (2006). Human resource management and its impact on innovation performance in companies. *International Journal of Technology Management, 35*(1), 11–28.

Camelo-Ordaz, C., Fernández-Alles, M., & Valle-Cabrera, R. (2008). Top management team's vision and human resources management practices in innovative Spanish companies. *The International Journal of Human Resource Management, 19*(4), 620–638.

Chang, H. T. & Chi, N. W. (2007). Human resource managers' role consistency and HR performance indicators: The moderating effect of interpersonal trust in Taiwan. *The International Journal of Human Resource Management, 18*(4), 665–683.

Chang, S., Gong, Y., & Shum, C. (2011). Promoting innovation in hospitality companies through human resource management practices. *International Journal of Hospitality Management, 30*(4), 812–818.

Chen, C. J. & Huang, J. W. (2009). Strategic human resource practices and innovation performance: The mediating role of knowledge management capacity. *Journal of Business Research, 62*(1), 104–114.

Chew, I. K. & Horwitz, F. M. (2004). Human resource management strategies in practice: Case-study findings in multinational firms. *Asia Pacific Journal of Human Resources, 42*(1), 32–56.

Chi, N. W., Huang, Y. M., & Lin, S. C. (2009). A double-edged sword?: Exploring the curvilinear relationship between organizational tenure diversity and team innovation: The moderating role of team-oriented HR practices. *Group & Organization Management, 34*(6), 698–726.

Clausen, T. H. (2013). External knowledge sourcing from innovation cooperation and the role of absorptive capacity: Empirical evidence from Norway and Sweden. *Technology Analysis & Strategic Management, 25*(1), 57–70.

Cohen, W. M. & Klepper, S. (1996). A reprise of size and R&D. *The Economic Journal, 106*(437), 925–951.

Cohen, W. M. & Levinthal, D. A. (1990). Absorptive capacity: A new perspective on learning and innovation. *Administrative Science Quarterly, 35*(1), 128–152.

Colbert, B. A. (2004). The complex resource-based view: Implications for theory and practice in strategic human resource management. *Academy of Management Review, 28*(3), 341–358.

Cooke, F. L. & Saini, D. S. (2010). (How) does the HR strategy support an innovation oriented business strategy?: An investigation of institutional context and organizational practices in Indian firms. *Human Resource Management, 49*(3), 377–400.

Cooke, P. & Wills, D. (1999). Small firms, social capital and the enhancement of business performance through innovation programmes. *Small Business Economics, 13*, 219–234.

Cosier, R. A. (1981). Dialectical inquiry in strategic planning: A case of premature acceptance. *Academy of Management Review, 6*(4), 643–648.

Daft, R. L. (1978). A dual-core model of organizational innovation. *Academy of Management Journal, 21*(2), 193–210.

Damanpour, F. & Evan, W. M. (1984). Organizational innovation and performance: The problem of "organizational lag." *Administrative Science Quarterly, 29*(3), 392–409.

Davenport, T. H. (1994). Process innovation. *Topics in Health Information Management, 14*(3), 87.

Dean, J. W. & Jr. (1987). Building the future: The justification process for new technology. In J. M. Pennings & A. Buitendam (Eds.), *New technology as organizational innovation: The development and diffusion of micro-electronics* (pp. 35–58). Cambridge, MA: Ballinger.

Deci, E. L. & Ryan, R. M. (1985). *Intrinsic motivation and self-determination in human behavior*. New York: Plenum.

Deephouse, D. L. (1999). To be different, or to be the same?: It's a question (and theory) of strategic balance. *Strategic Management Journal, 20*(2), 147–166.

De Jong, J. P. J. & Den Hartog, D. N. (2010). Measuring innovative work behaviour. *Creativity and Innovation Management, 19*(1), 23–26.

Delaney, J. T. & Huselid, M. A. (1996). The impact of human resource management practices on perceptions of organizational performance. *Academy of Management Journal, 39*(4), 949–969.

Delery, J. E. & Doty, D. H. (1996). Modes of theorizing in strategic human resource management: Tests of universalistic, contingency, and configurational performance predictions. *Academy of Management Journal, 39*(4), 802–835.

Delery, J. E. & Shaw, J. D. (2001). The strategic management of people in work organizations: Review, synthesis, and extension. In G. R. Ferris (Ed.), *Research in Personnel and Human Resources Management, 20*, 165–197.

Delmotte, J., De Winne, S., & Sels, L. (2012). Toward an assessment of perceived HRM system strength: Scale development and validation. *The International Journal of Human Resource Management, 23*(7), 1481–1506.

Dhanaraj, C. & Parkhe, A. (2006). Orchestrating innovation networks. *Academy of Management Review, 31*(3), 659–669.

Dougherty, D. (1992). A practice-centered model of organizational renewal through product innovation. *Strategic Management Journal, 13*(S1), 77–92.

Dul, J., Ceylan, C., & Jaspers, F. (2011). Knowledge workers' creativity and the role of the physical work environment. *Human Resource Management, 50*(6), 715–734.

Edwards, P. & Wright, M. (2001). High-involvement work systems and performance outcomes: The strength of variable, contingent, and context-bound relationships. *The International Journal of Human Resource Management, 12*(4), 568–585.

Edvardsson, B. & Olsson, J. (1996). Key concepts for new service development. *Service Industries Journal, 16*(2), 140–164.

Evans, W. R. & Davis, W. D. (2005). High-performance work systems and organizational performance: The mediating role of internal social structure. *Journal of Management, 31*(5), 758–775.

Fan, P. (2011). Innovation capacity and economic development: China and India. *Economic Change and Restructuring, 44*(1–2), 49–73.

Farr, J. L. & Ford, C. M. (1990). Individual innovation. In M. A. West & J. L. Farr (Eds.), *Innovation and creativity at work: Psychological and organizational strategies* (pp. 63–80). Chichester: Wiley.

Forum for the Future (2013). Retrieved from www.forumforthefuture.org/sites/default/files/images/GreenFutures/India/India_lowres_SPREADS. Pdf.

Frambach, R. T., Barkema, H. G., Nooteboom, B., & Wedel, M. (1998). Adoption of a service innovation in the business market: An empirical test of supply-side variables. *Journal of Business Research, 41*(2), 161–174.

Fredrickson, B. L. (2004). The broaden-and-build theory of positive emotions. *Philosophical Transactions-Royal Society of the Royal Society B: Biological Sciences, 359*(1449). London Series Biological Sciences, 1367–1378.

Freitas, K. & Pradeep, N. (2015, October 7) Practices that Wow! InMobi's innovative people practices. Retrieved from www.peoplematters.in/article/strategic-hr/practices-wow-inmobis-innovative-people-practices-12223.

Fu, X. (2012). How does openness affect the importance of incentives for innovation?. *Research Policy, 41*(3), 512–523.

Gautam, D. K. (2012). Changing perspective of managing human resources in Nepal. *Asia Pacific Journal of Business, 3*(2), 23–33.

Gittell, J. H., Seidner, R., & Wimbush, J. (2010). A relational model of how high-performance work systems work. *Organization Science, 21*(3), 490–506.

Goyal, M. (2015, August 2). Why InMobi may be India's most innovative company, *Economic Times Bureau*. Retrieved August 22, 2016, from http://articles.economictimes.indiatimes.com/2015-08-02/news/65129291_1_naveen-tewari-in-mobi-google-and-facebook.

Guthrie, J. P. (2001). High-involvement work practices, turnover, and productivity: Evidence from New Zealand. *Academy of Management Journal, 44*(1), 180–190.

Guzzo, R. A. & Noonan, K. A. (1994). Human resource practices as communications and the psychological contract. *Human Resource Management, 33*(3), 447–462.

Hammond, M. M., Neff, N. L., Farr, J. L., Schwall, A. R., & Zhao, X. (2011). Predictors of individual-level innovation at work: A meta-analysis. *Psychology of Aesthetics, Creativity, and the Arts, 5*(1), 90–105.

Han, J., Chou, P., Chao, M., & Wright, P. M. (2006). The HR competencies–HR effectiveness link: A study in Taiwanese high-tech companies. *Human Resource Management, 45*(3), 391–406.

Hartog, D. N. & Verburg, R. M. (2004). High performance work systems, organizational culture and firm effectiveness. *Human Resource Management Journal, 14*(1), 55–78.

Hirst, G., Knippenberg, D. V., & Zhou, J. (2009). A cross-level perspective on employee creativity: Goal orientation, team learning behavior, and individual creativity. *The Academy of Management Journal, 52*(2), 280–293.

Hope-Hailey, V. H. (2001). Breaking the mould? Innovation as a strategy for corporate renewal. *The International Journal of Human Resource Management, 12*(7), 1126–1140.

Hoskisson, R. E. & Hitt, M. A. (1988). Strategic control systems and relative R&D investment in large multiproduct firms. *Strategic Management Journal, 9*(6), 605–621.

Ishak, N. A. (2005). Promoting employees' innovativeness and organizational citizenship behavior through superior-subordinate relationship in the workplace. *Research and Practice in Human Resource Management, 13*(2), 16–30.

Jackson, S. E., Schuler, R.S., & Rivero, J. C. (1989). Organizational characteristics as predictors of personnel practices. *Personnel Psychology, 42*(4), 727–786

Jain, H., Mathew, M., & Bedi, A. (2012). HRM innovations by Indian and foreign MNCs operating in India: A survey of HR professionals. *The International Journal of Human Resource Management, 23*(5), 1006–1018.

Jiang, J., Wang, S., & Zhao, S. (2012). Does HRM facilitate employee creativity and organizational innovation?: A study of Chinese firms. *The International Journal of Human Resource Management, 23*(19), 4025–4047.

Jiménez-Jiménez, D. & Sanz-Valle, R. (2005). Innovation and human resource management fit: An empirical study. *International Journal of Manpower, 26*(4), 364–381.

Jiménez-Jiménez, D. & Sanz-Valle, R. (2008). Could HRM support organizational innovation? *The International Journal of Human Resource Management, 19*(7), 1208–1221.

Jiménez-Jiménez, D. & Sanz-Valle, R. (2011). Innovation, organizational learning, and performance. *Journal of Business Research, 64*(4), 408–417.

Kang, S. C., Morris, S. S., & Snell, S. A. (2007). Relational archetypes, organizational learning, and value creation: Extending the human resource architecture. *Academy of Management Review, 32*(1), 236–256.

Kanter, R. L. (1988). When a thousand flowers bloom: Structural, collective, and social conditions for innovation in organizations. In B. M. Staw & L. L. Cummings (Eds.), *Research in organizational behavior* (pp. 169–211). Greenwich, CT: JAI Press.

Katou, A. & Budhwar, P. (2006). Human resource management systems and organizational performance: A test of mediating model in the Greek manufacturing context. *The International Journal of Human Resource Management, 17*(7), 1223–1253.

Kelly, K. (1994). *Out of control: The rise of neo-biological civilization*. Reading, MA: Addison-Wesley.

Khanna, T. (2007). *Billions of entrepreneurs: How China and India are reshaping their futures and yours*. Boston, MA: Harvard Business School Press.

Khosla, V. & Dasgupta, B. (2015, September 11). Startups like Urban Ladder, FreshMenu make induction fun to keep fresh hires engaged. Retrieved from http://content.timesjobs.com/urban-ladder-freshmenu-make-induction-fun-for-new-hires/.

Kim, D. & Choi, Y. (2014, December). Social exchange model between human resource management practices and innovation in software engineering. *Seoul Journal of Business, 20*(2), 49–69.

Kimberly, J. R. (1981). Managerial innovation. In P. C. Nystrom & W. H. Starbuck (Eds.), *Handbook of organizational design* (pp. 84–104). New York: Oxford University Press.

Kogut, B. & Zander, U. (1992). Knowledge of the firm, combinative capabilities, and the replication of technology. *Organization Science, 3*(3), 383–397.

Kozlowski, S. W. J. & Klein, K. J. (2000). A multi-level approach to theory and research in organizations: Contextual, temporal, and emergent processes. In K. J. Klein & S. W. J. Kozlowski (Eds.), *Multilevel* theory, research, and methods in organizations: Foundations, extensions, and new directions (pp. 349–381). San Francisco, CA: Jossey-Bass.

Kumar, N. & Puranam, P. (2012). *India inside: The emerging innovation challenge to the West*. Boston, MA: Harvard Business Review Press.

Laursen, K. and Foss, N. (2003). New human resource management practices, complementarities and the impact on innovation performance. *Cambridge Journal of Economics, 27*(2), 243–263.

Leavy, B. (2014). India: MNC strategies for growth and innovation. *Strategy & Leadership, 42*(2), 30–39.

Lepak, D. & Snell, S. (1999). The human resource architecture: Toward a theory of human capital allocation and development. *Academy of Management Review, 24*(1), 31–48.

Lepak, D. P., Liao, H., Chung, Y., & Harden, E. (2006). A conceptual review of human resource management systems in strategic human resource management research. In J. Martocchio (Ed.), *Research in personnel and human resource management* (pp. 217–271). Stamford, CT: JAI Press.

Levitt, T. (1962). *Innovation in marketing: New perspectives for profit and growth*. New York: McGraw-Hill.

Li, X., Frenkel, S. J., & Sanders, K. (2011). Strategic HRM as process: How HR system and organizational climate strength influence Chinese employee attitudes. *The International Journal of Human Resource Management, 22* (9), 1825–1842.

Li, Y., Zhao, Y., & Liu, Y. (2006). The relationship between HRM, technology innovation and performance in China. *International Journal of Manpower, 27*(7), 679–697.

Ling, T. C. & Nasurdin, A. M. (2010). Human resource management practices and organizational innovation: An empirical study in Malaysia. *Journal of Applied Business Research, 26*(4), 105.

Lu, K., Zhu, J., & Bao, H. (2015). High-performance human resource management and firm performance. *Industrial Management & Data Systems, 115*(2), 353–382.

Michie, J. & Sheehan, M. (1999). HRM practices, R&D expenditure and innovative investment: evidence from the UK's 1990 workplace industrial relations survey (WIRS). *Ind Corp Change, 8*(2), 211–234.

Michie, J. & Sheehan, M. (2003). Labour market deregulation, "flexibility" and innovation. *Cambridge Journal of Economics, 27*(1), 123–143.

Mumford, M. D. (2000). Managing creative people: Strategies and tactics for innovation. *Human Resource Management Review, 10*(3), 313–351.

Nasscom. (2015a). *Perspective 2025: Shaping the digital revolution*. New Delhi: McKinsey & Company. Retrieved October 15, 2015, from www.business-standard.com/article/companies/india-s-tech-industry-to-touch-350-bn-by-2025-nasscom-mckinsey-study-115100500913_1.html.

Nasscom. (2015b). Start-up India—Momentous rise of the Indian start-up ecosystem. Retrieved from www.nasscom.in/startup-india-%E2%80%93-momentous-rise-indian-startup-ecosystem#sthash.Yh0HrfcC.dpuf.

Nonaka, I. & Takeuchi, H. (1995). *The knowledge-creating company: How Japanese companies create the dynamics of innovation*. New York: Oxford University Press.

Nord, W. R. & Tucker, S. (1987). *Implementing routine and radical innovations*. Lexington, MA: D.C. Heath.

Ostergaard, C. R., Timmermans, B., & Kristinsson, K. (2011). Does a different view create something new? The effect of employee diversity on innovation. *Research Policy, 40*(3), 500–509.

Ouchi, W. G. (1981). *Theory Z: How American business can meet the Japanese challenge* (pp. 577–594). Reading, MA: Addison-Wesley.

Özbağ, G. K., Esen, M., & Esen, D. (2013). The impact of HRM capabilities on innovation mediated by knowledge management capability. *Procedia-Social and Behavioral Sciences, 99*, 784–793.

Paul, A. K. & Anantharaman, R. N. (2004). Influence of HRM practices on organizational commitment: A study among software professionals in India. *Human Resource Development Quarterly, 15*(1), 77–88.

Penrose, E. T. (1959). *The theory of the growth of the firm*. Oxford: Basil Blackwell.

Prabhu, J. & Jain, S. (2015). Innovation and entrepreneurship in India: Understanding jugaad. *Asia Pacific Journal of Management, 32*(4), 843–868.

Prahalad, C. K. & Krishnan, M. S. (2008). *New age of innovation: Driving co-created value through global networks*. New York: McGraw Hill.

Prieto, I. M. & Pérez-Santana, M. P. (2014). Managing innovative work behavior: The role of human resource practices. *Personnel Review, 43*(2), 184–208.

Pudelko, M. & Harzing, A. W. (2010). Japanese human resource management: inspirations from abroad and current trends of change. In R. Bubenroth & T. Kanai (Eds.), *International human resource management in Japan*. London: Routledge.

Rai, S. (2014, February 17). From India, proof that a trip to Mars doesn't have to break the bank. *New York Times*.

Rogers, E. M. (1983). *Diffusion of innovations*. New York: Free Press.

Roland Berger. (2012). Retrieved from www.rolandberger.com/press_releases/512-press_archive2012_sc_content/Emerging_markets_drive_innovation.html.

Sanders, K., Moorkamp, M., Torka, N., Groeneveld, S., & Groeneveld, G. (2010). How to support innovative behavior?: The role of LMX and satisfaction with HR practices. *Technology and Investment, 1*(1), 59–68.

Schonberger, R. J. (1982). *Japanese manufacturing techniques: Nine hidden lessons in simplicity*. New York: Free Press.

Schumpeter, J. (1950). *Capitalism, socialism, and democracy*. New York: Harper & Row.

Schuster, F. E. (1986). *The Schuster report: The proven connection between people and profits*. New York: Wiley.

Scott, S. G. & Bruce, R. A. (1994). Determinants of innovative behavior: A path model of individual innovation in the workplace. *Academy of Management Journal, 37*(3), 580–607.

Scozzi, M., Carvelli, C., & Crowston, K. (2005). Methods for modeling and supporting innovation processes in SMEs. *European Journal of Innovation Management, 8*(1), 120–137.

Sekiguchi, T. (2013). Theoretical implications from the case of performance-based human resource management practices in Japan: Management fashion, institutionalization and strategic human resource management perspectives. *The International Journal of Human Resource Management, 24*(3), 471–486.

Shalley, C. E., Gilson, L. L., & Blum, T. C. (2009). Interactive effects of growth need strength, work context, and job complexity on self-reported creative performance. *Academy of Management Journal, 52*(3), 489–505.

Shipton, H., West, M., Dawson, J., Birdi, K., & Patterson, M. (2006). HRM as a predictor of innovation. *Human Resource Management Journal, 16*(1), 3–27.

Singh, R., Gupta, V., & Mondal, A. (2012). Jugaad—From "making do" and "quick fix" to an innovative, sustainable and low-cost survival strategy at the bottom of the pyramid. *International Journal of Rural Management, 8*(1–2), 87–105.

Som, A. (2006). Bracing for MNC competition through innovative HRM practices: The way ahead for Indian firms. *Thunderbird International Business Review, 48*(2), 207–237.

Som, A. (2007). What drives adoption of innovative SHRM practices in Indian organizations? *The International Journal of Human Resource Management, 18*(5), 808–828.

Som, A. (2008). *Organization redesign and innovative HRM*. New Delhi: Oxford University Press.

Som, A. & Bouchikhi, H. (2003). Adoption of innovative HRD in Indian companies. Paper presented at The Second Asian Conference of the Academy of HRD, Human Resource Development in Asia: National Policy Perspectives, November 29–December 2, 2003. National Institute for Development Administration (NIDA), Thailand.

Sparrow, P. (2012). Globalising the international mobility function: The role of emerging markets, flexibility and strategic delivery models. *The International Journal of Human Resource Management, 23*(12), 2404–2427.

Subramaniam, M. & Youndt, M. A. (2005). The influence of intellectual capital on the types of innovative capabilities. *Academy of Management Journal, 48*(3), 450–463.

Sundbo, J. (1997). Management of innovation in services. *Service Industries Journal, 17*(3), 432–455.

Takahiro, E., Delbridge, R., & Morris, J. (2015). Does Japan still matter? Past tendencies and future opportunities in the study of Japanese firms. *International Journal of Management Reviews, 17*(1), 101–123.

Takeuchi, R., Chen, G., & Lepak, D. P. (2009). Through the looking glass of a social system: Cross-Level effects of high-performance work systems on employees attitudes. *Personnel Psychology, 62*(1), 1–29.

Tolber, P. S. & Zucker, L. (1983). Institutional sources of change in the formal structure of organizations: The diffusion of civil service reform, 1880–1935. *Administrative Science Quarterly, 28*(1), 22–39.

Utterback, J. M. & Abernathy, W. J. (1975). A dynamic model of process and product innovation. *Omega, 3*(6), 639–656.

Venkatesan, R. (2013). *Conquering the chaos: Win in India, win everywhere*. Boston, MA: Harvard Business Review Press.

Verma, P. (2015, October 19). HCL begins shift from bell curve appraisals towards feedback-based system. *The Economic Times*. Retrieved from http://economictimes.indiatimes.com/articleshow/49446096.cms?utm_source=contentofinterest&utm_medium=text&utm_campaign=cppst.

Verma, P. (2015). *Infosys* bids goodbye to bell curve for performance assessment, attrition comes down. Retrieved from http://articles.economictimes.indiatimes.com/2015-09-26/news/66907661_1_bell-curve-vishal-sikka-attrition.

Von Krogh, G. (1998). Care in knowledge creation. *California Management Review, 40*(3), 133–153.

Wang, Z. & Zang, Z. (2005). Strategic human resources, innovation and entrepreneurship fit: A cross-regional comparative model. *International Journal of Manpower, 26*(6), 544–559.

Way, S. A. (2002). High performance work systems and intermediate indicators of firm performance within the US small business sector. *Journal of Management, 28*(6), 765–785.

Westphal, J. D., Gulati, R., & Shortell, S. M. (1997). Customization or conformity?: An institutional and network perspective on the content and consequences of TQM adoption. *Administrative Science Quarterly, 42* (2), 366–394.

Wiklund, J. & Shepherd, D. (2003). Knowledge-based resources, entrepreneurial orientation, and the performance of small- and medium-sized businesses. *Strategic Management Journal, 24*(13), 1307–1314.

Wolfe, R. A. (1994). Organizational innovation: Review, critique and suggested research directions. *Journal of Management Studies, 31*(3), 405–431.

Womack, J. P., Jones, D. T., & Roos, D. (1990). The machine that changed the world: Based on the Massachusetts Institute of Technology 5-million-dollar 5-year study on the future of the automobile. New York: Rawson Associates: Collier Macmillan Canada: Maxwell Macmillan International.

Woodman, R., Sawyer, J., & Griffin, R. (1993). Toward a theory of organizational creativity. *Academy of Management Review, 18*(2), 293–321.

Wright, P. M., Gardner, T. M., Moynihan, L. M., & Allen, M. R. (2005). The relationship between HR practices and firm performance: Examining causal order. *Personnel Psychology, 58*(2), 409–446.

Xerri, M. & Brunetto, Y. (2011). Fostering the innovative behavior of SME employees: A social capital perspective. *Research and Practice in Human Resource Management, 19*(2), 43–59.

Yu J. & Meyer-Ohle, H. (2008). Working for Japanese corporations in China: Qualitative study. *Asian Business & Management, 7*(1), 33–51.

Yu, K. P., Song, J. H, Yoon, S. W., & Kim, J. (2014). Learning organization and innovative behavior: The mediating effect of work engagement. *European Journal of Training and Development, 38*(1/2), 75–94.

Yuan, F. & Woodman, R. W. (2010). Innovative behavior in the workplace: The role of performance and image outcome expectations. *Academy of Management Journal, 53*(2), 323–342.

Zhang, Q., Lim, J. S., & Cao, M. (2004). Innovation-driven learning in new product development: A conceptual model. *Industrial Management & Data Systems, 104*(3), 252–261.

Zhou, Y., Hong, Y., & Liu, J. (2013). Internal commitment or external collaboration?: The impact of human resource management systems on firm innovation and performance. *Human Resource Management, 52*(2), 263–288.

Žnidaršič, J. & Jereb, E. (2011). Innovations and lifelong learning in sustainable organization. *Organizacija, 44*(6), 185–194.

10

LEADERSHIP AND LEADERSHIP DEVELOPMENT IN ASIA

Alexander Newman, Nathan Eva, and Kendall Herbert

Introduction

Over the course of the last two decades there has been growing empirical research on leadership in Asian organizational settings (Arvey, Dhanaraj, Javidan, & Zhang, 2015; Liden, 2012). Whilst one stream of research suggests that cultural and institutional factors have led Asian managers to adopt distinct leadership styles (Farh & Cheng, 2000), another stream of research has examined the differences and similarities in individuals' perceptions as to what constitutes effective leadership in Asia and the West (Kirkman, Chen, Farh, Chen, & Lowe, 2009), and whether Western models of leadership are applicable in the Asian context (Leong & Fischer, 2011). This work asserts that many leadership behaviors are universally accepted and effective in promoting positive work outcomes amongst followers (Arvey et al., 2015).

In this chapter, the extant literature on leadership in Asia will be reviewed. First, we will examine how the cultural and institutional environment has influenced the leadership styles practiced by managers in Asian workplaces. Second, we will review research on effective leadership in Asia, and highlight similarities and differences between what has been found to constitute effective leadership in Asia and the West. Following this, we will examine the implications of our findings for leadership development in Asian organizations. In doing this, we will examine the issues surrounding leadership talent identification and leadership development programs in Asia, and analyze the gap between current and best practice. Further, we will look specifically at the role that leadership development programs play in fostering female managers and nurturing young talent. Finally, we will highlight directions for future research.

What is leadership?

Although there is no agreed-upon definition of leadership, scholars generally assert that leadership is a process of social influence by which the leader influences others to achieve important objectives (House, Dorfman, Javidan, Hanges, & Sully De Luque, 2013). The definition of what constitutes effective leadership has been debated throughout the leadership literature (Avolio, Walumbwa, & Weber, 2009). In general terms, effective leaders stimulate positive behaviors and attitudes in employees as a direct result of their leadership approach. Positive employee behaviors of performing at a higher level (Newman, Kiazad, Miao, & Cooper, 2014) and creativity (Zhang & Bartol, 2010), and attitudes such as organizational commitment (Miao, Newman, Schwarz, & Xu, 2013a) are provoked when a leader fosters engagement and participation amongst their employees. More recently, scholars have examined ethical, moral, and service-focused leadership approaches, which have been found to drive citizenship behaviors (Newman et al., 2014) and to reduce employee unethical behaviors (Miao, Newman, Yu, & Xu, 2013b), whilst still ensuring high levels of job performance (Kang, Park, & Jung, 2013) and team effectiveness (Hu & Liden, 2011).

Scholars have adopted two main perspectives when looking at leadership from a cross-cultural angle: the culture-universal and culture-specific perspectives. First, those adopting the culture-universal perspective have argued that certain leadership practices are effective in all cultures. Second, those adopting the culture-specific perspective propose that some leadership practices are only applicable to certain cultural groups and are not universally effective (Singh, 2015). In essence, leadership researchers have found support for both perspectives. There are some leadership concepts that have been proven to be effective regardless of culture, and others that have been found to be culture-specific. In analyzing the research on Asia, scholars have used both perspectives to describe the impact of particular leadership styles on follower work outcomes in different cultural samples.

Leadership in Asian culture

Asian styles of leadership

Scholars have highlighted the importance of being aware of the cultural and institutional context in which leadership is enacted in order to understand the prevalence and effectiveness of different leadership styles by managers in Asia. According to Hofstede's (2001) cultural dimensions framework, research has revealed that Asian countries are characterized by cultures with medium to high levels of collectivism and power distance (Liden, 2012). In such cultures, leaders typically take group interests in account to a greater extent than in more individualistic cultures, and there is typically greater acceptance of the leader's authority by followers (Li & Sun, 2015). This results from the pervasive influence of Confucianism, which stresses the importance of hierarchical relationships and maintenance of harmony between individuals in society (Chen & Lee, 2008). The influence of Confucianism has arguably led to the prevalence of top-down leadership styles and limited participation by followers in the process of decision-making within Asian organizations. For example, researchers highlight the greater use of paternalistic leadership styles amongst managers in Asia than in the West (Chen & Kao, 2009; Farh & Cheng, 2000; Wu, Huang, & Chan, 2012).

Paternalistic leadership has been defined as a leadership style which combines strong discipline and authority with fatherly benevolence and the rule of morality (Pellegrini & Scandura, 2008). As well as exhibiting authoritarian leadership behaviors which involve asserting a high degree of control over their followers, and demanding absolute loyalty, paternalistic leaders also demonstrate benevolent leadership behaviors through the provision of care, support and protection to their followers, and act as ethical role models to their followers through the exhibition of moral leadership (Farh & Cheng, 2000; Redding, Norman, & Schlander, 1994). While empirical research has generally established that benevolent and moral styles of leadership have a positive impact on follower work outcomes and teamwork outcomes, authoritarian leadership has been found to have negative or non-significant effects (Chan & Mak, 2012; Chan, Huang, Snape, & Lam, 2013; Chen, Eberly, Chiang, Farh, & Cheng, 2014; Wu et al., 2012). More specifically, Chen et al.'s (2014) study of 601 supervisor–subordinate dyads in twenty-seven subsidiaries of a Taiwanese conglomerate found a positive relationship between the benevolence and morality dimensions of paternalistic leadership and both in-role and extra-role performance, yet the authoritarian paternalistic leadership dimension was found to be negatively related to subordinate performance. Similarly in their study of 223 leader-member dyads in a Chinese non-profit organization, Chan and Mak (2012) found a positive relationship between benevolent leadership and both follower task performance and organizational citizenship behavior toward the organization. These results point to the importance of paternalistic leaders emphasizing their role as a benevolent and a moral leader rather than focusing on dictating work to staff.

In addition to work outcomes, the literature has identified a relationship between paternalistic leadership and employee attitudes such as satisfaction, commitment, and loyalty (Cheng et al., 2004; Farh, Cheng, Chou, & Chu, 2006; Pellegrini et al., 2010). Research has also found that the meaning of paternalistic leadership is consistent across Asian cultures (Cheng et al., 2014). Furthermore, using a sample of 543 subordinates from Taiwanese businesses Cheng, Chou, Wu, Huang, and Farh (2004) established that paternalistic leadership explains a significant proportion of the variance in followers' work outcomes above and beyond that accounted for by transformational leadership developed in the West. Due to the prevalence of paternalism in China and in India, and the relative size of those two countries (alongside other Asian countries), paternalistic leadership may in fact be the most commonly practiced leadership style in the world (Aycan, Schyns, Sun, Felfe, & Sahers, 2013).

As well as highlighting the importance of Confucianism, researchers have also examined the influence of Daoism on leadership in Asia (Fernandez, 2004; Oc, Bashshur, Daniels, Greguras, & Diefendorff, 2015). Daoist conceptions of leadership reflect a strong humanistic, value-based approach to leadership which focuses on the maintenance of social harmony (Lee, Han, Byron, & Fan, 2008). For example, Daoism stresses the importance of serving others without expectation of personal gain and being humble, and rejects traits which are often valued in the West such as assertiveness, aggressiveness, and competition (Lee et al., 2008). In this respect, Daoist conceptions of leadership have significant overlap with Western theories of servant and authentic leadership, which will be introduced later in the chapter (Oc et al., 2015). The Daoist perspective has been highlighted in recent work linking humility in leadership to positive organizational outcomes (Oc et al., 2015; Ou et al., 2014). For example, Ou et al.'s mixed-method research involving fifty-one CEOs, 328 TMT members, and 645 middle managers from private companies in China established that CEO humility is positively related to empowering leadership behaviors, which in turn promote top-management team integration and middle managers' work engagement, commitment, and job performance.

Differences in leadership styles preferred by Asian employees

There are contrasting views on whether leadership preferences in Asia differ across countries. Major leadership studies have tended to group Asian countries together, rather than explore subtle differences between them in terms of preferred leadership styles. For example, the Global Leadership and Organizational Behavior Effectiveness (GLOBE) Research Program, which investigated the effectiveness of leadership behaviors across sixty-two cultures in a sample of more than 17,000 managers from 951 organizations (House, Hanges, Javidan, Dorfman, & Gupta, 2004), clustered Asian countries into either the Southern Asia Cluster (Iran, India, Thailand, Malaysia, Indonesia, and the Philippines) or the Confucian Asia cluster (China, Hong Kong, Japan, Singapore, South Korea, and Taiwan). Their findings indicated that charismatic/value-based, team-oriented, autonomous, and humane leadership were positively endorsed across the Asian clusters without significant variation from Anglo clusters (Australia, Canada,

Ireland, New Zealand, white South Africa, United Kingdom, and United States). However, the findings of the GLOBE project have been criticized due to inconsistencies between their findings and those from other research. For example, although the GLOBE study reported that the Middle East is characterized by high levels of power distance, prior research suggests Middle East employees reported a preference for leaders who exhibit low levels of power distance (Abdalla & Al-Homoud, 2001).

Unlike top-down leadership styles, which are seen in many Asian cultures, Fukushige and Spicer's (2007) exploratory study in Japan found that leadership styles, which focused on participation, building strong relationships with followers, protecting followers from those in power, and stressing meritocracy, were favored by employees. Comparing the preferred leadership styles of 125 UK and 226 Japanese employees, Fukushige and Spicer's (2011) study later found that while British followers favored transformational leadership styles that stressed idealized influence, inspirational motivation, and individual consideration, Japanese followers favored more transactional leadership styles which focused on provision of contingent rewards and management by exception. Researchers have also investigated preferred leadership styles amongst Thai employees. For example, in a study of 546 operators and professional staff in three manufacturing firms in Bangkok, Yukongdi (2010) found that Thai employees preferred leadership styles than stress consultation and participation of followers in decision-making.

These preferred styles of leadership in Japan and Thailand, differ significantly from those in the Indian culture, where top-down authoritarian styles of leadership are more commonly practiced, and culture is heavily affected by caste, religion, family, gender, language, nationality, and region of origin (Salminen-Karlsson, 2015). Case study research, conducted by Saini and Budhwar (2008) involving two SMEs based in north India, operating in the handloom sector found that the leader's impression of an employee, which was often driven by loyalty and family connections, is the most important aspect in performance approvals. This strong emphasis on relationships was also stressed in an exploratory study by Suri and Abbott (2013), who found that in the Indian IT industry employees were closely supervised by their leader and provided with limited autonomy and opportunities to take part in decision-making. Anecdotally, Pellegrini, Scandura, and Jayaraman (2010) argued that Indian men might enjoy paternalistic leadership more than women due to the patriarchal nature of Indian society, however, this hypothesis is yet to be tested.

As prior research has tended to either classify Asia as one cultural grouping and compare it to the West, or only focus on one specific country, there is still a significant gap in knowledge as to how leadership is practiced and the preferred leadership styles of individuals in different Asian countries. We believe further cross-cultural research is needed in this area.

Western leadership models in Asia

Although we earlier highlighted research which suggests there is greater use of more top-down authoritarian leadership styles in Asian cultures, other researchers have pointed out there are more similarities than disagreements over what constitutes effective leadership in both Asian and Western cultures (House et al., 2004; Kirkman et al., 2009). They argue that leadership styles, which provide followers with support and autonomy, as opposed to more control-based leadership styles, are preferred irrespective of cultural context. This may have strengthened over the last twenty years as a result of growing interaction between Asia and the West in the business, cultural, and educational spheres. Researchers have begun to examine whether such interaction has led to the dissemination of Western management principles and influenced the leadership styles adopted by managers in Asian business organizations. For example, researchers have highlighted the importance of business education, consulting, and management training to the dissemination of Western management ideas amongst Asian managers (Zhang, Chen, Liu, & Liu, 2008). As well as a growth in the number of MBA and executive education programs which offer leadership development content in Asian countries, we have witnessed increased investment in leadership training amongst the subsidiaries of multinational organizations based in Asian countries and Asian organizations looking to do business overseas. As a result, we expect to see a greater congruence between Asian and Western leadership styles over time, especially due to the proliferation of international business and travel (Liden, 2012).

Currently, the GLOBE study reports that only two of the six leadership dimensions are significantly different between Asia and the West (House et al., 2004). Perceptions of participative leadership effectiveness differed between the Anglo and the Southern and Confucian Asian clusters, in that the Anglo cluster endorsed participative leadership significantly more positively than either of the two Asian clusters. Perceptions of self-protective leadership effectiveness also differed between the Anglo and the Asian clusters, in that the Anglo cluster endorsed self-protective leadership significantly more negatively than either of the two Asian clusters. Although research confirms that Asia and the West vary in terms of their cultural values and practices, perceptions of leadership effectiveness however, vary only in the extent to which participative leadership is desired and self-protective leadership is undesired. In other words, there is general agreement as to the directional relationship between various leadership dimensions and leadership effectiveness across the cultural clusters. These findings support the idea of universal leadership practices. Although the GLOBE study, as a major cross-cultural research project, has generated significant insights about leadership across cultures, it has also received some criticism. For example, Graen (2006) argues that the GLOBE study claims too much cross-cultural ecological and construct validity and generalizability. Further Hofstede (2010) voiced concern about the usefulness of the GLOBE dimensions in that they exhibit weak external validity against other variables not part of the GLOBE study.

Relevance of Western models of leadership in Asia

In the past, researchers were generally skeptical as to the applicability of Western models of leadership to cultural contexts outside those in which they were developed (House et al., 2004; Swierczek, 1991), especially to Asian societies, which have been characterized by markedly different cultural values than those of the West (Hofstede, 2001). However, a growing body of research has begun to indicate that Western models of leadership might be effective in the Asian organizational context (Den Hartog et al., 1999; Leong & Fischer, 2011). In the following sections, we examine the findings of research which look at the effects of different leadership approaches on follower work outcomes in the Asian organizational context.

We start by examining three distinct leadership styles, which have been shown to have significant effects on individual and organizational performance: transformational (Bass, 1985), participative (empowering) leadership, and shared/distributed leadership. Such theories have dominated the Western leadership literature since their development. Following this, we examine literature on value-based theories of leadership such as ethical leadership, servant leadership, and authentic leadership, which have gained increasing popularity since the turn of the millennium. These leadership theories do not simply focus on leadership effectiveness as measured by financial performance, but examine the effectiveness of leadership in terms of its effectiveness in reducing unethical behavior and promoting pro-social behavior. Finally, we highlight work that has taken a contingency perspective to determine in which situations different leadership styles are effective. Contingency theories of leadership (Fielder, 1964; Hersey & Blanchard, 1969) suggest that the effectiveness of leadership is dependent on the situation in which it is enacted and the characteristics of followers.

Transformational leadership

Transformational leadership refers to a leadership style in which leaders act as role models to their followers (idealized influence), stimulate and encourage creativity in their followers (intellectual stimulation), provide followers with a sense of purpose in their job (inspirational motivation), and provide them with support and mentoring (individualized consideration) (Bass & Avolio, 1994; Bass, 1998). There is growing evidence that transformational leadership is universally accepted and effective across cultures (Bass, 1997; Den Hartog et al., 1999; Leong & Fischer, 2011). Research has shown transformational leadership is effective in enhancing follower work behavior and attitudes in countries such as China (Bai, Li, & Xi, 2012; Wang, Law, Hackett, Wang, & Chen, 2005), Singapore (Avolio, Zhu, Koh, & Bhatia, 2004; Koh, Steers, & Terborg, 1995), India (Cappelli, Singh, Singh, & Useem, 2010), Thailand (Mitchie & Zumitzavan, 2012), Hong Kong (Schaubroeck, Lam, & Peng, 2011), Malaysia (Jogulu & Ferkins, 2012) and Korea (Hur, van de Berg, & Wilderom, 2011; Shin & Zhou, 2003). For example, it has been found to enhance performance (Wang et al., 2005), organizational commitment (Koh et al., 1995), and creativity (Shin & Zhou, 2003).

However, recent research points out that transformational leadership may not be effective in all situations. For example, in a study of 318 supervisor–subordinate dyads from a manufacturing organization in China, Zhu, Newman, Miao, and Hooke (2013) established that as well as having positive effects on the work outcomes of followers through heightening their affective trust in their leader, transformational leadership might also have a negative effect on job performance through making them more dependent on their leader (as measured by cognitive trust). Moreover, using a sample of 112 R&D teams from seven industrial parts manufacturers in Japan, Ishikawa's (2012) survey findings revealed that transformational leadership led to team cultures in which divergence from group norms was discouraged. This, in turn, led to fewer innovative ideas and no performance increment. Finally, Palrecha Spangler, and Yammarino (2012) found that, when controlling for indigenous leadership styles, transformational leadership did not predict follower performance in an Indian rural development organization.

Currently limited research on transformational leadership has been undertaken in the Middle East. Transformational leadership, which requires employee involvement, was previously seen as inappropriate due to the hierarchical culture which arose from the Bedouin tribal codes of loyalty (Hickson & Pugh, 1995; Robertson, Al-Habib, Al-Khatib, & Lanoue, 2001). As a result, top-down leadership models (e.g., transactional, authoritarianism) have tended to be preferred in Middle Eastern organizations (Shahin & Wright, 2004). Scholars have started to argue that with the proliferation of expatriate employees in the Middle East and a growing younger globally aware workforce, the implementation of Western styles of leadership are becoming more common to cater for the individualistic values held by these groups (Murphy, 2002). Studies such as Sheikh, Newman, and Al Azzeh (2013) have demonstrated that transformational leadership can be used to increase job involvement in the Middle East. However, it should be noted that this relationship was stronger for those who have high levels of collectivism as well as low levels of uncertainty avoidance.

Recent meta-analytical research has also shown that societal culture influences the extent to which leaders engage in transformational leadership behavior (Leong & Fischer, 2011). More specifically, they found that transformational leadership behaviors were more widely used in countries with low levels of power distance than those with high levels of power distance (as in Asia).

Participative (empowering) leadership

Growing research has also examined the effectiveness of leadership styles which stress follower participation in decision-making in the Asian cultural context (Huang, Shi, Zhang, & Cheung, 2006; Huang, Iun, Liu, & Gong, 2010; Miao et al., 2013a; 2014; Newman et al., 2014; Zhang & Bartol, 2010). There is general agreement that a participative or empowering leadership style will lead employees to exhibit higher levels of commitment (Huang et al., 2006; Miao et al., 2013a), perform to a higher level (Huang et al., 2010; Newman et al., 2014), and be more creative (Zhang & Bartol, 2010). Participative leadership has also been shown to be beneficial in some Middle Eastern countries such as Qatar, Kuwait, and Turkey (Kabasakal & Dastmalchian, 2001; Pasa, Kabasakal, & Bodur, 2001). Amongst Indian employees, participative leadership has also found to be more effective than instrumental leadership (task oriented and close monitoring) in enhancing satisfaction with supervisor, but not job performance (Mulki, Caemmerer, & Heggde, 2015). Although some work has been conducted in other countries, most of the work on participative leadership has been conducted in the Chinese organizational context. As yet, limited work has been conducted in other countries to confirm the generalizability of research findings to other Asian cultures.

Shared/distributed leadership

Traditionally, leadership has been viewed as a role which is undertaken by just one individual. However, recent meta-analytical research suggests that shared leadership may account for the unique variance in team outcomes after taking into account vertical leadership (Nicolaides et al., 2014; Wang, Waldman, & Zhen, 2014b). In contrast to vertical modes of leadership, which take place through a top-down influence, shared leadership refers to a collaborative team process where leadership is carried out by the team as a whole, rather than solely by a designated individual (Ensley, Hmieleski, & Pearce, 2006; Zander & Butler, 2010).

Recent research by Herbert, Mockaitis, and Zander (2014) has revealed similarly positive perceptions of shared leadership in the East and West. The survey results drawn from 357 globally dispersed student team members revealed that despite significant differences across regional groupings on horizontal and vertical individualism and collectivism cultural values, differences in regards to perceptions about shared leadership were not that large. Although Asian respondents did not significantly differ in their preferences for shared leadership from Anglo and European respondents, they differed significantly from the African and Latin American groups, preferring shared leadership less than either of these groups. These findings suggest that Asians prefer shared leadership as much as Anglo and European team members do, but not to the extent of African and Latin American team members. The results of this study indicate that Asians and non-Asians should be willing to engage in shared leadership behaviors, allowing more efficient use of expertise and skills through increasing the effectiveness of leadership by distributing leadership roles to those most capable.

Servant leadership

Servant leadership refers to a leadership style in which leaders set aside their self-interest and altruistically work for the betterment of their followers (Parris & Peachey 2013). There is growing evidence highlighting the effectiveness of servant leadership styles in Asian cultures. Prior work has examined the effects of servant leadership in both China (Han, Kakabadse, & Kakabadse, 2010; Hu & Liden, 2011; Miao, Newman, & Huang, 2014; Zhang, Kwan, Everett, & Jian, 2012b) and Indonesia (Pekerti & Sendjaya, 2010; Sendjaya & Pekerti, 2010). Such work has been found to have a positive influence on followers' organizational commitment, team effectiveness, and work–family enrichment.

Ethical leadership

Ethical leadership has been defined as "the demonstration of normatively appropriate conduct through personal actions and interpersonal relationships, and the promotion of such conduct to followers through two-way communication, reinforcement, and decision-making" (Brown, Trevino, & Harrison, 2005: 120). Previous studies have found it to lead to positive work outcomes amongst employees in both China (Li, Xu, Tu, & Lu, 2014; Liu, Kwan, Fu, & Mao, 2013; Miao et al., 2013b; Newman et al., 2014; Tu & Lu, 2013) and Korea (Kang, Park, & Jung, 2013; Shin, 2012). For example, it has been found to lead to higher levels of job performance (Kang et al., 2013; Liu et al., 2013), innovative behavior (Tu & Lu, 2013), citizenship behavior (Newman et al., 2014; Shin, 2012), well-being (Li et al., 2014), and to reduce unethical behavior (Miao et al., 2013b).

Authentic leadership

Authentic leadership refers to a leadership style that is honest and ethical, and consistent with the leaders' personality and core values (George, 2003). Researchers have found strong evidence of its positive effects on work outcomes in countries such as China (Wang, Sui, Luthans, Wang, & Wu, 2014a), Singapore (Toor & Ofori, 2009), and Taiwan (Hirst, Walubwa, Aryee, Butarbu-tar, & Chen, 2015; Hsiung, 2012). Although researchers have noticed some differences as to how authentic leadership is practiced in Asia (Zhang et al., 2012a), it has been found to be positively related to followers' job performance (Wang et al., 2014a), citizenship behavior (Hirst et al., 2015), well-being (Toor & Ofori, 2009), and voice behavior (Hsiung, 2012).

Adopting a contingency perspective

As highlighted above, there is growing recognition that Western models of leadership might work effectively in Asian organizational settings. However, a growing body of research highlights the importance of adopting a contingency perspective to understand when and for whom different styles of leadership might be most effective. Contingency theories of leadership posit that successful leadership depends upon the characteristics of the situation and the characteristics of the follower (Fielder, 1964; Hersey & Blanchard, 1969). For example, drawing on survey data from 398 employees working in Chinese hotels, Newman and Butler (2014) found that the effects of transformational leadership on followers' organizational commitment were stronger for followers low in power distance and high in uncertainty avoidance and collectivism. Similarly, drawing on survey data from 560 followers and 174 leaders in China and United States, Kirkman et al. (2009) found that followers with low levels of power distance responded more positively to transformational leadership than those with high levels of power distance. Based on survey data from 171 subordinate–supervisor dyads in China, Chen and Aryee (2007) also highlighted the importance of adopting a contingency perspective. Their findings revealed that leadership styles, which stress follower participation, had stronger effects on the work outcomes of employees low in traditionality than those high in traditionality. Together such findings highlight the importance of taking into account within-culture variation in followers' cultural values, when examining the effectiveness of different leadership styles.

Leadership development in Asia

There is an increasing realization amongst Asian organizations that in order to compete effectively in a globalized market there needs to be a greater focus on leadership development in order for managers to build relevant leadership competencies. An increasing number of organizations are creating their own leadership development programs or encouraging their employees to take part in education and training outside of the organization. The following section will outline current leadership and management development practices in Asian organizations and current best practices. The research on leadership development in Asia is currently sparse, providing ample opportunities for scholars to address these gaps.

Current leadership development practice in Asia

Leadership development is incredibly important in Asia due to increased competition between domestic organizations and foreign multinationals establishing themselves in Asia (Huang, 2013; Tatli, Vassilopoulou, & Özbilgin, 2013). As local managers will generally have a greater understanding of the country's operating environment, a premium is put on hiring and developing local employees with leadership potential. One of the biggest issues facing Asian leadership development is the effective management of high-potential young executives to ensure that the most promising talent remains in the organization (Agrawal, Khatri, & Srinivasan, 2012). Having strong leadership development programs for young executives has been one strategy used to ensure the best talent stays within Asian companies (Kaye & Jordan-Evans, 2014). For example, Turner Broadcasting International, a television broadcaster in Asia, has developed a number of Asia-specific leadership development programs which allow senior executives to mentor and monitor the development of their high-potential employees to ensure they are given the right training before they are promoted into senior roles (Dunnagan, Maragakis, Schneiderjohn, Turner, & Vance, 2013).

Young Asian employees are now favoring leadership styles that are more similar to those valued in the West than their predecessors. This is driven from greater exposure to global business culture through a rise in social media and global news outlets, Western education, and the influence of the US MBA model (Cooke & Saini, 2012; Liden, 2012). This has meant the traditional Asian leadership approach of command and control will not be as effective as it has been in the past. In managing a generationally diverse workforce in Asia, managers also need to be aware of how they should engage differently with the younger generation of employees. As with the younger generation in the West, there is a tendency for the younger Asian generation to be impatient and demanding, and more willing to participate in decision-making and seek greater empowerment and autonomy than previous generations (Weldon & Chow, 2005).

To develop the younger generation, many leading Asian organizations focus on rotational assignments or "stretch" assignments, where employees are sent to an office in another country to learn the culture, language, customs, and business behaviors of that country (Huang, 2013; Stahl et al., 2012). The aim is to help aspiring leaders to develop a global perspective and foster diverse networks. These opportunities have been seen to be more effective than traditional classroom training programs. Organizations such as PricewaterhouseCoopers (PwC) are hiring young Chinese graduates and training them in the United States for two to three years, before sending them back to managerial positions in China (Stahl et al., 2012). This process has worked for younger employees partly because of the cultural convergence between East and West (Mahbubani, 2014).

Although great advances have been made in leadership development in Asia, where Asian organizations are falling behind Western organizations is in their dearth of investment in formal leadership development programs. Research by Mercer (2013) analyzed the difference in dollars spent by Asian companies on leadership development compared to that of US companies. Only a third of Asian companies surveyed were spending over US$5,000 per employee on leadership development, whereas US companies were spending over US$12,000 per employee on average. Seventy-one percent of the Asian companies surveyed stated that although funds were not a barrier to developing leaders, time constraints were a bigger hindrance (45 percent). Even though organizations across the globe have similar access to talent development methodologies, technology, and leadership development programs (Gentry, Eckert, Munusamy, Stawiski, & Martin, 2014), many Asian organizations do not prioritize the development of their people. This trend is consistent across studies that have shown senior leaders do not spend enough time developing employees underneath them (e.g., Choi, Yoon, & Jeung, 2012).

Key improvement areas in leadership development

Recent research from Gentry, Eckert, Munusamy, Stawiski, and Martin (2014) has shown that the challenges that Asian leaders need to be trained for do not differ significantly from those faced by Western leaders. In terms of leadership development, skills such as inspiring others, developing employees, leading a team, developing managerial effectiveness, and guiding change were needed in leaders regardless of the political, cultural, economic, and social contexts in which they were situated. In particular, leading a team was the most frequent leadership development competency that was needed regardless of culture. This is consistent with the findings of the GLOBE study, which demonstrated strong similarities in preferred leadership approaches in the West and the East (House et al., 2004). Similar findings have been reported across other studies showing that there is general agreement as to the required leadership skills and abilities between Asia and the rest of the globe (Choi et al., 2012; Fisher, 2011).

Despite these similarities in preferred leadership styles, there are differences between what is actually taught in leadership development programs in Asia and the West. Asian leadership development programs have tended to focus on tangible outcomes through the provision of classroom training, development plans, and overseas assignments. These practices are more regularly implemented in Asian organizations rather than practices aimed at the development of soft skills such as mentoring, and internal and external leadership coaching (Mercer, 2013). When looking at leadership research, coaching, developing an inspiring vision, and working with employees are seen as hallmarks of great leadership (Collins, 2005), and are required in leadership development programs (Eva & Sendjaya, 2013). Further, scholars have argued that leadership development programs do not have to be culture specific. Rather, it may be more important to tailor the leadership development program to the organization and the markets in which they operate, rather than a specific culture (Darby, 2015; Dunnagan et al., 2013). Overall, this research suggests that a shift in thinking in Asian leadership development may be required to focus more on the development of others first, rather than the development of the bottom line.

One of the key success factors in leadership development programs is mentoring from senior managers. Mentoring has been consistently shown as one of the major components of effective leadership and one-on-one mentoring can have a profound effect on employees (Lester, Hannah, Harms, Vogelgesang, & Avolio, 2011). However, the social and emotional distance between managers and employees due to cultural norms in Asian countries (Liden, 2012) has previously been a barrier to the success of these programs. A recent study from Choi et al. (2012) in Korea shows a shift in thinking, and Western-trialed forms of leadership development, which have previously been met with resistance from Asian employees, are now starting to have a significant effect on employees. Specifically, programs such as mentoring, 360-degree feedback, and action learning are now being utilized with positive outcomes in Asian organizations (Choi et al., 2012). An example of this is Citibank Asia which has an established leadership program that focuses on leadership training specific to the leadership challenges in their organization. Internal senior managers run the program and emphasize the importance of leaders developing leaders within the company. As part of their performance system, Citibank Asia managers must mentor at least one junior employee at any given time. Through this, they have been able to create a continuous culture of leadership mentoring throughout the organization (Dunnagan et al., 2013).

Finally, one of the key improvement areas in leadership development in Asia is the development of female leaders (Tatil et al., 2013). As with the rest of the world, the percentage of females in leadership positions is quite low in Asia (Stahl et al., 2012). There has been limited implementation of diversity practices that encourage women to seek leadership positions and support them once in such positions (Tatil et al., 2013). According to recent research, currently less than a third of Asian organizations have a strategy in place to foster the development of female leaders. In addition, those organizations that did have a strategy in place still had significant issues with female representation in the top 100 positions in the company, with most reporting that females hold less than 15 percent of these positions (Mercer, 2013). One of the key reasons behind this under-representation is that there are significant barriers preventing females from making the transition into leadership roles in Asian organizations. In response, scholars have argued that this is due to the patriarchal nature of Asian cultures (Thompson, 2002). For example, Confusion patriarchal values solidify traditional gender roles in China, which in turn shape work–life balance, recruitment, and promotion practices. These act as barriers for females to advance into leadership programs, and if they achieve a leadership position, can also hinder their opportunities to access further training (Leung, 2002; Turner, 2006).

Further, a recent exploratory study by Aaltio and Huang (2007) showed that the importance of *guanxi* in Chinese business hinders women's development into leadership positions as family commitments often conflict with the opportunity they have to build *guanxi*. These barriers also extend to Singapore (Chi-Ching, 1992), Thailand (Lawler, 1996), and Taiwan (Wua, Huang, & Khuang, 2010). Mixed-methods research in South Korea further showed that even when women reach managerial roles, being part of a patriarchal organization would significantly hinder their opportunities for training and development (Rowley, Kang, & Lim, 2016). Although this research sheds light on the lack of opportunities for females to move into leadership roles and then a lack of leadership development training, a greater understanding of how this can be rectified is needed in the literature.

Future research directions

Although research on leadership in Asia has grown over the last two decades (Avery et al., 2015; Liden 2012), there are still significant gaps in our understanding of how leadership is perceived, implemented, and developed in Asia. First, researchers should begin to accept that not all Asian employees are the same. Existing studies still tend to classify Asia as one entity and compare it to the West, or research a particular leadership model in one Asian county. Scholars need to start examining the differences between Asian countries in their preferred styles of leadership to help managers understand the differences between leading in one Asian country from another.

The research on Asian specific leadership approaches, such as paternalistic leadership, has been encouraging. However, one of the prominent issues in paternalistic leadership research going forward is that the existing studies are narrowly focused on China and Chinese values, with very few studies looking at other Asian countries (Salminen-Karlsson, 2015). As India is the seventh largest country by area and the second largest in population, we believe that more research needs to examine the effects of paternalistic leadership on Indian employees. This is in light of recent research, which shows that paternalistic leadership has been effective when used with young Indian software professionals (Salminen-Karlsson, 2015; Raghuram, 2011). Further, as Pellegrini et al. (2010) argued that female employees would prefer paternalistic leadership less than male employees, future research might examine whether females respond to the use of paternalistic leadership more negatively than males. Researchers might also look at whether Western leaders are able to effectively use Asian leadership approaches when managing Asian employees.

As transformational leadership has already been shown to be effective in many Asian cultures (e.g., Bai et al., 2012; Shin & Zhou, 2003), future research on this style of leadership might focus on specific countries such as the Middle East, as little leadership research has been conducted here relative to the rest of Asia. As top-down leadership styles have traditionally been preferred in the Middle East in the past (Shahin & Wright, 2004), understanding how leadership styles such as transformational or participative leadership are received in the Middle East would be of great interest.

Servant and ethical leadership are now starting to establish themselves as popular leadership approaches in the West. Although prior research has been conducted in organizational contexts outside of Asia, only a few studies have started to explore their effectiveness in Asian countries such as China (Miao et al., 2014; Newman et al., 2014), Indonesia (Sendjaya & Pekerti, 2010), and Korea (Shin, 2012). As these leadership approaches differ greatly from traditional top-down leadership approaches, future research needs to examine the applicability of these leadership approaches in greater detail across Asia. One such area of interest is the link between Daoism and the development of servant and authentic leaders. For example, as Daoism stresses the importance of serving others without expectation of personal gain and being humble (Lee et al., 2008), we would expect that Daoist values might foster the development of servant and authentic leaders.

Leadership development in Asia is currently under-researched and needs further attention from scholars. Longitudinal studies highlighting the effects of different approaches to leadership development in Asia will give greater insight into what is currently working in Asian countries and how the content of leadership development programs differs from that in the West. Specifically, it will be of interest to both scholars and organizations to examine how organizations can use leadership development programs to retain their most talented employees. As highlighted earlier, one successful element of Western leadership programs, mentoring and coaching, is not as widely used in Asian leadership development programs (Liden, 2012). As mentoring and coaching are seen as effective ways to develop the leadership capacities of employees (Collins, 2005; Lester et al., 2011), understanding how coaching and mentoring work in Asian organizations is an important area for future research. In addition, we call on leadership scholars to understand how organizations may reduce the barriers for female employees to access leadership training and be promoted into leadership positions.

Conclusion

This chapter has provided a snap shot of leadership and leadership development research in Asia. The chapter examined Asian styles of leadership such as paternalistic leadership and the influence of Confucianism and Daoism on leadership, and highlighted some key differences in leadership between Asian countries. Western leadership ideas that have been introduced in Asia were then reviewed, and it was found that many follower-oriented leadership styles, such as transformational, servant, ethical, and participative leadership are effective in the Asian cultural context. The chapter then went on to address how leaders are being developed in Asia and where key areas of improvement lie. Current examples of leadership development practice were discussed with a focus on mentoring and stretch assignments. Specifically, female leadership development and junior staff leadership development were stressed as key areas that need to be addressed by organizations and researchers alike. Finally, a summary of future research directions was provided with an emphasis placed on greater research on the differences between Asian countries, under-researched regions such as the Middle East and India, analyzing new leadership approaches, such as ethical and servant leadership, and the importance of research on leadership development in Asia.

References

Aaltio, I. & Huang, A. J. (2007). Women managers' careers in information technology in China: High flyers with emotional costs?. *Journal of Organizational Change Management, 20*(2), 227–244.

Abdalla, I. A. & Al-Homoud, M. A. (2001). Exploring the implicit leadership theory in the Arabian Gulf States. *Applied Psychology: An International Review, 50*(4), 506–531.

Agrawal, N. M., Khatri, N., & Srinivasan, R. (2012). Managing growth: Human resource management challenges facing the Indian software industry. *Journal of World Business, 47*(2), 159–166.

Arvey, R., Dhanaraj, C., Javidan, M., & Zhang, Z. X. (2015). Are there unique leadership models in Asia?: Exploring unchartered territory. *The Leadership Quarterly, 26*, 1–6.

Avolio, B. J., Zhu, W., Koh, W., & Bhatia, P. (2004). Transformational leadership and organizational commitment: Mediating role of psychological empowerment and moderating role of structural distance. *Journal of Organizational Behavior, 25*(8), 951–968.

Avolio, B. J., Walumbwa, F. O., & Weber, T. J. (2009). Leadership: Current theories, research, and future directions. *Annual Review of Psychology, 60*(1), 421–449.

Aycan, Z., Schyns, B., Sun, J., Felfe, J., & Sahers, N. (2013). Convergence and divergence of paternalistic leadership: A cross-cultural investigation of prototypes. *Journal of International Business Studies, 44*(9), 962–969.

Bai, Y., Li, P. P., & Xi, Y. (2012). The distinctive effects of dual-level leadership behaviors on employees' trust in leadership: An empirical study from China. *Asia Pacific Journal of Management, 29*(2), 213–237.

Bass, B. M. (1985). *Leadership and performance beyond expectations.* New York: Free Press.

Bass, B. M. (1997). Does the transactional–transformational leadership paradigm transcend organizational and national boundaries? *American Psychologist, 52*, 130–139.

Bass, B. M. (1998). *Transformational leadership: Industry, military, and educational impact.* Hillsdale, NJ: Lawrence Erlbaum.

Bass, B. M. & Avolio, B. J. (1994). *Improving organizational effectiveness through transformational leadership.* Thousand Oaks, CA: Sage.

Brown, M. E., Trevino, L. K., & Harrison, D. A. (2005). Ethical leadership: A social learning perspective for construct development and testing. *Organizational Behavior and Human Decision Processes, 97,* 117–134.

Cappelli, P., Singh, H., Singh, J. V., & Useem, M. (2010, March, 2–9). Leadership lessons from India. *Harvard Business Review.*

Chan, S. C. H., Huang, X., Snape, E., & Lam, C. K. (2013). The Janus face of paternalistic leaders: Authoritarianism, benevolence, subordinates' organization-based self-esteem, and performance. *Journal of Organizational Behavior, 34*(1), 108–128.

Chan, S. C. H. & Mak, W. M. (2012). Benevolent leadership and follower performance: The mediating role of leader–member exchange (LMX). *Asia-Pacific Journal of Management, 29*(2), 285–301.

Chen, C. C. & Lee, Y. T. (2008). Introduction: The diversity and dynamism of Chinese philosophies on leadership. In C. C. Chen & Y. T. Lee (Eds.), *Leadership and management in China* (pp. 239–271). Cambridge: Cambridge University Press.

Chen, H. Y. & Kao, H. S. R. (2009). Chinese paternalistic leadership and non-Chinese subordinates' psychological health. *The International Journal of Human Resource Management, 20,* 2533–2546.

Chen, X. P., Eberly, M. B., Chiang, T. J., Farh, J. L., & Cheng, B. S. (2014). Affective trust in Chinese leaders: Linking paternalistic leadership to employee performance. *Journal of Management, 40*(3), 796–819.

Chen, Z. X. & Aryee, S. (2007). Delegation and employee work outcomes: The cultural context of mediating processes in China. *Academy of Management Journal, 50*(1), 226–238.

Cheng, B. S., Boer, D., Chou, L. F., Huang, M. P., Yoneyama, S., Shim, D., Sun, J. M., Lin, T. T, Chou, W. J., & Tsai, C. Y. (2014). Paternalistic leadership in four East Asian societies: Generalizability and cultural differences of the triad model. *Journal of Cross-Cultural Psychology, 45*(1), 82–90.

Cheng, B. S., Chou, L. F., Wu, T. Y., Huang, M. P., & Farh, J. L. (2004). Paternalistic leadership and subordinate responses: Establishing a leadership model in Chinese organizations. *Asian Journal of Social Psychology, 7*(1), 89–117.

Chi-Ching, E. Y. (1992). Perceptions of external barriers and the career success of female managers in Singapore. *Journal of Social Psychology, 132,* 661–674.

Choi, M., Yoon, H. J., & Jeung, C. W. (2012). Leadership development in Korea: A delphi study. *Asia Pacific Journal of Human Resources, 50*(1), 23–42.

Collins, J. (2005). Level 5 leadership: The triumph of humility and fierce resolve. *Harvard Business Review, 83*(7–8), 136–146.

Cooke, F. L. & Saini, D. S. (2012). Managing diversity in Chinese and Indian organizations: A qualitative study. *Journal of Chinese Human Resources Management, 3*(1), 16–32.

Darby, R. (2015). Leadership development in the Asia-Pacific region: Building capacity in the Indonesia defense environment. *Journal of Management Development, 34*(5), 506–523.

Den Hartog, D. N., House, R. J., Hanges, P. J., Ruiz-Quintanilla, S. A., Dorfman, P. W., & 170 co-authors. (1999). Culture specific and cross-culturally generalizable implicit leadership theories: Are attributes of charismatic/transformational leadership universally endorsed?. *Leadership Quarterly, 10*(2), 219–256.

Dunnagan, K., Maragakis, M., Schneiderjohn, N., Turner, C., & Vance, C. M. (2013). Meeting the global imperative of local leadership talent development in Hong Kong, Singapore, and India. *Global Business & Organizational Excellence, 32*(2), 52–60.

Ensley, M. D., Hmieleski, K. M., & Pearce, C. L. (2006). The importance of vertical and shared leadership within new venture top management teams: Implications for the performance of startups. *Leadership Quarterly, 17*(3), 217–231.

Eva, N. & Sendjaya, S. (2013). Creating future leaders: An examination of youth leadership development in Australia. *Education + Training, 55*(6), 584–598.

Farh, J. L. & Cheng, B. S. (2000). A cultural analysis of paternalistic leadership in Chinese organizations. In J. T. Li., A. S. Tsui, & E. Weldon (Eds.), *Management and organizations in the Chinese context* (pp. 84–127). London: Macmillan.

Farh, J. L., Cheng, B. S., Chou, L. F., & Chu, X. P. (2006). Authority and benevolence: Employees' responses to paternalistic leadership in China. In A. S. Tsui, Y. Bian, & L. Cheng (Eds.), *China's domestic private firms: Multidisciplinary perspectives on management and performance* (pp. 230–260). New York: Sharpe.

Fernandez, J. A. (2004). The gentlemen's code of Confucius: Leadership by values. *Organizational Dynamics, 33*(1), 21–31.

Fielder, F. E. (1964). A theory of leadership effectiveness. In L. Berkowitz (Ed.), *Advances in experimental social psychology*. New York: Academic Press.

Fisher, E. (2011). What practitioners consider to be the skills and behaviors of an effective people project manager. *International Journal of Project Management, 29*(8), 994–1002.

Fukushige, A. & Spicer, D. P. (2007). Leadership preferences in Japan: An exploratory study. *Leadership & Organization Development Journal, 28*(6), 508–530.

Fukushige, A. & Spicer, D. P. (2011). Leadership and followers' work goals: A comparison between Japan and the UK. *The International Journal of Human Resource Management, 22*(10), 2110–2134.

Gentry, W. A., Eckert, R. H., Munusamy, V. P., Stawiski, S. A., & Martin, J. L. (2014). The needs of participants in leadership development programs: A qualitative and quantitative cross-country investigation. *Journal of Leadership & Organizational Studies, 21*(1), 83–101.

George, W. (2003). *Authentic leadership: Rediscovering the secrets to creating lasting value*. San Francisco, CA: Jossey-Bass.

Graen, G. B. (2006). In the Eye of the beholder: Cross-cultural lesson in leadership from project GLOBE: A response viewed from the third culture bonding (TCB) model of cross-cultural leadership. *Academy of Management Perspectives, 20*(4), 95–101.

Han, Y., Kakabadse, N. K., & Kakabadse, A. (2010). Servant leadership in the People's Republic of China: A case study of the public sector. *Journal of Management Development, 29*(3), 265–281.

Herbert, K., Mockaitis, A. I., & Zander, L. (2014). An opportunity for east and west to share leadership: A multicultural analysis of shared leadership preferences in global teams. *Asian Business & Management, 13*(3), 257–282.

Hersey, P. & Blanchard, K. H. (1969). An introduction to situational leadership. *Training and Development Journal, 23*, 26–34.

Hickson, D. & Pugh, D. (1995). *Management worldwide*. London: Penguin Books.

Hirst, G., Walumbwa, F., Aryee, S., Butarbutar, I., & Chen, C. J. H. (2015). A multi-level investigation of authentic leadership as an antecedent of helping behavior. *Journal of Business Ethics*. doi:10.1007/s10551-015-2580-x.

Hofstede, G. (2001). *Culture's consequences: Comparing values, behaviors, institutions and organizations across nations* (2nd ed. rev.). Thousand Oaks, CA: Sage.

Hofstede, G. (2010). The GLOBE debate: Back to relevance. *Journal of International Business Studies, 41*(8), 1339–1346.

House, R. J., Dorfman, P., Javidan, M., Hanges, P. W., & Sully De Luque, M. (2013). *Strategic leadership across borders: The GLOBE Study of CEO leadership behavior and effectiveness in 24 countries*. Thousand Oaks, CA: Sage.

House, R. J., Hanges, P. J., Javidan, M., Dorfman, P. W., Gupta, V., & GLOBE Associates. (2004). *Leadership, culture, and organizations: The GLOBE study of 62 societies*. Thousand Oaks, CA: Sage.

Hsiung, H. H. (2012). Authentic leadership and employee voice behavior: A multi-level psychological process. *Journal of Business Ethics, 107*(3), 349–361.

Hu, J. & Liden, R. C. (2011). Antecedents of team potency and team effectiveness: An examination of goal and process clarity and servant leadership. *Journal of Applied Psychology, 96*(4), 851–862.

Huang, J. (2013). Developing local talent for future leadership. *China Business Review, 40*(1), 28–30.

Huang, X., Shi, K., Zhang, Z., & Cheung, Y. L. (2006). The impact of participative leadership behavior on psychological empowerment and organizational commitment in Chinese state-owned enterprises: The moderating role of organizational tenure. *Asia-Pacific Journal of Management, 23*, 345–367.

Huang, X., Iun, J., Liu, A., & Gong, Y. (2010). Does participative leadership enhance work performance by inducing empowerment or trust?: The differential effects on managerial and non-managerial subordinates. *Journal of Organizational Behavior, 31*, 122–143.

Hur, Y., van den Berg, P. T., & Wilderom, C. P. (2011). Transformational leadership as a mediator between emotional intelligence and team outcomes. *The Leadership Quarterly, 22*(4), 591–603.

Ishikawa, J. (2012). Leadership and performance in Japanese R&D teams. *Asia Pacific Business Review, 18*(2), 241–258.

Jogulu, U. & Ferkins, L. (2012). Leadership and culture in Asia: The case of Malaysia. *Asia Pacific Business Review, 18*(4), 531–549.

Kabasakal, H. & Dastmalchian, A. M. (2001). Introduction to leadership and culture in the Middle Eastern Countries: Norms, practices and effective leadership attributes in Iran, Kuwait, Turkey and Qatar. *Applied Psychology: An International Review, 50*(4), 479–488.

Kang, S. W., Park, H. J., & Jung, D. (2013). Why does ethical leadership matter in workplace? Empirical evidence from South Korea. Academy of Management Proceedings 2013.

Kaye, B. & Jordan-Evans, S. (2014). *Love 'em or lose 'em: Getting good people to stay.* San Francisco, CA: Berrett-Koehler Publishers.

Kirkman, B. L., Chen, G., Farh, J. L., Chen, Z. X., & Lowe, K. B. (2009). Individual power distance orientation and follower reactions to transformational leaders: A cross-level, cross-cultural examination. *Academy of Management Journal, 52*(4), 744–764.

Koh, W. L., Steers, R. M., & Terborg, J. R. (1995). The effects of transformational leadership on teacher attitudes and student performance in Singapore. *Journal of Organizational Behavior, 16*(4), 319–333.

Lawler, J. J. (1996). Diversity issues in South-East Asia: The case of Thailand. *International Journal of Manpower, 17*(4/5), 152–167.

Lee, Y. T., Han, A. G., Byron, T. K. & Fan, H. X. (2008). Daoist leadership: Theory and application. In C. C. Chen & Y. T. Lee (Eds.), *Leadership and management in China* (pp. 239–271). Cambridge: Cambridge University Press.

Leong, L. Y. C. & Fischer, R. (2011). Is transformational leadership universal?: A meta-analytical investigation of multifactor leadership questionnaire means across cultures. *Journal of Leadership & Organizational Studies, 18*(2), 164–174.

Lester, P. B., Hannah, S. T., Harms, P. D., Vogelgesang, G. R., & Avolio, B. J. (2011). Mentoring impact on leader efficacy development: A field experiment. *Academy of Management Learning & Education, 10*(3), 409–429.

Leung, A. S. M. (2002). Sexuality at work. *Journal of Managerial Psychology, 17*, 506–522.

Li, Y. & Sun, J. M. (2015). Traditional Chinese leadership and employee voice behavior: A cross-level examination. *The Leadership Quarterly, 26*(1), 172–189.

Li, Y., Xu, J., Tu, Y., & Lu, X. (2014). Ethical leadership and subordinates' occupational well-being: A multi-level examination in China. *Social Indicators Research, 116*(3), 823–842.

Liden, R. C. (2012). Leadership research in Asia: A brief assessment and suggestions for the future. *Asia-Pacific Journal of Management, 29*, 205–212.

Liu, J., Kwan, H. H., Fu, P. P. & Mao, Y. (2013). Ethical leadership and job performance in China: The roles of workplace friendships and traditionality. *Journal of Occupational and Organizational Psychology, 86*(4), 564–584.

Mahbubani, K. (2014). *The great convergence: Asia, the West, and the logic of one world.* New York: Perseus Books Group.

Mercer. (2013). Asia pacific leadership development practices study. Marsh & McLennan Companies.

Miao, Q., Newman, A., & Huang, X. (2014). The impact of participative leadership on job performance and organizational citizenship behavior: Distinguishing between the mediating effects of affective and cognitive trust. *The International Journal of Human Resource Management, 25*(20), 2796–2810.

Miao, Q., Newman, A., Schwarz, G., & Xu, L. (2013a). Participative leadership and the organizational commitment of civil servants in China: The mediating effects of trust in supervisor. *British Journal of Management, 24*, S76-S92.

Miao, Q., Newman, A., Yu, J., & Xu, L. (2013b). The relationship between ethical leadership and unethical pro-organizational behavior: Linear or curvilinear effects? *Journal of Business Ethics, 116*(3), 641–653.

Mitchie, J. & Zumitzavan, V. (2012). The impact of "learning" and "leadership" management styles on organizational outcomes: A study of tyre firms in Thailand. *Asia Pacific Business Review, 18*(4), 607–630.

Mulki, J. P., Caemmerer, B., & Heggde, G. S. (2015). Leadership style, salesperson's work effort and job performance: The influence of power distance. *Journal of Personal Selling & Sales Management, 35*(1), 3–22.

Murphy, T. E. (2002). Market forces and the Middle East's new interest in HRM. *Business Horizons, 45*(5), 63–71.

Newman, A. & Butler, C. (2014). The influence of follower cultural orientation on attitudinal responses towards transformational leadership: Evidence from the Chinese hospitality industry. *The International Journal of Human Resource Management, 25*(7), 1024–1045.

Newman, A., Kiazad, K., Miao, Q., & Cooper, B. (2014). Examining the cognitive and affective trust-based mechanisms underlying the relationship between ethical leadership and organizational citizenship: A case of the head leading the heart? *Journal of Business Ethics, 123*(1), 113–123.

Nicolaides, V. C., LaPort, K. A., Chen, T. R., Tomassetti, A. J., Weis, E. J., Zaccaro, S. J., & Cortina, J. M. (2014). The shared leadership of teams: A meta-analysis of proximal, distal, and moderating relationships. *Leadership Quarterly, 25*(5), 923–942.

Oc, B., Bashshur, M. R., Daniels, M. A., Greguras, G. J., & Diefendorff, J. M. (2015). Leader humility in Singapore. *Leadership Quarterly, 26*(1), 68–80.

Ou, Y., Tsui, A. S., Kiniki, A. J., Waldman, D. A., Xiao, Z. X., & Song, J. W. (2014). A humble chief executive officers' connections to top management team integration and middle managers' responses. *Administrative Science Quarterly, 59*(1), 34–72.

Palrecha, R., Spangler, W. D., & Yammarino, F. J. (2012). A comparative study of three leadership approaches in India. *Leadership Quarterly, 23*, 146–162.

Parris, D. L. & Peachey, J. W. (2013). A systematic literature review of servant leadership theory in organizational contexts. *Journal of Business Ethics, 113*(3), 377–393.

Pasa, S. F., Kabasakal, H., & Bodur, M. (2001). Society, organizations and leadership in Turkey. *Applied Psychology: An International Review, 50*(4), 559–589.

Pekerti, A. A. & Sendjaya, S. (2010). Exploring servant leadership across cultures: Comparative study in Australia and Indonesia. *The International Journal of Human Resource Management, 21*(5), 754–780.

Pellegrini, E. K. & Scandura, T. A. (2008). Paternalistic leadership: A review and agenda for future research. *Journal of Management, 34*, 566–593.

Pellegrini, E. K., Scandura, T. A., & Jayaraman, V. (2010). Cross-cultural generalizability of paternalistic leadership: An expansion of leader-member exchange theory. *Group & Organization Management, 35*(4), 391–420.

Raghuram, S. (2011). Organizational identification among young software professionals in India. *The International Journal of Human Resource Management, 22*(18), 3913–3928.

Redding, S. G., Norman, A., & Schlander, A. (1994). The nature of individual attachment to theory: A review of East Asian variations. In H. C. Triandis, M. D. Dunnett, & L. M. Hough (Eds.), *Handbook of industrial and organizational psychology* (pp. 674–688). Palo Alto, CA: Consulting Psychology Press.

Robertson, C., Al-Habib, M., Al-Khatib, J., & Lanoue, D. (2001). Beliefs about work in the Middle East and the convergence versus divergence of values. *Journal of World Business, 36*(13), 223–235.

Rowley, C., Kang, H. R., & Lim, H. J. (2016). Female manager career success: The importance of individual and organizational factors in South Korea. *Asia Pacific Journal of Human Resources, 54*(1), 98–122.

Saini, D. S. & Budhwar, P. S. (2008). Managing the human resource in Indian SMEs: The role of indigenous realities. *Journal of World Business, 43*(4), 417–434.

Salminen-Karlsson, M. (2015). Expatriate paternalistic leadership and gender relations in small European software firms in India. *Culture & Organization, 21*(5), 409–426.

Schaubroeck, J., Lam, S. S. K., & Peng, A. C. (2011). Cognition-based and affect-based trust as mediators of leader behavior influences on team behavior. *Journal of Applied Psychology, 96*, 863–871.

Sendjaya, S. & Pekerti, A. (2010). Servant leadership as antecedent of trust in organizations. *Leadership & Organization Development Journal, 31*(7), 643–663.

Shahin, A. I. & Wright, P. L. (2004). Leadership in the context of culture: An Egyptian perspective. *Leadership and Organization Development Journal, 25*, 499–511.

Sheikh, A. Z., Newman, A., & Al Azzeh, S. A. F. (2013). Transformational leadership and job involvement in the Middle East: The moderating role of individually held cultural values. *The International Journal of Human Resource Management, 24*(6), 1077–1095.

Shin, S. J. & Zhou, J. (2003). Transformational leadership, conservation, and creativity: Evidence from Korea. *Academy of Management Journal, 46*, 703–714.

Shin, Y. (2012). CEO ethical leadership, ethical climate, climate strength, and collective organizational citizenship behavior. *Journal of Business Ethics, 108*(3), 299–312.

Singh, K. (2015). Leadership style and employee productivity: A case study of Indian banking organizations. *Journal of Knowledge Globalization, 8*(2), 39–67.

Stahl, G. K., Björkman, I., Farndale, E., Morris, S. S., Paauwe, J., Stiles, P., Trevor, J., & Wright, P. (2012). Six principles of effective global talent management. *MIT Sloan Management Review, 53*(2), 25–32.

Suri, G. S. & Abbott, P. Y. (2013). IT cultural enclaves and social change: The interplay between Indian cultural values and Western ways of working in an Indian IT organization. *Information Technology for Development, 19*(3), 193–214.

Swierczek, F. W. (1991). Leadership and culture: Comparing Asian managers. *Leadership & Organization Development Journal, 12*(7), 3–10.

Tatli, A., Vassilopoulou, J., & Özbilgin, M. (2013). An unrequited affinity between talent shortages and untapped female potential: The relevance of gender quotas for talent management in high growth potential economies of the Asia Pacific region. *International Business Review, 22*(3), 539–553.

Thompson, M. R. (2002). Female leadership of democratic transitions in Asia. *Pacific Affairs, 75*(4), 535–555.

Toor, S. & Ofori, G. (2009). Authenticity and its influence on psychological well-being and contingent self-esteem of leaders in Singapore construction sector. *Construction Management and Economics, 27,* 299–313.

Tu, Y. & Lu, X. (2013). How ethical leadership influence employees' innovative work behavior: A perspective of intrinsic motivation. *Journal of Business Ethics, 116*(2), 441–455.

Turner, Y. (2006). Swinging open or slamming shut? The implications of China's open-door policy for women, educational choice and work. *Journal of Education & Work, 19*(1), 47–65.

Wang, H., Law, K. S., Hackett, R. D., Wang, D., & Chen, Z. X. (2005). Leader–member exchange as a mediator of the relationship between transformational leadership and followers' performance and organizational citizenship behavior. *Academy of Management Journal, 48,* 420–432.

Wang, H., Sui, Y., Luthans, F., Wang, D., & Wu, Y. (2014a). Impact of authentic leadership on performance: Role of followers' positive psychological capital and relational processes. *Journal of Organizational Behavior, 35,* 5–21.

Wang, D., Waldman, D. A., & Zhen, Z. (2014b). A meta-analysis of shared leadership and team effectiveness. *Journal of Applied Psychology, 99*(2), 181–198.

Weldon, E. & Chow, M. (2005). A question of leadership: Are Western leadership development approaches appropriate in China, or might a Chinese approach be more effective? *Leadership in Action, 25*(5), 12–13.

Wu, M., Huang, X., & Chan, S. C. H. (2012). The influencing mechanisms of paternalistic leadership in Mainland China. *Asia Pacific Business Review, 18,* 631–648.

Wua, M., Chang, C. C., & Zhuang, W. L. (2010). Relationships of work–family conflict with business and marriage outcomes in Taiwanese copreneurial women. International. *Journal of Human Resource Management, 21,* 742–753.

Yukongdi, V. (2010). A study of Thai employees' preferred leadership style. *Asia-Pacific Business Review, 16*(1–2), 161–181.

Zander, L. & Butler, C. L. (2010). Leadership modes: Success strategies for multicultural teams. *Scandinavian Journal of Management, 26*(3), 258–267.

Zhang, H., Everett, A. M., Elkin, G., & Cone, M. H. (2012). Authentic leadership theory development: Theorizing on Chinese philosophy. *Asia-Pacific Business Review, 18*(4), 587–605.

Zhang, H., Kwan, H. K., Everett, A. M., & Jian, Z. (2012a). Servant leadership, organizational identification, and work-to-family enrichment: The moderating role of work climate for sharing family concerns. *Human Resource Management, 51*(5), 747–768.

Zhang, X. M. & Bartol, K. M. (2010). The influence of creative process engagement on employee creative performance and overall job performance: A curvilinear assessment. *Journal of Applied Psychology, 95*(5), 862–873.

Zhang, Z. X., Chen, C. C., Liu, L. A. & Liu, X. F. (2008). Chinese traditions and Western theories: Influences on business leaders in China. In C. C. Chen & Y. T. Lee (Eds.), *Leadership and management in China* (pp. 239–271). Cambridge: Cambridge University Press.

Zhu, W., Newman, A., Miao, Q., & Hooke, G. (2013). Revisiting the mediating role of trust on transformational leadership effects: Do different types of trust make a difference? *Leadership Quarterly, 24,* 94–105.

11

COMPENSATION SYSTEMS AND PAY PRACTICES IN ASIA

Tae-Youn Park and Jason D. Shaw

Introduction

Decision makers face a number of choices in setting compensation levels and establishing other pay practices. Some organizations appear to prefer "tried and true" practices, consulting specific, detailed, and well-accepted encyclopedias for designing compensation systems and adopting common approaches (e.g., Milkovich, Newman, & Gerhart, 2013). On the other hand, some organizations prefer to innovate and experiment with alternative forms for base pay, benefits, and different types of incentives. Recent years have seen a number of changes in compensation practices in Asia, as more organizations appear to be experimenting voluntarily or, in some cases involuntarily, with so-called Western or global-style compensation practices. These practices shift the historical emphasis away from seniority, status, hierarchy, and respect, and toward merit, effort, and performance measures (hereafter, pay-for-performance). For example, South Korean organizations had been known to rely mostly on a seniority-based compensation practices, but by 2005 nearly one-half of all Korean organizations adopted some form of pay-for-performance compared to 1.6 percent in 1996, according to the Korean Ministry of Labor (Yang & Rowley, 2008).

Despite the growing attention on performance-based compensation and human resource (HR) practices, a long-standing debate is whether Western-style compensation practices fit in with Asian countries' *culture*—"the collective programming of the mind which distinguishes the members of one group or category of people from another" (Hofstede, 1991: 5). Some argue that the newly adopted practices cause more problems (e.g., increased conflicts) than benefits (e.g., increased productivity) because of their misfit with Asian countries' cultures. In this vein, those who raise the cultural fit issues argue that, even though the national-level statistics report that Asian organizations widely adopted performance-based compensation practices, those adopted practices should not be labeled as Western-style performance-based pay practices as many Asian organizations do not manage and implement the practices in the same way as Western organizations. In contrast, others argue that the concern for the cultural fit may be exaggerated because, compared to organizational or group culture, national culture plays a relatively limited, or no, role in the design and implementation of compensation practices (e.g., Gerhart, 2008; Newman & Nollen, 1996; Schuler & Rogovsky, 1998).

The purpose of this chapter is to advance the debate on the effectiveness of (Western-style) performance-based compensation practices in Asian organizations. To do this, we first present a comprehensive review of the literature and discuss how compensation scholars have theorized the effects of culture on compensation practices. Second, we summarize the extant empirical evidence on the effects of culture. Third, we examine existing critiques and limitations of the empirical studies. Last, building on the limitations identified in prior studies, we suggest future research directions. In particular, we encourage future researchers to focus less on compensation practice preference differences across different countries, and instead focus more on how people's reactions on a given form of compensation practice (e.g., individual-performance-based pay) vary depending on their culture. In making this suggestion, we further encourage future researchers to reconceptualize culture as an individual's "way of knowing, of construing the world and others" (Bruner, 1993: 516), building on the cultural psychology literature (Greenfield, 2000; Heine, 2010; Shweder, 1990), rather than the cross-cultural psychology literature (Hofstede, 1980).

We made several important decisions in this chapter. First, we focused on a monetary form of compensation, not on other forms of compensation such as non-monetary (e.g., fringe benefits) and intrinsic (e.g., job design, career development opportunity) compensation. Second, in discussing the differences in compensation practices across countries and regions, we mainly focused on the effects of *culture* on compensation practices rather than other factors such as institutional and regulatory environmental forces (e.g., stock market maturity, unionization rates). Prior work (e.g., Rowley & Benson, 2004; Varma & Budhwar, 2014) and other chapters of this book present a thorough review of the regulatory environment differences amongst Asian countries. Those institutional forces are important determinants of an organization's compensation practice design, but are, for the most part, compliance rather than strategic choice issues. The effects of culture on compensation practices, however, seem to be a more nuanced, debatable topic. Third, in our review of the literature, we included studies that tested cultural differences in compensation issues, while excluding studies that investigated compensation issues within a single cultural context. We made this decision because we aimed to investigate the comparative differences in compensation in different cultures. Thus, although a number of interesting studies on international compensation have tested hypotheses in a single cultural context (e.g., Chang, 2006; Du & Choi, 2010; Greckhamer, 2015; Shin, Kang, Hyun, & Kim, 2014; Sun, Zhao, & Yang, 2010), we excluded them from our review. Last, we focused on compensation practices for general employees, not for expatriates or executives, a topic that has been extensively discussed in prior work (e.g., Hallock, 2012; Martocchio, 2013; Milkovich et al., 2013).

The effects of culture on compensation practices

Research has shown that national culture influences the way people understand the nature of work, their approach to it, and the way in which they expect to be treated (Hofstede, 1980, 1991, 1993, 2001; House, Hanges, Javidan, Dorfman, & Gupta, 2004). Bringing this perspective to the human resource (HR) management literature, researchers have posited that management practices that are not congruent with those deeply held values will likely be ineffective, as employees will feel dissatisfied, distracted, uncomfortable, and uncommitted and, thus, will not be productive (Gomez-Mejia & Welbourne, 1991; Newman & Nollen, 1996; Schuler & Rogovsky, 1998).

A seminal set of propositions on national culture and compensation practices was offered by Gomez-Mejia and Welbourne (1991). Although their study seems somewhat dated, it is important to review their main propositions because many later studies built their theories and empirical research design based on this study. Gomez-Mejia and Welbourne adopted Hofstede's cultural dimensions, which characterize national cultural differences using four continua: power distance, individualism/collectivism, uncertainty avoidance, and masculinity/femininity. Later, Hofstede and Bond (1988) added a fifth dimension—long-term orientation—but Gomez-Mejia and Welbourne focused primarily on the four dimensions of culture.

The effects of power distance on compensation practices

Power distance is the extent to which individuals expect and readily accept an unequal power distribution (Hofstede, 1980, 1993, 2001). High power distance means that class, authority, and power symbols are pronounced across people. According to Hofstede (2015), countries such as Malaysia, the Philippines, Mexico, and China are high power distance countries, whereas countries such as Denmark, Ireland, and Switzerland are low power distance countries. In an organizational setting, power is often reflected as job status, authority, and decision-making. Employees from a high power distance culture tend to put a high premium on organizational hierarchy (Child & Markoczy, 1993). Building on this conceptual background, Gomez-Mejia and Welbourne (1991) proposed that pay differentials across job levels are greater in high power distance countries than in low power distance countries. In addition, the researchers also suggested that, in low power distance countries, participatory pay practices (e.g., employee ownership plans, stock options) are more prevalent than in high power distance countries.

The effects of individualism (vs. collectivism) on compensation practices

Individualism refers to the extent to which people in a given society value independence over belonging to groups. The opposite end of the individualism continuum (i.e., low individualism) is labeled collectivism, in which people place a higher value on belonging to groups than on being independent. People in high collectivism (i.e., low individualism) cultures tend to value loyalty and harmony, and they pay attention to "saving face," as they attach greater importance to the views others hold of them (Bond & Hwang, 1986). In this vein, Gomez-Mejia and Welbourne (1991) suggested that organizations in highly individualistic countries are likely to: (a) use individual-performance-based pay, and (b) give more emphasis to external equity, whereas those in low individualism cultures are likely to: (a) use group-performance-based pay, (b) use seniority-based pay, and (c) give more emphasis to internal equity (as opposed to external equity). Many Asian countries (e.g., Singapore, South Korea, Indonesia, Japan, and Taiwan) are generally collectivistic.

The effects of uncertainty avoidance on compensation practices

Uncertainty avoidance reflects the degree to which instability and unpredictability are tolerated in a society. In countries where uncertainty avoidance is high, people tend to feel uncomfortable in unstructured or risky situations, and organizations tend to have many rules and procedures so that risky situations can be minimized. In this vein, Gomez-Mejia and Welbourne (1991) proposed that organizations in countries with a high uncertainty avoidance culture rely more on bureaucratic pay policies and avoid the use of variable pay, whereas those in a low uncertainty avoidance culture have a higher proportion of variable pay and give more discretion to supervisors and business units in pay allocation. Several Asian countries (e.g., Singapore, Hong Kong, China, and Indonesia) are low on uncertainty avoidance.

The effects of masculinity (vs. femininity) on compensation practices

Masculinity indicates that society promotes competition, achievement, and success along with assertive attitudes and behaviors. The opposite end of this dimension is femininity, in which societal caring for others and quality of life is promoted. Masculine countries are characterized by high emphasis on material possessions, rigidity in gender stereotypes, and acceptance of gender inequalities. Accordingly, men and women tend to have different, predetermined career roles and segregation of occupations, in such ways that fewer women are in upper-level management positions, while for men, work lives are emphasized and failure within a specific career results in significant stress. Building on this conceptual background, Gomez-Mejia and Welbourne (1991) suggested that organizations in a highly masculine country are likely to experience differentiated pay policies that allow for gender inequalities and to reward "male" traits more in promotions and other personnel decisions. These researchers also proposed that, in a highly masculine country, paternalistic benefits for women (e.g., paid maternity leave, day care) are less generous in masculine countries. Japan scores the highest in terms of masculinity, and other Asian countries such as China, the Philippines, and Australia are also masculine cultures.

Table 11.1 shows the summary of main propositions developed by Gomez-Mejia and Welbourne (1991).

Review of previous empirical studies

Since Gomez-Mejia and Welbourne (1991) introduced their propositions, HR and compensation researchers have made efforts to extend and empirically test them, using two different approaches. Some researchers have collected large-scale survey data from employees or managers in different countries and tested whether employees' or managers' thoughts on compensation practices differ meaningfully across regions. Other researchers have adopted an experiment-based, policy-capturing approach and investigated whether pay-related decisions are made differently when decision makers originate from different countries, typically one or two East Asian countries, such as China, Japan, or South Korea, and one or two North American countries, such as the United States or Canada.

Evidence from cross-country survey data

Newman and Nollen (1996) explored the effect of national culture on various forms of management practices (e.g., participatory decision-making, emphasis on individual responsibility) and merit-based reward practices, a type of pay-for-performance. Newman and Nollen hypothesized that merit-based reward practices would contribute to organizational performance in highly masculine countries but are detrimental to organizational performance in highly feminine countries. They found supportive evidence using data from global units of a US-based high technology company such that the work units in highly masculine cultures were high performing in terms of return on assets (ROA) and return on sales (ROS) when they used more merit-based rewards for pay and promotion. In contrast, the work units in highly feminine cultures showed higher performance (ROA and ROS) when they relied less on merit-based rewards. Interestingly, this is the only study, to date, that has directly examined the effects of congruence between culture and HR practices on organizational performance. As we discuss below to our knowledge, all the other studies have examined the effects of culture on employees' or managers' preferences for certain types of compensation practices or the prevalence of certain compensation practices.

Table 11.1 The effects of national culture on compensation practices

Cultural dimensions	Definitions	Proposed effects on compensation practices
Power distance	The extent to which individuals expect and readily accept an unequal power distribution.	In high power distance countries, hierarchical pay system (i.e., large differentials in pay and benefits between job levels) is likely.
		In low power distance countries, egalitarian pay system (i.e., small differentials in pay and benefits between job levels) is likely. In addition, participatory pay strategies (e.g., gain sharing) are more prevalent.
Individualism (vs. collectivism)	The extent to which people in a given society value independence over belonging to groups.	In individualistic countries, individual performance-based pay (especially for individual performance), external equity and short-term orientation are likely.
		In collectivistic countries, seniority, internal equity, and personal needs are key guiding principles in designing compensation practices.
Uncertainty avoidance	The degree to which instability and unpredictability are tolerated in a society.	In high uncertainty avoidance countries, bureaucratic and fixed-pay-based pay policies are prevalent. In addition, little discretion is given to supervisor in making pay allocation decisions.
		In low uncertainty avoidance countries, variable pay, external equity, and decentralized pay programs are prevalent.
Masculinity (vs. femininity)	The extent to which a society promotes competition, achievement, and success along with assertiveness attitudes and behaviors.	In high masculinity countries, "male" traits are rewarded in compensation decisions, and gender inequalities are allowed in terms of pay levels and paternalistic benefits intended to be geared primarily toward women (e.g. day care, paid maternity leave).
		In high femininity countries, "masculine" traits carry no special value for compensation decisions, and jobs are evaluated regardless of gender composition.

Source: Gomez-Mejia and Welbourne, 1991.

Mamman, Sulaiman, and Fadel (1996) focused specifically on the alignment of compensation practices and culture using data collected from employees in Australia, Hong Kong, Indonesia, and Malaysia. These authors found that Indonesian and Malaysian employees preferred seniority-based pay and education-based pay more than Australian employees did, controlling for the effects of industry and respondent characteristics. Their expectation that Australian employees would prefer performance-based pay more than Asian employees was not supported. Schuler and Rogovsky (1998) conducted the largest cross-country empirical study to date. The researchers used three different data sets: a worldwide survey of HR policies and practices conducted by IBM and Towers Perrin, the International Social Survey Programme (ISSP) data set, and another data set collected by Price Waterhouse-Cranfield (PW-CR). Using these data sets covering fourteen countries, Schular and Rogovsky tested whether and how Hofstede's four cultural dimensions—uncertainty avoidance, power distance, individualism, and masculinity—relate to the prevalence of compensation practices. The results showed that, as they expected, seniority-based or skill-based pay practices were prevalent in countries with high uncertainty avoidance countries, whereas individual performance-based pay was prevalent in low uncertainty avoidance countries. Uncertainty avoidance was not associated with the prevalence of pay-for-performance. Unexpectedly, the results showed that employee stock ownership plans (ESOP) were more prevalent in high uncertainty avoidance countries. In terms of individualism, Schuler and Rogovsky found that individualism culture score was positively related to the prevalence of performance-based pay and ESOP. They also found that ESOPs were less prevalent in high, rather than low, power distance cultures.

Another large-scale survey was conducted by Lowe, Milliman, De Cieri, and Dowling (2002). They used survey data from managers and engineers in each of nine countries and one region—Australia, Canada, China, Indonesia, Japan, Korea, Mexico, Taiwan, the United States, and a collection of Latin American countries—asking about the compensation practices currently used in their organizations. Compensation practices were classified into pay incentives, benefits, long-term focus in pay, and seniority-based pay. The data revealed patterns that were somewhat contrary to conventionally thinking, for example, pay-for-performance preferences were lowest in the United States. One consistent finding was that all respondents, regardless of countries, reported that individual pay-for-performance "should be" used more in the future.

Later, Chiang and Birtch (2005, 2006, 2007; also see Chiang, 2005) examined the effects of culture on pay practices by asking a sample of bank employees located in four different countries—United Kingdom, Canada, Hong Kong, and Finland—about their preferences for individual pay-for-performance, group pay-for-performance, and fixed (vs. variable) pay. The findings were again rather mixed. Contrary to their expectations, individual pay-for-performance was largely preferred; no differences across masculine, individualistic, and high uncertainty avoidance cultures were observed. In addition, regardless of culture, group performance-based pay was consistently rated as the least-preferred compensation practice. Moreover, variable pay (e.g., performance-, skill-, and competency-based pay) practices were consistently rated as more preferred than fixed pay that links pay with seniority and cost-of-living adjustments.

Evidence from policy-capturing, experiment-based studies

As the above review shows, the number of studies testing cross-national effects is limited and the results are inconsistent. The lack of studies in this area might be partly due to the difficulty in obtaining full access to cross-national-level compensation data. To overcome this difficulty, several researchers have adopted an experiment-based, policy-capturing method and examined the culture effects. Most of these studies tested the reward allocation preference differences between individuals in/from one country versus other individuals in/from other countries (e.g., American students/managers vs. Chinese students/managers). A common prediction has been that performance-based pay allocation is preferred for those from a high individualism culture (or low collectivism), whereas more equalized pay allocation is preferred by those from low individualism (or high collectivism) cultures.

Initial evidence was presented in Bond, Leung, and Wan's (1982) study. They compared pay allocation preferences between American students, who are presumably highly individualistic, and Hong Kong students, who are presumably highly collectivistic. Their hypothesis was that Hong Kong students are less likely to use individual performance information in making pay allocation decisions than their American counterparts. To test this, they gave research participants a scenario about a group of students working on a group project. In this scenario, they manipulated the students' contribution to the group project along two dimensions: task inputs (i.e., contributions for the project) and harmony maintenance inputs (i.e., contributions for the group members' interpersonal relationships) and the research participants were asked to assign peer evaluation ratings by taking the peer group members' perspective. The results showed that, as Bond et al. expected, American students gave more weight to the task inputs than did Hong Kong Chinese students. Bond et al. (1982) also hypothesized that Hong Kong Chinese students would give more weight to the harmony maintenance inputs than American students, but this hypothesis was not supported.

Two follow-up studies also compared pay allocation decisions amongst individuals in different countries. Murphy-Berman, Berman, Singh, Pachauri, and Kumar (1984) examined whether bonus allocation decisions differed between students in India and students in the United States. The scenario-based results showed that, on average, American students preferred more merit-based pay allocations, whereas Indian students preferred more need-based pay allocation (i.e., allocating the most to those who need most). Similarly, Marín (1985) showed that Indonesian students placed more weight on the recipient's need and concern for equality ("every employee should get the same raise") than American students.

Later, Kim, Park, and Suzuki (1990) attempted to constructively replicate Bond et al.'s (1982) findings in an expanded sample of individuals in three countries: United States, Japan, and South Korea. However, results showed no difference in task inputs or harmony maintenance inputs on the target person's grade outcome across the three countries. Although the researchers' hypotheses were largely unsupported, they did find a significant pattern from the data indicating that US students made the highest degree of pay differential between high and low performers, whereas Korean students made the smallest pay differentials.

Chen (1995) did not follow the conventional way of hypothesizing that individuals in the USA (an individualistic culture) prefer the performance-based pay allocation norm more than those in China do. Instead, Chen brought in a more contextualized perspective and argued that organizational goals precede cultural effects. Specifically, Chen hypothesized that Chinese business organizations give higher priority to performance-based pay allocation than US businesses because then (and probably persistent by now) the Chinese economic and social environment was transitioning toward more meritocratic practices, which led the country to place higher priority on economic goals than humanistic goals. To test this idea, Chen recruited employees in China and the United States and asked them to play the role of a newly appointed president who had initiated organizational changes, and evaluate the appropriateness of pay allocated to other top managers. The results showed that Chinese employees endorsed performance-based pay allocations significantly more than their American counterparts. It is important to note that Chen did not use this finding to refute any argument on culture effects but, instead, used it to develop a more nuanced proposition by including time dimensions. Specifically, in a follow-up study, Chen, Chen, and Meindl (1998) argued that, in an individualistic culture, performance-based pay allocation enhances cooperation in both short- and long-term work relations, whereas in a collectivistic culture performance-based pay allocation enhances cooperation in short-term relations but in long-term relations equality-based pay allocation enhances cooperation. Chen (1995) and Chen et al. (1998) explained that Chinese employees' strong preference for performance-based pay allocation, even compared with that of US employees, suggests a swinging social pendulum, such that equality had been emphasized to such a great extent in China in the past that employees highly desired change in the opposite direction.

Following Chen's (1995) study, Giacobbe-Miller, Miller, and Victorov (1998) argued that the Russian managers would place similar priority on the performance-based pay allocation as US managers because the societal reforms in Russia shifted people's preferences from the traditional collectivistic norm to a more individualized, meritocratic norm. In their role-play study, managers in both countries emphasized individual performance as a primary source of pay differentials, putting co-worker relations and equality as secondary factors. Their data showed further that, contrary to their expectations, US managers regarded harmonious co-worker relations as more important than did Russian managers and that, although both Russian and US managers highly emphasized individual performance, the managers made significant base allocations to everyone, meaning that the reward allocations were based primarily on equality norms.

Zhou and Martocchio (2001) argued that prior studies were limited because they forced respondents to consider one to three allocation norms—equity, equality, and need—while, in reality, managers had to consider various factors simultaneously. Accordingly, Zhou and Martocchio designed a scenario-based experiment and asked the study participants—working professionals from China and the United States—to make a bonus increase decision for an employee. The scenario described the employee's (i.e., potential bonus recipient's) performance, relationship with co-workers, relationship with managers, and needs at different levels. This way, Zhou and Martocchio were able to examine the within-individual variance in making bonus increase decisions. They found that, when considered simultaneously, Chinese professionals placed less emphasis on work performance and more emphasis on need when making bonus decisions compared to Americans.

Gully, Phillips, and Tarique (2003) found support for the conventional proposition that individualists tend to prefer high pay differentiations, whereas collectivists tend to prefer low pay differentiations. They recruited working professionals who were also part-time students in Singapore, Indonesia, and the United States. Gully et al. (2003) asked them to make merit pay raise decisions for four subordinates who showed different levels of performance. The data showed that, on average, Singaporeans and Indonesians gave higher levels of merit pay than did professionals from the United States regardless of the subordinate's performance; that is, the Asian professionals (i.e., collectivists) made less pay differentials based on subordinates' job performance. US professionals allocated a higher merit raise to high-performing subordinates. Gully et al. concluded that: "collectivists tend to protect the lower-performing members of their work group, which is consistent with the fact that collectivists place greater value on a collective identity and group harmony" (2003: 1385). Another notable finding from their data was that they measured each respondent's collectivism score. Individual differences in collectivism partially mediated the effects, but culture remained significant, implying that there may be other mechanisms that mediate the country effects on merit pay raise decisions.

Ramamoorthy, Gupta, Sardessai, and Flood (2005) also directly measured individualism–collectivism scores in a study of pay allocation preference differences among MBA students in three countries: United States, Ireland, and India. They showed that Indian students preferred highly differentiated reward allocation schemes than students in the United States and Ireland, which is contrary to the conventional proposition if interpreted based on Hofstede's culture scores; the United States scored much higher (91) than India (48) in terms of the individualism dimension (Ireland scored 70). Their survey results showed, however, that Indian students had higher individualism scores than US and Irish students which then explains their findings from the conventional individualism-pay allocation viewpoint. Finally, Fischer and Smith (2003) did not find evidence that individualism culture scores were meaningfully related to people's pay allocation decision patterns. Rather, they found that individuals in high power distance countries preferred highly differentiated pay allocation more than those in low power distance countries.

Limitations of previous studies

The review of previous empirical studies reveals inconsistent findings. As a result, several compensation scholars have recently suggested that it would be more beneficial to focus on proximal determinants of compensation practices, such as company and industry characteristics, and pay less attention to culture—a distal, country-level factor (e.g., Bloom, Milkovich, & Mitra, 2003; Chen, 1995; Chiang, 2005; Chiang & Birch, 2005, 2006, 2007; Gerhart, 2008; Long & Shields, 2005; Milkovich et al., 2013). However, some evidence does show statistically meaningful effects of culture on compensation practices. This suggests that we cannot make a conclusion that culture effects do exist nor can we conclude that they do not.

It is difficult to draw conclusions at this point because many of the previous studies suffer from notable methodological limitations. First, most previous studies have overlooked an individual-level, within-country variation in cultural values and relied largely on the assumption that individuals from a country have the same cultural value score as the country itself, often represented as one score per each of Hofstede's (1980) cultural dimensions. This assumption, however, can be problematic when individuals within one country have significantly different cultural values based on age, gender, community, organization, and other socio-economic characteristics. Indeed, it is noteworthy that two previous studies which directly measured an individual's cultural value showed that individual-level culture scores did not always correspond to a country's culture scores (Gully et al., 2003; Ramamoorthy et al., 2005). For example, Ramamoorthy et al. (2005) observed an unexpected finding from their data indicating that Indian students were more likely to follow performance-based pay allocation decisions than American students, but their data also showed that Indian students scored higher in individualism than American students, which informs us that their findings are not inconsistent with the well-regarded notion that an individualistic culture prefers pay-for-performance more than collectivist cultures. If Ramamoorthy et al. (2005) simply followed prior studies' paradigm of assigning Hofstede's cultural value scores to countries, their findings might have been interpreted as contrasting evidence.

Second, many of the prior studies explore managers' or employees' self-reported *preference* for various forms of compensation practice such as a pay-for-performance plan. Self-reported preference measures are limited in studying compensation issues (Rynes, Colbert, & Brown, 2002; Rynes, Gerhart, & Minette, 2004). Rynes et al. (2004) noted that when the self-report method is used, people report that they are not motivated by pay but by other intrinsic factors such as career development opportunities. This self-reported preference, however, does not correspond with a number of empirical studies demonstrating that people are motivated strongly by monetary incentives in terms of their behavioral outcomes (Jenkins, Mitra, Gupta, & Shaw, 1998; Shaw & Gupta, 2015). In this regard, it may not be surprising that people *report* that they prefer to be paid based on their individual performance regardless of their country and cultural values (e.g., Lowe et al., 2002). This self-report does not mean that people having different cultural values show the same cognitive, affective, and behavioral reactions when a pay-for-performance plan is actually implemented. Indeed, many of the prior studies that compared people's compensation practice *preference* levels across different countries have commonly reported that people simply prefer pay-for-performance regardless of cultural values (Chiang, 2005; Chiang & Birch, 2005, 2006, 2007; Lowe et al., 2002), whereas the study that examined behavioral outcomes of the interaction between cultural values and pay practice (Newman & Nollen, 1996) and the study that compared the prevalence of a certain form of pay practice across countries (Schuler & Rogovsky, 1998) did find significant culture effects.

In addition, studies that have adopted a scenario-based experiment method are limited in that they simply regarded culture effects as the function of a pay allocation decision maker's own cultural value—based on the decision maker's nationality—and overlooked another important cultural factor—the managing group's cultural climate—that can also influence the pay allocator's decision, independent of the decision maker's cultural value. Research has shown that managers' pay allocation decisions are significantly influenced by the managing group members' values and behaviors because managers bear the cognitive and emotional burdens of dealing with group members' constant attempts to influence the manager's decisions (Bartol & Martin, 1988). For example, previous studies have shown that when managers perceive that subordinates are likely to attempt to influence the manager's pay allocation decisions, they tend to minimize the pay differentials amongst subordinates (even if contrary to what they personally believe) so that they do not need to worry about subordinates' dissatisfaction with pay allocation decisions or their influence attempts (Bartol & Martin, 1989; Leventhal, Karuza, & Fry, 1980b; Leventhal, Michaels, & Sanford, 1972; Major & Adams, 1983). Accordingly, in examining the effects of culture on managers' pay allocation decisions, it is critical to consider the cultural climate of the group members (i.e., whether the group members, in general, have highly collectivistic values versus highly individualistic values) because this will significantly influence the manager's pay allocation decisions (to avoid causing dissatisfaction amongst group members).

Finally, effect sizes are an issue. Gerhart (2008) conducted a comprehensive re-examination of prior studies' findings on the effect of culture on pay allocation decisions compared to Cohen's (1992) benchmarks—r-square of 0.01 is small, r-square of 0.09 is medium, and r-square of 0.25 is large—after taking the square of the effect sizes and concluded that:

> the importance of national culture differences, as typically measured, may be less important than commonly believed … the practical significance of even statistically significant hypothesized effects may be overestimated … it may be mistakenly assumed that any observed relationship between national culture and compensation necessarily constrains firms to a significant degree in their choice of compensation practices and strategies.
>
> *(Gerhart, 2008: 155)*

In sum, we cannot make firm conclusions on the existence or meaningfulness of culture effects on compensation practices because previous studies suffer from the many methodological limitations summarized above.

Role of culture in compensation practice effectiveness

One conclusion we can draw from prior studies is that pay-for-performance is preferred regardless of cultural sphere, especially individualism versus collectivism (e.g., Chen, 1995; Giacobbe-Miller et al., 1998; Lowe et al., 2002). This evidence aligns with the recent trend of Asian organizations' compensation practice changes from seniority-based pay practices to pay-for-performance (e.g., Rowley & Benson, 2004; Varma & Budhwar, 2014). This increases the importance of investigating *how* Asian organizations can make an effective transition of their compensation practices than *whether* organizations prefer to adopt global, or Western-style, compensation practices. Below, we illustrate how compensation researchers can consider the role of culture in investigating compensation practice effectiveness in Asian countries.

We suggest that, instead of viewing culture as national culture differences on any type of dimension (e.g., Hofstede, 1980; House et al., 2004), the literature will benefit by viewing culture from the cultural psychology perspective as a shared pattern of construing self amongst individuals within a definable population that is distinct from that shared within other populations (Lehman, Chiu, & Schaller, 2004). As discussed above, it can be problematic to assume that everyone in the same country has similar levels and characteristics of culture. An alternative perspective is found in the cultural psychology literature, which "does not view culture as a superficial wrapping of the self, or as a framework within which selves interact, but as something that is intrinsic to the self" (Heine, 2001: 884). Instead of viewing culture as a country-level value which can be characterized by several dimensions such as those of Hofstede, we suggest viewing culture as individuals' shared form of self-construal, which emerges and is attuned by a cultural meaning practice within which the individuals develop (Shweder, 1990; Heine & Ruby, 2010).

When viewed as the way an individual construes self within an environment, culture can be defined in terms of whether individuals construe themselves as independent entities or interdependent entities (Markus & Kitayama, 1991). Independent self-construal refers to a "bounded, unitary, stable" self that is separate from social context (Markus & Kitayama, 1991: 230). The constellation of elements composing an independent self-construal includes an emphasis on: (a) internal abilities, thoughts, and feelings; (b) being unique and expressing the self; (c) realizing internal attributes and promoting one's own goals; and (d) being direct in communication. When thinking about themselves, individuals with highly developed independent self-construals have as referents their own abilities, attributes, characteristics, or goals rather than the thoughts, feelings, or actions of others. Similarly, when thinking about others, those others' individual characteristics and attributes become focal rather than relational or contextual factors (Markus & Kitayama, 1991).

An interdependent self-construal refers to a "flexible, variable" self (Markus & Kitayama, 1991: 230) that emphasizes: (a) external, public features such as status, roles, and relationships; (b) belonging and fitting in; (c) occupying one's proper place and engaging in appropriate action; and (d) being indirect in communication and "reading others' minds." When thinking about themselves or others, there is a sense that the self and others are intertwined. In addition, neither self nor other is separate from the situation but rather is molded by it. Harmonious interpersonal relationships and the ability to adjust to various situations are goals of the interdependent self-construal. Therefore, the interdependent self tends to communicate indirectly and to be attentive to others' feelings and unexpressed thoughts (i.e., "read others' minds"). Contrary to the independent self, the interdependent self depends on others, his or her relationships with those others, and contextual factors to regulate behavior. Because connecting with others and fitting in are primary sources of self-esteem, the situation and others present become "actively and continuously" integrated into the interdependent self (Markus & Kitayama, 1991).

Research has shown that North Americans tend to construe themselves as being highly independent, whereas Asians, especially East Asians, tend to construe themselves as being highly interdependent (e.g., see Oyserman, Coon, & Kemmelmeier's [2002] meta-analytic evidence). Indeed, many of the cultural psychology studies use "Westerners" as a label to refer to those who have independent self-construal and "(East) Asians" as a label to refer to those who have interdependent self-construal when characterizing differences amongst people in different cultural values. Following this approach, in suggesting future research avenues, we use the label "Westerners" to refer to those who have independent selves (representatively, North Americans) and "Asians" to refer to those who have interdependent selves (representatively, South Koreans, Japanese, Chinese, and Indonesians).

To illustrate how the interplay of culture and compensation practices can be theorized from the cultural psychological perspective, we present several exemplary research questions below. In doing so, we focus on a pay-for-performance only. Pay-for-performance refers to linking a cash reward to some form of performance measure. Various forms of pay-for-performance plans exist, such as merit increase, individual incentive or sales commission, gain-sharing, profit-sharing, and stock options, depending on: (a) the subjective vs. objective type; and (b) the individual- versus collective-level of performance measure used to determine pay (Gerhart & Rynes, 2003; Gerhart, Rynes, & Fulmer, 2009). By crossing the two dimensions, Gerhart et al. (2009) classified pay-for-performance plans into four types: individual-level behavioral performance-based pay (e.g., merit pay); individual-level objective performance-based pay (e.g., individual incentives, sales commissions); collective-level behavioral performance-based pay (e.g., merit pay for executives); and collective-level objective performance-based pay (e.g., gain-sharing, profit-sharing, stock plans). Below, in discussing the effectiveness of pay-for-performance plans in different cultures, we adopt Gerhart et al.'s (2009) pay-for-performance typology and present possible research questions.

Individual performance-based pay and the degree of pay differential

Individual-level, behavior-performance-based pay. The use of individual-level, behavior-based performance measures in designing a pay-for-performance plan offers several advantages. Those measures allow managers to factor in variables that are not under the employee's control but that nevertheless influence performance. In addition, by not simply emphasizing results as performance measures, behavior-based performance measures allow managers to consider whether the results are achieved through the right means and behaviors. Furthermore, they can also prevent employees from paying exclusive attention to easily measurable/quantifiable tasks or results at the expense of broader pro-social and pro-organizational behaviors such as organizational citizenship behaviors and extra-role performance (Lawler, 1971; Milgrom & Roberts, 1992; Wright, George, Farnsworth, & McMahan, 1993).

However, the use of individual behavior-based performance measures also bears some costs. By increasing the subjectivity of performance measures (and the following pay decisions), managers can become reluctant to make meaningful performance differentiations amongst subordinates, as high differentiations can produce undesirable consequences such as heightened conflict, increased political behaviors, and lowered cooperation and collaboration (Heneman & Judge, 2000; Shaw, 2014). In addition, behavior-based measures are not applicable in situations where the comprehensive observation of employee behaviors is not feasible. Indeed, a major issue in the merit-pay raise—a representative form of a behavioral performance-based pay plan—literature has been about how to encourage managers to make sufficient performance differentiation amongst subordinates (Heneman, 1992).

Given the subjective nature of behavior-based performance measures, the implementation of a behavioral performance-based pay plan becomes especially difficult when employees engage in excessive social comparison with each other. Because managers are highly likely to have limited information on subordinates' work behaviors, they will have difficulty in explaining and justifying the degree of performance (and pay) differential to each subordinate. In addition, when behavior-based measures are used, employees are more likely to question the fairness of the degree of performance and pay differentials (e.g., Cook & Yamagishi, 1983; Dunning, Johnson, Ehrlinger, & Kruger, 2003). Thus, the implementation of a behavioral performance-based pay plan becomes especially difficult when subordinates pay more attention to their *relative* pay standing among colleagues than their past pay levels.

Westerners have high independent self-construal and tend to focus on their own, intra-individual (i.e., internally oriented) thoughts, feelings, and goals, whereas Asians have high interdependent self-construal, tend to have an extra-individual (i.e., externally oriented) focus, and are more concerned with the thoughts, feelings, behaviors, and goals of others (Markus &

Kitayama, 1991; Oyserman et al., 2002). Building on this conceptual basis, Gibbons and Buunk (1999) showed that, as individuals with high interdependent self-construal tend to pay attention to and base behavior on the ways other behave, they are more likely to engage in social comparison than those with high independent self-construal. Similarly, White and Lehman posited that Asians make more social comparisons than Westerners because they are motivated to "(a) monitor the social environment, (b) evaluate the self in relation to the social context, (c) affiliate with or feel a sense of connectedness with others, and (d) improve the self" (2005: 233). Indeed, several other studies have found that Asians were more likely to engage in social comparisons than Westerners (e.g., Bordia & Blau, 2003; Chung & Mallery, 1999; White & Lehman, 2005). For example, Bordia and Blau (2003) showed that other employees' pay levels had a significant impact on a focal employee's satisfaction with pay only when the employee had high collectivistic values (but not with high individualistic values).

When employees engage in high levels of social comparison, behavioral performance pay plans will likely be difficult to implement, as managers bear a high social and emotional burden in sufficiently differentiating pay amongst employees. Also, when employees engage in social comparison and are concerned with their relative standing in their workgroup, managers need to justify their pay decisions based not only on the focal employee's own performance but also on the employee's relative performance (and pay) in relation to others. This increases the cognitive and emotional burden managers bear in making pay allocation decisions. Indeed, previous studies have shown that when managers believe that employees are likely to attempt to influence their decisions, they tend to minimize the pay differentials amongst employees (Bartol & Martin, 1989; Leventhal, Karuza, & Fry, 1980; Leventhal et al., 1972; Major & Adams, 1983). Accordingly, we expect that managers having Asian employees are likely to avoid making large performance and pay differentials more than managers having Western employees.

Individual-level, results-performance-based pay. One way to avoid the above-described managers' concerns is to link pay with objective (i.e., results) performance measures such as productivity and sales volumes, instead of subjective (i.e., behavioral) measures. When objective measures are used, managers are less likely to bear the cognitive and emotional burdens of dealing with employees' attempts to influence their pay decisions, as the objective measures help them explain and justify their decisions (Lawler, 1971). Indeed, previous studies have shown that the incentive effects of high pay differentials are highest when the pay differentials are based on objective and legitimate factors (Jenkins et al., 1998; Shaw, Gupta, & Delery, 2002; Trevor, Reilly, & Gerhart, 2012). Accordingly, we expect that when a pay-for-performance plan is designed based on objective performance measures, managers' burdens can be reduced, which in turn lead to a sufficient degree of pay differentials among employees for both managers with Asian subordinates and those with Western subordinates.

Individual performance-based pay and sorting

An important consequence of a pay-for-performance plan is sorting effects—changes in the workforce composition resulting from a pay-for-performance plan (Gerhart & Milkovich, 1992). Pay-for-performance may cause some people to stay and others to leave an organization. For example, Shaw and Gupta (2007) showed that high performance-based pay differentials amongst employees lead poor performers to be more likely to quit (while retaining high performers). Similarly, Lazear (2000) showed that, in a glass installation facility, the implementation of a pay-for-performance plan led to increased employee productivity, and about 50 percent of the productivity increase was attributable to the workforce composition changes—less productive workers quit and were replaced by more productive workers over time. A theoretical reasoning for this sorting effect is that individuals self-select to a right form of compensation plan (e.g., performance-based pay vs. fixed pay) based on relatively stable individual characteristics such as risk seeking (Cable & Judge, 1994), trait-like motivation (Amabile, Hill, Hennesey, & Tighe, 1994), and ability (Trank, Rynes, & Bretz, 2002). However, an individual's own perception of the stability or malleability of the self can be different, and this can influence the strength of turnover intention when pay-for-performance is implemented.

Cultural psychology research has shown that individuals have different implicit theories on the malleability of their selves and the world around them (Dweck, Hong, & Chiu, 1993; Dweck & Leggett, 1988). Asians tend to see themselves as malleable and the world as stable, whereas Westerners tend to see themselves as stable and the world as malleable (Heine, 2001; Su et al., 1999). Specifically, Heine and Ruby explain that:

> In hierarchical collectivistic cultures, such as in East Asia, the social world remains somewhat impervious to efforts by a lone individual to change things (e.g., Chiu, Dweck, Tong, & Fu, 1997), and people are more likely to have a flexible and incremental view of themselves (Heine et al., 2001; Norenzayan, Choi, & Nisbett, 2002). When the self is perceived as more mutable than the social world, it follows that people would be willing to adjust themselves to better fit the demands of their social worlds. In contrast, people from Western cultures tend to stress the malleability of the world relative to the self (Su et al., 1999) and the independent self is experienced as relatively immutable and consistent (Heine et al., 2001; Suh, 2002). This view that the self is an immutable entity, working within the context of a mutable world, sustains a perception of primary control.
>
> *(2010: 258)*

We posit that this cultural difference in the malleability of self-view versus world-view will strengthen/weaken the pay-for-performance plan effects on workforce composition change (i.e., sorting effects). When a pay-for-performance plan is implemented, and the pay differential between poor performers and high performers becomes greater, Asians are more likely to react by increasing their work efforts, placing the quit possibility as a last resort, based on the belief that they are malleable and can find ways to reduce the pay differentials within the organization. Accordingly, low performers will react by increasing work efforts rather than leaving their jobs to find better fitting jobs. Westerners will also react by increasing their work efforts, but at the same time, they will be less hesitant to change jobs (e.g., transfer or quit) than Asians, as they tend to believe that they are less malleable and it is relatively easier to change the environment around them. Hence, we expect that low-performing (and thus low-paid) Westerners are more likely to leave their current jobs (i.e., sorting effects) than their Asian counterparts when a pay-for-performance plan is implemented.

Collective performance-based pay and social loafing: moderating role of culture

Instead of using individual performance measures, a pay-for-performance plan can be designed by using collective-level performance measures such as organizational profit and team productivity increases. Linking pay to collective-level performance helps employees pay more attention to the interdependent nature of work in an organization (e.g., teamwork, cooperation). A potential problem of using an individual performance-based pay plan is that it may lead employees to compete with one another and attempt to attain personal success at the expense of other employees or the larger organization. Such undesirable effects on the social fabric can be prevented by using a collective performance-based pay plan, as employees will pay more attention to the collective interests than their self-interests. Despite those advantages, collective performance-based pay plans have potential drawbacks as well. Employees can be less motivated to work harder because collective performance can be influenced by many factors that are beyond each employee's control; thus, the link between their efforts and their pay becomes unclear. In a similar vein, a collective performance-based pay plan can cause a social loafing problem—"reduction in motivation and effort when individuals work collectively compared with when they work individually or coactively" (Karau & Williams, 1993: 681)—because some employees may strategically choose to rely on other employees' efforts and performance while not exerting their best work efforts. Thus, preventing undesirable social relational issues and social loafing problems is critical for the effectiveness of collective performance-based pay plans. Cultural psychology literature explains that Asians tend to emphasize conformity more than their Western counterparts because they define themselves in relation to others. For example, Asch's (1956) classic conformity study has been replicated well over 100 times in seventeen countries, and a meta-analysis of these studies revealed that people feel conformity pressure across all countries, but Asians conform even more than Westerners (Bond & Smith, 1996). Triandis explains this cultural difference as follows:

> In individualist cultures, most people's social behavior is largely determined by personal goals that overlap only slightly with the goals of collectives such as the family, the work group, the tribe, political allies, co-religionists, fellow countrymen and the state. When a conflict arises between personal and group goals, it is considered acceptable for the individual to place personal goals ahead of collective goals. By contrast, in collectivist cultures social behavior is determined largely by goals shared with some collective, and if there is a conflict between personal and collective goals, it is considered socially desirable to place collective goals ahead of personal goals.
>
> *(1990: 42)*

In addition, research has shown that Asians tend to engage in mutual monitoring behaviors more than Westerners because of their attention to group norms and conformity pressures (Puffer & Shekshnia, 1996; Triandis, Bontempo, Villareal, Asai, & Lucca, 1988). This implies that Asians are likely to engage less in social loafing than Westerners. More nuanced findings show that Asians' focus on interpersonal relationships and conformity pressure occurs only when they perceive others as their in-group (vs. out-group) members. In fact, Bond and Smith's (1996) meta-analysis, which quantitatively summarized the follow-up evidence of Asch's (1956) study, showed that Asians were more likely to show higher conformity behaviors than Westerners when other individuals were perceived as their peers, but in a situation with strangers their conformity behaviors were similar to Westerners and even showed some evidence of anti-conformity (Bond & Smith, 1996; Frager, 1970). This line of reasoning and evidence suggests that Asians perceive a higher level of pressure to conform to a group norm than Westerners only with their in-group members.

Linking individuals' pay to their group's or organization's performance sets a common goal for the group/organization members and incentivizes them to work together. This also makes the in-group boundary clear. For example, the use of organization-level performance measures sets the collective unit's boundary at the organization level, and the use of team-level performance measures sets the collective unit's boundary at the team level. Thus, the use of a collective performance-based pay plan helps employees to clearly identify their in-group members (and out-group members) and increases conformity pressure and mutual monitoring behaviors within the in-group boundary (Puffer & Shekshnia, 1996; Triandis et al., 1988). As described above, Westerners, having independent self-construal, tend to focus more on their own qualities and attributes as a unique member of the group and, thus, the in-group boundary may not have a large impact on their cognition or behaviors. In contrast, Asians, having interdependent self-construal, pay more attention to others' behaviors by giving/receiving conformity pressure and, thus, the in-group boundary has a relatively larger impact for them than for Westerners. Accordingly, when pay levels are determined based on collective performance measures, Asian work-groups suffer less from social loafing problems than Western workgroups. Indeed, Karau and Williams' (1993) meta-analysis on social loafing behavior presented supportive evidence of this notion that Asians (e.g., Japanese, Taiwanese, Chinese) tend to engage in social loafing behavior less than Westerners (e.g., people in the United States). Accordingly, we expect that Asians are less likely to show social loafing behaviors than Westerners when a collective performance-based pay plan is implemented.

Conclusion

In this chapter, we reviewed previous studies on the effects of culture on compensation practices and illustrated several research questions for future research building on the idea that the effects of a pay-for-performance plan on employee attitudes and behaviors is strengthened/weakened (i.e., moderated) by culture. In making those suggestions, we conceptualized culture using a broad term—Asians and Westerners—rather than a cross-country cultural difference score such as power distance, uncertainty avoidance, individualism, or masculinity (Hofstede, 1980), which has been used in most previous culture-compensation studies. We intentionally avoided defining culture based on a national boundary, as we conceptualized culture as a product of the interaction between self and an environment and, thus, as malleable and changeable over time. For example, in many Asian countries, younger generations (e.g., Millennials) are characterized as not having a different culture than the country's traditional culture (e.g., Confucianism) but as having a more Westernized culture. In addition, the Asian financial crisis, and the following regulatory and institutional changes, influenced many Asian people to adopt a more Western-ized lifestyle.

Accordingly, conceptualizing culture based on a national boundary seems to be less mean-ingful, and it is more reasonable to consider culture as individual differences—amongst those having independent self-construal (i.e., Westerners) and those having interdependent self-construal (i.e., Asians)—although those differences might still be shared among a societal unit such as a country, region, community, organization, or team. Thus, we expect that our above-presented expectations to apply to any unit that can be characterized as having a shared value (i.e., independent self-construal or interdependence self-construal) amongst the members. Despite this, studies have shown that many people in Asian countries still have high interde-pendent self-construal, and we expect that our propositions about interdependent self-construal will apply to many organizations in Asia (perhaps Australia and New Zealand might be exceptions).

The key argument we made in this chapter is that even though previous studies have not produced consistent evidence, it is still important to consider culture as a contextual/situational factor which influences the effectiveness of compensation practices. We believe that the sugges-tions made in this chapter provide guidance for future researchers who aim to investigate the interplay of culture and compensation practices.

Future research avenues

We suggest that the Asian, or more broadly international, compensation literature could be further advanced if researchers consider the following issues in their future research:

1   Paying more attention to individual-level variation in cultural values. Specifically, we suggest that researchers take the cultural psychological perspective rather than the cross-cultural perspective (Hofstede, 1980) and define culture as an individual's shared form of self-construal, which is emerged and attuned by a cultural meaning practice within which the individual develops.
2   Investigating the moderating role of culture in the effect of compensation on outcomes rather than investigating the direct effects of culture on compensation practice preferences.
3   Considering four distinctive forms of pay-for-performance practices (Gerhart et al., 2009) and making specific predictions on culture effects for the four forms of pay-for-performance.

We offer examples of research questions as follows: when individual-level, behavioral-performance-based pay plans are implemented, do Asians make more compressed pay differentials than Westerners? When individual-level, results-based pay plans are implemented, do Asians and Westerners make similar pay differentials? When individual performance-based pay plans are implemented, are Asian low performers less likely to quit than Western low performers? When collective performance-based pay plans are implemented, do Asians social loaf less than Westerners?

References

Amabile, T. M., Hill, K. G., Hennessey, B. A., & Tighe, E. M. (1994). The work preference inventory: Assessing intrinsic and extrinsic motivational orientations. *Journal of Personality and Social Psychology, 66*, 950–967.

Asch, S. (1956). Studies of independence and conformity: A minority of one against a unanimous majority. *Psychological Monographs, 70* (9, Whole No. 416).

Bartol, K. M. & Martin, D. C. (1988). Influences on managerial pay allocations: A dependency perspective. *Personnel Psychology, 41*, 361–378.

Bartol, K. M. & Martin, D. C. (1989). Effects of dependence, dependency threats, and pay secrecy on managerial pay allocations. *Journal of Applied Psychology, 74*, 105–113.

Bloom, M., Milkovich, G. T., & Mitra, A. (2003). International compensation: Learning from how managers respond to variations in local host contexts. *The International Journal of Human Resource Management, 14*, 1350–1367.

Bond, M. H. & Hwang, K. K. (1986). The social psychology of Chinese people. In M. H. Bond (Ed.), *The psychology of the Chinese people* (pp. 213–266). Hong Kong: Oxford University Press.

Bond, M. H., Leung, K., & Wan, K. C. (1982). How does cultural collectivism operate?: The impact of task and maintenance contributions on reward allocation. *Journal of Cross-Cultural Psychology, 13*, 186–200.

Bond, R. & Smith, P. B. (1996). Culture and conformity: A meta-analysis of studies using Asch's (1952b, 1956) line judgment task. *Psychological Bulletin, 119*, 111–137.

Bordia, P. & Blau, G. (2003). Moderating effect of allocentrism on the pay referent comparison-pay level satisfaction relationship. *Applied Psychology: An International Review, 52*, 499–514.

Bruner, J. (1993). Do we "acquire" culture or vice versa? *Behavioral and Brain Sciences, 16*, 515–516.

Cable, D. M. & Judge, T. A. (1994). Pay preferences and job search decisions: A person–organization fit perspective. *Personnel Psychology, 47*, 317–348.

Chang, E. (2006). Individual pay for performance and commitment HR practices in South Korea. *Journal of World Business, 41*(4), 368–381.

Chen, C. C. (1995). New trends in rewards allocation preferences: A Sino-US comparison. *Academy of Management Journal, 38*, 408–428.

Chen, C. C., Chen, X. P., & Meindl, J. R. (1998). How can cooperation be fostered? The cultural effects of individualism-collectivism. *Academy of Management Review, 23*, 285–304.

Chiang, F. F. T. (2005). A critical examination of Hofstede's thesis and its application to international reward management. *The International Journal of Human Resource Management, 16*, 1545–1563.

Chiang, F. F. T. & Birtch, T. (2005). A taxonomy of reward preference: Examining country differences. *Journal of International Management, 11*, 357–375.

Chiang, F. F. T. & Birtch, T. (2006). An empirical examination of reward preferences within and across national settings. *Management International Review, 46*, 573–596.

Chiang, F. F. T. & Birtch, T. (2007). The transferability of management practices: Examining cross-national differences in reward preferences. *Human Relations, 60*, 1293–1330.

Child, J. & Markoczy, L. (1993). Host-country managerial behaviour and learning in Chinese and Hungarian joint ventures. *Journal of Management Studies, 30*, 611–630.

Chiu, C., Dweck, C. S., Tong, J. U., & Fu, J. H. (1997). Implicit theories and conceptions of morality. *Journal of Personality and Social Psychology, 73*, 923–940.

Chung, T. & Mallery, P. (1999). Social comparison, individualism-collectivism, and self-esteem in China and the United States. *Current Psychology: Developmental, Learning, Personality, Social, 18*, 340–352.

Cohen, J. (1992). A power primer. *Psychological Bulletin, 112*, 155–159.

Cook, K. S. & Yamagishi, T. (1983). Social determinants of equity judgments: The problem of multidimensional input. In D. M. Messick & K. S. Cook (Eds.), *Equity theory: Psychological and social perspectives* (pp. 95–126). New York: Praeger.

Du, J. & Choi, J. N. (2010). Pay for performance in emerging markets: Insights from China. *Journal of International Business Studies, 41*(4), 671–689.

Dunning, D., Johnson, K., Ehrlinger, J., & Kruger, J. (2003). Why people fail to recognize their own incompetence. *Current Directions in Psychological Science, 12*, 83–87.

Dweck, C. S., Chiu, C., & Hong, Y. (1995). Implicit theories and their role in judgements and reactions: A world from two perspectives. *Psychological Inquiry, 6*, 267–285.

Dweck, C. S., & Leggett, E. (1988). A social-cognitive approach to motivation and personality. *Psychological Review, 95*, 256–273.

Fischer, R. & Smith, P. (2003). Reward allocation and culture: A meta-analysis. *Journal of Cross-Cultural Psychology, 34*, 251–268.

Frager, R. (1970). Conformity and anti-conformity in Japan. *Journal of Personality and Social Psychology, 15*, 203–210.

Gerhart, B. (2008). Compensation and national culture. In L. R. Gomez-Mejia & S. Werner (Eds.), *Global compensation: Foundations and perspectives*. New York: Routledge.

Gerhart, B. & Milkovich, G. T. (1992). Employee compensation: Research and practice. In M. D. Dunnette & L. M. Hough (Eds.), *Handbook of industrial & organizational psychology* (2nd ed.) (pp. 481–569). Palo Alto, CA: Consulting Psychologists Press.

Gerhart, B. & Rynes, S. L. (2003). *Compensation: Theory, evidence, and strategic implications.* Beverly Hills, CA: Sage.

Gerhart, B., Rynes, S. L., & Fulmer, I. S. (2009). Pay and performance: Individuals, groups, and executives. *Academy of Management Annals, 3*, 251–315.

Giacobbe-Miller, J. K., Miller, D. J., & Victorov, V. I. (1998). A comparison of Russian and U.S. pay allocation decisions, distributive justice judgments, and productivity under different payment conditions. *Personnel Psychology, 51*, 137–163.

Gibbons, F. X. & Buunk, B. P. (1999). Individual differences in social comparison: Development of a scale of social comparison orientation. *Journal of Personality and Social Psychology, 76*, 129–142.

Gomez-Mejia, L. R. & Welbourne, T. (1991). Compensation strategies in a global context. *Human Resource Planning, 14*(1), 29–41.

Greckhamer, T. (2015). CEO compensation in relation to worker compensation across countries: The configurational impact of country-level institutions. *Strategic Management Journal, 37*(4), 793–815.

Greenfield, P. M. (2000). Three approaches to the psychology of culture: Where do they come from? Where can they go? *Asian Journal of Social Psychology, 3*, 223–240.

Gully, S. M., Phillips, J. M., & Tarique, I. (2003). Collectivism and goal orientation as mediators of the effect of national identity on merit pay decisions. *The International Journal of Human Resource Management, 14*, 1368–1390.

Hallock, K. F. (2012). *Pay: Why people earn what they earn and what you can do now to make more.* New York: Cambridge University Press.

Heine, S. J. (2001). Self as cultural product: An examination of East Asian and North American selves. *Journal of Personality, 69*, 881–906.

Heine, S. J. (2010). Cultural psychology. In D. T. Gilbert, S. Fiske, & G. Lindzey (Eds.), *Handbook of social psychology* (5th ed.) (pp. 1423–1464). New York: Wiley.

Heine, S. J., Kitayama, S., Lehman, D. R., Takata, T., Ide, E., Leung, C., & Matsumoto, H. (2001). Divergent consequences of success and failure in Japan and North America: An investigation of self-improving motivations and malleable selves. *Journal of Personality and Social Psychology, 81*, 599–615.

Heine, S. J. & Ruby, M. B. (2010). Cultural psychology. *Wiley Interdisciplinary Reviews: Cognitive Science, 1*, 254–266.

Heneman, H. G. & Judge, T. A. (2000). Compensation attitudes. In S. L. Rynes & B. Gerhart (Eds.), *Compensation in organizations* (pp. 61–103). San Francisco, CA: Jossey-Bass.

Heneman, R. L. (1992). *Merit pay: Linking pay increases to performance ratings.* Reading, MA: Addison-Wesley.

Hofstede, G. (1980). *Culture's consequences: International differences in work-related values.* Beverly Hills, CA: Sage.

Hofstede, G. (1991). *Cultures and organizations: Software of the mind.* London: McGraw-Hill.

Hofstede, G. (1993). Cultural constraints in management theories. *Academy of Management Executive, 7*, 81–94.

Hofstede, G. (2001). *Culture's consequences: Comparing values, behaviors, institutions, and organizations across nations* (2nd ed.). Thousand Oaks, CA: Sage.

Hofstede, G. (2015). In the Hofstede centre. Retrieved November 10, 2015 from http://geert-hofstede.com/countries.html.

Hofstede, G. & Bond, M. H. (1988). Confucius and economic growth: New trends in culture's consequences. *Organizational Dynamics, 16*, 4–21.

House, R. J., Hanges, P. J., Javidan, M., Dorfman, P. W., & Gupta, V. (2004). *Culture, leadership, and organizations.* Thousand Oaks, CA: Sage.

Jenkins, D. G., Jr., Mitra, A., Gupta, N., & Shaw, J. D. (1998). Are financial incentives related to performance?: A meta-analytic review of empirical research. *Journal of Applied Psychology, 83*, 777–787.

Karau, S. J. & Williams, K. D. (1993). Social loafing: A meta-analytic review and theoretical integration. *Journal of Personality and Social Psychology, 65*, 681–706.

Kim, K. I., Park, H. J., & Suzuki, N. (1990). Reward allocations in the United States, Japan, and Korea: A comparison of individualistic and collectivistic cultures. *Academy of Management Journal, 33*, 188–198.

Lawler, E. E. III. (1971). *Pay and organizational effectiveness: A psychological view.* New York: McGraw-Hill.

Lazear, E. (2000). Performance pay and productivity. *American Economic Review, 90*, 1346–1361.

Lehman, D. R., Chiu, C. Y., & Schaller, M. (2004). Psychology and culture. *Annual Review of Psychology, 55*, 689–714.

Leventhal, G. S., Karuza, J. Jr., & Fry, W. R. (1980). Beyond fairness: A theory of allocation preferences. In G. Mikula (Ed.), *Justice and social interaction* (pp. 167–218). New York: Springer Verlag.

Leventhal, G. S., Michaels, J. W., & Sanford, C. (1972). Inequity and interpersonal conflict: Reward allocation and secrecy about reward as methods of preventing conflict. *Journal of Personality and Social Psychology, 23*, 88–102.

Long, R. J. & Shields, J. L. (2005). Performance pay in Canadian and Australian firms: A comparative study. *The International Journal of Human Resource Management, 16*, 1783–1811.

Lowe, K. B., Milliman, J., De Cieri, H., & Dowling, P. J. (2002). International compensation practices: A ten-country comparative analysis. *Human Resource Management, 41*, 45–66.

Major, B. & Adams, J. B. (1983). Role of gender, interpersonal orientation, and self-presentation in distributive-justice behavior. *Journal of Personality and Social Psychology, 45*, 598–608.

Mamman, A., Sulaiman, M., & Fadel, A. (1996). Attitudes to pay systems: An exploratory study within and across cultures. *The International Journal of Human Resource Management, 7*, 101–121.

Marín, G. (1985). The preferences for equity when judging the attractiveness and fairness of an allocator: The role of familiarity and culture. *Journal of Social Psychology, 125*, 543–549.

Markus, H. R. & Kitayama, S. (1991). Culture and the self: Implications for cognition, emotion, and motivation. *Psychological Review, 98*, 224–253.

Martocchio, J. J. (2013). *Strategic compensation* (7th ed.). Boston, MA: Pearson.

Milgrom, P. & Roberts, J. (1992). *Economics, organization, and management.* Englewood Cliffs, NJ: Prentice Hall.

Milkovich, G. T, Newman, J., & Gerhart, B. (2013). *Compensation* (11th ed.). New York: McGraw-Hill Irwin.

Murphy-Berman, V., Berman, J. J., Singh, P., Pachauri, A., & Kumar, P. (1984). Factors affecting allocation to needy and meritorious recipients: A cross-cultural comparison. *Journal of Personality and Social Psychology, 46,* 1267–1272.

Newman, K. L. & Nollen, S. D. (1996). Culture and congruence: The fit between management practices and national culture. *Journal of International Business Studies, 27,* 753–778.

Norenzayan, A., Choi, I., & Nisbett, R. E. (2002). Cultural similarities and differences in social inference: Evidence from behavioral predictions and lay theories of behavior. *Personality and Social Psychology Bulletin, 28,* 109–120.

Oyserman, D., Coon, H. M., & Kemmelmeier, M. (2002). Rethinking individualism and collectivism: Evaluation of theoretical assumptions and meta-analyses. *Psychological Bulletin, 128,* 3–72.

Puffer, S. M. & Shekshnia, S. V. (1996). The fit between Russian culture and compensation. *The International Executive, 38,* 217–241.

Ramamoorthy, N., Gupta, A., Sardessai, R. M., & Flood, P. C. (2005). Individualism/collectivism and attitudes towards human resource systems: A comparative study of American, Irish and Indian MBA students. *The International Journal of Human Resource Management, 16,* 852–869.

Rowley, C. & Benson, J. (2004). *The management of human resources in the Asia Pacific Region: Convergence reconsidered.* New York: Frank Cass.

Rynes, S. L., Colbert, A., & Brown, K. G. (2002). HR professionals' beliefs about effective human resource practices: Correspondence between research and practice. *Human Resource Management, 41,* 149–174.

Rynes, S. L., Gerhart, B., & Minette, K. A. (2004). The importance of pay in employee motivation: Discrepancies between what people say and what they do. *Human Resource Management, 43,* 381–394.

Schuler, R. S. & Rogovsky, N. (1998). Understanding compensation practice variations across firms: The impact of national culture. *Journal of International Business Studies, 29,* 159–177.

Shaw, J. D. (2014). Pay dispersion. *Annual Review of Organizational Psychology and Organizational Behavior, 1,* 521–544.

Shaw, J. D. & Gupta, N. (2007). Pay system characteristics and quit patterns of good, average, and poor performers. *Personnel Psychology, 60,* 903–928.

Shaw, J. D. & Gupta, N. (2015). Let the evidence speak again! Financial incentives are more effective than we thought. *Human Resource Management Journal, 25,* 281–293.

Shaw, J. D., Gupta, N., & Delery, J. E. (2002). Pay dispersion and workforce performance: Moderating effects of incentives and interdependence. *Strategic Management Journal, 23,* 491–512.

Shin, J. Y., Kang, S. C., Hyun, J. H., & Kim, B. J. (2014). Determinants and performance effects of executive pay multiples evidence from Korea. *Industrial and Labor Relations Review, 68*(1), 53–78.

Shweder, R. A. (1990). Cultural psychology: What is it? In J. W. Stigler, R. A. Shweder, & G. Herdt (Eds.), *Cultural psychology: Essays on comparative human development* (pp. 1–43). Cambridge: Cambridge University Press.

Su, S. K., Chiu, C. Y., Hong, Y. Y., Leung, K., Peng, K., & Morris, M. W. (1999). Self organization and social organization: American and Chinese constructions. In T. R. Tyler, R. Kramer, & O. John (Eds.), *The psychology of the social self* (pp. 193–222). Mahwah, NJ: Lawrence Erlbaum.

Suh, E. M. (2002). Culture, identity consistency, and subjective well-being. *Journal of Personality and Social Psychology, 83,* 1378–1391.

Sun, S. L., Zhao, X., & Yang, H. (2010). Executive compensation in Asia: A critical review and outlook. *Asia Pacific Journal of Management, 27*(4), 775–802.

Trank, C. Q., Rynes, S. L., & Bretz, R. D., Jr. (2002). Attracting applicants in the war for talent: Differences in work preferences among high achievers. *Journal of Business and Psychology, 16,* 331–345.

Trevor, C. O., Reilly, G., & Gerhart, B. (2012). Reconsidering pay dispersion's effect on the performance of interdependent work: Reconciling sorting and pay inequality. *Academy of Management Journal, 55,* 545–610.

Triandis, H. C. (1990). Cross-cultural studies of individualism and collectivism. In J. J. Herman (Ed.), *Nebraska symposium on motivation 1989: Cross-cultural perspectives* (Vol. 37, pp. 279–336). Lincoln, NE: University of Nebraska Press.

Triandis, H. C., Bontempo, R., Villareal, M. J., Asai, M., & Lucca, N. (1988). Individualism and collectivism: Cross-cultural perspectives on self-ingroup relationships. *Journal of Personality and Social Psychology, 54*, 323–338.

Varma, A. & Budhwar, P. S. (2014). *Managing human resources in Asia-Pacific.* New York: Routledge.

White, K. & Lehman, D. R. (2005). Culture and social comparison seeking: The role of self-motives. *Personality and Social Psychology Bulletin, 31*, 232–242.

Wright, P. M., George, J. M., Farnsworth, R., & McMahan, G. C. (1993). Productivity and extra-role behavior: The effects of goals and incentives on spontaneous helping. *Journal of Applied Psychology, 78*, 374–381.

Yang, H. & Rowley, C. (2008). Performance management systems in South Korea. In A. Varma, P. Budhwar & A. DeNisi (Eds.), *Performance management systems around the globe* (pp. 316–340). London: Routledge.

Zhou, J. & Martocchio, J. J. (2001). Chinese and American managers' compensation award decisions: A comparative policy-capturing study. *Personnel Psychology, 54*, 115–114.

12

HUMAN CAPITAL FLOWS AND TALENT MANAGEMENT IN ASIA

Anthony McDonnell and Ying Guo

Introduction

Asia is a vast continent encompassing three of the world's most competitive economies (Singapore, Japan, and Hong Kong SAR) with three more within the top twenty (World Economic Forum, 2015). Over the past couple of decades, Asia has emerged as a hotbed for business opportunity. Low-cost manufacturing, enhanced personal wealth, a larger middle class, an increasingly open and pro-business environment have all been strong contributors to this. The Asian economies appeared to buffer the most negative impacts of the 2007–2009 global financial crisis, relative to much of the Western world with economic growth continuing across much of the region. A concern that has surfaced over the past decade, and which shows little sign of changing, has been in relation to ensuring that there is a sufficient supply of talent. This threatens business and economic prosperity across many industries and countries. While each country has its strengths and limitations, the quality and supply of talent is seemingly a consistently pressing issue across most of the Asian countries, albeit not always for the same reasons. Vorhauser-Smith and Cariss (2014) suggest that of the Southeast Asian economies, only Singapore possessed the educational standards that multinational companies (MNCs) require for their skilled roles. Yet, on the other hand, Singapore has one of the more aging populations and workforces in Asia. Consequently, talent shortages may be a concern in Singapore albeit for potentially different reasons to other countries in the region, that is, countries with youthful populations but which are less educated and qualified. Similar talent availability concerns, as will be articulated in the chapter, exist in other Asian economies, most notably in China.

Talent challenges in Asian countries exist with respect to both attraction and retention of skilled staff. In other words, organizations are grappling with how to attract and retain talent. This is of consequence beyond an industry or organization but goes to the national level. With the significant changes in international migration flows over the past few decades, the working populations of many countries are increasingly diverse. This has led to concerns in some countries of the negative impact of brain drain. Cooke (2011) has noted that the opening up of the Chinese economy and the rise of globalization has led to a brain drain of local talent through migration and also from Chinese firms to foreign owned MNCs. A more diverse labor pool can be a critical success factor for organizations and countries alike. Diversity does, however, raise challenges.

Concern over the ability to attract and retain sufficient levels and caliber of human capital was a central reason behind the emergence of talent management as a topic of interest to senior organizational leaders and academics. The rise of talent management as a concept has been ascribed to the McKinsey consultancy group tabling that a "war for talent" was taking place, one that was going to be increasingly intense (Michaels, Handfield-Jones, & Axelrod, 2001). Over the past two decades, talent management has established itself across the world as a critical senior management activity (Sparrow, Scullion, & Tarique, 2014). It also appears to give organizational leaders considerable distress. Skills shortages appear to be continuing as an unrelenting worry for organizations across much of the world (Deloitte, 2013; Manpower, 2013). In spite of the great awareness and interest in talent management by organizational leaders, it appears to be an activity that they view themselves as not being especially effective in. For example, a recent report by PricewaterhouseCoopers (PwC, 2014) found that 93 percent of the surveyed CEOs recognized their organization needed to change their talent strategy. Of more concern to this high perceived need for change was the fact that only 34 percent responded that human resources (HR) was well prepared to deal with the talent challenges.

In this chapter, we consider the context of human capital flows and talent management in Asia. We commence by considering the rise of the Asian world and the emerging talent challenges that have resulted. Then the chapter provides a synthesis of the talent management literature that focuses on Asian countries. As will become evident, there is a limited empirical base in this area. Specifically, little to nothing exists on talent management in domestic Asian firms, or at least, not which have been published in the leading international (English) academic journals. The chapter then moves to considering talent attraction and retention issues from the domestic and multinational company perspective, before considering the challenge for foreign talents working in Asia.

The rise of Asia and the emerging talent challenge

The last decade, which included a major global financial crisis (2007–2009), has seen the economic power move somewhat away from the developed world to developing countries. This has seen the ascent of China and India as two of the most dynamic economies attracting significant swathes of foreign direct investment (FDI), along with building strong indigenous industrial sectors. Overall, Asia contributes significantly to global economic growth and takes a key role in shaping the global market. The forecast for GDP growth in developing Asia was 5.8 percent and 6 percent in 2015 and 2016 (Asian Development Bank, 2015), with the global economy expected to grow 3 percent and 3.3 percent in these two years respectively (World Bank, 2015). Stable growth and development has helped Asia become one of the most important FDI recipients and contributors. FDI inflows to the Asian area grew to $541 billion in 2015, a 15.6 percent increase from 2014; and the FDI outflows from Asia achieved $332 billion in 2015 (UNCTAD, 2016). Five host economies out of the top twenty FDI recipients are from Asian areas and Japan, China, Hong Kong (China), Singapore, and the Republic of Korea were ranked in the top twenty home economies of FDI outflows (UNCTAD, 2016).

FDI flows can provide benefits in terms of finance, technology, and managerial knowledge (for example, through MNCs establishing) while also boosting talent mobility amongst Asian counties and the talent flows between Asia and the rest of the world. Human capital has been examined in terms of its impact on attracting FDI (Noorbakhsh, Paloni, & Youssef, 2001). The rapid rise of some Asian economies (in particular China) has led to real difficulties in terms of talent supply. Asia has a relatively large population, especially China and India; however, attracting skilled talent is still important given that the local talent supply is arguably viewed as somewhat weak. Although there are a large number of university graduates coming through every year, it continues to be difficult for companies to find qualified employees (Diez, 2014). Cooke (2011) points to a paradoxical situation whereby there has been a substantial increase in the number of graduates from the Chinese education system, yet, significant shortages of managerial and skilled workers are evident. She notes that the employment data for these graduates as underwhelming (e.g., 70 percent of graduates in 2008 found employment within one year). Accentuating this situation is the brain drain issue whereby many graduates are looking overseas for opportunities. The ability to attract talent back to Asia will, in the future, be a competitive necessity.

The Global Talent Competitiveness Index 2014 provides a ranking of each country's ability to create competitive advantage through the quality of human capital. The index is based on two core dimensions. First, *Inputs*—define a country's ability to attract, grow, and retain talent within its regulatory, market, and business landscape. Second, *outputs*—define the knowledge capabilities and vocational skills these inputs produce. The index is then composed of sixty-five factors to produce the index. As shown in Table 12.1, the Asian economies are typically low in the ranking with Singapore the outlier in second. Japan is twentieth, China is forty-first, and India is seventy-eighth. Overall, the index appears to highlight talent competitiveness as an area of potential angst for Asian states in improving their economic and social development.

Table 12.2 further supports the contention of there being some significant challenges in attracting skilled employees. This table articulates the ease of finding skilled staff amongst organizations in the Southeast Asian Nations (ASEAN). Malaysia, Singapore, and the Philippines received the strongest scores in terms of companies evaluating the ease of finding skilled employees. The World Economic Forum (2016) briefing paper notes that there is a very strong variation between organizations on how they perceive the quality of training programs across and within countries in this region.

Table 12.1 Selection of countries ranking on the Global Talent Competitiveness Index 2014

Country	Rank
Switzerland	1
Singapore	2
Luxembourg	3
United States	4
Canada	5
Sweden	6
United Kingdom	7
Denmark	8
Australia	9
Ireland	10
Japan	20
Malaysia	35
China	41
Philippines	54
Thailand	61
Vietnam	75
India	78
Cambodia	83

Source: Lanvin and Evans (2014).

Table 12.2 Labor market conditions in ASEAN

Country	Ease of finding skilled employees
Myanmar	2.4
LAO PDR	3.1
Vietnam	3.4
Cambodia	3.4
Thailand	3.8
Indonesia	4.3
Philippines	4.4
Singapore	4.8
Malaysia	5.3

Source: World Economic Forum (2016).

Note
Mean values provided. 1 = hardest; 7 = easiest.

Talent management: a brief review

The introduction to this chapter highlighted the relatively recent emergence of talent management as a concept of interest. Despite its recent heritage, many tracing it to the late 1990s, the area has seen an impressive outlay of articles and special issues, which are increasingly published in high-ranking international journals. An interesting and common thread across much of the current literature is that there has been a failure to agree on a consistent definition of talent management that is shared by researchers (Lewis & Heckman, 2006). While it is argued here that the need for a consistent and shared definition is not necessarily critical to the development of the field, the need for greater agreement over the parameters of the concept is especially important. Cappelli and Heller (2014) suggest that, due to the lack of consensus on the boundaries of the field, its development has been quite haphazard.

There appears to be four strands of thought in the extant literature that depicts talent management as a concept. For some, talent management is merely a repackaging of human resource management (HRM). Under this perspective, talent management is focused on the same activities as HRM, namely, attraction, selection, development, and retention of the entire workforce. The second viewpoint is where the objective is to fill all organizational roles with "A players" and in so doing, poorly performing staff should be managed out. This has been referred to as top-grading and is intrinsically linked to the forced distribution approach made famous at General Electric under Jack Welch's regime. The third perspective centers on identifying high potentials and developing these in the talent pools to take on future leadership positions (Kara-evli & Hall, 2003).

More recently, a paper by Collings and Mellahi (2009) has had a significant impact on the field. They proposed a fourth approach that brings in the identification of strategic positions as the starting point of effective talent management. Strategic or pivotal positions refer to those roles that can have a disproportionate impact on the achievement of the corporate objectives. It refers to roles whereby variation in the level or quality of work displayed by an incumbent can have a significant impact on organizational performance. Huselid, Beatty, and Becker (2005) made a similar argument suggesting "A positions" were those roles where poor performance leads to substantial negative organizational outcomes. While not universally agreed, the definition proposed by Collings and Mellahi appears to be the most commonly used in the literature:

activities and processes that involve the systematic identification of key positions which differentially contribute to the organization's sustainable competitive advantage, the development of a talent pool of high potential and high performing incumbents to fill these roles, and the development of a differentiated human resource architecture to facilitate filling these positions with competent incumbents and to ensure their continued commitment to the organization. In this regard, it is important to note that key positions are not necessarily restricted to the top management team (TMT) but also include key positions at levels lower than the TMT and may vary between operating units and indeed over time.

(2009: 304)

Talent management in Asia: a review of the literature

So what do we know about talent management in Asia? The most appropriate answer appears to be little but it is something that is changing. Typical of much of the management literature in international journals, the overwhelming focus is on the Western, developed world context. Of note in the context of talent management has been a special issue of the *Asia Pacific Journal of Human Resources* that focused on the topic and region (see McDonnell, Collings, & Burgess, 2012). A systematic literature review of the top international journals saw fifty empirically based articles (see McDonnell, Collings, Mellahi, & Schuler, 2017). The review found that this field of research has been snowballing at an exceptional rate over the past decade. Of interest, was that the review demonstrated a significant focus of empirical efforts incorporated the Asian context. Indeed, the overly US focus of the field does not appear as strong as some have previously suggested (Collings, Scullion, & Vaiman, 2011), a point also recently emphasized by Gallardo-Gallardo and Thunnissen (2016).

Table 12.3 provides a summary of the empirical papers in the review conducted by McDonnell et al. (2017) and which we supplement with some more recent additions that incorporate Asia in the data.[1] These papers are specifically those that are viewed as engaging with the concept of talent management as opposed to merely using the term for perhaps "packaging" reasons.[2] The articles depicted in Table 12.3 may to some only be a small microcosm of the talent management literature which does not include published works in languages other than English while there is an Anglo-bias in terms of journals included. Notably and unsurprisingly, the overwhelming focus has been on the Chinese and Indian contexts with a number of key works published in the *Journal of World Business* and *The International Journal of Human Resource Management* (both have also published special issues which partly explain the high number of publications).

Arguably, the most notable research on talent management in Asia stems from a large-scale quantitative study of employees in India (see Tymon, Stumpf, & Doh, 2010; Doh, Tymon Jr., & Stumpf, 2011b). In this research, there is evidence found of sophisticated talent management systems in Indian industry and the authors, notwithstanding the cross-sectional survey, foresee this as a growing trend. There was a positive finding between talent management practices and employee pride, and satisfaction with their organization. Interestingly, there was also a positive relationship to retention, although the effect was less significant than those of pride and satisfaction.

The other key published works focused on talent management in the Chinese subsidiaries of foreign MNCs. Preece, Iles, and Chuai (2011) suggest that there wasn't a particularly strong emphasis on talent management in Chinese subsidiaries, while Iles Chuai, and Preece (2010) suggested that there were very strong similarities in views of what talent management and HRM

Table 12.3 Summary of articles focused on talent management with an Asian empirical component

Reference	Paper aim	Research methods	Findings
Bhatnagar (2007)	How does talent management relate to employee engagement?	Mixed method case studies: employee questionnaires in four business process outsourcing firms in India. Focus groups entailing thirty team managers, project heads, technical heads, and seventy-two exit interviews from one of the case studies.	Employee dissatisfaction with career paths and incentive schemes were linked to higher turnover. Low engagement early in an employee's career linked to high turnover.
Chadee and Raman (2012)	How talent management impacts performance in knowledge-intensive organizations?	Quantitative: online questionnaires of executives in Indian-based offshore IT service providers.	Talent management may be a key mechanism to exploiting knowledge into enhanced organizational performance.
Cooke, Saini, and Wang (2014)	How do non-HR managers perceive talent management practices and challenges in their organization?	Qualitative survey: collected electronic qualitative survey from non-HR managers based in India (121 responses) and China (74 responses).	Talent management practices should be more particularistic in the international context as they are influenced by various factors such as culture, industry, and institutional environment.
Iles, Chuai, and Preece (2010)	Explores perspectives of talent management in China.	Qualitative case studies: seven case studies foreign MNCs in China. Data collection encompasses twenty-two interviews with senior and functional managers, HR specialists, and non-managerial employees.	Talent management did not appear to be treated different to human resource management (HRM). HRM appeared to be viewed as a boarder concept and more in promotion of egalitarianism, while talent management promoted segmentation.
Lehmann (2009)	Examination of the content and direction of the talent development process, and how social, organizational, and managerial practices impacts this.	Semi-structured interviews: fifteen interviews with individuals from eight Thai organizations and eleven interviews from seven Malaysian firms. Cross-industry study.	Greater need for adaption of social and firm structures to fit with the HRM practices implemented to aid attraction, development and retention of individual talents.
Kim, Froese, and Cox (2012)	Analysis of the effects of individual values on applicant attraction to employment in Japanese firms.	Quantitative: undergraduate student survey in three prestigious Vietnamese universities.	Individual values moderate the relationship between organizational characteristics and applicant attraction. Students who were work-centric, collectivist, and money-oriented were more attracted to Japanese MNCs.

continued

Table 12.3 Continued

Reference	Paper aim	Research methods	Findings
Doh, Smith, Stumpf, and Tymon Jr. (2011a)	Analyses how professional talent perceives their firm's talent management activities.	Quantitative: large online employee survey from twenty-eight companies in India. Sample encompasses foreign MNCs, Indian MNCs, and Indian domestic firms.	The employee value proposition can provide a competitive edge to an organization (vis-à-vis its competitors) in attracting and retaining talent. Meaningful and responsive talent management approaches appear central to a strong employee value proposition.
Hartmann, Feisel, and Schober (2010)	Examines the influence of institutional and cultural factors in diffusing talent management practices from Western HQs to their Chinese subsidiaries.	Qualitative case studies: seven case studies of US and European MNCs in China. Data are from interviews with senior- and middle-level HR managers and employees viewed as talent.	The talent management system was transferred from the headquarters with little consideration of institutional and cultural differences. There was little to suggest talent management was strategic and integrated with the rest of the organization's activities.
Poocharoen and Lee (2013)	Examines how talent management is practiced in the public sector in three Asian countries.	Comparative case studies: over twenty semi-structured interviews with public service officers across a range of public sector organizations in Malaysia, Singapore, and Thailand. Secondary data from official documentation and public sources were also used.	Talent management viewed from perspective of having scholarship schemes, special training programs for high potentials, and differentiated pay scales for talents. Definitions of talent varied across the research sites.
Preece, Lies, and Chuai (2011)	Is talent management a new fad or fashion or a discrete concept?	Qualitative case studies: seven case studies foreign MNCs in China. Data collection encompassing interviews with senior and functional managers, HR specialists, and non-managerial employees.	There was evidence that talent management appeared to display traits of a management fashion. However, there was more to talent management than a fad.
Preece, Iles, and Jones (2013)	Examines the talent management challenge in establishing regional MNC structures in the Asia Pacific.	Qualitative case study: five interviews with senior managers at the regional level followed by three interviews with senior managers at a second visit with one follow-up in a Japanese MNC seeking to establish a regional HQ in Asia.	Subsidiaries did not appear to be taking talent management very seriously. There was an increasing concern about developing subsidiary talent to take on key regional headquarters roles.

Table 12.3 Continued

Reference	Paper aim	Research methods	Findings
Raman, Chadee, Roxas, and Michailova (2013)	Investigates the effect of partnership quality, talent management, and global mindset on Indian offshore IT service providers.	Survey of a random sample of Indian IT service. Survey completed by a member of top management team— sixty-nine responses equating to an 8% response rate.	Talent management strongly mediates the effects of global mindset on partnership.
Shi and Handfield (2012)	Examines the underlying causes behind the difficulty in recruiting and retaining Chinese talent.	Semi-structured interviews along with participant observation (in one MNC). Interviews with: (1) eleven Western logistic MNC representatives with operations in China; (2) Professors and administrators from five Chinese universities with logistics/supply chain programs; and (3) eleven highly qualified Chinese managers working for MNCs in China.	A significant gap exists between the expectations of Chinese talent and the perceived reality of foreign managers.
Tymon, Stumpf, and Doh (2010)	Analyses of the role of intrinsic rewards and retention, career success and organizational satisfaction.	Quantitative: stratified random sample of almost 5,000 employees drawn from twenty-eight companies in India.	Employee perceptions of their organization as being socially responsible are strongly linked to pride in the firm which has a direct relationship to increased satisfaction and lower turnover intentions.
Vance, Siu Chow, Paik, and Shin (2013)	Examines perceptions of training fit of Korean expatriates and local staff and the implication for global talent management.	Quantitative: convenience survey of sixty-seven Korean expatriates in MNC subsidiaries in China and survey of 202 non-managerial local staff from Chinese and US MNCs in China.	The approach to training in Korean subsidiaries stems from the headquarters. There is strong similarity in trainer and learner views on career development and trainee ownership.
Wang-Cowham (2011)	Explores the relationship between talent development and knowledge sharing.	Semi-structured interviews: twenty Chinese HR practitioners.	Knowledge sharing socialization methods when integrated with talent development practices can lead to organizational knowledge sharing while supporting both individual- and firm-led talent development.

continued

Table 12.3 Continued

Reference	Paper aim	Research methods	Findings
Zheng (2009)	Examines how HR practices and talent impact service delivery and organization expansion.	Quantitative: survey of 281 service sector MNCs in Indonesia, Malaysia, Philippines, Singapore, Taiwan and Singapore.	There are significant links between HR practices, talent retention and service delivery.
Zheng, Soosay, and Hyland (2007)	Examines the challenge for MNCs in Asian countries in recruiting highly skilled managerial and professional staff.	Quantitative: survey of 529 MNCs in Singapore, Taiwan, Indonesia, Malaysia, Philippines, and Thailand.	MNCs in the Asian Tiger economies are significantly more aggressive in fighting for talent than elsewhere. Manufacturing MNCs appear especially challenged with talent attraction.

were. The key differentiation that they found was around exclusivity and inclusivity with HRM a more encompassing activity in terms of employees and the practices included. On the other hand, talent management was an approach that was centered on segmentation rather than egalitarianism (Chuai, Preece, & Iles, 2008). Hartmann, Feisel, and Schober (2010) examined the extent to which foreign MNCs considered the unique host country environments in seeking to transfer headquarter devised talent management systems to their subsidiaries. Notably, there was little evidence to suggest the case study MNCs gave much consideration of institutional and cultural differences. Further, the research provided little indication that talent management was a strategic activity that was integrated with other core organizational activities and processes.

An overarching conclusion that one can make with respect to published works with an Asian focus is the significant variation in terms of how talent management is conceptualized and measured. It was not always evident as to how talent management was differentiated from HRM. For example, Raman, Chadee, Roxas, and Michailova operationalize talent management through five items on a five-point scale. The example item provided is "our company's recruitment and selection processes are (1: substantially below industry standard … 5: substantially above industry standard)" (2013: 338). Such a measure appears to be more akin to HRM. It is important to note that this concern is not necessarily an Asian focused research issue but one that impacts the talent management field. The need for clearer parameters as to what talent management is and how it is operationalized and measured are key issues that need to be addressed to advance the field beyond its current state. As will become evident in the remaining sections, the challenges that organizations in Asia face with respect to attracting and retaining skilled talent make effective talent management especially important.

Attracting talent in Asia

Attracting skilled talent is dependent on the cultural, economic, institutional, and societal environment of the host countries (Cooke, 2011). The economic growth and transitioning in Asia brings increasing business and employment opportunities, which drives experienced and skilled talent to relocate to Asia and also bring migration return to the region. However, the uneven distribution of talent is obvious as the talents tend to work in large, international cities.

For example, most Chinese people prefer living in first-tier cities such as Beijing, Shanghai, and Guangzhou, which provides higher living standards, good salaries, but also with higher living costs. As a result, the underdeveloped areas in China experience brain drain as they are less attractive to both local and foreign talents compared to big cities (Bhatnagar, 2008). This is an issue that needs consideration at a national level because a continuance is likely to lead to significant problems around balanced economic and social development.

Cultural issues are another factor influencing talent flow with people tending to work in an environment with less cultural distance from their home country. For example, many people moved back to Hong Kong for work after becoming Canadian citizens (DeVoretz & Ma, 2002), while some Chinese MNCs are willing to recruit lots of highly skilled migrants with Chinese background such as overseas-born Chinese or Chinese immigrants (Tung, 2016). Some Asian countries share a similar cultural tradition and social values such as the Confucianism heritage in East Asia, which also drives the talent mobility amongst these countries. In the Japanese context, it is difficult for foreign expatriates to engage and communicate with their local colleagues due to the language barriers and culture distance; hence, there are negative impacts on their work as Japanese culture highlights the importance of teamwork (Kamibayashi, 2006). In contrast, the English language becomes a potential competitive advantage in recruiting and retaining foreign talents in Singapore and India.

Another factor related to cultural issues is the lifestyle and quality of life in the host country. Housing, facilities, living environment, pollution, schooling, and health care all influence foreign talent's relocation decision. Moreover, the talent policy/immigration policy is another factor that can drive or inhibit talent relocation or return to Asia. China experienced brain drain in the 1990s as significant numbers of talents moved to developed countries such as the USA and European countries after they finished study overseas. However, more overseas Chinese have recently decided to return due, in part, to the national talent attraction policy incorporating promotion, economic incentives, and long-term career plans. For example, the national government provides the "thousand talent program" to help attract talent to work in Chinese universities and research institutions (Harvey, 2014).

Singapore introduced the strategy of importing foreign talent and provides more immigration opportunities (Yahya & Kaur, 2010). Moreover, Japan has signed an agreement on the mutual recognition of qualifications, which has simplified the working visa application procedure (Kamibayashi, 2006). The Indian government meanwhile has implemented a number of financial incentives such as the use of the Person of Indian Origin (PIO) and Overseas Citizen of India (OCI) Card to change the situation from brain drain to brain circulation. Initiatives such as this have been viewed as instrumental to attracting returning professionals who work in IT, business process outsourcing, and financial service industries (Chanda & Screenivasan, 2006). In addition, the free trade area and agreement such as ASEAN helps to remove the barriers across national borders and enhance talent mobility in this area.

The talent challenges of organizations operating in Asia

The growth of the Asian economies shapes the global talent pool and also raises challenges for local companies and MNCs in relation to talent management. Both domestic and international companies face challenges in talent recruitment, retention, and development. Thus, talent management is an ongoing concern for most firms across the Asian region.

The talent challenges amongst local companies in Asia

Considering the issue of talent flow in Asia, how to attract and retain talent is a primary concern of local companies. For example, Chinese MNCs are experiencing management skills shortages in their global operations (Iwasaki, 2010). The challenge is especially acute in the service sector as the tacit knowledge transfer in this sector is different from the traditional manufacturing industry. The lack of skilled and experienced managers has become a key obstacle to internationalization of domestic firms (Chuai et al., 2008; Iles, Chuai, & Preece, 2010).

With more involvement in the global marketplace, local companies are willing and seeking to hire managers who have experience and skills in operating in an international environment. This is, however, proving to be extremely difficult which appears to be related to three aspects. First, the imbalanced economic growth in different areas makes for an uneven distribution of talent between developed and rural/developing areas in Asia. For example, foreign and returning talents tend to work in the largest and developed regions such as Mumbai, Bangalore, and New Delhi, which are also the destinations of business process outsourcing hubs in India (Chanda & Screenivasan, 2006). Second, although there are a large number of graduates each year in Asia, local companies appear to experience the greatest degree of difficulty in recruiting talent. Young professionals are considered to be the main sources of qualified talent, which are required by local Chinese companies (Hartmann et al., 2010). However, the skills learned from university and required by the company do not always appear to match (Diez, 2014). Third, there are global concerns about the availability of internationally competent managers with it being commonly reported that organizations have been facing increasing difficulty in locating suitable managerial talent (e.g., Scullion & Collings, 2006; Shen & Darby, 2006). Consequently, there is considerable competition for talent amongst different types and sizes of organizations across industrial sectors and countries. This is arguably all the more acute in countries such as India and China due to Western headquartered MNCs looking to invest in increasing numbers and scale.

According to Kuczera and Field (2012), the vocational training and planning system and standard is limited and inadequate in China. Domestic firms tend to recruit highly skilled employees from the external labor market rather than selecting individuals internally and developing them. This situation is leading to two emerging problems in local firms. First, it is increasingly difficult to find suitably skilled and experienced managers that meet person–organization fitness. For example, Poocharoen and Lee (2013) conducted interviews with officers from public service sector firms in Singapore, Malaysia, and Thailand and found that all of three countries are struggling with recruiting and retaining sufficient numbers to take on senior management roles. Similarly, Downing, Rouleau, and Stuber (2008) argue that the new generation graduates are not well prepared and trained to take on the important roles in local and international company's management and operation processes. Second, the insufficient attention to training and leadership development plans for talent tends to create a high turnover rate. This high turnover, coupled with aging society concerns in countries such as Japan, Singapore, and China, extenuates the talent management problems given there are a decreasing number of potential employees in the talent pool (Diez, 2014; Tung, 2007). Consequently, such a strong reliance on the external labor market for talent management may prove to be increasingly problematic when significant supply challenges exist.

There has been much interest over the past decade in the fact that the workforce is now made up of multiple generations. Generation Y employees (those born between 1980 and 2000) have had considerable research attention. These individuals have been moving into more senior and strategic roles. Those who argue that generational differences are visible and acute have argued that the younger generations have much less organizational commitment and higher turnover intentions than older generations (D'Amato & Herzfeldt, 2008). They are also depicted as possessing a greater learning orientation. The vast nature of the Asian region and the changing cultural and institutional contexts make for interesting and particularly challenging contexts in which organizations will operate. Arguably, the differences in perspectives and expectations amongst the newer and older generations in emerging, and recently open, economies will be magnified to a greater extent than generational differences in a mature, developed economy. The political, institutional, and cultural backgrounds of many of the different countries that make up the Asian region can be described as undergoing development and change. For example, the move away from communist regimes to more open and outward-looking societies is likely to impact on the effectiveness of particular organizational structures and management practices. Consequently, the actual influence of such evolving economic and social contexts on management practice will also be ongoing. The sophistication of talent management in domestic firms may be quite limited especially in domestic firms that have not been open to the international marketplace. Evidence from the Polish economy as it has moved on from its communist past has demonstrated that human capital and HRM related matters were quite underdeveloped (Skuza, Scullion, & McDonnell, 2013). It has only been in very recent times that HRM issues have started to gain prominence but they remain lower on the level of managerial priorities. Such issues may also be expected in a number of Asian countries.

The talent challenges to MNCs in Asia

Moving to the MNC context, the literature also indicates challenges in competent talent recruitment, retention, motivation, and career development (Collings, Scullion, & Morley, 2007; Scullion & Collings, 2006). With the rising economic and political status of Asian countries, the demand for competent and skilled talent of local companies is increasing and the talent pool for MNCs in Asia appears to have been scaled down. Of note is that some have suggested that Western MNCs appear to have become somewhat less attractive compared to domestic firms (Schmidt, 2011). This needs to be considered in the context that domestic firms themselves have reported significant recruitment difficulties. The previous advantages of MNCs such as higher salary, international assignment opportunities, and career development are beginning to narrow compared to some domestic firms that are becoming increasingly visible in the regional market. The time whereby Western-based MNCs arrived in Asia with undisputed brand appeal leading to a strong pull effect with respect to local talent appears to be less common. Essentially, the monopoly once held by MNCs on brand attractiveness is less evident. The natural increase in competition for employees is also very important to acknowledge. Inevitably, as domestic firms internationalize and increase in size, there is a corresponding increase in competition for talent that established MNCs are seeking. There is also evidence of the increasing level of entrepreneurial behavior with some skilled talents deciding to establish their own businesses (Dejoux & Thévenet, 2012).

The ability of MNCs to transfer their people management systems and practices to their overseas operations has been one of the most long-standing areas of research. Doh, Tymon, and Stumpf (2011b) have a word of caution to those seeking to transfer Western-styled talent management practices to India suggesting that it can lead to worker resentment and other negative feelings. This is likely to be most acute where employees feel that these practices are being forced upon them and are counter to their beliefs and Indian culture (Jaeger, 1990). It is suggested that even a mindset focused on "managing" rather than "assisting" employees may cause difficulty. The concerns stemming from the Indian research are reinforced by Cooke in the

Chinese context in making the point that the "enduring cultural and institutional factors are likely to make it difficult for MNCs to implement a [global talent management] system" (2011: 148).

Such issues raise challenges for MNCs seeking to ensure their performance appraisal and reward system are consistent across their global operations (Minbaeva & Collings, 2013). The desire for global consistency in performance management and talent management systems needs to be tempered by considering the cultural influence of the local environment on such activities (Evans, Smale, Björkman, & Pucik, 2011). Additionally, a well-established training system has been an important factor influencing individual's tendency to work in a large MNC. However, some management level employees may choose to move to a local company after having several years working experience and training in MNCs due to improving salary packages and higher job positions. This has led to key concerns on talent "poaching" with employees seemingly often willing to move organizations and roles for relatively minor increases in salary (Bennington & Habir, 2003; Wellins, Liu, & Tang, 2008).

Further, it is important to recognize the importance of "status" and "face" in many Asian cultures. The attractiveness of the potential position might vary in Western and Asian countries. For example, Jiang and Iles (2011) found that economic value, development value, and social value are the most important factors for job applicants in China. Wang (2008) also highlights the importance of the harmonious working environment and personal relations with colleagues for Chinese employees.

The challenges for foreign talent working in Asia

The international HRM literature was established on the back of the use of expatriate assignments in international business. The use of expatriates does not appear to be waning, although there is greater acknowledgement of the difficulties in getting individuals to take on international assignments, and particularly to where many Western expatriates perceive as less desirable locations. Notwithstanding the difficulties in getting sufficient numbers of expatriates to undertake international assignments, there are also significant challenges in being effective in these roles. The attraction of foreign talent has been a key issue for some time in the main Asian economies. For example, Lane and Pollner (2008) have previously raised the need for Chinese firms to look overseas to attract talent. However, there are key challenges related to expatriate work and life when they conduct international assignments in such a different cultural, social, and institutional environment.

Expatriates may experience liabilities of foreignness when they relocate and commence work in a new environment, which is considered as the key disadvantage of foreign talents compared to host country national (HCN) employees (Fang, Samnani, Novicevic, & Bing, 2013; Matsuo, 2000). The adjustment to the host country and engagement with the local environment has impacts on expatriate performance and assignment success (Osman-Gani & Rockstuhl, 2008). Black, Mendenhall, and Oddou (1991) proposed the adjustment model, which includes general adjustment, work adjustment, and interaction adjustment; this model has been widely empirically applied (though also received much criticism, e.g., Hippler, Caligiuri, Johnson, & Baytalskaya, 2014) in cross-cultural adjustment studies (see, e.g., Froese, Peltokorpi, & Ko, 2012; Kim & Slocum Jr, 2008). Considering the limited application of Black et al.'s (1991) model on different types of expatriation assignments, a recent study proposes and examines two dimensions called the work and family role adjustment (both considering task and relationship orientation) to global professionals (Shaffer et al., 2016). In addition, a number of studies have examined the factors influencing expatriate adjustment such as expatriate personality, organization context,

HCNs co-worker's support, and attitudes toward foreign talents (for examples, see Harrison, Shaffer, & Bhaskar-Shrinivas, 2004; Mahajan & Toh, 2014; Selmer, Lauring, Normann, & Kubovcikova, 2015; Toh & Denisi, 2007). Froese and Peltokorpi (2013) found that self-initiated expatriates in Japan experience a lower level of job satisfaction compared with organizational assigned expatriates because their supervisors are generally HCNs. Selmer et al.'s (2015) study found self-initiated expatriates working in local organizations achieve a higher level in general and interaction adjustment than those working in foreign organizations from China or Taiwan. The challenge for expatriates is to interact and build work-related relationships with their co-workers as well as with the HCNs, if there is a large cultural and institutional distance between their home country and the host country. Take China as an example, relationship building plays a key role in doing business in China (Fan, 2002); and the initiation and development of relationship building requires a relationship base and time investment which is difficult for foreigners.

These challenges are extenuated by the impacts of the family on expatriate work performance and satisfaction with their international assignment (Lazarova, Westman, & Shaffer, 2010). The relocation to a new environment especially with a different culture and social system has become a challenge for expatriate families in relation to health care, children's education, and potential work opportunities for the expatriate's partner. The requirements for the English-speaking service, international school, and Western-style food are difficult to achieve in some developing Asian countries. For example, Shanghai and Beijing in China were ranked as the top two cities where expatriates were willing to stay due to its food, lifestyle, innovation, business opportunities, and tourist attractions but more regional cities are less popular (Zhao, 2015).

Another issue, linked to the difficulty in getting sufficient numbers of individuals to take on expatriate assignments is that of the dual-career couple. Although some companies provide career support to the expatriate's accompanying partner, there are barriers in the host country such as visa permission and mutually recognized qualifications. The lack of spousal support has negative impacts on expatriate performance and leads to their early return (Bhaskar-Shrinivas, Harrison, Shaffer, & Luk, 2005), which is costly to MNCs.

Conclusions

The chapter has shown that there is continuing, persuasive evidence that talent shortages and managing talent is a considerable concern to organizations in Asia. The emerging evidence suggests that the demand for managerial and professional positions is outstripping supply (Di Gropello, Kruse, & Tandon, 2011; Deloitte, 2013). For example, professionals are commonly ranked amongst the top ten talent shortages in the Asia Pacific region (Manpower, 2013). While there is variation across countries in the region in terms of how challenging an environment exists for the supply and demand for talent, overall there are significant concerns for organizations and governments in terms of future business and economic prosperity.

The talent management research focused on Asia suffers from many of the same issues that encompass the broader literature in that there has been little coherence on the focus of research undertaken to date. This makes it difficult to discern patterns or themes of a distinct approach to talent management in Asia. Indeed, to adopt a critical perspective on papers that were found in the systematic review of Asian focused research studies on talent management, you would have to note that there are few papers that attempt to engage with the topic to a significant degree. A significant proportion of the published works appear to take the perspective of talent management practices as being nothing more than human resource management rebranded.

While the literature base is limited, there appears little doubt that talent management is a central issue in the region and that this is likely to continue and grow. Report after report support the view that talent shortages are particularly important, with continued organizational expansion likely to be impacted by the ability to attract and retain talent. How organizations compete for and manage their human capital is likely to be a competitive differentiator. This not only refers to being able to attract sufficient talent but also requires culturally and institutionally appropriate practices. For foreign MNCs, there should be strong consideration of the appropriateness of transferring talent management systems from headquarters without taking into account the impact of cultural and institutional difference. There is also a need for consideration on how the strong individualist overtones of talent management fit with the more collectivist cultures that embody many of the Asian countries.

Notes

1 Unlike the McDonnell et al. (2017), our updates are not systematic in terms of searching the relevant databases.
2 From discussion with scholars in the field, there is concern over how the terminology is often used in papers but which doesn't really attempt to engage with relevant works.

References

Asian Development Bank. (2015). Asian development outlook 2015 update: Growth outlook. Retrieved October 2, 2015, from www.adb.org/news/infographics/asian-development-outlook-2015-update-growth-outlook.

Bennington, L. & Habir, A. D. (2003). Human resource management in Indonesia. *Human Resource Management Review, 13*(3), 373–392.

Bhaskar-Shrinivas, P., Harrison, D. A., Shaffer, M. A., & Luk, D. M. (2005). Input-based and time-based models of international adjustment: Meta-analytic evidence and theoretical extensions. *Academy of Management Journal, 48*(2), 257–281.

Bhatnagar, J. (2007). Talent management strategy of employee engagement in Indian ITES employees: Key to retention. *Employee Relations, 29*(6), 640–663.

Bhatnagar, J. (2008). Managing capabilities for talent engagement and pipeline development. *Industrial and Commercial Training, 40*(1), 19–28.

Black, J. S., Mendenhall, M., & Oddou, G. (1991). Toward a comprehensive model of international adjustment: An integration of multiple theoretical perspectives. *The Academy of Management Review, 16*(2), 291–317.

Cappelli, P. & Keller, J. R. (2014). Talent management: Conceptual approaches and practical challenges. *Annual Review of Organizational Psychology and Organizational Behavior, 1*, 305–331.

Chadee, D. & Raman, R. (2012). External knowledge and performance of offshore IT service providers in India: The mediating role of talent management. *Asia Pacific Journal of Human Resources, 50*(4), 459–482.

Chanda, R. & Screenivasan, N. (2006). India's experience with skilled migration. In K. Christiane & P. E. Fong (Eds.), *Competing for global talent* (pp. 215–255). Geneva: International Institute for Labour Studies.

Chuai, X., Preece, D., & Iles, P. (2008). Is talent management just "old wine in new bottles"? The case of multinational companies in Beijing. *Management Research News, 31*(12), 901–911.

Collings, D. G. & Mellahi, K. (2009). Strategic talent management: A review and research agenda. *Human Resource Management Review, 19*(4), 304–313.

Collings, D. G., Scullion, H., & Morley, M. J. (2007). Changing patterns of global staffing in the multinational enterprise: Challenges to the conventional expatriate assignment and emerging alternatives. *Journal of World Business, 42*(2), 198–213.

Collings, D. G., Scullion, H., & Vaiman, V. (2011). European perspectives on talent management. *European Journal of International Management, 5*(5), 453–462.

Cooke, F. L. (2011). Talent Management in China. In. H. Scullion and D. G. Collings (Eds.), *Global Talent Management* (pp. 132–154). London: Routledge.

Cooke, F. L., Saini, D. S., & Wang, J. (2014). Talent management in China and India: A comparison of management perceptions and human resource practices. *Journal of World Business, 49*(2), 225–235.

D'Amato, A. & Herzfeldt, R. (2008). Learning orientation, organizational commitment and talent retention across generations: A study of European managers. *Journal of Managerial Psychology, 23*(8), 929–953.

Dejoux, C. & Thévenet, M. (2012). The shift in talent management for French MNCs in Asia. *Revue de Gestion Des Ressources Humaines, 86*(4), 36–51.

Deloitte. (2013). *Business trends 2013: Adapt, evolve, transform*. Westlake, TX: Deloitte University Press.

DeVoretz, D. J. & Ma, J. (2002). Triangular human capital flows between sending, entrepot and the rest of the world regions. *Canadian Studies in Population, 29*(1), 53–69.

Diez, F. (2014). Human capital management in Asia: The war for talent continues in this high-growth region. In A. Manuti & P. Davide de Palma (Eds.), *Why human capital is important for organizations: People come first* (pp. 137–150). Basingstoke: Palgrave Macmillan.

Di Gropello, E., Kruse, A., & Tandon, P. (2011). *Skills for the labor market in Indonesia: Trends in demand, gaps, and supply*. New York: World Bank Publications.

Doh, J. P., Smith, R. R., Stumpf, S. A. & Tymon Jr., W. G. (2011a). Pride and professionals: Retaining talent in emerging economies. *Journal of Business Strategy, 32*(5), 35–42.

Doh, J. P., Tymon Jr., W. G. & Stumpf, S. A. (2011b). Talent management in India. In H. Scullion & D. G. Collings (Eds.), *Global talent management* (pp. 115–131). London: Routledge.

Downing, J., Rouleau, W., & Stuber, S. (2008). *The war for the talent in China*. Retrieved October 11, 2015, from www.worldconcertrpo.com/GIM_China_paper_Downing_Stuber_Rouleau. pdf.

Evans, P., Smale, A., Björkman, I., & Pucik, V. (2011). Leadership development in multinational firms. In J. Storey (Ed.), *Leadership in organizations: Current issues and key trends* (pp. 207–222). London: Routledge.

Fan, Y. (2002). Questioning guanxi: Definition, classification and implications. *International Business Review, 11*(5), 543–561.

Fang, T., Samnani, A. K., Novicevic, M. M., & Bing, M. N. (2013). Liability-of-foreignness effects on job success of immigrant job seekers. *Journal of World Business, 48*(1), 96–109.

Froese, F. J. & Peltokorpi, V. (2013). Organizational expatriates and self-initiated expatriates: Differences in cross-cultural adjustment and job satisfaction. *The International Journal of Human Resource Management, 24*(10), 1953–1967.

Froese, F. J., Peltokorpi, V., & Ko, K. A. (2012). The influence of intercultural communication on cross-cultural adjustment and work attitudes: Foreign workers in South Korea. *International Journal of Intercultural Relations, 36*(3), 331–342.

Gallardo-Gallardo, E. & Thunnissen, M. (2016). Standing on the shoulders of giants? A critical review of empirical talent management research. *Employee Relations, 38*(1), 31–56.

Harrison, D. A., Shaffer, M. A., & Bhaskar-Shrinivas, P. (2004). Going places: Roads more and less traveled in research on expatriate experiences. *Research in Personnel and Human Resources Management, 23*, 199–248.

Hartmann, E., Feisel, E. & Schober, H. (2010). Talent management of Western MNCs in China: Balancing global integration and local responsiveness. *Journal of World Business, 45*(2), 169–178.

Harvey, S. W. (2014). Winning the global talent war: A policy perspective. *Journal of Chinese Human Resource Management, 5*(1), 62–74.

Hippler, T., Caligiuri, P. M., Johnson, J. E., & Baytalskaya, N. (2014). The development and validation of a theory-based expatriate adjustment scale. *The International Journal of Human Resource Management, 25*(14), 1938–1959.

Huselid, M. A., Beatty, R. W., & Becker, B. E. (2005). "A players" or "A positions"?: The strategic logic of workforce management. *Harvard Business Review, 83*(12), 110–117.

Iles, P., Chuai, X. & Preece, D. (2010). Talent management and HRM in multinational companies in Beijing: Definitions, differences and drivers. *Journal of World Business, 45*(2), 179–189.

Iwasaki, Y., (2010). Lessons from the People's Republic of China and India. In K. Gerhaeusser, Y. Iwasaki, & V. B. Tulasidhar (Eds.), *Resurging Asian giants: Lessons from the People's Republic of China and India* (pp. 1–40). Manila: Asia Development Bank.

Jaeger, A. J. (1990). The applicability of Western management techniques in developing countries: A cultural perspective. In A. M. Jaeger & R. N. Kerning (Eds.), *Management in developing countries* (pp. 131–145). London: Routledge.

Jiang, T. & Iles, P. (2011). Employer-brand equity, organizational attractiveness and talent management in the Zhejiang private sector, China. *Journal of Technology Management in China, 6*(1), 97–110.

Kamibayashi, C. (2006). Current migration of IT engineers to Japan: Beyond immigration control and cultural barriers. In K. Christiane & P. E. Fong (Eds.), *Competing for global talent* (pp. 171–185). Geneva: International Institute for Labour Studies.

Karaevli, A. & Hall, D. T. (2003). Growing leaders for turbulent times: Is succession planning up to the challenge?. *Organizational Dynamics, 32*(1), 62–79.

Kim, S., Froese Prof., F. J., & Cox, A. (2012). Applicant attraction to foreign companies: The case of Japanese companies in Vietnam. *Asia Pacific Journal of Human Resources, 50*(4), 439–458.

Kim, K. & Slocum Jr, J. W. (2008). Individual differences and expatriate assignment effectiveness: The case of US-based Korean expatriates. *Journal of World Business, 43*(1), 109–126.

Kuczera, M. & Field, S. (2012), *Learning for jobs: OECD reviews of vocational education and training: Options for China.* Paris: OECD.

Lane, K. & Pollner. F. (2008). How to address China's growing talent shortage. *The McKinsey Quarterly, 3,* 32–40.

Lanvin, B. & Evans, P. (Eds.) (2014). *Global talent competitiveness index 2014.* Retrieved March 4, 2015, from http://global-indices.insead.edu/documents/INSEADGTCIreport2014.pdf.

Lazarova, M., Westman, M., & Shaffer, M. A. (2010). Elucidating the positive side of the work–family interface on international assignments: A model of expatriate work and family performance. *Academy of Management Review, 35*(1), 93–117.

Lehmann, S. (2009). Motivating talents in Thai and Malaysian service firms. *Human Resource Development International, 12*(2), 155–169.

Lewis, R. E. & Heckman, R. J. (2006). Talent management: A critical review. *Human Resource Management Review, 16*(2), 139–154.

McDonnell, A., Collings, D. G., & Burgess, J. (2012). Talent management in the Asia-Pacific. *Asia Pacific Journal of Human Resources, 50*(4), 391–398.

McDonnell, A., Collings, D. G., Mellahi, K. & Schuler, R. S. (2017). Talent management: A systematic review and future prospects. *European Journal of International Management, 11*(17), 85–128.

Mahajan, A. & Toh, S. M. (2014). Facilitating expatriate adjustment: The role of advice-seeking from host country nationals. *Journal of World Business, 49*(4), 476–487.

Manpower Group. (2013). *Talent shortage survey.* Milwaukee, WI: Manpower Group.

Matsuo, H. (2000). Liability of foreignness and the uses of expatriates in Japanese multinational corporations in the United States. *Sociological Inquiry, 70*(1), 88–106.

Michaels, E., Handfield-Jones, H., & Axelrod, B. (2001). *The war for talent.* Boston, MA: Harvard Business School.

Minbaeva, D. & Collings, D. G. (2013). Seven myths of global talent management. *The International Journal of Human Resource Management, 24*(9), 1762–1776.

Noorbakhsh, F., Paloni, A., & Youssef, A. (2001). Human capital and FDI inflows to developing countries: New empirical evidence. *World Development, 29*(9), 1593–1610.

Osman-Gani, A. M. & Rockstuhl, T. (2008). Antecedents and consequences of social network characteristics for expatriate adjustment and performance in overseas assignments: Implications for HRD. *Human Resource Development Review, 7*(1), 32–57.

Poocharoen, O. O. & Lee, C. (2013). Talent management in the public sector: A comparative study of Singapore, Malaysia, and Thailand. *Public Management Review, 15*(8), 1185–1207.

Preece, D., Iles, P., & Jones, R. (2013). MNE regional head offices and their affiliates: Talent management practices and challenges in the Asia Pacific. *The International Journal of Human Resource Management, 24*(18), 3457–3477.

Preece, D., Lies, P., & Chuai, X. (2011). Talent management and management fashion in Chinese enterprises: Exploring case studies in Beijing. *The International Journal of Human Resource Management, 22*(16), 3413–3428.

PwC. (2014). *17th Annual Global CEO Survey: The talent challenge.* London: PricewaterhouseCoopers.

Raman, R., Chadee, D., Roxas, B., & Michailova, S. (2013). Effects of partnership quality, talent management, and global mindset on performance of offshore IT service providers in India. *Journal of International Management, 19,* 333–346.

Schmidt, C. (2011, March). The battle for China's talent. *Harvard Business Review,* 25–27.

Scullion, H. & Collings, D. G. (2006). *Global staffing.* Abingdon: Routledge.

Selmer, J., Lauring, J., Normann, J., & Kubovcikova, A. (2015). Context matters: Acculturation and work-related outcomes of self-initiated expatriates employed by foreign vs. local organizations. *International Journal of Intercultural Relations, 49,* 251–264.

Shaffer, M. A., Reiche, B. S., Dimitrova, M., Lazarova, M., Chen, S., Westman, M., & Wurtz, O. (2016). Work- and family-role adjustment of different types of global professionals: Scale development and validation. *Journal of International Business Studies, 47*(2), 113–139.

Shen, J. & Darby, R. (2006). Training and management development in Chinese multinational enterprises. *Employee Relations, 28*, 342–362.

Shi, Y. & Handfield, R. (2012). Talent management issues for multinational logistics companies in China: Observations from the field. *International Journal of Logistics: Research and Applications, 15*(3), 163–179.

Skuza, A., Scullion, H., & McDonnell, A. (2013). An analysis of the talent management challenges in a post-communist country: The case of Poland. *The International Journal of Human Resource Management, 24*(3): 453–470.

Sparrow, P., Scullion, H., & Tarique, I. (2014). *Strategic talent management: Contemporary issues in the international context.* Cambridge: Cambridge University Press.

Toh, S. M. & Denisi, A. S. (2007). Host country nationals as socializing agents: A social identity approach. *Journal of Organizational Behavior, 28*(3), 281–301.

Tung, R. L. (2007). The human resource challenge to outward foreign direct investment aspirations from emerging economies: The case of China. *The International Journal of Human Resource Management, 18*(5), 868–889.

Tung, R. L. (2016). New perspectives on human resource management in a global context. *Journal of World Business, 51*(1), 142–152.

Tymon, W. G., Stumpf, S. A., & Doh, J. P. (2010). Exploring talent management in India: The neglected role of intrinsic rewards. *Journal of World Business, 45*(2), 109–121.

UNCTAD. (2016). *World investment report 2016, Investor nationality: Policy challenges.* Geneva: United Nations Publication.

Vance, C. M., Siu Chow, I. H., Paik, Y., & Shin, K.-Y (2013). Analysis of Korean expatriate congruence with Chinese labor perceptions on training method importance: Implications for global talent management. *The International Journal of Human Resource Management, 24*, 985–1005.

Vorhauser-Smith, S. & Cariss, K. (2014). *Talented Southeast Asia.* Singapore: PageUp People.

Wang, Y. (2008). Emotional bonds with supervisor and co-workers: Relationship to organizational commitment in China's foreign-invested companies. *The International Journal of Human Resource Management, 19*(5), 916–931.

Wang-Cowham, C. (2011). Developing talent with an integrated knowledge-sharing mechanism: An exploratory investigation from the Chinese human resource managers' perspective. *Human Resource Development International, 14*(4), 391–407.

Wellins, R., Liu, L. & Tang, Q. (2008). *The talent management imperative: Fueling China's business growth.* Pittsburgh, PA: DDI International.

World Economic Forum. (2015). *Global competitiveness report 2015–2016.* Retrieved August 1, 2015, from http://reports.weforum.org/global-competitiveness-report-2015-2016/.

World Economic Forum. (2016). *Human Capital Outlook Association of Southeast Asian Nations (ASEAN): Regional community briefing.* Kuala Lumpur: World Economic Forum.

World Bank. (2015). *Global economic prospects: The global economy in transition.* Washington, DC: International Bank for Reconstruction and Development/The World Bank.

Yahya, F. B. & Kaur, A. (2010). Competition for foreign talent in Southeast Asia. *Journal of the Asia Pacific Economy, 15*(1), 20–32.

Zhao, X. (2015, March 9). Shanghai tops expat desirability list. *China Daily.* Retrieved October 4, 2015, from www.chinadaily.com.cn/business/2015-03/09/content_19753059_2.htm.

Zheng, C. (2009). Keeping talents for advancing service firms in Asia. *Journal of Service Management, 20*(5), 482–502.

Zheng, C., Soosay, C., & Hyland, P. (2007). Manufacturing to Asia: Who will win the emerging battle for talent between Dragons and Tigers? *Journal of Manufacturing Technology Management, 19*(1), 52–72.

13

MANAGING MULTINATIONAL COMPANIES IN ASIA

Yu Zheng and Chris Smith

Introduction

The economic, political, and social landscape of Asia has been changing rapidly as we witness the continuous flow of multinational companies (MNCs) into and from Asian countries over the past few decades. Much research attention has therefore been devoted to exploring MNCs' pursuit of internationally and locally competent management models, policies, and practices as the engagement between Asia and the global economy deepens (Dowling & Donnelly, 2013). However, as often as Asia is referred to in multinational's published regional strategic statements as a geographic term, it is extremely difficult, if not impossible, to generalize precisely about what such a regional strategy would entail in terms of managing the workforce in the subsidiaries across Asian countries. The complexity of Asia's institutional environment means that MNCs are exposed to divergent and often conflicting institutional pressures. Managing the workforce in Asia is more likely to be based on hybrid and programmatic decisions instead of unified and coherent strategies and policies. This chapter aims to offer an overview of the dynamic intersection between MNCs and institutions.

Active inward and outward foreign direct investment (FDI) in Asia has far from reduced diversity in the national institutional arrangements across Asian countries. At the extremes, Asia is constituted by such countries as North Korea, which is remote from any influence of MNCs, and countries that are highly integrated into the global economy, like Singapore. Some countries have taken constant and incremental steps to regulate the entry and impact of MNCs. East Asian developmental states are known for their industrial policies to accommodate as well as restrict FDI in order to protect domestic industry (Kasahara, 2013). Japan, being the forerunner of industrialization and internationalization, only removed the legislative barriers for MNCs to invest in all industrial sectors after the mid-1990s (Kushida & Shimizu, 2013). Some countries are much more progressive in terms of integrating MNCs into the local economy. China and India, for example, have introduced several rounds of legislative reforms and policy reinterpretations since 1990s, aiming to promote FDI inflow at first and then FDI outflow in more recent years (Hsueh, 2012). This has seen the shift of MNCs being treated as separate business entities to being integrated into the national legal framework. Some other countries, such as the United Arabic Emirates (UAE), have kept MNCs at bay by setting up "special economic zones" and MNCs remain separated from the rest of the host country economy (Ewers, 2016). Against generalizations about globalization, convergence, or the dominance of neoliberal practices (such as shareholder value, open capital markets, and flexible labor markets), there persists the power of the past, which continues to deliver significant national differences within Asian societies. This is why we have been repeatedly reminded to adopt a transformational approach in applying theories and to develop a contextualized frameworks to capture both common themes and nuanced differences that underline management of MNCs in Asia (Meyer, 2006).

Management in Asia has experienced drastic transitions in the past three decades. Although the pace of change varies across countries, such transitions often allow space for management experiments and innovations (Morgan, 2009). The once celebrated "Japanese model" has been challenged and undermined by MNCs from both the developed and emerging economies. New and hybrid forms of management have been observed across industrial sectors as the result of restructuring and revitalizing the Japanese firms (Fitzgerald & Rowley, 2015). The newly industrialized economies (first Hong Kong, Singapore, South Korea and Taiwan, and then Indonesia, Malaysia, Philippines, and Thailand) have been on the search for effective management models through alliances and competition with MNCs from both within and outside Asia (Zhu, Warner, & Rowley, 2007). What China has undergone, in contrast, is not incremental change. Rather, the country has experienced a systemic shift from state socialism to market capitalism, producing what some refer to as management with Chinese characteristics (Zhu & Warner, 2002). Structural transitions from a centrally planned economy to a market oriented economy in China have been followed by changes in many aspects of employment relations. Companies in the non-state sector, including the MNCs, have gained growing importance as employers, and lifetime employment and firm-centered welfare have been largely replaced by short-term contractual relations. China's transition was buttressed by MNCs diffusing and modifying management practices brought from their home countries. And the transition also requires MNCs to make further adaptations and generate new practices to manage their local workforce as they develop alongside change in China (Zheng, 2013). The enactment or agential side of management, therefore, is central to understanding MNCs in Asia.

Last but not least, regional collaboration and competition across Asian countries have created opportunities for new MNCs to emerge. Some of these MNCs are more like their counterparts from the developed countries, having a clear home base and carrying the national characteristics of their country of origins in their management practices. Nevertheless, these MNCs may well depart from the home country institutional imprints because one of the drivers for these firms' internationalization is to obtain what their home institutions were not able to provide (Child & Rodrigues, 2005). Faced with rivalry from well-established MNCs, emerging MNCs from Asian countries are likely to take different approaches to managing their international subsidiaries, although this may lead to both constructive management inventions (Govindarajan & Ramamurti, 2011) and disruptive behaviors such as hostile competition that undermines the creation of organizational capabilities (Luo, Rui, & Maksimov, 2013). Besides, some MNCs in Asia are part of a new trend of organizing and coordinating global activities through transactional and informal networks in addition to the conventional ownership-based internalization (Knight & Cavusgil, 2004). Creation and diffusion of innovative management processes and practices are embedded in some "transnational communities" rather than engraved in formalized organizational structures (Saxenian, 2002). In light of the growing numbers and varieties of MNCs in Asia, we are able to widen the scope of examining the developmental aspect of managing the workforce across countries.

In order to make sense of the differences and diversity between Asian countries, MNCs are obliged to observe and adapt to the specific institutional environment where the associated management are located. At the same time, such a diverse environment also allows MNCs to navigate across institutions and negotiate with the relevant agencies to introduce new management practices. While changes of management across Asia are driven by multiple forces, MNCs remain very active players amongst them. Encounters between MNCs and the national institutions within Asia offer the opportunity for advancing our knowledge of the context-dependency of work organizations and employment practices adopted by MNCs. More importantly, it also presents challenges to what we know about MNCs, which carry strong heritage to those from Western countries. In this chapter, we will discuss how studying the management of MNCs in Asia will advance our knowledge by considering Asian countries as both the host and source of the growing number of MNCs.

Asia as the host of MNCs: a vision from the center and a view from the frontier

There is a well-established body of literature that stresses the key to managing MNCs is to address the tension between integrating international operations and achieving local responsiveness (Ferner, 2010). Following some influential works in strategic analysis of multinationals (Porter, 1986; Prahalad & Doz, 1987; Bartlett & Ghoshal, 1989), MNC-based HRM research has explored how employment policies and practices can facilitate the allocation of resources, distribution of subsidiary roles, and coordination of knowledge transfer across countries (for a review, see Tarique & Schuler, 2010). At heart of this body of literature, a key concern of managing people in MNCs is the consistency and coherence between staffing and the overall corporate strategy (see, for example, Milliman, von Glinow, & Nathan, 1991; Schuler, Dowling, & De Cieri, 1993; Brewster, Sparrow, & Harris, 2005; and (Thite, Wilkinson, & Shaha, 2012). A shared common theme amongst these studies is a headquarters (HQ) centered view, reflecting an underlining functionalist assumption that MNCs operate as a coherent entity when managed top-down. In keeping with this wider literature, one of the most widely debated issues in the literature of managing MNCs in Asia is whether and how established management models, systems, or practices are diffused in the host countries.

Diffusion of established management practices in Asia

Much effort has been developed to scrutinize the continuum of standardization and localization by comparing subsidiary employment practices to those of the parent firms and local firms from the host country. A general consensus is that subsidiary management reflects selective adoption and creative adaptation: resonating de-institutionalization and re-institutionalization of existing management practices that prevail within and beyond the host country, which is extensively discussed in the international HRM literature (Edwards & Ferner, 2004; Edwards, Colling, & Ferner, 2007; Ferner & Edwards, 1995; Ferner & Temple, 2006; Ferner, Edwards, & Tempel, 2012). This developmental nature is sometimes referred to as "hybridization," which has become a key agenda in studying the management of MNCs and sparked the wider debate of "cross-country management transfer" (for a review, see Gamble, 2010).

The Asian host countries have offered ample evidence of the diffusion of management practices brought by MNCs from more developed countries. Amongst the Asian developed economies, Japan and Korea present distinctive and robust national systems of employment practices, and the adopting of new management paradigms or practices has been slow (Bae & Rowley, 2001; Dirks, Hemmert, Legewie, Meyer-Ohle, & Waldenberger, 2001; Kim & Briscoe, 1997). Recent research based in Japanese MNCs suggests that greater HR integration between the HQ and subsidiaries will facilitate changes in employment practices in Japan (Sekiguchi, Froese, & Iguchi, 2016). Emerging countries in Asia have opened the doors to MNCs as part of their structural reform. China has attracted the largest scale of FDI and diffusion of established management has been both in terms of standardization in manufacturing and the introduction of the concept of human resource management into public and private sectors, although significant industrial sector and regional differences remain (Cooke, 2012; Friedman & Lee, 2010). Likewise, discretionary adoption of the concept of HRM is observed in India under the backdrop of national institutional complexity, regional differences in economic and political infrastructures, and much stronger union power compared to China (Budhwar & Varma, 2011; Cooke & Saini, 2010). In recent years, a number of South East Asian countries like Vietnam, Sri Lanka, and Cambodia have absorbed growing investment from MNCs. Some forecast that regional integration will see more established employment practices being embraced locally (Rowley & Warner, 2010).

Diffusion of established management practices is often met by institutional resistance. Drawing heavily from culturalist and institutionalist frameworks, the concept of "institutional distance" between the home and host countries has been developed to assess why and how subsidiaries could import existing HR practices, adapt to local HR practices, and create hybrid forms of HR practices (Kostova, 1999). While the concept of cultural and institutional distance suggests objective and subjective constraints that undermine the applicability and effectiveness of the management practices developed in a different country context, it also endorses the coherency-seeking assumption that HRM in MNCs is there to serve the purpose of guiding the MNC through challenging external conditions, and against other internal claims to leadership and directive-capability within the MNC. Studies of MNCs in Asia, however, have offered some counter-evidence to this narrative.

The view from the Asian subsidiary side challenges a simple and static interpretation of institutions. Empirical findings show that subsidiary initiatives often reshape management within MNCs. Drawing upon the resource-based view, subsidiary management is also embedded in the host countries, follow context specific agendas, and build knowledge and capabilities that are not necessarily transferable to the rest of the MNC (Rugman, Verbeke, & Yuan, 2011). Resource allocation, a subsidiary's strategic roles and performance targets, are often contested between headquarters and subsidiaries, which in turn affect the management on both sides. Hong, Easterby-Smith, and Snell's (2006, 2008, 2009) program of research on knowledge transfer shows that conflicting interests between HQs and subsidiaries in controlling new product development has undermined the local staff's contribution to new product design. They believe that subsidiary managers are likely to take initiatives in the so-called "peripheral" areas such as the product modification because that is where local knowledge is valued. Likewise, Fitzgerald and Lai (2015) observe the critical role played by the local management team to establish the subsidiary as a "global factory" in the parent firms' networks. As the issue of managing people is sensitive to the labor market institutions bounded to the host country's society, subsidiaries have distinctive employment concerns that may not be shared or even relevant to the other units of MNCs (Sheldon & Li, 2013). In order to fence off HQs' influence that may be seen as disruptive or undesirable, subsidiary managers are found to have sought to redirect wider social economic and social political tensions rooted in host country, highlighting the significance of subsidiary agency (Zheng, 2013, 2016). Such heterogeneity observed in the managing of MNCs in Asia has supported the new direction in theorizing MNCs as a contested terrain, away from the conventional vision that MNCs act as a coordinated conglomerate (Edwards & Kuruvilla, 2005; Ferner et al., 2012; Kristensen & Zeitlin, 2005; Morgan & Kristensen, 2006).

Adding to the view from the frontier of MNCs, researchers also start to re-evaluate the theoretical implications of collaborations and conflicts between subsidiaries observed across Asian countries. Diffusion of knowledge between subsidiaries occurs, and not necessarily through the coordination by the HQ. Information sharing and learning between sister-subsidiaries enhances subsidiary capability in knowledge creation (Miao, Zeng, & Lee, 2016). It is also possible that competition between subsidiaries can be used constructively, although what comes out of such "coopetition" is subject to HQ intervention and sometimes beyond the control of subsidiary management (Luo, 2005). Such political dynamics in subsidiary–subsidiary relationship can influence and alter the power relations within MNCs, and sometimes affect sister-subsidiaries located outside Asia (Elger & Smith, 2005). As MNCs become multi-centric and attention shifts from the center to the frontier of MNCs, it is possible that future Asia-based research will lead to the renewal or possibly an overhaul of the notion of hybridization. To this end, examining new regimes of managing MNCs in Asia will potentially offer some insight.

Emergent new regimes of managing MNCs in Asia

As the interaction between MNCs increases, pinning down the "origin" of management practices is becoming more complex (Pudelko & Harzing, 2007). This is because workplace management practices derive from the systemic forces of capitalism, societal pressures for conformity, and trends set by a dominant lead-country (Smith & Meiksins, 1995; Smith, 2008). In consequence, discussion of the management of MNCs in Asia has started to look beyond the pick and mix of employment practices, and separate respective system, societal, or dominance effects. The focus moves to the potential of management paradigms or employment regimes evolving from the complex intersection between diffusion, reproduction, and transformation. As discussed in the previous section, subsidiary management is a *contested* process, in which management practices are enacted and constructed at the workplace, and innovative management policies and practices emerge (Boisot & Child, 1999; Edwards et al., 2007; Gamble, 2010; Geppert & Williams, 2006; Kristensen & Zeitlin, 2005; Zheng, 2016).

Some distinctive models of organizing and disciplining workforces providing standard products or services have flourished in Asia. Foxconn's "factory cities" in a number of locations in China is an example. China has become the home base for the JVs and wholly owned subsidiaries (WOSs) of MNCs from the Greater China region—Hong Kong, Taiwan, and Singapore. Some of them are loop-line Chinese investors: often FDI is from the People's Republic of China but badged as FDI to gain benefits that go to FDI in China (Henderson, Appelbaum, & Ho, 2013). Some other firms have developed their production regimes in China. Foxconn is arguably the most successful one, although it is only one case and perhaps an extreme one that can be labeled as enacting "bloody Taylorism" (Lipietz, 1987). Nevertheless, it typifies manufacturing contractors, emphasizing the control of cost and productivity, surviving and thriving in the highly competitive and low profit margin segments of global production networks. Another example is the growth of call centers, mainly in India. Moving customer services overseas promotes "standard" phrases, wordings, and accent (which Mirchandani [2009] calls "scripted Taylorism") as part of a management control strategy by MNCs. And call-center-based research has shed light on the socio-political implications of service standardization to the identity of the host country workforce (Mirchandani, 2004, 2009, 2015; Nath, 2011; Russell & Thite, 2008; Sonntag, 2009).

Over time, MNCs in Asian countries have promoted the diversification of employment practices as well. Zhang's (2008, 2015) study the management of the workforce in the automobile industry in China compares the joint venture firms and the local firms. She used the term employment "dualism" to capture the fact that workers performing the same tasks were under distinctive employment terms and hence their employment relations with the firms varied. Such dualism has also been observed in the Japanese manufacturing plants in China

(Zheng, 2013) and foreign invested retail stores (Gamble & Huang, 2009). Such types of employment dualism are not new. However, it differs from the dualism based on gender, age, or skill formation differences (Emmenegger et al., 2012) and reveals how the inequality embedded in the social transition infiltrates into the fragmentation of employment relationships. China presents a ready dualism through the operation of the internal passport (*hukou*) system, and legalistic divides between migrant and urban local residents. In the Gulf States, such citizen–non-citizen polarities are extensively used to manage workforces. Hence, such dualisms have deep *political* and not just social or demographic roots in some Asian societies. The renewed meaning of such political dualism, as well as the wider implications to workplaces outside Asia, warrant further investigation.

A number of new concepts that underpin significant transformation of employment relations have also generalized from empirical research of managing MNCs in Asia. Smith (2003) conceptualized the dormitory labor regime based on observations at a Hong Kong owned jewelry factory based in Guangdong, China. He highlights the obscured boundaries between the space of working and the space of living, which transformed the way labor is attached to employment and work organizations. Dormitory labor regimes demonstrate the power struggle between employers for control and workers for autonomy, with the heavy use of internal migrants, an internal passport (*hukou*) system, casualization of labor contracts, and radical breaks from former long-term bonds between worker and workplace (Friedman & Lee, 2010; Kuruvilla, Lee, & Gallagher, 2011). Many have reported managerial domination inside factories, with unfettered power to discipline workers, and control recreation relations, not just work lives in the factories (Chan & Pun, 2010; Lee, 1998; Lüthje, Luo, & Zhang, 2013; Smith, 2003; Smith & Pun, 2006). Smith and Chan (2015) conceptualized the term "student-labor," which reveals the added layer of control as teacher–student relations transform when teachers follow their student interns into the workplace to manage them. This transformed relationship, as Smith and Chan argue, will potentially undermine vocational schools as an institution that prepares human capital. These observations lead to reconsidering the impacts of MNCs on some wider social issues in the destination countries.

Broader management issues for MNCs in Asia

MNCs' influence over the social and economic development is mixed and uneven across Asian countries. Subsidiaries are capable of upgrading and changing their functions by drawing on local resources, especially when the host countries offer market opportunities for the upgraded products and services (Birkinshaw & Ridderstråle, 1999). Some more optimistic views suggest that Asian countries will achieve "social upgrading" in terms of wage level, skill development, and improvement of workplace conditions as they move up the global value chain (Gereffi, Humphrey, & Sturgeon, 2005). However, very limited evidence has been found to support the so-called "social upgrading" (Butollo, 2014). To what extend the presence of MNCs will improve the quality of work in Asian countries remains a very open-ended question. This is partly because the so-called "social upgrading" depends on the extent to which the subsidiaries in a country are integrated into the networks of MNCs (Edwards, Ahmad, & Moss, 2002), and partly due to MNCs' ability to stratify, reshuffle, and reintegrate production and service networks and relocate to different countries (Fröbel, Heinrichs, & Kreye, 1981).

The demand for MNCs to put more resources into enhancing the general well-being of the host country's societies has gained increasing academic and public attention (Dou & Sarkis, 2010; Matten & Moon, 2008; Shen, 2011). Scandals involving the MNCs subcontracting to factories under poor/unsafe working conditions and not complying with international labor codes have raised the concerns over the ethical responsibilities of MNCs in Asia. Equally important are agencies other than the national state in raising and monitoring the standard of MNCs' social responsibilities to the host country people and society (Oka, 2016). As the power relation between the home and host countries shifts, such agencies as NGOs from within the host country societies are likely to play stronger roles in pushing the ethical agenda amongst the MNCs.

Asia as the origin of MNCs

The perception that developed countries are homes of MNCs, and the Asian developing countries are hosts of MNCs has been long held in studies of international business and management (Dunning, 2000). MNCs from developed countries generate their competence by linking up managing people with gaining strategic resources, such as accessing local knowledge bases, building relationship with industrial and national institutions, as well as creating locally embedded expertise. Developing countries offer the resources, and cost-efficient sites for production. Research in Japanese MNCs, and later Korean MNCs, has enriched this line of enquiry. This scenario, nonetheless, is changing as a result of shifts in the global industrial structure.

MNCs from the more developed Asia: enriching and extending existing debates

Some research of MNCs from the developed countries in Asia, such as Japan and South Korean, has built upon and extended a vision of organizational coherence—a theme discussed in previous section. It is possible because established MNCs in Asia were once regarded as a source of "best practice." In fact, some of the constituent elements of what are sometimes referred to as a set of coherent "high performance work practices" (Pfeffer, 1994) bear substantial resemblance to what Dore (1973) defines as "welfare corporatism" in large Japanese firms: employment security, firm-organized skill acquisition, and career advancement within the firm. Experiences of the Japanese and South Korean MNCs have also offered support for HR being a strategic partner of transferring such home-grown best practices overseas. Based on the experiences of Japanese MNCs' expansion to the USA and Europe, Taylor, Beechler, and Napir (1996) suggest that HRM in MNCs is an interactive and selective cycle, in which established management practices are selected, modified, and retained at subsidiaries. This framework, proposed by the authors as "integrative," highlights that the relevance of HR policies and practices is assessed, negotiated, exercised, and reviewed by managers from both the center (HQ) and frontier (subsidiaries) of MNCs. They have proposed a series of forces that drive and enable such a process-based HR to generate organizational capabilities. Similarly, South Korean MNCs in general, echo a centrally guided HR approach with some space for subsidiary contributions, although specific practices vary across industrial sectors (Chung, Sparrow, & Bozhurt, 2014).

As part of MNCs' efforts in maintaining organizational congruency, employment practices adopted to coordinate between headquarters and subsidiaries have been well documented. In particular, the role played by expatriates and HR practices in support of expatriation have drawn heavily from empirical studies of Japanese MNCs. Research such as by Tung (1981, 1984, 1987) on expatriate management has addressed the general issues concerning the relationship between expatriates' tenure and performance of MNCs. Her work has inspired comparisons and discussions on expatriate use in MNCs from different country-of-origins and HR policies to support expatriates taking an assignment overseas (Harzing, 2001). Empirical research conducted in MNCs in Asia generally offers affirmation of the multiple and crucial roles played by expatriates in the diffusion of organizational techniques, management practices, and training and learning within the societies of the overseas subsidiaries to achieve organizational consistency (Belderbos & Heijltjes, 2005).

Since the 1990s, however, the employment practices to promote centrally coordinated knowledge transfer and a headquarters oriented staffing policies seem to have lost its appeal as the parent firms' growth slowed down or stalled in some cases. Many Japanese and South Korean MNCs started to review employment practices and restructure their business at home and overseas. Some suggest restructuring has created a more open approach in managing HR amongst Japanese and South Korean MNCs (Chung et al., 2014; Sekiguchi et al., 2016). Increasingly, there are signs that the notion of "global talent management" has been introduced into employment practices at the parent firms and subsidiaries. Others, however, warn of the risks of losing valuable human and social resources, especially when restructuring involves employment redundancy (Kawai, 2015). As MNCs seek to look beyond the extension of home country management regimes, the usefulness of the "country-of-origin" effect as a concept needs to be reassessed. This can be achieved by comparing the experiences of the more developed and the emerging MNCs from Asia.

Emerging MNCs from Asia: reassessing the "country-of-origin" effect

Recent years have seen a growing recognition that multinational corporations (MNCs) from Asia play a crucial role as facilitators of economic growth and management innovations. Asian MNCs are not only key contributors to growing regional trade, investment and employment, but also, many have started to play a major role in connecting with the developed countries through their ever-expanding global networks and capability to draw on resources embedded in the region. However, while this increasing activeness is noted and their crucial roles recognized, the theoretical implications and its connection to wider debates remain underdeveloped (Meyer, 2006).

The experiences of the Asian emerging MNCs are often compared to the internationalization of the Japanese MNCs, which have been well documented and debated. However, the frameworks built on the example of Japanese MNCs needs rethinking when we do this comparison. This is because the internationalization of Japanese MNCs was set against the backdrop of the rise of the Japanese economy, growth of Japanese MNCs' global outreach, and the distinctiveness and strength (as well as resilience) of the management model represented by the large-scale Japanese firm. This is hardly the background for the emerging MNCs from Asia to go global. To explore alternative research frameworks, a reconsideration of what constitutes the "country-of-origin" effect is on the agenda of many emerging MNCs-based studies.

Early research into the MNCs from emerging Asian countries focused on the strategic issues, and particularly, the factors that drive internationalization of emerging MNCs. The Chinese MNCs, as one of the most actively international investors, have received extensive research attention. Some emphasize the home country institutional environment as being an important "push factor" for emerging MNCs to go global. The intra-provincial diversity and regional protectionism within China are believed to have increased the cost of internal expansion and made international expansion a viable alternative for growth (Boisot & Meyer, 2008). Governmental support has been found to be significant for emerging MNCs to migrate into new territories (Cooke, 2014), although the effect of such support varied between MNCs under different ownership structures (Wei, Clegg, & Ma, 2014). In order to compete with the MNCs from more developed countries, MNCs from the emerging Asian economies are considered to be more able to draw on locally embedded resources (Thite et al., 2012). Asset and knowledge seeking—for brands and technology—are said to motivate emerging MNCs' internationalization strategies. These interpretations have built on Mathews's (2006) reconceptualization of "latecomer theory," which argued that emerging MNCs try to get strategic assets from mature countries in order to overcome their ownership disadvantages. The distinctiveness of emerging MNCs suggest the novelty of strategic motivation for internationalization—integrating knowledge seeking and internationalization as a strategy to "overcome competitive disadvantages" (Child & Rodrigues, 2005: 390) rather than consolidating home-country corporate advantages (internal to the firm) as OLI (ownership, location, and internalization advantages) theory would suggest (Deng, 2004, 2009, 2013; Buckley et al., 2007; Liu & Buck, 2009). Subsidiary management ranges from a strong sense of centralized control (Chang, Mellahi, & Wilkinson, 2009) to a "light-touch" approach, which is defined by Liu and Woywode (2013) as parent firms being detached from subsidiaries' business activities.

As MNCs from emerging economies become more active and visible in today's global economy, more are interested in finding out how they manage their global workforce. This stream of enquiry has offered a new lens to view the "transferability" of employment practices originated in some emerging countries. One observation is that emerging MNCs are changing traditional norms whereby expatriated staffs act as managers and local recruits as workers. For example, in the large construction project organized by the Chinese firms in a number of countries in Africa, Asia, and Central and Eastern European countries, the Chinese MNCs have shown strong preference for importing their own workforce, instead of employing local people (Zheng, 2008). Similar observations are reported in the Chinese-run mining facilities and manufacturing plants in a number of Asian and African countries (Cooke, 2012; Lee, 2009; Scott, 2013). Some suggest that Chinese investment in Africa is a case of a "Chinese practice of 'national self-exploitation' by importing their labor" (Mohan, 2013: 1263). However, comparative studies of employment practices adopted by the African subsidiaries of established MNCs from Europe and emerging MNCs from India suggest that emerging MNCs are less likely to be able to "export" management practices considered to be "bad practices" (Gomes, Sahadev, Glaister, & Demirbag, 2015). The use of contingent forms of labor observed in Chinese and Indian MNCs is more an indicator of the renewed mobility of capital and labor, which is changing the way "work" is organized and labor is deployed and reproduced in MNCs under a neoliberal wave of global political economy.

The mechanism of transferring the employment practices developed in emerging MNCs from Asian countries also shed light on the theoretical problems with the existing frameworks. Compared to MNCs with an established home base that are the source of funding, models of production or service provision, as well as management expertise, emerging MNCs' "home" is less integrated. This disintegration of MNCs' "home country" may be best reflected in the case of Foxconn, a Taiwanese electronic contractor with the production base in China. The company carries with it imprints from its Taiwanese origins, expanding the business and production model honed within Mainland China, and its internationalization dovetails with the generic movements of neoliberalism and more casualized and fragmented labor markets across the world. The Foxconn case cannot simply be read through the institutional origins of either Taiwan or China. Rather, unpacking the more complicated "country-of-origin" effect will be a useful starting point for us to better understand the employment practices being adopted by emerging MNCs (see Andrijasevic & Sacchetto, 2016).

Also highlighted by research on emerging MNCs are the spaces for producing a model of "catching-up" with existing MNCs and the actions of actors involved in creating such space. While national institutional regulations are comparatively robust across the developed countries, some level of reproducing casualized employment practices has been flagged up in the subsidiaries of emerging MNCs. In Europe, for example, new developments, such as "posted workers" and "social dumping," allow workers to slip through regulatory cracks, and for new segmented labor markets to be created (Caro, Berntsen, Lillie, & Ines, 2015; Friberg, Arnholtz, Eldring, Hansen, & Thorarins, 2014; Refslund, 2016). These new spaces can create segments for migrant workers, brought from low-wage economies within or outside the European Union (EU) through employer or contractor or employment agency dependent routes that mean they are living in marginal conditions and institutionally separate from their host society. For example, in Prato, local firms in the town initially imported Chinese workers to compete with Far East producers, only to find these workers leaking out of Italian SMEs and setting up rival businesses, and creating a significant Chinese presence in the town (Johanson, Smyth, & French, 2009). These new structures to the labor market of Europe mean that when new capital comes—such as Chinese firms—they can utilize these new practices, and reproduce marginalization and seg-mentation. A common reaction to these firms—especially new arrivals that stand out in the society, such as the Chinese—is to stigmatize and nationalize/ethnicize the practices they apply as something alien and different, when in fact they are only reproducing (and perhaps extending or adding their own color) to what already exists or is emerging in new regional spaces of more differentiated European labor markets. Therefore, when we are assessing the work and employ-ment practices of newcomers, we must always be careful not to confuse the application of practices, with the new arrival, and not emergent practices with the structure of the labor market. The distinctions between who constitutes parent, a local, or a third country national are increasingly blurred. The language used to distinguish MNCs' international HR practices becomes inadequate to capture the growing diversity of labor markets, the increased use of international employment agencies, and the dispatching of labor on a global scale (Coe, Johns, & Ward, 2010; Peck, Theodore, & Ward, 2005; Smith & Zheng, 2016).

Management practices observed in the emerging MNCs in developed countries reminds us to be cautious about how to interpret the "country-of-origin effect" in order to avoid stereo-typing. We would also argue that there is a need for case-by-case sensitivity to avoid the blanket label of "emerging MNCs."

As Deng argued in his recent review, research on the international expansion of emerging MNCs "offers a unique opportunity to extend and develop extant theorizing" (2013: 413). He recommends four primary research areas for future exploration: the latecomer perspective; Chinese state and government influences; the dynamics of firms and institutions; and the liab-ility of foreignness. So far, theory building based on emerging MNCs remains an underdevel-oped area, especially in the field of human resource management. Spatial and institutional territory is a created and politicized space, bounded by state or political actors. Various tech-nologies try to remove MNCs from national state controls through such territorial vehicles as special economic zones (SEZs), and to facilitate greater freedom for the MNCs to move and remove themselves. Resource-based investments by large multinational firms, such as Chinese state-owned enterprises (SOEs), are not simply a question of profit maximization, but also involve political considerations. On a separate account, the internationalization of small- and medium-sized firms from Asian countries offers opportunities to review the network theories and particular knowledge creation in new forms of global production or service networks. In summary, future theorization of managing emerging MNCs from Asia will have to deconstruct and rebuild existing foundations of international business and draw on multi-disciplinary refer-ences for research design.

Conclusions: emerging HRM issues and new challenges

Asia, as a site of growth for established MNCs and an incubator of emerging MNCs, has pro-vided a scholarly forum, from which some old ideas have been refined and new ones developed.

Empirical research use approaches such as large-scale and longitudinal questionnaires, grounded ethnographic case studies, and mixed method enquiries. Testing theory in detailed contexts, these richly comparative studies uncover the emergent and transcendent character of reflexive actors, who challenge the reality imposed upon them, but with divergent outcomes due to the uneven powers. It is also possible that researchers will design and operationalize new empirical studies beyond the dominant frameworks in the international business.

Studies of managing MNCs in Asia have not only addressed the issue of how to interpret "context," which is central for HRM (Jackson & Schuler, 1995), but have also exposed the problems with some assumptions proposed by existing theories. Internationalization of Asian MNCs poses questions about the feasibility of transferring "whole country" practices from country A to country B through the integrating vehicle of the MNC (see Elger & Smith, 2005; Peck, Theodore, & Ward, 2005; Peck & Zhang, 2013). And as such, the single "integrated" national models or national business systems (Whitley, 1999), which imply that MNCs are somehow representative of one "national business system," has to be revisited when applied to the cases in Asia. In particular, China and India do not present one single integrated business model, but several, based on ownership structure, regional development models, and connections with political cliques. Therefore, with regard to the "transfer question" in the case of emerging Asian MNCs, we are dealing with an empirically more complicated story. The idea of the national also implies a level of "integration" and a focus on "function" that is unrealistic when there can be increased divisions within and between national and other actors. Contradictions between layers/levels or different "scales," as geographers like to emphasize, are increasingly important for all MNCs within a more globalizing context. The functionalist view central to traditional international business, which looks for maintenance of systems and integration—the MNC as an integrated or integrating actor—is misplaced when it is possible to identify layers of contradictory and conflicting actions within the MNC and the contexts in which it operates.

References

Andrijasevic, R. & Sacchetto, D. (2016). Foxconn beyond China: Capital–labour relations as co-determinants of internationalization. In M. Liu, & C. Smith (Eds.), *China at work: A labour process perspective on the transformation of work and employment in China* (pp. 337–360). London: Palgrave.

Bae, J. & Rowley, C. (2001). The impact of globalization on HRM: The case of South Korea. *Journal of World Business, 36*(4), 402–428.

Bartlett, C. A. & Ghoshal, S. (1989). *Managing across borders: The transnational solution*. Boston, MA: Harvard Business Press.

Belderbos, R. A. & Heijltjes, M. G. (2005). The determinants of expatriate staffing by Japanese multinationals in Asia: Control, learning and vertical business groups. *Journal of International Business Studies, 36*(3), 341–354.

Birkinshaw, J. M. & Ridderstråle, J. (1999). Fighting the corporate immune system: A process study of peripheral initiatives in large, complex organizations. *International Business Review, 8*(2), 149–180.

Boisot, M. & Child, J. (1999). Organizations as adaptive systems in complex environments: The case of China. *Organization Science, 10*(3), 237–252.

Boisot, M. & Meyer, M. W. (2008). Which way through the open door? Reflections on the internationalization of Chinese firms. *Management and Organization Review, 4*(3), 349–365.

Bräutigam, D. & Tang, X. (2011). African Shenzhen: China's special economic zones in Africa. *The Journal of Modern African Studies, 49*(1), 27–54.

Brewster, C., Sparrow, P., & Harris, H. (2005). Towards a new model of globalizing HRM. *The International Journal of Human Resource Management, 16*(6), 949–970.

Buckley, P. J., Clegg, J. L., Cross, A. R., Liu, X., Voss, H., & Zheng, P. (2007). The determinants of Chinese outward foreign direct investment. *Journal of International Business Studies, 38*(4), 499–518.

Budhwar, P. S. & Varma, A. (2011). Emerging HR management trends in India and the way forward. *Organizational Dynamics, 40*(4), 317–325.

Butollo, F. (2014). *The end of cheap labour? Industrial transformation and "social upgrading" in China.* Chicago, IL: Chicago University Press.

Caro, E., Berntsen, L., Lillie, N., & Ines, W. (2015). Posted migration and segregation in the European construction sector. *Journal of Ethnic and Migration Studies, 41*(10), 1600–1620.

Chan, J. & Pun, N. (2010). Suicide as protest for the new generation of Chinese migrant workers. *The Asia-Pacific Journal: Japan Focus.* Retrieved from http://japanfocus.org/-jenny-chan/3408/article.html.

Chang, Y. Y., Mellahi, K., & Wilkinson, A. (2009). Control of subsidiaries of MNCs from emerging economies in developed countries: The case of Taiwanese MNCs in the UK. *The International Journal of Human Resource Management, 20*(1), 75–95.

Chen, C. & Orr, R. J. (2009). Chinese contractors in Africa: home government support, coordination mechanisms, and market entry strategies. *Journal of Construction Engineering and Management, 135*(11), 1201–1210.

Child, J. & Rodrigues, S. B. (2005). The internationalization of Chinese firms: A case for theoretical extension? *Management and Organization Review, 1*(3), 381–410.

Chung, C., Sparrow, P., & Bozhurt, O. (2014). South Korean MNEs' international HRM approach: Hybridization of global standards and local practices. *Journal of World Business, 49*(1), 549–559.

Coe, N., Johns, J., & Ward, K. (2010). The business of temporary staffing: A developing research agenda. *Geography Compass, 4*(8), 1055–1068.

Cooke, F. L. (2012). *Human resource management in China new trends and practices.* London: Routledge.

Cooke, F. L. (2014). Chinese multinational firms in Asia and Africa: Relationships with institutional actors and patterns of HRM practices. *Human Resource Management, 53*(6), 877–896.

Cooke, F. L. & Saini, D. S. (2010). (How) does the HR strategy support an innovation oriented business strategy? An investigation of institutional context and organizational practices in Indian firms. *Human Resource Management, 49*(3), 377–400.

Deng, P. (2004). Outward investment by Chinese MNCs: Motivations and implications. *Business Horizons, 47*(3), 8–16.

Deng, P. (2009). Why do Chinese firms tend to acquire strategic assets in international expansion? *Journal of World Business, 44*(1), 74–84.

Deng, P. (2013). Chinese outward direct investment research: Theoretical integration and recommendations. *Management and Organization Review, 9*(3), 513–539.

Dirks, D., Hemmert, M., Legewie, J., Meyer-Ohle, H., & Waldenberger, F. (2001). The Japanese employment system in transition. *International Business Review, 9*(5), 525–553.

Dore, R. (1973). *British factory–Japanese factory.* London: Allen & Unwin.

Dou, Y. & Sarkis, J. (2010). A joint location and outsourcing sustainability analysis for a strategic offshoring decision. *International Journal of Production Research, 48*(2), 567–592.

Dowling, P. J. & Donnelly, N. (2013). Managing people in global markets—The Asia Pacific perspective. *Journal of World Business, 48*(2), 171–174.

Dunning, J. H. (2000). The eclectic paradigm as an envelope for economic and business theories of MNE activity. *International Business Review, 9*(1), 163–190.

Edwards, R., Ahmad, A., & Moss, S. (2002). Subsidiary autonomy: The case of multinational subsidiaries in Malaysia. *Journal of International Business Studies, 33*(1), 183–191.

Edwards, T. & Ferner, A. (2004). Multinationals, reverse diffusion and national business systems. *Management International Review, 44*(1), 49–79.

Edwards, T. & Kuruvilla, S. (2005). International HRM: National business systems, organizational politics and the international division of labour in MNCs. *The International Journal of Human Resource Management, 16*(1), 1–21.

Edwards, T., Colling, T., & Ferner, A. (2007). Conceptual approaches to the transfer of employment practices in multinational companies: An integrated approach. *Human Resource Management Journal, 17*(3), 201–217.

Elger, T. & Smith, C. (2005). *Assembling work: Remaking factory regimes in Japanese multinationals in Britain.* Oxford: Oxford University Press.

Emmenegger, P., Häusermann, S., Palier, B., and Seeleib-Kaiser, M. (2012). *The age of dualization: The changing face of inequality in deindustrializing societies.* Oxford: Oxford University Press.

Ewers, M. C. (2016). Oil, human capital and diversification: The challenge of transition in the UAE and the Arab Gulf States. *The Geographical Journal, 182*(3), 236–250.

Ferner, A. (2010). HRM in multinational companies. In A. Wilkinson, N. Bacon, T. Redman, & S. Snell (Eds.), *The SAGE handbook of human resource management* (pp. 541–560). London: Sage.

Ferner, A. & Edwards, P. (1995). Power and the diffusion of organizational change within multinational enterprises. *European Journal of Industrial Relations, 1*(2), 229–257.

Ferner, A. & Temple, A. (2006). Multinationals and national business systems: A "power and institutions" perspective. In P. Almond & A. Ferner (Eds.), *American multinationals in Europe: Managing employment relations across national borders* (pp. 10–33). Oxford: Oxford University Press.

Ferner, A., Edwards, T., & Tempel, A. (2012). Power, institutions and the cross-national transfer of employment practices in multinationals. *Human Relations, 65*(2), 163–187.

Fitzgerald, R. & Lai, J. (2015). Strategic capabilities and the emergence of the global factory: Omron in China. *Asia Pacific Business Review, 21*(3), 333–363.

Fitzgerald, R. & Rowley, C. (2015). Japanese multinationals in the post-bubble era: New challenges and evolving capabilities. *Asia Pacific Business Review, 21*(3), 279–294.

Friberg, J. H., Arnholtz, J., Eldring, L., Hansen, N. W., & Thorarins, F. (2014). Nordic labour market institutions and new migrant workers: Polish migrants in Oslo, Copenhagen and Reykjavik. *European Journal of Industrial Relations, 20*(1), 37–53.

Friedman, E. & Lee, C. (2010). Remaking the world of Chinese labour: A thirty-year retrospective. *British Journal of Industrial Relations, 48*(3), 507–533.

Fröbel, F., Heinrichs, J., & Kreye, O. (1981). *The new international division of labour: Structural unemployment in industrialised countries and industrialisation in developing countries.* Cambridge: Cambridge University Press.

Gamble, J. (2010). Transferring organizational practices and the dynamics of hybridization: Japanese retail multinationals in China. *Journal of Management Studies, 47*(4), 705–732.

Gamble, J. & Huang, Q. (2009). One store, two employment systems: Core, periphery and flexibility in China's retail sector. *British Journal of Industrial Relations, 47*(1), 1–26.

Geppert, M. & Williams, K. (2006). Global, national and local practices in multinational corporations: Towards a sociopolitical framework. *The International Journal of Human Resource Management, 17*(1), 49–69.

Gereffi, G., Humphrey, J., & Sturgeon, T. (2005). The governance of global value chains. *Review of International Political Economy, 12*(1), 78–104.

Gomes, E., Sahadev, S., Glaister, A. J., & Demirbag, M. (2015). A comparison of international HRM practices by Indian and European MNEs: Evidence from Africa. *The International Journal of Human Resource Management, 26*(21), 2676–2700.

Govindarajan, V. & Ramamurti, R. (2011). Reverse innovation, emerging markets, and global strategy. *Global Strategy Journal, 1*(3–4), 191–205.

Harzing, A.-W. (2001). Who's in charge? An empirical study of executive staffing practices in foreign subsidiaries. *Human Resource Management, 40*(2), 139–158.

Henderson, J., Appelbaum, R. P., & Ho, S. (2013). Globalization with Chinese characteristics: Externalization, dynamics and transformations. *Development and Change, 44*(6), 1221–1253.

Hong, J. F., Easterby-Smith, M., & Snell, R. S. (2006). Transferring organizational learning systems to Japanese subsidiaries in China. *Journal of Management Studies, 43*(5), 1027–1058.

Hong, J. F. & Snell, R. S. (2008). Power inequality in cross-cultural learning: The case of Japanese transplants in China. *Asia Pacific Business Review, 14*(2), 253–273.

Hong, J., Snell, R. S., & Easterby-Smith, M. (2009). Knowledge flow and boundary crossing at the periphery of a MNC. *International Business Review, 18*(6), 539–554.

Hsueh, R. (2012). China and India in the age of globalization: Sectoral variation in postliberalization reregulation. *Comparative Political Studies, 45*(1), 32–61.

Jackson, S. E. & Schuler, R. S. (1995). Understanding human resource management in the context of organizations. *Annual Review of Psychology, 46*, 237–264.

Jacoby, W. (2014). Different cases, different faces: Chinese investment in Central and Eastern Europe. *Asia Europe Journal, 12*(1–2), 199–214.

Johanson, G., Smyth, R., & French, R. (2009). *Living outside the walls: The Chinese in Prato.* Chicago, IL: University of Chicago Press.

Kasahara, S. (2013). *The Asian developmental state and the flying geese paradigm.* Geneva: UNCTAD Discussion Papers.

Kawai, N. (2015). Does downsizing really matter? Evidence from Japanese multinational in the European manufacturing industry. *The International Journal of Human Resource Management, 26*(4), 501–519.

Kim, S. & Briscoe, D. R. (1997). Globalization and a new human resource policy in Korea. *Employee Relations, 19*(4), 298–308.

Knight, G. A. & Cavusgil, T. S. (2004). Innovation, organizational capabilities, and the born-global firm. *Journal of International Business Studies, 35*(2), 124–141.

Kostova, T. (1999). Transnational transfer of strategic organizational practices: A contextual perspective. *Academy of Management Review, 24*(2), 308–324.

Kristensen, P. H. & Zeitlin, J. (2005). *Local players in global games.* Oxford: Oxford University Press.

Kuruvilla, S., Lee, C. K., & Gallagher, M. E. (2011). *From iron rice bowl to informalization: Markets, workers and the state in a Changing China.* New York: Cornell University Press.

Kushida, K. E. & Shimizu, K. (2013). Introduction: Corporate restructuring and political reform in Japan. In K. E. Kushida, K. Shimizu, & J. Oi (Eds.), *Syncretization: Corporate restructuring and political reform in Japan* (pp. 1–30). Stanford, CA: Shorenstein APARC/Brookings Press.

Lee, C. (1998). *Gender and the South China miracle: two worlds of factory women.* Berkeley, CA: University of California Press.

Lee, C. (2009). Raw encounters: Chinese managers, African workers and the politics of casualisation in Africa's Chinese Enclaves. *The China Quarterly, 199*, 647–666.

Lipietz, A. (1987). *Mirages and miracles: Crisis in global Fordism.* London: Verso.

Liu, X. & Buck, T. (2009). The internationalisation strategies of Chinese firms: Lenovo and BOE. *Journal of Chinese Economic and Business Studies, 7*(2), 167–181.

Liu, Y. & Woywode, M. (2013). Light-touch integration of Chinese cross-border M&A: The influences of culture and absorptive capacity. *Thunderbird International Business Review, 55*(4), 469–483.

Luo, Y. (2005). Toward coopetition within a multinational enterprise: A perspective from foreign subsidiaries. *Journal of World Business, 40*(1), 71–90.

Luo, Y., Rui, H., & Maksimov, V. (2013). Tales of rivals: Inter-Chinese attacks in international competition. *Organizational Dynamics, 42*(2), 156–166.

Lüthje, B., Luo, S., & Zhang, H. (2013). *Beyond the iron rice bowl: Regimes of production and industrial relations in China.* Chicago, IL: University of Chicago Press.

Mathews, J. A. (2006). Catch-up strategies and latecomer effect in industrial development. *New Political Economy, 11*(3), 313–335.

Matten, D. & Moon, J. (2008). "Implicit" and "explicit" CSR: A conceptual framework for a comparative understanding of corporate social responsibility. *Academy of Management Review, 33*(2), 404–424.

Meyer, K. E. (2006). Asian management research needs more self-confidence. *Asia Pacific Journal of Management, 23*(2), 119–137.

Miao, Y., Zeng, Y., & Lee, J. Y. (2016). Headquarters resource allocation for inter-subsidiary innovation transfer: The effect of within-country and cross-country cultural differences. *Management International Review, 56*(5), 665–698.

Milliman, J., von Glinow, M. A., & Nathan, M. (1991). Organizational life cycles and strategic international human resource management in multinational companies: Implications for congruence theory. *The Academy of Management Review, 16*(2), 318–339.

Mirchandani, K. (2004). Practices of global capital: Gaps, cracks and ironies in transnational call centres in India. *Global Networks, 4*(4), 355–373.

Mirchandani, K. (2009). Transnationalism in Indian call centres. In M. Thite, & B. Russell (Eds.), *The next available operator: Managing human resources in Indian business process outsourcing industry* (pp. 83–111). London: Sage.

Mirchandani, K. (2015). Flesh in voice: The no-touch embodiment of transnational customer service workers. *Organization, 22*(6), 909–923.

Mohan, G. (2013). Beyond the enclave: Towards a critical political economy of China and Africa. *Development and Change, 44*(6), 1255–1272.

Morgan, G. (2009). Globalization, multinationals and institutional diversity. *Economy and Society, 38*(4), 580–605.

Morgan, G. & Kristensen, P. H. (2006). The contested space of multinationals: Varieties of institutionalism, varieties of capitalism. *Human Relations, 59*(11), 1467–1490.

Nath, V. (2011). Aesthetic and emotional labour through stigma: National identity management and racial abuse in offshored Indian call centres. *Work Employment & Society, 25*(4), 709–725.

Oka, C. (2016). Improving working conditions in garment supply chains: The role of unions in Cambodia. *British Journal of Industrial Relations, 54*(3), 647–672.

Peck, J. & Zhang, J. (2013). A variety of capitalism ... with Chinese characteristics? *Journal of Economic Geography, 13*(3), 357–396.

Peck, J., Theodore, N., & Ward, K. (2005). Constructing markets for temporary labour: employment liberalization and the internationalization of the staffing industry. *Global Networks, 5*(1), 3–26.

Pfeffer, J. (1994). *Competitive advantage through people.* Boston, MA: Harvard Business School Press.

Porter, M. E. (1986). *Competition in global industries.* Boston, MA: Harvard Business School Press.

Prahalad, C. K. & Doz, Y. L. (1987). *The multinational mission: Balancing local demands and global vision.* London: The Free Press.

Pudelko, M. & Harzing, A.-W. (2007). Country-of-origin, localization, or dominance effect? An empirical investigation of HRM practices in foreign subsidiaries. *Human Resource Management, 46*(4), 535–559.

Quer, D., Claver, E., & Rienda, L. (2012). Political risk, cultural distance, and outward foreign direct investment: Empirical evidence from large Chinese firms. *Asia Pacific Journal of Management, 29*(4), 1089–1104.

Refslund, B. (2016). Intra-European labour migration and deteriorating employment relations in Danish cleaning and agriculture: Industrial relations under pressure from EU8/2 labour inflows? *Economic and Industrial Democracy,* 37(4), 597–621.

Rowley, C. & Warner, M. (2010). Management in South-East Asia: Key findings, conclusions and prospects. *Asia Pacific Business Review, 16*(1–2), 259–267.

Rugman, A., Verbeke, A., & Yuan, W. (2011). Re-conceptualizing Bartlett and Ghoshal's classification of national subsidiary roles in the multinational enterprise. *Journal of Management Studies, 48*(2), 253–277.

Russell, B. & Thite, M. (2008). The next division of labour: Work skills in Australian and Indian call centres. *Work Employment & Society, 22*(4), 615–634.

Saxenian, A. (2002). Transnational communities and the evolution of global production networks: The cases of Taiwan, China and India. *Industry and Innovation, 9*(3), 183–202.

Schuler, R. S., Dowling, P. J., & De Cieri, H. (1993). An integrative framework of strategic international human resource management. *Journal of Management, 19*(2), 419–459.

Scott, E. (2013, August 2). China goes global in Egypt: a special economic zone in Suez. *Centre of Chinese Study Discussion Paper* (pp. 2–36). Retrieved February 19, 2015, from www.sun.ac.za/ccs.

Sekiguchi, T., Froese, F. J., & Iguchi, C. (2016). International human resource management of Japanese multinational corporations: Challenges and future directions. *Asian Business & Management, 15*(2), 83–109.

Sheldon, P. & Li, Y. (2013). Localized poaching and skills shortages of manufacturing employees among MNEs in China. *Journal of World Business, 48*(2), 186–195.

Shen, J. (2011). Developing the concept of socially responsible international human resource management. *The International Journal of Human Resource Management, 22*(6), 1351–1363.

Smith, C. (2003). Living at work: Management control and the dormitory labour system in China. *Asia Pacific Journal of Management, 20*(3), 333–358.

Smith, C. (2008). Work organization within a dynamic globalising context: A critique of national institutional analysis of the international firm and an alternative perspective. In C. Smith, B. McSweeney, & R. Fitzgerald (Eds.), *Remaking management between global and local* (pp. 25–60). Cambridge: Cambridge University Press.

Smith, C. & Chan, J. (2015). Working for two bosses: Student interns as constrained labour in China. *Human Relations, 68*(2), 305–326.

Smith, C. & Meiksins, P. (1995). System, society and dominance effects in cross-national organizational analysis. *Work Employment & Society, 9*(2), 241–267.

Smith, C. & Pun, N. (2006). The dormitory labour regime in China as a site for control and resistance. *The International Journal of Human Resource Management, 17*(8), 1456–1470.

Smith, C. & Zheng, Y. (2016). The management of labour in Chinese MNCs operating outside of China: A critical review. In M. Liu & C. Smith (Eds.), *China at work: A labour process perspective on the transformation of work and employment in China* (pp. 361–388). London: Palgrave.

Sonntag, S. K. (2009). Linguistic globalization and the call center industry: Imperialism, hegemony or cosmopolitanism? *Language Policy, 8*(1), 5–25.

Tarique, I. & Schuler, R. S. (2010). Global talent management: Literature review, integrative framework, and suggestions for further research. *Journal of World Business, 45*(2), 122–133.

Taylor, S., Beechler, S., & Napier, N. (1996). Toward an integrative model of strategic international human resource management. *Academy of Management Review, 21*(4), 959–985.

Thite, M., Wilkinson, A., & Shaha, D. (2012). Internationalization and HRM strategies across subsidiaries in multinational corporations from emerging economies—A conceptual framework. *Journal of World Business, 47*(2), 251–258.

Tung, R. L. (1981). Selection and training of personnel for overseas assignments. *Columbia Journal of World Business, 16*(1), 68–78.

Tung, R. L. (1984). Strategic management of human resource in the multinational enterprise. *Human Resource Management, 23*(2), 129–134.

Tung, R. L. (1987). Expatriate assignments: Enhancing success and minimizing failure. *The Academy of Management Executive (1987–1989), 1*(2), 117–125.

Wei, T., Clegg, J., & Ma, L. (2014). The conscious and unconscious facilitating role of the Chinese government in shaping the internationalization of Chinese MNCs. *International Business Review, 24*(2), 331–342.

Whitley, R. (1999). *Divergent capitalisms. The social structuring and change of business systems.* Oxford: Oxford University Press.

Zhang, L. (2008). Lean production and labor controls in the Chinese automobile industry in an age of globalization. *International Labor and Working Class History, 73*(1), 24–44.

Zhang, L. (2015). *Inside China's automobile factories: The politics of labor and worker resistance.* Cambridge: Cambridge University Press.

Zheng, C. (2008). China's investment in Africa: Expanding the "Yellow River Capitalism" and its implications. Melbourne: 31st African Studies Association of Australasia and Pacific.

Zheng, Y. (2013). *Managing human resources in China: Perspectives from inside MNCs.* Cambridge: Cambridge University Press.

Zheng, Y. (2016). Building from below: Subsidiary management's moderation of employment practices in MNCs in China: Subsidiary management moderation of employment practices in MNCs in China. *The International Journal of Human Resource Management, 27*(19), 2275–2303.

Zheng, Y. & Smith, C. (2015). The capital and labour functions in Chinese companies overseas: Overturning the orthodoxy on expatriate use in MNCs. *The 33rd International Labour Process Conference.* Athens, Greece.

Zhu, Y. & Warner, M. (2002). Human resource management "with Chinese characteristics": A comparative study of the People's Republic of China and Taiwan. *Asia Pacific Business Review, 9*(2), 21–42.

Zhu, Y., Warner, M., & Rowley, C. (2007). Human resource management with "Asian" characteristics: A hybrid people-management system in East Asia. *The International Journal of Human Resource Management, 18*(5), 745–768.

14

EQUAL OPPORTUNITY AND WORKFORCE DIVERSITY IN ASIA

Ahu Tatli, Mustafa Bilgehan Ozturk, and Maryam Aldossari

Introduction

Asia is subject to a wide array of diversity issues and challenges, ranging from deep and persistent inequalities with respect to gender and sexual orientation to problems of religious intolerance to clashes based on race/ethnicity as well as caste/tribal affiliation, to enumerate a few. Providing a coherent picture of the similarities and disparities observable in such a vast terrain would be an intractable task without conceiving of the continent in regional configurations. Therefore, in this chapter rather than a diffuse, transcontinental focus, we structure our analysis around sub-continental areas, such as the Middle East, South Asia, and East Asia. We provide a review of the relevant literature pertaining to a variety of countries in these areas, while we calibrate our efforts to display both intra and across regional convergences and divergences in employment practices and patterns of diversity and equal opportunity. Critiquing the one-size-fits-all approaches based on direct transposition of Western-based diversity ideas in a variety of non-Western contexts, Kamenou (2007) draws attention to the need to understand the norms, values, national, and cultural narratives as well as the social contexts of divergent geographies when tackling the task of addressing diversity challenges through management scholarship. We present a context-attentive overview of diversity and equal opportunity challenges in different parts of Asia through the adoption of an emic approach (Tatli & Özbilgin, 2012), where our exploration of equality and diversity issues is informed by historical and structural inequalities in specific contexts across Asia.

This chapter covers a wide geographical region and as a result demonstrates both divergence and convergence in the area of equality and diversity at work. As we shall discuss, the region faces several common challenges in achieving equality of opportunity but there are also equality issues that are more pressing in some countries than the others. Recognizing the potentially diverging fault lines of inequality in this vast geography, the chapter starts with three sections that provide the broad equality and diversity context in Middle East, South Asia, and East Asia. The second half of the chapter is devoted to a more in-depth exploration of the some of the key equality and diversity issues in the region. We have particularly chosen three strands of equality to depict the inequality challenges somewhat unique to the region in terms of their manifestations. Thus, in three sections, the chapter focuses three strands of equality, that is, sexual orientation, nationality and tribal affiliations, and gender, in three different country context, Turkey,

Saudi Arabia, and China respectively. To illustrate inequality dynamics and experiences pertaining to sexual orientation, nationality and tribal affiliations, and gender, we use interview extracts from empirical research we have conducted ourselves in the region. Finally, the conclusions section presents a brief summary, provides policy recommendations to achieve greater levels of equality of opportunity at work, and identifies future areas of research.

The Middle Eastern context of equality and diversity

Gender equality is increasingly recognized as the predominant diversity challenge in the employment sphere in the Middle East. Syed, Burke, and Acar (2010) suggest that although full gender equality is not yet achieved in Western societies, the Middle East offers a particularly challenging context, as women have historically been locked into strict social role identities revolving around the private sphere. Not only are women viewed first and foremost as wives and mothers, but also, as Syed (2010) explains, there is an overt Islamic emphasis on female modesty in many societies within the region, which has over time come to serve as justification for gender segregation in public life, with significantly negative consequences for female participation in the labor market. Thus, the issue of gender equality, one of the central questions that inform the diversity problematic in the Middle East (ME), can only be fully understood at its intersection with a patriarchal cultural framework sustained by the dominant religion of the region.

While Islam is often perceived as a cultural monolith, interpretations and practices of Islam vary widely in the ME countries, and this alone results in noticeable differences in country-specific gender ideologies with a wide range of outcomes in terms of women's right to participate in the labor market without suffering from discrimination in terms of rank, industry, or sector (Syed, 2008). Similarly, Charrad (2011) argues that Islam does not shape the women's social condition in a static manner across ME countries. One of the most important sources of variation in gender inequality in the region is the degree of integration between the state, religion, and society. For example, some countries such as Saudi Arabia, Iran, and UAE, observe the principles of Islamic jurisprudence, which is termed *Sharia*, and which actively shapes the employment rights of women often in narrow, restrictive bounds (Metcalfe, 2008). Yet, even within that cluster, there is variation. On the one hand, Saudi Arabia displays a highly discriminatory outlook where women are simply disenfranchised from the electorate, and they are unable to claim full citizenship rights, with almost no formal capacity to exert pressure on the body politic to challenge the severe curtailment of their employment opportunities. On the other hand, in Iran, which is also governed by *Sharia* law, women are to some extent able to negotiate gendered boundaries that limit their access to employment, and seek progressive societal change (Bahramitash, 2007). As well, in a study of female managers, Metcalfe (2006) finds that in Bahrain and Oman, career advancement is possible for women, although this is moderated by significant constraints based on still rigid perceptions of gender-based role divisions informed presumably by literal interpretations of some Islamic texts.

In yet other ME countries, a relatively less formal integration exists between the workings of religion and society with a concomitantly greater space and possibility for women to pursue life outside the private sphere. In this context, exclusion is often not explicitly integrated into the legal corpus, and yet there is either little effort to put in place equality-enhancing regulations or socio-normative backdrop evolves too slowly to achieve the full equality of women in employment. For example, in a study focused on delineating the key success factors for women's managerial careers in the Turkish context, Aycan (2004) notes that women have experienced some progress in securing female managerial employment, yet also finds that cultural norms that disadvantage women in the workplace remain resistant to change. Similarly, in Lebanon, Jamali,

Sidani, and Safieddine (2005) report that women's career development is negatively impacted by an accentuated patriarchy built upon cultural beliefs that relegate women to a subordinate status.

South Asian context of equality and diversity

One of the major issue areas for diversity and equal opportunity in South Asia is that of gender equality. While Bangladesh, Pakistan, and India all have equal opportunities laws and regulations in support of gender equality to varying extents, there is a strong implementation gap between discourse and actual action. Ali (2010) suggests that women face a complex pattern of discrimination in Pakistan due to the patriarchal cultural norms in conjunction with conservative religious outlook that actively devalue their contributions at work. A particularly conservative interpretation of Islam that requires *Purdah*, the separation of men and women in social spheres, and the veiling of women in "protection" from presumed male threat to their virtue, creates a dislocation for women employees that render them interlopers in the work environment. Further, Ali (2013) finds in her qualitative study involving thirty female employees in the banking, telecommunications, and education industries in Pakistan, that organizational interventions may not be sufficient to remedy the disadvantage faced by women workers. The deep and broad societal disapproval of women working in what is considered the male domain results in widespread sexual harassment, social stigmatization, and women's alienation within but also outside the organizational sphere. Often, marital status intersects with employment status in a compounding manner, which increases the likelihood of being at the receiving end of sexually threatening behavior for unmarried female employees (Ali, 2013; Ali & Kramar, 2015).

However, even in what may be considered a relatively more culturally liberal and legally protective context, India, the situation is far from satisfactory, with only about 20 percent of women occupying posts in the urban formal economy (Cooke & Saini, 2010). Conversely, women's share in the informal, low-paid, agricultural work remains significant, as women often face strong access barriers to non-agricultural work in many Indian states (Pio & Syed, 2013). Another reason for women's limited participation in the formal, urban, higher wage paying jobs is the traditional under-investment of families in the female offspring, which engenders a female labor force that is artificially kept low-skilled and sometimes even illiterate. Not surprisingly, in this difficult context, Budhwar, Saini, and Bhatnagar (2005) note that although women in management posts are almost always a small minority across the world, this numerical imbalance is especially in India, where only 3–5 percent of managers at various ranks are women. For Punia (2005), Indian women's under-representation in management positions often relates to domestic factors, as household responsibilities for Indian women are highly burdensome. As social change remains slow in terms of what is expected of women regarding their double shift, companies fail to make work–life balance a major concern, contributing to the perpetuation of barriers to women's advancement. Yet, India has long established constitutional protections regarding equal pay, maternity, and prohibitions on discrimination in recruitment (Budhwar et al., 2005), certainly more so than in the case of Bangladesh or Pakistan, whose constitutions provide far more equivocal protections against gender discrimination. In India, gender inequality, which is widespread in the private domain, often seeps strongly into the public domain, and women's participation in urban professional jobs remain at 20 percent (Cooke & Saini, 2010). Despite equality legislation designed to protect women from discrimination, women's participation in the labor force is limited, and female employees often suffer from horizontal and vertical occupational segregation. Situated as they are in deeply and historically gendered societies, work organizations in South Asian countries often achieve slow progress in combatting the unfavorable treatment of all women at different levels of employment and in a variety of industries.

In addition to the issue of gender inequality, ethnic, religious, and tribal intolerances permeate the South Asian subcontinent. In fact, the intersectionality of several areas of disadvantage is a key challenge in addressing inequalities. For example, in India, disadvantage experienced by a woman who is a scheduled tribe member is qualitatively more complex and far harder to address, without paying due attention to both gender and class as well as tribal relations within the work sphere and communities (see Haq, 2013). India requires particular attention in this region for its vast geography with a plethora of languages, wide-ranging cultural and religious traditions, and a societal context complicated by the caste system, a long-standing exclusionary order of socio-religious stratification, all of which intersect in complex and counter-intuitive configurations to complicate how human resources are understood and how diversity can be managed (Budhwar, 2009; Venkata Ratnam & Chandra, 1996). Caste forms the major social fault line in India, which is reflected in strong and enduring patterns of inequalities in the employment sphere. For example, in their study on the influence of caste in producing discriminatory outcomes in the labor market, Madheswaran and Attewell (2007) analyze national statistical survey data to find evidence that that scheduled castes and tribes earn on average 15 percent less than their equally qualified higher caste counterparts, suffer from occupational segregation, and face cross-sectoral discrimination, although this is moderated slightly by public sector reservations and quotas to support access.

South Asia is also characterized by a vast array of religious diversity with implications for equality at work. Syed and Pio give the examples of "Ahmadi and Shia Muslims, Christians and Hindus in Pakistan, Muslims and Christians in India, Tamils in Sri Lanka" (2013: 240) and suggest that many ethnic and religious minorities remain deeply excluded, and are both discriminated against and even persecuted, within a range of social contexts, including employment. For example, in India religious harmony at the societal level is insecure, and the lack of reconciliation of divergent religious traditions, particularly Islam and Hinduism, have in the recent past manifested themselves in riots fueled by an often intractable intolerance entailing tragic losses. In his study on the impact of religion on management and business practices in India, Rao (2012) finds evidence that his participants are aware that the wider social context of India is marred by historical clashes between Hinduism and Islam, and some explain the lack of religious tolerance at work by reference to the numerical dominance of Hindu workers in their organization.

East Asian context of equality and diversity

In countries such as Thailand, South Korea, and Japan ethnic and racial divisions are not perceived as immediate diversity concerns due to greater ethnic homogeneity, yet gender remains a major equal opportunities issue. Cooke (2010) suggests that gender is the critical strand of diversity in this particular geography, where women systematically face gender-based segregation with respect to occupation and industry, and in many cases, they are pushed into relatively less secure jobs, with low pay, and decreased opportunities for advancement.

For example, in Thailand, despite the strong female labor market participation, women face unfair treatment at work, and while women may have access to management positions, this is highly limited in many industries (Napasri & Yukongdi, 2015; Picavet, 2005). Others, whilst recognizing the improvements made as a result of legislative and educational reforms in the country, note that women continue to encounter occupational segregation, gender pay penalty, and a glass ceiling (Cheaupalakit, 2014; Tatli, Vassilopoulou, & Özbilgin, 2013; Yukongdi, 2005). As well, in East Asia, women's career progress may be hampered by the specific institutional practices as well as the unique employment strategies that are preferred by work organizations. For example, in Japan, work organizations have traditionally relied on internal labor markets in shaping their workforces, and provided lifelong employment to their core workforce. Yet, female employment patterns in Japan are significantly influenced by their marital and parental status, with women employees often switching to part-time contracts after marriage (Cooke, 2010). In a society, which emphasizes lifelong employment, part-time work as well as career breaks are perceived as indicators of a low level of commitment to work and to the organization, pushing women to the periphery of their organizations, and penalizing them through lack of promotion and equal pay (Benson, Yuasa, & Debroux, 2007; Nemoto, 2013). Research shows that one career strategy for Japanese women has been to find employment in international firms, however, this is a limited solution because such firms cannot accommodate the volume of women who may wish to accelerate their career progress by avoiding employment in the highly masculinist domestic company environment (Bozkurt, 2012). For Benson, Yuasa, and Debroux (2007), one source of hope is that growing skills shortages in the country may force Japanese organizations to promote greater gender equality in order to tap into the skills of female employees, which are currently under-utilized.

Similarly, in South Korea, many women work in irregular jobs as regular labor posts are implicitly reserved for men, and women's employment patterns change drastically after marriage, and the decision to keep a job revolves around the husband's social position (Cooke, 2010). In addition, the lack of effective regulatory safeguards for gender equality at work, women's lack of organization against the status quo distribution of power in work organizations, and gender-biased organizational cultural norms are seen as key problems that sustain the gender discrimination regime in Korean workplaces (Patterson & Walcutt, 2014). In Malaysia, women also experience exclusion and devaluation at work on a number of levels ranging from the individual, where their peers or supervisor may withhold support or appreciation for their work, to the organizations, which discriminate against women in recruitment for key positions, to the wider society, which portrays them as not simply employees, but actually workers who must be mother and wife first (Ismail & Ibrahim, 2008). Despite gains in tertiary education outcomes, female graduates are at a substantial disadvantage as compared with their male counterparts, often having to accept low-paid work or remain unemployed even when they have invested heavily in their human capital (Nagaraj, Goh, Cheong, Tey, & Jani, 2014). What complicates the situation further in this context is that the dimensions of gender and ethnicity may work together to form intersectional challenges for women's career prospects. While some East Asian societies are highly homogenous as mentioned above, Malaysia is a racially and ethnically heterogeneous society and ethnicity figures as an important dimension in employee relations (Rowley & Bhopal, 2005, 2006). Ethnic Malays, who also mainly subscribe to Islam as their religious affiliation, receive various affirmative action benefits, although they form the majority proportion in the wider population, which is a policy that does not often receive full support by Malaysian citizens of Chinese descent. However, affirmative action programs in Malaysia are designed to transform historical imbalances that limit access to higher education, management and leadership roles, and organizational ownership and control by the majority of the population, and social and economic life is still far from equal (Lee, 2012). Similarly, in Indonesia, Efferin and Hopper (2007) point out that the presence of ethnicity-based diversity challenges between employers and employees in the Indonesian private sector, with Chinese Indonesians, who are a tiny minority in the overall Indonesian population, owning most private firms in the country and employing mainly Javanese Indonesians. Furthermore, in terms of gender inequality, Indonesia has a significant pay gap problem, with women earning 30 percent less than male workers in a variety of waged labor contexts as well as self-employment (Sohn, 2015).

Unique equality and diversity challenges

In this section, we take Turkey, Saudi Arabia, and China as exemplar countries, which are unique spaces of contestation for a variety of diversity strands. Specifically, in the case of Turkey, we consider the causes and outcomes of sexual orientation discrimination, which is a strongly observed dynamic in the work and employment sphere. Saudi Arabia is chosen as one of the cases in this chapter in order to unpack the equality impact of nationality and tribal affiliations. Finally, we examine the gender inequality in China, where a Confucian socio-historical backdrop intersects with a process of rapid modernization and liberalization.

Sexual orientation equality and diversity: the case of Turkey

Turkey is a G20 country as well as an emerging market economy with a complex, multi-ethnic society that combines competing elements of modernity and tradition. At the intersection of the West and the East, and subject to contrasting socio-historical pull and push forces, Turkey is also a country of enduring anxieties about its national identity as well as its specific place in the world. Since its inception as a republic in 1923, Turkey has been shaped by a strong modernization project, which had the aim of creating a secular, technocratic economic order that would sustain long-term growth, prosperity, and stability as part of the Western world. The decades-long dream of Turkish accession into the European Union can be seen as part of this struggle to project a progressive and economically advanced national self-identity.

Gender equality was one of the flagship projects of the new republic in the country's attempt to severe its links with the Ottoman past and locate itself amongst modern Western states. In that scene, women were seen as the symbols of the new, modern, secular republic. This early era of modernization was marked by progressive gender equality legislation in the 1920s and 1930s. Yet, such legislative reforms did not translate into a radical change in the country's strongly gendered culture (Tatli, Özbilgin, & Küskü, 2008).

A growing feminist outlook and an increased questioning of gender hierarchies in the 1980s and 1990s offered fresh promises for change in the calcified gender order. However, with the exception of some positive steps such as the state's contingent recognition of transgender identity and the flourishing of Lesbian, Gay, Bisexual, and Transgender (LGBT) movement as exemplified by the formation of KAOS GL in the capital city Ankara and Lambda in Istanbul, the process of change which was experienced in this latter period was of a co-opted type, failing to result in major equality gains for women and sexual and gender identity minorities. Worryingly, over the past two decades, the conditional success of the modernization project has been heavily counter-balanced by a resurgence of a market-oriented, religious conservatism. The neo-conservative social forces at play in the contemporary Turkish context are increasingly and more explicitly patriarchal in terms of the norms and values projected by the political elites as well as the main institutions of society, such as the family, school, courts, and military (Acar & Altunok, 2013).

In a 2013 survey conducted by the Pew Research Centre on global attitudes and trends regarding homosexuality, only 9 percent of the respondents in Turkey have said that homosexuality is acceptable. Although homosexuality is not considered a crime by law, equality for sexual orientation minorities is not addressed in laws and regulations, and there is no legislation against discrimination on grounds of gender identity at work and beyond (Öner, 2015). Ironically, homosexuality is often taken as a moral crime, and in some circles a dishonorable status that besmirches the family name. More conservative communities within the society have strong negative reactions to young people coming out as non-heterosexual, often disowning their children, and rarely even engaging in opprobrious violence in the form of honor killing (Ataman,

2011). Ozturk (2011: 1111) found that LGBT employees experience a great degree of porosity between work and life, which then informed their decisions to disclose at work:

> My family wouldn't understand what gay means. They would think I am no longer a man. Being out could result in my family disowning me, excluding me from their surname, acting like I am dead to them. But taking life—it wouldn't come to that, unless transsexual-transvestite sexual change happened.
>
> *(Sales Associate, thirty years old)*

Such a deeply biased outlook toward their sexual identity in Turkey puts lesbian, gay, and bisexual individuals on the defensive in social contexts, forcing them to continually engage in heavy identity management strategies (Bakacak & Oktem, 2014). Not surprisingly, in this context, the workplace, along with many other spaces in the public sphere, stands as a highly marginalizing environment. In Turkey, employees who are sexual orientation minorities are often forced to conceal their identities, and those who come out or who are found out to be gay face a variety of negative outcomes, ranging from entry barriers to employment in a wide variety of industries to bullying and harassment on the job and job termination (Ozturk, 2011).

Constrained and excluded by the homophobic formal employment context, sexual minorities view informal sector work as a prized alternative for survival (Korkman, 2015). Noting the extreme difficulties faced by a gay refugee who fled from Iran to Turkey in search of a safe haven, Grungras, Levitan, and Slotek (2009) discuss the rampant sexual orientation discrimination in employment. While the study participant initially found a job at a restaurant, his contract was terminated after only four months on the job once the restaurant owner discovered that he was gay, and the participant had to resort to sex work for subsistence.

There are striking cases where football referees are denied their licenses and teachers are thrown out of the profession (Öztürk & Özbilgin, 2014). As well, in Turkey, serving in the military is prohibited for sexual minorities. This can have severe consequences for two categories of people. First, those who wish to serve in the military but are found to be gay, lesbian, or bisexual are immediately discharged from the military. Second, many gay male citizens attempt to avoid the Turkish compulsory military service requirement by declaring their sexual minority status when they are called into the recruitment office. Yet, those who seek exemption on the basis of homosexuality often have to undergo humiliating and long-discredited medical and psychological interrogations to prove their homosexuality (Basaran, 2014). Those gay men who are able to gain an exemption are given discharge papers, which state that they are exempt from military service on the basis of psychosexual disorder. As many employers wish to verify that job candidates do not have any unfulfilled military service requirement, gay men run the danger of outing themselves if they are asked to provide details on their exemption, a situation which can potentially result in revocation of job offers (Öztürk & Özbilgin, 2014). For instance, a twenty-nine-year-old civil engineer, who participated in Ozturk's research stated:

> I started dating, and in the heat of first love—this was my first proper gay relationship—I stupidly allowed him to hold my hand briefly on Istiklal Street as we were walking to a gay club. A work colleague and his wife walked past us. I was terrified, and I desperately hoped he didn't see me … Nobody said a word about it when I got to work on Monday. Just as I relaxed, right before lunchtime, my boss took me in his office and told me they didn't need people like me there and asked me to leave the job. I couldn't believe my whole world went upside down just like that. I hated myself for being so indiscreet; I kept thinking I should've been more careful.
>
> *(Ozturk, 2011: 1112)*

One of the key areas for improving equality of opportunity at work for LGBT individuals is extending anti-discrimination regulation to explicitly include sexual orientation and gender identity amongst the protected diversity strands. Furthermore, the lack of equal opportunities is often rendered invisible due to heteronormative cultural norms and values that legitimize LGBT discrimination at work. Work organizations, as entities embedded in the wider societal fabric, operate on the basis of the unspoken and unwritten homophobic assumptions that also inform the wider social relationships. As such, sexual orientation is implicitly linked to merit, where sexual minority status is treated as a deficit, generating multiplicity of barriers for career entry and progress (Ozturk, 2011).

Nationality and tribalism as equality and diversity challenges: the case of Saudi Arabia

In addition to severe gender inequalities, Saudi Arabia's diversity scene is also dominated by the impact of nationality and tribalism on work experiences and access to opportunities in the workplace. Accordingly, this section focuses on the equality and diversity effects of nationality in the context of localization (i.e., Saudization) and of *wasta*, which is a system of privilege based on tribal affiliations.

The Kingdom of Saudi Arabia is recognized as the largest producer of oil and one of the richest countries in the world (Torofdar, 2011). The economic development of Saudi Arabia was marked by the discovery of oil and oil-generated revenue in the country throughout the 1970s. This relatively sudden economic boom in Saudi Arabia had an impact on the overall structure of society at all levels, including extensive investment in public services and infrastructure (Mellahi, 2000, 2007). The rapid economic development created severe skill shortages in the country, leading to a still continuing reliance on migrant labor (Looney, 2003) whilst at the same time creating rising levels of unemployment for the local population, whose skills and expertise were misaligned with the requirements of the economy (Ramady, 2013). According to the International Monetary Fund, the unemployment rate was at 12 percent in 2012 with over 30 percent youth unemployment (IMF, 2013). As a response, the government introduced the Saudization policy in late 1980s (Al-Dosary & Rahman, 2005; Looney, 2004). This policy aims to develop, recruit, and retain qualified, trained, and knowledgeable local labor with a view to decrease the reliance on an expatriate labor force (Kamal & Al-Harbi, 1997; Mellahi & Al-Hinai, 2000). Yet, the Saudization policy has not resulted in significant employment gains for the local population, particularly in the private sector. In fact, research evidence shows that some organizations manipulated the system to avoid punitive consequences. One common strategy was to register family members and relatives as staff in order to meet the state imposed quotas (Mustafa, 2013). The equality and diversity impact of national origin in Saudi Arabia ensues in this unique setting.

Aldossari's (2014) case study research found that nationality had a strong determining effect on the levels of remuneration. She carried out her research in a large partially government-owned Saudi Arabian corporation, which receives subsidies from the government to support localization, and 81 percent of whose internal workforce is comprised of Saudi nationals. Yet, there were clear differences in terms of pay and rewards between employees from different nationalities (see Table 14.1).

As shown in Table 14.1, employees from Western countries are paid significantly higher than other groups whereas Asian passport holders are paid the lowest range of salaries. These figures are also aligned with the national trends, where Western expatriates earn 33 percent more than Saudi nationals (Mellahi & Al-Hinai, 2000). These disparities are likely to be due to

Table 14.1 Salary ranges for engineers

Nationality	Approximate salary per month
Indian/Pakistani/Bengali	5,500–6,500 SR
Filipino	6,500–7,000 SR
South African	9,000–11,000 SR
Arabs (Lebanon, Jordan, etc.)	11,000–11,500 SR
Saudi	14,000–15,000 SR
European (British, German, etc.)	20,000–22,000 SR
American/Canada/Australia	22,000–25,000 SR

Source: Aldossari (2014).

a combination of over-reliance on Western expatriate workforce for high-level posts and colonial remnants of racialized assumptions about skills and ability, for example, the assumed superiority of the white man. Nevertheless, the pay inequities left the Saudi employees feeling devalued and discriminated on the grounds of nationality. The words of a participant in Aldossari's (2014: 141) research exemplifies the emotional impact of nationality-based pay inequities:

Employees who have Canadian, American or British citizenships are treated differently from the rest. I call this discrimination, because salaries are being differentiated based on the citizenship … This kind of environment makes you feel that you don't have a value in your own country. Salaries should be determined based on one's qualifications and not on citizenship.

(Scientist, thirty years old)

Another interviewee, who is a twenty-eight-year-old engineer, who holds a PhD degree, shared similar feelings:

I am not fairly paid when I compare myself to others, like European and American expatriates who are paid triple salaries although they don't even have a masters' degree. My secretary, who has a British passport, is paid more than me!

(Aldossari, 2014: 157)

Another marker of privilege and disadvantage is the tribe affiliation. Saudi Arabia is a monarchy based on a tribal system, which determines the governance structures in the country (Torofdar, 2011). Tribes are nomadic groups defined by patrilineal lineage that unify individuals into larger social/societal segments and members of a tribe claim higher social status and the purity of blood and origin (Al-Rasheed, 2010). Tribal tradition and the collectivistic culture engenders mutual solidarity and support amongst extended tribe members (Abdalla & Al-Homoud, 2001; Barakat, 1993) with important implications for career opportunities (Javidan & House, 2002). An outcome of tribalism is nepotism, known locally as *wasta*. *Wasta* can be defined as the involvement of a supporter in favor of an individual to achieve benefits and/or resources from a third party. The concept refers to the process whereby individual goals are achieved, often through personal links with people in high-status positions derived from family relationships or close friendships (Cunningham & Sarayrah, 1993; Hutchings & Weir, 2006a). In the limited literature on *wasta*, the concept has been related to the Chinese notion of *guanxi* (Chen, Chen, & Xin, 2004; Hutchings & Weir, 2006a, 2006b; Smith, Huang, Harb, & Torres, 2012).

Aldossari (2014) conducted a case study in a large multinational company in Saudi Arabia, which describes itself as "the engine of change" and a major contributor to Saudization. Aldossari's (2014: 166) research shows that most HR practices, including the selection criteria, promotion opportunities, and career advancement were largely influenced by *wasta*:

> In the selection process, the preference is for the candidates who have *wasta*, and then, if there is an extra slot, they pass it to the rest.
>
> *(Geologist, twenty-eight years old)*

> There are many parts of the company where we know that you don't get promoted by merit; you get promoted by who you are, or how you are related to others or to whoever is in charge of promotion. That sort of thing is extremely de-motivating.
>
> *(Petroleum engineering, thirty-two years old)*

As the above quotes highlight, the lack of formalized and transparent HR policies create a space where decisions are shaped by *wasta*, and where career success is contingent on "who you know" (see also Aldossari & Robertson, 2016). In Saudi Arabia, the salience of *wasta* is taken for granted and it significantly influences organizational decision-making and beyond with implications for career development from university entrance to obtaining a job or securing a promotion (Hutchings & Weir, 2006a). As a result, *wasta* enables those who belong to powerful social networks, particularly associated with family and tribe, to maintain personal privilege and perpetuate inequalities in organizations. In a context where human resource management processes are strongly shaped by *wasta*, the higher an individual's status in the extended family, and the stronger their links to powerful tribes, the greater the likelihood that he or she will achieve career development through *wasta* (Cunningham & Sarayrah, 1993; Rice, 2004). Some scholars suggest that the widespread application of *wasta* has generated a workforce where employees are recruited and promoted on the basis of social ties instead of merit and potential (Abdalla, Maghrabi, & Raggad, 1998; Al-Saggaf & Williamson, 2006). Thus, a key equality implication of *wasta* is that it confers undue advantages to groups or individuals who may not necessarily merit them (Metcalfe, 2006).

Gender equality and diversity: the case of China

Research shows that employment patterns in the Chinese labor market are gendered, and the traditional value system has a significant role in shaping and maintaining gendered inequalities in organizations (Cooke & Xiao, 2014; Tao, Zheng, & Mow, 2004; Woodhams, Xian, & Lupton, 2015). The research evidence demonstrates that female employees are over-sexualized and consequently positionally diminished in various aspects of organizational life (Leung, 2002), their age, appearance, and clothing are subjected to surveillance with implications as to what job roles they can perform (Woodhams, Lupton, & Xian, 2009), their earning power is constrained (Meiyan, 2005), and their managerial experiences and careers are burdened with pressures from male colleagues (Aaltio & Huang, 2007; Bowen, Wu, Hwang, & Scherer, 2007; Cooke, 2005; Liu, Comer, & Dubinsky, 2001; Zhang, Hannum, & Wang, 2008).

Several scholars argue that cultural conditions and historical traditions are important factors in gendering patterns of work and employment in China (Cooke & Xiao, 2014; Leung, 2002; Woodhams et al., 2015; Zhang et al., 2008). This literature focuses on macro-level societal factors, such as gendered culture and history, and traces the negative impact of these factors variously on women employees and women managers. Particularly, Confucian cultural values and the resultant traditional gender hierarchies are prominently reflected in socio-economic policy-making and as well as organizational HR decisions.

Despite China's dynamic growth in the past two decades and the concomitantly greater valuation that Chinese commercial organizations ascribe to ostensibly gender-free constructs of employee skills, knowledge, and experience as key drivers of competitiveness in the world markets, women's ability to achieve recognition in the workplace and attain pay parity has been deteriorating (Shi, Jin, & Xiaochuan, 2011; Zhang, Han, Liu, & Zhao, 2008). Even when controlled for human capital, there is a large gender pay disparity in China (Meiyan, 2005). Additionally, although liberalization modernized many aspects of the economic order in fundamental ways, the conventional conception of women's place and purpose in society as well as at work has not been addressed at the policy level (Turner, 2006). In a recent research conducted by Tatli, Ozturk, and Woo, a twenty-nine-year-old female manager in a manufacturing company stressed the slow pace of change in traditional gender norms: "In China, women always have lower status than men. Change is difficult. Even now, people say a woman should be at home. But women have been out working" (2016: 10).

In the Chinese context, occupational role expectations are gendered in line with Confucian cultural codes and role divisions regarding men and women. Even in occupational roles traditionally sex-typed as women's positions such as those in the retail sales departments, as women progress upward on the career ladder they are subjected to negative attitudinal pressures from male employees (Liu et al., 2001). Similarly, organizational HRM practices are still strongly informed by Confucian understandings (Ngo, Lau, & Foley, 2008). In China, women are expected to prioritize domestic sphere over work and career due to gendered cultural traditions (Woodhams et al., 2015). This creates a tension for female managers who have strong career aspirations, due to a degree of mismatch between their career ambitions and traditional norms and expectations, which are strongly gendered. Interviewees, who took part in Tatli et al.'s (2016: 13) research talked about the ways in which traditional gender norms lead to differential interpretations the career motivations of male and female managers:

> Men can get a senior job easier. Men can move jobs and people just say they are ambitious and they want something better. When they apply for another job, that new place just says he is very good to think of improving himself. When a woman applies for a different job, people say she does this because she is about to lose her job, that she is not good.
>
> *(Manager, manufacturing, twenty-nine years old)*

Furthermore, women who are outside of the traditional family structure remain stigmatized. There is even a commonly used derogatory term, *shengnu* ("leftover" women), in reference to educated, high-earning women who are in their late twenties or older and who decide to remain single in presumed pursuit of professional career advancement (Fincher, 2014). Unsurprisingly, no so such corresponding term exists for men of similar situation and circumstances. This is but one example of the social pressure women may face if they prioritize their career aspirations. From a policy standpoint, it is necessary to contest the gendered views of "how things are done" in organizations and redress historical conditions that support gender disparity in the labor market. Organizations need to provide a strong value base that promotes gender equality so as to make sure that equality, instead of inequality, becomes legitimized and normalized. The state policy, on the other hand, may promote a positive cultural shift in gender norms, values, and expectations through social investment in all aspects of life (Jonsen, Tatli, Özbilgin, & Bell, 2013).

In order to promote equality of opportunity in employment, gender equality policies need to gain structural durability. For organizations, this means instating systems and processes that expressly promote gender equality in all aspects of organizational life, including the distribution of resources (Tatli & Özbilgin, 2012). Achieving gender equality in the context of Chinese work organizations requires a large-scale structural change, which hinges on a corresponding ex ante change in the redistribution of resources. Therefore, the state policy also needs to ensure that economic, social, and political resources are redistributed to maximize gender equality.

Conclusions

The preceding sections laid out a comprehensive snapshot of a large and complex continent. The chapter focused on a variety of workplace equality topics, such as gender inequality, sexuality, race/ethnicity, nationality, religion, etc., to name but a few. What seems striking is that patriarchy, an enduring social order, which systematically privileges men over women in the public and private life, is ubiquitous across the continent, resulting in gender inequalities at work. As noted in this chapter, patriarchy often works in conjunction with other forms of social power such as the Confucian system of thought in China, different interpretations of Islam in the Middle East or the caste system in India. As our discussion of the case of Turkey shows, there are severe disadvantages that still accrue to women professionals simply because of their gender status. Women continue to experience barriers in recruitment and selection which calcify horizontal segregation. Where women find a foothold in work organizations, they face vertical limitations due to work–life balance issues, sexual harassment, and glass ceilings. To be sure, gender is but one element of difference affected by patriarchy. In fact, patriarchal tradition, values, and norms have an inimical impact on equality along the dimension of sexual orientation, and LGBT individuals experiences at work are characterized by exclusion and inequality.

One issue we have not considered in detail in this chapter, which may be useful to tackle in future research, is to look at the impact of globalization on the Asian continent when it comes to creating more inclusive organizations and to promoting equal opportunities at work. Global organizations need to share best practices and engage in strategic diffusion of ideas for equality and inclusion based on their relatively longer experience in implementing change agendas outside Asia. To be sure, any such effort needs to be sensitively aligned with the population and cultural characteristics of the countries in question, and must take into account the unique challenges that crop up in particular geographies (for instance, *wasta* in the Middle East, as we considered in this chapter). Öztürk, Tatli, and Özbilgin (2015) suggest that a key pillar of global diffusion is local tailoring of policies and measures, which should be informed by equality and diversity diagnostic procedures, identified through strong interaction with multiple actors in local units, and pushed forward by the support of management in these contexts.

Future research could also consider the centrality of intersectionality in work lives. Individuals in work organizations may experience simultaneous identity-based disadvantages whose combined effects may be more than simply a sum of the different types of disadvantages. For example, a low-income woman from a scheduled caste in India may have a relatively more disadvantageous experience at work than a middle-income woman who is a Brahmin, although both would suffer in absolute terms as compared with a middle-income man who is a Brahmin. As intersectionality is highly complex in its workings and effects, and thus difficult to measure and easy to miss, there is a need for interview-based future research, which is relatively lacking in the field of workplace equality research in Asia. This kind of in-depth research can lead the way in informing equality and diversity practice and provide leads for more holistic organizational culture change strategies rather than piecemeal, one-size-fits-all solutions to equality challenges.

There is a very strong tendency toward individualization of responsibility for gender equality at work (for further discussion, see Tatli et al., 2016). What this means in practice is that work organizations are increasingly seen by their workers as well as governments and regulatory bureaucracies solely as engines of wealth accumulation and thus stand absolved of the task of promoting equality. This is indicative of a worrying trend which is reflected not only in China or even Asia, but also across the world where neoliberal values have come to privilege work organizations as a separate world, driven mainly by market forces. The new orthodoxy is that equality is a value that should be recognized conditional on its currency in the marketplace. Therefore, in the Asian context, both organizations and governments have crucial roles to play in conjunction with each other. The state and governments are the key actors in bringing in progressive legislation and then ensuring its implementation, whilst organizations need to design policies and programs that are tailored to the specific labor market and industry contexts within which they operate. In addition, awareness raising campaigns at both the industry level and the organizational level need to be initiated to diagnose and document the nature and shape of discriminatory barriers, disseminate information of existing problems, and finally respond to lapses in equality practice by favoring more collective means. The motivation to engage in this type of root and branch review and reformation will be absent without parallel efforts to introduce a stronger regulatory framework which can push industries/organizations out of complacency.

References

Aaltio, I. & Huang, J. (2007). Women managers' careers in information technology in China: High flyers with emotional costs? *Journal of Organizational Change Management, 20*, 227–244.

Abdalla, H. F., Maghrabi, A. S., & Raggad, B. G. (1998). Assessing the perceptions of human resource managers toward nepotism: A cross-cultural study. *International Journal of Manpower, 19*(8), 554–570.

Abdalla, I. A. & Al-Homoud, M. A. (2001). Exploring the implicit leadership theory in the Arabian Gulf States. *Applied Psychology, 50*(4), 506–531.

Acar, F. & Altunok, G. (2013). The "politics of intimate" at the intersection of neo-liberalism and neo-conservatism in contemporary Turkey. *Women's Studies International Forum, 41*, 14–23.

Al-Dosary, A. S. & Rahman, S. M. (2005). Saudization (localization): A critical review. *Human Resource Development International, 8*(4), 495–502.

Aldossari, M. (2014). *Repatriation and the psychological contract: A Saudi Arabian comparative study*. Doctoral dissertation, Queen Mary University of London.

Aldossari, M. & Robertson, M. (2016). The role of wasta in repatriates' perceptions of a breach to the psychological contract: A Saudi Arabian case study. *The International Journal of Human Resource Management, 27*(16), 1854–1873.

Ali, F. (2010). A comparative study of EEO in Pakistan, India and Bangladesh. In M. Özbilgin & J. Syed (Eds.), *Managing gender diversity in Asia: A research companion* (pp. 32–53). New York: Edward Elgar.

Ali, F. (2013). A multi-level perspective on equal employment opportunity for women in Pakistan. *Equality, Diversity and Inclusion: An International Journal, 32*(3), 289–309.

Ali, F. & Kramar, R. (2015). An exploratory study of sexual harassment in Pakistani organizations. *Asia Pacific Journal of Management, 32*(1), 229–249.

Al-Rasheed, M. (2010). *A history of Saudi Arabia*. Cambridge: Cambridge University Press.

Al-Saggaf, Y. & Williamson, K. (2006). Doing ethnography from within a constructivist paradigm to explore virtual communities in Saudi Arabia. *Qualitative Sociology Review, 2*(2), 5–20.

Ataman, H. (2011). Less than citizens: Lesbian, gay, bisexual and transgender question in Turkey. In R. O. Dönmez & P. Enneli (Eds.), *Societal peace and ideal citizenship for Turkey* (pp. 125–158). Plymouth: Lexington Books.

Aycan, Z. (2004). Key success factors for women in management in Turkey. *Applied Psychology, 53*(3), 453–477.

Bahramitash, R. (2007). Iranian women during the Reform Era (1994–2004): A focus on employment. *Journal of Middle East Women's Studies, 3*(2), 86–109.

Bakacak, A. G. & Oktem, P. (2014). Homosexuality in Turkey: Strategies for managing heterosexism. *Journal of Homosexuality, 61*(6), 817–846.

Barakat, H. (1993). *The Arab world: Society, culture, and state.* Berkeley, CA: University of California Press.

Basaran, O. (2014). "You are like a virus": Dangerous bodies and military medical authority in Turkey. *Gender & Society, 28*(4), 562–582.

Benson, J., Yuasa, M., & Debroux, P. (2007). The prospect for gender diversity in Japanese employment. *The International Journal of Human Resource Management, 18*(5), 890–907.

Bowen, C. C., Wu, Y., Hwang, C. E., & Scherer, R. F. (2007). Holding up half of the sky?: Attitudes toward women as managers in the People's Republic of China. *The International Journal of Human Resource Management, 18*, 268–283.

Bozkurt, Ö. (2012). Foreign employers as relief routes: Women, multinational corporations and managerial careers in Japan. *Gender, Work & Organization, 19*(3), 225–253.

Budhwar, P. (2009). Managing human resources in India. In J. Storey, P. Wright, & D. Ulrich (Eds.), *The Routledge companion to strategic human resource management* (pp. 435–446). London: Routledge.

Budhwar, P. S., Saini, D. S., & Bhatnagar, J. (2005). Women in management in the new economic environment: The case of India. *Asia Pacific Business Review, 11*(2), 179–193.

Charrad, M. M. (2011). Gender in the Middle East: Islam, state, agency. *Annual Review of Sociology, 37*, 417–437.

Cheaupalakit, P. (2014). Women leaders in the Thai education: Career paths and the glass ceiling. *International Journal of Behavioral Science, 9*(1), 1–14.

Chen, C. C., Chen, Y.-R., & Xin, K. (2004). Guanxi practices and trust in management: A procedural justice perspective. *Organization Science, 15*(2), 200–209.

Cooke, F. L. (2005). Women's managerial careers in China in a period of reform. *Asia Pacific Business Review, 11*, 149–162.

Cooke, F. L. (2010). Women's participation in employment in Asia: A comparative analysis of China, India, Japan and South Korea. *The International Journal of Human Resource Management, 21*(12), 2249–2270.

Cooke, F. L. & Saini, D. S. (2010). Diversity management in India: A study of organizations in different ownership forms and industrial sectors. *Human Resource Management, 49*(3), 477–500.

Cooke, F. L. & Xiao, Y. (2014). Gender roles and organizational HR practices: The case of women's careers in accountancy and consultancy firms in China. *Human Resource Management, 53*, 23–44.

Cunningham, R. & Sarayrah, Y. K. (1993). *Wasta: The hidden force in Middle Eastern society.* Westport, CT: Praeger.

Efferin, S. & Hopper, T. (2007). Management control, culture and ethnicity in a Chinese Indonesian company. *Accounting, Organizations and Society, 32*(3), 223–262.

Fincher, L. H. (2014). *Leftover women: The resurgence of gender inequality in China.* London: Zed Books.

Grungras, N., Levitan, R., & Slotek, A. (2009). Unsafe haven: Security challenges facing LGBT asylum seekers and refugees in Turkey. *Praxis: The Fletcher Journal of Human Security, 24*, 41–61.

Haq, R. (2013). Intersectionality of gender and other forms of identity: Dilemmas and challenges facing women in India. *Gender in Management: An International Journal, 28*(3), 171–184.

Hutchings, K. & Weir, D. (2006a). Guanxi and wasta: A comparison. *Thunderbird International Business Review, 48*(1), 141–156.

Hutchings, K. & Weir, D. (2006b). Understanding networking in China and the Arab world: Lessons for international managers. *Journal of European Industrial Training, 30*(4), 272–290.

IMF (2013). *Saudi Arabia: Selected issues.* Washington, DC: International Monetary Fund.

Ismail, M. & Ibrahim, M. (2008). Barriers to career progression faced by women: Evidence from a Malaysian multinational oil company. *Gender in Management: An International Journal, 23*(1), 51–66.

Jamali, D., Sidani, Y., & Safieddine, A. (2005). Constraints facing working women in Lebanon: An insider view. *Women in Management Review, 20*(8), 581–594.

Javidan, M. & House, R. J. (2002). Leadership and cultures around the world: Findings from GLOBE: An introduction to the special issue. *Journal of World Business, 37*(1), 1–2.

Jonsen, K., Tatli, A., Özbilgin, M. F., & Bell, M. P. (2013). The tragedy of the uncommons: Reframing workforce diversity. *Human Relations, 66*, 271–294.

Kamal, M. & Al-Harbi, A. S. (1997). Markov analysis of Saudization in engineering companies. *Journal of Management in Engineering, 13*(2), 87–91.

Kamenou, N. (2007) Methodological considerations in conducting research across gender, "race," ethnicity and culture: A challenge to context specificity in diversity research methods. *The International Journal of Human Resource Management, 18*(11), 1995–2009.

Korkman, Z. K. (2015). Feeling labor commercial divination and commodified intimacy in Turkey. *Gender & Society, 29*(2), 195–218.

Lee, H. A. (2012). Affirmative action in Malaysia: Education and employment outcomes since the 1990s. *Journal of Contemporary Asia, 42*(2), 230–254.

Leung, A. S. (2002). Sexuality at work: Female secretaries' experiences in the context of Chinese culture. *Journal of Managerial Psychology, 17*, 506–522.

Liu, S. S., Comer, L. B., & Dubinsky, A. J. (2001). Gender differences in attitudes toward women as sales managers in the People's Republic of China. *The Journal of Personal Selling and Sales Management, 21*, 303–311.

Looney, R. (2003). The Gulf Co-operation Council's cautious approach to economic integration. *Journal of Economic Cooperation, 24*(2), 137–160.

Looney, R. (2004). Saudization: A useful tool in the kingdom's battle against unemployment? *Journal of South Asian and Middle Eastern Studies, 27*(3), 13–33.

Madheswaran, S. & Attewell, P. (2007). Caste discrimination in the Indian urban labor market: Evidence from the National Sample Survey. *Economic and Political Weekly, 42*(41), 4146–4153.

Meiyan, W. (2005). Gender wage differentials in China's urban labor market. *Economic Research Journal, 12*, 35–44.

Mellahi, K. (2000). Human resource development through vocational education in Gulf Cooperation Countries: The case of Saudi Arabia. *Journal of Vocational Education and Training, 52*(2), 329–344.

Mellahi, K. (2007). The effect of regulations on HRM: Private sector firms in Saudi Arabia. *The International Journal of Human Resource Management, 18*(1), 85–99.

Mellahi, K. & Al-Hinai, S. M. (2000). Local workers in Gulf co-operation countries: Assets or liabilities? *Middle Eastern Studies, 36*(3), 177–190.

Metcalfe, B. D. (2006). Exploring cultural dimensions of gender and management in the Middle East. *Thunderbird International Business Review, 48*(1), 93–107.

Metcalfe, B. D. (2008). Women, management and globalization in the Middle East. *Journal of Business Ethics, 83*(1), 85–100.

Mustafa, H. (2013, September 5). Saudization program not helping Saudi Arabia's economic "competitiveness." *Al Arabiya*. Retrieved from http://english.alarabiya.net/en/business/economy/2013/09/05/Saudization-program-not-helping-Saudi-Arabia-s-economic-competitiveness-.html.

Nagaraj, S., Goh, K., Cheong, K., Tey, N. & Jani, R. (2014). Gender imbalance in educational attainment and labor market dynamics: Evidence from Malaysia. *Malaysian Journal of Economic Studies, 51*, 127–145.

Napasri, T. & Yukongdi, V. (2015). A study of Thai female executives: Perceived barriers to career advancement. *Review of Integrative Business and Economics Research, 4*(3), 108–120.

Nemoto, K. (2013). When culture resists progress: Masculine organizational culture and its impacts on the vertical segregation of women in Japanese companies. *Work, Employment and Society, 27*(1), 153–169.

Ngo, H. Y., Lau, C. M., & Foley, S. (2008). Strategic human resource management, firm performance, and employee relations climate in China. *Human Resource Management, 47*, 73–90.

Öner, A. (2015). *Beyaz Yakalı Eşcinseller: İşyerinde Cinsel Yönelim Ayrımcılığı ve Mücadele Stratejileri*. Istanbul: Iletisim.

Özturk, M. B. (2011). Sexual orientation discrimination: Exploring the experiences of lesbian, gay and bisexual employees in Turkey. *Human Relations, 64*(8): 1099–1118.

Öztürk, M. B. & Özbilgin, M. (2014). From cradle to grave. In F. Colgan & N. Rumens (Eds.), *Sexual orientation at work: Contemporary issues and perspectives* (pp. 152–165). London: Routledge.

Öztürk, M. B., Tatli, A., & Özbilgin, M. (2015). Global diversity management: Breaking the local impasse. In R. Bendl, I. Bleijenbergh, E. Henttonen, & A. Mills (Eds.), *The Oxford handbook of diversity in organizations* (pp. 370–387). Oxford: Oxford University Press.

Patterson, L. & Walcutt, B. (2014). Explanations for continued gender discrimination in South Korean workplaces. *Asia Pacific Business Review, 20*(1), 18–41.

Pew Research Center (2013). *The global divide on homosexuality. The Pew Global Attitudes Project*. Washington, DC.

Picavet, M. (2005). Thai women: Key players in the country's economic and social development. *ABAC Journal, 25*(3), 29–52.

Pio, E. & Syed, J. (2013). Our bodies, our minds, our men: Working South Asian women. *Gender in Management: An International Journal, 28*(3), 140–150.

Punia, B. K. (2005). Emerging gender diversity and male stereotypes: The changing indian business scenario. *Indian Journal of Industrial Relations, 41*(2), 188–205.

Ramady, M. (2013). Gulf unemployment and government policies: Prospects for the Saudi labor quota or Nitaqat system. *International Journal of Economics and Business Research, 5*(4), 476–498.

Rao, A. (2012). Managing diversity: Impact of religion in the Indian workplace. *Journal of World Business, 47*(2), 232–239.

Rice, G. (2004). Doing business in Saudi Arabia. *Thunderbird International Business Review, 46*(1), 59–84.

Rowley, C. & Bhopal, M. (2005). The role of ethnicity in employee relations: The case of Malaysia. *Asia Pacific Journal of Human Resources, 43*(3), 308–331.

Rowley, C. & Bhopal, M. (2006). The ethnic factor in state-labor relations: The case of Malaysia. *Capital & Class, 30*(1), 87–115.

Shi, L., Jin, S., & Xiaochuan, L. (2011). Evolution of the Gender Wage Gap among China's urban employees. *Social Sciences in China, 32*, 161–180.

Smith, P. B., Huang, H. J., Harb, C., & Torres, C. (2012). How distinctive are indigenous ways of achieving influence? A comparative study of *guanxi*, *wasta*, *jeitinho*, and "pulling strings." *Journal of Cross-Cultural Psychology, 43*(1), 135–150.

Sohn, K. (2015). Gender discrimination in earnings in Indonesia: A fuller picture. *Bulletin of Indonesian Economic Studies, 51*(1), 95–121.

Syed, J. (2008). A context-specific perspective of equal employment opportunity in Islamic societies. *Asia Pacific Journal of Management, 25*(1), 135–151.

Syed, J. (2010). An historical perspective on Islamic modesty and its implications for female employment. *Equality, Diversity and Inclusion: An International Journal, 29*(2), 150–166.

Syed, J., Burke, R. J., & Acar, F. P. (2010). Re-thinking *tanawo* (diversity) and *musawat* (equality) in the Middle East. *Equality, Diversity and Inclusion: An International Journal, 29*(2), 144–149.

Syed, J. & Pio, E. (2013). Rediscovering "*Anekta mein ekta*" or "*kasrat mein wahdat*" South Asian management through unity in diversity. *Equality, Diversity and Inclusion: An International Journal, 32*(3), 236–244.

Tao, J., Zheng, B., & Mow, S. L. (Eds.). (2004). *Holding up half the sky: Chinese women past, present and future.* New York: Feminist Press.

Tatli, A. & Özbilgin, M. F. (2012). An emic approach to intersectional study of diversity at work: A Bourdieuan framing. *International Journal of Management Reviews, 14*, 180–200.

Tatli, A., Özbilgin, M. & Küskü, F. (2008). Gendered occupational outcomes: The case of professional training and work in Turkey. In J. Eccles & H. Watt (Eds.), *Explaining gendered occupational outcomes* (pp. 406–449). Ann Arbor, MI: APA Press.

Tatli, A., Ozturk, M. B., & Woo, H. S. (2016). Individualization and marketization of responsibility for gender equality: The case of female managers in China. *Human Resource Management, 56*,(3), 407–430. doi:10.1002/hrm.21776.

Tatli, A., Vassilopoulou, J., & Özbilgin, M. (2013). An unrequited affinity between talent shortages and untapped female potential: The relevance of gender quotas for talent management in high growth potential economies of the Asia Pacific region. *International Business Review, 22*, 539–553.

Torofdar, Y. (2011). *Human Resource Management (HRM) in Saudi Arabia: A closer look at Saudization.* Riyadh: Institute of Public Administration.

Turner, Y. (2006). Swinging open or slamming shut?: The implications of China's open door policy for women, educational choice and work. *Journal of Education and Work, 19*, 47–65.

Venkata Ratnam, C. S. & Chandra, V. (1996). Sources of diversity and the challenge before human resource management in India. *International Journal of Manpower, 17*(4/5), 76–108.

Woodhams, C., Lupton, B., & Xian, H. (2009). The persistence of gender discrimination in China: Evidence from recruitment advertisements. *The International Journal of Human Resource Management, 20*, 2084–2109.

Woodhams, C., Xian, H., & Lupton, B. (2015). Women managers' careers in China: Theorizing the influence of gender and collectivism. *Human Resource Management, 54*(6), 913–931.

Yukongdi, V. (2005). Women in management in Thailand: Advancement and prospects. *Asia Pacific Business Review, 11*, 267–281.

Zhang, J., Han, J., Liu, P. W., & Zhao, Y. (2008). Trends in the gender earnings differential in urban China, 1988–2004. *ILR Review, 61*(2), 224–243.

Zhang, Y., Hannum, E., & Wang, M. (2008). Gender-based employment and income differences in urban China: Considering the contributions of marriage and parenthood. *Social Forces, 86*, 1529–1560.

PART IV

HRM in selected Asian countries

15

HUMAN RESOURCE MANAGEMENT IN JAPAN AND SOUTH KOREA

Fabian Jintae Froese, Tomoki Sekiguchi, and Mohan Pyari Maharjan

Introduction

This chapter provides an overview of human resource management (HRM) in Japan and South Korea (henceforth Korea) and discusses the recent globalization challenges that enterprises from both countries face. Given the importance of large enterprises in these countries, though the importance of small medium enterprises (SMEs) has been emphasized recently, we focus on the HRM issues of large enterprises. Moreover, we provide the managerial implications of how Japanese and Korean enterprises can respond to the current globalization challenges, as well as suggesting avenues for future research.

Japan and Korea, located in East Asia, are successful countries that have experienced so-called miraculous economic growth in the post-World War II period. Japan's economic boom started in the 1950s and by the 1960s, the country had become the world's second largest economic giant. Korea is one of the Four Asian Tigers, or Four Asian Dragons, along with Taiwan, Singapore, and Hong Kong. These highly free-market and developed economies experienced rapid industrialization between the early 1960s and the 1990s. Simultaneously, both Japan and Korea experienced severe economic downturns. For example, Japan suffered from a long-term recession after the collapse of the bubble economy in the early 1990s and Korea's economy was heavily influenced by the Asian financial crisis in the late 1990s, but recovered quickly.

Corresponding with their economic success, Japan and Korea have many distinctive multi-national enterprises (MNEs), including Toyota, Honda, Sony, Panasonic, and Mitsubishi (Japan) and Samsung, LG, Hyundai, and Posco (Korea). Most of these successful enterprises are organized into diversified business groups, so-called *keiretsu* (Japan) or *chaebols* (Korea). While both *keiretsu* and *chaebols* are characterized as conglomerates with cross-ownership amongst the various member enterprises, they also differ on several dimensions: the central role of banks in *keiretsu*, the hierarchical and centralized leadership of *chaebols*, and the stronger family bonds in *chaebols* (Hemmert, 2012).

As neighboring countries, Japan and Korea have experienced cultural exchange, trade, war, and political contact for more than 1,500 years. The cultivation of rice, Buddhism, Chinese foods, Chinese characters, and other technology came to Japan via Korea. Therefore, Japan and Korea share a similar cultural background. For example, Confucianism has influenced the culture of both countries, resulting in industrialization because the philosophy values stability, hard work, and loyalty and respect toward authority figures. Confucianism also influences the management style of companies in both countries.

Because of Japanese companies' great success in the world market before the economic crisis in the 1990s, Japanese management techniques, including Japanese-style HRM, have been studied extensively by international scholars. Indeed, Japanese-style HRM and US-style HRM are held up as "best practices" (Smith & Meiksins, 1995; Pudelko & Harzing, 2008). On the other hand, Korean HRM has received comparatively less attention from researchers (Tung, Paik, & Bae, 2013). Nonetheless, both Japanese and Korean HRM are worth studying and should be well understood because companies from Japan and Korea have both similarities and differences that contribute to their organizational success. Comparing and contrasting HRM practices of Japanese and Korean firms will help academic researchers and practitioners understand how the historical and cultural backgrounds of Japan and Korea have influenced their HRM, identify the source of their competitive advantage in terms of HRM, and explore the nature of the global challenges these companies face.

The remainder of this chapter is structured as follows. In the next section, we provide an overview of the HR systems in both countries. In the following section, we discuss the major challenges arising from globalization. Both Japanese and Korean MNEs are highly globalized, yet still often pursue very domestic HRM. We then provide managerial recommendations as well as avenues for future research.

HR systems of Japan and Korea

Both Japan and Korea are well known for their distinctive HR practices (Rowley, Benson, & Warner, 2004). As a result of Japanese companies' rapid economic success after World War II, Korean companies benchmarked and largely adopted the Japanese HR system (Bae & Rowley, 2003). However, in response to the Asian financial crisis in 1997 and the US financial crisis in 2008, Korean companies sought inspiration elsewhere (Tung et al., 2013). Japanese companies also modified their HR practices given the long domestic recession that started in the 1990s. For instance, while lifetime employment used to be the norm in the past, in recent years, poorly performing Japanese companies laid off people to reduce costs (Ahmadjian & Robinson, 2001). Notwithstanding certain similarities, several distinct differences have emerged between Japanese and Korean HR practices (Rowley et al., 2004). Table 15.1 provides an overview of the similarities and differences between HR practices in Japan and Korea, and also contrasts these with

Table 15.1 Comparison of HR systems

	Japan	*Korea*	*Western approach*
Organizational culture	Collectivistic, relationship focused	Collectivistic, hierarchical	Individualistic, flat hierarchies
Recruitment and retention	College recruiting, long-term employment	Entry and mid-career recruiting	Flexible
Training and development	Firm specific, long term	Extensive training, more focus on specialist skills	Focus on specialist skills
Compensation and rewards	Seniority and ability based	Seniority and performance-based, financial incentives	Performance and job based

typical Western approaches. In the following, we discuss Japanese and Korean HR practices in more depth. We organize HR practices into organizational culture, recruitment and retention, training and development, and compensation and rewards. For each subsection, we first describe the situation in Japan and Korea separately, and then provide a comparative summary.

Organizational culture

Organizational culture in Japan. Organizational culture in Japan is deeply rooted in the national culture (Marsh & Mannari, 1976). Japanese culture is characterized by collectivism, moderate power distance, strong uncertainty avoidance, masculinity, and a long-term orientation (Hofstede, 2001). Collectivism manifests in Japanese companies in the way they organize work in teams. Also, considering the moderate power distance, teams are usually decentralized and have the autonomy to make decisions and to conduct the tasks assigned to the team. Japanese employees are known for their attachment to their organization and their long working hours (Froese, 2013; Jakonis, 2009; Li-Ping Tang, Kim, & O'Donald, 2000).

Japan is a mono-cultural, mono-racial, and mono-lingual country. In the organizational culture, Japanese firms have incorporated the notion of "in" (*uchi*) and "out" (*soto*) (Doi, 1971). They prefer group membership. This in turn creates a strong distinction between in-groups and out-groups (Gudykunst & Nishida, 2001). The way Japanese workers communicate to in-groups and out-groups is also distinctive. They hesitate to express contrasting opinions (Peltokorpi, 2008). They identify themselves mainly in terms of groups and try to fit into groups by displaying the right attitudes, behavioral patterns, and values (Nakane, 1972). Many mechanisms exist to help employees fit in with the groups and the organization (Sekiguchi, 2006).

Japanese people tend to find relief and comfort in hierarchical structures (Hofstede, 2001) and their organizational culture is strongly bonded by the relations between seniors and subordinates (Haghirian, 2010). Japanese managers are more likely to link success and failure to effort and dedication rather than employees' abilities and financial performance, as in the USA (Baba, Hanaoka, Hara, & Thompson, 1984). Moreover, in Japan, the employee–employer relationship is largely based on verbal contracts (Peltokorpi, 2008).

The organizational conditions in Japan are favorable for knowledge creation. Indeed, some scholars have called Japanese organizations knowledge-creating companies (Nonaka & Takeuchi, 1995). *Kaizen* (continuous improvement) is the basis for creating knowledge as it deals with interactive learning and problem solving (Sadler, 1997).

Organizational cultures in Korea. The organizational cultures of Korean companies have several unique features rooted in Confucianism and the military regime (Hemmert, 2012). Collectivism, work ethic, hierarchy, and paternalistic leadership are typical traits (Froese, 2013; Hemmert, 2012; Jöns, Froese, & Pak, 2007). Collectivism is highly regarded in Korean society and companies. Teamwork and socialization within teams and companies are important to build trust and loyalty. Thus, training, company trips (e.g., trip to Cheju Island), and outings (e.g., mountain climbing) are an integral part of their work. Colleagues usually have lunch, coffee, and dinner together. Socialization even extends beyond the organizational boundaries and it is common for colleagues to attend each other's family gatherings (e.g., weddings, funerals).

In terms of work ethic, several studies have reported Koreans' high work motivation and willingness to work long hours (e.g., Froese, 2013). Thus, it is not surprising that Korea has amongst the longest working hours in the world (Bader, Froese, & Kraeh, 2016). In 2014, Koreans worked on average 2,124 hours per year. In comparison, Germans only worked 1,371 hours per year, while Japanese and US employees worked around 1,700 hours per year. Koreans not only work longer hours each day than their European counterparts, but they also take fewer holidays. Even though they are entitled to fifteen to twenty-five days of paid holidays a year, Korean labor laws and peer pressure result in most employees doing "holiday work" instead of taking their holidays (Suk, 2013).

Korean organizations are well known for their centralized and hierarchical structures rooted in Confucianism (Jöns et al., 2007). The several-decades-long military regime and mandatory military service for all Korean men have further enforced the hierarchical organizational culture (Chang, Chang, & Jacobs, 2009). Supervisor–subordinate relationships are also very hierarchical. Subordinates are expected to follow almost blindly the instructions of their supervisors. Supervisors in turn are expected to be benevolent leaders and provide guidance to their subordinates (Hong, Cho, Froese, & Shin, 2016).

Comparative summary of organizational cultures. Both Japanese and Korean enterprises are well known for their strong organizational cultures. Influenced by their national cultures, the organizational cultures in both Japan and Korea are characterized by collectivism, emphasizing teamwork, and personal relationships. However, the specific manifestations and interpretations vary somewhat. For instance, Korean companies tend to have a short-term orientation in contrast to the long-term orientation of Japanese companies. Another major difference between the countries is that work relationships and personal relationships in Korean organizations tend to be much more hierarchical than in Japanese organizations. Work and personal relationships are also more strongly interwoven in Korea than in Japan. The tendency to work long hours and sacrifice holidays is also more pronounced in Korea than in Japan (Froese, 2013). The strong sense of collectivism and strict hierarchies contradict the Western understanding of individualism and flat hierarchies, thus providing grounds for potential conflict between Korean and Western employees (Froese, Pak, & Chong, 2008).

Recruitment and retention

Recruitment and retention in Japan. Japanese companies have a periodic hiring system (JILPT, 2003). They focus on entry-level recruiting and prefer to hire new graduates directly from schools and colleges (Froese & Peltokorpi, 2011; Peltokorpi & Froese, 2015; Robinson, 2003). There is low mid-career movement in Japan (Auer & Cazes, 2000; JILPT, 2012), in part because of employees' firm-specific skills (Jacoby, 2005; Ono, 2007) and the limited pension portability (Ono, 2007). Because Japanese companies look for employee attitudes and whether applicants would fit into their organization, there is less emphasis on technical expertise (Peltokorpi, 2013) during the recruitment process.

The employment relationship in Japan is long term in nature (Peltokorpi, Allen, Froese, 2015). The organization is bonded by the employee–employer relationships and hence downsizing is the last option that Japanese companies consider in difficult economic periods (Kato, 2001). As a consequence, Japanese employees are embedded in their organization and the turnover rate is much lower than in other countries (Peltokorpi et al., 2015). However, due to the long-term recession, poorly performing Japanese companies also have started to lay off employees (Ahmadjian & Robinson, 2001).

Recruitment and retention in Korea. In the past, Korean MNEs relied on college recruiting and then slowly promoted these recruits internally. However, since the Asian financial crisis in 1997/1998 and in response to scarcity in certain areas (e.g., engineering), Korean MNEs have expanded their recruiting sources and now actively seek talent at all levels from the external labor market (Yu & Rowley, 2009). For instance, amongst Samsung's domestic workforce of 110,000, 36 percent were recruited from other organizations (Tung et al., 2013). However, traditional selection criteria such as the prestige of the university, personality traits, fit with the organization, and personal relationships still play important roles in the recruitment process. Korean companies heavily emphasize the selection of candidates that best fit their needs and organizational culture. Thus, applicants go through multiple rounds of tests and interviews before a final employment decision is made. Large Korean MNEs have developed their own aptitude tests for the initial screening for entry-level positions.

While long-term careers within the same organization are still common for core employees in large, well-known Korean chaebols, there has been a change toward more flexible careers crossing different organizations. Since the Asian financial crisis in 1997, the Korean labor market has become much more flexible (Lim & Jang, 2006). As a consequence, Korean researchers have lamented the associated risks of reduced job security and reduced morale amongst Korean employees (e.g., Bae & Rowley, 2002).

Comparative summary of recruitment and retention. Although traditional recruitment and retention practices were relatively similar between Japan and Korea, Korean organizations adopted flexible employment systems more aggressively after the Asian financial crisis. A good fit between organizational values and (potential) employees remains an important criterion for recruiting channels in both countries. Thus, selection is an important function. However, the source of talent has changed more dramatically in Korea than in Japan. Whereas large Japanese MNEs still rely on colleges to recruit their core employees (Peltokorpi & Froese, 2015), Korean MNEs have increasingly broadened their recruitment channel mix and hired at the middle and senior level through external sources (Tung et al., 2013). This also implies that turnover rates in Korea are higher than in Japan. The flexible employment system in Korea is more in line with the Western approach.

Training and development

Training and development in Japan. The training in Japanese companies is largely firm-specific. Because companies in Japan promote the fit of their employees with the company, the entry-level training programs and socialization processes encourage embeddedness in the organization. The firm-specific training is largely conducted based on job rotation and on-the-job training and the accumulation of skills continues throughout employees' entire career (Peltokorpi, 2013). Indeed, the formal orientation programs and socialization efforts in Japanese companies are continuous (Morishima, 1995). These socialization efforts further help establish person–organization fit between newcomers and organizations (Cable & Parsons, 2001). Employee orientation and training of new employees are also often extensive (Ichniowski & Shaw, 1999).

Japanese organizations are characterized as learning organizations, and they place significant emphasis on employee learning and skill development throughout employees' careers (Sekiguchi, 2006). Japanese companies also emphasize job rotation to increase flexibility in employee skills and abilities (Morishima, 1995; JILPT, 2003) and to develop employees' firm-specific skills. Employees are rotated through different functions and locations. Holzhausen (2000) said that the long-term development of human capital within the firm is the core objective of the Japanese employment system. Hence, the internal labor market is the main source of knowledge and skills.

Training and development in Korea. Korean companies provide extensive training and development opportunities for their staffs. Once new employees enter the company, they usually receive one to several months of orientation training. The training focuses on firm-specific knowledge, socialization, and to a limited extent, job-specific content. Training and development then continue throughout the whole career.

279

Korean chaebols have sophisticated training programs, including various on- and off-the-job programs, tailored to specific groups of employees. The programs range from in-house training in the companies' own training facilities to sponsored MBA programs at major domestic and US business schools. Korean companies also embraced online and blended learning formats early on (Yu & Rowley, 2009). Action and experiential learning (e.g., volunteering) have become popular as well. Annual corporate training trips to domestic destinations (e.g., Cheju Island) as well as to exotic destinations (e.g., the Philippines) are also common. In recent years, however, in an attempt to reduce costs, Korean companies have concentrated their training efforts on a select group of high performers and special functions like engineering (Tung et al., 2013).

Comparative summary of training and development. Training and development are emphasized in both Japan and Korea. While large enterprises in both countries emphasize training and development, Korean companies tend to use a greater variety of external training methods, such as sponsored MBA programs and external executive training. Korean companies have also earlier and more aggressively adopted online and blended learning formats. In accordance with selection practices, person–organization fit is an important aspect in training and development, for instance, new recruits will be socialized into the existing corporate cultures through lengthy orientation programs. While the focus of training in Japan is on firm-specific knowledge and skills, often including rotations through different functions, Korean companies have a more balanced approach and also focus on specialist skills and knowledge. In line with the shifted focus of training, job rotations have become less common in Korea.

Compensation and rewards

Compensation and rewards in Japan. Compensation is determined on the basis of a combination of tenure and assessment results (Sekiguchi, 2006; Holzhausen, 2000). The assessment of employees in Japanese companies is based on an ability grading system (Sekiguchi, 2006) or a qualification grading system (Holzhausen, 2000). This system includes not only performance but also a supervisor's assessment of the employee's attitudes, abilities, and future potential (Sekiguchi, 2006; Holzhausen, 2000). Holzhausen (2000) argued that this grading system is not a tool to replace seniority-based pay but to develop competent human capital. The ability grading system is assumed to lead to more productivity than the seniority compensation system because it rewards learning efforts and contributes to knowledge creation in the company.

Usually, the total compensation package in Japanese firms consists of base pay, bonuses, and benefits. Under the ability grading system, base pay is determined by a combination of seniority and ability. Bonuses account for about 30 percent of total cash compensation and are based primarily on firm profitability and individual or group performance. Thus, seniority, ability grade, and the firm's economic prosperity affect the larger fraction of total compensation, and intra-firm individual differences in pay related to short-term job performance are relatively small (Sekiguchi, 2006).

Compensation and rewards in Korea. The traditional Korean compensation and rewards system was based on seniority. Compensation and rewards would automatically increase with tenure in the organization. The compensation was composed of base salary, benefits, and bonus, though the bonus was more or less guaranteed. However, in response to the Asian financial crisis, Korean companies adopted a performance-based compensation and reward system (Tung et al., 2013). While in 2000, only one-fifth of Korean companies had performance-based compensation systems, now more than two-thirds do (Korea Employment Information Service, n.d.).

Performance-based compensation is more widespread amongst large companies and more often applied to white-collar employees in higher positions. However, the performance-based compensation systems vary substantially across industries and organization in Korea (Yu &

Rowley, 2009). On the one hand, some companies, in particular banks, have transferred typical performance-based pay systems from the USA. The performance-based component of pay can be substantial. On the other hand, many Korean companies still use a combination of Western-style performance-based compensation and seniority. In addition to individual-level performance-based compensation, Korean companies increasingly consider group-level performance-based compensation as well as profit-sharing agreements, based on financial criteria (e.g., economic value added, stock price).

Comparative summary of compensation and rewards. In the past, compensation and rewards were mainly driven by seniority, length of time spent at the organization, and age, however, that system has been greatly under attack since the long recession in Japan, and the Asian crisis in Korea. Enterprises in both countries have sought inspiration from US performance-oriented HR practices. Even though companies in both Japan and Korea have adopted performance-based merits, the degree of implementation varies substantially. In contrast to most Japanese companies that have only reluctantly adopted performance-based merits, many Korean companies have implemented performance-based merits to a much larger extent. The performance-orientation is relatively well perceived in Korea (Froese et al., 2008), whereas the sentiments in Japan remain mixed. Some Japanese companies aggressively adopted US-style performance-based systems but converted back to traditional Japanese seniority-based systems due to the fierce opposition of their employees.

HR challenges in Japan and Korea: moving from ethnocentrism to global HR integration

Japan and Korea face similar HR challenges as other industrialized countries, for example, digitalization, and gender inequality. In this chapter, we focus on global HR integration, as this is a particularly pressing issue for both Japan and Korea due to the high degree of international-ization of their economies and the historically homogenous make-up of their societies. The demographic shift in industrialized countries, including Japan and Korea, has created serious challenges in meeting their current and prospective global talent demand. This has led to a vivid practical and scholarly debate about the need to increase the participation of formerly under-represented groups of employees, such as females, older workers, and foreigners, in the workforce (e.g., Kulik, Ryan, Harper, & George, 2014). Despite the need for talent and the high degree of business globalization, Japan and Korea still struggle to integrate foreign talent in their workforces at home and abroad. The vast majority of large Korean MNEs generates more than 50 percent of sales abroad and has substantial foreign direct investments abroad. However, for their subsidiaries abroad, Japanese and Korean organizations tend to utilize parent country nationals (PCNs) in key management positions, in contrast to US and European MNEs (Harzing, 2001; Kopp, 1994). In addition, the existence of a glass ceiling has created difficulty in attracting and retaining the most talented local individuals for their overseas operations (Keeley, 2001; Kopp, 1994). This, in turn, has reinforced Japanese organizations' inclination to send Japanese expatriates to top management positions at their overseas subsidiaries, and a vicious circle has been created. This ethnocentric global staffing in Japanese MNEs is considered to be their *Achilles' heel* (Bartlett & Yoshihara, 1988). However, given the increased size of operations abroad, the challenges, and the high cost of expatriates, Japanese and Korean firms can no longer rely exclusively on PCNs in their operations abroad. Thus, MNEs must seriously reconsider their global staffing approach to remain successful in the years to come.

In addition to their challenges abroad, Japanese and Korean organizations face a shortage of labor in their home country. Due to demographic changes resulting from low fertility rates and aging societies, their working populations are shrinking rapidly. With a median age of about 46.1 years, Japan is amongst the oldest populations in the world, and Korea has a median age of about 40.8 years (CIA, 2015). Life expectancy at birth has risen to 83.3 years in Japan, while the fertility rate has dropped to 1.4 births per woman (World Bank, 2015a). In Korea, the situation appears to be similar; on average, people are expected to live slightly shorter lives (81.5 years), while the Korean birth rate of 1.2 is amongst the lowest worldwide (World Bank, 2015b). As a consequence, the working population is not only aging but also shrinking. These developments have tremendous consequences for organizations operating in these "aging societies." To stay competitive in the long run, organizations must attract new target groups, such as foreign appli-cants and female candidates, to fill the talent pipeline (Collings & Mellahi, 2009; Kemper, Bader, & Froese, 2016).

The ethnocentric management practices of Japanese and Korean MNEs and the countries' homogenous societies make the integration of foreign workers into their talent pool difficult. Traditionally, Japan has not been diverse; rather, 99 percent of the country's population is ethni-cally homogenous (Nishii & Özbilgin, 2007). Today, approximately two million foreign nationals—the official registered number in 2014 was 2,121,831—are residing in Japan (Statis-tics Bureau Japan, 2016). This number, however, accounts for only 1.66 percent of the entire Japanese population (Statistics Bureau Japan, 2016) and is the smallest figure amongst all indus-trialized countries. The number of foreigners has not changed much during the last thirty years, partly due to strict immigration laws. The situation in Korea is similar. Korea is a homogenous society and emphasizes its own cultural heritage. However, Korea has seen a huge influx of foreigners since 2000, from less than 200,000 to approximately 1.4 million today (3.2 percent of the Korean population). The vast majority of foreigners come from China. Furthermore, it should be noted that the majority of working-aged foreigners are comprised of low-skilled workers (547,300) in contrast to the small portion of highly skilled workers (47,100) (OECD, 2013). Even though the total population of foreigners has rapidly increased, the number of highly skilled foreign workers has largely remained constant.[1] Because of a relatively high number of highly skilled Korean emigrants, Korea actually suffers from brain drain. In summary, both Japan and Korea face a serious talent shortage and must find ways to meet their global talent demand. However, prior empirical research has shown that Japanese and Korean com-panies are not attractive employers abroad (Froese & Kishi, 2013).

In the following sections, we illuminate how Japanese and Korean companies deal with their respective global HR challenges. We provide an overview of the main challenges that Japanese and Korean companies face in their overseas operations and their domestic markets and suggest some tentative solutions.

Global HR challenges in Japan

Many Japanese companies are expanding their business globally and the only way to successfully compete in the global market is to recruit, develop, and retain global talent. However, the unique characteristics of the Japanese management system are making it difficult to internation-alize their HR practices in both the domestic context and foreign subsidiaries. Many Japanese companies are becoming more diverse and adopting several measures to cope with the chal-lenges created by internationalization (Sekiguchi, Froese, & Iguchi, 2016). However, many companies still lag behind in appropriately integrating the global workforce into their overall organizational structure.

In foreign subsidiaries, as mentioned earlier, this circumstance is partly due to the centraliza-tion strategy of Japanese companies; they prefer to have a control mechanism based on Japanese expatriate managers. Many have argued that Japanese companies rely on expatriates due to the unique nature of Japanese management, as well as cultural and linguistic barriers, to convey the Japanese way of doing business. Many Japanese practices are not written down but are informally managed. This kind of management system is difficult to convey to local managers. Since Japanese MNEs are usually controlled by their headquarters, they need to have frequent communication with regard to the day-to-day operation of the subsidiary. For this, someone who is familiar with the subsidiary management and the way of doing things in the headquarters is needed. Hence, Japanese expatriate managers in subsidiaries are the solution to balance these demands. The subsidiary decisions are mostly made by expatriate managers in consultation with the headquarters. Host country national (HCN) managers and employees of the subsidiary are often left out of the decision-making process (Maki & Sekiguchi, 2016).

Japanese companies strongly believe that the homogeneity of their society is the key factor to their success and thus they tend to preserve such homogeneity and employ ethnocentric international policies and practices (Fernandez & Barr, 1993). This might create discrimination and treatment of non-Japanese employees as outsiders; it might also create a feeling of the "unique us" versus "non-Japanese them." Japanese even tend to think that their unique culture cannot be fully understood by non-Japanese. Apparently, this attitude hinders smooth communication between Japanese and foreign employees (Keeley, 2001).

The low level of English proficiency amongst Japanese managers also impedes communication and thus reinforces the non-Japanese employees as an out-group. However, some research has shown that this miscommunication is not only a matter of language proficiency. For example, Keeley (2001) acknowledged that foreign employees hired in the headquarters in Japan, fluent in Japanese, having a good understanding of Japanese culture, and even having gained experience at headquarters, nevertheless do not feel integrated into the in-groups when they work at the foreign subsidiaries in their home country.

In Japan, foreign employees are not well integrated because of the unique Japanese culture, working environment, and traditional Japanese-style HR practices. We mentioned earlier in the organizational culture section that Japanese society emphasizes the practice of in-groups and out-groups and this is heavily reflected in the organizational culture. Foreign employees working in Japanese companies are regarded as out-groups and not included in the core structure of the company (Maki, Ebisuya, & Sekiguchi, 2014). It is quite rare for them to be promoted to the senior managerial levels. They are considered a minority group and the glass ceiling is virtually impermeable. Furthermore, there are many unwritten rules. Foreign employees find it difficult to cope with the non-verbal organizational communication and to read between the lines. The low English proficiency of Japanese employees makes it much more difficult for foreigners to communicate and become members of in-groups. Moreover, the traditional Japanese HR system is incompatible with global HR trends. Foreign employees aiming for global careers are less attracted by seniority or long-term-based employment systems.

Maki, Ebisuya, and Sekiguchi (2015) found that foreign employees working in traditional Japanese companies in Japan perceive the long-term-based employment system and job rotation as attractive. However, most of them are localized, live a Japanese lifestyle, and wish to have permanent residence in Japan (Maki et al., 2015). These foreigners were carefully selected and socialized into their Japanese companies so that they fit the Japanese and firm-specific mindset. Therefore, this kind of recruitment and training system might create more foreign employees with Japanese-like mindsets than global mindsets. While this is one way to integrate foreign employees, we need to acknowledge that only a few foreigners are willing and able to integrate into traditional, ethnocentric Japanese companies.

Possible global HR solutions for Japan

Positive changes have appeared in recent years. The companies that have a high percentage of global (local) sales and supply networks are promoting a "rapid growth" scheme for HCNs in foreign subsidiaries. They pay attractive performance-based salaries and develop common practices that help these employees move transnationally (Maki & Sekiguchi, 2016).

Yamao and Sekiguchi (2015) recommended implementing HR practices that promote learning a foreign language. They argued that such HR practices have direct and interactive effects on employees' affective and normative commitment to their firm's globalization. Therefore, Japanese companies considering the internationalization of their business operations should consider introducing such HR practices.

Maki, Ebisuya, and Sekiguchi (2015) provided three recommendations for how Japanese companies could better integrate their foreign employees. First, in addition to teaching English language skills, Japanese companies should provide training to Japanese employees to improve their cross-cultural skills. Second, Japanese companies should develop and utilize employees with cross-cultural competencies, who can help facilitate smooth communication between Japanese and foreign employees. Third, Japanese companies should educate foreign employees on the core features of Japanese management, including the features embedded in Japanese culture and society (Sekiguchi et al., 2016).

Case study: Rakuten

Rakuten is the largest Internet service company in Japan, with aspirations to become number one in the world. Hiroshi Mikitani, the CEO of Rakuten, recognized that the most challenging task is to make his employees "speak English" so that they are able to communicate to the world. In 2010, Mikitani announced a new policy specifying that, within the next two years, all Rakuten employees must improve their English proficiency or be demoted. With mixed responses from both internal and external sources, Rakuten successfully implemented this policy.

Rakuten was the first Japanese company to formally pursue such steps. With massive coverage in the international business press, Rakuten attracted many new customers as well as global talent. When it announced its English policy in 2010, it had around 2 percent foreign employees, but after five years, this number increased to 10 percent. As the company put special effort into recruiting engineers from all over the world, about 70 percent of newly hired engineers in Japan are now foreigners. The company has been extremely successful in attracting fresh graduates from the top universities in the world.

English is not only critical to attract global talent, but it is also imperative to share information and the latest technology amongst business groups. Due to Rakuten's English language policy, cross-border mergers and acquisitions (M&As) and other forms of international cooperation have become effective. As a consequence of the English policy, the company's employees do not need to use interpreters to communicate to their business groups around the world (Sekiguchi, 2016), thus saving cost and facilitating communication.

Other Japanese companies are also pursuing a similar direction. For example, First Retailing (fashion) and Panasonic (electronics) have started recruiting non-Japanese as their core global staff. Bridgestone (tires), Nippon Sheet Glass (industrial glass), and Nissan have started using English as their official language.

Source: Sekiguchi (2016); Yamao and Sekiguchi (2015)

Global HR challenges in Korea

As a consequence of the Asian financial crisis in 1997, the International Monetary Fund (IMF) imposed changes in the regulatory system and liberalized the market. The influx of foreign direct investment had a huge impact on Korean management (e.g., Froese et al., 2008). This led to major changes in the recruitment, retention, compensation, and rewards systems, converging toward US systems (Bae & Rowley, 2001; Tung et al., 2013), as described in the previous section. The US-style HR practices of Korean companies have the potential to provide an attractive work environment for foreign workers. However, several features of the traditional Korean HR system still prevail and present major challenges for foreign talent.

Korean companies have been highly successful in entering foreign markets. While they adopted a global strategy during the early phase of internationalization, several companies have now adopted a more polycentric or geocentric approach (Tung et al., 2013). In line with their strategic orientation and following the Asian financial crisis, Korean MNEs also modified their global HR systems. Based on a case study of nine Korean MNEs, Chung, Sparrow, and Bozkurt (2014) found that Korean MNCs used a hybrid approach in their foreign subsidiaries (i.e., implementing global HR standards and adapting certain HR elements to local needs). An intriguing finding of that study is that Korean MNCs felt somewhat ashamed of their origin and instead of traditional Korean HR practices, tried to implement global best (US) practices in their overseas subsidiaries. Notwithstanding the idea of global HR, most Korean companies still maintain an ethnocentric staffing orientation and rely heavily on Korean expatriates for their key positions in their foreign subsidiaries (Tung et al., 2013). These Korean expatriate managers in turn transfer traditional Korean values such as strict hierarchies to the foreign subsidiaries (Kim & Tung, 2013; Yang & Kelly, 2008). These traditional Korean cultural features are not well perceived in foreign subsidiaries and may lead to frustration, distrust, and tension between Korean expatriate managers and local employees (Yang & Kelly, 2008). Furthermore, pay inequality and limited career opportunities further reduce the morale amongst local employees in Korean subsidiaries abroad.

Another key challenge is communication. Even though several Korean MNCs have announced English as their corporate language, Korean still remains the de facto business language. Given the centralized nature of most Korean companies where decisions are made at the headquarters, communication and coordination with the Korean headquarters are essential. However, with the limited number of Korean speakers outside Korea, key positions in foreign subsidiaries need to be staffed with Korean expatriates. This limits the career prospects of local employees. Moreover, even though Korean headquarters are able to communicate with their Korean expatriate managers abroad, Korean expatriate managers may not sufficiently communicate with local employees due to linguistic challenges and cultural differences (Yang & Kelly, 2008). The tendency of Korean expatriate managers to spend considerable time amongst themselves, not including local employees, further results in the negative stereotyping of "us" versus "them."

The traditionally homogenous Korean society makes it difficult to integrate foreign workers in Korea. Some Korean companies have started to recruit foreign workers for their operations in Korea. They have used two common approaches. First, large Korean MNCs transfer their foreign subsidiary employees to Korea, so-called inpatriation (Froese, Kim, & Eng, 2016). This trend can be observed in certain industries and highly qualified jobs that are in high demand but lack local talent (e.g., IT professionals, engineers). These highly qualified professionals are well paid and come from countries across the globe, though mostly from other Asian countries (Kraeh, Froese, & Park, 2015). Korean MNCs usually provide housing and other benefits to help with the integration. Second, Korean companies of various sizes and industries hire foreigners who already live in Korea. These people have various qualifications and mostly come from China and other Asian countries. Although most Chinese immigrants work in low-paid jobs in the service industry, Chinese people also represent the number one foreign student population in Korea (more than 40,000 students, more than 70 percent of the total foreign student population). Even though university-educated Chinese graduates could be a major source to fill the talent gap in Korea, more than 90 percent have no intention of finding work in Korea (Kim & Oh, 2015). University graduates from prestigious Korean universities can easily find jobs in major Korean MNCs. However, in a follow-up survey, Kim and Oh (2015) found that Chinese students wanted to leave Korea because they felt discrimination and cultural problems.

Even though most foreign workers in Korean companies have some prior experience with Korean and/or Korean companies, a majority report dissatisfaction with the working conditions and have a high tendency to leave Korea (Kraeh et al., 2015). In a survey of foreign professionals in Korea, Kraeh, Froese, and Park (2015) found that strict hierarchies, time pressure, and the lack of English communication at work were their main sources of dissatisfaction. Approximately two-thirds of respondents expressed their desire to leave Korea within the next three years. Not only foreign professionals from Western countries but also those from Asian countries had difficulty accepting the hierarchical organizational culture and leadership style in Korean companies. The group-oriented culture, particularly the separation between Korean and foreign employees, creates further tension between Korean and foreign employees (Froese, 2010). Time pressures in the form of long working hours and the *bbali, bbali* (quickly, quickly) working style also place burdens on foreign employees (Bader et al., 2016). Foreign workers are not accustomed to these unique Korean organizational cultural characteristics and cannot adapt to them.

In another study, Froese, Kim, and Eng (2016) found that not using English and the lack of understanding of cultural differences were the main reasons for the turnover intentions of foreign professionals in Korea. Only those who spoke Korean and possessed cultural intelligence could deal with the situation. The findings of this study also implied that foreign professionals who were working in a multicultural and English-speaking environment were more satisfied than those who were not. For example, foreign professors in globalized Korean universities were largely well adjusted and satisfied with their situation (Froese, 2012). By and large, differences in language and communication style are central problems for foreign workers in Korea (Froese, 2013; Froese, Jommersbach, & Klautsch, 2013; Froese, Peltokorpi & Ko, 2015).

Possible global HR solutions for Korea

As a traditional homogenous society and latecomer to the internationalization of business, Korean companies have had a difficult start but are making progress toward global HR and global talent management. While Korean companies have swiftly modified their production and marketing to meet global demands, their HR function is somewhat lagging. Several large MNCs, such as Samsung (see Case Study), have spearheaded several promising initiatives to better respond to global HR challenges. One promising step was the implementation of a hybrid approach to HR practices around the global, balancing both global best HR practices and local needs (Chung et al., 2014).

Korean companies have been fairly successful in recruiting foreign talent; however, they should put more emphasis on retaining this talent (Froese, 2010). An important step toward that goal is to adopt a geocentric approach (Tung et al., 2013). Korean companies should consider modifying their traditional Korean organizational cultures and adopting an organizational climate that does not discriminate between Koreans and foreigners but embraces multiculturalism (Froese, 2010; Froese et al., 2016). Consistent with the geocentric approach, Korean companies should also create global talent programs, which are particularly important for highly qualified and ambitious foreign talent.

Improving the communication situation is a major challenge that cannot be solved by Korean companies alone. The Korean government should increase the English component and emphasize the value of multiculturalism in the curriculum of schools and universities and promote international exchange (Froese et al., 2012; Kraeh et al., 2015). Korean companies should also establish English as the corporate language. While such changes are recommended, the success of such initiatives hinges on their actual implementation. For instance, LG hastily introduced English as the corporate language. However, it is impossible for employees who cannot speak English to suddenly be expected to communicate in English from the next day on. Not surprisingly, the suddenly introduced policy created inconvenience and dissatisfaction amongst Korean employees. Instead, such initiatives should be well planned and carefully implemented (e.g., rolling out gradually, providing English lessons, and using English as a selection criterion for job candidates).

Case study: Samsung

Samsung is the largest chaebol in Korea with more than US$300 billion in sales annually and employing almost 500,000 worldwide. Amongst its various subsidiaries, Samsung Electronics, well known for mobile phones and flat-screen TVs, is the flagship. Samsung Electronics is highly internationalized with more than 80 percent of sales and numerous production and R&D centers abroad.

In response to the Asian financial crisis in 1997, Samsung introduced global HR practices. Samsung has several structured programs to recruit and develop global talent. First, it has dedicated global development programs primarily for Korean employees, tailored to the different hierarchical levels and corresponding purposes. The CEO Development Program is aimed at senior managers to help them develop the capability to better understand the business opportunities and challenges of a specific country. Middle managers will be sent on expatriate assignments. For lower level managers, the company introduced the Overseas Regional Specialist Program in 1990, a one-year expatriate assignment. The aim of the program is to develop experts on specific countries. Participants in this program learn the language and culture of the host country.

Second, Samsung operates dedicated programs primarily for foreigners and primarily targeting entry-level and lower level positions. In an attempt to attract and recruit excellent foreign university graduates, Samsung offers internship and scholarship programs. Samsung offers a Global Internship Program in their Korean headquarters targeting foreign master and doctoral students from prestigious universities around the world, preferably in business and engineering. In 2002, Samsung Electronics introduced the Global Scholarship Program mainly targeting Chinese and other Asian students. Students receive a two-year scholarship to study in the graduate programs at Seoul National University for engineering students or Sungkyunkwan University for business students. Upon graduation, they are supposed to work for two years for Samsung in Korea. In addition, foreign employees in Samsung's foreign subsidiaries have the opportunity to be dispatched to the Korean headquarters, which is particularly common for engineering and information technology professionals due to the labor shortage for those jobs in Korea.

Samsung is further determined to fully pursue a geocentric approach, to develop and promote employees regardless of national origin. Currently, senior positions in Korea and abroad are still predominantly filled by Koreans. As it takes time to develop global leaders, the coming years will show whether Samsung is serious about its geocentric approach.

Source: Paik and Pak, 2009; www.samsung.com[2]

Comparative summary

As Japanese and Korean MNEs are becoming increasingly globalized, they need to better respond to global HR challenges. However, the ethnocentric management approach of Japanese and Korean MNEs and the homogenous societies at home present severe challenges for attracting and integrating foreign workers. Korean MNEs have more aggressively adopted Western HR practices than Japanese MNEs, thereby providing more attractive work environments for foreign employees. However, even in the case of Korean MNEs, the traditional organizational cultures and the ethnocentric orientation and decision-making processes cause conflicts with foreign talent (Froese, 2010; Kraeh et al., 2015; Tung et al., 2013). To overcome the current difficulties, Japanese and Korean organizations should fully integrate foreign workers into their organizations by adopting a more geocentric HRM approach. To make that happen, Japanese and Korean MNEs should create multicultural organizational cultures, install English as their business language, and add foreign employees to the global talent pool. These initiatives might help in attracting and retaining a great pool of talented workers from all over the world. Several companies have already made progress down that road (see our Case Studies for examples) and others might follow. The efforts of Japanese and Korean companies should be supported by their governments since changes toward a more global mindset and increasing the English levels of the population are strategic long-term goals that also benefit the society as a whole. In addition to embracing foreigners, Japanese and Korean companies can also embrace other under-utilized segments of the labor market, in particular women and older employees (Kemper et al., 2016).

Conclusions

Japan and Korea are two highly performing economies in Asia that have developed many successful enterprises. In this chapter, we provided a comparative overview of the unique HR systems of large enterprises within these two countries. While the HR systems resembled each other in the past, economic recessions and globalization have led Korean enterprises to modify their HR systems more aggressively, mostly in line with Anglo-Saxon practices, in contrast to Japanese enterprises which have been more reluctant to implement changes. Due to increased globalization and declining demography, Japanese and Korean enterprises need to find ways to attract a sufficient number of highly and lowly skilled employees, in order to remain competitive in the long run. Homogenous societies, male-dominated cultures, centralized, unique, and ethnocentric management styles present a difficult starting point for Japanese and Korean MNEs to meet the demands of global talent. Below, we offer some indications for future research on HRM in Japan and Korea.

First, Japan and Korea share similar backgrounds, for example, geographic location, industrialized countries, homogenous societies, highly internationalized enterprises, and have developed similar HR systems in the past. However, in response to economic recessions and globalization, HRM has changed in both countries during the past twenty years, though at different speeds and magnitude. While Korean enterprises aggressively modified their HR practices, mostly adopting US-style HR practices, Japanese enterprises were much more cautious and resistant to change. Prior research has well covered the changes and corresponding challenges in HR practices in both countries during the last decades. However, prior research was mostly confined to either Japanese HR or Korean HR. Comparative research would be recommended to better understand the underlying mechanisms, enrich our theoretical understanding, and develop managerial implications of which specific HR practices can be implemented and under what conditions. Such research could focus on how the macro-level, for example, cultural environment, influences the *meso* (organizational) and/or micro (individual) level. Future research could also focus on the success of implemented changes in specific HR areas. More than twenty years ago, Japanese electronics and car companies dominated the world market, whereas Korean companies were largely unknown. Meanwhile, Samsung has overtaken Sony, and Hyundai has become a serious competitor in the car industry. To what extent have changes in HR contributed to the recent success of Korean MNEs? More research could also explore the resistance to change of Japanese HR and how that can be overcome.

Second, in this chapter we focused on challenges related to the globalization of HR, because both Japan and Korea are facing severe challenges in managing a global workforce, yet are increasingly dependent on global talent due to their high level of internationalized MNEs and shrinking workforces at home (Froese et al., 2016; Kemper et al., 2016). The homogeneous societies coupled with the strong need for global talent make Japan and Korea fascinating countries to study global talent challenges. Sekiguchi, Froese, and Iguchi (2016) distinguish between "internal internationalization" at headquarters and "external internationalization" in foreign subsidiaries. Despite the strong need for internal internationalization in both Korea and Japan, research is still scarce but clearly needed not only from a practical point of view but also from a theoretical point of view. Although prior research has looked at internal internationalization in the USA and Europe, the cultural and regulatory environments in Japan and Korea differ substantially, requiring a replication of prior work and/or completely new investigation. Such inquiries could enrich our understanding of existing theories or could develop new theories. Discrimination, communication, and socializing foreign newcomers into Japanese or Korean headquarters seem to be key challenges (e.g., Froese et al., 2016, Keeley, 2001; Maki et al., 2014) and need further research attention. Focusing on language issues would be another promising area, particularly in Japan given the uniqueness and difficulty of learning Japanese and the low English proficiency of Japanese employees (Froese, 2010; Froese et al., 2012). For example, will Japanese MNEs introduce English as their business language? How would they do it and how would employees respond? Both Japanese and Korean MNEs have maintained their unique, tight corporate cultures, have carefully selected, and socialized foreigners into them. Will they continue to do so, or modify their corporate culture and embrace multiculturalism as recommended by some scholars (e.g., Kraeh et al., 2015)? To what extent and how do they integrate foreign university students who study in Japan and Korea, respectively? These are just a few tentative research questions that deserve attention.

Third, prior research on internal internationalization is scarce; substantial research has investigated the external internationalization of Japanese MNEs. Those studies often had a strategic HRM perspective and focused on the (intended) transfer of Japanese practices to overseas subsidiaries (e.g., Beechler & Yang, 1994), and ethnocentric staffing policies (Harzing, 2001; Kopp, 1994). Extending this line of research, future research is recommended to investigate which specific HR practices could be transferred around the globe, or meanwhile, whether a mix of global and localized practices for MNE subsidiaries from Japan and Korea would be preferable. Such an investigation could also pay attention to differences across industries and firm characteristics (Chung et al., 2014). Sekiguchi et al. (2016) propose a conceptual model that defines the degree of path dependence and competitive advantage of Japanese style HRM practices as predictors of adoption of global HR practices. Empirical research to test this framework is encouraged. Comparatively, the HRM of Korean companies has received much less research attention (Tung et al., 2013). Given the outstanding performance of several Korean MNEs such as Samsung and Hyundai in recent years, more research on Korean companies' HRM is warranted. Insightful as prior studies on strategic HRM are, we still know relatively little about the challenges individuals face inside Japanese and Korean foreign subsidiaries. Little is known about the situation of PCN expatriates and HCNs working in foreign subsidiaries of Japanese and Korean MNEs. Prior research suggests major challenges between Japanese/Korean expatriates and HCN employees due to ethnocentric management styles, communication difficulties, and the separation between expatriates and HCN employees (Keeley, 2001; Kim & Tung, 2013; Yang & Kelly, 2008). As Japanese and Korean MNEs extend their value generation abroad, HR in foreign subsidiaries gain in importance. Thus, more research is needed to increase our understanding of the interaction between PCN expatriates and HCN employees and how Japanese and Korean companies can better attract, motivate, develop, and retain HCNs abroad. Future research could also focus on how Japanese and Korean MNEs can facilitate knowledge transfer from the headquarters to the foreign subsidiaries and vice versa.

Finally, global talent is only one source of meeting the demand for labor. Instead, Japanese and Korean enterprises could tap into segments of the existing domestic labor force that has been under-utilized. In both countries, the labor participation rate of women is still very low compared to other industrialized nations (Kemper et al., 2016). Prior research indicates that women are discriminated against in the workplace, for example, lower pay, insecure jobs, and do not receive sufficient support (Cooke, 2010; Rowley, Kang, & Lim, 2016). Although governments in both countries have started various initiatives to support women (Cooke, 2010; Mackie, Okano, & Rawstron, 2014), more research is needed to better understand how governments, enterprises, supervisors, and colleagues can better support women to start and continue their careers, even after maternity leave. Instead of a one-size-fits-all approach, future research and management practice should also consider the different career identities and objectives of women and offer tailored solutions. We hope that this chapter has provided a good overview of HRM in Korea and Japan and inspired more researchers, policy makers, and managers to tackle the HRM challenges arising from globalization and declining demography.

Notes

1 Kostat, the Korean Statistical Institute, provides the following statistics for highly skilled foreigners in Korea (E1–E7). Retrieved from http://kostat.go.kr/portal/korea/kor_nw/2/3/4/index.board?bmode=read&bSeq=&aSeq=356794&pageNo=1&rowNum=10&navCount=10&currPg=&sTarget=title&sTxt=.
2 Further details can be found at: https://news.samsung.com/kr/386; and https://news.samsung.com/kr/398.

References

Ahmadjian, C. L. & Robinson, P. (2001). Safety in numbers: Downsizing and the deinstitutionalization of permanent employment in Japan. *Administrative Science Quarterly, 46*(4), 622–654.
Auer, P. & Cazes, S. (2000). The resilience of the long-term employment relationship: Evidence from the industrialized countries. *International Labor Review, 139*(4), 379–404.
Baba, M., Hanaoka, M., Hara, H., & Thompson, R. (1984). *Managerial behavior in Japan and the USA.* Tokyo: Japan Productivity Center.

Bader, K., Froese, F. J., & Kraeh, A. (2016). Clash of cultures? German expatriates' work–life boundary adjustment in South Korea. *European Management Review.*

Bae, J. & Rowley, C. (2002). The impact of globalization on HRM: The case of South Korea. *Journal of World Business, 36*(4), 402–428.

Bae, J. & Rowley, C. (2003). Changes and continuities in South Korean HRM. *Asia Pacific Business Review, 9*(4), 76–105.

Bartlett, C. A. & Yoshihara, H. (1988). New challenges for Japanese multinationals: Is organization adaptation their Achilles heel? *Human Resource Management, 27*(1), 19–43.

Beechler, S. & Yang, J. Z. (1994). The transfer of Japanese style management to American subsidiaries: Contingencies, constraints and competencies. *Journal of International Business Studies, 25*(3), 467–491.

Cable, D. M. & Parsons, C. K. (2001). Socialization tactics and person-organization fit. *Personnel Psychology, 54*(1), 1–23.

Chang, J. H, Chang, W. S., & Jacobs, R. (2009). Relationship between participation in communities of practice and organizational socialization in the early careers of South Korean IT employees. *Human Resource Development International, 12*(4), 407–427.

Chung, C., Sparrow, P., & Bozkurt, Ö. (2014). South Korean MNEs' international HRM approach: Hybridization of global standards and local practices. *Journal of World Business, 49*(4), 549–559.

CIA (2015). *The world factbook: Median age.* Retrieved July 29, 2016, from www.cia.gov/library/publications/the-world-factbook/fields/2177.html.

Collings, D. G. & Mellahi, K. (2009). Strategic talent management: A review and research agenda. *Human Resource Management Review, 19*(4), 304–313.

Cooke, F. L. (2010). Women's participation in employment in Asia: A comparative analysis of China, India, Japan, and South Korea. *The International Journal of Human Resource Management, 21*(12), 2249–2270.

Doi, T. (1971). *Amae no kozo* [*The anatomy of dependence*]. Tokyo: Kôbundô.

Fernandez, J. P. & Barr, M. (1993). *The diversity advantage: How American business can out-perform Japanese and European companies in the global marketplace.* New York: Jossey-Bass.

Froese, F. J. (2010). Acculturation experiences in South Korea and Japan. *Culture & Psychology, 16*(3), 333–348.

Froese, F. J. (2012). Motivation and adjustment of self-initiated expatriates: The case of expatriate academics in South Korea. *The International Journal of Human Resource Management, 23*(6), 1095–1112.

Froese, F. J. (2013). Work values of the new generation of business leaders in Shanghai, Tokyo and Seoul. *Asia Pacific Journal of Management, 30*(1), 297–315.

Froese, F. J., Jommersbach, S., & Klautsch, E. (2013). Cosmopolitan career choices: A cross-cultural study of job candidates' expatriation willingness. *The International Journal of Human Resource Management, 24*(17), 3247–3261.

Froese, F. J., Kim, K., & Eng, A. (2016). Language, cultural intelligence, and inpatriate turnover intentions: Leveraging values in multinational corporations through inpatriates. *Management International Review, 56*(2), 283–301.

Froese, F. J. & Kishi, Y. (2013). Organizational attractiveness of foreign firms in Asia: Soft power matters. *Asian Business & Management, 12*(3), 281–297.

Froese, F. J., Pak, Y. S., & Chong, L. C. (2008). Managing the human side of cross-border acquisitions in South Korea. *Journal of World Business, 43*(1), 97–108.

Froese, F. J. & Peltokorpi, V. (2011). Recruiting channels of foreign subsidiaries in Japan. *Zeitschrift für Betriebswirtschaft* [*Journal of Business Economics*], *81*(3), 101–116.

Froese, F. J., Peltokorpi, V., & Ko, K. A. (2012). The influence of intercultural communication on cross-cultural adjustment and work attitudes: Foreign workers in South Korea. *International Journal of Intercultural Relations, 36*, 331–342.

Gudykunst, W. B. & Nishida, T. (2001). Anxiety, uncertainty, and perceived effectiveness of communication across relationships and cultures. *International Journal of Intercultural Relations, 25*(1), 55–71.

Haghirian, P. (2010). *Understanding Japanese management practices.* New York: Business Expert Press.

Harzing, A. W. (2001). Who's in charge?: An empirical study of executive staffing practices in foreign subsidiaries. *Human Resource Management, 40*(2), 139–158.

Hemmert, M. (2012). *Tiger management: Korean companies on world markets.* New York: Routledge.

Hofstede, G. (2001). *Culture's consequences: Comparing values, behaviors, institutions, and organizations across nations* (2nd ed.). Thousand Oaks, CA: Sage.

Holzhausen, A. (2000). Survey article. Japanese employment practices in transition: Promotion policy and compensation systems in the 1990s. *Social Science Japan Journal, 3*(2), 221–235.

Hong, G., Cho, Y., Froese, F. J., & Shin, M. (2016). The effect of leadership styles, rank, and seniority on organizational commitment: A comparative study of U.S. and Korean employees. *Cross-cultural and Strategic Management, 23*(2), 340–362.

Ichniowski, C. & Shaw, K. (1999). The effects of human resource management systems on economic performance: An international comparison of U.S. and Japanese plants. *Management Science, 45*(5), 704–721.

Jacoby, S. M. (2005). *The embedded corporation: Corporate governance and employment relations in Japan and the United States.* Princeton, NJ: Princeton University Press.

Jakonis, A. (2009). Culture of Japanese organization and basic determinants of institutional economy. *Journal of Intercultural Management, 1*(2), 90–104.

JILPT (Japan Institute for Labor Policy and Training) (2003). *Guide to human resource management: Comparative HRM between Japan and the US.* Retrieved December 5, 2012, from www.jil.go.jp/english/laborinfo/library/documents/hrm_us.pdf.

JILPT (Japan Institute for Labor Policy and Training) (2003). *Guide to human resource management: Comparative HRM between Japan and the US.* Retrieved December 5, 2012, from www.jil.go.jp/english/laborinfo/library/documents/hrm_us.pdf

Jöns, I., Froese, F. J., & Pak, Y. S. (2007). Cultural changes during the integration process of acquisitions: A comparative study between German and German–Korean acquisitions. *International Journal of Intercultural Relations, 31*(5), 591–604.

Kato, T. (2001). The end of lifetime employment in Japan?: Evidence from national surveys and field research. *Journal of the Japanese and International Economies, 15*(4), 489–514.

Keeley, T. D. (2001). *International human resource management in Japanese firms: Their greatest challenge.* New York: Palgrave Macmillan.

Kemper, L., Bader, K., & Froese, F. J. (2016). Diversity management in aging societies: A comparative study of medium to large corporations in Germany and Japan. *Management Revue, 27*(1/2), 29–49.

Kim, H. D. & Tung, R. L. (2013). Opportunities and challenges for expatriates in emerging markets: An exploratory study of Korean expatriates in India. *The International Journal of Human Resource Management, 24*(5), 1029–1050.

Kim, J. & Oh, S. S. (2015). A pathway of knowledge transfer from Korea to Asian countries: Korea's policies on foreign-born students in science and engineering. In A. D'Costa (Ed.), *After development economics* (pp. 201–220). Seoul: Oxford University Press.

Kopp, R. (1994). International human resource policies and practices in Japanese, European, and United States multinationals. *Human Resource Management, 33*(4), 581–599.

Korea Employment Information Service (n.d.). Retrieved from www.wage.go.kr/real/real_view.jsp?sub=04.

Kraeh, A., Froese, F. J., & Park, H. (2015). Foreign professionals in South Korea: Integration or alienation? In A. D'Costa (Ed.), *After development economics* (pp. 185–200). Seoul: Oxford University Press.

Kulik, C. T., Ryan, S., Harper, S., & George, G. (2014). Aging populations and management. *Academy of Management Journal, 57*(4), 929–935.

Lim, H. C. & Jang, J. H. (2006). Neo-liberalism in post-crisis South Korea: Social conditions and outcomes. *Journal of Contemporary Asia, 36*(4), 442–463.

Li-Ping Tang, T., Kim, J. K., & O'Donald, D. A. (2000). Perceptions of Japanese organizational culture employees in non-unionized Japanese-owned and unionized US-owned automobile plants. *Journal of Managerial Psychology, 15*(6), 535–559.

Mackie, V., Okano, K., & Rawstron, K. (2014). Japan: Progress towards diversity and equality in employment. In A. Klarsfeld, L. A. E. Booysen, E. Ng, I. Roper, & A. Tatli (Eds.), *International handbook on diversity management at work: Country perspectives on diversity and equal* (pp. 137–161). Northampton, MA: Edward Elgar.

Maki, M., Ebisuya, A., & Sekiguchi, T. (2014). Gurōbaruka suru Nihon Kigyō ni okeru Gaikokujin Hōsetsu Mondai [Social inclusion of foreign employees in globalizing Japanese firms]. *Osaka Economic Papers, 64*(2), 287–302.

Maki, M., Ebisuya, A., & Sekiguchi, T. (2015). Nihon Kigyō Honsha ni okeru Jinji Kokusaika no Genjo to Kadai. [The internationalization of human resource practices in Japanese headquarters]. *Multinational Enterprises, 8*(1), 93–113.

Maki, M. & Sekiguchi, T. (2016). Nihon Kigyō Kaigai Kogaisha ni okeru Jintekisigen Kanri no Jishō Kenkyu [An empirical investigation of human resource management in Japanese foreign subsidiaries]. *Journal of International Business, 8*(1), 89–105.

Marsh, R. M. & Mannari, H. (1976). *Modernization and the Japanese factory.* Princeton, NJ: Princeton University Press.

Morishima, M. (1995). Embedding HRM in a social context. *British Journal of Industrial Relations, 33*(4), 617–640.

Nakane, C. (1972). *Japanese society.* Berkeley, CA: University of Berkeley Press.

Nishii, L. H. & Özbilgin, M. F. (2007). Global diversity management: Towards a conceptual framework. *The International Journal of Human Resource Management, 18*(11), 1883–1894.

Nonaka, I. & Takeuchi, H. (1995). *The knowledge-creating company: How Japanese companies create the dynamics of innovation.* Oxford: Oxford University Press.

OECD (Organisation for Economic Co-operation and Development) (2013). *International Migration Outlook 2013.* OECD Publishing. doi: 10.1787/migr_outlook-2013-en

OECD (Organisation for Economic Co-operation and Development). (2014). OECD statistics. Retrieved July 29, 2016, from https://stats.oecd.org/Index.aspx?DataSetCode=ANHRS.

Ono, H. (2007). Careers in foreign-owned firms in Japan. *American Sociological Review, 72*(2), 267–290.

Paik, Y. & Pak, Y. S. (2009). The changing face of Korean management of overseas affiliates. In C. Rowley & Y. Paik (Eds.), *The changing face of Korean management* (pp. 165–188). New York: Routledge.

Peltokorpi, V. (2008). Cross-cultural adjustment of expatriates in Japan. *The International Journal of Human Resource Management, 19*(9), 1588–1606.

Peltokorpi, V. (2013). Job embeddedness in Japanese organizations. *The International Journal of Human Resource Management, 24*(8), 1551–1569.

Peltokorpi, V., Allen, D., & Froese, F. J. (2015). Organizational embeddedness, turnover intentions, and voluntary turnover: The moderating effects of employee demographic characteristics and value orientations. *Journal of Organizational Behavior, 36*(2), 292–312.

Peltokorpi, V. & Froese, F. J. (2015). Recruiting source practices in domestic and foreign-owned firms: A comparative study in Japan. *Asia Pacific Journal of Human Resources, 54*(4), 421–444.

Pudelko, M. & Harzing, A. W. (2008). The Golden Triangle for MNCs: Standardization towards headquarters practices, standardization towards global best practices and localization. *Organizational Dynamics, 37*(4), 394–404.

Robinson, P. A. (2003). The embeddedness of Japanese HRM practices: The case of recruiting. *Human Resource Management Review, 13*(3), 439–465.

Rowley, C., Benson, J., & Warner, M. (2004). Towards an Asian model of human resource management?: A comparative analysis of China, Japan, and South Korea. *The International Journal of Human Resource Management, 15*(4–5), 917–933.

Rowley, C., Kang, H. R., & Lim, H. J. (2016). Female manager success: The importance of individual and organizational factors in South Korea. *Asia Pacific Journal of Human Resources, 54*(1), 98–122.

Sadler, D. (1997). The role of supply chain management in the "Europeanisation" of the automobile production system. In R. Lee & J. Wills (Eds.), *Geographies of economies* (pp. 311–320). London: Arnold.

Sekiguchi, T. (2006). How organizations promote person-environment fit: Using the case of Japanese firms to illustrate institutional and cultural influences. *Asia Pacific Journal of Management, 23*(1), 47–69.

Sekiguchi, T. (2016). Kukusai Jinteki Shigen Kanri towa Nanika [What is international human resource management?]. In T. Sekiguchi, N. Takeuchi, & C. Iguchi (Eds.), *Kokusai Jinteki Shigen Kanri* [*International human resource management*]. Tokyo: Chuo-Keizai Sha.

Sekiguchi, T., Froese, F. J., & Iguchi, C. (2016). International human resource management of Japanese multinational corporations: Challenges and future directions. *Asian Business & Management, 15*(2), 110–136.

Smith, C. & Meiksins, P. (1995). System, society and dominance effects in cross-national organizational analysis. *Work, Employment and Society, 9*(2), 241–267.

Statistics Bureau Japan (2016). *Japan statistical yearbook 2016.* Retrieved June 9, 2017, from www.stat.go.jp/english/data/nenkan/65nenkan/1431-02.htm.

Suk, G. H. (2013, October 9). Working hours cut faces rough ride. *The Korea Herald.* Retrieved November 5, 2013, from http://khnews.kheraldm.com/view.php?ud=20131009000304&md=20131012004158_AT.

Tung, R., Paik, Y., & Bae, J. (2013). Korean human resource management in the global context. *The International Journal of Human Resource Management, 24*(5), 905–921.

World Bank. (2015a). *World development indicators: Japan.* Retrieved August 4, 2015, from http://data.worldbank.org/country/japan.

World Bank. (2015b). *World development indicators: Korea.* Retrieved December 8, 2015, from http://data. worldbank.org/country/korea-republic.

Yamao, S. & Sekiguchi, T. (2015). Employee commitment to corporate globalization: The role of English language proficiency and human resource practices. *Journal of World Business, 50*(1), 168–179.

Yang, I. & Kelly, A. (2008). Avoidance as the first choice of default management: Challenges in overseas Korean organizations. *Journal of Asia Business Studies, 2*(2), 61–67.

Yu, G. C. & Rowley, C. (2009). The changing face of Korean human resource management. In R. Chris & P. Yongsun (Eds.), *The changing face of Korean management* (pp. 29–48). New York: Routledge.

16

HUMAN RESOURCE MANAGEMENT IN CHINA AND VIETNAM

Jie Shen and Anne Cox

Introduction

China and Vietnam are two neighboring socialist countries. Both have been experiencing a successful transition from socialist planned economies to socialist market economies, resulting in remarkable economic, social, and cultural changes. As a result of the adoption of favorable investment policies, large markets and relatively cheap workforces, China and Vietnam have been attractive destinations for foreign investment over recent decades. In many significant respects, Vietnam and China can be regarded as a pair. Factors influencing their similarities include geographical proximity, historical traditions of Confucianism, similar domestic economies, and similarity between the two parties' senior leaderships.

Economically, Vietnam and China both commenced their paths to economic reforms from a broadly similar point of departure, in the sense that they had previously adopted from the Soviet Union, a common Marxist-Leninist ideology and a Leninist political framework. In the process of economic reform, both countries have broadly followed parallel paths: moving away from the command economy and toward a market economy; reforming the state sector; allowing private enterprises to emerge in almost all areas of the economy; and turning vigorously toward the world market and successfully opening their doors to investment by foreign firms (Kerkvliet, Chan, & Unger, 1999).

Politically, both have maintained centralized political control in the hands of their respective communist parties, unlike other transitional economies in Europe, which have seen the demise of their communist governments. There is still a lack of democratic institutions in both countries, and political pluralism is certainly not on the agenda. The two countries have shown a combination of economic liberalism with political conservatism. Furthermore, international organizations exert similar pressure for a standardization of labor conditions. Indeed, both the Trade Union Law and the Labor Law were encouraged and assisted by the International Labour Organization (ILO) in an attempt to implement ILO standards (Unger & Chan, 1995, cited in Zhu & Warner, 2000). On the other hand, foreign investments are constituting powerful if not coercive elements of being benchmarks as regard employment practices (Chen & Wilson, 2000).

Observing China and Vietnam's reform processes and strategies, Turley and Selden (1993) suggested the emergence of a distinctive Asian, or at least Sino-Vietnamese, socialism. Similarly, based on their analysis of China and Vietnam, Chan and Nørlund (1999) questioned whether there exists an Asian socialist reform model. In both countries, the change to the economic environment has entailed somewhat similar alterations in state-owned enterprise (SOE)'s employment practices toward a convergent model more closely resembling Western HRM. This chapter examines and compares the HRM practices under the socialist market economies in China and Vietnam respectively in order to ascertain similarities and differences in HRM between these two economies.

The economic reform in China and Vietnam

China's reform: from a socialist planned economy to a socialist market economy

From 1949 to 1976, the Chinese Communist Party under Mao Tse-Tung instituted, according to socialist ideologies and the examples of the Soviet Union's economic collectivization under Joseph Stalin, a socialist wholly centrally planned economy (Urio, 2010). All industries were owned by the state and operated through regional and local government bureaucracies which then planned and managed all resources (Shen, 2007). Industrial enterprises were not responsible for production, marketing, pricing, sales, or management of employees. The state was all-powerful and took everything under its control. The socialist planned economy developed the system of the so-called "three irons" including the "iron rice-bowl" (*tie fan wan*), "iron wage" (*tie gong zi*), and "iron chair" (*tie yi zi*) to ensure that all employable Chinese had lifetime employment and cradle to grave welfare (Ding, Goodall, & Warner, 2000; Warner, 2004).

In the late 1970s, under the leadership of Deng Xiaoping, China launched an unprecedented economic reform with the objective to transform the poor, Soviet-style centrally planned socialist economy to a modern socialist market economy (Goodall & Warner, 1999). The Third Plenary Session of the eleventh Chinese Communist Party (CCP) Central Committee passed a set of policies regarding reforming the economy and opening its doors to the outside world. In contrast to rapid economic restructuring in Russia following the collapse of the Soviet system, the Chinese economic reform has been a gradual process. The Chinese Government allowed both the planned and market economy to coexist for a period with market mechanisms gradually taking over the planned economy and dominating the nation's economy (Cooke, 2012; Shen, 2007).

The first wave of reforms, between the late 1970s and the early 1980s, consisted of instituting the household contract responsibility system in agriculture, by which farmers began being responsible for individual plots of land; they could sell their surplus crops on the open market and were allowed to establish township village enterprises (TVEs) (Shen, 2007). When the Chinese Communist Party (CCP) came to power in 1949, the state took over the land owned by individual landlords and established communes. A commune consisted of a number of Great Production Teams; each included few production teams. Production teams were given quotas of goods that had to be produced in a collective work system and members of production teams were allocated food equally within team excepting the differences between men and women. Farmers were not allowed to sell products in the market or take part in any commercial activities. This period of agricultural productivity was very low and farmers lived extremely poor lives (Lin, 1992). With the household contract responsibility system, farmers were granted the right to use the land for a period of fifteen years (later extended), enjoyed considerable production autonomy and were allowed to sell the surplus after agricultural tax in the open market. The household contract responsibility not only greatly increased agricultural productivity but also freed a large number of farmers who became available to work in other industries. The large surplus rural labor provided opportunities to develop TVEs and industries in urban areas (Ding et al., 2000).

In the early stage of the enterprise reform, China decentralized enterprise management and marketized the pricing system, giving enterprises autonomy to do business including managing people. For some years, the Chinese government adopted a dual-tract pricing system, in which some goods and services were allocated at the state-controlled prices, with others allocated at market prices. This dual-track pricing system disappeared when market mechanisms prevailed in the mid-1990s. During this period, economic liberalization occurred and this applied particularly to state-owned enterprises and state-owned enterprises (SOEs), where the Chinese government scaled down or even withdrew the Chinese Communist Party administrative apparatuses at the microeconomic management level (Ding et al., 2000). Enterprises were given the autonomy to determine their production, prices, and investments subject to the market and the "invisible hand," and were required to be responsible for profits, losses, and employment of human resources. The 1988 Enterprise Law stipulated the rights and obligations of enterprises. This marked the most critical step in the process of the Chinese economic reform as this movement has in fact changed Chinese employment relations. At the same period, China opened its doors to the outside world, allowing foreign-owned enterprises (FOEs) to operate in China and encouraging Chinese firms to compete overseas. Consequently, foreign multinationals have brought in modern HRM practices that have impacted considerably people management of Chinese indigenous firms over the last few decades (Björkman, Smale, Sumelius, Suutari, & Lu, 2008; Easterby-Smith, Malina, & Lu, 1995).

Much of the Chinese economic reform and development can be attributed to the rapid development of non-SOEs, including privately owned enterprises (POEs), TVEs, joint ventures (JVs), and foreign investment enterprises (FIEs). Prior to the reform, the private economy was virtually non-existent. In 1980, only 0.8 percent of urban employment was in the private sector. Since the early 1980s, non-SOEs have expanded rapidly due to the removal of barriers to entry and a relaxation on the monopoly of several important economic sectors such as manufacturing (Shen, 2010). Non-SOEs, especially TVEs, owned by village and township governments and individuals, have been important in the development of the Chinese economy as they contributed significantly to the rising GDP as well as having been the major providers of job opportunities; absorbing surplus labor from the SOE and rural sectors that made the enterprise reform more achievable (Cooke, 2012).

Vietnam's economic reform

Two contrasting economic systems had coexisted in Vietnam before 1975. In 1945, after the defeat of the French at the battle of Dien Bien Phu, the Vietnamese communists took control of North Vietnam. This effectively resulted in a fragmented Vietnam with two sovereign states—the Democratic Republic of Vietnam in the North and the Republic of Vietnam, supported by the United States of America, in the South. The North and the South developed along two very different paths in terms of politics and economics. The North's economy developed all the characteristics of a Soviet-style socialist centralized economic system, while the South's economy was decentralized and heavily dependent on America (Beresford, 1988). After the unification, a communist-style constitution was enacted which formally committed the country to the development of a socialist economic system. Under this system, the state and collective sectors, which were highly subsidized by the state budget, were the foundation of the economy. Large-scale private economic organizations were forced or encouraged to join the state or collective sectors. This process effectively eliminated the market mechanism except in small-scale (household) activities.

However, as early as 1977, it became clear that the economic strategy was not working, with the economy witnessing steady declines in production and productivity in vital industries, including agriculture (Le & McCarty, 1995). During the period of 1976–1980 (the Second Five-Year Plan), the growth rate of national income was only 0.5 percent, agricultural production 1.9 percent, and industrial production 0.6 percent, instead of the targeted 13 to 14 percent, 8–10 percent, and 16–18 percent per year respectively (Fforde & Vylder, 1996: 167). Vietnam suffered from an economic crisis in 1979, which had both domestic and foreign causes. On the one hand, Vietnam faced unusually bad luck with the weather, which cut agricultural output, and from the over-hasty collectivization of the South, which caused depression in industrial, commercial, and agricultural activities. On the other hand, after the Vietnamese invasion of Cambodia in late December 1978, most Western and Chinese aid and trade was cut off, though a number of European countries did not adhere to the American embargo.

By the mid-1980s, the Vietnamese economy was only sustainable thanks to significant assistance from the Eastern bloc. The lowest point was reached in 1985, when a miscalculated currency reform plan was introduced, which effectively re-valued the Dong, in a bid to reduce the amount of money circulating and to encourage an import-reliant economy, but in fact it resulted in an escalating inflation rate. This monetary miscalculation may have been the final contributory factor in Vietnam's decision to re-evaluate its economic policies, and paved the way for the *Doi Moi* period. As Wurfel puts it: "Economic necessity was the mother of [Vietnamese] reformist invention" (1993: 23).

At the Sixth National Congress of the Communist Party in December 1986, the Vietnamese government formally introduced a comprehensive reform program, known as *Doi Moi*, with the objective of liberalizing and deregulating the economy. This was the major turning point in the economic development of the country. The reform's focus was on five main areas: (1) the market economy was accepted; (2) an "open door policy" in foreign economic relations was adopted; (3) private ownership was allowed in all activities; (4) the industrialization model giving top priority to heavy industry at the expense of agriculture and light industry was dismantled and reversed; and (5) SOEs were downsized and restructured (Tran, 1997: 11–13). A series of laws were enacted to implement the new direction of the economy. The new economic system was firmly established when the National Assembly adopted a new Constitution in 1992. The results of the economic reforms were remarkable. The GDP growth rate has increased gradually since 1986. In 2014, Vietnam's Gross National Income per capita was US$1,890, classified by the World Bank as a lower middle-income country (World Bank, 2016a). Vietnam's economy continued to strengthen in 2015, with an estimated GDP growth rate of 6.7 percent (World Bank, 2016b).

It is important to note that the core premise of socialism has remained in place throughout the economic reform storms. The revised Constitution still holds socialism as a long-term goal, stresses the leading role of the Communist Party, and maintains state and collective ownership of business as the foundation of the economic system. The economic reforms have been understood as to "correct the nature of socialism," while avoiding a political discontinuity (Fforde, 1999).

Employee management in China and Vietnam

Employee management in China under the socialist market economy

HR planning, recruitment, and selection. Since the economic reform, the Chinese government has shifted its responsibility for utilizing the workforce to enterprises (Cooke, 2011; Warner, 2010). Enterprises became responsible for their employees, including the workforce size, the types of employees, and the issues of hiring, firing, and remuneration. As a result, human resources have strategic and financial implications for enterprises. As labor costs have become a major part of operational costs, enterprises that emphasize profits and competition have put controlling the workforce at the top of management's agenda, and Chinese workers have constantly faced the danger of being made redundant in all kinds of enterprises. Chinese enterprises, especially POEs, do not usually make long-term HR plans. Instead, they are flexible and responsive to the firm's short-term needs and market situations (Shen, 2008). Such a system usually lacks long-term vision, strategic integration, and sustainability.

The reform in employment relations has been a gradual process and did not start until 1986, since then the *tie fan wan* (lifelong employment) system has been step by step replaced by flexible employment contracts (Shen, 2010). Labor contracts have two forms, individual and collective, covering many aspects of labor terms, such as the period of employment, wages, production tasks, labor discipline, and penalties (Shen, 2007). The years between 1986 and 1995—the year when the 1994 Labor Law came into effect—marked the trial period for labor contracts as the government was worried about the opposition of the majority of workers in SOEs and COEs. During that period, enterprises only required new recruits to sign labor contracts and the existing employees were still guaranteed of *tie fan wan*. Contracts could be terminated by the employer on the grounds of poor performance, violation of company rules, or enterprise poor financial performance during the probationary period (Shen, 2007). Often, contract and temporary (those have not signed a contract but are not permanent) workers were not entitled to a range of enterprise welfare benefits, such as organizational contributions to superannuation (Shen, 2007).

The 1994 Labor Law legitimized the massive dismissal of workers in enterprises that were declared bankrupt (enterprise bankruptcy was popular in the early 1990s in China) or in extreme financial difficulties.

> In case it becomes necessary for the employer to reduce the workforce during the period of legal consolidation on the brink of bankruptcy or when it experiences business difficulties, then the employer should explain the situation to its workers' union or all employees thirty days in advance.
>
> *(1994 Labor Law, Chapter 3, Article 27)*

Since the promulgation of the 1994 Labor Law, the labor contract system has been widely implemented and by the end of 1996, it had become compulsory in both public and private sectors (Shen, 2010). However, there is a need to note that although the Labor Law requires the compulsory signing of labor contracts, many companies do not comply fully with this policy and, in fact, the signing of labor contracts does not prevent the termination of employment relations.

Many employees had been forced to retire before they reached the legal retirement ages in order for the enterprise to control the size of its workforce. Such early retirement is better called "internal retirement" (*nei tui*). According to the 1994 Labor Law, employees were allowed to take jobs outside of their own companies for a certain period, but retain employee status within the enterprise without receiving salaries (*ting xing liu zhi*). *Ting xing liu zhi* was practiced in most SOEs and COEs in the late 1900s, but declined in the wake of widespread privatization. The government maintained a great deal of control over employment relations, but such influence greatly diminished since the implementation of the 1994 Labor Law. The law also virtually eradicated the "*iron rice bowl*" system, as there were literally no remaining permanent workers in any Chinese industry (Morris, Sheehan, & Hassard, 2001; Urio, 2010). It is important to note that increasing unemployment resulting in poverty and loss of social security is a major threat to social stability in China (Shen, 2010).

The central government's role in dictating employment relations at the local level has gradually diminished. While business management can make its own decisions on the quantity and quality of the workforce, employees can choose their own employers. This is better called "two-way selection" and is becoming more common. Since the 1980s, large numbers of peasants have left rural areas to work or live in cities closer to industries. This influx of cheap labor has been the engine of China's capitalist miracle and facilitated employers' free selection of workers (Shen, 2007; Zhu, Zhang, & Shen, 2012). The widespread closure of loss-making SOEs and COEs and massive job losses gave significant rise to unemployment in the late 1990s and the early 2000. By the end of 2004, the number of registered unemployed stood at 8.27 million, while in rural areas the number of unemployed people was estimated at more than 150 million (United Nations, 2005). Job losses in SOEs and COEs became a major cause of growing labor disputes (Shen, 2007). The unemployment problem has been relieved in the 2010s due to rapid economic growth. In fact, currently, there is a serious labor shortage in Chinese industries (Cooke, 2012).

Chinese enterprises now use multiple channels to recruit employees, including individual recommendations, job fairs organized by local labor authorities or employment centers (belonging to local personnel authorities), media advertising, recruitment agencies, and employment services at universities. When recruiting managers or skilled employees, they tend to use job fairs or media advertising; when recruiting unskilled workers, they normally use recruitment agencies or word of mouth (Shen, 2008). The criteria for selecting and promoting cadres have shifted from pure political ideology and seniority to youth, education, demonstrated technical skills and managerial capability, job-person fit factor (Chow, 2004; Cooke, 2012; Shen and Edwards, 2004; Zhu, C. J., 2005), *guanxi* (interpersonal relations), and a willingness for long-term service (Chow, 2004). Recently face-to-face interviews—previously a non-preferred selection method—have become very popular in China.

Training and development. The training system for workers has been transformed from compulsory apprenticeships to optional professional training (Zhu et al., 2012). Training is usually run by vocational training schools, and enterprises usually encourage employees to choose particular courses and pay their employees' expenses. Firms typically give priority to improving technical skills, preparing for future jobs, and providing orientation to new employees. Teaching employees about organizational values and culture, business or organizational procedures, and understanding of business and behavioral training techniques such as team building and interpersonal skills often receive low priority, particularly in TVEs (Chow, 2004). Enterprise management usually regards training as costly and disruptive to production. On-the-job training is provided only when it is unavoidable (e.g., when the authorities have issued new regulations). There is usually no training plan, analysis, or audit (Shen, 2008). Overall, due to China's rapid economic expansion, firms do not have enough resources and time to implement systematic training, which results in a lack of high-caliber or properly trained and mentored employees (Cooke, 2012; Shen, 2008; Zhu, C. J., 2005). Also, due to the high level of turnover, Chinese enterprises are generally not interested in investing in employee training.

In SOEs, the Communist Party within the enterprise is responsible for managerial development, while in non-SOE sectors management development is the responsibility of senior enterprise managers. In general, *De* (political and moral attitudes), *Neng* (ability and educational background), *Qing* (working attitudes), and *Ji* (performance and achievement) have become the criteria for promotion (Shen & Darby, 2006). However, the emphasis has recently shifted from political attitudes to work performance, leadership, and management ability. This is especially so in non-SOEs. Nonetheless, there is still much concern about how candidates behave, such as moral behavior and engaging in interpersonal relationships. When promotion does occur, especially for middle- or lower-level managers, it is dealt with on a pragmatic basis: the promotion criteria focus purely on experience and competency, such as having *guanxi* with government authorities. Promotion is also heavily influenced by *guanxi* with senior management (Cooke, 2012). Hence, these companies take no heed of career development and cultivating the talented and potential managers who work for them. The most economical way to obtain skilled workers and capable managers is "buying," which means in effect dismissing unqualified personnel and recruiting qualified employees or managers (Zhu et al., 2012).

Performance management. Since the economic reform, performance appraisal is regarded as one of the most important HRM practices by Chinese firms. Performance appraisals are used mainly for determining pay and improving efficiency of the firm but have little to do with employees' personal development (Shen, 2007). However, contrary to the Western literature, performance appraisal in TVEs does not serve the purpose of communication, as there is a lack of open discussion and giving feedback (Chow, 2004). Appraisal criteria for workers are preset goals or quantity and quality of production units (*Ji*) and behavior (*Qing*), and for senior managers this may also include political attitudes (*De*) and ability (*Neng*). There is also an emphasis on "democratic" soundings of opinions, but in the context of Chinese culture, this means striving for harmonious peer and supervisor–subordinate relationships. Moreover, Chinese firms underline sound moral practices and good personal relationships. The performance appraisal procedure includes self-assessment, peer group discussion, and a superior's final comments (Shen, 2010; Zhu & Dowling, 1998). One-on-one face-to-face appraisal used to be uncommon in China. Recently, peer assessment has become diminishing, and instead, one-on-one face-to-face interviews between the supervisor or line manager and employees have been increasingly conducted. In order to create efficiency and encourage competition within the company, appraisals are sometimes conducted in a "cruel" manner: revealing appraisal results to all employees (Zhu et al., 2012). Under normal circumstances, the worst-performing employee is likely to be fired and, not surprisingly, such practices put a lot of pressure on employees (Shen, 2008).

Generally, however, the results of performance appraisal usually remain confidential because management feels reluctant to pass on negative information to appraisees so that direct confrontation is avoided and "face" can be saved. Feedback is given only when problems have been identified or not provided at all. The lack of openness, transparency, influence on management development, and objective standards in Chinese performance-appraisal practices has provoked large-scale skepticism and resistance to the implementation of performance appraisals (Shen, 2004a). Moreover, Chinese firms often focus on conformity and compliance with rules by emphasizing discipline, punishment, restrictions, and personal loss of face rather than cultivating employee commitment (Benson, Debroux, Yuasa, & Zhu, 2000).

Rewards and benefits. Since the mid-1980s, firms have been gradually given the autonomy to devise their own remuneration systems within the given state guidelines. By the 1990s, a performance-based reward system (equitable pay) linking compensation with achievement was introduced to replace the grade-based system, which was on a "post-plus skills" (PPS) basis

(Zhu et al., 2012). Changes in the compensation system include the introduction of higher wage differentials and a shift in the relative weight of various compensation components in order to end the egalitarian mentality and provide sufficient incentives so as to motivate employees (Ding, Akhtar, & Ge, 2006). In addition, job responsibility (position wages) and education (including skill wages) have replaced seniority as the most significant predictors of pay (Cooke, 2005, 2012; Shen, 2004b; Zhu, C. J., 2005). Bonuses and profit sharing are also incorporated into compensation structures (Ding et al., 2006). In a large number of firms, pay is completely performance-based, which is reflected in that the bonus has become the major part of remuneration and is mainly concerned with short-term fluctuations in individual production and sales. These changes have resulted in inequality in income distribution. Income gaps between executives and lower employees are continuously widening, and the gap between the rich and poor in China has now reached an unprecedented level. Widening income gaps have become a major cause of social instability (Shen, 2007).

Pay is also competitive, which makes the pay in one firm level with the competitors in the same industry. It has been recognized that the level and structure of compensation systems change over time, vary according to the ownership of the firm, and differ across firms from different industries (Chow, 2004; Ding et al., 2006; Shen, 2004b). For example, Chow (2004) argued that the situation in TVEs is different, where long-term orientation and seniority rather than strong benefits and incentives are considered important in designing the pay system. Nevertheless, it is widely agreed that Chinese workers are no longer entitled to comprehensive social benefits including housing, medical, and children's education as they were under the planned economy (Cooke, 2012; Zhu et al., 2012). In the early stage of the economic reform, firms were obliged to pay the superannuation installments only for employees who had signed employment contracts. At present, however, firms have to contribute to superannuation for all employees. During the last decade, the Chinese government has taken some measures in order to reduce income gaps. These measures include the implementation of minimum wages and monitoring and limiting executive salaries in large SOEs.

Differences in HRM amongst different economic ownerships. The adoption of HRM in China appears to be uneven and fragmented (Zheng, Morrison, & O'Neill, 2006), largely due to government policy, the diversity of economic ownership systems, and the nature of management styles that exist in China's transitional economy (Zhu, Cooper, De Cieri, & Dowling, 2005). POEs tend to have their own unique way of managing human resources. Some enterprise managers in the largest SOEs may be aware that the central government relies on them, more than on any other type of firm, and for this reason managers implement measures to avoid large-scale redundancies. Owners of POEs, however, only care about the profit that their firms must make in order to stay viable in a cut-throat, competitive marketplace. Increasingly, more POEs are not complying with government labor regulations regarding labor contracts, or committing to career and management development of talented employees. In seeking efficiency, POEs are pushing employees to the limit in appraisals and pay (e.g., production unit-based appraisal and pay, releasing appraisal results to the public). The income gaps between workers and managers are often considerable, and egalitarianism no longer exists in the pay system or, indeed, in the workplace. Pay and appraisal processes are no longer concerned with "saving face," and, as a result, employees are subject to the pressures of job insecurity. In this context, despite the central government's rhetoric concerning workers' rights, they cannot be protected in practice. In general, industrial relations are more intense and labor disputes are increasing much faster in POEs than in other sectors (Shen, 2008; Zhu, C. J., 2005; Zhu & Warner, 2005). However, it is worth noting that HRM practices in SOEs and non-SOEs are converging due to massive privatization and changes to HRM styles in non-SOEs.

Employee management in Vietnam under the socialist market economy

HR planning, recruitment, and selection. Since *Doi Moi*, HR planning, recruitment, and the selection of employees at the workplace level have witnessed some slow yet fundamental changes. First, the government has loosened control in labor allocation. Enterprises were allowed to hire new employees in light of their business needs and labor control by residence permit was abandoned. Second, SOEs made their own recruitment and selection decisions based only on the quality of candidates.

In practice, SOEs focus strongly on internal promotions and personal recommendations. To a much lesser extent, they also utilize advertisements in newspapers to attract more candidates. The selection criteria are mainly based on educational qualifications and harmonious personal characteristics and do not reflect specific requirements of the organizations and the specific job (Quang & Dung, 1998). As in a similar manner to *guanxi*, Vietnamese personal networks influence much of the business conducted in Vietnam. Those who are in charge of recruitment and selection functions in Vietnam are normally under an incredible level of pressure directly from their own social circles and indirectly from those who belong to the social circles of the candidates. Visits are paid, phone calls are made, and even money changes hands to ensure that certain persons will be on the candidate list and/or selected (Vo, 2009). A typical process for selecting white-collar and blue-collar workers is very simple and consists of reading a written application to make the first cut, then interviews, health checks, and a probation period for the newly recruited employee. For blue-collar workers, a manual dexterity test is also normally required. SOEs rely heavily on unstructured interviews as a selection method, which has a low level of reliability and validity, and thus is not a sufficient or appropriate method to identify the best candidates. Furthermore, top-level positions are normally appointed rather than selected. This situation implies the need for objective selection criteria and sophisticated selection methods in the state sector (cf. Vo, 2009). Furthermore, although prohibited by labor laws and other regulations, recruitment advertisements frequently specify "male candidates only," even when the jobs can clearly be done by both sexes, for example, accountancy, marketing, or human resource jobs. So far, this practice has not been subjected to any reprimand or penalty from local authorities (Vo & Strachan, 2008).

In terms of the non-state sector, HRM systems diverge (Thang & Quang, 2005; Zhu, Collins, Webber, & Benson, 2008). Kauanui, Ngoc, and Cotleur's (2006) study of private SMEs in Vietnam find that 76 percent of these organizations had no formal HR department per se. Similarly, Bartram, Stanton, and Thomas (2009) confirm that Vietnamese SMEs' HRM system is characterized by the pragmatic use of HRM practices, particularly in the use of performance appraisal and incentive payments. However, according to Nguyen and Bryant (2004), SMEs in Vietnam face the need to formalize HR practices not only because of government regulations (Marlow & Patton, 2002), but also from a need to stay competitive and attract and keep good employees. According to Vo (2010), recruitment and selection in SMEs tends to be informal. This process tends to be simple and fast. As SMEs rely heavily on personal relationship in their recruitment and selection, potential employees are normally interviewed by people they know such as friends and family members. This may reduce the formality of the selection process and affect the real quality of this process (Vo, 2010).

On the other hand, due to the constraints of the Vietnamese labor market, which is short of highly skilled labor, MNCs utilize all channels of recruitment and maintain a balance between internal and external labor markets. Recruitment through personal networks is also very popular in foreign invested firms despite the fact that it has been criticized to be biased and subjective. However, attempts to achieve fairness and reduce the influence of nepotism in the selection process is ensured by maintaining a high level of professionalism, where only qualified interviewers are allowed to conduct interviews with job applicants and using highly standardized selection processes. With regard to the selection criteria, some MNCs use their global "competence list," emphasizing the job applicants' capability, work experience, and job performance (Vo, 2009). It is noted that there has been an ongoing "domestic brain drain," where the foreign invested sector attracts more talented employees out of the domestic labor market than SOEs, as they offer higher salaries, benefits and better training opportunities (cf. Vo, 2009).

Training and development. According to Collins (2009), there are industry sectors in Vietnam in desperate need of semi-skilled workers, however, there is little or no training available in vocational colleges to address this need. A survey carried out by the Ministry of Labor, Invalids and Social Affairs (MOLISA) showed that about 13% of graduates must be retrained or supplemented with more skills, 40% of graduates must be closely supervised at work and more than 41% of graduates need more probation time before they can actually perform their job (Luong, 2010).

Along the same line of argument, a study by CIEM (2006) points out that the quality of the national education and training system is low, failing to meet the labor input requirements of companies.

At the organizational level, Vietnamese SOEs have poor training and development systems that lead to poor employee attitudes, low commitment, and high levels of employee turnover (Neupert, Baughn, & Dao, 2005). Thang and Quang (2007) stated that whilst most Vietnamese organizations are aware of the link between training and performance, they often lack resources to implement it (Cox & Warner, 2013; Nguyen, Bryant, & Buyens, 2011). After *Doi Moi*, workforces with low skill levels still are a common situation in SOEs. SOEs only invest limited resources in training and development for their managerial staff. These activities suffer from limited financial resources, low quality training courses, out-of-date training methods and lack of systematic training systems. Workers are offered further technical on-the-job training and are required to pass technical grade examinations, which are held every year. Management training courses are still primarily concerned with familiarizing managers with the government's law and regulations rather than offering them opportunities to learn modern management concepts and methods. Management development is a process reserved for a selected few. High-potential employees are nominated by their supervisors to attend courses as part of their preparation for career advancement. The nomination process normally lacks clear standards but is done arbitrarily by the supervisor, whose fairness is sometimes questionable (Quang & Dung, 1998). Finally, SOEs demonstrate a lack of a systematic approach to training with no training need analysis, poor training design and implementation, and no training evaluation process (Vo, 2009).

In the context of SMEs, Kauanui et al.'s (2006) research on training initiatives in 200 Vietnamese manufacturing corporations determined a positive correlation between higher levels of spending on training and higher levels of SME performance. Nevertheless, whilst most of the SMEs participating in the study provided some form of training for their employees, it is largely informal—a common feature of SMEs. Furthermore, SME's put limited resources into training.

Research suggests that MNCs invest more into training initiatives than either SMEs or SOEs (Friedman, 2004; Thang & Quang, 2007). According to Thang and Quang (2007), foreign investors understand the lack of skills and qualifications in the labor market and make training a priority. Geib (1999), in interviewing Vietnamese managers of US subsidiaries in Vietnam, found that it is used as a key strategic management tool. Joint ventures and foreign-owned corporations offer training facilities and highly skilled expatriates to help (Thang & Quang, 2007, Thang & Buyens, 2008). Training may thus be considered as a means of supporting organizational strategy.

Performance management. Performance management (PM) has not been fully recognized by Vietnamese enterprises as a critical managerial tool (Kamoche, 2001; Kauanui et al., 2006; Truong, 2006; Stanton & Pham, 2014). However, PM in SOEs is in a gradual transition from a politically oriented bureaucratic assessment toward an equitable system that aims to break egalitarianism by linking performance to compensation and placing stronger emphasis on merit and achievements. The PM process has been separated from the intervention of mass organizations, although trade union representatives are still informed of the final performance rating decisions. Employees can no longer take for granted that they will receive the same treatment regardless of their productivity. Instead, the new performance appraisal system placing emphasis on competence and performance criteria, which are used to evaluate an employee's work effectiveness and real contributions to the organization, has been given much more attention since the economic reforms. Although solid attempts to link performance to pay have been recorded, it is evident that the old practice of egalitarianism still lingers. Vietnamese employees have a non-confrontational style of communication, as they try to minimize the loss of face and preserve harmonious relations. Negative feedback and areas for improvement are normally provided and recorded in vague terms only (e.g., working attitude needs to be improved, performance can be enhanced, etc.), where more detailed feedback is preferably given in informal talks in private, usually out of the working hours (cf. Kamoche, 2001; Truong, 2006; Stanton & Pham, 2014).

PM systems still serve more of an evaluation purpose rather than a developmental purpose. Although SOEs use PM systems to justify pay for performance, salary increases, and identify candidates for promotion, all of which are considered to be short-term goals, they do not use this tool to implement any long-term goals. It is evident that SOEs show more emphasis on the assessment of past performance than on planning future development. There is a very weak link, if any, between the results of an employees' performance appraisal and any training and development opportunities they might receive in the near future. In practice, career planning and development are hardly discussed during the performance appraisal process.

Kauanui et al. (2006) suggested that the rapport between performance appraisal and PM in Vietnamese SMEs is still weak. Nguyen and Bryant (2004) suggested that firms should give high priority to introducing clear criteria for performance appraisals. Along the same line of argument, Ying Zhu (2005) argued that although corporate culture in Vietnamese firms emphasizes harmony, this makes it difficult to implement such practices as individual performance-based pay and developing new ways of maximizing employee potential needs to happen if firms are to stay competitive. Finally, Stanton and Pham (2014) exploring PM in the service industry found an increasing use of PM practices and that Vietnamese managers considered PM to be a useful tool to manage and improve employee attitudes and behavior. However, such practices had to be tailored to the company's strategic goals and HR plan and, importantly, had to be culturally acceptable to employees and managers.

In the foreign invested sector, MNCs are able to design and implement their own PM policies and practices, often leading to SOEs and private Vietnamese firms looking to MNCs' PM for practices to emulate as they attempt to build competitiveness through developing a highly skilled and committed workforce (Thang & Quang, 2005; Zhu, Collins, Webber, & Benson, 2008). A wide range of advanced PM tools and techniques, including the use of self-evaluation, peer evaluation, 360-degree feedback, Balanced Scorecards, SMART objectives, and forced distributions are found in American and European firms (Kamoche, 2001; Truong, 2006; Vo, 2009). Vo and Stanton (2011) also found evidence of successfully transferred PM practices in US MNCs. However, in Asian MNCs, PM is characterized by a top-down performance objective setting, an informal and regular performance review, and performance appraisals conducted strictly top-down, and allegedly suffering from favoritism and a lack of openness (Vo, 2009).

Rewards and benefits. In the wake of the *Doi Moi* period, the government has given special attention to the remuneration policies in order to make them more relevant to the new economic situation. The new salary system has been in operation since April 1, 1993 with two Decrees by the Government No. 25/CP and 26/CP dated on May 23, 1993. While the salary system remained centrally controlled by the government, SOEs are now responsible for the design of their own reward systems, in line with their operating situation, and on the principle of remunerating according to performance. They, however, must pay and promote their workers in conformity with the government's policy on salaries and wages. Every worker now earns an income corresponding to his or her work performance in the enterprise. The government only imposed a floor income but not an income ceiling (Le, 1997; Nguyen & Tran, 1997). Wage differentials within the state sector between skilled and unskilled workers have been increased. This shows that the government has recognized the necessity to widen the gap between unskilled and highly skilled labor. These changes were seen as a big move toward monetizing salary, replacing and abolishing the system of subsidized distribution, and toward reproducing the labor force (Vo, 2009).

A number of researchers (e.g., Nguyen, 2002, 2005) have pointed out constraints in the salary system. These include, for example, the complex salary system, with far too many salary schemes, grades, and steps; automatic increment without performance improvement, in which employees can gradually proceed through salary schemes and ladders without the need to improve their performance; seniority orientation, in which salary ratios do not reflect precisely the characteristics, complexity, and work nature of each job. More importantly, the SOE salary is insufficient for employees to maintain an average living standard. A survey on the actual expenditure of a household of civil servants has shown that the official income is only VND2,888,000 per month whereas the minimal living cost required is VND4,178,000. Thus, the income only meets approximately 69 percent of the living costs (GTZ, 2006: 32, cited in Vo, 2009: 92). In this situation, SOE employees must find other jobs to supplement their income, leading to low productivity and limited work stimulation in the state sector. For many employees, supplementary income from additional jobs provides an important contribution to the level of income necessary to satisfy their families' living needs. Coupled with a much lower salary when compared to the private and foreign invested sectors, it is difficult for SOEs to attract and retain talent. Corruption is a direct consequence (Vo, 2009).

Differences in HRM amongst different economic ownerships. In terms of non-state sectors, in her study of US MNCs operating in the automotive industry in Vietnam, Vo (2004) finds that US firms follow their global compensation and benefit strategies. This global view is reflected in what US MNCs offer in Vietnam—they are amongst market leaders, who have a reputation of providing highly competitive pay and benefits. They are considered to be leaders in terms of establishing and influencing pay levels, benefit levels, and HR practices.

There are signs of foreign investors, especially though coming from newly developed countries such as Hong Kong, South Korea, and China violating the salary-related legislation, leading to waves of labor strikes, especially in industrial zones (Cox, 2015). Some delicate techniques have been developed by these companies to lower the real minimum salary paid to the Vietnamese employees. One of these techniques is to ignore the signing of a labor contract.

According to a MOLISA report (2002: 23), only 70 percent of foreign invested enterprises have signed labor contracts—approximately 30 percent of them have not. The simple reason for this is that firms do not want to increase their costs. A labor contract would compel the companies to contribute monthly wage expenditure to the government's social security and health insurance funds. Within this 70 percent, some deliberately sign extremely basic contracts, neglecting essential terms such as job descriptions, trial time, working and resting time, working conditions, and terms which relate to ending contracts. Some repeating seasonal contracts or short-term contracts significantly reduce the labor rights and salary level of employees and the companies' financial responsibility to the Vietnamese government. Some of them pay lower than the minimum level without the approval of the relevant authority. Some apply the minimum salary to trained workers or skilled workers. Some include all fringe benefits in the salary package to say that they pay higher than the minimum level. Some illegally prolong the trial time, training time, or increase the required productivity to reduce the real salary paid to employees. These situations continue despite the Labor Law explicitly mandating wages, insurance, and other conditions. They reveal that the enforcement of labor law regarding salary issues and trade unions can only be seen as extremely ineffective (Cox, 2015).

Discussion

This chapter has provided an overview of Chinese and Vietnamese late twentieth-century reforms toward the "liberalization" of their economies, and the impacts of such reforms on managing workforces in enterprises. Though incremental and still well entrenched in a socialist framework, these reforms have induced ample social re-engineering, especially in the management of labor. China has successfully transformed a socialist command economy to a socialist market economy beginning in the late 1970s, while Vietnam started a similar reform about a decade later. China and Vietnam have taken similar paths to economic reform including the management of labor, that is, gradually marketized people management by giving firms the right to manage their workforce by playing market rules.

As shown in Table 16.1, it becomes obvious that there are a range of similarities in HRM practices in enterprises between the two countries. There is evidence that the market-oriented HRM practices indicate considerable progress in adopting modern HRM concepts in these two economies. More specifically, HRM practices in Chinese and Vietnamese firms are, to a great extent, adaptable to the internal and external environments and geared to the firm's business goals and objectives. The adoption of marketized HRM practices has contributed to greater efficiency and the rapid development of these two socialist market economies.

Nevertheless, there is variation in the HRM practices adopted by enterprises in the two countries. For example, different from Vietnam, training in China is usually run by vocational training schools, and enterprises usually encourage employees to take particular courses and pay their employees' expenses. Performance appraisals are sometimes conducted in a "cruel" manner by revealing appraisal results to all employees in the Chinese firm. Chinese firms have more freedom to determine wages than their Vietnamese counterparts. Wages are more competitive in China. The adoption of best practices and the transformation of HRM systems in Vietnam are weak. Instead of adopting best practices systematically, firms are still dependent upon government guidelines and regulations, and tend to use fairly universalistic forms of common-sense management.

Obviously, Vietnam has taken a similar path of people management in enterprises to what China has. There has been a shift from the "old" employment practice paradigm—distinguished

Table 16.1 Similarities in HRM between China and Vietnam

HR functions	Similarities
Overall	HR is increasingly being viewed as having strategic and financial implications, and is marketized.
Recruitment and Selection	The responsibility for HR planning, recruitment, and selection has shifted from the government to enterprises. Multiple recruitment channels are used and two-way selection is popular. Selection criteria have shifted from pure political ideology to education, demonstrated technical skills, managerial capability, and job–person fit factor. *Guanxi* influences Chinese managers' decisions about recruitment and selection, while nepotism plays a significant role in Vietnam.
Training and Development	Enterprises are not interested in investing in employee training and do not have training resources and expertise. Limited training is provided about regulations and policies. The importance of political attitudes has declined in affecting the chances of promotion.
Performance Management	Performance appraisals are widely implemented and are related to remuneration. Appraisals focused on merit and performance and the importance to political attitudes have diminished. Appraisals are conducted mainly for the purpose of determining pay rather than employment development. Negative feedback is rarely provided. There is a lack of transparency and objective standards in performance appraisals.
Reward and Benefits	Pay is, to a great extent, performance based. The government sets minimum wages.
Differences across ownership forms	Foreign MNCs comply with labor laws better than SOEs, and SOEs comply with labor laws better than non-SOEs relatively speaking.

by centrally planned job allocation, jobs for life, work assignment, egalitarian and highly standardized pay system, and an in-house welfare state, to a newer approach—characterized by labor mobility, labor contracts, job choice, performance-based wages, and contributory social insurance. At this point in history, based on the evidence presented, we argue that there is a convergence in HRM practices adopted by Chinese and Vietnamese enterprises. We understand that the major contributing factors are the similar political systems, economic structures, and cultures. In terms of HRM development, although taking the same transformational path, Chinese enterprises are more advanced than their Vietnamese counterparts, as reflected in the differences mentioned above. These differences only indicate that China began its labor reform earlier than Vietnam did, and these two countries are currently at different stages of development and are rather diverging in their HRM reforms.

HRM practices in Chinese and Vietnamese firms have serious limitations resulting from organizational inertia, ideological legacies of socialism, the lack of financial resources, and a general lack of knowledge about the "modern" concept of HRM amongst those responsible for the HR function. Specifically, HRM is pragmatic in nature rather than showing a commitment to human resource development. Typically, the bulk of business management in China and Vietnam shares the common philosophy of not investing much in their employees. Firms are not interested in personal and management-oriented training, which is generally regarded as an expense. There is a lack of management and career development for ordinary employees, resulting in performance appraisals being used mainly to establish rates of pay and not for personal or professional development. Moreover, employee participation in decision-making is both lacking and discouraged. While it can be argued that workers working in such conditions may not see much of a future for themselves, research shows that HRM practices that care about all employees' commitment and involvement will have a positive impact on organizational performance (Wright, Gardner, Moynihan, & Allen, 2005). The current Chinese HRM system has been described by Warner (2008) as "HRM with Chinese characteristics." Similarly, we suggest that the Vietnamese HRM system can also be called "HRM with Vietnamese characteristics." Due to the similarities, it may be appropriate to describe such HRM systems as "the Sino-Vietnamese HRM model."

While the Sino-Vietnamese HRM model has contributed significantly to the rapid economic development in China and Vietnam, unfortunately, HRM is currently being performed in a such way that it will inevitably lead to low morale, low job satisfaction, and low employee organizational commitment in the long term. There is a real need for Chinese and Vietnamese firms to learn quickly from MNCs in order to survive and develop in the increasingly intense competition in their own land. This is because a well-developed HRM system is essential to attract and retain talented employees in labor markets that are restricted by severe skill shortages and other related issues. Skill shortages leads to tough competition amongst firms for skilled and managerial employees and an augmentation of salaries for the workforce. Apparently, MNCs often offer models of "better practices," which local firms could choose to benchmark. Foreign-owned firms, without doubt, have important implications for the future development of HRM practices in China and Vietnam.

Conclusions

Nankervis, Compton, and Baird state that: "strategic HRM emphasizes the need for HR plans and strategies to be formulated within the context of overall organizational strategies and objectives, and to be responsive to the changing nature of the organization's external environment" (2008: 13). This definition emphasizes a long-term focus for strategic HRM and a linkage between HRM, business strategies, and the external environment. Examining the HRM practices adopted by Chinese and Vietnamese firms, this chapter points out that, currently, the "Sino-Vietnamese HRM model" has serious limitations due to political, economical, social, and cultural constraints. The macro environment for the operation of HRM is complex, and marked by uncertainty. In the middle of a radical transformation process, the Chinese and Vietnamese economic systems as a whole contain features of both centrally planned economies and market-oriented ones. The transformation process in both countries is far from being completed. The adoption of strategic HRM at the organizational level is still weak. The low degree of transformation might also be attributed to the perceived lack of necessity and assumptions about the importance of particular HRM practices and a lack of financial resource. The "Sino-Vietnamese HRM model" is expected to further develop by learning from better practices adopted by foreign MNCs.

References

Bartram, T., Stanton, P., & Thomas, K. (2009). Good morning Vietnam: New challenges for HRM. *Management Research News, 32*(10), 891–904.

Benson, J., Debroux, P., Yuasa, M., & Zhu, Y. (2000). Flexibility and labor management: Chinese manufacturing enterprises in the 1990s. *The International Journal of Human Resource Management, 11*(2), 183–196.

Beresford, M. (1988). *Vietnam politics, economics and society*. London and New York: Pinter Publishers.

Björkman, I., Smale, A., Sumelius, J., Suutari, V., & Lu, Y. (2008). Changes in institutional context and MNC operations in China: Subsidiary HRM practices in 1996 versus 2006. *International Business Review, 17*(2), 146–158.

Chan, A. (1998). Labor standards and human rights: The case of Chinese workers under market socialism. *Human Rights Quarterly, 20*(4), 886–904.

Chan, A. & Nørlund, I. (1999). Vietnam and Chinese labor regimes: On the road to divergence. In A. Chan, B. J. T. Kerkvliet, & J. Unger (1999). *Transforming Asian Socialism: China and Vietnam compared.* Sydney: Allen & Unwin in association with ANU.

Chen, S. & Wilson, M. (2000). Standardization and localization in the human resource management of Sino-foreign joint ventures: An inductive model and research agenda. Paper for Paris AGRH Conference. Retrieved November 13, 2016, from www.agrh.fr/assets/actes/2000chen-wilson021.pdf.

Chow, I. H. S. (2004). Human resource management in China's township and village enterprises: Change and development during the economic reform era. *Asia Pacific Journal of Human Resources, 42*, 318–335.

CIEM (Central Institute for Economic Management). (2006). *Vietnam's economy in 2005.* Hanoi: Central Institute of Economic Management.

Collins, N. (2009). *Economic reform and employment relations in Vietnam.* London and New York: Routledge.

Cooke, F. L. (2005). *HRM, work and employment in China.* London: Routledge.

Cooke, F. L. (2009). A decade of transformation of HRM in China: A review of literature and suggestions for future studies. *Asia Pacific Journal of Human Resource Management, 47*(1), 6–40.

Cooke, F. L. (2011). The role of the state and emergent actors in the development of human resource management in China. *The International Journal of Human Resource Management, 22*, 3830–3848.

Cooke, F. L. (2012). *Human resource management in China new trends and practices.* New York: Routledge.

Cox, A. (2015). The pressure of wildcat strikes on the transformation of industrial relations in a developing country: The case of the garment and textile industry in Vietnam. *Journal of Industrial Relations, 57*(2), 271–290.

Cox, A. & Warner, M. (2013). Whither "training and development" in Vietnam?: Learning from United States and Japanese MNCs' practice. *Asia Pacific Journal of Human Resources, 51*(2), 175–192.

Ding, Z. D., Akhtar, S., & Ge, L. G. (2006). Organizational differences in managerial compensation and benefits in Chinese firms. *The International Journal of Human Resource Management, 17*, 693–715.

Ding, Z. D., Goodall, K., & Warner, M. (2000). The end of the iron rice-bowl: Whither Chinese human resource management?. *The International Journal of Human Resource Management, 11*(2), 217–236.

Ding, Z. D., Goodall, K., & Warner, M. (2002). The impact of economic reform on the role of trade unions in Chinese enterprises. *The International Journal of Human Resource Management, 13*(3), 431–449.

Easterby-Smith, M., Malina, D., & Lu, Y. (1995). How culture sensitive is HRM?: A comparative analysis of practices in Chinese and UK companies. *The International Journal of Human Resource Management, 6*(1), 31–59.

Fforde, A. (1999). From plan to market: The economic transition in Vietnam and China compared. In A. Chan, B. J. T. Kerkvliet, & Unger, J. (Eds.), *Transforming Asian socialism: China and Vietnam compared.* Sydney: Allen & Unwin in association with ANU.

Fforde, A. & de Vylder, S. (1996). *From plan to market: The economic transition in Vietnam.* Boulder, CO: Westview Press.

Friedman, J. (2004). Firm ownership and internal labor practices in a transition economy: An exploration of worker skill acquisition in Vietnam. William Davidson Institute Working Papers Series 2004–696, William Davidson Institute at the University of Michigan.

Geib, P. (1999). U.S. strategic management in Vietnam's transition economy. *Competitiveness Review, 9*(1), 40–53.

Goodall, K. & Warner, M. (1999). Enterprise reform, labor–management relations and human resource management in a multinational context. *International Studies of Management and Organization, 29*(3), 21–36.

Kamoche, K. (2001). Human resources in Vietnam: The global challenge. *Thunderbird International Business Review, 43*(5), 652–668.

Kauanui, S., Ngoc, S., & Cotleur, A. (2006). Impact of human resource management: SME performance in Vietnam. *Journal of Developmental Entrepreneurship, 11*(1), 79–96.

Kerkvliet, B. J. T., Chan, A., Unger, J. (1999). Comparing Vietnam and China: An introduction. In A. Chan, B. J. T. Kerkvliet, & J. Unger (Eds.), *Transforming Asian socialism: China and Vietnam compared.* Sydney: Allen & Unwin in association with ANU.

Le, D. D. (1997). Legal consequences of state-owned enterprise reform. In N. C. Yuen, N. J. Freeman, & F. H. Huynh (Eds.), *State-owned enterprise reform in Vietnam Lessons from Asia*. Singapore: Institution of Southeast Asian Studies.

Le, D. D. & McCarty, A. (1995). Economic reform in Vietnam: Achievements and prospects. In S. F. Naya & J. L. H. Tan (Eds.), *Asian transitional economies* (pp. 99–153). Singapore: Institute of Southeast Asian Studies.

Lin, Y. F. (1992). Rural reforms and agricultural growth in China. *The American Economic Review, 82*(1), 34–51.

Luong, Brian (2010, February 16). Students in Ho Chi Minh City Are Weak in Soft Skills. *OneVietnam Talking Points*. Retrieved from http://talk.onevietnam.org/?p=2205.

Marlow, S. & Patton, D. (2002). Minding the gap between employers and employees: The challenge for owner-managers of smaller manufacturing firms. *Employee Relations, 24*(5), 523–539.

Ministry of Labor, Invalids, & Social Affairs (MOLISA). (2002). Statistical Yearbook of labor-invalids and social affairs 2002, Labor Social Publishing House, Vietnam.

Morris, J., Sheehan, J., & Hassard, J. (2001). From dependency to defiance? Work-unit relationships in China's state enterprise reforms. *Journal of Management Studies, 38*(5), 697–717.

Nankervis, A., Compton, R. L., & Baird, M. (2008). *Human resource management: Strategies and processes* (6th ed.). Melbourne: Thomson.

Neupert, K., C. Baughn, & T. Dao. (2005). International management skills for success in Asia: A needs-based determination of skills for foreign managers and local managers. *Journal of European Industrial Training, 29*(2), 165–180.

Nguyen, T. D. (2005). Co so ly luan va thuc tien cho viec xay dung he thong thang, bang luong moi [Theoretical and Practical Foundation for the Development of a New Salary and Allowances system] Code: DTDL-2003/24. Hanoi: MOHA (unpublished paper).

Nguyen, V. T. (2002). Xac dinh tien luong toi thieu tren co so dieu tra nhu cau muc song dan cu lam can cu cai cach tien luong o Viet Nam giai doan 2001–2010 [Determining the Basic Salary on the Basis of the Living Standard Requirements Survey as the Foundation for Salary Reform in Vietnam in the Period of 2001–2010]. Hanoi: MOET (unpublished paper).

Nguyen, T. V. & Bryant, S. E. (2004). A study of the formality of human resource management practices in small- and medium-size enterprises in Vietnam. *International Small Business Journal, 22*(6), 595–618.

Nguyen, T. N., Truong, Q., & Buyens, D. (2011). Training and firm performance in economies in transition: A comparison between Vietnam and China. *Asia Pacific Business Review, 17*(1), 103–119.

Nguyen, V. H. & Tran, V. N. (1997). Government policies and state-owned enterprises. In N. C. Yuen, N. J. Freeman, & F. H. Huynh (Eds.), *State-Owned enterprise reform in Vietnam, lesson from Asia*. Singapore: Institute of Southeast Asian Studies.

Quang, T. & Dung, H. K. (1998). Human resource development in state-owned enterprises in Vietnam. *Research and Practice in Human Resource Management, 6*(1), 85–103.

Shen, J. (2004a). A model of international performance appraisal: Policies, practices and determinates in the case of Chinese MNEs. *The International Journal of Manpower, 25*, 547–563.

Shen, J. (2004b). Compensation in Chinese MNEs. *Compensation and Benefits Review, 36*(1), 15–24.

Shen, J. (2007). *Labor disputes and their management in China*. Oxford: Chandos Publishing.

Shen, J. (2008). HRM in Chinese privatized enterprises. *Thunderbird International Business Review, 50*(2), 91–104.

Shen, J. (2010). Employees' satisfaction with HRM in Chinese privately owned enterprises. *Asia Pacific Business Review, 16*, 339–354.

Shen, J. & Darby, R. (2006). International training and management development in Chinese multinational enterprises. *Employee Relations, 28*(4), 342–362.

Shen, J. & Edwards, V. (2004). Recruitment and selection policies and practices in Chinese MNEs. *The International Journal of Human Resource Management, 15*, 814–835.

Stanton, P. & Pham, H. (2014). Managing employee performance in an emerging economy: Perceptions of Vietnamese managers. *Asia Pacific Business Review, 20*(2), 269–285.

Thang, N. N. & Buyens, D. (2008). Training organizational strategy and firm performance. *Asia Pacific Business Review, 11*(2), 176–183.

Thang, N. N. & Quang, T. (2007). International briefing 18: Training and development in Vietnam. *International Journal of Training and Development, 11*(2), 139–149.

Thang, L. C. & Quang, T. (2005). Human resource management practices in a transitional economy: A comparative study of enterprise ownership forms in Vietnam. *Asia Pacific Business Review, 11*(1), 25–47.

Tran, V. H. (Ed.) (1997). *Economic development and prospects in the ASEAN: Foreign investment and growth in Vietnam, Thailand, Indonesia, and Malaysia.* Basingstoke: Macmillan.

Truong, Q. (2006). Human Resource Management in Vietnam. In A. Nankervis, S. Chatterjee, & J. Coffey (Eds.), *Perspectives of human resource management in the Asia Pacific* (pp. 31–252). Sydney: Pearson Prentice Hall.

Turley, W. S. & Selden, M. (Eds.). (1993). *Reinventing Vietnamese socialism, Doi Moi in comparative perspective.* Boulder, CO: Westview Press.

United Nations. (2005). The national human development reports for China. Retrieved August 17, 2006, from www.undp.org.cn/modules.php?op=modloadand name=Newsand file=articleand topic=40and sid= 228.

Urio, P. (2010). *Reconciling state, market and society in China: The long march toward prosperity.* Abingdon: Routledge.

Vo, A. N. (2004), The interaction of home and host country effects in a low power host environment: The case of industrial relations and human resource management in US and Japanese multinational subsidiaries in Vietnam. PhD thesis, De Montfort University, Leicester.

Vo, A. N. (2009). *The transformation of human resource management and industrial relations in Vietnam.* Oxford: Chandos Publishing.

Vo, A. & Stanton, P. (2011). The transfer of HRM policies and practices to a transitional business system: The case of performance management practices in US and Japanese MNEs operating in Vietnam. *The International Journal of Human Resource Management, 22*(17), 3513–3527.

Vo, A. & Strachan, G. (2008, September 30). Gender equity in a transforming economy, paper presented at Ninth International women in Asia conference. University of Queensland, Brisbane.

Vo, T. T. (2010). *Selection matters: Predicting intrinsic motivation and employee commitment in small Vietnamese firms,* submitted in partial fulfillment of the requirements for the degree of Master of Science (administration) at the Concordia University. Montreal, Quebec, Canada.

Warner, M. (2004). Human resource management in China revisited: Introduction. *The International Journal of Human Resource Management, 15*(4/5), 617–634.

Warner, M. (2008). Reassessing human resource management "with Chinese characteristics": An overview. *The International Journal of Human Resource Management, 19*(5), 771–801.

Warner, M. (2010). In search of Confucian HRM: Theory and practice in greater China and beyond. *The International Journal of Human Resource Management, 21*(12), 2053–2078.

World Bank. (2016a). Data, Vietnam. Retrieved May 25, 2016, from http://data.worldbank.org/country/vietnam.

World Bank (2016b). Vietnam overview. Retrieved May 25, 2016, from www.worldbank.org/en/country/vietnam/overview.

Wright, P. M., Gardner, T. M., Moynihan, L. M., & Allen, M. R. (2005). The relationship between HR practices and firm performance: Examining causal order. *Personnel Psychology, 58*(2), 409–447.

Wurfel, D. (1993). Doi Moi in comparative perspective. In W. S. Turley & M. Selden (Eds.), *Reinventing Vietnamese socialism, Doi Moi in comparative perspective.* Boulder, CO: Westview Press.

Zheng, C., Morrison, M., & O'Neill, G. (2006). An empirical study of high performance of HRM practices in Chinese SMEs. *The International Journal of Human Resource Management, 17,* 1772–1803.

Zhu, C. J. (2005). *Human resource management in China: Past, current and future HR practices in the industrial sector.* London and New York: Routledge.

Zhu, C. J. & Dowling, P. J. (1994). The impact of economic system on HRM practices in China. *Human Resource Planning, 17*(4), 1–21.

Zhu, J. H., Cooper, B., De Cieri, H., & Dowling, P. (2005). A problematic transition to a strategic role: Human resource management in industrial enterprises in China. *The International Journal of Human Resource Management, 16,* 513–531.

Zhu, J. H. & Dowling, P. J. (1998). Performance appraisal in China. In J. Selmer (Ed.), *International management in China: Cross-cultural issues* (pp. 115–136). London: Routledge.

Zhu, J. H., Zhang, M., & Shen, J. (2012). Paternalistic and transactional HRM: The nature and transformation of HRM in contemporary China. *The International Journal of Human Resource Management, 23*(19), 3964–3982.

Zhu, Y. (2005). The Asian crisis and the implications for Human Resource Management in Vietnam. *The International Journal of Human Resource Management, 16*(7), 1261–1276.

Zhu, Y., Collins, N. Webber, M., & Benson, J. (2008). New forms of ownership and human resource practices in Vietnam. *Human Resource Management, 47*(1), 157–175.

Zhu, Y. & Warner, M. (2005). Changing Chinese employment relations since WTO accession. *Personnel Review, 34*(3), 354–369.

Zhu, Z. & Warner, M. (2000). Changing approaches to employment relations in the People's Republic of China (PRC). In G. J. Bamber, F. Park, C. Lee, P. K. Ross, & K. Broadbent (Eds.), *Employment relations in the Asia-Pacific changing approaches*. Singapore: South Wind Productions.

17

HUMAN RESOURCE MANAGEMENT IN HONG KONG, MACAU, AND TAIWAN

Shu-Yuan Chen and David Ahlstrom

Introduction

Widely accepted as a source of competitive advantage (Boswell, 2006; Choi, 2014; Combs, Liu, Hall, & Ketchen, 2006; Pfeffer, 2007), management systems, including human resource management (HRM) are now seen as particularly crucial to the development and competitiveness of the firms and economies (Aghion & Howitt, 1998; Ahlstrom, 2010; Bloom & Van Reenen, 2011; Schuler & Jackson, 2014). This chapter examines human resource management (HRM) in the newly developed economies of Hong Kong, Macau, and Taiwan, which have been undergoing major changes in their industrial and institutional environments in recent years (Ahlstrom, Chen, & Yeh, 2010; Mutlu, Zhan, Peng, & Lin, 2015). Hong Kong, Macau, and Taiwan share cultural values (Ahlstrom, Levitas, Hitt, Dacin, & Zhu, 2014; Chen, 2001) but have also developed some distinct characteristics (Varma & Budhwar, 2013). With the growth and industrial transformations in Taiwan as well as in China's two Special Administrative Regions (SARs) of Hong Kong and Macau, HRM has been changing due to increasing competition and globalization (Varma & Budhwar, 2013). As such, this chapter reviews human resources research in these economies over the last quarter century and their ongoing impact.

This chapter contains four main sections in addition to the introduction and conclusion. First, this chapter provides the background to the development of HRM in Hong Kong, Macau, and Taiwan to give a general idea of how HRM developed in those three economies. Second, it provides the cultural, economic, and industrial structure of those three economies. Third, this chapter discusses the HRM practices in Hong Kong, Macau, and Taiwan to provide a general idea of the HRM practices that are widely adapted and implemented as well comparing HR practices in the three economies. Finally, based on the research and evidence regarding HRM practices and fairly recent changes in Hong Kong, Macau, and Taiwan, this chapter suggests future trends in HRM to discuss changes in HR and their effects in the three economies.

Background of HRM in Hong Kong, Macau, and Taiwan

HRM is increasingly important in Asia, as firms have reduced their focus on maximizing production, while looking more to HR development (Li, Ashkanasy, & Ahlstrom, 2010; Ahlstrom, 2014; Briscoe, Schuler, & Tarique, 2014; Cooke, Saini, & Wang, 2014; Cooke, Cooper,

Bartram, Wang, & Mei, 2016). Although often described as relatively homogeneous, Hong Kong, Macau, and Taiwan all have some differences in terms of formal institutions and industrial environment (Ahlstrom et al., 2014; Chan, 2000; Gong, Chow, & Ahlstrom, 2011; Kwon, 2012). Hong Kong was a British colony for 150 years before the return to China in 1997. Its economy has been ranked as the freest economy in the world for two decades by the Index of Economic Freedom (2015). Hong Kong became a SAR under the "one country, two systems" policy and retained its existing capitalist economy and legal system starting in 1997. The presence of foreign multinational corporations (MNCs) has also exerted influence on Hong Kong's institutional structure through contract law and commercial conventions brought from other countries and accepted locally (Ahlstrom & Bruton, 2006; Tung, 2016).

Macau is also a territory of China on her south coast. Administered by Portugal from the sixteenth century through to 1999, Macau is one of the most densely populated regions in the world. Also under the one country, two systems policy, Macau also maintains its own legal and monetary system with China responsible for its defense. Macau is one of the world's richest cities, owing to the large and active travel and hospitality sector (The World Bank Factbook, 2015). Moreover, it is one of the very few regions in Asia with a "very high Human Development Index" as primary and tertiary education and training along with public health have all received a great deal of attention in recent years (Human Development Report, 2014).

Situated about 225 kilometers off China's east coast, Taiwan is populated by 23 million ethnic Chinese. Administratively separate from Mainland China, Taiwan's formal institutions have been significantly influenced by more developed countries such as Japan, Germany, and the United States (Liu, Wang, Zhao, & Ahlstrom, 2013). For half a century, from 1895 to 1945, Taiwan was a colony of Japan, which introduced a number of new laws there, including property rights and criminal codes (Myers & Peattie, 1983). Other formal institutions, similar to those in the USA, were also later imported (Berger & Lester, 2005; Liu, Ahlstrom, & Yeh, 2006).

Culture, and the economic and industrial structure of Hong Kong, Macau, and Taiwan

Culture

A prominent informal institution in Hong Kong, Macau, and Taiwan is Confucianism, which forms a major basis of other aspects of Chinese culture (Chen, 2001). HR practices in the earlier commercial development of the three regions were strongly influenced by Chinese cultural values such as recruiting criteria based more on propinquity, loyalty, and the reliance on referrals from personal connections (Chen, 2001). Similarly, formal training was traditionally less likely to be provided by companies that held to traditional Chinese cultural values, as training was seen as a cost not an investment, and Chinese culture holds that self-disciplined individuals should be responsible for their own development (Varma & Budhwar, 2013). In addition, HR practices aligned with Chinese culture tend to make less effort on performance appraisals; in order to avoid conflicts amongst managers and employees, employees tend to be given middling ratings (Chen, 2001). Pay would be based more on seniority rather than performance, and wage structure was generally compressed to maintain staff harmony (Ahlstrom, Young, Chan, & Bruton, 2004), though this been changing recently. Chinese culture tends to emphasize authority and conformity, resulting in fewer participatory decisions and self-directed teams, sometimes negatively impacting innovation and change (van Someren & van Someren-Wang, 2013; Wang, Ahlstrom, Nair, & Hang, 2008).

Economic development

The economies of Hong Kong, Macau, and Taiwan have changed dramatically since the 1990s (Berger & Lester, 2005; Schuman, 2010). Taiwan enjoyed much economic prosperity in the 1970s and the 1980s, with economic growth ranging from 8 percent to 12 percent annually during that time (DGBAS, 2009) (see Figure 17.1). However, in the 1990s, the business environment in Taiwan became more challenging with slowing economic growth rates and increased competition from other developing economies (Steinfeld, 2005). During the same period, Hong Kong enjoyed similar growth, while Macau enjoyed a growth takeoff somewhat later, after its return to China in 1999. The enlarging scope of globalization created pressures on firms such that they could no longer compete primarily on the basis of cost or absorbing cheap labor from the agricultural sector (Piazza, 2014; Steinfeld, 2005).

Upon China's reforms in the 1980s, the growing competition and cost pressures got Hong Kong firms moving. Some companies moved north into Mainland China, and more recently some have moved south to Vietnam, Malaysia, and Cambodia to seek lower wage costs and good supply chains, while finance, design, and logistics firms remained in Hong Kong and fueled a transformation of the economy (Berger & Lester, 1997; Rowley & Fitzgerald, 2000).

Macau had few factories to pull up stakes for the Mainland (Yeh & Xu, 2011). Yet after Macau's 1999 handover, economic and legal reforms proceeded smartly with the hospitality and gaming industries opening up and growing very quickly (Yeh & Xu, 2011). Macau also had to fill an increasingly large number of construction and service jobs. Many new workers arrived from Mainland China and the Philippines, land reclamation proceeded in earnest to fill in swampy areas, and the University of Macau was even given a brand new campus just outside of

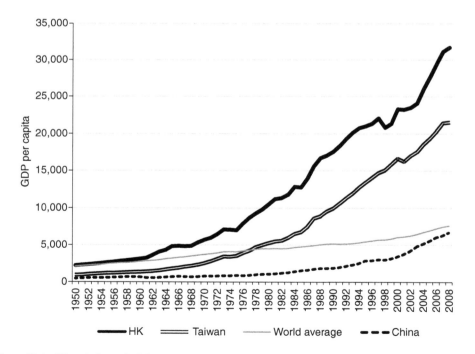

Figure 17.1 Historical trend of GDP 1950–2008, Hong Kong, Taiwan, and China

Source: Angus Maddison database, accessed through www.quandl.com.

Macau in Zhuhai. At the same time, however, a slowing of investment from China and a reduction in tourism has yielded increased unemployment problems in Macau, which has highlighted the need for diversification in the economy (Chen, Lawler, & Bae, 2005; Cheung, Lai, & Wong, 2012).

However, many firms in this region have realized that it is inevitable that they become more flexible and innovative to enhance competitiveness by making organizational and governance changes (Chan & Lui, 2004; Studwell, 2014).[1] Although Chinese cultural norms emphasizing loyalty and harmony are quite important, particularly in many smaller or traditional firms, other types of enterprises such as MNCs and the newer high-technology firms are introducing modern HR and governance reforms more rapidly (Budhwar, 2004; Lin & Liu, 2011; Liu et al., 2013; Varma & Budhwar, 2013).

The role of HR has become more crucial as economic and institutional transitions have accelerated in Taiwan and MNCs are bringing different and attractive HR systems, influencing local firms (Chen et al., 2005). These include practices that emphasize employee development, offer more autonomous jobs, and link performance evaluations to rewards, thus promoting organizational attractiveness (to prospective employees) and competitiveness (Schuler & Jackson, 2014). HR development in Hong and Macau has followed a similar path of change as both Hong Kong and Macau were heavily influenced by Anglo-American and (to a lesser extent) European management conventions (Li & Bray, 2007).

Industry structure

The industrial environment of Hong Kong, Macau, and Taiwan also experienced shifts in the 1990s, further expediting the transformation of HRM (Berger & Lester, 2005; Cheong, 2012; Enright, Scott, & Chang, 2005). Hong Kong and Macau have several very competitive firms and a vibrant small- and medium-enterprise (SME) sector in which HR plays a major role (Chan & Lui, 2004; Pfeffer, 2007). In Hong Kong, a large proportion of businesses involve foreign investment and multinational trading business as well as finance and tourism; recent data suggest these figures have remained high as foreign direct investment (FDI) into Hong Kong has increased and tourism has risen substantially (Census and Statistics Department, 2015; Magretta, 1998). In Macau, the hospitality, tourism, and gaming industries dominate the industry landscape (Chan & Kuok, 2011; Wan, 2010). Many gaming and hotel firms are foreign invested enterprises, often from North America, Hong Kong, and other parts of East Asia. Even accounting for cyclical slowdowns in the gaming and tourism sector, Macau has a tight labor market (Macao Government Information Bureau, 2009). The labor force of the three pillars of Macau's economy: gaming, restaurants, and hotels, increased almost threefold from 37,800 in 2003 to 106,400 in 2009. The total number of hotels and rooms roughly doubled over the same period making Macau a major hotel and hospitality purveyor (Government of Macau DSEC, 2009, 2010).

In Taiwan, manufacturers of textile, shoes, and chemicals, whose products have relatively low value added, accounted for a major industrial share there before the 1980s. However, the high-technology sector, which was established in the early 1980s, began prospering in the 1990s as key sub-assemblies to products were increasingly built in Taiwan, or in factories managed by Taiwan entrepreneurs in Mainland China or Southeast Asia (Enright et al., 2005). The rapid growth of high-tech companies has given Taiwan a high percentage of export trade and a worldwide reputation of providing good quality electrical products. Taiwanese enterprises, particularly those in the electronic industries, are well recognized: Taiwan Semiconductor Manufacturing Company is the world's largest semiconductor foundry. HRM in high-technology industries is distinct from that in other industries, often more closely following Anglo-American models brought to Taiwan by managers who have studied overseas. HRM in the service context also learned from mainstream HR practices from the USA and the UK. This is important as service-oriented business accounts for more than 70 percent of GDP in Taiwan (Uen, Ahlstrom, Chen, & Tseng, 2012).

HRM practices in Hong Kong, Macau, and Taiwan

Recruitment and selection

Recruitment and selection management play a key role in attracting the necessary talent in the services and SME sectors, which are so important in Hong Kong and Macau. The common mindset in Hong Kong has typically sought to focus more on finding the "top talent," as opposed to selecting employees for their educational credentials or emphasizing subsequent training, (Khilji, Tarique, & Schuler, 2015). In terms of talent, employers tend to emphasize the résumés and initial screening over other selection approaches. Recently social media screening and interviews have started to be ranked high in Hong Kong and Macau for initial selection, with less emphasis being placed on work samples and situational interviews. In addition, it was found that candidates emphasizing industry experience were very helpful in being short-listed for an interview (Chan & Kuok, 2011; Moody, Stewart, & Bolt-Lee, 2002; Ryan & Tippins, 2004).

With the increasing levels of FDI, international experience has also been seen as important in Hong Kong and Macau (Tung, 2016). Special sections of local newspapers are devoted to job notices and include numerous articles on regional firms with growing HR requirements. Foreign invested enterprises are particularly aggressive in this regard, and at most levels of the employment spectrum. The increasing number of MNCs going to Hong Kong and Macau has enhanced the demand for talent and the attention given to selection has stayed high in China's SARs (Khilji et al., 2015; Tarique & Schuler, 2010). Recognizing the importance of global talent management and overseas experience, firms in Hong Kong and Macau have quickly realized that a fast way of having a good talent pool is to attract members of the Chinese diaspora to return to the region (Khilji et al., 2015; Tung & Chung, 2010). Hong Kong and Macau (as well as Mainland China) have both official and unofficial programs to encourage the diaspora from the region back to southern China, especially the skilled diaspora; the governments in southern China have recently been aggressive in supporting these programs (Ragazzi, 2014).

Recruitment and selection management plays a key role in attracting talent in Taiwan as well (Uen, Ahlstrom, Chen, & Liu, 2015). Shortages of skilled workers have proved to be a major concern in Taiwan such that firms have been rethinking their strategies to attract talented employees (Khilji et al., 2015). Much like Hong Kong and Macau, Taiwan firms are increasingly using social media platforms, and not just conventional ones like LinkedIn and Facebook, but other lesser-known sites to introduce the firm and build its reputation with employees and perspective hires as a good place to work (Uen et al., 2015). Researchers have also suggested the key role of integrating organizational strategies or goals with recruitment and selection policies and practices in order to achieve better results from recruiting and attracting talent (Hsu & Leat, 2000; Uen et al., 2012). In addition, performance- and skill-based promotion practices highlighted in the recruitment information have proven helpful in attracting the targeted talent (Tsai, Huang, & Yen, 2008). Moreover, recruitment and selection studies in Taiwan hold that several effective recruitment and selection sources such as realistic job reviews are able to positively influence interviewees' evaluation (Chen, Tsai, & Hu, 2008; Tsai, Chen, & Chiu, 2005).

Interviewers also play a key role affecting employment image as well as candidates' job choice intention. Taiwanese firms reportedly put more effort and perhaps place more faith and emphasis on the interview process and building firm reputation vis-à-vis job seekers, which has not been mentioned much in research on Hong Kong and Macau (Tsai, Yang, & Lin, 2009; Uen et al., 2015).

Training practices

Compared with recruitment and selection, traditionally less attention has been given to the training and evaluation of staff in Hong Kong and Macau (Lam, Lo, & Chan, 2002). Hong Kong managers in particular were skeptical of spending money on training and management development (Verma, Kochan, & Lansbury, 1995), though this has been changing in recent years. Traditionally, in-house training in Hong Kong and Macau focused narrowly on technical and vocational abilities, while management development or leadership skills received little or no attention (Kirkbride & Tang, 1989). As turnover problems for service establishments—especially hotels, restaurants, and other tourist enterprises which are so important to the economies in Hong Kong and Macau—often occur in the first few months of worker employment, firms have slowly started to invest more in training and development, in order to retain employees and reduce the turnover (Barron, 2008; Chan & Kuok, 2011; Lam et al., 2002). As early as Hong Kong's 1997 return to Mainland China, Ng and Chiu (1997) observed that training was being provided to junior staff across a variety of firms, some for the first time, and this has increased in recent years (Yonezawa, 2014; Zhou, 2012).

Training has received increased attention recently in Macau as well. Employees' interpersonal communication is expected to enhance a better service quality. The attributes of employees are vital factors for return visits. Thus, Macau HR managers expect the applicants to have good people skills, including various communication, verbal, and listening skills perceived as important to prospective employers for the personnel needs in the travel and hospitality industry, as well as for retaining quality employees in such high-turnover industries (Barron, 2008; Okeiyi, Finley, & Postel, 1994; Tas, 1988). Consequently, employers carefully identify and hire those with communication competencies (good verbal, listening, and human relation skills) to provide quality service, instead of just hiring employees with job-related knowledge or requisite degrees. Communication competencies allow the new hire to work cooperatively with others in the organization and more training is given accordingly today (Cheong, 2012).

Training practices have been getting more attention from both practitioners and scholars in Taiwan as well, since these help employers to develop employee necessary skills and evaluate employee performance (Briscoe et al., 2014). Teambuilding training methods were supported for the effectiveness of employee behavior and performance (Lin, Wang, & Sheu, 2010) To further explore the effects of training practices, several studies found that the training practices effectively influence organizational performance through developing human capital in an organization (Chi, Wu, & Lin, 2008; Han & Shen, 2007; Young & Tsai, 2008; Lin, Chen, & Chiang, 2003).

Appraisal and compensation

In terms of appraisal and compensation, Kirkbride and Tang (1989) conducted an early review in Hong Kong and found they were not very sophisticated compared with those in more developed economies (cf. Rowley & Fitzgerald, 2000). Although formal appraisal systems were common, they were often accompanied by management–employee collusion—gaming of the appraisal systems were a common problem (Saha & Rowley, 2015). Previous research has also showed that employers in Hong Kong and Macau strongly emphasize financial compensation to attract, retain, and motivate employees to achieve organizational goals as opposed to job satisfaction and engagement programs (Cheong, 2012; Heskett, Sasser, & Wheeler, 2008; Saha & Rowley, 2015). Snape, Thompson, Yan, and Redman (1998) noted that the use of performance appraisal was more widespread in Hong Kong than in Britain, but it was more directive and less participative. McCormick (2001) further added the need to use more term-based appraisals to suit the local collectivist-oriented culture, but there was not that much innovation in compensation regarding group appraisals, for example (Milkovich, Newman, & Gerhart, 2013). Supplementary appraisal approaches that have received much attention in recent years, such as giving praise and coaching, were also seldom reported in Hong Kong and in other parts of East Asia (Chan & Kuok, 2011; Milkovich et al., 2013; Sun, Zhao, & Yang, 2010).

Similarly, appraisal and compensation in Macau were fairly basic and generally thought to be not very imaginative (Cheong, 2012; Wan, 2010). The insufficient workforce due to the rapid development of the hospitality and tourism industry in Macau has encouraged many employees to change jobs to gain higher salaries. Previous research suggested that pay satisfaction and organizational commitment are positively related and pay dissatisfaction is a major reason for the turnover in Hong Kong and Macau (Chan & Lui, 2004; Tang & Chiu, 2003). Indeed, Macau employers report low commitment from employees and a high level of turnover, often on short notice (Chan & Kuok, 2011).

In Taiwan, benefit and compensation practices have received more attention from researchers and the press as they are considered to be effective incentives. Compensation packages including direct payments, benefits, and profit-sharing plans are suggested to affect employee attitudes, motivation, and performance (Chu, Chi, & Lee, 1998; Lee, Hsu, & Lien, 2006). Research in North America has questioned the value of traditional financial rewards in favor of alternative methods of motivation and compensation (e.g., Latham, 2011; Pfeffer & Sutton, 2006). Recent work in Taiwan has also shown that cash-based profit-sharing plans have had little impact on employee extra-role behavior but that the stock-based or combined-total profit-sharing plans did positively influence employee citizenship behavior (Chiu & Tsai, 2007). Amongst other benefit plans, severance plans positively affected employee turnover rate, while the retirement plans and fringe benefits did not show significant effects in Taiwan firms. In addition, pension plans had differing impacts such as negative effects on employee turnover rate from more highly educated employees to positive effects on firms with lower average educational levels (Lee et al., 2006).

Strategic HRM

A 1991 survey of more than 1,000 medium and large companies in Hong Kong showed that a third of the companies employed full-time HR personnel. Of these, 3.9 percent had some responsibility for strategy (Hong Kong Vocational Training Council, 1992). Two subsequent large-scale surveys conducted in 1995 by the Hong Kong Institute of HRM (Cheung, 1998; Tang, Lai, & Kirkbride, 1995) showed the increasing, though still limited influence of HR in Hong Kong companies on strategic issues such as staffing plans, changes in work culture of the organization, and the introduction of new HR systems and their link with firm strategy (Chan & Lui, 2004; Uen et al., 2012).

A number of HR studies in Macau have similarly focused on HR practices or systems and the relationship with firm performance (such as high-performance work systems [HPWS], e.g., Gong, Shenkar, Luo, & Nyaw, 2005; Law, Tse, & Zhou, 2003; Sun, Aryee, & Law, 2007).

There is also a growing body of work on MNCs examining various HR and employee relations in foreign invested enterprises in China because of the ineffective people management they have encountered (Cooke, 2009; Zheng & Lamond, 2009). Characteristics of HR systems in Macau tended to combine some of Hong Kong's HR system and some of Mainland China's (and a little from Portugal, particularly in the Macau civil service), and has yielded HR research that accounts for the institutional context as well as the task environment (gaming and hospitality services) in Macau (Shen, 2007).

In Taiwan, research on strategic management and its link to HR has also focused attention on strategic HRM development and particularly the systematic perspective of HR practices. Early work held that when HR systems are line with major organizational strategies and goals, improved organizational effectiveness is the result (Huang, 2003; Shih & Huang, 2005). Amongst those strategic HRM-related studies, HPWS represents a widely adopted approach to building an internally consistent HR system with an eye on organizational effectiveness (Cooke et al., 2016; Huang, Ahlstrom, Lee, Chen, & Hsieh, 2016; Schuler & Jackson, 2014). Several studies found a positive relationship between HPWS and organizational performance and in a range of industries from high technology to the services industry (Chang & Huang, 2005; Chuang & Liao, 2010; Lin & Shih, 2008; Shih & Hsu, 2006; Tsai, 2006; Yang & Lin, 2009). Chuang and Liao (2010) found well-constructed HR systems help service organizations to improve the organizational climate for both employees and customers, while reducing costly employee turnover and customer defection (Heskett et al., 2008).

HRM in the MNC context

Work conducted regarding Hong Kong HR has also examined culture, expatriate issues, and organizational performance (Tung, 2016). The cultural differences of HR practices between Hong Kong and Britain (Snape et al., 1998) have been one focus with the large amount of cross-border business. The HRM of MNCs operating in Hong Kong and how MNCs impact HRM in their host location in Hong Kong is also an important area of research (e.g., Ngo, Turban, Lau, & Lui, 1998). In addition, HR has been influenced by research on the service businesses, given the emphasis in Hong Kong industry on the financial, trading, and hospitality and tourism sectors (Rowley & Fitzgerald, 2000; Zhu, Warner, & Rowley, 2007). Generally speaking, Hong Kong has (albeit slowly) adopted more Anglo-American HR practices from the UK and the USA, particularly in the areas of selection, training, and pay for performance (Tsui & Lai, 2009). For example, British and American firms tended to use formal performance appraisal, fairly standardized methods of job evaluation, female-friendly HR practices, and merit-based pay (Fields, Chan, & Akhtar, 2000; Ng & Chiu, 1997; Shaw, Tang, Fisher, & Kirkbride, 1993) as opposed to less-formal evaluations, seniority-based compensation and promotion, as has traditionally been more common in East Asia (Ngo et al., 1998). The former practices have influenced Hong Kong's HR environment, though more slowly in certain areas. For example, certain changes have been slow to develop regarding merit-based (or non-family) promotions, corporate governance reform, and generational-ownership transfers in family firms (Ahlstrom et al., 2004; Au, Chiang, Birtch, & Ding, 2013).

In Macau, in recent years, HRM research and practice alike have focused more on the fusion of Chinese management practices and HR practices suitable for firms in ethnic Chinese communities, in part because of large numbers of customers and invested firms from Mainland China (Wan, 2010). In Macau, as in Hong Kong, there is also a lot of Western influence, particularly with respect to the MNCs in hospitality and gaming (Chan & Kuok, 2011; Chan & Lui, 2004; Zhao & Du, 2012). Formal and informal institutions also play a role in influencing foreign entry strategies and the subsequent HR systems, which MNCs choose to set up (Ahlstrom, Bruton, & Chan, 2001; Meyer, Estrin, Bhaumik, & Peng, 2009). Some HR systems will be brought from the MNC's home country, but the system must be localized to some extent to account for local laws and customs in Macau, and must be consistent with Chinese cultural values (Zhu et al., 2007).

With economic development and foreign investment into Taiwan as well, HRM has also taken on a cross-cultural character. The influence of cultural factors are the major concern and the HR system comparison between countries are the mainstream in this line of studies such as reward allocation decisions of Taiwanese versus US managers, employee financial participation in Korea and Taiwan, and a cross-national comparison of personnel selection practices (Bruton, Ahlstrom, & Wan, 2003; Cin, Han, & Smith, 2003; Huo, Huang, & Napier, 2002; Hu, Hsu, Lee, & Chu, 2007). In addition, the similarities and differences between locally owned companies and MNC subsidiaries has also become a focus for international HRM. Training and development for example, tend to borrow directly from home in order to keep a global consistency in MNCs (Bartlett, Lawler, Bae, Chen, & Wan, 2002). Otherwise, MNCs tend to adopt more flexible HRM systems in order to adapt home-country practices to local cultural or institutional factors (Chen et al., 2005).

New trends in HRM in Hong Kong, Macau, and Taiwan

This section will examine new trends in HRM in Hong Kong, Macau, and Taiwan with a focus on the increased cultural convergence in those three economies on the one hand, and the continuing institutional and task-economic differences on the other.

Crossvergence between Eastern values and Western-style management

Chinese cultural values are rooted in the management styles of many more traditional companies in Taiwan. For example, many Taiwanese businesses are family-controlled SMEs. When it comes to the core management staffing issues, the major positions in SMEs are nearly all held exclusively by close family members, since non-family members are usually not well trusted by the principal owner. This fact is reflected in staffing practices; these enterprises hire close relatives or close friends as workers to ensure loyalty. Similarly, Taiwan firms try to stock the board with family members or close associates, though this practice has been changing in recent years, particularly in the newer high-technology firms (Liu et al., 2013). However, this approach is not only restricted to the more traditional Taiwan SMEs. Loyalty and the "right" personality qualities, such as being a conscientious, hard-working employee are also major concerns for larger enterprises when they hire workers. For example, Uni-President Enterprises, the biggest food company in Taiwan, traditionally placed much importance on key Chinese cultural values such as loyalty when hiring (e.g., Chen, 1997). In addition, the recruitment approaches focus more on employee referrals that are consistent with the view that close relatives and friends are good to hire and minimize turnover. Employers tended not to put much faith on employee training in Taiwan, especially in SMEs (Lam, Lo, & Chan, 2002; Varma & Budhwar, 2013). This reflects that many SMEs in this region still tend to see HR as a traditional administrative function than embracing more recent HR evidence and practice that can enhance competitiveness (Pfeffer, 2007; Bloom & Van Reenen, 2011).

Yet there is evidence that in recent years, compensation and evaluation practices in Taiwan have moved closer to more Anglo-American HR practices (Huang et al., 2016), even those that seem to be at odds with traditional Chinese culture (Ahlstrom et al., 2010; Chen et al., 2005).

Compensation strategies have been changed much in firms in order to enhance employee performance. For example, instead of seniority-based incentives, many of the newer Taiwanese firms (often in electronics and information technology) tend to compensate employees based on their performance such as R&D professionals in order to encourage employees' better performance, (Chien, Lawler, & Uen, 2010; Liu et al., 2013). However, with the new performance-based incentives, the employee often receives a performance bonus based on performance evaluations (i.e., Grade A, B, etc.). However, in order to maintain the harmony in an organization, more than 80 percent of employees in SOEs and the public sector can be ranked as Grade A in their performance evaluation and receive one-month-base-wage performance bonus. If they are ranked as Grade B, they can receive half-month-base-wage performance bonus. It is not common for the employees to receive a "below-average" (Grade C or below) evaluation (Ahlstrom, Foley, Young, & Chan, 2005; Chen, 1997).

Over the last decade, HR scholars in Taiwan have tended to look into a sort of crossvergence between East value and West management practices. This could be in part related to the extensive attention given to HR amongst Taiwan universities, the government, and the large, active private and public HR research institutes (Huang et al., 2016). For example, family-owned business as well as SME issues have been getting more attention in recent years in Taiwan from both the government and academia in attempts to improve the sector's competitiveness (Liu, Chen, & Wang, 2017; Uen et al., 2015). HR scholars assisted in this effort in focusing more on HR practice effectiveness especially in family business in Taiwan (Tsai, 2010). For example, Gatfield and Youseff (2001) further indicated that HRM practices with special emphasis on employee compensation and performance appraisal were able to affect firm performance significantly. Zheng, O'Neill, and Morrison (2009) suggested that innovative HR practices development is able to enhance SME firm performance. Other recent research has looked at innovation, improving corporate governance in part through personnel practices, and strategic HRM (Lin & Liu, 2011; Liu et al., 2013; Uen et al., 2012).

The HR development in Hong Kong and Macau, on the other hand, has been showing a somewhat different developmental pattern. Firms in Hong Kong and Macau adopted more Anglo-American HR practices earlier than in Taiwan did. In the late 1990s, practices such as regular performance appraisals, varied compensation plans, and more coherent and consistent HR systems were experimented with and were widely adopted (Snape et al., 1998; Ngo et al., 1998). Even the heretofore-sacrosanct thirteenth-month bonus (usually automatically given to many workers in Hong Kong and Macau around Chinese New Year) was done away with or modified—often linked to performance (Ahlstrom & Bruton, 2009). Somewhat differently from Taiwan, HR development in Hong Kong and Macau suggests that HR practices were evolving based on the influence of MNCs and international cultural influences, particularly from North America and the UK, as well as more internationalized university education, which entered Hong Kong and Macau earlier than in Taiwan, resulting in it holding to a more local focus for longer.

Institutional permissiveness

The free market principles underlying the economy, coupled with the weak bargaining power of labor unions and the Chinese culture of paternalism has engendered what Ng (2002) speaks of as institutional permissiveness in the workplace in Hong Kong. Institutional permissiveness refers to loose and informal regulatory institutions in the labor market that help to maintain harmonious industrial relations. This is reflected in the relatively weak legal regulations. The Hong Kong government has so far regulated the labor market and employment mainly through the Employment Ordinance of Hong Kong. While there is a trend of government intervention, it is still on the mild side, compared with most Western countries. The introduction of the MPF scheme and the minimum wage law in Hong Kong are amongst the strictest HR-related regulations introduced. According to government statistics, there were 824 registered trade unions in Hong Kong in 2010. Of these, only 107 unions had declared a membership of more than 1,000 (Chan & Man, 2013). The role of trade unions in Hong Kong has remained weak due to the small size of establishments in manufacturing and many service firms (Snape & Chan, 1999).

HR systems have often emphasized family-friendly issues and women-friendly HR practice issues. In Hong Kong, a stream of research has appeared on women in management, family-friendly management, and flextime (e.g., Chiu & Ng, 1999; Lau & Ngo, 2004). Chiu and Ng (1999) suggested that HR systems emphasizing female employee friendly management are able to enhance female workers' performance and increase their engagement.

Firms in Hong Kong, Macau, and (more slowly) in Taiwan have gradually adopted Anglo-American HR practices with increased inward foreign direct investment but also have adapted those practices to fit with the local Chinese cultural milieu in order to manage Chinese employees better (Lau & Ngo, 2004). The question is not what are cultural or institutional differences amongst economies and regions, but rather, which cultural or institutional aspects matter the most and how can these aspects be properly accounted for in a modified or adapted HR system?

Implications and future research

Although HR development in Hong Kong, Macau, and Taiwan have all made some cultural crossvergence with Chinese cultural values and Anglo-American HR practices, new and varied industrial and economic forces have still produced some differences in these individual economies, which require additional research. In Taiwan, the major focus of HRM is on better management of high-technology and service industries as these industries have accounted for about three-quarters of Taiwan's GDP recently (Uen et al., 2012). For example, HRM in the high-tech industry is thought to emphasize a more sophisticated and creative approach toward HR (Ramirez & Fornerino, 2007) and is impacting top management by reducing the reliance on family members in favor of managers with technical backgrounds. In that context, HR practices seek to focus on proper selection, the facilitation of knowledge activities, and incentivizing innovation (Collins & Smith, 2006; Jackson, Chuang, Harden, & Jiang, 2006; Wang et al., 2008). Additional research is needed in the services industry as well as HRM seeks to address both customer needs and to manage the employee–organization relationship to facilitate a positive customer–organization relationship (Batt, 2002; Chuang & Liao, 2010; Liao & Subramony, 2008).

As noted before, HR development in Hong Kong is strongly influenced by Anglo-American educational practices regarding HR and multinational trading and financial businesses (Magretta, 1998), while in Macau, the hospitality and tourism industries as well as the gaming industry are major influencers along with MNCs and Anglo-American education (Chan & Kuok, 2011). Thus, HR development in Hong Kong, instead of focusing on specific industry characteristics, has tended to co-evolve around the needs of MNCs based in Hong Kong or doing business there (Chow, 2004). HR practices development in the context of MNCs working to cope with the parent cooperation as well as local needs. As for HR development in Macau, there needs to be more focus on the basics such as on recruitment, selection, and retention issues in the hospitality, tourism, and gaming industries, which is where future research should focus (Chan & Kuok, 2001).

Future research may also investigate how Macau's HR requirements might be better met through utilizing the abundance of human resources across the borders in Mainland China. Such research might help to provide answers to unresolved issues concerning local HR needs in tight labor markets through both guest workers and formal migration programs—a considerable amount of research is needed, given the large numbers of migrant workers and refugees moving around in recent years.

Conclusion

After a slow start, HRM in Asia has become well researched in recent years, particularly in East Asia (Bruton, Ahlstrom, & Chan, 2000; Huang et al., 2016; Zhu & Warner, 2001; Zhu et al., 2007) and effective HR practices have become increasingly widespread (Schuler & Jackson, 2014; Huang et al., 2016). HR research (and increasingly its practice) has become fairly well developed and is playing a key role in the fairly well-developed economies of Hong Kong, Macau, and Taiwan (Uen et al., 2012; Varma & Budhwar, 2013).

These important economies of East Asia are grounded in Chinese culture and linked through close commercial ties with each other and with the economy of Mainland China (Ahlstrom et al., 2010). The development of HRM in Asia has further undergone some shifts in the past two decades as the local firms have become more influenced by Anglo-American management practices, and have sought to cope with the dramatic competitive changes in the business and institutional environments. This has included the introduction of new high-tech industries, reformed commercial law and governance standards, globalization, and the weakening of the relative influence of family business as more MNCs, start-up firms, educational institutions, and venture capitalists have brought new standards to East Asian economies (Ahlstrom & Bruton, 2006; Uen et al., 2015). This chapter has reviewed the related HRM studies covering Hong Kong, Macau, and Taiwan to provide a discussion and comparison of the development of HRM in those three economies. With elements of traditional Chinese culture, Western management (and business school) influence, and changing the institutional environment, HRM has been developing to fit with the increasingly competitive and fast-changing environments in those three economies (Huang et al., 2016; Liu et al., 2013).

Concerns have long been raised about the ability of more traditional SMEs and family firms to respond to global competition (Liu et al., 2017; Rajan & Zingales, 2003) and to introduce effective management and HR practices (Ahlstrom, 2014; Ahlstrom et al., 2004; Bloom & Van Reenen, 2010; Carney, 1998). Indeed, there is much evidence that family firms, which continue to be controlled by the established (subsequent) family generations, are less profitable and innovative than in their early days, when they were controlled by the founder-entrepreneurs, and are also resistant to change (Bennedsen, Nielson, Pérez-González, & Wolfenzon, 2007; Miller, Le Breton-Miller, Lester, & Cannella, 2007).

Yet recent empirical research has shown that traditional family businesses can reform in several ways, ranging from the introduction of new management systems to (more) careful stewardship of resources and their application to innovation (Gedajlovic, Carney, Chrisman, & Kellermanns, 2012; Liu et al., 2017; Miller, Le Breton-Miller, & Scholnick, 2008). Related to HR, the traditional family firm in ethnic Chinese communities is proving slowly able to further adopt and develop modern HR systems, enhancing incentives for employees, improving selection and training, and cultivating corporate governance by bringing in outside managers and directors (Jiang & Peng, 2011; Liu et al., 2006, 2013). Those management reforms are slowly being embraced to produce sorts of *hybrid HR policies* that can function well in the institutional and cultural environments that have developed in Hong Kong, Macau, and Taiwan (Saha &

Rowley, 2015; Zhu et al., 2007). Even select outsourcing of HR in this region has led to consultancy firms developing specialties in HR activities such as compensation systems (Chiang, Chow, & Birtch, 2010). This all has to be achieved consistently with different institutions as well as with the differing task environments which are developing in the region with the changes in industrial structures and new positions in global value chains. Culture and informal institutions are surely important, but formal institutions, technology, and the task environment are also impacting firms in this region (Acemoglu, 2002; Bloom, Propper, Seiler, & Reenen, 2010). Firms are able to hire top management and board members from outside the family and are moving beyond basic seniority for promotion and compensation (Liu et al., 2013; Varma & Budhwar, 2013). Firms in those Chinese societies, and increasingly in Mainland China, are proving to be reasonably agile in their ability to modify HR systems consistent with the cultural and institutional conditions in their respective local and regional environments (Ahlstrom & Ding, 2014; Varma & Budhwar, 2013). Researchers and HR practitioners alike can likely learn much from the systems that are emerging with the increased development and competition in the region (Abrahamson, 2008; Ahlstrom et al., 2010), particularly in terms of their successful innovations with respect to HR and the adaptation to and application in the growing economies of East Asia.

Note

1 For example, when firms in East Asia provide more protection to minority shareholders, thus minimizing the principal–principal problem (Young, Peng, Ahlstrom, Bruton, & Jiang, 2008), and bring in outsiders, their performance will improve (Jiang & Peng, 2011).

References

Abrahamson, E. (2008). 22 things I hate mini rants on management research. *Journal of Management Inquiry, 17*(4), 422–425.

Acemoglu, D. (2002). Technical change, inequality, and the labor market. *Journal of Economic Literature, 40*(1), 7–72.

Aghion, P. & Howitt, P. (1998). *Endogenous growth theory*. Cambridge, MA: MIT Press.

Ahlstrom, D. (2010). Innovation and growth: How business contributes to society. *Academy of Management Perspectives, 24*(3), 11–24.

Ahlstrom, D. (2014). The hidden reason why the First World War matters today: The development and spread of modern management. *Brown Journal of World Affairs, 21*(1), 201–218.

Ahlstrom, D. & Bruton, G. D. (2006). Venture capital in emerging economies: Networks and institutional change. *Entrepreneurship Theory and Practice, 30*(2), 299–320.

Ahlstrom, D. & Bruton, G. D. (2009). *International management: Strategy and culture in the emerging world*. Mason, OH: Cengage.

Ahlstrom, D., Bruton, G. D., & Chan, E. S. (2001). HRM of foreign firms in China: The challenge of managing host country personnel. *Business Horizons, 44*(3), 59–68.

Ahlstrom, D., Chen, S. J., & Yeh, K. S. (2010). Managing in ethnic Chinese communities: Culture, institutions, and context. *Asia Pacific Journal of Management, 27*(3), 341–354.

Ahlstrom, D. & Ding, Z. (2014). Entrepreneurship in China: An overview. *International Small Business Journal, 32*(6), 610–618.

Ahlstrom, D., Foley, S., Young, M. N., & Chan, E. S. (2005). Human resource strategies in post-WTO China. *Thunderbird International Business Review, 47*(3), 263–285.

Ahlstrom, D., Levitas, E., Hitt, M. A., Dacin, M. T., & Zhu, H. (2014). The three faces of China: Strategic alliance partner selection in three ethnic Chinese economies. *Journal of World Business, 49*(4), 572–585.

Ahlstrom, D., Young, M. N., Chan, E. S., & Bruton, G. D. (2004). Facing constraints to growth?: Overseas Chinese entrepreneurs and traditional business practices in East Asia. *Asia Pacific Journal of Management, 21*(3), 263–285.

Au, K., Chiang, F. F. T., Birtch, T. A., & Ding, Z. (2013). Incubating the next generation to venture: The case of a family business in Hong Kong. *Asia Pacific Journal of Management, 30*(3), 749–767.

Barron, P. (2008). Education and talent management: Implications for the hospitality industry. *International Journal of Contemporary Hospitality Management, 20*(7), 730–742.

Bartlett, K. R., Lawler, J. J., Bae, J., Chen, S. J., & Wan, D. (2002). Differences in international human resource development among indigenous firms and multinational affiliates in East and Southeast Asia. *Human Resource Development Quarterly, 13*(4), 383–405.

Batt, R. (2002). Managing customer services: Human resource practices, quit rates, and sales growth. *Academy of Management Journal, 45*(3), 587–597.

Bennedsen, M., Nielsen, K. M., Pérez-González, F., & Wolfenzon, D. (2007). Inside the family firm: The role of families in succession decisions and performance. *Quarterly Journal of Economics, 122*, 647–691.

Berger, S. & Lester, R. K. (1997). *Made by Hong Kong*. Hong Kong: Oxford University Press.

Berger, S. & Lester, R. K. (2005). Globalization and the future of the Taiwan miracle. In S. Berger & R. K. Lester (Eds.), *Global Taiwan: Building competitive strengths in a new international economy* (pp. 3–32). Armonk, NY: M. E. Sharpe.

Bloom, N. & Van Reenen, J. (2010). Why do management practices differ across firms and countries? *The Journal of Economic Perspectives, 24*(1), 203–224.

Bloom, N. & Van Reenen, J. (2011). Human resource management and productivity. In O. Ashenfelter & D. Card (Eds.), *Handbook of labor economics* Vol. 4B (pp. 1697–1767). Amsterdam: Elsevier and North-Holland.

Bloom, N., Propper, C., Seiler, S., & Van Reenen, J. (2010). *The impact of competition on management quality: Evidence from public hospitals* (No. w16032), Cambridge, MA: National Bureau of Economic Research.

Boswell, W. R. (2006). Aligning employees with the organization's strategic objectives: Out of "line of sight," out of mind. *The International Journal of Human Resource Management, 17*(9), 1489–1511.

Briscoe, D., Schuler, R., & Tarique, I. (2014). *International human resource management: Policies and practices for multinational corporations* (4th ed.). New York: Routledge.

Bruton, G. D., Ahlstrom, D., & Chan, E. S. (2000). Foreign firms in China: Facing human resources challenges in a transitional economy. *SAM Advanced Management Journal, 65*(4), 4–11.

Bruton, G. D., Ahlstrom, D., & Wan, J. C. (2003). Turnaround in East Asian firms: Evidence from ethnic overseas Chinese communities. *Strategic Management Journal, 24*(6), 519–540.

Budhwar, P. S. (2004). Introduction: HRM in the Asia-Pacific context. In P. S. Budhwar (Ed.), *Managing human resources in Asia-Pacific* (pp. 1–16). London: Routledge.

Carney, M. (1998). A management capacity constraint? Obstacles to the development of the overseas Chinese family business. *Asia Pacific Journal of Management, 15*(2), 137–162.

Census and Statistics Department-Hong Kong SAR. (2015). Retrieved March 1, 2016, from www.censtatd.gov.hk/hkstat/sub/sp260.jsp?tableID=048&ID=0&productType=8.

Chan, A. & Lui, S. (2004). HRM in Hong Kong. In P. S. Budhwar (Ed.), *Managing human resources in Asia-Pacific* (pp. 75–92). London: Routledge.

Chan, A. & Man, D. (2013). Human resource management in Hong Kong. In A. Varma & P. S. Budhwar (Eds.), *Managing human resources in Asia-Pacific* (2nd ed.) (pp. 82–97). New York: Routledge.

Chan, D. (2000). Understanding adaptation to changes in the work environment: Integrating individual difference and learning perspectives. In G. R. Ferris (Ed.), *Research in personnel and human resources management* (pp. 1–42). Stamford, CT: JAI Press.

Chan, S. H. & Kuok, O. M. (2011). A study of human resources recruitment, selection, and retention issues in the hospitality and tourism industry in Macau. *Journal of Human Resources in Hospitality & Tourism, 10*(4), 421–441.

Chang, W. J. A. & Huang, T. C. (2005). Relationship between strategic human resource management and firm performance: A contingency perspective. *International Journal of Manpower, 26*(5), 434–449.

Chen, M. J. (2001). *Inside Chinese business: A guide for managers worldwide*. Boston MA: Harvard Business School Publishing.

Chen, S. J. (1997). The development of HRM practices in Taiwan. *Asia Pacific Business Review, 3*(4), 152–169.

Chen, S. J., Lawler, J. J., & Bae, J. (2005). Convergence in human resource systems: A comparison of locally owned and MNC subsidiaries in Taiwan. *Human Resource Management, 44*(3), 237–256.

Chen, Y. C., Tsai, W. C., & Hu, C. (2008). The influences of interviewer-related and situational factors on interviewer reactions to high structured job interviews. *The International Journal of Human Resource Management, 19*(6), 1056–1071.

Cheong, W. M. (2012). *Human resource development for knowledge-based economies and its implementation for Macao.* Macau: Research and Statistics Department, Monetary Authority of Macao.

Cheung, M., Lai, T. M., & Wong, C.-S. (2012). Factors that influence the level of problem gambling: A Macao case. *The Journal of Gambling Business and Economics, 6*(1), 49–64.

Cheung, S. (1998). *Human resource management practices in Hong Kong survey report 1998.* Hong Kong: Hong Kong Institute of Human Resource Management.

Chi, N.-W., Wu, C.-Y., & Lin, C. Y.-Y. (2008). Does training facilitate SME's performance? *The International Journal of Human Resource Management, 19*(10), 1962–1975.

Chiang, F., Chow, I. H. S., & Birtch, T. (2010). Examining human resource management outsourcing in Hong Kong. *The International Journal of Human Resource Management, 21*(15), 2762–2777.

Chien, M. S., Lawler, J. S., & Uen, J. F. (2010). Performance-based pay, procedural justice and job performance for R&D professionals: Evidence from the Taiwanese high-tech sector. *The International Journal of Human Resource Management, 21*(12), 2234–2248.

Chiu, S. F. & Tsai, W. C. (2007). The linkage between profit sharing and organizational citizenship behaviour. *The International Journal of Human Resource Management, 18*(6), 1098–1115.

Chiu, W. C. & Ng, C. W. (1999). Women-friendly HRM and organizational commitment: A study among women and men of organizations in Hong Kong. *Journal of Occupational and Organizational Psychology, 72*(4), 485–502.

Choi, J-H. (2014). The HR-performance link using two differently measured HR practices. *Asia Pacific Journal of Human Resources, 52*(3), 370–387.

Chow, I. H. S. (2004). The impact of institutional context on human resource management in three Chinese societies. *Employee Relations, 26*(6), 626–642.

Chu, C., Chi, S., & Lee, C. (1998). A study on relationships among pay factors, task characteristics, and employee attitudes: The theory and empirical analysis on the two-dimensional contingency model of pay design. *Taiwan Journal of Management, 15*(4), 561–585.

Chuang, C. H. & Liao, H. (2010). Strategic human resource management in service context: Taking care of business by taking care of employees and customers. *Personnel Psychology, 63*(1), 153–196.

Cin, B. C., Han, T. S., & Smith, S. C. (2003). A tale of two tigers: Employee financial participation in Korea and Taiwan. *The International Journal of Human Resource Management, 14*(6), 920–941.

Collins, C. J. & Smith, K. G. (2006). Knowledge exchange and combination: The role of human resource practices in the performance of high-technology firms. *Academy of Management Journal, 49*(3), 544–560.

Combs, J., Liu, Y., Hall, A., & Ketchen, D. (2006). How much do high-performance work systems matter?: A meta-analysis of their effect on organizational performance. *Personnel Psychology, 59*(3), 501–528.

Cooke, F. L. (2009). HRM in China. In J. Storey, P. Wright, & D. Ulrich (Eds.), *The Routledge companion to strategic HRM* (pp. 447–461). London: Routledge.

Cooke, F. L., Cooper, B., Bartram, T., Wang, J., & Mei, H. (2016). Mapping the relationships between high-performance work systems, employee resilience and engagement: A study of the banking industry in China. *The International Journal of Human Resource Management,* 1–22. DOI: 10.1080/09585192. 2015.1137618.

Cooke, F. L., Saini, D. S., & Wang, J. (2014). Talent management in China and India: A comparison of management perceptions and human resource practices. *Journal of World Business, 49*(2), 225–235.

Directorate-General of Budget, Accounting and Statistics Report (DGBAS) (2009). Government of Macau SAR.

Enright, M. J., Scott, E., & Chang, K-m. (2005). *Regional powerhouse: The Greater Pearl River Delta and the rise of China.* New York: John Wiley.

Fields, D., Chan, A., & Akhtar, S. (2000). Organizational context and human resource management strategy: A structural equation analysis of Hong Kong firms. *The International Journal of Human Resource Management, 11*(2), 264–277.

Gatfield, T. & Youseff, M. (2001). A critical examination of and reflection on the Chinese family business unit and the Chinese business clan. *Family Business Review, 14*(2), 153–158.

Gedajlovic, E., Carney, M., Chrisman, J. J., & Kellermanns, F. W. (2012). The adolescence of family firm research: Taking stock and planning for the future. *Journal of Management, 38*(4), 1010–1037.

Gong, Y., Chow, I. H. S., & Ahlstrom, D. (2011). Cultural diversity in China: Dialect, job embeddedness, and turnover. *Asia Pacific Journal of Management, 28*(2), 221–238.

Gong, Y., Shenkar, O., Luo, Y., & Nyaw, M. K. (2005). Human resources and international joint venture performance: A system perspective. *Journal of International Business Studies, 36*(5), 505–518.

Government of Macau Special Administrative Region Statistics and Census Service (DSEC, 2009). *Yearbook of Statistics 2008*. Retrieved from www.dsec.gov.mo/getAttachment/7a7fece9-fe72-4bac-a2d3-f1c05b96b346/E AE PUB 2008 Y.aspx.

Government of Macau Special Administrative Region Statistics and Census Service (DSEC, 2010). *Yearbook of Statistics 2009*. Retrieved from www.dsec.gov.mo/getAttachment/7c6ec555-4dba-440d-8992-251e3c6e7949/E AE PUB 2009Y.aspx.

Han, T. S. & Shen, C. H. (2007). The effects of bonus systems on firm performance in Taiwan's high-tech sector. *Journal of Comparative Economics, 35*(1), 235–249.

Heskett, J. L., Sasser, W. E., & Wheeler, J. (2008). *Ownership quotient: Putting the service profit chain to work for unbeatable competitive advantage.* Boston, MA: Harvard Business School Publishing.

Hong Kong Vocational Training Council (1992). *1991 survey report on manpower and training needs of human resources management personnel.* Hong Kong: Vocational Training Council.

Hsu, Y. R. & Leat, M. (2000). A study of HRM and recruitment and selection policies and practices in Taiwan. *The International Journal of Human Resource Management, 11*(2), 413–435.

Hu, H. H., Hsu, C. T., Lee, W. R., & Chu, C. M. (2007). A policy-capturing approach to comparing the reward allocation decisions of Taiwanese and US managers. *Social Behavior and Personality: An International Journal, 35*(9), 1235–1250.

Huang, C. (2003). Human resource management, employment relationships and employees' response: Psychological contract perspective. *Taiwan Journal of Management, 20*(3), 483–514.

Huang, L. C., Ahlstrom, D., Lee, A. Y. P., Chen, S. Y., & Hsieh, M. J. (2016). High performance work systems, employee well-being, and job involvement: An empirical study. *Personnel Review, 45*(2), 296–314.

Human Development Report (2014). United Nations Development Programme. New York: United Nations.

Huo, Y. P., Huang, H. J., & Napier, N. K. (2002). Divergence or convergence: A crossnational comparison of personnel selection practices. *Human Resource Management, 41*(1), 31–44.

Index of Economic Freedom (2015). Retrieved December 1, 2015, from www.heritage.org/index/ranking.

Jackson, S. E., Chuang, C. H., Harden, E. E., & Jiang, Y. (2006). Toward developing human resource management systems for knowledge-intensive teamwork. In J. Martocchio (Ed.), *Research in personnel and human resources management* (pp. 27–70). Oxford: Elsevier.

Jiang, Y. & Peng, M. W. (2011). Are family ownership and control in large firms good, bad, or irrelevant? *Asia Pacific Journal of Management, 28*(1), 15–39.

Khilji, S. E., Tarique, I., & Schuler, R. S. (2015). Incorporating the macro view in talent management. *Human Resource Management Review, 25*(3), 236–248.

Kirkbride, P. S. & Tang, S. F. (1989). Personnel management in Hong Kong. *Asia Pacific Journal of Human Resources, 27*(2), 43–57.

Kwon, J. W. (2012). Does China have more than one culture?: Exploring regional differences of work values in China. *Asia Pacific Journal of Management, 29*(1), 79–102.

Lam, T., Lo, A., & Chan, J. (2002). New employees' turnover intentions and organizational commitment in Hong Kong's hotel industry. *Journal of Hospitality & Tourism Research, 26*(3), 217–234.

Latham, G. P. (2011). *Becoming the evidence-based manager: Making the science of management work for you.* Boston, MA: Nicholas Brealey.

Lau, L. J. (2012). *The long-term economic growth of Taiwan.* Shatin, Hong Kong: Institute of Global Economics and Finance. The Chinese University of Hong Kong.

Lau, C. M. & Ngo, H.-Y. (2004). The HR system, organizational culture, and product innovation. *International Business Review, 13*(6), 685–703.

Law, K. S., Tse, D. K., & Zhou, N. (2003). Does human resource management matter in a transitional economy?: China as an example. *Journal of International Business Studies, 34*(3), 255–265.

Lee, C. H., Hsu, M. L., & Lien, N. H. (2006). The impacts of benefit plans on employee turnover: A firm-level analysis approach on Taiwanese manufacturing industry. *The International Journal of Human Resource Management, 17*(11), 1951–1975.

Li, M. & Bray, M. (2007). Cross-border flows of students for higher education: Push–pull factors and motivations of Mainland Chinese students in Hong Kong and Macau. *Higher Education, 53*(6), 791–818.

Li, Y., Ashkanasy, N. M., & Ahlstrom, D. (2010). A multilevel model of affect and organizational commitment. *Asia Pacific Journal of Management, 27*(2), 193–213.

Liao, H. & Subramony, M. (2008). Employee customer orientation in manufacturing organizations: Joint influences of customer proximity and the senior leadership team. *Journal of Applied Psychology, 93*(2), 317.

Lin, H. C. & Shih, C. T. (2008). How executive SHRM system links to firm performance: The perspectives of upper echelon and competitive dynamics. *Journal of Management, 34*(5), 853–881.

Lin, W. J., Chen, P. S., & Chiang, W. Y. (2003). Using Solomon four-group design to evaluate the effectiveness of a team-building training: A case of a large size of insurance company. *Taiwan Journal of Management, 20*(5), 899–928.

Lin, W. J., Wang, Y. S., & Sheu, J. S. (2010). Evaluating the training effectiveness by using different training methods: A comparison of teambuilding training between indoor lecture and outdoor experiential training. *Journal of Management and Systems, 17*(2), 229–254.

Lin, W. T. & Liu, Y. (2011). The impact of CEO succession on top management teams and the degree of firm internationalisation. *European Journal of International Management, 5*(3), 253–270.

Liu, Y., Ahlstrom, D., & Yeh, K. S. (2006). The separation of ownership and management in Taiwan's public companies: An empirical study. *International Business Review, 15*(4), 415–435.

Liu, Y., Chen, Y-J., & Wang, L. C. (2017). Family business, innovation and organizational slack in Taiwan. *Asia Pacific Journal of Management, 34*(1), 193–213.

Liu, Y., Wang, L. C., Zhao, L., & Ahlstrom, D. (2013). Board turnover in Taiwan's public firms: An empirical study. *Asia Pacific Journal of Management, 30*(4), 1059–1086.

Macao Government Information Bureau (2009). *Macau yearbook 2009.* Macao: The Government Information Bureau of the Macao Special Administrative Region.

McCormick, I. (2001). Performance appraisals in Asia. *HR Focus, 4*, 20–21.

Magretta, J. (1998). Fast, global, and entrepreneurial: Supply chain management, Hong Kong style—an interview with Victor Fung. *Harvard Business Review, 76*(5), 102–115.

Meyer, K. E., Estrin, S., Bhaumik, S. K., & Peng, M. W. (2009). Institutions, resources, and entry strategies in emerging economies. *Strategic Management Journal, 30*(1), 61–80.

Milkovich, G., Newman, J., & Gerhart, B. (2013). *Compensation.* New York: McGraw-Hill.

Miller, D., Le Breton-Miller, I., Lester, R. H., & Cannella, A. A. (2007). Are family firms really superior performers? *Journal of Corporate Finance, 13*, 829–858.

Miller, D., Le Breton-Miller, I., & Scholnick, B. (2008). Stewardship vs. stagnation: An empirical comparison of small family and non-family businesses. *Journal of Management Studies, 45*(1), 51–78.

Moody, J., Stewart, B., & Bolt-Lee, C. (2002). Showcasing the skilled business graduate: Expanding the tool kit. *Business Communication Quarterly, 65*(1), 21–33.

Mutlu, C. C., Zhan, W., Peng, M. W., & Lin, Z. J. (2015). Competing in (and out of) transition economies. *Asia Pacific Journal of Management, 32*(3), 571–596.

Myers, R. H. & Peattie, M. R. (1983). *The Japanese colonial empire, 1895–1945.* Princeton, NJ: Princeton University Press.

Ng, C. W. & Chiu, W. (1997). Women-friendly HRM good for QWL? The case of Hong Kong based companies. *The International Journal of Human Resource Management, 8*(5), 644–659.

Ng, R. M-C. (2002). Culture and modernization: The case of the People's Republic of China. In X. Lu, W. Jia, & D. R. Hailey (Eds.), *Chinese communication studies: Contexts and comparisons* (pp. 33–45). Westport, CT: Ablex Publishing.

Ngo, H. Y., Turban, D., Lau, C. M., & Lui, S. Y. (1998). Human resource practices and firm performance of multinational corporations: Influences of country origin. *The International Journal of Human Resource Management, 9*(4), 632–652.

Okeiyi, E., Finley, D., & Postel, R. T. (1994). Food and beverage management competencies: Educator, industry, and student perspectives. *Hospitality & Tourism Educator, 6*(4), 37–40.

Pfeffer, J. (2007). Human resources from an organizational behavior perspective: Some paradoxes explained. *The Journal of Economic Perspectives, 21*(4), 115–134.

Pfeffer, J. & Sutton, R. I. (2006). *Hard facts, dangerous half-truths and total nonsense: Profiting from evidence-based management.* Boston, MA: Harvard Business School Publishing.

Piazza, R. (2014). Growth and crisis, unavoidable connection? *Review of Economic Dynamics, 17*(4), 677–706.

Ragazzi, F. (2014). A comparative analysis of diaspora policies. *Political Geography, 41*, 74–89.

Rajan, R. & Zingales, L. (2003). The great reversals: The politics of financial development in the twentieth century. *Journal of Financial Economics, 69*(1), 5–50.

Ramirez, J. & Fornerino, M. (2007). Introducing the impact of technology: A "neo-contingency" HRM Anglo-French comparison. *The International Journal of Human Resource Management, 18*(5), 924–949.

Rowley, C. & Fitzgerald, R. (Eds.) (2000). *Managed in Hong Kong: Adaptive systems, entrepreneurship and human resources*. London: Frank Cass Publishers.

Ryan, A. M. & Tippins, N. T. (2004). Attracting and selecting: What psychological research tells us. *Human Resource Management, 43*(4), 305–318.

Saha, J. M. & Rowley, C. (2015). *The changing role of the human resource profession in the Asia Pacific region*. Amsterdam: Elsevier.

Schuler, R. & Jackson, S. E. (2014). Human resource management and organizational effectiveness: Yesterday and today. *Journal of Organizational Effectiveness: People and Performance, 1*(1), 35–55.

Schuman, M. (2010). *The miracle: The epic story of Asia's quest for wealth*. New York: Harper Business.

Shaw, J. B., Tang, S. F., Fisher, C. D., & Kirkbride, P. S. (1993). Organizational and environmental factors related to HRM practices in Hong Kong: A cross-cultural expanded replication. *The International Journal of Human Resource Management, 4*(4), 785–815.

Shen, J. (2007). Labour contracts in China: Do they protect workers' rights? *Journal of Organisational Transformation & Social Change, 4*(2), 111–129.

Shih, H. A. & Hsu, C. C. 2006. Can High Performance Work Systems really lead to better performance? *International Journal of Manpower, 27*(8): 741–763.

Shih, H. & Huang, J. (2005). The relationship between knowledge management and human resource management in Taiwanese high-tech corporations. *Sun Yat-sen Management Review, 13*(4), 925–958.

Snape, E. & Chan, A. W. (1999). Hong Kong trade unions: In search of a role. In P. Fosh, A. W. Chan, W. W. S. Chow, E. Snape, & R. Westwood (Eds.), *Hong Kong management and labour: Change and continuity* (pp. 255–270). London: Routledge.

Snape, E. D., Thompson, D., Yan, F. K. C., & Redman, T. (1998). Performance appraisal and culture: practice and attitudes in Hong Kong and Great Britain. *The International Journal of Human Resource Management, 9*(5), 841–861.

Steinfeld, E. S. (2005). Cross-Straits integration and industrial catch-up. In S. Berger & R. K. Lester (Eds.), *Global Taiwan: Building competitive strengths in a new international economy* (pp. 228–279). New York: Routledge.

Studwell, J. (2014). *How Asia works: Success and failure in the world's most dynamic region*. New York: Grove Press.

Sun, L. Y., Aryee, S., & Law, K. S. (2007). High-performance human resource practices, citizenship behavior, and organizational performance: A relational perspective. *Academy of Management Journal, 50*(3), 558–577.

Sun, S. L., Zhao, X., & Yang, H. (2010). Executive compensation in Asia: A critical review and outlook. *Asia Pacific Journal of Management, 27*(4), 775–802.

Tang, S. F., Lai, E. W., & Kirkbride, P. S. (1995). *Human resource management practices in Hong Kong: Survey report*. Hong Kong Institute of Human Resource Management.

Tang, T. L. P. & Chiu, R. K. (2003). Income, money ethic, pay satisfaction, commitment, and unethical behavior: Is the love of money the root of evil for Hong Kong employees?. *Journal of Business Ethics, 46*(1), 13–30.

Tarique, I. & Schuler, R. S. (2010). Global talent management: Literature review, integrative framework, and suggestions for further research. *Journal of World Business, 45*(2), 122–133.

Tas, R. F. (1988). Teaching future managers. *The Cornell Hotel and Restaurant Administration Quarterly, 29*(2), 41–43.

The World Factbook (2015). East & Southeast Asia: Macau. Retrieved August 1, 2016, from www.cia.gov/library/publications/the-world-factbook/geos/mc.html.

Tsai, C. J. (2006). High performance work systems and organizational performance: An empirical study of Taiwan's semiconductor design firms. *The International Journal of Human Resource Management, 17*(9), 1512–1530.

Tsai, C. J. (2010). HRM in SMEs: Homogeneity or heterogeneity? A study of Taiwanese high-tech firms. *The International Journal of Human Resource Management, 21*(10), 1689–1711.

Tsai, W. C., Chen, C. C., & Chiu, S. F. (2005). Exploring boundaries of the effects of applicant impression management tactics in job interviews. *Taiwan Journal of Management, 31*(1), 108–125.

Tsai, W. C., Huang, C. H., & Yen, L. C. (2008). The main and joint influences of human resource management practices on organizational attractiveness to prospective employees. *NTU Management Review, 19*(1), 1–28.

Tsai, W. C., Yang, W. F., & Lin, C. W. (2009). The Effects of interviewer behavior and corporate employment image on applicant job choice intention: The case of applicants for the defense military service. *NTU Management Review, 19*(2), 295–320.

Tsui, A. P. & Lai, K. T. (Eds.). (2009). *Professional practices of human resource management in Hong Kong: Linking HRM to organizational success* (Vol. 1). Hong Kong University Press.

Tung, R. L. (2016). New perspectives on human resource management in a global context. *Journal of World Business, 51*(1), 142–152.

Tung, R. L. & Chung, H. F. L. (2010). Diaspora and trade facilitation: The case of ethnic Chinese in Australia. *Asia Pacific Journal of Management, 27*(3), 371–392.

Uen, J. F., Ahlstrom, D., Chen, S., & Liu, J. (2015). Employer brand management, organizational prestige and employees' word-of-mouth referrals in Taiwan. *Asia Pacific Journal of Human Resources, 53*(1), 104–123.

Uen, J. F., Ahlstrom, D., Chen, S. Y., & Tseng, P. W. (2012). Increasing HR's strategic participation: The effect of HR service quality and contribution expectations. *Human Resource Management, 51*(1), 3–23.

Van Someren, T. C. & Van Someren-Wang, S. (2013). *Innovative China: Innovation race between East and West.* Heidelberg: Springer.

Varma, A. & Budhwar, P. S. (Eds.) (2013). *Managing human resources in Asia-Pacific* (2nd ed.). New York: Routledge.

Verma, A., Kochan, T. A., & Lansbury, R. D. (Eds.). (1995). *Employment relations in the growing Asian economies.* London: Routledge.

Wan, Y. K. P. (2010). Exploratory assessment of the Macao casino dealers' job perceptions. *International Journal of Hospitality Management, 29*(1), 62–71.

Wang, L. C., Ahlstrom, D., Nair, A., & Hang, R. Z. (2008). Creating globally competitive and innovative products: China's next Olympic challenge. *SAM Advanced Management Journal, 73*(3), 4–15.

Yang, C. C. & Lin, C. Y. Y. (2009). Does intellectual capital mediate the relationship between HRM and organizational performance?: Perspective of a healthcare industry in Taiwan. *The International Journal of Human Resource Management, 20*(9), 1965–1984.

Yeh, A. G. O. & Xu, J. (Eds.). (2011). *China's Pan-Pearl River Delta: Regional cooperation and development.* Hong Kong: Hong Kong University Press.

Yonezawa, A. (2014). Japan's challenge of fostering "Global Human Resources": Policy debates and practices. *Japan Labor Review, 11*(2), 37–52.

Young, C. S. & Tsai, L. C. (2008). The sensitivity of compensation to social capital: Family CEOs vs. nonfamily CEOs in the family business groups. *Journal of Business Research, 61*(4), 363–374.

Young, M. N., Peng, M. W., Ahlstrom, D., Bruton, G. D., & Jiang, Y. (2008). Corporate governance in emerging economies: A review of the principal–principal perspective. *Journal of Management Studies, 45*(1), 196–220.

Zhao, S. & Du, J. (2012). Thirty-two years of development of human resource management in China: Review and prospects. *Human Resource Management Review, 22*(3), 179–188.

Zheng, C. & Lamond, D. (2009). A critical review of human resource management studies (1978–2007) in the People's Republic of China. *The International Journal of Human Resource Management, 20*(11), 2194–2227.

Zheng, C., O'Neill, G., & Morrison, M. (2009). Enhancing Chinese SME performance through innovative HR practices. *Personnel Review, 38*(2), 175–194.

Zhou, Y. (2012). Research on the high-skilled talents' training mechanism: In reference to the experience of Hong Kong VTC talents training mechanism (in Chinese). *Journal of Suzhou College of Education, 29*(6), 68–70.

Zhu, Y. & Warner, M. (2001). Taiwanese business strategies vis-à-vis the Asian financial crisis. *Asia Pacific Business Review, 7*(3), 139–156.

Zhu, Y., Warner, M., & Rowley, C. (2007). Human resource management with "Asian" characteristics: A hybrid people-management system in East Asia. *The International Journal of Human Resource Management, 18*(5), 745–768.

18

HUMAN RESOURCE MANAGEMENT IN INDONESIA, MALAYSIA, AND THAILAND

Chaturong Napathorn and Sarosh Kuruvilla

Introduction

Although very different in terms of culture and ethnicity, Indonesia, Malaysia, and Thailand share some common features. They are the three largest economies in the Association of Southeast Asian Nations (ASEAN), which was established in 1967 to promote cooperation amongst its members, and is now on the brink of realizing the goal of an ASEAN Economic Community (AEC), established on December 31, 2015. Thus, Indonesia, Malaysia, and Thailand collaborate with one another as part of ASEAN, and there are flows of labor amongst them, especially between Indonesia and Malaysia. Their collaboration can be seen in the establishment of a regional growth triangle—the 1993 Indonesia-Malaysia-Thailand Growth Triangle (IMT-GT)—to encourage tripartite economic cooperation amongst the southern part of Thailand, the northern part of Malaysia, and Indonesia's Sumatra Island. The aim of the IMT-GT is to maximize the utilization of resources and emphasize the development of agriculture, fisheries, livestock, forestry, agro-food processing, and tourism amongst the three countries. Additionally, the countries compete with one another in the production and export of palm oil and rubber products and in the tourism industry, as well as in the export of lower skilled manufactured goods and in auto parts.

Our modest goal in this chapter is to provide an overview of the evolution of human resource management (HRM) systems in the three countries, while spotlighting firm-level HRM practices in each country. We do not claim to provide a comprehensive survey of HRM practices across establishments in these countries. We rely primarily on prior literature to draw out distinctively national features and issues in HRM. The next section provides a brief history and basic data about the three countries (see Table 18.1). Section Three focuses on employment relations and cultural contexts (primarily according to Hofstede's dimensions), while Section Four discusses the evolution of HRM systems. Section Five highlights some firm-level HRM practices in those countries. We pay attention to dominant HRM practices, including recruitment and selection, training and development, and pay and reward practices in this section. Section Six focuses on changes in the role of the HR function, whereas Section Seven discusses trends in strategic HRM and some new HRM practices. Finally, Section Eight concludes the chapter by highlighting some likely future challenges in HRM and their implications for the three countries.

Table 18.1 Indonesia, Malaysia, and Thailand's economies at a glance

Indicators	Indonesia		Malaysia		Thailand	
	2000	2014	2000	2014	2000	2014
Population (million)[1]	208.94	252.81	23.49	30.26	62.34	67.22
Labor Force (million)[2]	98.83	122.13 (in 2013)	9.81	13.04 (in 2013)	34.70	39.87 (in 2013)
GDP, PPP (current billion international dollars)[3]	973.48	2,676.11	291.36	746.09	441.72	985.53
GDP per capita, PPP (current international dollars)[4]	4,601.8	10.517.0	12,440.1	24,951.1	7,045.7	14,551.7
GDP by sector[5]						
Agriculture	15.6%	13.7%	8.6%	9.1%	9.0%	11.6%
Industry	45.9%	42.9%	48.3%	40.5%	42.0%	42.0%
Services	38.5%	43.3%	43.1%	50.4%	49.0%	46.3%
Unemployment (% of total labor force) (modeled ILO estimate)[6]	6.1%	6.3% (in 2013)	3.0%	3.2% (in 2013)	2.4%	0.7% (in 2013)
Inflation, Consumer Prices (annual %)[7]	3.7%	6.4%	1.5%	3.1%	1.6%	1.9%
Trade Union Density (% of total employment)	–	14.0% (in 2005)[8]	–	7.6% (in 2007)[9]	–	1.4% (in 2007)[9]
Collective Bargaining Coverage (% of total employment)[10]	–	4.0% (in 2005)	–	1.8% (in 2007)*	–	1.4% (in 2007)

Sources: 1 Worldometers (2015) and IndexMundi (2015); 2–5 World Bank (2015); 6–7 World Bank (2015); 8 Hall-Jones (2007); and 9–10 Hayter and Stoevska (2011).

Note

* Todd and Peetz (2001) noted that the collective bargaining coverage rate in Malaysia during 1994–1996 was approximately 6%.

Background and history

Indonesia

Indonesia is the fourth-most populous country in the world, after China, India, and the USA, with approximately 259.9 million people in the year 2016. The size of the labor force is approximately 124.1 million (World Bank, 2016). Consisting of approximately 17,508 islands and islets, it has the world's largest population of Muslims, although it is not officially an Islamic state. The primary language is Bahasa Indonesia, but there are 250 other regional languages and dialects (Bishop & McNamara, 1997). The government officially recognizes six religions: Islam, Protestantism, Roman Catholicism, Hinduism, Buddhism, and Confucianism (Thorat, 2013). The country has more than 300 ethnic groups, all of which have distinct cultural traditions that have been developed over centuries and that have been influenced by Arabic, Chinese, Malay, and European sources. Indonesia is thus a country with enormous diversity and faces a variety of HRM challenges. Until recently, Indonesia was one of the least addressed countries in the business and HRM literatures (Bennington & Habir, 2003; Chandrakumara, 2013; Rhodes, Walsh, & Lok, 2008).

The Indonesian economy grew rapidly before the Asian economic crisis of 1997. Its gross domestic product (GDP) growth during the period of 1985–1996 exceeded 7 percent per year (Munandar, 2003). The reasons for this rapid economic growth included both political and economic stability and continued deregulation efforts to foster investment activities (Munandar, 2003; Prijadi & Rachmawati, 2002). After the 1997 Asian economic crisis, economic growth slowed, and unemployment increased (Munandar, 2003; Wengel & Rodriguez, 2006). Nevertheless, unlike several more export-dependent neighboring countries, Indonesia attempted to avoid recession by stimulating domestic demand and implementing a government fiscal stimulus package (Thorat, 2013). During the 1997 crisis, Indonesia transformed from an authoritarian regime dominated by a powerful presidency to a fledgling democracy with an intention to recover from the excesses of the Soeharto government (Emmerson, 1999). The year 1998 was considered to mark the end of Soeharto's "new order" era and the beginning of the period of reformation. Bacharuddin Jusuf Habibie, who served as president of Indonesia after the fall of Soeharto, moved the country onto a more liberal trajectory, repealing restrictive press laws, permitting the creation of new media, releasing political prisoners, allowing the foundation of new political parties, and preventing the military from playing political roles (Emmerson, 1999; Kim & Haque, 2002; Liddle, 2000; Hill & Shiraishi, 2007). A more democratic environment has arisen in Indonesia since this change of regime, as successive Indonesian presidents (Abdurrahman Wahid, Megawati Soekarnoputri, Susilo Bambang Yudhoyono, and Joko Widodo) have been elected democratically.

Malaysia

Malaysia is a pluralistic, multi-ethnic, multi-religious, and multicultural society. Its population in the year 2016 was 30.6 million, with 75.5 percent of the total population living in urban areas (Worldometers, 2016a). The size of its labor force is approximately 13.3 million (World Bank, 2016). Malaysia is a federal democratic state with a constitutional monarchy. It consists of thirteen large states and three different federal territories. Geographically, Malaysia is divided into two parts: Peninsular Malaysia and East Malaysia, comprising the northern part of Borneo. The two parts are separated by the South China Sea. Of the total population, more than 60 percent are Malays called "Bumiputra or sons of the soil." The remaining population is varied but the largest ethnic groups are Chinese and Indian. In this regard, British colonial capitalist activities and expansion played a crucial role in the social formation of the population of Malaysia. For instance, rubber cultivation and tin mining during the colonial era relied on labor imported from China and India, while the Malays were not incorporated into these colonial activities (Abdul-Rahman & Rowley, 2008). This issue has implications for the role of the state and HRM challenges in Malaysia (Abdul-Rahman & Rowley, 2008). In terms of religion, Islam is the official religion of the country because Malays, who are the majority group, are Muslims. The Chinese are mostly Buddhists, and the Indians are mostly Hindus.

In the 1960s, British colonial expansion also influenced the economic and political context in Malaysia. During this period, the Chinese had greater economic power than the Malays because the transformation of economy along the path of capitalism excluded most Malays from participation in the modern economy, as they were mostly farmers. The Chinese were active in business and commerce in urban areas, while the Indians primarily served as the wage labor in rubber and oil palm cultivation, leading to the unequal development of these ethnicities (Abdul-Rahman & Rowley, 2008). Subsequently, the government attempted to restructure society by promoting the participation of Malays in economic activities via affirmative action policies. The New Economic Policy (NEP) was implemented during the period of 1971–1990 to achieve this goal (Malaysia, 1971). The NEP attempted to improve the economic circumstances of Malays through various means, including policies providing preferential employment and preferential educational policies for Malays, and through reservation of ownership in companies (Malays must hold at least 30 percent of stock in private companies) (Policy Brief 13, 2006).

In 1982, the government attempted to imitate factors that contributed to the success of the Japanese economy by implementing the "Look East" policy (for further details, see Section Three). These factors included discipline, patriotism, and a strong work ethics (Abdul-Rahman & Rowley, 2008). During the period of 1980–1990, coinciding with this policy, Malaysia thus experienced its most rapid rate of progress and development. Subsequently, in 1990, Malaysia launched Vision 2020, a long-term plan for the country's further development, with an attempt to achieve two main goals: modernizing the country to achieve self-sufficient developed country status by 2020 and developing the country along several dimensions including economic, political, social, spiritual, psychological, and cultural (Abdul-Rahman & Rowley, 2008). To achieve Vision 2020 in the next three to four years, however, Malaysia still needs to overcome several challenges such as establishing a scientific and progressive society and creating a psychologically liberated, secure, and developed Malaysian society.

Thailand

The total population of Thailand in 2016 was approximately 68.1 million (Worldometers, 2016b). The size of the labor force was approximately 40.1 million (World Bank, 2016). The country consists of seventy-seven provinces. The Thai population is rather homogeneous, most of the Thai people are ethnic Thais and Sino-Thais (progeny of ethnic Thais married to Chinese-Thais) (Lawler & Suttawet, 2000). The intermarriage between Thais and Chinese is quite unlike the case of Malaysia and Indonesia, where the Chinese and local populations have remained separate. Other ethnic groups in Thailand include Indians, Muslims (mainly in the southern part of the country), and members of various hill tribes in the northern part of Thailand, along with immigrants, particularly from Myanmar and Cambodia. However, these groups of people play a rather limited role in Thai society (Lawler & Atmiyanandana, 2003).

Unlike Malaysia and Indonesia, Thailand was never quite colonized, although there was a period of Japanese occupation during the war. Thailand reached a turning point in 1932, when it changed from an 800-year-old absolute monarchy to a constitutional monarchy (Gullaprawit, 2002). It then changed its name from "Siam" to "Thailand." However, since the change in regime, military dictators have ruled Thailand for much of the time.

Thailand had a predominantly agricultural economy for many years. However, it became more involved in trade, business, and economic and industrial development after World War II. Thailand enjoyed very high rates of economic growth from the late 1980s through to 1997. The average economic growth rate during the period of 1960–1990 was approximately 7.5 percent, the highest rate amongst developing countries (Akrasanee, Dapice, & Flatters, 1991). The optimism surrounding Thailand's economy, however, drastically changed for the worse in 1997. The financial and economic crisis that began in July 1997 resulted from the fact that capital inflows (in the form of short-term loans from foreign countries) following financial deregulation and liberalization had a substantial impact on Thailand's economy (Chiengkul, Kamoltrakul, Prasertchareonsuk, & Leelawattanun, 1998). Currently, Thailand has fallen into the middle-income trap, with low economic and productivity growth, low rates of research and development (R&D) investment, and innovation. Total productivity growth in Thailand between 1990 and 2008 was only 0.7 percent, which is much lower than that in China (4.7 percent), South Korea (1.6 percent), and Taiwan (1.3 percent) (Asian Productivity Organization, 2011). Additionally, relatively low rates of economic growth (3–5 percent per year) during the past decade have done little to improve the well-being of the majority of Thais.

Employment relations and cultural contexts

Indonesia

Globalization has led to an open trade and investment regime and an outward/export orientation in countries in Southeast Asia, including Indonesia. It has also led to greater state intervention in Indonesia (Narjoko & Putra, 2015). In broad terms, the employment relations context in Indonesia has long been dominated by politico-bureaucrats and corporate executives. Specifically, the government pursued a policy of deregulation and opened up several sectors to facilitate massive inflows of foreign direct investment (FDI). To provide foreign capital with workplace flexibility, unions have been suppressed, and the establishment of labor unions, except those sanctioned by the state, has been prohibited (Caraway, 2004; Hadiz, 1997; Manning, 1993). According to Lange, the new Indonesian manpower law (Law No. 13/2003):

> legalized outsourcing, specific time contract, restricted the right to strike to specific types of labor disputes, and gave authority to employers to terminate their workers for the alleged commission of a crime without the need to await a binding criminal conviction to be handed down by the relevant court of law.
>
> *(Lange, 2010: 34)*

The Indonesian parliament passed the new manpower law in 2003 to balance the protection of worker rights and the concerns of private companies regarding their competitiveness in the era of globalization (van der Eng, 2004). Manning and Roesad (2007: 65) noted that the provisions of this new manpower law have led to important changes in employment relations with respect to hiring and firing, contractual employment, and minimum wage setting.

While it is always hazardous to attempt to characterize a country's culture, we provide a brief description below to be consistent with the other chapters in this volume, and to be consistent with the literature on HRM. According to Habir and Rajendran (2008) and Hofstede (1983),

Indonesian culture can be characterized as follows. The relationship between employers and employees in Indonesia is recognized as moral rather than calculative. This implies mutual agreement between employers who need to protect their employees and employees who need to be loyal to their employers. In Indonesia, relationships take priority over tasks. Although its society has been described as paternalism with status-oriented relationships, there has been some evidence to support the notion that such cultural dimensions have eroded over time and that more strategic- and performance-oriented relationships have gradually replaced the former system (Thorat, 2013).

Malaysia

Unsurprisingly, employment relations in Malaysia represent a hybrid of institutions inherited from the colonial era and those that emerged from the period of the developmental state during the 1980s (Carney & Andriesse, 2014). Centralized trade unions emerged in Malaysia after World War II and reflected efforts by the colonial authorities to install a British-style reformist labor movement, consisting of institutions rather similar to the British Labor Party's industrial unions (Wad, 2001) and legislation providing for collective bargaining and minimum standards, with a focus on containing conflict to support the promotion of national economic development (Kuruvilla & Arudsothy, 1995; Kuruvilla, 1996a). Later, as part of the "Look East" policy in the 1980s, the government introduced a Japanese-style model of enterprise unions in Malaysia because it believed that this Japanese approach would foster loyalty amongst employees to their firms and promote productivity-oriented employee relations. The low-cost labor intensive export-oriented model coincided with some degree of suppression of union rights in Malaysia (Kuruvilla, 1996a), but the transition to a more advanced export-oriented industrialization (EOI) strategy resulted in employment relations policies to improve workplace flexibility, the importation of guest workers to alleviate labor shortages, and training and development designed to foster a better quality workforce. Since the 1990s, the government has thus attempted to accomplish two main goals: furnishing foreign investors with a peaceful and cooperative employment relations climate; and enhancing its legitimacy as a champion of ethnic Malays' rights and opportunities amongst the majority of people in Malaysia (Bumiputra) (Rasiah, Crinis, & Lee, 2015; Carney & Andriesse, 2014; Kuruvilla, 1996a; Frenkel & Kuruvilla, 2002).

Malaysian cultures should be understood as a mixture of local Confucian, Islamic, and Western values (Mansor & Ali, 1998). As noted by Noordin, Williams, and Zimmer (2002), Malaysia is a collectivistic society. Thus, self-sacrifice, social relations, and family integrity are quite strong. Hofstede (1991) and Mellahi and Wood (2004) also classified Malaysia as a country with high power distance, strong uncertainty avoidance, and low individualism. These cultural dimensions can be exemplified from the fact that most junior employees are less willing to make decisions without reference to the most senior executives in their firms. Additionally, Mellahi and Wood (2004) noted that Malaysian cultures, similar to many Asian cultures, place a strong emphasis on maintaining face and on obedience to leaders. Moreover, humility, courtesy, non-assertiveness and compliance, tactfulness, harmony, and avoidance of conflicts are emphasized in Malaysian cultures. Mellahi and Wood (2004) also differentiate between Malaysian cultures and Chinese Malaysian cultures, in that the former exhibit stronger entrepreneurial drive.

Thailand

Because Thailand was never colonized and its institutional domains have primarily been dominated by business elites, employment relations in Thailand are characterized by weak and fragmented institutions (Frenkel & Yu, 2014). Most employment protections in the country are attributable to customary values and norms. In particular, labor unions have played a less important role in the Thai employment relations system. The shift in the country's economic development from an import substitution industrialization (ISI) to an EOI strategy did not allow unions to play a role in labor processes during the wave of globalization. The labor regime under an EOI strategy can be characterized by 3Ls, that is, low wages, long working hours, and low productivity (Mounier & Charoenloet, 2010). Further liberalization of the economy in the 1990s attracted competitive pressures from other countries such as Bangladesh and Cambodia, especially in the textile and clothing industry. Many firms in Thailand have begun to reduce production costs by increasingly relying on contract workers or outsourcing work to home-workers. This so-called "putting-out" system has forced homeworkers to be exposed to precarious work and has reduced the bargaining power of labor unions (Charoenloet, 2015), aggravating the weakness and fragmentation of labor unions in employment relations contexts. In this regard, it is not surprising that most private sector workers are not unionized due to the highly paternalistic labor–management relations existing in these companies, the difficulties associated with unionizing workers in the era of globalization, and the limited size of Thai companies; the number of micro-companies or companies employing 1–20 workers in Thailand is approximately 319,000, accounting for approximately 1,650,000 workers as of July 6, 2010, and labor unions cannot be established within these companies. Unsurprisingly, the rate of unionization in Thailand remains very low (Napathorn & Chanprateep, 2011). Napathorn and Chanprateep (2011: 68) found that less than 5 percent of workers in Thailand are members of labor unions. Additionally, Thailand's employment relations system is highly fragmented because there are too many labor federations and councils that have diluted the capacity of trade unions to effectively mobilize support to organize workers in Thailand (Charoenloet, 2015). Napathorn and Chanprateep (2011) found that the fragmentation and lack of solidarity amongst Thai laborers, the labor movement, and labor organizations have been persistent.

In terms of culture, Buddhism plays an important role in shaping cultural dimensions in Thailand. Approximately 95 percent of the population belongs to this religion (Lawler & Atmiyanandana, 2003). Theravada Buddhism encourages Thai people to believe in passive and contemplative ways of coping with life events or challenges (Siengthai & Vadhanasindhu, 1991). This religious practice is one of the reasons that Thai people are passive and unambitious in asserting their rights. They attempt to avoid conflicts with others if possible. Thai people focus on values and attitudes such as *Mai Pen Rai* (never mind), *Jai Yen Yen* (take it easy), *Kreng Jai* (be self-effacing, respectful, humble, and extremely considerate), and *Boon Khun* (reciprocity). These values and attitudes tend to favor patron–client relationships within the workplace (Siengthai, Tanlamai, & Rowley, 2008). Another important Thai value is *Sa Nuk* (fun) (Lawler & Atmiyanandana, 2003). Thai people do not accept the value of high levels of stress at work. Instead, they believe that fun should be a part of their life and work. Thus, it is the responsibility of employees to incorporate "fun" into employees' working life. Thailand also ranks "high" in the power-distance dimension (Hofstede, 1980). That is, Thai people accept the imbalance of power and authority between groups of people within their society. For instance, employees are willing to defer their employers and tend to avoid conflict. Thai employees do not express their true opinions, if they contradict those of their employers.

Evolution of the HRM system

Indonesia

Historically, HRM did not play a crucial role in management in Indonesia. It has not been regarded as a high-status field. Companies typically have viewed HRM as an administrative function (Thorat, 2013). Although there have been some changes in recent years such as in departments' names, for instance, from the personnel management (PM) department to the HRM department, especially in state-owned enterprises (Sitalaksmi & Zhu, 2010), HRM departments have not been considered of equal status to other management functions such as finance or marketing (Rowley & Abdul-Rahman, 2008). The main duties and responsibilities of the HRM department are "keeping records, complying with regulations, processing pay, leave, and training, and organizing company gatherings and outings" (Rowley & Abdul-Rahman, 2008: 21). HRM departments have been unable to solve problems related to gender-, ethnicity-, and race-based discrimination in the workplace. These problems persist in Indonesia. However, Rowley and Warner (2010) and Sitalaksmi and Zhu (2010) argue that the HRM practices, especially in state-owned enterprises, have, to some extent, shifted toward "best practices" and a market-oriented approach due to transformation initiatives to survive in the global era. In this regard, Indonesian firms' HRM practices should probably be understood as a hybrid model (Zhu, Warner, & Rowley, 2007), which means that the HRM practices incorporate both traditional PM activities and market-based or competency-based HRM activities. Nevertheless, as approximately 70 percent of Indonesian workers are employed in the informal sector, there may be limits to how typical and prevalent any HRM practices could be regarded (Habir & Rajendran, 2008).

Malaysia

Since the late 1980s, managers have increasingly employed the term "HRM" instead of "personnel management (PM)" because of the introduction of the new economic model and the move from "labor-intensive, primary commodity and agro-based sectors toward more capital-intensive, manufacturing, hi-tech, and service sectors" (Rowley & Abdul-Rahman, 2008: 21–22). Todd and Peetz (2001) found evidence of the increasing strategic integration of HRM with other management functions. Additionally, Zhu, Warner, and Rowley (2007) noted that more "hard" HRM policies and practices, such as retrenchment and individual performance-oriented pay and promotion, have been adopted by the majority of firms since the 1997 Asian financial crisis, reflecting the move toward internationally standardized HRM practices. HRM has, thus, played an increasingly important role in transforming the Malaysian work culture from "one of some complacency to one of greater competitiveness" (Abdul-Rahman & Rowley, 2008: 60). Indeed, the importance of HRM in both national development and within firms is evinced in the renaming of the Ministry of Labor to the Ministry of Human Resources in 1990 (Abdul Malek, Varma, & Budhwar, 2014). This ministry is primarily responsible for every aspect related to human resources and the production of an adequately skilled, knowledgeable workforce, including the development of formal human resource development (HRD) policies and skills development policies. In this regard, the Ministry of Human Resources attempted to foster the training and multi-skilling of the workforce in the 1990s (Todd & Peetz, 2001). Although the government spent a large share of its budget on skills development according to the Ninth Malaysia Plan (2006–2010), Malaysia faces various HRM challenges, including a chronic shortage of skilled labor (Carney & Andriesse, 2014) and skills mismatches (World Bank, 2009).

Thailand

Rowley and Abdul-Rahman (2008), Siengthai, Tanlamai, and Rowley (2008), and Siengthai (2014) noted that most firms were familiar only with traditional PM until the 1990s. Since then, and particularly after the financial crisis in 1997, business operations began to change. The influx of FDI from multinational corporations (MNCs) and joint ventures during the wave of globalization, the availability of advanced information and communication technologies, and the shift away from labor-intensive industries in economic development led to the spread of modern HRM practices. However, ownership structure plays an important role in differentiating HRM practices across firms in this country (Lawler & Atmiyanandana, 1995; Lawler, Jain, Ratnam, & Atmiyanandana, 1995; Lawler, Siengthai, & Atmiyanandana, 1997; Lawler & Siengthai, 1997). Studies on this subject classify the ownership structures of firms into four different types (i.e., Thai family enterprises, publicly owned Thai corporations, Western MNCs, and Japanese MNCs) and use these four classifications to understand the different HRM practices of each type of firm. Siengthai and Bechter (2005) reported that the majority of firms have not yet developed their HR functions into the firms' "strategic partner," closest to the idea of strategic HRM or the progressive HRM model proposed by Kamoche (2000). However, as globalization becomes increasingly significant in the twenty-first century, the development of HRM as a strategic partner in large organizations must finally be realized.

Firm-level HRM practices

At the outset, we would like to highlight that there has yet to be any systematic study of HRM practices in all of the three countries that would allow us to make generalizations about the state of HRM in each country. Consequently, we are dependent on limited prior literature in our examination of HRM in these countries.

Indonesia

Recruitment and selection. Challenges in recruiting employees include high attrition rates amongst employees due to low levels of loyalty, the poaching of high-skilled employees, shortages of quality employees in marketing, finance, and IT functions due to the low quality of education and training, and workplace discrimination in terms of age, gender, and disability (Thorat, 2013). Firms have employed multiple recruitment methods such as word-of-mouth, print advertisements, newspapers, magazines, recruitment consultants, and the Internet (Habir & Rajendran, 2008). Companies utilize advertisements in newspapers only when they realize that doing so is worth the cost because advertising in newspapers is very expensive (Bennington & Habir, 2003). Chandrakumara (2013) noted that word-of-mouth is the most common method for recruiting blue-collar workers. Typically, the recruitment process for blue-collar workers is less complicated than that for white-collar workers because the supply of blue-collar labor exceeds demand (Prijadi & Rachmawati, 2002; Rachmi, 2013). Regarding personnel selection, most large organizations, especially in the private sector, have employed several selection tools, including behavioral interviews, assessment centers, knowledge tests, and motivational fit inventories. Behavioral interviews are considered a common selection tool amongst firms (Habir & Rajendran, 2008). Some large organizations have established their own assessment centers to determine the potential of employees who are due for promotion. These centers, however, have primarily been employed to select candidates for senior positions because such assessment is costly. One of the unique features of recruitment and selection practices in Indonesia is that personnel selection is typically based on the following qualifications: age (the most important consideration), educational background, gender, marital status, personal appearance, aptitude, temperament, character, work experience, skills, and training (the least important consideration) (Bennington & Habir, 2003; Lange, 2010). The main argument here is that age can influence workers' psychological and mental ability and workers' responsibilities.

Training and development. Training and development practices in various Indonesian companies differ, depending on a variety of factors (Soetjipto, Sadeli, & Nayaputera, 2012). For instance, at the industry level, all banks must allocate a percentage of their budget to training employees. At the firm level, however, training initiatives depend on factors such as the company's financial status, its leaders, and the strategic position of its HRM department. Nevertheless, in large domestic organizations and MNCs in Indonesia, training is conducted by internal bodies and is well planned, from needs-based analysis, training design, and training execution, to post-training evaluation, to ensure a strong quality-oriented culture for their staff (Habir & Larasati, 1999; Rachmi, 2013). By contrast, state-owned enterprises are more likely to implement regular training activities intended to foster the culture of government (Sutiyono, 2007). When conducting trainings to foster new employee behaviors, few Indonesian organizations use competency assessments and performance appraisals to monitor the development of such behaviors. Moreover, several organizations have generally conducted training without a stated purpose or plan (Habir & Rajendran, 2008; Rachmi, 2013). Training, particularly external training, has been viewed as a type of reward for employees rather than as a means of developing employees according to needs-based analysis (Chandrakumara, 2013). Additionally, on-boarding programs to socialize new recruits to the organizational context are considered the most neglected area of HRM (Habir & Rajendran, 2008). Most organizations offer such programs; however, they are more likely to be ritualistic rather than programs intended to help those new recruits to be successful in the organizations over the long run. Finally, firm-level training programs are highly influenced by economic turbulence (Thorat, 2013). For instance, when inflation is high and consumers' purchasing power declines, Indonesian companies' training programs are typically reduced or removed from the list of HRM practices to save operating costs.

Characteristics of pay and reward practices. In general, the compensation structure of large firms in Indonesia consists of basic pay (basic wages, which are usually linked to regional minimum wages, allowances for family responsibilities, and allowances for the length of service), variable allowances (e.g., meal allowances, transportation allowances, health allowances, performance bonuses, shift work allowances, coffee allowances, weekday overtime, and holiday overtime), deductions (*Jamsostek* [social security]), income taxes, and union dues), and benefits (e.g., medical reimbursements for outpatient medical care) (Lange, 2010). Legally, there is a minimum wage policy in Indonesia. In practice, however, minimum wages vary across regions. Some scholars have argued that minimum wages have been set at a level insufficient to cover the "minimum physical needs for a single person," and the amount is lower than that in other neighboring countries, such as Thailand (Bennington, 2001; Habir & Rajendran, 2008). Additionally, there are extreme and obvious differences between the lowest- and highest-paid employees. Chandrakumara (2013) noted that those differences range from $1:7$ in the public sector (Rohdewohld, 1995; Bennington & Habir, 2003) to $1:20-1:150$ in the private sector (Bennington & Habir, 2003). Moreover, pay levels differ between men and women, despite the fact that the constitution states that women are equal to men with regard to rights, obligations, and opportunities (Habir & Rajendran, 2008; Lange, 2010). Women in the manufacturing sector still receive lower wages than men, and they are often hired as day laborers instead of full-time, permanent employees. One of the unique features of the pay and reward system in

Indonesia is the common "thirteenth-month" pay. This type of pay is "the sum of basic pay and fixed allowances" and is typically paid out to all employees on either Idul Fitri or during the Christmas holidays (Habir & Rajendran, 2008: 41).

Malaysia

Recruitment and selection. Recruitment and selection practices are generally standardized. Most firms prefer to use external recruitment (Abdul-Rahman & Rowley, 2008). Newspaper advertisements seem to be the most popular recruitment method for recruiting employees at all levels, according to Chew (2005). Other recruitment methods are also employed, such as web-based recruitment agencies, employee referrals, personal applications, and to a lesser extent, direct recruitment from universities or schools. Malaysia has had a labor shortage since the 1980s, hence making recruitment a competitive activity. Regarding selection, it is unsurprising that firms typically recruit mid-career employees who are immediately able to perform specialized duties. This is consistent with the concept of external recruitment mentioned above. Abdul-Rahman and Rowley (2008) noted that selection processes consist of two main stages: analysis of curriculum vitae (the shortlisting process) and interviews (Abdul Ghani Azmi, 2015). Abdul Ghani Azmi (2015) proposed that the main criteria for selecting Muslim workers, who constitute the majority of the population in Malaysia, are piety and competence in terms of qualifications, skills, and experience. Additionally, proficiency in speaking and writing English is important for administrative and managerial jobs. Chew (2005) noted that one of the main selection criteria for foreign-owned MNCs is person and organization fit, while that for locally owned firms is person and job fit. One of the unique features of recruitment and selection practices in Malaysia is the role of ethnicity. Although some large firms have attempted to recruit graduates directly from universities, managers often turn to specific ethnic groups when they attempt to fill certain positions. In particular, Chinese are preferred for supervisory positions, and people from the countryside are preferred when recruiting production workers (Mellahi & Wood, 2004; Abdul-Rahman & Rowley, 2008), and the Malaysian affirmative action program described above also requires affirmative action for Malay citizens. In state-owned banks, for instance, ethnic Malays (Bumiputra) are more desirable due to the affirmative action policies, whereas in privately owned banks, Chinese employees are more favored.[1]

Training and development. Malaysia aims to become a developed nation by the end of 2020 (Abdul Malek et al., 2014). Training and development practices have become significant tools to contribute to achieving this objective. However, it is well known that Malaysia has faced a problem regarding the growing mismatches between the supply of workers' skills and the requirements of various industries (Carney & Andriesse, 2014). The Malaysian government has recognized the importance of this problem and has attempted to invest considerable funds in increasing the appreciation for vocational/technical education by establishing ten skills-training institutes and upgrading sixteen existing institutes under the Ninth Malaysia Plan (Abdul Malek et al., 2014: 196). The number of trainees who have attended vocational/technical colleges has increased, however, the number of graduates has decreased, and this problem needs to be solved as quickly as possible. Additionally, to encourage the private sector to devote greater attention to training and development practices, the Human Resource Development Act of 1992 requires that organizations employing more than fifty employees must contribute at least 1 percent of their monthly wage bill to training (Abdul Malek et al., 2014; Abdul-Rahman & Rowley, 2008). Only registered employers have received training assistance. This initiative was initially promoted only for firms in the manufacturing sector, but it was subsequently expanded to the service sector, including banks. In several MNCs, such as Panasonic and Nestlé, corporate universities have been established to provide in-house training programs and develop employees internally. In general, training in Malaysia focuses on four main areas: management training, functional training, engineering and operations management training, and e-learning programs (Wan, 2006; Abdul-Rahman & Rowley, 2008). At the firm level, on-the-job training and multi-skilling are primarily conducted to upgrade existing employees and their skills (Abdul Malek et al., 2014; Kuruvilla, 1996b; Zhu et al., 2007). Jantan and Honeycutt Jr. (2013) noted that sales training has become more important in the banking industry in Malaysia to support the growth of new financial products in this industry. Chew (2005) also proposed that training in foreign-owned MNCs is typically beyond the scope of the current job, while training in locally owned firms is primarily job specific. Finally, according to Abdul Ghani Azmi (2015), the training and development of Muslim workers should pay attention to both physical training (e.g., training workers to be more competent in their work) and spiritual training (e.g., understanding the wisdom of Allah). The latter training is more important than the former in that the latter might influence behavior during the former training.

Characteristics of pay and reward practices. In general, the basic compensation structure is composed of a basic salary, allowances, and bonuses and is quite simple (Abdul-Rahman & Rowley, 2008). Occupation-level wages, annual salary increases, and contractual bonuses represent the majority of compensation. Performance-related bonuses are also included in pay packages (Todd & Peetz, 2001; Chew, 2005), although to a lesser extent. Annual salary increases depend on the length of service and individual performance. Allowances are primarily job related and variable and cover expenses such as housing, transportation, overtime, night shifts, and entertainment. Wan (2008) argued that the current compensation system in the private sector is too rigid and does not reward productivity gains. Rather, the system places greater emphasis on seniority. Additionally, the system does not foster reward differentiation between high and poor performers (the so-called kopi-gang culture), leading to the resignation of star performers instead of poor performers (Hay Group, 2010). One of the unique features of the pay and reward system in Malaysia is a recent and radical change in the minimum wage policy. The minimum wage law was announced on May 1, 2012. The poverty line is set at RM740; thus, the National Wage Advisory Council stated that the minimum wage should be higher than this amount (Abdul Malek et al., 2014). Starting salaries in Malaysia have typically been fixed at RM800 and RM900. Some have argued that the minimum wage should be higher than RM1,200. Studies by the World Bank and others, however, have noted that this amount is likely to be too high and may impact the Malaysian economy as a whole by increasing the risks of inflation, reducing competitiveness, and increasing unemployment.

Thailand

Recruitment and selection. For publicly owned Thai corporations (some of which originated from Thai family enterprises and are now managed and controlled by the founders and their families), campus recruitment, walk-in applications, employee referrals, and newspaper advertisements are the most popular recruitment methods. In terms of selection methods, an interview is the most frequently used approach to screen applicants (Siengthai, Dechawattana-paisal, & Wailerdsak, 2009). Both HRM and line managers are involved in the selection processes. Prominent companies, such as banks, rarely have any difficulty in recruiting high-profile applicants (Lawler & Siengthai, 1997). Currently, most companies engage in e-recruiting as an efficient way to recruit applicants in this age of information technology (Siengthai, 2014). Recruitment and selection methods employed by firms in the manufacturing and service sectors do not differ significantly. In Western MNCs, the recruitment of skilled employees from the external labor market is preferable (Lawler et al., 1997). Siengthai, Tanlamai, and Rowley (2008) noted that US and European MNCs use outside recruitment services more frequently than Thai companies do. For Japanese companies, recruiting from within the internal labor market is both preferable and typical. In Australian firms, the recruitment of Australian expatriates who wish to relocate to Thailand involves an interview and other types of assessment of the applicants' spouses, as these firms believe that the spouse plays an important role in the success of expatriates in Thailand (Clegg & Gray, 2002; Siengthai et al., 2008). One of the notable features of the recruitment and selection practices in Thailand is that familism, nepotism, and/ or favoritism still play a role (Roongrerngsuke, 2010). Specifically, familism influences the recruitment and selection practices of many local businesses and some MNCs that originate in Thailand such as the Charoen Pokphand Group (Roongrerngsuke, 2010). A personal relationship is important for Thai family enterprises in the recruitment and selection of employees. This process is known in Thai as "*Mee Sen*" (to have connections with firms) (Lawler et al., 1997). Such an approach is usually not a significant problem because the employee turnover rate is low (Siengthai & Bechter, 2004). Roongrerngsuke (2010) noted that nepotism and/or favoritism still play a role, albeit to a lesser extent than in the past, in recruiting and selecting employees. Because the final decisions to hire employees are made by particular employees, it is unavoidable that employees will be hired based on social networks or personal relationships, not on the results of employment tests.

Training and development. New employees are usually obliged to attend the company's orientation program (Lawler & Siengthai, 1997; Siengthai et al., 2009). Most companies expect new employees to be acculturated into their new work environment through on-the-job training. Only employees at the supervisory level or above participate in formal training programs offered by companies (Siengthai et al., 2008). In a positive development, most firms now invest more in training and developing human capital than they did previously (Siengthai et al., 2009). Catalysts for this development may be globalization and increasing competition within the market. However, in Thai family enterprises that do not have formal HR functions, training programs are problematic because they incur a cost while offering what may be seen as uncertain future benefits. Siengthai, Dechawattanapaisal, and Wailerdsak (2009) found that many large and high-profile organizations have their own training centers and provide training programs for their employees; one such example is the Panyapiwat Institute of Management (PIM) managed by the Charoen Pokphand Group (Suehiro & Yabushita, 2014). Some organizations prepare their high-potential employees by providing in-house executive development training programs, offering scholarships to those employees to study abroad (Yabushita & Suehiro, 2014), or, at times, sending these employees abroad for short-term training programs. However, since the financial crisis, most large organizations have relied on in-house training programs and on-the-job training to reduce training expenses (Siengthai et al., 2009). During the financial crisis, tactics such as job rotation and redeployment of the workforce were also utilized. Lay-offs were treated as a last resort for most companies during that time. Thai firms in the manufacturing and service sectors differ somewhat with respect to training and development activities. Most firms in the manufacturing sector have both short-term and long-term training programs for employees, but those in the service sector provide only short-term training programs for their employees (Rowley & Abdul-Rahman, 2008). In the banking sector, some banks provide a "mini MBA" program for their employees (Lawler & Siengthai, 1997), particularly for managerial employees. This program is usually run jointly between renowned university business schools and the banks. These programs may require approximately 300 hours of intensive training before issuing the students university certificates. Overall, a variety of management development programs have become more available and widespread in Thailand (Siengthai, 2014).

Characteristics of pay and reward practices. Siengthai, Dechawattanapaisal, and Wailerdsak (2009) found that most private firms pay market rates to remain competitive. Those firms' compensation levels tend to be proportional to the minimum wage levels. Previously, the minimum wage varied across regions, but the highest rate was in Bangkok (Lawler & Suttawet, 2000). The new nationwide minimum wage of 300 Baht was introduced by the previous government, which was led by a female prime minister (Siengthai, 2014). Employers are expected to implement more highly automated technologies in the workplace, outsource work to homeworkers, or invest more in training their existing employees. Currently, the Ministry of Labor is in the process of conducting a feasibility study of a floating wage system, however, the minimum wage is still fixed at 300 Baht (Dailynews, 2015). Thai companies also offer bonuses and other incentives, such as diligence allowances, complimentary lunches, compensated travel expenses, profit sharing, and employment tenure awards. Pay in this country has increasingly become performance-based (Siengthai et al., 2008), although some Japanese companies continue to apply seniority-based pay. Many firms, including airlines and banks, incorporated "broad-banding" into the pay system and used job evaluations according to the Hay system to retain equity within the firms after re-engineering their business processes in the wake of the financial crisis. Some public and private enterprises are now applying the "balanced scorecard" concept to the pay system (Siengthai et al., 2009). Most organizations provide welfare and benefits, although some pay only the minimum required by law. Compensation systems do not differ significantly between Thai companies and MNCs (Kongchan, 2001; Siengthai et al., 2008). Companies in both the manufacturing and service sectors tend to offer compensation on an individual basis (not a group basis). Generally, Western MNCs tend to provide higher salaries than Thai companies and Japanese MNCs, making them more attractive to job seekers (Siengthai, 2014). Japanese MNCs have long provided less compensation than other types of firms, but they offer greater job security (Lawler et al., 1997). Finally, Thai people commonly believe that while the public sector offers lower salaries than the private sector, the welfare and benefits it provides are much better than those in the private sector, including such benefits as healthcare expense reimbursement.

Changes in the role of the HR function

Indonesia

Mamman and Somantri (2014) analyzed the roles of HR function in a very large state-owned organization spread across Indonesia and concluded that the HR function in Indonesia has been changing toward a more strategic focus. Specifically, HRM practitioners typically play a facilitating and strategic role in the strategic planning process and play more strategic than operational roles such as the HR function ensuring that HRM strategies are aligned with business strategies. Previously, Habir and Larasati (1999) conducted a study in three leading Indonesian companies and indicated a changing orientation of HRM toward a more strategic focus. Another study conducted by a high-reputation management magazine titled *SWA* in 2006 demonstrated the strategic role of the HR function in forty-nine major companies, consisting of eleven state enterprises and thirty-eight Indonesian private companies. These organizations view employees as human capital and a value-added factor of production (SWA, 2006; Habir & Rajendran, 2008). A small number of organizations in Indonesia, however, have experienced difficulties in gaining sufficient financial support for implementing strategic roles for HRM (Thorat, 2013). These organizations may believe that HRM is a cost center instead of a center for investment in human capital. In this regard, these organizations did not perform some HRM strategies and practices well such as the follow-up on performance appraisal. Thorat noted, "HRM managers indicated it was not easy to wipe the negative image of HRM out from the people's minds" (2013: 6). Hence, the HR function needs to provide concrete evidence that its function really contributes to the firm's business strategies.

Malaysia

The HR function in Malaysia is in the process of transforming toward a more strategic orientation (Abdul Malek et al., 2014; Todd & Peetz, 2001). However, although the HRM role is gradually gaining in importance, the HR function still largely plays an administrative role rather than a strategic role (Abdul Malek et al., 2014; Chew, 2005). In line with this argument, Long and bin Wan Ismail (2008) conducted a study involving thirty-two manufacturing companies in Malaysia and concluded that HR professionals lack the capacity to play a role as a strategic partner and change agent. Abdul Malek, Varma, & Budhwar (2014), Todd and Peetz (2001), and Yong (1996) noted that HR professionals in Malaysia are typically people who have general qualifications such as a social science degree with four–five years of work experience and are able to communicate in Bahasa Malaysia and English. Thus, to improve the role of the HR function, HR managers and professionals in Malaysia should devolve some of HRM activities to line managers and formulate HRM policies and practices that can be effectively communicated to the line managers as requirements to perform their role (Mat, Hazimah, Zabidi, & Salleh, 2015). In particular, HR professionals may feel overworked, if they have to perform both strategic and operational roles. Thus, if some of HRM activities, especially operational ones, are devolved to line managers, those HR professionals should have greater time and resources to perform the strategic roles of HRM (Abdul Malek et al., 2014).

Thailand

The role of the HR function in Thailand has been undergoing a process of constant change for several reasons such as globalization, the establishment of the AEC, and labor migration within the region (Siengthai, 2014). Firms, especially large firms, are expected to implement policies and practices of strategic HRM such as the alignment of the pattern of planned HRM policies and practices intended to enable the organization to achieve its goals (Kokkaew & Koompai, 2012). In other words, the role of the HR function should become more proactive and involve serving as a strategic partner. This means that the duties and responsibilities of both HR professionals and line managers in those firms have to be altered to respond to a new strategic view that people are not costs but are a key to the success and achievement of organizational goals (Visitchaichan, 2004). Siengthai (2014) noted that one of the key challenges currently facing the HR function is to be able to increase job satisfaction and productivity amongst employees and to generate sustainable competitive advantages for firms. In this regard, the alignment between HRM strategies and practices, and corporate strategies and practices is crucial. Siengthai (2014) also proposed that the role of the HR function in Thailand should be to help to facilitate the fierce competition amongst firms to attract and retain talents over the long run. Additionally, the HR function would play a role in organizational innovation, knowledge transfer amongst employees, and productivity improvement, especially in the era of technological improvement (Boonyarith & Siengthai, 2014; Siengthai, 2014). To be able to fulfill these roles, however, the HR function of firms in Thailand should focus more on performance management. Specifically, more objective performance management should be implemented to facilitate alignment between firms' business strategies and HRM strategies.

Trends in strategic HRM and new HRM practices

Indonesia

To strengthen the position of strategic HRM, Electronic HRM (eHRM) has been increasingly adopted in companies, especially subsidiaries of MNCs, in Indonesia. Bondarouk, Schilling, and Ruël (2016) noted that management support and the availability of resources play important roles in such adoption. The HR function, however, continues to be poorly regarded by enterprises in Indonesia. There are several regulations that might complicate or facilitate the adoption of eHRM in those enterprises to support the alignment of their business strategies with their HRM strategies. In this regard, managers must find a way to make their voices heard in the decision-making process of eHRM adoption to overcome those problems.

In terms of HRM practices, one of the increasingly important practices in Indonesia is talent management (Bruning & Tung, 2013; Habir & Rajendran, 2008). Research conducted by PageUp People noted that in Indonesia, the labor market rapidly absorbs qualified talent, leading to the problem of talent shortages. In this regard, firms in Indonesia should implement talent management and retention strategies and practices to alleviate this problem (PageUp People, 2012). For instance, firms should build a talent pipeline that will allow them to identify, develop, and retain talent efficiently and effectively. Additionally, firms in Indonesia have devoted greater attention to managing diversity within the workplace (Jalal, 2013). Here, management support and recognition of differences within an organization are crucial to the successful implementation of diversity management practices by firms.

Malaysia

Green HRM systems have been implemented in some organizations in Malaysia to promote cleaner sustainability strategies within organizations, leading to improved employee well-being and long-term organizational performance (Gholami, Rezaei, Saman, Sharif, & Zakuan, 2016). A Green HRM system involves the alignment of HRM practices with environmental goals. In this respect, HRM practices play a crucial role in implementing and maintaining environmental management systems. One of the most important start-up tools for a Green HRM system is the adoption of eHRM in Malaysia (Yusliza & Ramayah, 2012). Additionally, HR outsourcing is considered a new trend in Malaysia (Abdul-Halim & Che-Ha, 2010). Several manufacturing firms in Malaysia are likely to outsource recruitment and training functions because they would like to gain access to expert services and obtain excellent service quality in those HR functions from external vendors. Several firms, however, do not outsource their HR functions to external vendors because HR outsourcing may not be appropriate for their business operations. Nevertheless, HR outsourcing will become more common in Malaysia in the future.

With respect to HRM practices, because Malaysia aims to become a high-income and developed nation by 2020, the issue of talent management has become an important agenda for several organizations in Malaysia (Azmen, Sirat, & Pang, 2016). Talent management has been viewed as the strategy of an organization to retain employees over the long run (Abdul Hamid, Hashim, Omar, Kamil, & Akmal, 2011). In this regard, HR professionals need to explain to both management and employees in their organizations the importance of talent management, its benefits to organizations and participants, and its specific processes. Similar to the case of Indonesia, workforce diversity and HRM practices have become a significant issue in Malaysia—a multi-racial and multi-ethnic country (Salleh & Sulaiman, 2012). Organizations in

Malaysia thus need to develop strategic plans to enhance and promote such workforce diversity. Here, diversity training and diversity evaluation are crucial for an organization to manage that diversity.

Thailand

Because climate change has become a serious concern for the global community, firms in Thailand are expected to demonstrate their corporate social responsibility to the environment and surrounding contexts. In this respect, the movement toward Green HRM processes is one of the emerging trends in the field of HRM in Thailand (Siengthai, 2014). One of the transformations here is the adoption of eHRM amongst firms in Thailand. The so-called eHRM has been introduced in several large organizations such as Michelin and the Hong Kong & Shanghai Banking Corporation to foster the efficiency and effectiveness of HRM practices (Siengthai, 2014). Additionally, research on strategic HRM in Thailand that has been conducted in recent years (e.g., Pongpearchan, 2015; Popaitoon & Siengthai, 2014; Tangthong, Trimetsoontorn, & Rojniruttikul, 2015) demonstrates that HRM practices aligned with organizational strategies play a crucial role in fostering firms' performance. Hence, the practices of strategic HRM are expected to be implemented amongst a larger number of firms in Thailand in the near future.

Regarding new HRM practices, some leading organizations in Thailand have implemented several selection tools such as horoscopes, face reading, the "Go" game, and fingerprint and footprint analysis (Napathorn, 2017) to select their managerial and professional employees. Confucianism or Chinese-Thai cultures inform these practices. Such practices are likely to complement standardized selection practices such as interviews, employment tests, psychological tests, and assessment centers and are implemented to ensure that the selected candidates demonstrate "fit" with organizational culture and contexts. Talent management is another emerging HRM practice in many organizations in Thailand. Piansoongnern (2014) noted that firms should first implement equal employment opportunity practices for the successful implementation of talent management. Specifically, the processes of talent identification, development, rewarding, and retention should be equally implemented amongst talented employees at all levels in those firms to foster the higher level of engagement by those talented employees over the long term.

Conclusions

This chapter has provided a brief overview of the evolution of HRM systems in three countries: Indonesia, Malaysia, and Thailand. It highlights firm-level HRM practices, specifically recruitment and selection, training and development, and characteristics of pay and reward practices in each country. Although there is considerable variation in the HRM practices at the firm level in each of the three countries, we have attempted to report on the unique and dominant HRM practices within each country.

In Indonesia, although HRM has been regarded as important generally, it cannot be said that HRM is seen as a strategic issue by national governments or by most firms in Indonesia, except large firms that have experienced successes in implementing strategic HRM systems and internationally recognized HRM practices (Habir & Rajendran, 2008). Nevertheless, a highly uncertain environment will likely influence the general adoption of strategic views on HRM and the implementation of the best HRM practices by firms. In this regard, the progress toward a more strategic approach to HRM within firms should be based on support from the HR professionals and top management of those firms.

One of the most fundamental problems in Malaysia will be a chronic skill shortage in certain areas, such as the engineering, life sciences, pharmaceutical, information and communication technology, and retail sectors (Abdul Malek et al., 2014). The Ministry of Human Resources should thus play a more important role in shaping HRM policies and practices in the future, but to its credit, it has developed national HRD policies consistent with Vision 2020. At the firm level, HRM policies and practices should progress toward strategic HRM with a focus on maintaining a supply of multi-skilled workers that responds to the requirements of industries and firms in each sector, thereby fostering employee productivity and promoting employee welfare in general.

Finally, it is important for firms in Thailand to upgrade the skills of their workers to survive in a globally competitive environment, particularly after the implementation of the new minimum wage rate. The government should play a more active role in alleviating chronic skill shortages and mismatches because graduates do not have skills that respond to the needs of industries or firms. At the firm level, we believe that the role of the HR function should be consistently transformed from an administrative role to a more strategic role, although most small- and medium-sized firms in Thailand still perceive the HR function as having the former role. Currently, many large-sized firms have adopted talent management, succession planning, and employee engagement strategies to attract and retain talented employees over the long term. Additionally, HRM analytics will be increasingly employed, particularly for strategic decision-making amongst large-sized firms. Finally, it is important for HR professionals to be able to address the issue of diversity amongst people from different generations and the issue of an aging society at the firm level.

Note

1 From interviews conducted by the first author from July 27–28, 2015.

References

Abdul Ghani Azmi, I. (2015). Islamic human resource practices and organizational performance: Some findings in a developing country. *Journal of Islamic Accounting and Business Research, 6*(1), 2–18.
Abdul-Halim, H. & Che-Ha, N. (2010). HR outsourcing among Malaysian manufacturing companies. *Business Strategy Series, 11*(6), 363–370.
Abdul Hamid, Z., Hashim, J., Omar, A., Kamil, M., & Akmal, B. (2011). A study on the implementation of talent management practices at Malaysia companies. *Asian Journal of Business and Management Sciences, 1*(4), 147–162.
Abdul-Rahman, S. & Rowley, C. (2008). The changing face of management in Malaysia. In C. Rowley & S. Abdul-Rahman (Eds.), *The changing face of management in Southeast Asia* (pp. 59–96). London: Routledge.
Abdul Malek, M., Varma, A., & Budhwar, P. S. (2014). Human resource management in Malaysia. In A. Varma & P. S. Budhwar (Eds.), *Managing human resources in Asia-Pacific* (2nd ed.) (pp. 191–208). New York and London: Routledge.
Akrasanee, N., Dapice, D., & Flatters, F. (1991). Thailand's export-led growth: Retrospect and prospects. *TDRI Quarterly Review, 6*(2), 24–26.
Asian Productivity Organization (2011) *APO productivity databook 2011*. Tokyo: Keio University Press.
Azman, N., Sirat, M., & Pang, V. (2016). Managing and mobilizing talent in Malaysia: Issues, challenges and policy implications for Malaysian universities. *Journal of Higher Education Policy and Management, 38*(3), 316–332.
Bennington, L. (2001). Indonesia. In M. Patrickson & P. O'Brien (Eds.), *Managing diversity: An Asian and Pacific focus*. Milton, QLD: John Wiley & Sons Australia.
Bennington, L. & Habir, A. D. (2003). Human resource management in Indonesia. *Human Resource Management Review, 13*(3), 373–392.

Bishop, B. & McNamara, D. (1997). *The Asia-Australia Survey 1997–1998*. South Melbourne: Macmillan Education Australia.

Bondarouk, T., Schilling, D., & Ruël, H. (2016). eHRM adoption in emerging economies: The case of subsidiaries of multinational corporations in Indonesia. *Canadian Journal of Administrative Sciences/Revue Canadienne des Sciences de l'Administration, 33*(2), 124–137.

Boonyarith, S. & Siengthai, S. (2014). The headquarters' strategy in knowledge transfer effectiveness: An empirical study in Thailand. *International Journal of Innovation and Learning, 15*(1), 65–94.

Bruning, N. S. & Tung, R. L. (2013). Leadership development and global talent management in the Asian context: An introduction. *Asian Business & Management, 12*(4), 381–386.

Caraway, T. (2004). Protective repression, international pressure, and institutional design: Explaining labor reform in Indonesia. *Studies in Comparative International Development, 39*(3), 28–49.

Carney, M. & Andriesse, E. (2014). Malaysia: Personal capitalism. In M. A. Witt & G. Redding (Eds.), *The Oxford handbook of Asian business systems* (pp. 144–168). Oxford: Oxford University Press.

Chandrakumara, P. (2013). *Human resources management practices in small and medium enterprises in two emerging economies in Asia: Indonesia and South Korea*. Annual SEAANZ Conference (pp. 1–15). Small Enterprise Association of Australia and New Zealand.

Charoenloet, V. (2015). Industrialization, globalization and labor force participation in Thailand. *Journal of the Asia Pacific Economy, 20*(1), 130–142.

Chew, Y. T. (2005). Achieving organizational prosperity through employee motivation and retention: A comparative study of strategic HRM practices in Malaysian institutions. *Research and Practice in Human Resource Management, 13*(2), 87–104.

Chiengkul, K., Kamoltrakul, K., Prasertchareonsuk, T., & Leelawattanun, N. (1998). *Thai financial crisis: Impacts from IMF and solutions* (translated from Thai), Bangkok: Pra-Pun-San Press.

Clegg, B. & Gray, S. J. (2002). Australian expatriates in Thailand: Some insights for expatriate management policies. *The International Journal of Human Resource Management, 13*(4), 598–623.

Dailynews (2015). Ministry of Labor confirmed that the minimum wage at 300 Baht would not be repealed (in Thai). Retrieved August 26, 2015, from www.dailynews.co.th/politics/326746.

Emmerson, D. K. (Ed.) (1999) *Indonesia beyond Suharto: Polity, economy, society, transition*. New York: M. E. Sharpe.

Frenkel, S. J. & Kuruvilla, S. C. (2002). Logics of action: Globalization and changing employment relations in China, Malaysia, India, and the Philippines. *Industrial and Labor Relations Review, 55*(3), 387–412.

Frenkel, S. J. & Yu, K.-H. (2014). Employment relations and human resource management in Asia. In M. A. Witt & G. Redding (Eds.), *The Oxford handbook of Asian business systems* (pp. 383–418). Oxford: Oxford University Press.

Gholami, H., Rezaei, G., Saman, M. Z. M., Sharif, S., & Zakuan, N. (2016). State-of-the-art Green HRM system: Sustainability in the sports center in Malaysia using a multi-methods approach and opportunities for future research. *Journal of Cleaner Production, 124*, 142–163.

Gullaprawit, C. (2002). Thailand. In M. Zanko (Ed.), *The handbook of human resource management policies and practices in Asia-Pacific economies, Vol. 1*. Northampton, MA: Edward Elgar.

Habir, A. D. & Larasati, A. B. (1999). Human resource management as competitive advantage in the new millennium: An Indonesian perspective. *International Journal of Manpower, 20*(8), 548–562.

Habir, A. D. & Rajendran, K. (2008). The changing face of human resource management in Indonesia. In C. Rowley & S. Abdul-Rahman (Eds.), *The changing face of management in Southeast Asia* (pp. 30–58). London: Routledge.

Hadiz, V. (1997). *Workers and the state in New-Order Indonesia*. London: Routledge.

Hay Group (2010). Fight or flight: Performance and reward in Malaysia. Retrieved May 20, 2016, from www.haygroup.com/downloads/sg/misc/haygroup_rewarding_malaysia_july2010.pdf.

Hill, H. & Shiraishi, T. (2007). Indonesia after the Asian crisis. *Asian Economic Policy Review, 2*(1), 123–141.

Hofstede, G. (1980). *Culture's consequences: International differences in work-related values*. Beverly Hills, CA: Sage.

Hofstede, G. (1983). Cultural pitfalls for Dutch expatriates in Asia. *Euro-Asia Business Review, 2*(1).

Hofstede, G. (1991). *Culture's consequences: Software of the mind*. London: McGraw-Hill.

Jalal, O. M. (2013). *Diversity in the workplace*. Retrieved June 2, 2016, from https://manajemenppm.word press.com/2013/04/22/diversity-in-the-workplace/.

Jantan, M. A. & Honeycutt Jr, E. D. (2013). Current sales training practices in the commercial retail banking industry in Malaysia. *Services Marketing Quarterly, 34*(1), 1–17.

Kamoche, K. (2000). From boom to bust: The challenges of managing people in Thailand. *The International Journal of Human Resource Management, 11*(2), 452–468.

Kim, S. H. and Haque, M. (2002). The Asian Financial Crisis of 1997: Causes and policy responses. *Multinational Business Review, Spring*, 37–44.

Kokkaew, N. & Koompai, S. (2012). Current practices of human resource management (HRM) in Thai construction industry: A risk and opportunity perspective. *Review of Integrative Business and Economics Research, 1*(1), 1.

Kongchan, A. (2001). *Human resource management in Thai firms and multinational corporations in Thailand* (translated from Thai). Research Report, Chulalongkorn University.

Kuruvilla, S. & Arudsothy, P. (1995). Economic development strategy, government labor policy and firm level industrial relations practices in Malaysia. In A. Verma, T. A. Kochan, & R. Lansbury (Eds.), *Employment relations in the growing Asian economies* (pp. 158–193). London: Routledge.

Kuruvilla, S. (1996a). The relationship between economic development strategies and industrial relations: India, Malaysia, Singapore and the Philippines. *Industrial and Labor Relations Review, 49*(4), 635–657.

Kuruvilla, S. (1996b). National industrialization strategies and their influence on patterns of HR practices. *Human Resource Management Journal, 6*(3), 26–41.

Lange. J. S. (2010). *Human resource management in Indonesia: important issues to know before establishing a subsidiary in Indonesia.* Hamburg: Diplomica Verlag GmBH.

Lawler, J. J. & Atmiyanandana, V. (1995). Human resource management in Thailand. In L. F. Moore & P. D. Jennings (Eds.), *Human resource management on the Pacific rim: Institutions, practices, and attitudes.* Berlin: de Gruyter.

Lawler, J. J. & Atmiyanandana, V. (2003). HRM in Thailand: A post-1997 update. *Asia Pacific Business Review, 9*(4), 165–185.

Lawler, J. J., Jain, H. C., Ratnam, C. S. V., & Atmiyanandana, V. (1995). Human resource management in developing economies: A comparison of India and Thailand. *The International Journal of Human Resource Management, 6*(2), 319–346.

Lawler, J. J. & Siengthai, S. (1997). Human Resource Management and strategy in the Thai banking industry. *Research and Practice in Human Resource Management, 5*(1), 73–88.

Lawler, J. J., Siengthai, S., & Atmiyanandana, V. (1997). HRM in Thailand: Eroding traditions. *Asia Pacific Business Review, 3*(4), 170–196.

Lawler, J. J. & Suttawet, C. (2000). Labor unions, globalization and deregulation in Thailand. *Asia Pacific Business Review, 6*(3–4), 214–238.

Liddle, R. (2000). Indonesia in 1999: Democracy restored. *Asian Survey, 40*(1), 32–42.

Long, C. S. & bin Wan Ismail, W. K. (2008). Human resource competencies: A study of the HR professionals in manufacturing firms in Malaysia. *International Management Review, 4*(2), 65.

Malaysia (1971). *First Outline Perspective Plan, 1971–1990.* Kuala Lumpur: National Printing Department.

Mamman, A. & Somantri, Y. (2014). What role do HR practitioners play in developing countries: An exploratory study in an Indonesian organization undergoing major transformation. *The International Journal of Human Resource Management, 25*(11), 1567–1591.

Manning, C. (1993). Structural change and industrial relations during the Soeharto period: An approaching crisis? *Bulletin of Indonesian Economic Studies, 29*(2), 59–95.

Manning, C. & Roesad, K. (2007). The Manpower Law of 2003 and its implementing regulations: Genesis, key articles and potential impact. *Bulletin of Indonesian Economical Studies, 43*(1), 59–86.

Mansor, N. & Ali, M. (1998). An exploratory study of organizational flexibility in Malaysia: A research note. *The International Journal of Human Resource Management, 9*(3), 506–515.

Mat, N., Hazimah, N., Zabidi, Z. N., & Salleh, M. (2015). Linking the line managers' human resource management role to human resource management effectiveness: Some evidence from Malaysia. *Advanced Science Letters, 21*(5), 1439–1443.

Mellahi, K. & Wood, G. (2004). HRM in Malaysia. In P. Budhwar (Ed.), *Managing human resources in Asia Pacific.* London: Routledge.

Mounier, A. & Charoenloet, V. (2010). New challenges for Thailand: Labor and growth after the crisis. *Journal of Contemporary Asia, 40*(1), 123–143.

Munandar, A. S. (2003). Culture and management in Indonesia. In M. Warner (Ed.), *Culture and management in Asia.* London: RoutledgeCurzon.

Napathorn, C. (2017). Thailand: How selection practices make a difference: A case study of a global Thai company. In L. C. Christiansen, E. Farndale, M. Biron, & B. Kuvaas (Eds.), *Global human resource management casebook* (2nd ed.). New York: Routledge.

Napathorn, C. & Chanprateep, S. (2011). Recent labor relations and collective bargaining issues in Thailand. *Interdisciplinary Journal of Research in Business, 1*(6), 66–81.

Narjoko, D. & Putra, C. T. (2015). Industrialization, globalization, and labor market regime in Indonesia. *Journal of the Asia Pacific Economy, 20*(1), 57–76.

Noordin, F., Williams, T., & Zimmer, C. (2002). Career commitment in collectivist and individualist cultures: A comparative study. *The International Journal of Human Resource Management, 13*(1), 35–54.

PageUp People (2012). New research highlights: Talent management challenges in Indonesia. Retrieved May 28, 2016, from www.pageuppeople.com/news_item/new-research-highlights-talent-management-challenges-in-indonesia/.

Piansoongnern, O. (2014). Talent Management in ASEAN: A Study of Thailand. In Al Ariss, A. (Ed.), *Global talent management: Challenges, strategies, and opportunities* (pp. 171–181). Geneva: Springer International Publishing.

Policy Brief 13. (2006). Inter-regional inequality facility: Sharing ideas and policies across Africa, Asia, and Latin America—Affirmative Action: Malaysia. Retrieved October 31, 2016, from www.odi.org/resources/docs/4078.pdf.

Pongpearchan, P. (2015). Effect of transformational leadership on strategic human resource management and firm success of Toyota's dealer in Thailand. *The Business & Management Review, 7*(1), 256.

Popaitoon, S. & Siengthai, S. (2014). The moderating effect of human resource management practices on the relationship between knowledge absorptive capacity and project performance in project-oriented companies. *International Journal of Project Management, 32*(6), 908–920.

Prijadi, R. and Rachmawati, R. (2002). Indonesia. In M. Zanko (Ed.), *The handbook of human resource management policies and practices in Asia-Pacific economies* (pp. 260–293). Asia Pacific Economic Corporation-APEC HRD Working Group, Northampton, MA: Edward Edgar Publishing.

Rachmi, A. (2013). *The HRM practices of Indonesian medium-sized companies in the textile industry in Java.* DBA thesis, Southern Cross University, Lismore, NSW.

Rasiah, R., Crinis, V., & Lee, H. (2015). Industrialization and labor in Malaysia. *Journal of the Asia Pacific Economy, 20*(1), 77–99.

Rhodes, J., Walsh, P. & Lok, P. (2008). Convergence and divergence issue in strategic management: Indonesia's experience with the Balanced Scorecard in HR Management. *The International Journal of Human Resource Management, 19*(6), 1170–1185.

Rohdewohld, R. (1995). *Public administration in Indonesia.* Melbourne: Montech.

Roongrerngsuke, S. (2010). *Best HR Practices in Thailand.* Bangkok: Nation News Network Company Limited.

Rowley, C. & Abdul-Rahman, S (2008). Introduction. In C. Rowley & S. Abdul-Rahman (Eds.), *The changing face of management in Southeast Asia.* London: Routledge.

Rowley, C. & Warner, M. (2010). Management in South-East Asia: Key findings, conclusions and prospects. *Asia Pacific Business Review, 16*(1–2), 259–267.

Salleh, K. M. & Sulaiman, N. L. (2012). Diversity and the changing role of human resource in Malaysian organization. *The International Journal of Human Resource Management and Research, 2*(4), 1–8.

Siengthai, S. (2014). Human resource management in Thailand. In A. Varma & P. S. Budhwar (Eds.), *Managing human resources in Asia-Pacific* (2nd ed.) (pp. 150–165). New York and London: Routledge.

Siengthai, S. & Bechter, C. (2004). Human resource management in Thailand. In P. Budhwar (Ed.), *HRM in Southeast Asia and the Pacific Rim.* London: Routledge.

Siengthai, S. & Bechter, C. (2005). Human resource management in Thailand: A Strategic Transition for Firm Competitiveness. *Research and Practice in Human Resource Management, 13*(1), 18–29.

Siengthai, S., Dechawattanapaisal, D., & Wailerdsak, N. (2009). Human resource management: Future trends. In T. G. Andrews & S. Siengthai (Eds.), *The changing face of management in Thailand.* London: Routledge.

Siengthai, S., Tanlamai, U., & Rowley, C. (2008). The changing face of human resource management in Thailand. In C. Rowley & S. Abdul-Rahman (Eds.), *The changing face of management in Southeast Asia* (pp. 155–184). London: Routledge.

Siengthai, S. & Vadhanasindhu, P. (1991). Management in a Buddhist society—Thailand. In J. M. Putti (Ed.), *Management: Asian context.* Singapore: McGraw-Hill.

Sitalaksmi, S. & Zhu, Y. (2010). The transformation of human resource management in Indonesian state-owned enterprises since the Asian Crisis. *Asia Pacific Business Review, 16*(1–2), 37–57.

Soetjipto, B. W., Sadeli, J., and Nayaputera, M. (2012). Indonesia: Performance and talent management in Indonesia: The case of XYZ Company. In J. C. Hayton, M. Biron, L. C. Christiansen, & B. Kuvaas (Eds.), *Global human resource management casebook* (pp. 289–298). New York and London: Routledge.

Suehiro, A. & Yabushita, N. (2014). Thailand: Post-developmentalist capitalism. In M. A. Witt & G. Redding (Eds.), *The Oxford handbook of Asian business systems* (pp. 260–282). Oxford: Oxford University Press.

Sutiyono, W. (2007). Human resource management in state-owned and private enterprises in Indonesia. *Bulletin of Indonesian Economic Studies, 43*(3), 377–394.

SWA (2006, November, 15). *Para Kampium SDM (The HR Champions).* 30–38.

Tangthong, S., Trimetsoontorn, J., & Rojniruttikul, N. (2015). The effects of HRM practices on firm performance in Thailand's manufacturing industry. *Journal for Global Business Advancement, 8*(3), 250–282.

Thorat, P. (2013). HRM in Indonesia. *International Journal of Enterprise and Innovation Management Studies, 4*(1), 1–9.

Todd, P. & Peetz, D. (2001). Malaysian industrial relations at century's turn: Vision 2020 or a spectre of the past? *The International Journal of Human Resource Management, 12*(8), 1365–1382.

van der Eng, P. (2004). Businesses in Indonesia: Old problems and new challenges. In M. C. Basri & P. van der Eng (Eds.), *Businesses in Indonesia: New challenges, old problems* (pp. 1–22). Singapore: Institute of Southeast Asian Studies.

Visitchaichan, S. (2004). Strategic human resource management in Thailand. *AU Journal of Management, 2*(1).

Wad, P. (2001). *Transforming industrial relations: The case of the Malaysian auto industry.* Clara Working Paper 12. Amsterdam: IISG.

Wan, H. L. (2006). Implementing e-HRM: The readiness of small and medium sized manufacturing companies in Malaysia. *Asia Pacific Business Review, 12*(4), 465–485.

Wan, H. L. (2008). Current remuneration practices in the multinational companies in Malaysia: A case study analysis. *Research and Practice in Human Resource Management, 16*(1), 78–103.

Wengel, J. T. & Rodriguez, E. (2006). SME export performance in Indonesia after the crisis. *Small Business Economics, 26*(1), 25–37.

World Bank (2009). *Malaysia economic monitor: Repositioning for growth.* Bangkok: World Bank.

World Bank (2016). *Labor Force, Total.* Retrieved March 15, 2016, from http://data.worldbank.org/indicator/SL.TLF.TOTL.IN.

Worldometers (2016a). *Population of Malaysia.* Retrieved April 2, 2016, from www.worldometers.info/world-population/malaysia-population/.

Worldometers (2016b). *Population of Thailand.* Retrieved April 8, 2016, from www.worldometers.info/world-population/thailand-population/.

Yabushita, N. W. & Suehiro, A. (2014). Family business groups in Thailand: Coping with management critical points. *Asia Pacific Journal of Management, 31*(4), 997–1018.

Yong, A. K. (1996). *Malaysian human resource management.* Kuala Lumpur: Eagle Trading Sdn Bhd, Malaysian Institute of Management.

Yusliza, M. & Ramayah, T. (2012). Determinants of attitude towards E-HRM: An empirical study among HR professionals. *Procedia-Social and Behavioral Sciences, 57*, 312–319.

Zhu, Y., Warner, M., & Rowley, C. (2007). Human resource management with "Asian" characteristics: A hybrid people-management system in East Asia. *The International Journal of Human Resource Management, 18*(5), 745–768.

19

HUMAN RESOURCE MANAGEMENT IN CITY STATES
Dubai and Singapore

Julia Connell, John Burgess, and Peter Waring

Introduction: why compare Dubai and Singapore?

Dubai and Singapore serve as interesting cases for the comparative examination of HRM processes and systems. Both are small city states (Dubai is part of the United Arab Emirates—UAE) with extensive government regulation alongside a liberal approach to trade and investment, high rates of economic growth, and a dependence on short-term foreign labor. Both depend upon and encourage trade and investment with low rates of taxation and supportive programs for foreign investment. Singapore is ranked number one (and has done so for nine consecutive years) and the UAE twenty-second out of 189 countries on the Ease of Doing Business Scale (World Bank, 2015). A high Ease of Doing Business ranking means the regulatory environment is more conducive to the starting and operation of a local firm. As a result, many MNEs have situated their regional headquarters in the respective cities.

Dubai and Singapore are also hubs for tourism and banking services in their regions with international airports in Dubai and Singapore being amongst the largest and busiest in the world. Deregulation and the growth of air transport networks have enabled these small, low-populated cities to develop into major international tourism destinations using combined airline, airport, and tourism strategies to achieve these goals (Lohmann, Albers, Koch, & Pavlovich, 2009). Each has invested in and developed global airlines: Singapore Airlines and Emirates Airlines. Singapore has an AAA sovereign debt rating and is regarded as one of the least corrupt locations in which to do business and is also listed as one of the major locations for international tax minimization (Shunko, Do, & Tsay, 2014). Against this, Singapore ranks lowly for freedom of speech and assembly (Foley, 2013). Unlike Singapore, the UAE comprises a hereditary monarchy with constraints on civil liberties, political rights, and freedom of speech (Vora, 2012).

Singapore possesses no natural resources but is advantaged by its location on the Malay Peninsula, and consequently, is one of the world's busiest shipping routes. Dubai as an Emirate of the UAE has access to oil and gas revenues. However, unlike other members of the UAE, Dubai has relatively small oil reserves and its economy is driven by other industries such as tourism, banking, and logistics. Like Singapore, Dubai is located on a busy shipping route that provides advantages in regard to the location of its port in relation to a number of industries.

Both city states were originally part of the British Empire and as a result, the English language and elements of the British legal system can still be found in both cities. Both cities are also diverse in their culture and ethnicity. In terms of labor market regulation, the following features are common: there is a high dependence on foreign labor, both skilled and unskilled; there are extensive regulations concerning work and workplaces, although they tend to apply to the core workforce of local and professional expatriate workers; and both house the regional head-quarters of MNEs, which means that they have access to international HRM systems. However, as Thite, Wilkinson, and Shah point out the theories and practices relevant for Western MNCs are giving way to new economic and management paradigms that are adapted according to the host country (2012: 256). For example, Dubai has an Emiratization policy designed to reserve places for local workers in the formal private sector of the economy, a strategy intended to reduce the dependence of locals on public sector employment (Forstenlechner & Rutledge, 2011). Whereas, Singapore has recently introduced hiring policies designed to advantage Singapore citizens, and parties such as the National Solidarity Party have frequently called for a "Singaporean First" policy in the workplace. This refers to Singaporeans being offered job vacancies before any other groups (Lim, 2015).

Both city states recognize the strategic importance of nurturing and developing human capital as a means of supporting future economic growth. To this end, both have invested in education and training, and have supported the migration of skilled labor. For example, Singapore recently introduced the Skills Future initiative, which provides funding to Singaporean citizens over twenty-five years old. Funding can be spread throughout their working life as long as it is used with approved education providers (Harris, 2016). The UAE ranks relatively highly on the Knowledge Economy Index (World Bank, 2012) and this is partly due to the widespread introduction of Freezones, which are industry clusters, such as Knowledge Village which currently hosts more than 450 educational partners—including a range of well-known international universities. Freezones support trading and business development for non-UAE citizens (discussed later), which encourage the strong reliance on an expatriate labor force and the consequent low participation of the local population in the workforce, particularly in the private sector (Thorpe & Connell, 2013). It has been estimated by *The Economist* Intelligence Unit that approximately 90 percent of the workforce in Dubai are expatriates (Barnett, Malcolm, & Toledo, 2015), while the figure is about 40 percent in the case of Singapore. Despite successes as trading centers, there are challenges associated with the HRM processes and practices that are prevalent in both countries, which will be outlined throughout this chapter.

Dubai and Singapore have both achieved economic transformation growing from small and regional city states to hubs of international business over a relatively short period of time. This success has been built on national development programs that have facilitated human resource development and supported the recruitment of expatriate labor across all segments of the workforce. In both city states, there are ongoing challenges around managing large expatriate workforces, assimilating locals into the workforce (in the case of Dubai), and in meeting ongoing skills shortages.

Accordingly, the next section of the chapter will focus on HRM in the City State of Dubai, before considering HRM in the City State of Singapore. Relevant HRM developments and challenges in each will be discussed before comparing and contrasting the two.

Background, labor conditions, and HRM in the city state of Dubai

Dubai is one of seven emirates in the United Arab Emirates (UAE). Abu Dhabi is the capital of the UAE and the largest of the emirates and Dubai the second largest (Abdulla, Djebarni, & Mellahi, 2011). In terms of both income and population, Dubai has grown rapidly over the last few decades evolving "from a trading enclave to become the leading Middle East business/ leisure center, aiming to become a hybrid East/West economic, social and religious model that may act as a catalyst for change" (Iles, Almhedie, & Baruch, 2012: 465).

Prior to the financial crisis of 2008, the UAE regularly exceeded 7 percent annualized GDP growth largely due to oil exports. In the wake of the economic crisis and the slow depletion of natural resources in oil rich Arab countries, Arab governments have begun to recognize that they must adapt to sustain competitiveness (Al-Esia & Skok, 2014). Shayah and Qifeng (2015) point out that economic diversification is one of the most important aims of the UAE's strategy according to Vision 2021, which was launched in February 2010, and outline the need for the UAE to maintain its drive toward sustainable development in a future that is less reliant on oil expanding strategic sectors and to channel energy into industries and services where a long-term competitive advantage can be built (The UAE Vision, 2021). In an effort to meet such expectations, developmental policy agendas have been published throughout the Gulf—such as the *Abu Dhabi Vision 2030* and *Dubai Vision 2020* that are intended to propagate the transition to a knowledge society as a foundation for a sustainable future states (Kolb, 2015).

Dubai has adopted an economic development model, which has been described as strongly pro-business, emphasizing market liberalism, economic openness, and globalization, taking a different approach to the economic models applied in other countries in the Gulf Cooperation Council (GCC) (Hvidt, 2011; Roper & Barria, 2014). The GCC is a regional intergovernmental political and economic union comprising all the Arab states of the Persian Gulf apart from Iran, comprising Bahrain, Kuwait, Oman, Qatar, Saudi Arabia, and the UAE.

With some of the largest migrant populations worldwide according to the percentage of the total population, the resource-rich states of the Gulf Cooperation Council (GCC) have an extended historical record of migrant entrepreneurship, pre-dating that of the modern state (Kolb, 2015). The current guest worker system adopted by the UAE has prevented import-competing industries from collapsing in the presence of foreign competition. Survival of these industries would not have been possible without the supply of a relatively cheap migrant labor force (Toledo, 2013). Despite the tangible benefits arising from labor immigration, creating and preserving jobs for the native population has become a major issue dominating economic and political debates in the UAE—thus, while Emiratization is intended to increase the employment quota for natives it can also reduce industry production and employment (Marchon & Toledo, 2014).

In the UAE, regulations governing employment are extensive and cover the registration of expatriate workers and the content of the employment contract (Mahdavi, 2013). There are a number of segmented labor regulations, which govern UAE nationals employed in the public sector, expatriates/other workers, and domestic service workers (Connell & Burgess, 2013; Lillie, Çaro, Berntsen, & Wagner, 2013). There are also regulations concerning special free trade zones (free zones) that may be exempt from some labor law regulations or involve special conditions that only apply to the specified zones (Davis, 2006). The UAE free zones are designated areas that eliminate traditional trade barriers, such as tariffs, and minimize bureaucratic regulations. The target of a free zone is to enhance global market presence by attracting new business and foreign investments, usually from MNEs. One hundred percent foreign ownership is permitted in all sectors and additional benefits include exemption from corporate or personal taxes, low import duties except on tobacco and alcohol, and no exchange restrictions (Mitra & Thorpe, 2010). The UAE Government has established over forty free zones with the highest number in Dubai (Shayah & Qifeng, 2015). The free zones are often based on the clustering of like industries, for example, Internet City. This allows firms in the same industry to access and observe best practice in the industry since the clusters attract leading MNEs. In addition, the government supports human resource development through a number of agencies. The Knowledge and Human Development Authority, established in 2006, has as its task to monitor training, education, and human resource development (Siddique, 2012), and the Mohammed Bin Rashid Al Maktoum Foundation, established in 2017, has US$10 billion in funding to support research and technology development (Siddique, 2012).

Many foreign multinational enterprises (MNEs) operate in the UAE, including US Fortune 500 companies such as Microsoft and MasterCard. Many of these MNEs use Dubai as their regional headquarters for operations in the Middle East and North African (MENA) region and Southeast Asia (Cherrayil, 2015). According to Mina,

> The total number of U.S. MNEs' affiliates in the UAE with assets, sales or net income greater than US$25 million amounted to 113 in 2010, according to U.S. Bureau of Economic Analysis data, and 95 of them were majority-owned affiliates. Those majority-owned affiliates employed about 19,500 employees, of whom 4,400 were in professional, scientific and technical services, 4,300 in manufacturing, 1,900 in wholesale, and 1,900 in mining.
>
> *(2014: 6)*

The "Dubai Model" has relied on importing labor, both skilled and unskilled, on a significant scale, creating an economic infrastructure base and support industries, where previously very little existed (Connell & Thorpe, 2010). The limited skills and work experience of many UAE nationals (Emiratis) has meant that there has been a heavy reliance on migrant labor to achieve the country's high growth rate. Migrant workers tend to be attractive because they cost less than the locals and also because they are more easily controlled and, in some cases, exploited (Hertog, 2014). The sponsorship system in Dubai (until it was changed recently) prevented most foreign workers from changing employers without the consent of their current employer. Hertog (2014) points out that this regulation gave foreign employees a weak bargaining position and generates wages that lie below marginal productivity.

The population of Dubai was estimated to be 2,327,350 at the end of 2014 with 1,613,175 males and 714,175 females (69.3 percent and 30.7 percent) respectively of the total population (Dubai Statistics Centre, 2015). The higher proportion of males in the Dubai community (226 males per 100 females) is attributed to the majority of expatriate workers being males, who do not have accompanying family members for various reasons. The population growth rate increased, on average, by 5.11 percent from 2011–2013. As Levitt (2013: 45) points out, as "more people live transnational lives, their hard-won earnings move across borders as well."

Table 19.1 illustrates the percentage distribution of workers aged fifteen years and over by nationality, gender, and occupation in the Emirate of Dubai in 2015. The majority of Emirati nationals are employed as professionals, technicians, and managers with the majority of females occupied as professionals and clerks. The majority of non-Emiratis are employed in craft and related occupations, followed by sales and services, with most non-Emirati females employed in elementary occupations and as professionals.

The GCC countries rely on two main types of migrant workers: low- to mid-skilled workers in construction, low-tech industries and services (such as domestic workers), and mid- to high-skilled workers in high value-added services such as banking and education (Roper & Barria, 2014). This has resulted in a three-tier labor market (Connell & Burgess, 2013). In the top tier are the local Emiratis, where due to their preference of working in local government, the government has introduced quotas in some private sectors that require selected industries to employ a minimum share of native workers (Marchon & Toledo, 2014). In tier two are the professional

Table 19.1 Percentage distribution of employed fifteen years and over by nationality, gender, and occupation: Emirate of Dubai, 2015

Nationality	Gender	Armed forces	Skilled agric/ fishery	Elementary occupations	Craft and related occupations	Plant and machinery operators	Service and sales	Clerks	Technicians and assistant profs	Professionals	Managers	Total
Emirati	Male	11.5	0.4	0.2	0.8	0.8	19.8	10.2	29.3	12.4	14.6	100
	Female	0.6	0.0	0.7	0.3	0.0	8.1	25.3	23.2	29.0	13.5	100
	Total	7.4	0.2	0.1	0.6	0.5	15.4	15.9	27.0	18.6	14.2	100
Non–Emirati	Male	0.0	0.8	13.0	28.2	11.6	18.1	4.3	6.7	10.3	7.0	100
	Female	0.0	0.0	36.0	0.4	0.3	14.3	7.9	8.4	24.8	7.0	100
	Total	0.0	0.7	16.9	23.7	9.8	17.4	4.9	7.0	12.6	7.0	100
Total	Male	0.4	0.8	12.6	27.3	11.3	18.1	4.5	7.4	10.3	7.3	100
	Female	0.1	0.0	33.4	0.4	0.3	13.7	9.5	9.8	25.2	7.6	100
	Total	0.3	0.6	16.2	22.7	9.4	17.4	5.4	7.8	12.9	7.3	100

Source: Dubai Statistics Center—Bulletin of Labor Force Survey Results, 2015.

expatriates, highly skilled migrants who generally enjoy much better working conditions than those workers in tier three, who are the low-skilled migrants (Vora, 2012). Tier three workers are largely construction workers (listed as elementary occupations in Table 19.1), from South Asia and comprise 42 percent of the UAE's workforce. Also in tier three are the domestic workers, who are mostly female (Connell & Burgess, 2013).

In terms of formal labor rights, the ILO indicates that the UAE outlaws unions and collective action and is a signatory to six out of the eight core ILO conventions. The UAE has also ratified two out of the 177 technical conventions (these cover working hours, work conditions, occupational health and safety [OH&S], minimum working ages, workers compensation, and employment contracts) (ILO, 2015). Dubai has been criticized for the abuse of migrants, especially domestic and construction workers, who often work under oppressive conditions (Connell & Burgess, 2013). Those migrants working in tier three of the Dubai labor market have low-skilled jobs that are not socially acceptable to the local Emiratis.

Most of the MNEs employ professionals for highly skilled jobs (tier two). PricewaterhouseCoopers (PwC) undertook a survey of UAE CEOs, who reported that 94 percent were dependent on expatriate workers and only 12 percent were "satisfied" with the number of skilled Emiratis available for positions, indicating a lack of human capital amongst local workers (Barnett et al., 2015). Finding meaningful employment for UAE nationals led to the introduction of the Emiratization policy, which imposes quotas on sectors such as banking and insurance to ensure that they employ local staff (Forstenlechner, Madi, Selim, & Rutledge (2012).

The UAE government introduced the Emiratization program in 2004 to encourage employment for its citizens in both the public and private sectors and to reduce dependence on migrant workers (Latham & Watkins, 2014). Under the UAE Labour Law, employers must prioritize UAE nationals (followed by other Arab nationals) over any other nationalities when seeking to recruit employees—apart from those based in Free Zones—(Latham & Watkins, 2014).

Several studies have reported that the Emiratization policy has not been successful to date. For example, Randeree (2009) stated that in 2006, over 52 percent of the workforce was employed in the private sector with only 2 percent comprising UAE nationals, indicating that most Emiratis consider public sector jobs to be the most desirable. Forstenlechner, Madi, Selim, and Rutledge (2012) surveyed approximately 250 UAE-based HRM personnel to identify which factors (social, cultural, economic, regulatory, educational, and motivational) influence employers' decisions to recruit UAE nationals. Their findings suggest that, given the complexities of social and cultural issues, the UAE labor nationalization policy should focus on motivation and regulation as ways to improve the employment opportunities of native workers (Forstenlechner et al., 2012: 12).

In addition, as nationals are not subject to sponsorship and can bargain and move freely within the private labor market, this can, according to Hertog (2014) make them less attractive to businesses who are used to docile and dependent migrant workers. The lack of labor rights for foreign workers in relation to dismissal procedures, pensions, and other social security regulations can also contribute to making nationals less attractive to businesses and their employment more costly overall (Hertog, 2014: 6).

Background, labor conditions, and HRM in the city state of Singapore

In 1965, Singapore withdrew from the Malayan Federation and became an independent state. Few commentators gave the 700 square kilometer city state a strong chance to survive, let alone flourish. The island at the tip of what is now Peninsular Malaysia had no permanent water supply, no mineral resources, and only a modest industrial base. It also faced declining economic contributions from the withdrawing British military that returned to the city following the Japanese occupation. In addition, there were a wide range of social challenges including racial tension and industrial disharmony. While it is an error of modern-day observers to suggest that Singapore was at its birth, a third-world society (see Lee, 2015; Lim, 2015), it was also far from being a self-sustaining sovereign nation. From a resource-based perspective, the newly minted republic had only its advantageous geographic position and the hard work and ingenuity of its people from which to forge its competitive advantages.

From the outset, the indomitable Prime Minister Lee Kuan Yew (a labor lawyer) set about recasting the republic through a highly pragmatic policy mix of free market policies combined with heavy government intervention into economic, political, social, and private domains. Tight regulation of trade union activity and the absence of a minimum wage was unusually combined with the establishment of many government-linked corporations and a highly interventionist industry policy. Foreign capital and multinational corporations were enticed to set up in Singapore through generous tax breaks, subsidies, and the prospect of a compliant labor force, while Singaporeans were provided with subsidized public housing and expanded educational opportunities.

This atypical policy blend helped the Singaporean republic evolve from a low-middle-income country to a high-income country in the relatively short period of five decades. Its economic progress is evidenced by the steep increase in its GDP per capita, growing from $24,898 in 1991 to $63,050 in 2011 (World Bank, 2015b). There was also significant growth in its national income from $38.9 billion in 1990 to $95.8 billion in 2000, and to $297.9 billion by 2013; and GDP per capita from $12,766 in 1990 to $55,182 in 2013 (World Bank, 2015a). Additionally, Singapore has become globally renowned for its expertise and prowess in water technology, oil and gas technologies, as well as pharmaceutical and bio-medical products. Lim and Leong reinforce the dramatic transformation of the economy and living standards:

> Singapore is a thriving, modern city-state, running like a well-oiled machine. From an initial per capita income of US$511 in 1965 (source: World Development Indicators database) which at the time was the third highest among Southeast Asian countries, Singapore now boasts a per capita income of US$56,498, making it the third richest country in the world in 2013. The city-state is also home to the world's busiest port and world's best airline, and named the best place to do business in the world in 2013 by the World Bank.
>
> *(2016: 324)*

While the heterodox policies of Singapore's ruling party have produced a record of strong economic growth, they also appear to be responsible for a range of economic and social challenges including burgeoning inequalities, growing urban congestion, and poor productivity. Total factor productivity's contribution to GDP growth has been anemic over the last several decades with a brief spike during the sharp upswing of the economic cycle following the global financial crisis. The foundation of Singapore's impressive economic credentials have stemmed therefore, not from the rising productivity of inputs, but rather from accretive factors of production—most notably capital and labor. Through its astute government agencies, especially the Economic Development Board (EDB), Singapore has skillfully attracted external capital flows by focusing on ensuring that it remains an attractive business location that is deeply integrated within the global economy. As a result, it has greatly benefited from global trade, technologies, investment, and manpower flows, and has come to rely heavily on its external sector. There is a strong local pride and affinity with organizations that have international recognition and standing such as

Singapore Airlines, Changi Airport, DBS Bank, and the National University of Singapore (Lim & Leong, 2016).

Singapore has become a host for the regional headquarters of thousands of MNEs as well as large government linked companies (GLCs) that were nurtured by the state in strategic sectors of the economy. Companies such as DBS Bank, Singtel, Singapore Airlines, and ST Engineering have allowed the state to develop the economy as well as invest in the region (Tan & Bhaskaran, 2015: 1550030–30). These organizations have sophisticated and extensive HRM systems to support regional and international competitiveness. For example, the international success of Singapore Airlines is supported by a comprehensive HRM program around recruitment, training, and a focus on service delivery (Wirtz, Heracleans, & Panarakan, 2008). Contrary to free market principles, the Singapore Government also intervenes extensively in the domestic economy through its control of two sovereign wealth funds—Temasek Holdings and the Government Investment Corporation (GIC). While the latter does not disclose its funds under management, Temasek Holdings had a net portfolio value of S$266 billion.

In common with Dubai, Singapore's economic success and modest local population has also given rise to perennial manpower shortages, which it has addressed by relying on foreign labor. The growth of foreign labor (which now stands at just under 40 percent of the labor force) has in itself produced concerns over congestion externalities, particularly in transport, housing, and recreational facilities. These acute concerns surfaced at the General Election in 2011 and focused on the perceived social problems created through the influx of foreign workers. Unfettered access and reliance on cheap foreign labor to fill Singapore's manpower shortages has also been associated with declining productivity from 3.4 to 1.1 percent during 2001–2011 (Pang & Lim, 2015).

This is not a new phenomenon; Singapore has a long history of attracting foreign workers to augment its local labor supply, particularly with respect to low-skilled positions. Since colonial times, the authorities have relaxed or tightened the flow of migrant labor depending upon the perceived needs of the labor market and the broader economy. The most significant period of growth in the number of foreign workers occurred during the period between 2006 and 2014, when the migrant workforce doubled in size (Waring, Bali, McKiernan, & Vas, 2015). For policy makers, the issue of foreign labor is sometimes regarded as a "wicked problem." On the one hand, there is evidence that those sectors of the economy which are most dependent on foreign labor are also those with the worst productivity records. These sectors include construction, retail, and hospitality as well as manufacturing. On the other hand, businesses in Singapore have become highly dependent on this cheap source of labor and, as a result of Singapore's falling birth rate (presently tracking at 1.1), it seems likely that these sectors will continue to need foreign workers for the foreseeable future.

To address the challenges produced by the foreign workforce and flagging productivity growth, the Singapore government is pursuing a multi-pronged effort designed to enhance workforce skills and raise productivity levels. Complementing these initiatives is a focus on the pursuit of high value-added industries especially high performance computing, bio-technology, and additive manufacturing.

In December 2014, the total resident workforce stood at just over 2.18 million people (62 percent of the total employed workforce), while foreigners made up the balance (38 percent) or just under 1.35 million people (Ministry of Manpower [MOM], 2015a). Unemployment stood at 2.6 percent of the total labor force, while the total labor force participation rate was 67 percent—higher for males (75.9 percent) than for females (58.6 percent) (MOM, 2015a). The majority of the workforce are employed in manufacturing (2.1 million workers), while the service sector employs 1.73 million workers in spite of the sector contributing 75 percent to Singapore's GDP. Table 19.2 provides an overview of the occupational structure of the resident workforce.

Table 19.2 Singapore's occupational categories (2015)

Occupation	Total	Males	Females
Total	2,103.5	1,161.0	942.5
Managers and Administrators	267.5	173.2	94.3
Working Proprietors	74.8	53.2	21.6
Professionals	290.7	170.4	120.4
Associate Professionals and Technicians	483.4	236.0	247.4
Clerical Support Workers	265.3	64.8	200.5
Service and Sales Workers	256.4	121.2	135.3
Craftsmen and Related Trade Workers	82.2	75.2	6.9
Plant and Machine Operators and Assemblers	146.4	125.9	20.4
Cleaners, Laborers and Related Workers	166.0	72.1	93.8
Others	70.8	68.9	1.9

Source: Ministry of Manpower (2015b).

The gross median monthly income for employed male residents of Singapore was S$3,770 in 2014 (which included Central Provident Fund employer contributions) and for females the figure was S$3,087 or S$45,240 per annum. There is a culture in Singapore of paying a variable wage component or bonus as part of a worker's remuneration. This varies by industry and the economic performance of firms from a month's pay in accommodation and food services through to over three months' pay in the Financial & Insurance Services. Singaporeans tend to work long hours with average weekly paid hours registering at forty-six per week. Those employees holding a degree tend to work higher average weekly hours than those with other educational attainment levels. Overtime hours (weekly average) were recorded as 3.7 hours, however, average overtime can accrue to more than eight hours per week in industries such as construction, transport equipment, and manufacturing (MOM, 2015b: C.3).

As noted previously, the proportion of foreigners in employment in Singapore has grown from 30 percent in 2006 to 38 percent in 2014. As Table 19.3 notes, the single largest employer

Table 19.3 Pass types, workforce numbers, and types of employment in Singapore

Pass type	Workforce numbers	Explanation/comments
Employment Pass	180,800	For professionals and executives
S Pass	173,800	Largely for diploma holders and those with a technical skill base
Work Permit (Total)	993,900	Work permits for unskilled/semi-skilled foreign guest workers
Work Permit (Foreign Domestic Workers)	227,100	Mostly female domestic workers
Work Permit (Construction)	322,400	22% of the foreign workforce
Other Work Passes	19,700	Includes holders of training work permits and letters of consent
Total Foreign Workforce	1.368 million	

Source: Ministry of Manpower (2015b): as at June 2015.

of foreign labor is the construction industry, which in 2014, employed just over 23 percent of the total foreign labor pool of 1.355 million workers. These workers are typically employed through recruitment agencies and come from low-wage developing countries in the region such as Bangladesh, India, China, and Indonesia. Other work permit holders (visa for unskilled or semi-skilled foreign workers), work as cleaners, in marine and offshore engineering, road maintenance, manufacturing, and in other industries where local workers are typically not found. A significant number (225,500) of foreign workers are female domestic workers from countries such as the Philippines, Indonesia, and Myanmar. Table 19.3 outlines the type of employment permits, workforce numbers, and whom they relate to in Singapore as of June 2015.

Of the resident Singaporean labor force comprising some 2.285 million people, some 32 percent held a degree qualification, while a further 19.4 percent held a diploma level qualification (MOM, 2015b: A.4).

Reflecting a pro-business policy mix, the Employment Relations system in Singapore can be described as being "lightly regulated." There is no minimum wage in Singapore and the key labor law statute, The Employment Act 1968 only regulates the employment of those earning less than S$4,500 per month, and managers and executives earning below S$2,500 per month. The employment of those excluded from the coverage of the Employment Act is subject to the common law. The Employment Act 1968 "lightly" regulates termination of employment, hours of work, rest days, annual leave, and other basic conditions of employment. Additionally, the government has only fairly recently sought to improve occupational health and safety protection through the enactment of the Workplace Safety and Health Act 2006. Singapore has ratified twenty ILO conventions, including the five core conventions, but is yet to ratify ILO Convention 181 dealing with Temporary Employment (MOM, 2009). Singapore has dispute resolution machinery in place, which includes the Ministry of Manpower's "Advisory Services and Dispute Management" service that provides both employees and employers with advice on employment issues as well as a complaints and claim management service for alleged breaches of the Act. More serious disputes are heard by the Industrial Arbitration Court, while collective bargaining is regulated by the Industrial Relations Act 1960.

Employment relations in Singapore are characterized by the strong tripartite relationship between the government and the peak union body, the National Trade Union Congress (NTUC). The NTUC and its affiliate unions have tended to place emphasis on a "servicing" rather than "organizing" model of trade unionism in which collective bargaining and industrial action is downplayed in favor of establishing businesses offering discounted goods and services for union members. Its close relationship with the government has meant that its policy positions are rarely in serious conflict with that of the Government. Trade unions in Singapore are regulated by the Trade Unions Act.

The act defines Trade Unions as associations of workers who have the purpose of:

1   Promoting good industrial relations;
2   Improving the working conditions of workers or enhancing their economic and social status; and
3   Raising productivity for the benefit of workers, employers, and the overall economy.

In total, there were sixty-five registered trade unions in 2014 in Singapore with just under one-third of these (eighteen) which have memberships exceeding 10,000 employees. In total, there were 686,676 trade union members or a density of around 32 percent, with the majority of these (141,688) working in the manufacturing sector (MOM, 2015b: E.6).

Industrial disputation is very low in Singapore with the last industrial stoppage recorded in 2012. There were, however, 106 trade disputes referred to MOM for conciliation—the majority of these (sixty-six) were related to wages or conditions of service. A much larger number (8,013 in 2014) of individual disputes were recorded by MOM. Just twelve trade disputes were referred to the Industrial Arbitration Court for resolution in 2014 (MOM, 2015b).

Although Singapore's employment relations system is only lightly regulated, there have been some progressive developments in the last decade which have sought to address some of the more acute Human Resource Management issues that have surfaced in recent times. Perhaps the most important of these has been the growing attention paid to occupational health and safety. The poor safety record of foreign workers operating in industries such as construction and manufacturing prompted a more concerted effort by the authorities, and the Ministry of Manpower in particular, to implement a robust approach to regulation. In Singapore, health and safety in the workplace is now regulated by the progressive Workplace Safety and Health Act (2006) that places greater emphasis on employer's obligations and duty of care, and establishes improved monitoring and enforcement. The new framework has improved Singapore's safety record especially in construction where workplace fatalities have halved since the introduction of the Act. In 2014, Singapore recorded an average fatality injury rate of 1.8 persons per 100,000 employed persons and a workplace injury rate of 405 injuries per 100,000 workers (MOM, 2015b: F.1).

Another prominent workplace issue stems from broader national concern over Singapore's low birth rate (as previously mentioned, Singapore has a total fertility rate of 1.1—lower than that of Japan); the Singapore Government has undertaken a series of initiatives to support reproduction, including four months maternity leave for women and the introduction of paternity leave for fathers. Parents also receive a "baby bonus" to assist with the cost of raising children in addition to enjoying tax benefits that grow with the size of the family. More recently, the authorities have also improved childcare leave entitlements. So far these efforts have not led to desired improvements in the birth rate, which many believe requires a multi-pronged policy response that additionally addresses concerns over workplace stress and work–life balance (see, for example, Galovan, Feistman, Stowe, & Hill, 2015).

Workplace discrimination is another area of HRM, which remains "conspicuously unregulated" (Waring, 2010: 55) in Singapore and has also garnered increasing attention in recent years. The Ministry of Manpower introduced "The Tripartite Alliance for Fair and Progressive Employment Practices" (TAFEP) in 2006, which led to guidelines on discrimination issues being promulgated in 2007. Employees who believe they have been discriminated against can seek assistance from TAFEP, who will undertake an investigation. Where there is sufficient evidence that an employer has not complied with the guidelines, MOM may take action against the employer but the sanctions are rather modest with MOM either issuing warnings to noncompliant employers, or withdrawing work pass entitlements. According to MOM, TAFEP received less than eighty race-, language-, or religion-related complaints each year, in the period 2010–2015. In 2014, MOM took action against nine employers for race-, language-, or religion-based discriminatory practices.

These guidelines have been somewhat augmented by the introduction of the "Fair Consideration Framework," which requires firms to be open to employing Singaporeans and to advertise certain jobs on a "jobs bank" maintained by the "Singapore Workforce Development Agency" before foreign workers are considered. These guidelines were developed in response to the 2011 general election in which sensitivity over the growing foreign workforce became a political issue.

Most recently, and in response to lagging productivity, the Singapore government launched a national program in 2015 called Skills Future. Described as a "national movement," Skills

Future is a multifaceted and multi-billion dollar commitment to broadening and deepening skills acquisition and development. Involving all elements of the education and training eco-system, Skills Future fosters lifelong learning by providing financial support to Singaporeans at various stages of their life. A key component of Skills Future is the provision of $500 worth of "credit" to all Singaporeans aged twenty-five years and above in 2015, which they may use with registered training and education providers to acquire new skills. The Government has announced that this "credit" will be "topped up" at regular intervals. However, this is just the centerpiece of a number of targeted programs and initiatives, including work integrated learning opportunities for vocational and university students, career guidance programs, mid-career enhanced course subsidies, mentor schemes for SMEs, funding for modular course develop-ment, and many others. It is too early to evaluate the success or otherwise of Skills Future but it is another example of the government's pragmatism and its willingness to galvanize national efforts in response to national economic challenges.

Comparing Dubai and Singapore

Dubai, in common with the government in Singapore has, and continues to have, an overarch-ing influence on its country's economic development. A common, though superficial view, of Singapore's remarkable rise is that it can be solely attributed to the adoption of free market principles. However, this belies a more complex reality of extensive state intervention through the management of labor and the development of Government Linked Corporations and statu-tory agencies such as the Housing Development Board of Singapore and the Central Provident Fund (national savings agency).

In the case of Singapore, while the government has maintained labor market policy settings that are undeniably pro-business and designed to maintain the flow of foreign direct investment, we can also detect a growing awareness of the HRM issues that have surfaced over the last ten years (such as safety, discrimination, work–life balance, productivity, and skills) and a growing willingness to act pragmatically in response to these challenges.

However, there is still a need for more change both in the workplace and in relation to the government's approach to migrant workers. With regard to the former, Stanton and Nankervis cite Choo, who argues that the "Singaporean workplace culture is control-based, managerial, highly bureaucratic, and aligned with overriding government imperatives—resulting in similar private and public sector management styles, in ways that are unparalleled in most other regional countries" (Stanton & Nankervis, 2011: 83). Turning to the latter—the government's approach to migrant workers—a fatal accident in December 2013 sparked a spontaneous outbreak of rioting by migrant workers. This led to fifty-seven workers being deported and others being detained in police custody. Under Article 9 of Convention 143, migrant workers are entitled to the right of appeal regarding any expulsion orders, however, as mentioned previously, Singa-pore has not yet ratified the Convention dealing with temporary workers. Consequently, as Neo (2015) points out the need for an inclusive and integrationist approach toward the migrant workers, who contribute to Singapore's economy but who have been "left out of both state rhetoric and society" (Hamid, 2015: 5).

Migrant workers who protest their working conditions have also been deported from Dubai. As Human Rights Watch (2006: 24) maintains, there are no organizations that are independent of the government to advocate for migrant workers' rights and no mechanism to systematically report the abuses of workers. In 2007, workers building the Burj Khalifa (the world's tallest building) protested their working conditions—2,500 migrants banded together to protest their working conditions as they were dissatisfied with their low wages, living conditions, and delayed payments (Janardhan, 2011). The government responded with threats of mass deportation and reportedly a new rule that any expatriates who provoked riots would be deported and unable to return to work for a year (Janardhan 2011: 109).

As a global city state, Singapore is often "outward looking" and judges its position relative to other prominent global cities, especially those with major financial centers such as Dubai, New York, Hong Kong, and London. As such, it increasingly sees itself participating in a global war for talent, which the authorities understand is necessary for Singapore to continue to flourish. However, the liberal augmentation of the domestic workforce with expatriate labor continues to produce tension amongst the citizenry. How this tension is managed is likely to influence the operationalization of HRM in Singapore in the decades ahead.

As small city states with strategic locations, Dubai and Singapore represent examples of where state-directed development has attracted foreign investment and developed the cities as trading and tourist hubs in their respective regions. In both cases, investors and multinationals have been attracted by an array of inducements. As such, in both cities there is a major MNE presence and with them comes the opportunity to transmit best practice HRM policies and programs. However, the respective labor markets and regulatory systems do differ and incorporate different types and degrees of regulation. This applies to the use of foreign labor, where there is clear segmentation between professionals and service workers (Europeans and North Americans) and workers in hotels, domestic service, and construction (from Asia and the Middle East). In both cities, there has been an emphasis on human capital development through heavy investment in education and training, and through attracting international universities, schools, teaching, and research staff. Emirati nationals have, to date, largely worked in the public sector whereas, in Singapore, nationals can be found across most sectors with the exception of domestic service, hospitality, and construction sectors that are low paid and have poor conditions. In both countries, there are HRM challenges around effective diversity management programs given the large differences across the respective workforces by ethnicity, nationality, and religion.

The strong service culture evident in both countries' national airlines (Singapore Airlines and Emirates Airlines) is a testament to the strong focus each airline has on recruitment, selection, and the development and retention processes. Singapore Airlines (SIA) is consistently highly ranked (Wirtz et al., 2008) and is the world's second largest operator of the type after Emirates of the UAE. Singapore Airlines investment in training covers not just functional skill development but also interpersonal skills, in addition to team building and empowerment to support effective service delivery (Wirtz et al., 2008). Emirates Airlines flies to more than 130 destinations in more than seventy countries, and new destinations are constantly being added. In July 2016, Emirates Airlines was named the World's Best Airline 2016 at the Skytrax World Airline Awards. Skytrax awards are based on a total of 19.2 million completed surveys covering 280 airlines, by customers from more than 104 countries (Skytrax, 2016). The Skytrax survey measures quality standards across forty-one key performance indicators of front-line products and services in the airline industry. However, Emirates Airlines, in common with the rest of the UAE, is dependent on expatriate workers, who are given short-term contracts compliant with the UAE Labour Law.

While conditions for business are relatively free, especially in terms of attracting investment and start-ups, there are extensive regulations in both city states governing employment that have to be observed. As discussed previously, Dubai has "no unions and no strike" policies, regulations governing workplace conditions, and laws concerning religious observance especially during Ramadan (such as shorter hours for fasting workers), and the Emiratization policy which encourages the employment of nationals in the private sector.

To date, the record of economic growth in both city states has been impressive. However, we suggest that there are major HR challenges ahead. For Singapore, there is the challenge of an aging population, growing political opposition to immigration, and an ongoing dependence on cheap foreign labor in key competitive sectors such as hospitality and manufacturing. In the case of Dubai, the population profile suggests that population aging will not be an immediate problem. However, the immediate problem is absorbing the large numbers of nationals who are graduating and seeking professional jobs. No longer will they be able to be absorbed into the public sector and the Emiratization program is an attempt to open up private sector job opportunities for nationals. Singapore is extending the domain of its HR programs to include gender equity and equal employment opportunity (EEO), largely in response to the challenges of an aging population. In both cities, there are large pockets of immigrant labor, who are employed under conditions that locals would not accept. Consequently, there are human rights and OH&S issues evident, particularly in the domestic service and construction sectors.

In general, the labor conditions are sector and nationality dependent. It appears that Singapore is more attentive to ILO standards than Dubai. However, as outlined in this chapter, in both cities low-paid migrants often have their labor and human rights violated. To date, Singapore has taken up many more of the technical standards than has Dubai and has extended the domain of HRM beyond the core issues of recruitment and pay. However, Singapore needs to work to better protect its migrant workers, particularly unskilled laborers and domestic workers. Dubai has developed a centrally regulated employment system that systematically segregates the workforce and excludes basic labor rights (Connell & Burgess, 2013). As the ILO (2011) states, with reference to the unrest in the Middle East, the popular uprisings result from exacerbated poverty, inequality, and exclusion, arising from long-term deficits of democratic governance, essential freedom, and social dialogue.

In both cities, government labor market regulation is again sector and worker dependent. Nationals in general receive rights and protections in both countries. Regulations concerning religious observance are also important in Dubai. There are also some changes taking place as in August 2010 the Dubai Labour Ministry introduced a new classification system for companies ranking them as either A, B, or C (A being the highest) with the intention that the move will regulate the job market. This strategy arose from the implementation of a Cabinet Resolution governing the classification of establishments into groups in accordance with the degree of their compliance with labor legislation, systems and standards, cultural diversity approaches, on-time payment of salaries, provision of accommodation, and Emiratization quotas. Firms were given until January 2011 to comply, but apart from the salary aspects of this regulation (discussed later), it is difficult to find any reports concerning the effectiveness of this system; the UAE Labour Minister intends to provide mechanisms that put in place a safe and stable environment and to protect rights of all categories in the community.

Unions and collective action are illegal in Dubai, with the Dubai Ministry acting as the adjudicator in any contract disputes. In Singapore, there is an accord between the government and unions to promote harmonious workplace relations, although in both countries there are very low levels of recorded disputation, Singapore has an extensive system of formal dispute resolution. In Dubai, employee rights are the responsibility of the Ministry of Labour. However, the Wage Protection System (WPS) was introduced in 2009 with the intention that it would penalize those responsible for the non-payment of salaries in the private sector (mainly construction, retail, and small businesses). Since the WPS began, approximately 2.9 million workers and 205,000 of the UAE's 250,000 registered businesses have registered, and more than 600 employers have been penalized (Malit Jr & Al Youha, 2013).

In both countries, their labor markets and regulatory segmentation mitigates against a uniform HRM system. Differences are present according to the sector and the nationality of workers and active HRM programs tend to be limited to national citizens and MNE professional workers. However, in Singapore, there is an emerging recognition of the need to address EEO and discrimination, and to broaden the domain of HRM, and in the UAE, new laws came into effect on January 1, 2016 intended to improve the transparency of job terms and employment contracts, specifying how contracts can legally be terminated, and making it easier for workers to change employers. Although McGeehan, a UAE researcher at Human Rights Watch (cited in Lemon, 2015), said the reforms are to be applauded, he warned that some might be less serious than they seem and could be a "rehash" of others, so it remains to be seen how the reforms are enacted.

Conclusion

The aim of this chapter was to investigate HRM in relation to the city states of Dubai and Singapore. As discussed, there are local rules, customs, and pressures that constrain the application of universal models of HRM practice (Björkman, Budhwar, Smale, & Sumerlius, 2008). While both city states attract foreign investment and emphasize free trade and market-led growth, there remain in place extensive government regulations and controls across all aspects of commerce. In both, the development of human capital has been a priority with heavy investments in the education system being supplemented by migration and, in the case of Singapore, an extensive national training system. We have pointed out the similarities between the two states that focus on the extensive use of migrant workers and the challenges around diversity management, protecting unskilled and low-paid migrant workers, talent management, and providing opportunities for nationals, especially within the private sector. In both locations, there are diverse workforces and dependence on expatriate professionals, especially in MNEs. In both cities, the strong presence of MNEs can result in the adaptation of best practice HRM programs to local conditions; although to date, they have been largely directed to professional and expatriate workers. Dubai operates in an environment where unions and collective actions are illegal. In Singapore, unions form part of a tripartite consensus with government and employers. Singapore faces potential labor shortages with an aging population; in Dubai, the challenge is to address the unemployment of large numbers of graduates. These factors are likely to remain the key HRM challenges for each city state for the foreseeable future.

References

Abdulla, J., Djebarni, R., & Mellahi, K. (2011). Determinants of job satisfaction in the UAE: A case study of the Dubai police. *Personnel Review, 40*(1), 126–146.

Al-Esia, Z. & Skok, W. (2014). Arab knowledge sharing in a multicultural workforce: A dual case study in the UAE. *Arabian Journal of Business and Management Review, 4*(4), 1–10.

Barnett, A. H., Malcolm, M., & Toledo, H. (2015). Shooting the goose that lays the golden egg: The case of UAE employment policy. *Journal of Economic Studies, 42*(2), 285–302.

Björkman, I., Budhwar, P., Smale, A., & Sumerlius, J. (2008). Human resource management in foreign-owned subsidiaries: China versus India. *The International Journal of Human Resource Management, 19*(5), 964–978.

Cherrayil, N. K. (2015). *Multinationals see multifold benefits in setting up Dubai base, Gulf News Investment.* Retrieved November 13, 2015, from http://gulfnews.com/business/sectors/investment/multinationals-see-multi-fold-benefits-in-setting-up-dubai-base-1.1434945.

Connell, J. & Burgess, J. (2013). Vulnerable workers in an emerging Middle Eastern economy: What are the implications for HRM? *The International Journal of Human Resource Management, 24*(22), 4166–4184.

Connell, J. & Thorpe, M. (2010). Regional development and the "Dubai Model": Some observations and experiences. In C. Jayachandran, M. Thorpe, R. Subramanian, & V. Nagadevera (Eds.), *Business clusters, partnering for strategic advantage* (pp. 231–259). New Delhi and Oxford: Routledge.

Davis, M. (2006, September–October). Fear and money in Dubai. *New Left Review, 46,* 47–69. Retrieved November 19, 2015, from https://newleftreview.org/II/41/mike-davis-fear-and-money-in-dubai.

Dubai Statistics Centre. (2015). Retrieved July 30, 2016, from www.dsc.gov.ae/en-us.

Economist Intelligence Unit. (2015). *UAE country analysis, Economist Intelligence Unit.* Retrieved November 30, 2015, from http://country.eiu.com/united-arab-emirates.

Foley, J. A. (2013). Freedom from the press: Journalism and state power in Singapore. *Asian Journal of Literature, Culture and Society, 7*(2).

Forstenlechner, I., Madi, M. T., Selim, H. M. & Rutledge, E. J. (2012). Emiratisation: Determining the factors that influence the recruitment decisions of employers in the UAE. *The International Journal of Human Resource Management, 23*(2), 406–421.

Forstenlechner, I. & Rutledge, E. J. (2011). The GCC's "demographic imbalance": Perceptions, realities and policy options. *Middle East Policy, 18*(4), 25–43.

Galovan, A. M., Feistman, R. E., Stowe, J. D., & Hill, E. J. (2015). Achieving desired family size in dual-working households: Work and family influences among Singaporean couples. *Journal of Family Issues, 36,* 1377–1401.

Hamid, W. (2015). Feelings of home amongst Tamil migrant workers in Singapore's Little India. *Pacific Affairs, 88*(1), 5–25.

Harris, C. W. (2016). Lifelong learning and earning: The changing landscape of higher education in Singapore. In M. Scerri & L. K. Hui (Eds.), *CAUTHE 2016: The changing landscape of tourism and hospitality: The impact of emerging markets and emerging destinations.* Sydney: Blue Mountains International Hotel Management School, 1151–1160. Retrieved May 31, 2016, from http://search.informit.com.au.ezproxy.lib.uts.edu.au/documentSummary;dn=936422733502169;res=IELBUS ISBN: 9780987050793.

Hertog, S. (2014). *Arab Gulf states: An assessment of nationalisation policies.* Retrieved November 19, 2015, from http://cadmus.eui.eu/bitstream/handle/1814/32156/GLMM%20ResearchPaper_01-2014.pdf?sequence=1&isAllowed=y.

Human Rights Watch (2006). *Building towers, cheating workers, exploitation of migrant construction workers in the United Arab Emirates.* New York: Human Rights.

Hvidt, M. (2011). Economic and institutional reforms in the Arab Gulf countries. *The Middle East Journal, 65*(1), 85–102.

Iles, P., Almhedie, A., & Baruch, Y. (2012). Managing HR in the Middle East: Challenges in the public sector. *Public Personnel Management, 41*(3), 465–492.

International Labour Organization. (2011). *Questions and answers on the ILO response to challenges in the Arab World.* Retrieved September 14, 2015, from www.ilo.org/global/about-the-ilo/press-and-,ediacentre/insight/WCMS_1594.

ILO. (2015). *Labour Inspection United Arab Emirates Labour Inspection Country Profile: UNITED ARAB EMIRATES.* Retrieved November 30, 2015, from www.ilo.org/labadmin/info/WCMS_150919/lang-en/index.htm.

Janardhan, N. (2011). *Boom amid gloom: The spirit of possibility in the 21st century Gulf.* Reading: Ithaca Press.

Kolb, J. (2015). Expatriate entrepreneurship in the Gulf region between informality and a globalized knowledge society. *American Journal of Entrepreneurship, 8*(2), 89–107.

Latham & Watkins, LLP (2014). *Employment issues in the United Arab Emirates* (2nd ed). Retrieved November 15, 2016 from www.lw.com/thoughtleadership/employment-issues-in-uae.

Lee, S. A. (2015). Governance and economic change in Singapore. *Singapore Economic Review, 60*(3), 1550028.

Lemon, J. (2015). *HRW Researcher says UAE Labor Reform could be "Huge Improvement."* Retrieved August 29, 2016 from http://stepfeed.com/more-categories/big-news/hrw-researcher-says-uae-labor-reform-huge-improvement/#.V8VNT1t95aQ.

Levitt, P. (2013). A new social contract social welfare in an era of transnational migration. *Tikkun, 28*(3), 44–46.

Lillie, N., Çaro, E., Berntsen, L., & Wagner, I. (2013). Migration and human resource management. In M. Martínez Lucio (Ed.), *International human resource management: An employment relations perspective* (pp. 220–237). London: Sage Publications.

Lim, L. Y. C. (2015). Fifty years of development in the Singapore economy: An introductory review. In L. Y. C. Lim (Ed.), *Singapore's economic development: Retrospection and reflections* (pp. 1–15). Singapore, World Scientific Publications. Reprinted from *Singapore Economic Review, 60*(3).

Lim, S. & Leong, C. (2016). Casting the shadow of our past to illuminate the future of Singapore. *International Journal of Social Science and Humanity, 6*(5), 324–331.

Lohmann, G., Albers, S., Koch, B., & Pavlovich, K. (2009). From hub to tourist destination: An explorative study of Singapore and Dubai's aviation-based transformation. *Journal of Air Transport Management, 15*(5), 205–211.

Mahdavi, P. (2013). Gender, labour and the law: The nexus of domestic work, human trafficking and the informal economy in the United Arab Emirates. *Global Networks, 13*(4), 425–440.

Malit Jr, F. T. & Al Youha, A. (2013). Labor migration in the United Arab Emirates: Challenges and responses. *The Online Journal of the Migration Policy Institute.* Retrieved November 19, 2015, from www.migrationpolicy.org/article/labor-migration-united-arab-emirates-challenges-and-responses.

Marchon, C. and Toledo, H., 2014. Re-thinking employment quotas in the UAE. *The International Journal of Human Resource Management, 25*(16), 2253–2274.

Mina, W. (2014). United Arab Emirates FDI outlook. *The World Economy, 37*(12), 1716–1730.

Ministry of Manpower. (MOM) (2009). Workplace Relations and Standards. Retrieved September 15, 2009, from www.mom.gov.sg.

Ministry of Manpower. (MOM) (2015a). *Labour Force in Singapore, 2014.* Retrieved May 23, 2015, from www.mom.gov.sg.

Ministry of Manpower. (MOM) (2015b). Singapore Yearbook of Manpower Statistics 2015, Singapore: Ministry of Manpower. Retrieved March 24, 2016, from www.mom.gov.sg.

Mitra, S. & Thorpe, M. W. (2010). Government policy, clusters and the "Dubai Model." *International Journal of Globalization and Small Business, 4*(1), 73–91.

Neo, J. L. (2015). Riots and rights: Law and exclusion in Singapore's migrant worker regime. *Asian Journal of Law and Society, 2*(01), 137–168.

Pang, E. F. & Lim, L. (2015). Labour, productivity and Singapore's development model. *The Singapore Economic Review, 60*(3), 155033–1–1550033–30.

Randeree, K. (2009). Strategy, policy and practice in the nationalisation of human capital: Project Emiratisation. *Research and Practice in Human Resource Management, 17*(1), 71–91.

Roper, S. D. & Barria, L. A. (2014). Understanding variations in Gulf migration and labor practices. *Middle East Law and Governance, 6*(1), 32–52.

Shayah, M. H. & Qifeng, Y. (2015). Development of Free Zones in United Arab Emirates. International Review of Research in Emerging Markets and the Global Economy (IRREM), *An Online International Research Journal, 1*(2), 286–294.

Shunko, M., Do, H., & Tsay, A. A. (2014, September 28). Should a multinational firm place part of its supply chain in a tax haven?: Strategies to enable international tax arbitrage. *SSRN.* Retrieved from http://ssrn.com/abstract=2502534; or http://dx.doi.org/10.2139/ssrn.2502534.

Siddique, C. (2012). Knowledge management initiatives in the United Arab Emirates: A baseline study. *Journal of Knowledge Management, 16*(5), 702–723.

Skytrax (2016). *World's Top Ten Airlines 2016.* Retrieved August 10, 2016, from www.airlinequality.com/review-pages/top-10-airlines/.

Stanton, P. & Nankervis, A. (2011). Linking strategic HRM, performance management and organizational effectiveness: Perceptions of managers in Singapore. *Asia Pacific Business Review, 17*(01), 67–84.

Tan, K. & Bhaskaran, M. (2015). The role of the State in Singapore: Pragmatism in pursuit of growth. *The Singapore Economic Review, 60*(3), 1550030–1550030–30.

Thite, M., Wilkinson, A., & Shah, D. (2012). Internationalization and HRM strategies across subsidiaries in multinational corporations from emerging economies: A conceptual framework. *Journal of World Business, 47*(2), 251–258.

Thorpe, M. & Connell, J. (2013). Industry clusters, Dubai and the GCC: The antidote for growth and innovation after the GFC? In K. Brown, J. Burgess, M. Festing, & S. Royer (Eds.), *Resources and competitive advantage in clusters* (pp. 97–112). Munich: Rainer Hampp Verlag.

Toledo, H. (2013). The political economy of Emiratization in the UAE. *Journal of Economic Studies, 40*(1), 39–53.

UAE Government Strategy. (2007). Retrieved December 3, 2008, from www.dubai.ae/en.portal?topic,hm_uaegovstrategy,1,&_nfpb=true&_pageLabel=2.

The UAE Vision 2021. Retrieved May 5, 2014, from www.vision2021.ae/home-page.html.

Vora, N. (2012). Free speech and civil discourse: Producing expats, locals, and migrants in the UAE English-language blogosphere. *Journal of the Royal Anthropological Institute, 18*(4), 787–807.

Waring, P. (2010). Developments in employee relations in the Asia Pacific. In J. Connell & S. Teo (Eds.), *Strategic HRM: Contemporary issues in the Asia Pacific Region*. Prahran, VIC: Tilde University Press Victoria.

Waring, P., Bali, A., McKiernan, P., & Vas, C. (2015) Kicking the habit: Business responses to the Singapore government's efforts to reduce the foreign worker dependency. Second International Conference on Public Policy, Milan, Italy, July 1–4.

Wirtz, J., Heracleans, L., & Panarakan, L. (2008). Managing human resources for service excellence and cost effectiveness at Singapore Airlines. *Managing Service Quality, 18*(1), 4–19.

World Bank (2012). Knowledge Assessment Methodology. Retrieved November 19, 2015, from knhttp://web.worldbank.org/WBSITE/EXTERNAL/WBI/WBIPROGRAMS/KFDLP/EXTUNIKAM/0,,menuPK:1414738~pagePK:64168427~piPK:64168435~theSitePK:1414721,00.html.

World Bank. (2015a). *Doing business: Measuring business regulations*. Retrieved November 30, 2015, from www.doingbusiness.org/rankings.

World Bank. (2015b) World Development Indicators. Retrieved June 8, 2015, from http://wdi.worldbank.org/table/4.2.

20

HUMAN RESOURCE MANAGEMENT IN INDIA AND THE PHILIPPINES

Jennifer Ann L. Lajom, Simon Lloyd D. Restubog,
Mendiola Teng-Calleja, Raymund Habaradas, and
Ma Cristina Esquivel-Saldivar

Introduction

India and the Philippines are currently at the forefront of economic development. Both countries are heavily influenced by Western management approaches (Neelankavil, Mathur, & Zhang, 2000). In particular, the British system of management has been the foundation of current Indian management style, while the Philippines have adopted management styles that have been originated from multinational companies that settled in the country after World War II (Tiglao, 1992). Such exposure also enabled India and the Philippines to learn and utilize English as a mode of communication for business transactions (Malhotra, Ulgado, Agarwal, Shainesh, & Lan, 2005).

While it is recognized that India and the Philippines are both collectivistic in nature (Malhotra et al., 2005), each country's own inherent cultural imprints have been a salient influence in their management styles (Neelankavil et al., 2000). India has developed its own flavor where organizations are typically paternalistic in nature with an emphasis on personal relationships (Neelankavil et al., 2000). In the Philippines, the management system is infused with various indigenous practices such as *pakikisama* (i.e., the choice to conform to avoid conflict and maintain positive relations) and *utang na loob* (i.e., reciprocal obligation) (Restubog & Bordia, 2007; Roffey, 1999).

Indeed, both countries share similarities as a developing nation, having historical, cultural, and political influences in management styles, human resource management (HRM) policies, and practices. Despite these similarities, subtle but distinct differences remain salient. In particular, variations between the two countries' political influence over workers, economic status, and conditions of industrial relations impact HR policies and practices (Kuruvilla, 1996). It is worthwhile examining how the two countries forged their way toward promoting HR practices as a means of competitive advantage for business (Frenkel, Restubog, & Bednall, 2012; Hamel & Prahalad, 1990; Pfeffer, 1994; Wright, McMahan, & McWilliams, 1994) and superior organizational performance (Edralin, 2010; Hayton, 2005; Jain, Mathew, & Bedi, 2012; Singh, 2003).

The chapter is organized in four sections. First, we provide a general overview of the institutional context of each country. Second, we discuss three HRM themes within each country to identify areas of convergence and distinction. Third, we identify key HRM issues and challenges faced by both countries. Finally, we examine the extent to which the two countries have embraced strategic HRM.

Institutional and cultural context of India and the Philippines

India and the Philippines are emerging economies with large populations. In 2014, India had a population of 1.267 billion, making it the second most populous country in the world. The Philippines, on the other hand, exceeded the 100 million mark in 2014, and was ranked twelfth in the world in terms of population. Both countries are classified by the World Bank as lower middle-income countries. India had a GDP of US$2.067 trillion in 2014, while the Philippines had a GDP of US$284.6 billion in the same year. The relatively rapid economic growth rates of the two countries have resulted in a general improvement in their respective GDP per capita from 2010 to 2014. It is interesting to note that while India has succeeded in reducing the poverty headcount ratio (percentage of population) from 37.2 percent in 2004 to 21.9 percent in 2011 (World Bank, India Development Indicators 2015), the Philippines did not make any headway in reducing poverty, which even increased slightly from 24.9 percent in 2003 to 25.2 percent in 2012 (World Bank, Philippines Development Indicators 2015). The dynamic economic growth rates of India and the Philippines can be attributed to the structural adjustments that resulted from policy initiatives that led to the opening up of the economies of these two countries.

India's institutional context

The personnel function in India arose from a strong concern toward the welfare of factory laborers in the 1920s. Workers' unions were recognized through the Trade Unions Act established in 1926 and the establishment of the Royal Commission in 1932 (Budhwar, Varma, Singh, & Dhar, 2006). In 1947, the Industrial Disputes Act (IDA) was implemented and ensured social justice to both employers and employees through negotiations arbitrated by the Boards of Conciliation, Labor Courts, and Industrial Tribunals. The IDA further reinforced the government's role in approving establishment closure, worker retrenchment, as well as providing remuneration of affected workers of unfair labor practices (Hill, 2009). The Factories Act in 1948 further paved the way for the recognition of labor personnel's qualification and appointments (Budhwar et al., 2006).

Generally, HR practices in India were heavily influenced by the liberalization of the Indian economy (Guchait & Cho, 2010). The Indian government introduced economic reforms in

Table 20.1 GDP growth rate and GDP per capita (current US$) of India and the Philippines, 2010–2014

Country and key figures	2010	2011	2012	2013	2014
India					
GDP growth	10.3	6.6	5.1	6.9	7.4
GDP per capita	1,417.10	1,503.30	1,481.20	1,486.90	1,630.80
Philippines					
GDP growth	7.6	3.7	6.8	7.2	6.1
GDP per capita	2,135.90	2,358.10	2,587.60	2,765.10	2,843.10

Source: World Bank, India and Philippines Development Indicators (2015).

1991 after decades of protectionism, extensive regulation, and state ownership of large monopolies. The liberalization of economic policies and the closure of public monopolies led to substantial investments by foreign firms, raising the level of competition amongst Indian businesses. Domestic firms suddenly had to keep up with foreign firms not only in terms of improving operational efficiency but also in employee development (Singh, 2003). Indian businesses had "to undergo transformations in their human resource management (HRM) systems with supporting management values" (Amba-Rao, Petrick, Gupta, & Von Der Embse, 2000: 60). Clearly, HR managers had to adopt a strategic orientation in implementing the different HR functions.

In order to remain competitive, local firms developed their workforce, and changed routine human resource practices to a more strategic approach. The establishment of two professional bodies in India, namely, the National Human Resource Development Network (NHRDN) in 1985 and the Academy of Human Resource Development (AHRD) in 1990, "accelerated the shift of the personnel function towards the human resource management and development orientation" (Singh, 2003: 531). Since economic reforms were introduced in the early 1990s, the strategic role of the HR function has been highlighted because competitive pressures pushed domestic companies to develop their employees to match the skills and performance of those employed by their multinational counterparts (Budhwar & Sparrow, 1997; Singh, 2003; Sparrow & Budhwar, 1997; Nankervis, Cooke, Chatterjee, & Warner, 2013). The transformation from a regulated to a free market environment opened doors for growth, paving the way to competition with overseas firms in terms of available skilled workers and capacity to attain organizational efficiency and effectiveness.

The Philippines' institutional context

The establishment of the Personnel Management Association of the Philippines (PMAP) in the mid-1950s led to the institutionalization of personnel management in the country (Selmer & De Leon, 2001). Initially, HR practices were unstructured and informal, focusing on clerical tasks with limited involvement in actual recruitment and selection, hiring, promotion, and termination. Over the past sixty years, the practice of HRM evolved and adapted an intricate legal system. The laws revolve around work hours (e.g., overtime and holiday pay), employee benefits, labor relations (e.g., unionization and collective bargaining agreement), and manpower development (Selmer & De Leon, 2001).

The political reforms in the Philippines took place after the 1986 People Power Revolution against the dictatorship of former president Ferdinand Marcos. The following year, the Corazon Aquino administration came into power and focused on rebuilding democratic institutions, starting with the ratification of the 1987 Constitution. Institutional reforms accelerated in the 1990s with focus on legislation for the liberalization of the economy, the dismantling of monopolies, the deregulation of service industries, the privatization of state corporations, and the approval of tax-enhancement measures (Aldaba, 2013). As Philippine firms strived to recover from the effects of the Asian financial crisis in 1998, a strategic approach to HRM enabled firms to train their employees to utilize new production technologies and techniques to enhance their competitiveness (Audea, Teo, & Crawford, 2005).

Similar to India, there has been a shift from a traditional HRM model to a more strategic HRM approach. Filipino HR managers became more aware of their strategic role within their organizations (Benson & Rowley, 2003), and recognized the importance of linking HR with business planning (Ulrich, 1997). The role of HR in executive-level planning and execution also became salient (Teng-Calleja & Franco, 2013). Specifically, HR provides support for cost approximation of additional manpower and portrays an advisory role to various departments in times of conflicting policy issues. It also communicates the organization's vision and goals to its employees. This reflects the fact that the people management function in the Philippines has been evolving from personnel administration to a more strategic HRM approach (Audea & Crawford, 2005; Selmer & De Leon, 2001).

Human resource management practices

In this section, we describe and compare HR practices in India and the Philippines. We focus on three HRM areas, namely: (1) recruitment and selection, (2) performance management, and (3) training and development. The final section describes the utility of strategic HRM in India and the Philippines.

Recruitment and selection

Recruitment and selection practices in India and the Philippines involve sourcing potential applicants both from within and outside of the organization. Indian and Philippine organizations also resort to recruitment agencies, billboard advertisements, and networking as forms of external recruitment and employee referrals for both internal and external recruitment (Rao, 2010; Selmer & De Leon, 2001). Résumés, personality tests, and behavioral interviews have various aims in the selection process (Rao, 2010). Résumés of potential employees are used to identify whether the applicant possesses the required knowledge, skills, and abilities (KSA). Personality testing identifies key individual characteristics such as creativity, dynamism, working style, team-player orientation, and emotional intelligence. Behavioral interviews include one-on-one and panel interviewing that enables the organization to probe an applicant's background to determine its relevance to a job.

Various industries such as business process outsourcing (BPO), manufacturing, and information technology in India and the Philippines utilize these strategies. India is one of the leading providers of knowledge-based service industries (e.g., BPO), due to the availability of low-cost labor force with above-standard English proficiency and high levels of scientific and technical skills (Budhwar et al., 2006). Internal recruitment is a common practice for entry-, junior-, and upper-level management in the BPO industry, but those requiring technical expertise amongst its customer service representatives seek out prospective employees through external recruitment (Pereira & Anderson, 2012). The selection criteria emphasizes above-average English communication skills, voice tone and modulation, energy levels and overall attitude. Other criteria include educational background, prior work experience, and personality (Budhwar et al., 2006). Prospective candidates undergo an extensive ninety-minute interview and personality assessment (Pereira & Anderson, 2012).

The Philippines is also one of the world's largest providers of offshore outsourcing, second only to India (Beerepoot & Hendriks, 2013). The rise of the BPO industry in the Philippines has pushed call center firms to take an aggressive approach to recruitment practice. BPO firms tap into different outlets to inform prospective candidates of the vacancies and employment packages on offer (Hechanova, 2013). For instance, full-page print ads containing job information are released and re-advertised on a weekly basis. Some call center firms also participate in job fairs, hosted by universities, while other BPO companies resort to shopping-mall-based applicant centers for broader access to prospective applicants. Attractive bonus packages such as referral and sign-on bonuses are also offered to make call center jobs more appealing. In some cases, rival firms also offer lucrative and competitive benefits as a form of "labor poaching"

(Beerepoot & Hendriks 2013: 836) in order to attract prospective employees to transfer to their organization.

Similar to India, the selection criteria for BPO employment in the Philippines includes a university degree, some level of computer literacy, and fluency in English communication (Beerepoot & Hendriks, 2013). English proficiency is assessed via expression of precise grammar, coherence, and sharpness of thought and response (Lockwood, 2012). The applicants' command of English is evaluated throughout the interviews and written tests where the use good grammar is critically scrutinized.

Amongst Indian manufacturing firms, recruitment strategies include direct or walk-in applicants, utilizing placement consultants and head hunters, advertising through job portals, company websites, and print media outlets, personal contacts within the organization and referrals from current employees (Kundu, Rattan, Sheera, & Gahlawat, 2012; Singh, Singh, & Yadav, 2013). Employee referrals are preferred because it is perceived to guarantee accurate knowledge, capabilities, and the work ethic of prospective candidates (Singh et al., 2013). Selection practices are also employed such as behavioral interviews and psychological testing in order to assess specific skills and educational background.

Varied recruitment strategies and selection criteria are implemented amongst manufacturing firms in the Philippines such as those in the Mactan Export Processing Zone (MEPZ) (Chant, 1995). Unless a company prioritizes extensive expertise, a younger cohort is generally preferred as they are more physically able (e.g., better eyesight for electronic work) and can easily assimilate organizational values and culture. Recruitment practices include employee referrals and "walk-in" application. Denoted as the "backer system" (Chant, 1995: 158), current employees recommend potential applicants befitting of the job vacancy. Applicants are vouched for by another employee, a supervisor, or manager, and when hired, applicants are likely to do what it takes to do well in their new jobs out of respect for the referee and in order to return the favor (Chant, 1995; Selmer & De Leon, 2001). "*Compadre nepotism*" (Selmer & De Leon, 2001: 137) is the counterpart phenomenon for applicants, where they take advantage of personal connections or internal links with the organization, thus, having a greater chance of being offered a job. Companies also accept "walk-in" applicants as a form of recruiting potential employees. Applicants approach the companies and submit their résumé without necessarily responding to any job advertisement, rendering vacancy advertising unnecessary. Selection practices include the provision of relevant documents such as a school diploma and transcripts, police clearance, and referral letters. Prospective applicants also undergo psychological testing that assesses their intelligence and practical skill sets such as visual acuity, manual dexterity, and sewing skills (Chant, 1995).

The information technology and software industry in India also uses internal and external recruitment and selection procedures. Entry-level positions such as software trainees and programmers are recruited externally through campus placements and media advertisements, while middle- and senior-level vacancies such as project leaders or managers are filled through internal recruitment (Prasad & Kamalanabhan, 2010). Prospective applicants are selected on the basis of technical ability and soft skills such as leadership, problem-solving, and decision-making. Technical knowledge is a vital criterion amongst entry-level applicants, whereas technical and soft skills are important criteria for higher-level positions. Applicants are screened using personality tests, and structured and unstructured interviews (Prasad & Kamalanabhan, 2010; Rao, 2010). Finally, employee referrals are used for both internal and external recruitment procedure, either for entry-level positions or for senior and middle management staff. Employee referrals are beneficial because current employees are able to provide a sufficient and realistic preview of the vacancy to prospective applicants, thus ensuring a person–organization/person–fit component.

The "insider knowledge" which internal applicants receive enables them to adapt easily in the new role and eventually display optimum performance (Rao, 2010).

Selmer and De Leon (2001) report similar patterns of recruitment and selection practices amongst industrial firms in the Philippines. Employee referral is also a prominent practice in recruiting for prospective employees. Formal guarantees in the form of pertinent school documents, police clearance, and other relevant certifications enable the application process to proceed. Test administration and interviews are common selection practices amongst various manufacturing and industrial firms (Chant, 1995; Selmer & De Leon, 2001).

A salient characteristic of the recruitment and selection practices between India and the Philippines is depicted in its similarities. Both countries practice internal and external recruitment strategies in attracting prospective employees across different industries. In certain cases, the Philippines display a more aggressive and varied approach in applicant recruitment such as extending recruitment in schools and entertaining informal, "walk-in" applicants. Both countries also use personality and skills assessment strategies as a means to select qualified applicants. More importantly, some of these practices are driven by each country's respective cultural background. For instance, a notable recruitment strategy demonstrated in both countries is the use of employee referrals. While there is practical merit such as providing favorable recommendations toward the capabilities of the prospective candidate, other reasons that are culturally grounded still exist.

The idea behind Indian firms' preference to hire "one of their own" as an internal recruitment strategy reflects the Indian's culture of in-group collectivism (House, Hanges, Javidan, Dorfman, & Gupta, 2004). Organizational members are preferred to benefit from hiring opportunities rather than outsiders. In the Philippines, the more culturally salient aspect of employee referral is evident in external recruitment, with emphasis on the backer system and "*compadre nepotism*" (i.e., hiring based on applicant's personal connection within the organization, Chant, 1995; Selmer & De Leon, 2011). The concept of "*utang na loob*" (debt of gratitude), an implicit form of gratitude or contractual obligation to return a favor (Kaut, 1961; Pe-Pua & Protacio-Marcelino, 2000), and "*pakikisama*" (getting along with others), a way of avoiding conflict and maintaining positive relations (Roffey, 1999) could be factors why referred applicants in Philippine organizations are perceived to demonstrate high levels of performance.

Finally, some recruitment strategies are more apparent in one country than the other. For example, foreign firms in India partner with universities in order to gain access to a talented pool of manpower (Holtbrügge, Friedman, & Puck, 2010). In the Philippines, various industries (e.g., BPO, manufacturing, ship manning, automotive, and business retailing) that provide work–life balance programs, such as family welfare programs, are regarded as an important recruitment strategy (Nierras, 2012). Indeed, encouraging and enabling working conditions is vital in recruiting and retaining organizational staff (Adeyemo, Sehoole, & Cueno, 2015).

Performance management

The parallelisms between India and the Philippines provide an interesting backdrop for describing and comparing the performance management practices of organizations in these two countries. Our review of the existing literature revealed the following: (a) there is a diversity in the performance appraisal practices of firms; (b) performance appraisals are undertaken for their evaluative rather than a developmental purpose; and (c) the subjectivity and bias of line managers may undermine the effectiveness of the performance appraisal process.

In India, performance appraisal practices vary across firms. For instance, Sanyal and Biswas (2014) found that multinational companies in the software industry conduct employee assessments annually despite reporting to do so biannually or quarterly. Techniques used also vary amongst multinational firms and big Indian firms where highly sophisticated techniques are utilized, such as management-by-objectives (MBO), 360-degree appraisal, forced-choice method, and self-evaluations done electronically through portals. Smaller firms use the traditional supervisory report and the formal peer and self-evaluation method.

In the Philippines, performance management in most companies are driven by management-by-objectives (MBO) and competency-based assessments. Based on the 2008 Benchmark Survey conducted by PMAP, "at least 12 percent of Philippine companies are still trait-based in their appraisals," signifying the misalignment of performance management systems (PMS) with business goals (Moya, n.d.).

Indian businesses, whether these are multinational companies (MNCs) or joint ventures (JVs), private investor corporations (PIs) or private family firms (PFs), are more likely to use performance appraisal results for evaluative purposes compared to their public sector (PS) counterparts. Public sector organizations tend to maximize public value rather than market value, and emphasize procedural fairness rather than efficiency. This is in contrast with private sector firms that deal with intense levels of competition that render them pressed to reward effective performance and sanction under-par performance (Amba-Rao et al., 2000). Public sector managers also value hierarchy and authority, contractual obligations, and bureaucratic procedures that are believed to nurture public trust and welfare (Petrick & Quinn, 1997)

Performance management has taken root as a result of a mandate by the Philippine Congress, as expressed in the Governing Principles of the Modified Compensation and Position Classification System and Base Pay Schedule of the Government (Civil Service Commission, 2012). This encourages the establishment of a PMS that aligns personnel performance with organizational performance to safeguard performance orientation within the compensation system and sets the stage for the Performance Based Incentive System (PBIS). Apart from the established alignment, civil servants are now assessed using the following standards: (a) effectiveness/quality, (b) efficiency, and (c) timeliness (Civil Service Commission, 2012).

Government incentives used to be uniformly given to all civil servants regardless of the quality and quantity of their performance. Under the PBIS, exemplary government employees receive two incentives: (a) the productive enhancement incentive (PEI), which is annually distributed to all government employees across the board, and; (b) the performance-based bonus (PBB), which is given to employees based on actual performance and contributions to the accomplishment of their respective agencies' targets (Malacanang Administrative Order No. 25, 2011).

The 2008 PMAP benchmark survey (Moya, n.d.) described performance appraisal in the private sector as being closely linked to rewards. An employee's performance ratings determines the year-end bonus or annual salary increase that he or she receives, which drives employee performance and consequently achieves business objectives. However, the 2008 PMAP benchmark survey suggests that Philippine companies view performance management as a tool to influence behavior rather than for training needs analysis. Indeed, most companies have a section on areas for improvement and/or career track in their appraisal forms, but the developmental scope of performance management remains largely ignored. Further, customized development programs might be feasible for smaller organizations, but more difficult to carry out for organizations employing thousands of workers. While exceptional individuals are given an opportunity to undergo a more customized program or take highly specialized courses, the rest of the workforce undergo the standard training and development programs (Moya, n.d.).

HR practices of Indian firms were found to be more personalized and subject to the whims of top management, in contrast to the impersonally institutionalized and stable practices of Western firms (Mendonca & Kanungo, 1990; Shenkar, 1995). This seems to be the case for performance appraisal (PA) practices which are biased and disconnected from a strategic and globally competitive HRM system (Amba-Rao et al., 2000). Indian managers face value-laden dilemmas such as reconciling their professional role that requires objectivity and rationality, with their social hierarchical role; its expectations of conformity and paternalism become diffi- cult, leading to a superficial commitment to the performance appraisal process (Parikh & Garg, 1990). Further, when performance appraisals do not distinguish between employee contribu- tions and the social, technical, and environmental constraints on performance, employees tend to perceive performance appraisals as unfair and withhold productive efforts (Amba-Rao et al., 2000; Sparrow & Budhwar, 1997; Varma & Budhwar, 2014). While gradual exposure to modern management philosophies elevated the recognition of merit and equity in performance manage- ment systems, initiatives to reform PA practices remain deterred by inertia, social expectations, and practical delivery system constraints (Amba-Rao et al., 2000).

In the Philippines, HR professionals acknowledge that line managers view performance appraisals as tedious, routine-based, and highly bureaucratic (Moya, n.d.). This mindset dis- regards the relevant areas of the appraisal, and superficial approaches in performance evaluation are implemented. Since business units interact with a host of clients, varied sources for feedback and performance should also be considered; however, immediate supervisors typically have the authority to provide performance ratings. This myopic approach renders the appraisals biased and devoid of a holistic portrait of the employee (Moya, n.d.).

Training and development

Training and development plays an essential role in sustaining a twenty-first century com- petitive organization. Acquiring new competencies increases the efficiency and effectiveness of an organization and highlights the relevance of HR in enabling the organization to stay com- petitive in a highly globalized environment (Benson, 2014; Hamid, 2011; Hub, 2015; Supangco, 2012; Yu, Kim, & Restubog, 2015). In this section, we discuss how both the Philippines and India developed these new competencies through training and development.

Training and development initiatives in Philippine organizations have been implemented since the 1990s. For instance, San Miguel Corporation, one of the largest conglomerate of food and beverages in the Philippines, built two training centers to provide courses on marketing, finance, operations management, leadership, communications skills, and foreign languages (Selwyn, 1992). However, the 1992 Philippine Labor Flexibility Survey (PLFS) reported that out of 1,311 Philippine organizations, about 47 percent provided initial training for newly hired employees, 30 percent provided retooling programs to improve employee performance, and only 25 percent had retooling programs for employees to upgrade their skills, grade, or status. Similarly, only 21 percent of these firms provided all three types of training, typically within the electronics industry, large-scale, and foreign-owned firms. Training programs were least fre- quent in construction, wood products, and small-scale enterprises. Most firms with fifty or fewer employees did not carry out any training at all. In contrast, large corporations allocated more than 45 percent of their total HR budget to personnel development and encouraged their leaders to undertake training courses locally and abroad (Selmer & De Leon, 2001).

However, an overlap on skill development initiatives from various public and private sector agencies paved the way for a more streamlined technical-vocational education and training (TVET) system. Through the enactment of the Technical Education and Skills Development Act (1994), the Technical Education and Skills Development Authority (TESDA) was estab- lished and signed into law by the then President Fidel V. Ramos. This Act aims to formulate a comprehensive development plan and to reform industry-based training programs, which include apprenticeships, dual training systems, and other similar programs. Not long after in 1997, domestic firms in the private sector began using HRM practices that enhance firm effectiveness. Large firms have either invested in establishing their own training centers or have started sending their employees to training programs outside their company and were required to provide "echo sessions" (Skene, 2003: 119) to share what they have learned.

Furthermore, training programs in the Philippines reflect training needs assessment from various sources like job competency requirements, departmental performance, employee feedback, and performance appraisal results (Edralin, 2011). Commonly used types of training methods include lectures accompanied by educational technologies such as CD-ROM, the Internet, and their company's intranet/portal, followed by team trainings and on-the-job training. Team teaching and adopting a core-curriculum approach are also used to nurture and sustain innovation efforts of manufacturing and non-manufacturing industries to uphold standards of employee skills development (Edralin, 2011).

Edralin (2011) identified several best practices to stimulate and generate innovation in Philippine organizations. These include: (a) the implementation of extensive, continuing training development programs on technical competencies and the promotion of work behaviors aligned with the company's values and philosophy; (b) conducting training needs assessment focusing on competencies needed for successful job performance; (c) promoting cross training, coordination training, and team leader training in conjunction with the utility of new learning technologies (e.g., internet resources) and simulation exercises; and (d) a genuine interest and determined stance from company executives to engage in training and development to promote a positive organizational climate. These practices and innovations resulted in increased organizational commitment, creativity, and productivity (Cooke & Saini, 2010; Edralin, 2011; also see Chapter 9 in this volume).

Recognizing the need to nurture the professional development of Indian workers at the time of India's economic reformation marked the changing priorities of policy makers in the government. It was a significant step that guaranteed that all Indian workers from various sectors would receive adequate training in managing the challenges of the twenty-first century (Sharma, 1992). The need to advance meaningful, relevant, and effective training programs in India became salient with liberalization, spurring the entry of foreign companies, and the need to become globally competitive (Hamid, 2011; Sharma, 1992).

Yapadithaya and Stewart (2003) explored various aspects of training and development initiatives. In terms of corporate commitment to training and development, 71 percent of training programs are managed by the HR personnel or training specialist while only a little above 10 percent is managed by line managers, supervisors, or foremen. While 13 percent reported that both HR specialists and supervisors manage the training initiatives in their organization, 4.8 percent of the respondents reported that nobody from their organization manages the training and development function. These results suggest an incongruence between services provided by HR personnel and training specialists and those solely being handled by line managers (Yapadithaya & Stewart, 2003).

The trends and status of conducting training needs analysis and evaluation also show that while 66 percent of the Indian organizations reported conducting training needs, nearly 10 percent reported that they do not evaluate the effectiveness of their training initiatives and only 14 percent of the organizations claimed that they evaluate the impact of training at the organizational level. Overall, these indicators suggest the low level of corporate commitment devoted to the training and development function (Yapadithaya & Stewart, 2003).

Given the large population in India with a projected 986 million workers to join the workforce by the year 2030, the ability to create new jobs at an unprecedented rate will pose a challenge. Effective training programs should involve matching the job profiles of various categories of employees in order to accommodate the requirements of both national and international clientele. An evaluation of the current skills base is recommended to identify the gaps, formulate training programs and plans, and to develop performance assessment criteria based on job requirements (Hamid, 2011). Sultana, Devi, and Navyteja (2014) also suggest that training and development programs need to be tailored to the unique needs of each organization. Hiring training specialists who can offer high quality training programs may not accurately meet the unique needs of the employees and the organization. In addition, Indian firms are also giving importance to the role of HR consultants and HRM professional networks in disseminating new HRM practices when adopting Western approaches and conforming to the general trend in order to maintain a competitive global stance (Cooke & Saini, 2010).

After the liberalization of economic policies in India and the Philippines, both countries experienced an increased level of competition with international firms. This exerted a tremendous impact on both countries as domestic industries needed to better prepare and develop their workforce to be more competitive (Benson & Rowley, 2003; Kramar & Parry, 2014; Tayeb, 1996). Training and development programs of both countries share similar designs, while sufficiently divergent to address the unique cultural elements present in both countries. Indeed, Kramar and Parry (2014) observed that despite the similarities in the HR practices, variations can be attributed to the unique cultures of these countries. Thus, there is a need to provide culturally sensitive HRM practices that can be converged with current global practices.

Key issues and challenges

Building on the insights derived from theoretical and empirical work on HRM practices in India and the Philippines, we identify key issues and challenges that HRM professionals in these two countries must confront.

Recruitment and selection practices in India and the Philippines determine the kind of employees that organizations hire, with implications to performance outcomes at work. While there are adequate descriptive reports of the specific recruitment and selection strategies that are used in Indian and Philippine organizations, there is little information on the extent to which these strategies are valid and effective. For instance, the prevalence of the use of employee referrals only pertains to its advantages, but does not recognize its limitations (e.g., potentially preventing the organization from acquiring the optimum knowledge, skills, and abilities necessary for the job).

Table 20.2 Summary of key issues and challenges

Recruitment and selection	1 Unclear rationale and link of practices to organization's overall strategic business plan 2 Validity and effectiveness of strategies 3 Cultural and social influence as potential deterrents to effective practice
Performance management	1 Line-support divide 2 De-emphasis of the developmental role of performance appraisals 3 Cultural misfit of performance appraisals
Training and development	1 Lack of legislation and financing 2 Limited manpower for provision and implementation 3 Underdeveloped indicators of successful training outcomes

Cultural and social influences are also inherent in the recruitment and selection practices in the Philippines (Restubog & Bordia, 2006; Restubog & Bordia, 2007). For instance, the referral system benefits the organization by reducing monitoring costs as immediate supervisors or managers vouch for a new employee (Selmer & De Leon, 2001). However, extreme cases of nepotism abound in certain situations, where political connections can also dictate hiring over and above the required qualification (Ishii, Rohitarachoon, & Hossain, 2013). Such practices undermine the presence of a personnel selection board and delegitimize prescribed recruitment procedures. Clearly, inadequate recruitment and selection strategies are bound to result in a mismatch between the job requirements and the prospective candidate, consequently leading to lowered employee performance, increased dissatisfaction, and attrition (Gonzales, 2014).

To address these issues, recruitment and selection strategies must be aligned with the strategic goals of the organization. For instance, offering attractive compensation packages (e.g., bonuses), is a common practice in the Philippines, particularly in the BPO industry (Joint Foreign Chambers of the Philippines, 2010). However, while this may attract prospective employees for one organization, it may signify attrition to another contributing to additional recruitment cost. The Joint Foreign Chambers of the Philippines (2010) suggests that highlighting the career progression and growth and development opportunities could be used to attract a broader labor pool.

Holtbrügge and colleagues (2010) also propose that while focusing on the personal characteristics of prospective job candidates, the firms could also package themselves as an attractive option for employment. For instance, Indian firms establish affiliations with relevant groups, such as educational institutions that produce talented managers and specialists, or those that highlight the organization's reputation and desirable features such as location, wage level, and corporate culture. Moreover, Indian companies in the manufacturing, IT, infrastructure, and heavy industries subscribe to detailed recruitment and selection policies and appropriate selection criteria, and involved line managers in the selection procedures. Consequently, this has a positive influence on financial (e.g., market share, profit growth, and sales) and non-financial (e.g., employee satisfaction and productivity) organizational performance (Chanda, Bansal, & Chanda, 2010).

In the domain of performance management, there is a need to address the "line-support divide." HR professionals must establish partnerships with the line functions that they support by communicating the value of the performance management system, calibrating their expectations, and streamlining appraisal process in order to minimize the negative connotations associated with performance appraisals. HR professionals must also pay attention to the developmental aspects of performance appraisal. Instead of simply reducing performance appraisals to its evaluative purpose and perceiving employees as mere human capital, employees could be perceived as possessing human dignity and having the right to flourish in their work ("work is for man" rather than "man for work"; Pontifical Council for Justice and Peace, 2012). Indeed, the developmental and evaluative uses of performance reviews seem intertwined (Boswell & Boudreau, 2002), and thus, merits the potential in utilizing performance appraisals for such purposes.

HR professionals must also implement HR practices (including the performance appraisal process) that are culturally fit (Frenkel et al., 2012). In India, Rao (2010) suggests that in consideration of the high power distance within Indian workspaces, managers must facilitate performance management processes that imbibe a performance culture. Unit, functional, and department heads must take the initiative in establishing awareness of company objectives and its alignment with departmental and individual goals. In the Philippines, the PMAP has attempted to build an HR framework that is rooted in values that approximate the Filipino's characteristics at work. These concepts include *malasakit* (care), *pananagutan* (responsibility), and *bayanihan* (spirit of community), which highlight how Filipino employees work and achieve goals (Moya, n.d.; Tang, Restubog, Rodriguez, & Cayayan, 2006). Integrating these values, as well as the corporate values espoused by organizations into the appraisal system serves an important function in culture building.

There are also several critical challenges that prevent Indian and Philippine organizations from capitalizing on training and development initiatives. First, despite efforts on the part of employees to engage in training and development programs, a climate that nurtures successful acquisition and transfer of knowledge and skills is not maintained. In the case of the Philippines, a specific provision in the Labor Code on National Manpower Development Program (Department of Labor and Employment, 2009) stipulated the need for training and development, however, specific and concrete performance outcomes are less explicit. The lack of specific and documented training and development policies was also reflected in Indian organizations (Yapadithaya & Stewart, 2003; Sultana et al., 2014). A second challenge pertains to the individuals responsible for providing and implementing training and development programs. There is a need for training specialists who can work closely with line managers to ensure that the training provided is relevant and that training goals are achieved. It is also important to have qualified training specialists who understand the fundamental needs of their clients. Indeed, training specialists should utilize a stimulating learning environment and a customized design and delivery of training programs rather than using a singular training approach (Sultana et al., 2014). Last, although many Indian and Philippine organizations have increasingly provided training and development to bring about the needed positive changes for the organization, there is still an urgent need to develop more accurate success indicators. Effective indicators can identify how training initiatives foster organizational commitment and boost organizational performance and innovation for both the organization and its constituents.

The issues and challenges noted above across different areas of HR practice indicate the extent to which strategic HR is apparent amongst Indian and Philippine organizations. A country's cultural background and the lack of explicit strategic HR policies of the organization are salient factors in various HR practices that determine the successful organizational performance. This highlights the importance of HRM in the execution of an organization's strategic planning process (Teng-Calleja & Franco, 2013). In the next section, we discuss how Indian and Philippine organizations embrace the practice of strategic HRM.

Strategic HRM in India and the Philippines

Human resource management in both India and the Philippines has evolved from the traditional personnel administration to having a strategic role in organizations (Bhatnagar, 2007; Teng-Calleja & Franco, 2013). Although HR practitioners continue to fight for their place in the boardroom, studies in both countries have shown how strategic HRM creates an impact on firm performance, and employee attitudes and behaviors (Bhatnagar & Sharma, 2005; Edralin, 2013; Som, 2008; Supangco, 2012).

Strategic HRM roles, practices, and outcomes

A number of studies in both countries used David Ulrich's original articulation of Strategic HR Roles as descriptor of strategic HRM practice in organizations (e.g., Bhatnagar, 2007 in India; Villaluz, Fernandez, Salvosa, & Ilac, 2011 in the Philippines). This seems to be a reflection of the significant influence of Western frameworks in HR practice in both countries (Amante, 1997; Bhatnagar, 2007).

Ulrich (1997) described the four strategic HR Roles as: (1) Administrative Expert or the responsibility of HR to efficiently design and deliver various HR systems, practices, and processes; (2) Employee Champion or the HR practitioner's responsibility to attend to the daily needs and concerns of employees as well as promote employee well-being; (3) Change Agent or HR's role in determining organization issues and managing change; and (4) Strategic Partner which involves aligning HR strategies to strategic organizational directions and partnering with line managers in achieving objectives.

Studies by Bhatnagar (2007) and Bhatnagar and Sharma (2005) showed moderate to high agreement amongst managers in fifty Indian firms that Strategic HR Roles are evident in their organizations. These studies established positive relationships between strategic HR Roles and psychological empowerment, organizational learning, organization commitment, and firm performance. Research on strategic HR Roles conducted in the Philippines, on the other hand, showed that HR practitioners rated themselves higher in being employee champions and administrative experts compared to the more strategic HR roles of being change agents and strategic partners (Hechanova, 2013; Villaluz et al., 2011). Studies conducted on HR units demonstrating strategic HR roles in Philippine organizations showed significant positive associations with employee commitment and engagement (Glarino, 2013) as well as perceptions of organizational effectiveness (Calleja, 2006).

Strategic HRM can also be described through the different HR practices in organizations. The economic liberalization policy implemented by the Indian government, beginning in 1991, intensified competition amongst local and foreign firms and pushed HR practitioners to innovate HRM practices that translate to their firm's competitive advantage (Som, 2008). Findings showed that improvements in recruitment and selection as well as compensation and reward practices have significant and positive relationships with perceived organizational performance. Innovative recruitment and selection practices include selecting better-qualified managers and supervisors, making information about job vacancies easily available, and having formal onboarding processes. Flexible work hours, perceived equity between performance and rewards, as well as effective communication and implementation of remuneration policies comprise innovations in compensation and rewards practices (Som, 2008).

Globalization and continuing migration due to economic concerns and changing employee values exemplify the trends and issues affecting organizations in the Philippines (Villaluz et al., 2011). HR practitioners in organizations respond to these challenges by facilitating change and enhancing the effectiveness of HR systems through innovations. A study was conducted by Edralin (2013) on innovative HR practices amongst thirty organizations in the Philippines. Using the model employers' questionnaire adapted from Hewitt Asia's Model of Best Employers in 2005, the study explored which innovations implemented within six HR functions—Recruitment and Selection, Training and Development, Compensation, Performance Management, Work–Family Balance, and Employee Relations—were perceived to give the organization a competitive advantage. Findings showed that innovations in Training and Development in the context of strategic HRM is the most significant determinant of achieving competitive advantage. Innovations include aligning development efforts to the vision and mission, crafting core curricula as guide for competency development, the use of ICT in training, and adequate investment in both technical and behavioral programs.

A study conducted by Supangco (2012) involving thirty-three organizations described the state of HRM in the Philippines and compared how HRM practices have evolved from 2003 to 2008. For instance, the use of technology through the use of Human Resource Information Systems (HRIS) in payroll administration and monitoring of work time and attendance increased. However, there is a decline in the use of HRIS in recruitment and selection. The study also reported greater use of performance appraisal systems. In 2003, performance evaluation was generally utilized to assess professional/technical workers and managers, while in 2008, performance evaluation covered all employee categories. The sourcing of HR Heads from amongst HR specialists outside of the organization and the shared responsibility between HR and line managers in making people management decisions, however, remained unchanged. Specifically, HR takes the lead in major policy decisions pertaining to recruitment and selection, as well as pay and benefits. Line managers, on the other hand, take the primary role in decisions pertaining to expanding or reducing the workforce. HR practitioners in the Philippines disengage from the outsourcing of highly administrative HR functions such as payroll and benefits computation, preventing its capacity to devote more attention to activities with more strategic impact.

The research presented above describes the state of strategic HRM in India and the Philippines. The findings specifically point to how HRM practice in both countries strives to be on a par with and to improve based on established Western standards. This may be influenced by best practices introduced by foreign multinational corporations operating in these countries and/or the efforts of the MNCs to establish a strong alignment between the HR systems of the parent company to local subsidiaries (Amante, 1997; Jain et al., 2012). The strategic HRM efforts proved to have positive employee and organizational outcomes. However, there is evident recognition of the need to evolve from having a largely operational to a more strategic HR role and practice. This is to be achieved in the context of challenges brought about by the increasing employee expectations, and the war for talent.

Challenges to strategic HRM

Both the Philippines and India are beset with problems related to migration and increasing employee expectations. Globalization and technological advancements have made exposure to various job opportunities locally and abroad more accessible to employees. For example, India is known for its strong software industry and although companies operating in this area put an emphasis on retaining technical talent, voluntary attrition remains a significant problem. Employees in this industry were observed to prioritize career growth over company loyalty and familial influence pushes employees to seek employment abroad or in organizations that offer higher compensation (Agrawal & Thite, 2003).

Similar observations are seen in the Philippines. For example, young Filipino workers primarily work to support and help their families and look for good salary and benefits as well as opportunities for career growth (Hechanova, Alampay, & Franco, 2006). A culture of migration has likewise evolved in the Philippines (Asis, 2006), wherein Filipinos continuously seek employment abroad for better economic benefits as well as social security (Ang, 2008).

Voluntary attrition is also a growing concern in the BPO industries in both countries. BPO industry leaders reported an annual attrition average of 55 percent amongst the major players in the country (Destacamento, 2013). Dhal and Nayak (2015) suggests that a lack of career prospects, better remuneration, stressful lifestyle, and dissatisfying interpersonal relationships with peers and supervisors as reasons for leaving their organizations. In the Philippines, low salary, lack of opportunities for growth, non-competitive benefits, unfair treatment by management, lack of job security, a poor relationship with bosses, routine or boring job, and a poor relationship with peers are factors that influence the employees' decision to leave the organization (Hechanova-Alampay, 2010).

The retention factors in the major industries of both India and the Philippines highlight the importance of strategic HRM systems pertaining to rewards management, employee relations and well-being, and career development, as well as leadership development to improve superior–subordinate relationships. Strategic HRM practitioners are challenged to understand the needs of employees, and enhance the overall talent management system in organizations. To be able to effectively address these challenges, it is critical for HR practitioners to relinquish highly administrative HR functions through outsourcing or maximum use of technology so it can focus on more strategic concerns.

Conclusions

Decades of historical, political, and social transitions shaped the HRM practices in India and the Philippines that we know today. These practices also bear the cultural stamp that makes some practices uniquely Indian and Filipino. Indeed, the evolution of HRM practices brought about sophisticated transformation in the areas of recruitment and selection, performance management, and training and development in Indian and Filipino organizations. However, the development within the areas of HRM carries red flags that both countries contend and overcoming these shortcomings is imperative in fostering long-term productivity and organizational effectiveness.

Both countries are evidently implementing strategic HRM initiatives with India gradually setting the pace over the Philippines. However, there is ample room for both countries to fully embrace strategic HRM. Organizations must take the initiative in recognizing the alignment between HR practices and the strategic goals of the organization. Organizations should assess whether their once prospective applicants are developing their KSAs in order to enable optimum work outcomes eventually leading to firm performance. Thus, successful strategic HRM practice does not merely involve a select group of individuals within an HR department, but should involve the top management, line managers, and the employees working together toward a common goal. Finally, it is also important to recognize that organizations are embedded in a broader social context (Bordia, Restubog, Bordia, & Tang, 2010; Restubog & Bordia, 2006; Restubog & Bordia, 2007). Cultural and political factors also play a role in shaping how strategic HRM can be implemented in both Indian and Philippine organizations. While culture may remain an intricate part of strategic HRM practice, adequate legislation to support strategic HRM could further reinforce its implementation in both countries.

References

Adeyamo, K. S., Sehoole, C., & Cueno, C. G. (2015). The use of the job enrichment technique for decision-making in higher education: The case of the Philippines. *SA Journal of Human Resource Management, 13*, 1–9.

Agrawal, N. M. & Thite, M. (2003). Human resource issues, challenges and strategies in the Indian software industry. *International Journal of Human Resource Development and Management, 3*, 249–264.

Aldaba, R. M. (2013). Twenty years after Philippine trade liberalization and industrialization: What has happened and where do we go from here?. Retrieved from http://dirp3.pids.gov.ph/ris/dps/pidsdps1321.pdf.

Amba-Rao, S., Petrick, J., Gupta, J., & Von Der Embse, T. (2000). Comparative performance appraisal practices and management values among foreign and domestic firms in India. *The International Journal of Human Resource Management, 11*, 60–89.

Amante, M. S. (1997). Converging and diverging trends in HRM: The Philippine "halo-halo" approach. *Asia Pacific Business Review, 3*, 111–132.

Ang, D. (2008). Philippine international migration: Causes and consequences. Retrieved from www.cfo.gov.ph/pdf/.../DAA%20speech%20at%20Dalhousie%20U.pdf.

Asis, M. M. (2006). Living with migration: Experiences of left-behind children in the Philippines. *Asian Population Studies, 2*, 45–67.

Audea, T., Teo, S., & Crawford, J. (2005). HRM professionals and their perceptions of HRM and firm performance in the Philippines. *The International Journal of Human Resource Management, 16*, 532–552.

Beerepoot, N. & Hendriks, M. (2013). Employability of offshore service sector workers in the Philippines: Opportunities for upward labor mobility or dead-end jobs?. *Work, Employment and Society, 27*, 823–841.

Benson, B. (2014). Importance of employee training: 6 reasons why it saves money. Retrieved from http://lineshapespace.com/importance-of-employee-training/.

Benson, J. & Rowley, C. (2003). Changes in Asian HRM: Implications for theory and practice. *Asia Pacific Business Review, 9*, 186–195.

Bhatnagar, J. (2007). Predictors of organizational commitment in India: Strategic HR roles, organizational learning capability and psychological empowerment. *The International Journal of Human Resource Management, 18*, 1782–1811.

Bhatnagar, J. & Sharma, A. (2005). The Indian perspective of strategic HR roles and organizational learning capability. *The International Journal of Human Resource Management, 16*, 1711–1739.

Bordia, P., Restubog, S. L. D., Bordia, S., & Tang, R. L. (2010). Breach begets breach: Trickle-down effects of psychological contract breach on customer service. *Journal of Management, 36*, 1578–1607.

Boswell, W. R. & Boudreau, J. W. (2002). Separating the developmental and evaluative performance appraisal uses. *Journal of Business and Psychology, 16*, 391–412.

Budhwar, P. S. & Sparrow, P. R. (1997). Evaluating levels of strategic integration and devolvement of human resource management in India. *The International Journal of Human Resource Management, 8*, 476–494.

Budhwar, P. S., Varma, A., Singh, V., & Dhar, R. (2006). HRM systems of Indian call centers: An exploratory study. *The International Journal of Human Resource Management, 17*, 881–897.

Calleja, M. (2006). The relationship of human resource management roles and practices and organizational effectiveness. *Philippine Journal of Psychology, 39*, 15–37.

Chanda, A., Bansal, T., & Chanda, R. (2010). Strategic integration of recruitment practices and its impact on performance in Indian enterprises. *Research and Practice in Human Resource Management, 18*, 1–15.

Chant, S. (1995). Gender and export manufacturing in the Philippines: Continuity or change in female employment?: The case of the Mactan Export Processing Zone. *Gender, Place and Culture: A Journal of Feminist Geography, 2* (2), 47–176.

Civil Service Commission Memorandum Circular no. 6 (2012). Guidelines in the Establishment and Implementation of Agency Strategic Performance Management System (SPMS). Retrieved from www.hrdo.upd.edu.ph/MC6.pdf.

Cooke, F. L. & Saini, D. S. (2010). Diversity management in India: A study of organizations in different ownership forms and industrial sectors. *Human Resource Management, 49*, 477–500.

Department of Labor and Employment (2009). *National manpower development program.* Retrieved from www.dole.gov.ph/labor_codes/view/3

Destacamento, J. (2013, April 10). BPO players told, tame attrition rates to stay in the game. *The Freeman.*

Dhal, S. K. & Nayak, A. C. (2015). A study on employee attrition in BPO industries in India. *International Journal of Science and Research, 4*, 2242–2249.

Edralin, D. M. (2010). Human resource management practices: Drivers for stimulating corporate entrepreneurship in large companies in the Philippines. *DLSU Business & Economics Review, 19*(2), 25–41.

Edralin, D. M. (2011). Training and development practices of large Philippine companies. *Asia Pacific Business Review, 17*, 225–239.

Edralin, D. M. (2013). Work and life harmony: An exploratory case study of entrePinays. *DLSU Business & Economics Review, 22*(2), 15–36.

Frenkel, S., Restubog, S. L. D., & Bednall, T. (2012). How employee perceptions of HR policy and practice influence discretionary work effort and co-worker assistance: Evidence from two Australian organizations. *The International Journal of Human Resource Management, 23*, 4193–4210.

Glarino, G. G. (2013). Strategic human resource management: Influences on perceived organizational support and job attitudes. *International Journal of Business and Social Science, 4*, 6–15.

Gonzales, S. J. L. (2014). Labor turnover of a manufacturing firm in Tarlac City, Philippines. *Review of Integrative Business and Economics Research, 4*, 103–116.

Guchait, P. & Cho, S. (2010). The impact of human resource management practices on intention to leave of employees in the service industry in India: The mediating role of organizational commitment. *The International Journal of Human Resource Management, 21*, 1228–1247.

Hamel, G. & Prahalad, C. K. (1990). The core competence of the organization. *Harvard Business Review, 90*, 79–93.

Hamid, S. (2011). A study of effectiveness of training and development programmes of UPSTDC, India: An analysis. *South Asian Journal of Tourism and Heritage, 4*(1), 72–82.

Hayton, J. (2005). Promoting corporate entrepreneurship through human resource management practices: A review of empirical research. *Human Resource Management Review, 15*, 21–41.

Hechanova-Alampay, M. R. (2010). *1–800-Philippines: Understanding and managing the Filipino call center worker.* Institute of Philippine Culture, Ateneo de Manila University: Quezon City.

Hechanova, M. R. M. (2013). The call center as a revolving door: A Philippine perspective. *Personnel Review, 42*, 349–365.

Hechanova, M. R., Alampay, R. B., & Franco, E. F. (2006). Psychological empowerment, job satisfaction and performance among Filipino service workers. *Asian Journal of Social Psychology, 9*, 72–78.

Hill, E. (2009). The Indian industrial relations system: Struggling to address the dynamics of a globalizing economy. *Journal of Industrial Relations, 51*, 395–410.

Holtbrügge, D., Friedman, C. B., & Puck, J. F. (2010). Recruitment and retention in foreign firms in India: A resource-based view. *Human Resource Management, 49*, 439–455.

House, R. J., Hanges, P. J., Javidan, M., Dorfman, P. W., & Gupta, V. (2004). *Culture, leadership, and organizations: The GLOBE study of 62 societies.* Thousand Oaks, CA: SAGE Publications.

Hub, N. (2015). *Importance of training and development.* Retrieved from www.naukrihub.com/trainings/importance-of-training.html.

Ishii, R., Rohitarachoon, P., & Hossain, F. (2013). HRM reform in decentralised local government: Empirical perspectives on recruitment and selection in the Philippines and Thailand. *Asian Journal of Political Science, 21*, 249–267.

Jain, H., Mathew, M., & Bedi, A. (2012). HRM innovations by Indian and foreign MNCs operating in India: A survey of HR professionals. *The International Journal of Human Resource Management, 23*, 1006–1018.

Joint Foreign Chambers of the Philippines. (2010). Business Process Outsourcing (BPO). *Arangkada Philippines 2010: A Business Perspective*, 73–90.

Kaut, C. (1961). Utang na loob: A system of contractual obligation among Tagalogs. *Southwestern Journal of Anthropology, 17*, 256–272.

Kramar, R. & Parry, E. (2014). Strategic human resource management in the Asia Pacific region: Similarities and differences?. *Asia Pacific Journal of Humans Resources, 52*, 400–419.

Kundu, S. C., Rattan, D., Sheera, V. P., & Gahlawat, N. (2012). Recruitment and selection techniques in manufacturing and service organizations operating in India. *Journal of Strategic Human Resource Management, 1*, 9–19.

Kuruvilla, S. (1996). The relationship between economic development strategies and industrial relations: India, Malaysia, Singapore, and the Philippines. *Industrial and Labor Relations Review, 49*, 635–657.

Lockwood, J. (2012). Are we getting the right people for the job?: A study of English language recruitment assessment practices in the Business Processing Outsourcing sector India and the Philippines. *Journal of Business Communication, 49*, 107–127.

Malacanang Administrative Order no. 25 S. (2011). Inter-Agency Task Force on the Harmonization of National Government Performance Monitoring, Information and Reporting Systems. Retrieved from www.gov.ph/downloads/2011/12dec/20111221-AO-0025-BSA.pdf.

Malhotra, N. K., Ulgado, F. M., Agarwal, J., Shainesh, G., & Wu, L. (2005). Dimensions of service quality in developed and developing economies: Multi-country cross-cultural comparisons. *International Marketing Review, 22*, 256–278.

Mendonca, M. & Kanungo, R. N. (1990). Work culture in developing countries: Implications for performance management. *Psychology & Developing Societies, 2*, 137–164.

Moya, D. (n.d.). Pinoy performance management: Issues and prospects. Retrieved from www.pmap.org.ph/content/research/pinoy-performance-management-issues-and-prospects-2/.

Nankervis, A., Cooke, F. L., Chatterjee, S. & Warner, M. (2013). *New models of human resource management in China and India.* London: Routledge.

Neelankavil, J. P., Mathur, A., & Zhang, Y. (2000). Determinants of managerial performance: A cross-cultural comparison of the perceptions of middle-level managers in four countries. *Journal of International Business Studies, 31*, 121–140.

Nierras, E. M. (2012). Strategic human resource management practices of work–life balance and labor relations and its prevalence on selected Filipino firms. *International Journal of Information Technology and Business Management, 7*, 1–16.

Parikh, I. & Garg, P. (1990). Indian organizations: Value dilemmas in managerial roles. In A. Jaeger & R. Kanungo (Eds.), *Management in developing countries* (pp. 175–190). London: Routledge

Pe-Pua, R. & Protacio-Marcelino, E. A. (2000). Sikolohiyang Pilipino [Filipino psychology]: A legacy of Virgilio G. Enriquez. *Asian Journal of Social Psychology, 3*, 49–71.

Pereira, V. & Anderson, V. (2012). A longitudinal examination of HRM in a human resources offshoring (HRO) organization operating from India. *Journal of World Business, 47*, 223–231.

Petrick, J. A. & Quinn, J. F. (1997). *Management ethics: Integrity at work*. Thousand Oaks, CA: Sage.

Pfeffer, J. (1994). *Competitive advantage through people: Unleashing the power of the workforce*. Boston, MA: Harvard Business School Press.

Pontifical Council for Justice and Peace. (2012). *Vocation of the business leader: A reflection.*

Prasad, P. A. & Kamalanabhan, T. J. (2010). Human resource excellence in software industry in India: An exploratory study. *International Journal of Logistics Economics and Globalisation, 2*, 316–330.

Rao, P. (2010). A resource-based analysis of recruitment and selection practices of Indian software companies: A case study approach. *Journal of Indian Business Research, 2*, 32–51.

Restubog, S. L. D. & Bordia, P. (2006). Workplace familism and psychological contract breach in the Philippines. *Applied Psychology: An International Review, 55*, 563–585.

Restubog, S. L. D. & Bordia, P. (2007). One big happy family: Understanding the role of workplace familism in the psychological contract dynamics. In A. I. Glendon, B. Myors, & B. M. Thompson (Eds.), *Advances in organizational psychology: An Asia-Pacific perspective* (pp. 371–387). Brisbane: Australian Academic Press.

Roffey, B. (1999). Filipina managers and entrepreneurs: What leadership models apply?. *Asian Studies Review, 23*, 375–405.

Sanyal, M. & Biswas, S. (2014). Employee motivation from performance appraisal implications: Test of a theory in the software industry in West Bengal (India). *Procedia Economics and Finance, 11*, 182–196.

Selmer, J. & De Leon, C. (2001). Pinoy-style HRM: Human resource management in the Philippines. *Asia Pacific Business Review, 8*, 127–144.

Selwyn, M. (1992). *The Secrets of San Miguel's Sparkle, 28*(11), 28–35.

Sharma, R. D. (1992). Management training in India: Its nature and extent. *International Journal of Manpower, 12*, 41–55.

Shenkar, O. (1995). *Global perspectives of human resource management*. New York: Prentice Hall.

Singh, K. (2003). Strategic HR orientation and firm performance in India. *The International Journal of Human Resource Management, 14*, 530–543.

Singh, B., Singh, R., & Yadav, C. (2013). State of human factors in small manufacturing sectors of India. *International Journal of Social, Behavioral, Educational, Economic, Business and Industrial Engineering, 7*, 2981–2986.

Skene, C. (2003). Change and continuity: Recent developments in HRM in the Philippines. *Asia Pacific Business Review, 9*, 106–128.

Som, A. (2008). Innovative human resource management and corporate performance in the context of economic liberalization in India. *The International Journal of Human Resource Management, 19*, 1278–1297.

Sparrow, P. R. & Budhwar, P. S. (1997). Competition and change: Mapping the Indian HRM recipe against world-wide patterns. *Journal of World Business, 32*, 224–242.

Sultana, A., Devi, P. N., & Navyateja. (2014). Training and development: Issues in the Indian context. *Global Journal of Finance and Management, 6*, 599–608.

Supangco, V. (2012). Strategic HR practices in some organizations in the Philippines. *Philippine Management Review, 19*, 35–48.

Tang, R. L., Restubog, S. L. D., Rodriguez, J. A. C., & Cayayan, P. L. T. (2006). The impact of human resource management practices on organization commitment: Investigating the mediating roles of perceived organizational support and Procedural Justice. *Philippine Journal of Psychology, 39*, 146–174.

Tayeb, M. (1996). *The management of a multicultural workforce*. New York: Wiley.

Technical Education and Skills Development Act (1994). An act creating the technical education and skills development authority, providing for its powers, structure and for other purposes. Retrieved from www.tesda.gov.ph/uploads/File/REPUBLIC%20ACT%20NO.%207796.pdf.

Teng-Calleja, M. & Franco, E. P. (2013). Positioning analysis of HR's participation in top-level management planning and execution. *Philippine Journal of Psychology, 46*, 15–37.

Tiglao, R. (1992). Focus: Philippines—new, upwardly mobile tycoons. *Far Eastern Economic Review, 155* (35), 44–45.

Ulrich, D. (1997). *Human resource champions: The next agenda for adding value and delivering results.* Boston: MA: Harvard Business School Press.

Varma, A. & Budhwar, P. (2014). *Performance management and motivation.* London: SAGE Publications.

Villaluz, V., Fernandez, P., Salvosa, H., & Ilac, E. (2011). *HR & OD trends and practices: 2011 and beyond.* Monograph, Ateneo Center for Organization Research and Development.

World Bank, India Development Indicators. (2015). Retrieved from data.worldbank.org/country/india.

World Bank, Philippines Development Indicators (2015). Retrieved from data.worldbank.org/country/philippines.

Wright, P., McMahan, G., & McWilliams, A. (1994). Human resource and sustained competitive advantage: A resource-based perspective. *The International Journal of Human Resource Management, 5,* 301–326.

Yapadithaya, P. S. & Stewart, J. (2003). Corporate training and development policies and practices: A cross-national study of India and Britain. *International Journal of Training and Development, 7,* 108–123.

Yu, K., Kim, S. & Restubog, S. L. D. (2015). Transnational contexts for professional identity development in accounting. *Organization Studies, 36,* 1577–1597.

21

HUMAN RESOURCE MANAGEMENT IN BANGLADESH AND SRI LANKA

Vathsala Wickramasinghe and Monowar H. Mahmood

Introduction

Bangladesh and Sri Lanka are two developing countries in the South Asia. Bangladesh is located in the South East Asia of the South Asian subcontinent, whereas Sri Lanka is an island located in the Indian Ocean on the seaways between the East and West. Both countries have similar historical and cultural roots due to the colonial past and dependence on foreign direct investment (FDI) for economic development.

This chapter is devoted to discussing human resource management (HRM) in Bangladesh and Sri Lanka. The term HRM is used to incorporate main systems for recruitment and selection, performance management, rewards management and human resource development (HRD), and concerned with the management of all levels of personnel in the organizational hierarchy. This chapter contains five main sections. The next section presents an introduction to the country contexts of Bangladesh and Sri Lanka. This will be followed by an outline of the HRM practices in state sector. Section 4 presents HRM practices in the private sector, including multinational companies (MNCs), and small- and medium-sized enterprises (SMEs). Section 5 is devoted to discuss the strategic focus of HRM in the two countries.

Background of Bangladesh and Sri Lanka

Socio-economic context

Sri Lanka is a country with a unique and proud historical record of an impressive civilization, which spans over a period of several centuries before the Common Era (Sri Lanka Tourism Development Authority, n.d.). Sri Lanka was a colony of the Portuguese, the Dutch, and the British from 1505 to 1948. A Portuguese colonial mission was the first to arrive in Sri Lanka in 1505, followed by the Dutch and then the British. Sri Lanka became independent in 1948; since 1972, the country has officially been known as the Democratic Socialist Republic of Sri Lanka. In contrast, Bangladesh was a part of Bengal province of India, which comprised of West Bengal and Assam during the British colonial period (1747–1945). Thereafter, it was a part of Pakistan from 1945 to 1971. The country became independent in 1971. Both countries have gone through considerable changes in economic activities since the independence. In this regard,

Budhwar (2007) states that the social sector in Sri Lanka showed a strong development compared to other countries in the South Asia, which is clearly visible in most human development indicators. However, the main economic development in the South Asia was initiated in the 1980s, when the markets of Sri Lanka and later India, Pakistan, and Bangladesh were opened to FDI (Budhwar, 2007).

The Sri Lankan government introduced an array of far-reaching policy reforms in 1977. Since then, the country's economic growth has been mainly driven by the private sector led expansion of the manufacturing and service sectors. The five key economic sectors which have contributed to the Gross Domestic Product (GDP) since 2012 in the order of importance were wholesale and retail trade, manufacturing, transport and communication, agriculture, livestock and forestry, and construction (Central Bank of Sri Lanka, 2014). Investments in public infrastructure, the establishment of industrial zones, the prevalence of capital market infrastructure, and the flexibility of labor market have influenced the growth of foreign and local investments. According to the World Bank (2010), the future of Sri Lanka as a middle-income country depends on the knowledge-intensive services of banking and finance, information technology (IT), communications, insurance, and hospitality and leisure.

Bangladesh has initiated economic reforms since 1980s to attract FDI by promoting private sector involvement and global economic integration through trade liberalization. The country has taken steps for global economic integration through trade liberalization policies and the promotion of export-oriented manufacturing industries. Accordingly, Bangladesh created export-processing zones with minimal government interventions and various incentives for investors. Today, the industrial sector is considered to be the engine of growth, with its specialization in export-oriented apparel production. Employing around 40 percent of manufacturing labor force and generating over 80 percent of total export revenue, Bangladesh has been rated as the second largest apparel exporter in terms of export volume after China (Curran & Nadvi, 2015). This impressive growth can mainly be attributed to the comparatively lower wage rate of the Bangladeshi workers (International Labour Organization [ILO], 2013). In addition to apparel production, the country has made a considerable progress in the pharmaceutical, leather, and electronic industries during the recent past. As a result, the share of employment in the manufacturing sector has gradually increased, while the share of employment in the agricultural sector has gradually decreased.

The population and size of labor force of the two countries are shown in Table 21.1. One of the significant observations in Sri Lanka is the increasing number of educated women entering

Table 21.1 Labor force—Sri Lanka and Bangladesh

	Sri Lanka	*Bangladesh*
Population	21.9 million	168.95 million
GDP Contribution	Agriculture: 10.6%, industry: 32.4%, services: 57%	Agriculture: 15.9%, industry: 27.9%, services: 56.2%
Labor force	Total: 8.53 million. Agriculture: 31.8%, industry: 25.8%, services: 42.4%	Total: 80.27 million. Agriculture: 47%, industry: 13%, services: 40%
Labor force participation rate	Total: 53.3%. By gender—male 74.6%, female 34.7%. By residential sector: urban 48.9%, rural 54.2%	Total: 59.3%. By gender—male 82.5%, female 36%. By residential sector: urban 57.3%, rural 60%

Source: CIA World Fact Book, 2014.

the economically active population and this trend is projected to continue. In Bangladesh, changes in the sectoral composition of employment can be observed with increased importance to industry and services (ILO, 2013).

It is expected that the next decade will bring economic opportunities and challenges for both countries locally and globally on various fronts, and that HRM will continue to play a significant role in this regard.

Cultural context

In comparison to many Asian countries such as China, India, and Japan, Sri Lanka and Bangladesh have limited empirical literature to integrate cultural context with the HRM. The following sections review the literature that could have some implications on the development of HRM in the two countries.

Sri Lanka

Sri Lankans exhibit Asian traits in their family and social interactions; the decision-making system of a typical Sri Lankan family is hierarchical (Nanayakkara, 1984). Sri Lankans are oriented predominantly toward the collective (Freeman, 1996; Niles, 1998). Still, Sri Lankans are also oriented toward individual goals such as good education and secure employment (Niles, 1998).

In business management, Sri Lankans depict a mixture of Asian values and Western philosophies and practices (Nanayakkara, 1984). This is mainly a result of it having been a colony of the Portuguese, the Dutch, and the British until 1948. Reward systems are based on individual performance, reflecting individualistic cultural values (Nanayakkara, 1984; Wickramasinghe & Dabere, 2012). Business managers are oriented predominantly toward the collective. They prefer to maintain status and distance from their subordinates, and could be classified at the higher end of power distance continuum (Gunasekera, 1994). Further, managers are oriented toward more managerial and administrative styles than the entrepreneurial style of leadership (e.g., low risk taking and preference toward not challenging the status quo). Furthermore, employees see work as a way of living rather than as a way of life. Employees believe work is good in itself but is meaningful only if it relates to an organization and a job position, rather than believing and depending on entrepreneurship (Chandrakumara & Sparrow, 2004).

When participation is considered as a part of the organizational culture, non-managerial employees' involvement in decision-making enhances job performance (Wickramasinghe & Liyanage, 2013). However, employees perceive that their level of participation is moderate and managers perceive that their commitment to share decision-making with employees is far from satisfactory; managers perceive organizational culture as a barrier to adopting participative management techniques (Wickramasinghe & Wickramasinghe, 2011). Employees' work value orientation influences their expectation of HRM policy-practice design choices relating to empowerment, performance management, job-focused training, career development, and teamwork (Chandrakumara & Sparrow, 2004).

Bangladesh

The Bangladeshi culture inherited elements from ancient Indian tradition that embodies a combination of Buddhist, Hindu, and Muslim religious values, a partial influx of British culture during the colonial period, and the continual adoption of Western cultures in the recent past.

Religion-based mutually exclusive social groups such as *"Ashraf"* (high esteem) and *"Atrar"* (low status) amongst Muslims as well as occupation-based (caste) social groups amongst Hindus still prevail in the country (Bhuiyan, 2008). These social groups have contributed to the growth and continuance of functionality, status, and authority-related value systems of the Bangladeshi organizations.

Despite the high level of religious, ethnic, and linguistic homogeneity, social stratification is steeply hierarchical due to the influence of colonial and religious values and norms (Bhuiyan, 2012; Chowdhury & Mahmood, 2012; Sarker, 2012). Family is the basic unit of social life, and it cements all the members of two to five generations like a nucleus. In an extended family system, individuals are expected to act toward the welfare of the family. The eldest male family member is the leader and is responsible for the overall guidance and maintenance of the family. Seniority and old age are regarded as synonymous with wisdom and experience.

The British-originated administrative structure has developed a high power distance—hierarchical—authority relationship in organizations, with a reciprocal response between the rulers and the ruled. Obedience to seniors is considered to be the most important part of one's duty. Power, social position, and personal status determine the nature of interpersonal relationships (Bhuiyan, 2008; Mahmood, 2011). Therefore, opposing a superior's decision or raising a question is often considered as *"beyadobi"* (ill-manners), whereas a proper manner is considered as obedience and deference, which are vital in gaining access to patronage and favor (Bhuiyan, 2012). The senior–junior relationship is characterized by protection, patronage, and favor on the part of the senior and respect, loyalty, and compliance on the part of the junior (Bhuiyan, 2012).

Owing to this hierarchical relationship orientation, organizational roles are personalized, peer competition is avoided, and the approval of one's behavior is often sought within social or peer groups. Therefore, social relationships acquire more salience than work itself. Accordingly, performance evaluation depends more on subjective criteria than on objective criteria; norms aim at maintaining harmonious social relationships more than getting the job done (Miah & Hossain, 2014). In traditional Bangladeshi society, people spend much of their time interacting, discussing, and sharing ideas with social and peer groups (Chowdhury & Mahmood, 2012). As a result, the line between their personal and professional lives usually becomes blurred (Bhuiyan, 2012). Personalized relationships assume priority in the organizational context and create opportunities for favoritism, nepotism, and bias in selection, promotion, and the HRD-related decision-making (Hoque, 2009; Miah & Hossain, 2014).

Overall, both countries depict the Asian cultural values, which have been conditioned by the colonial legacy. These cultural characteristics seem to influence the way employees are managed at work and the institutionalization of HRM in the two countries.

HRM in the state sector

HRM practices are frequently differentiated on the basis of ownership (Budhwar & Boyne, 2004). This differentiation is viable for the state and private sectors since the private sector is owned by entrepreneurs or shareholders, while the state sector is managed by administrators from different levels of government. It is visible in both Bangladesh and Sri Lanka that the state sector is encouraged to emulate the management practices of the private sector as a part of privatization programs, implying that the private sector has superior management practices. Based on this premise, this section provides a description of HRM in the state sector.

HRM in the state sector: Sri Lanka

The state sector employment accounts for 15 percent of Sri Lanka's total labor force. Of the total labor force in this sector, 3.5 percent were managerial employees while the rest belonged to the category of non-managerial (Department of Census and Statistics, n.d.). All employees in the state sector operate in a highly regularized environment. The Public Services Commission (PSC) of Sri Lanka regulates employment relations in the state sector. Its Establishment Code provides guidance in carrying out employment related functions across state sector organizations. According to PSC of Sri Lanka, the purpose of Establishment Code is to provide a single source of reference specifying uniform set of practices for people management.

However, due to the existence of Establishment Code, each state sector organization is not in a position to customize the HRM activities to address its own circumstances. In selecting employees for entry level jobs, vacancies are gazetted and placement tests are conducted; job descriptions are too general and vague; promotions are given based on seniority and efficiency bar examinations; an effective performance management system does not exist for both managerial and non-managerial employees; rewards are not integrated with job performance—government financial circulars issued time to time specify basic salary levels and entitlement for allowances such as the cost of living.

However, training in the state sector had several achievements since 1955, and the year 1982 witnessed the establishment of a public corporation named the Sri Lanka Institute of Development Administration to cater for the training needs of this sector. However, the magnitude of the target group of the institution made it difficult to effectively impart training embracing all state sector organizations and job grades. As a result, several public corporations set up their own institutions to provide pre-service, in-service, and specialized HRD programs (Chinniah, 1986). Examples of few of these institutions are the Management Development and Productivity Centre established in 1968 currently known as National Institute of Business Management, the National Institute of Plantation management, and the Central Bank Training Institute that cater for the needs of public and private sectors on request.

Employees in the state sector have the right to form a trade union and to become members of the trade union. They also have the right to engage in trade union activities. If these rights are violated in the state sector, it becomes a violation of fundamental rights guaranteed by the Constitution (Sarveswaran, 2011).

In 2006, the government of Sri Lanka issued an administrative circular to establish a specialized unit in each state sector organization under the direct monitoring of Presidential Secretariat. The purpose of this unit was to enhance proper resource utilization, the eradication of corruption, the improvement of employee relations, and to seek non-managerial employees' cooperation in decision-making, ultimately enhancing productivity across state sector organizations. Several governments have been changed since then and these units do not seem to be active in the present day. Although the expectation is to create a uniform set of practices across state sector organizations, governments encourage each state sector organization to develop its own mission, vision, and goal statements. This incompatibility created issues in the achievement of action plans of each state sector organization. State sector organizations are, in general, identified as being the most unproductive organizations in the country.

HRM in the state sector: Bangladesh

The Bangladesh Public Service Commission (PSC) recruits and selects managerial and executive level employees on behalf of the government. In doing so, the PSC recruits entry-level managerial officials through a competitive examination known as the Bangladesh Civil Service (BCS) examination that comprised of a written test, which assesses applicants' knowledge on various compulsory and elective subjects, a psychological test, and an interview (PSC, 2013). The Ministry of Establishment prescribes the methods of recruitment, the qualifications of candidates, age limit, the syllabi of examination, and all other aspects of the entire selection process to be adopted in hiring BCS cadre officials. For non-managerial employees, respective departments conduct all recruitment and selection activities with the permission of relevant ministries.

The Bangladesh Public Administration Training Centre (PATC), on behalf of the government, imparts all training programs for entry, mid-, and senior-level employees. In addition to the PATC, there are few other training institutions that undertake the training of government employees. In addition, a few government organizations conduct well-structured internal training programs for their own employees. However, in the public sector, hierarchical career progression is not linked to training and the acquisition of qualifications but rather is linked to seniority and intervention from canvassers and peers. As a result, training and the acquisition of qualifications rarely bring any benefit to employees in terms of hierarchical career progression, and they do not have any scope to bypass the "seniority list" for promotions (Mahmood & Absar, 2015).

The compensation, salary, and other benefits for public sector employees are determined by the National Pay Commission (NPC) of Bangladesh. Although the basis of the pay structure is not explicitly clear, the NPC adopts the historical categorization of jobs originated by the British Government with four broad categorizations (Islington Commission, 1917, cited in Obaidullah, 1995), that is, Class I (Officer/Executives: pay grades 1–9), Class II (Junior Officers: pay grade 10), Class III (Clerical/Secretarial: pay grades 11–16), and Class IV (Custodial: pay grades 17–20), with respective four direct entry-level tiers, three promotion tiers, and two conversion tiers. Of these classifications, Class II jobs require entry-level educational qualifications, Class III jobs require the Higher Secondary Certificate (twelve years of full-time education) or equivalent qualifications, while Class IV jobs do not require any recognized qualifications other than some literacy or numerical ability. While the government declares pay structures for the entire public sector, individual organizations determine pay structures for the non-managerial employees in consultation with respective officials in corporations and ministries.

The government determines a single set of uniform pay scales and allowances for all the public sector enterprises. Therefore, collective bargaining and pay negotiations take place between the government and trade unions rather than between enterprise management and worker representatives (Mahmood & Absar, 2015). Trade unions are also involved in industrial conflict resolution, the application of labor law, the improvement of working conditions, the adoption of welfare programs, and the education and training of workers (Mamun, 2009).

Overall, over the last four decades, several reform initiatives were taken to modernize the HRM practices for the efficient and effective management of state sector organizations in Bangladesh and Sri Lanka. But resistance from bureaucracy and the lack of political will constrain the implementation of these reform programs. Therefore, HRM in the state sector of Bangladesh and Sri Lanka still remain as highly centralized, rigid, rule-based, and non-responsive to the needs of the global economic environment compared to dynamic, flexible, and performance-focused HRM in the private sector of the two countries.

HRM in the private sector

HRM in the private sector of Sri Lanka

The most common criterion used to classify private sector is the number of employees engaged. Enterprises with fewer than ten employees are identified as micro, 10–49 as small sized; 50–99 as medium sized; and those with more than 100 as large sized (Department of Census and Statistics, n.d.). In general, 91.8 percent of the establishments were micro; 7 percent were small sized, 1 percent was medium sized, and the balance of 0.2 percent was large sized; 44 percent of the labor force was engaged in micro-enterprises, 18 percent were in small-sized enterprises, 13 percent were in medium-sized enterprises, and 25 percent were in large-sized enterprises. Further, sole ownership is the dominant legal status of 94 percent of micro-enterprises and 66 percent of small-sized enterprises, whereas it is 37 percent in medium-sized enterprises and 20 percent in large-sized enterprises (Department of Census and Statistics, 2015). The following sections review the main HRM practices under four subheadings, namely, recruitment and selection, performance management, HRD, and rewards, based on the literature available on large-sized enterprises. HRM in MNCs and SMEs, the two subsets of the private sector, are discussed separately.

Recruitment and selection. Firms hire people for different employment status. Permanent employment, which is understood as a contract for an indefinite term, has been installed as the dominant form and standard entry-point for access to a comprehensive set of industrial rights and benefits. Outside this framework lays non-standard employment status, such as, casual, probationary, seasonal, fixed-term, and apprenticeships.

Firms give preference to educational/professional qualifications, experience and job-related competencies in selecting candidates across employment status (Wickramasinghe, 2007; Wickramasinghe & Kumara, 2009). However, the highest preference is for job-specific skills and experience across job categories and business sectors, and the premium on industry experience is very high in compensation decisions. Firms' high preference for an external labor market implies a move away from the internal labor market, and creates an environment for employees to hop from one workplace to another to maximize their future employability. As a result, HRM practices often focused on short-term job performance with short-term productivity targets. Existing research conducted in new business sectors, such as business process outsourcing (BPO), suggests that with a longer tenure in the present workplace employees become less satisfied, feel loss of interest, and intend to leave their present workplaces (Wickramasinghe, 2009). Therefore, firms' preference for the external labor market may not represent a strategic approach to employee resourcing.

As an external flexibility strategy, firms hire people through non-standard arrangements, such as casuals (Wickramasinghe & Chandrasekara, 2011). The use of casuals reflects a desire of firms to increase the alignment of workforce to economic gains rather than a commitment to meeting equal or fair opportunity motivation to assist employees. Firms, especially those in industrial sectors that are not traditionally associated with casual work, seem to be in a process of converting existing non-casual jobs into casual jobs. The intention of the use of "long-term casuals" is to reduce workforce non-unionization and operational costs. However, casual employees felt that they were being treated as second-class citizens by both employers and by fellow permanent workers, and depict different work-related attitudes and behavior based on the specifics of their exchange relationship. The rise and flourishing of such inferior job offers are mainly due to sizeable gaps in the regulatory system.

To increase the likelihood of attracting the best possible candidates, firms have adopted an internal flexibility strategy of flexible working hours. This provides considerable discretion over timing for employees and the effective utilization of an existing workforce for firms (Wickramasinghe & Jayabandu, 2007). Flexible working hours have helped to create a women-friendly work environment to attract and retain women into the active labor force. Firms also make variations in the amount of work by hiring employees for shift work—a quantitative or numerical flexibility strategy (Wickramasinghe & De Silva, 2011). Shift-work schedules allow employees to succeed each other at the same workstation in shifts that range from seventeen-hour or twenty-four-hour time-span on some regular basis as directed by the firm. However, shift work causes negative effects on the rhythm of minds and bodies, families, and social lives, and the routines of rest of the community. This calls for improvements in working conditions of shift-based workforce to help industries to flourish at large.

When considering the methods of recruitment, the highest preference is for various forms of advertising across business sectors (Wickramasinghe, 2007; Wickramasinghe & Kumara, 2009). A selection interview was rated as the most frequently used method for hiring. A written examination, psychometric test, and assessment centers were also used when hiring for managerial jobs. Despite the apparent confidence some firms demonstrated in employee retention, many new hires leave due to the lack of person–job fit, which implies the importance of generating realistic expectations on the job context (Wickramasinghe & Wickramanayake, 2013). This further implies the need for further investigations into the perceptions of new hires on employee resourcing practices and their decision-making in the selection process.

Performance management. Formalized job-based performance evaluation with opportunities for two-way communication guides employees to achieve higher levels of performance outcomes, serving both administrative and motivational purposes (Wickramasinghe & Liyanage, 2013). Performance targets were linked to individual, departmental, and corporate levels. The main performance criteria used were technical, business, personal, and intellectual capabilities, and these were used across job categories. Performance criteria and the procedure used for the implementation of performance appraisal were high in quality (Ali & Opatha, 2008). However, performance appraisal policy, feedback, storing, and the retrieval of performance data for managerial decision-making were moderate in quality whereas the content and appearance of appraisal form, the training of appraisers, and review and renewal process were low in quality.

The utilization, relevance, and acceptability of performance management practices were identified as the key areas of performance management effectiveness. Performance management focus, target setting, administrative work procedures, interdependency, and integration with other HRM functions significantly predict performance management effectiveness (Wickramasinghe, 2016b). Although considerable improvements are needed in the level of adoption of performance management practices, firms had devoted considerable energy in adopting the practices. It is a very positive signal for the practice of HRM, since performance management is one of the key areas designed to manage, support, and develop workforce of any organization.

The effective utilization of performance management information fosters post-promotion managerial performance (Wickramasinghe & Samaratunga, 2016). Specially, performance management rating plays a significant role in identifying the potential and development needs of personnel in managerial positions. Performance management practices adopted by firms during an economic recession significantly impact on employees' willingness to pursue job targets, utilize skills and talents to perform job tasks, and their overall happiness at work (Wickramasinghe & Perera, 2012).

Human resource development. Organizational strategy is directed to identify the HRD needs (Akuratiyagamage, 2006; Wickramasinghe & Garusinghe, 2010). For example, when importing new forms of product and process technologies in accordance with corporate strategy, firms provide specific HRD programs for the application and subsequent maintenance of these new technologies in the workplace (Wickramasinghe & Garusinghe, 2010). When planning business mergers, firms provide various types of HRD programs for the effective management of interests and expectations of employees (Wickramasinghe & Karunaratne, 2009). Firms also identify HRD needs through daily/weekly activity meetings of project teams and while handling problems on the job (Wickramasinghe & Widyaratne, 2012). However, the main intention of the provision of HRD programs is to enhance short-term productivity, and skills upgrades to complete projects at hand, instead of long-term commitment for the betterment of firms and employees (Akuratiyagamage, 2006; Wickramasinghe & Liyanage, 2013).

Widely used HRD programs include in-house activities by adding more job-related responsibilities, learning from feedback, self-study, learning blogs, and customized programs provided by vendors on specific project-related topics (Akuratiyagamage, 2006; Wickramasinghe & Kumara, 2009). Mentoring, action learning, coaching, learning logs, and guided reflection were rarely used, even for the managerial-level employees. There is an increased use of e-learning solutions such as blackboard, videos, search engines, and social networking to improve procedural, administrative, and job-related technical knowledge and skills (Wickramasinghe & Nisaf, 2013). This suggests firms' reliance on tacit knowledge, and the promotion of communities of practice. Although knowledge sharing is a natural function that takes place automatically, it could very much be controlled at the level of individuals. Unless steps were taken to facilitate intentionally the sharing of knowledge, either the full extent of knowledge may not be realized and utilized or organizations may experience a loss of knowledge once employees leave the workplace (Wickramasinghe & Widyaratne, 2012).

Firms use job rotation and horizontal mobility as a qualitative or functional flexibility strategy. Multi-skilling through on-the-job activities increases the number of potential alternative uses for which skills can be applied on consecutive tasks, whether upstream or downstream (resource flexibility), and alternative mechanisms to redeploy employees in different capacities (coordination flexibility) on a day-to-day basis in the lean production (Wickramasinghe & Wickramasinghe, 2016). Multi-skilling allows flexibility for firms when quantitative flexibility becomes inappropriate due to quality requirements, customization, continuous innovation, and product differentiation.

Firms design sophisticated HRD programs for the effective transfer of imported technology (Wickramasinghe & Garusinghe, 2010). These programs were designed to be delivered at the overseas technology transferor's environment as well as at the transferee's environment. When the technology transferor is from a non-English speaking country, firms highly prefer to hold these at the technology transferor's environment. Programs at the transferee's environment were delivered either by an in-house expert who was trained abroad or newly hired to the firm locally, by the local agent of the technology transferor or by an expert hired as a consultant.

Firms make inquiries into transfer, validation, and evaluation of programs (Wickramasinghe, 2006; Wickramasinghe & Garusinghe, 2010). Validation occurs by obtaining feedback at three levels, that is, at the level of participants, participants' immediate superiors and resource persons. Still, the most popular source is obtaining feedback from the participant. The programs were evaluated at the reaction level by obtaining feedback, at the learning level by giving tests, at the behavioral level by observing how skills are applied, and at the results level by comparing present and past performance (Wickramasinghe & Garusinghe, 2010). Criteria such as improvements in production efficiency, quality, wastage, and the consistency of operational efficiency were used at the results level.

However, firms face problems in the transfer of training (Wickramasinghe, 2006). The main reasons that prevent transfer were insufficient control over the transfer process, a non-supportive work environment to apply the new skills learned, and the difference between work environment and training environment. The main reasons that prevent transfer in the context of e-learning were the lack of personal contact, the lack of relevance of material for specific job contexts, and the lack of direction in finding specific materials from a collection of hundreds of online documents.

Rewards. The state stipulates minimum wages to be followed by the private sector. In many manufacturing sectors, wages boards are established as per the Wages Boards Ordinance of 1941. Salaries and wages are paid not earlier than on twenty-fifth day of a given month and not later than tenth day of the following month, fulfilling the labor regulations of the country. Working hours and overtime are regulated by the Shop and Office Employees Act of 1954 and Factories Ordinance of 1942.

Firms pay market-based rewards maintaining internal equity. Salaries enjoyed by employees attached to the IT sector can be identified as the best of all industries. However, reduction in financial rewards and benefits during an economic recession significantly impact on their happiness at work, negatively influencing their willingness to pursue job targets and the use of skills and talents (Wickramasinghe & Perera, 2012).

Performance-based financial incentives were paid across business sectors (Wickramasinghe & Dabere, 2012). These were paid for meeting or exceeding performance goals, as a percentage of monthly salary, as an increasing rate on performance, or on profit-sharing basis. Most widely utilized incentive schemes were individual based. The goals of incentive schemes, reward-based (e.g., surpassing a score), calculation-based (e.g., a percentage of monthly salary), incentive scheme-type (e.g., individual-based), employee participation in setting goals, and pay-out frequency have significant effects on job performance. In contrast, employees mainly experience team-based variable pay plans in the lean production, where variable pay was delivered subject to achieving targets, and calculated based on each unit of efficiency (Wickramasinghe & Wickramasinghe, 2016). When firms find difficulties in quantifying work output, variable pay was delivered as a flat rate calculated as a percentage of base pay, if the final product was rated as a prime quality product in lean production.

Employees' expectations of rewards not only include payments in financial terms, but also include promotion, job security, the perceptibility of expertise, and identification with the organization (Wickramasinghe & Wickramanayake, 2013). However, opportunities for promotion were limited due to the standardization of jobs to facilitate rapid replacement and the adoption of flatter organization structures (Wickramasinghe, 2016a). However, hierarchical career plateau did not make a significant contribution to the career satisfaction of employees in new business sectors since hierarchical plateauing is an inevitable part of the organizational life (Wickramasinghe & Jayaweera, 2010). Employees attached to new business sectors did not experience job content plateau due to the use of a project-based work environment, and lateral and cross-functional moves. These measures meet both firms' needs for flexibility and individuals' need for broad-based career experience. However, increased levels of voluntary working time extensions beyond normal working hours, holidays, and weekends to fulfill daily workloads decreased job satisfaction and increased turnover intention (Wickramasinghe, 2010b).

HRM in MNCs versus local private sector of Sri Lanka

Yeung, Warner, and Rowley (2008) reported that the employment practices in developing countries tend to be less institutionalized, less structured, and less impactful. However, only the dated literature in the Sri Lankan context (Nanayakkara, 1992) supports such claims while recent findings did not support them (Akuratiyagamage, 2006; Mamman, Akuratiyagamage, & Rees, 2006; Wickramasinghe, 2006; Wickramasinghe and Gamage, 2011).

When firms are categorized into local, foreign, and joint venture, these firms were established in either government initiated export processing zones/industrial parks, sector specific privately owned industrial parks, or outside export processing zones/industrial parks on government owed or privately owned lands (Board of Investment, n.d.). Akuratiyagamage (2006), Mamman et al. (2006), and Wickramasinghe (2006) investigated export-oriented apparel firms of local, foreign, and joint ventures established in all the above location options, and found that the firms had adopted relatively sophisticated HRM systems that reflect the global best practices. Further, Akuratiyagamage (2006) and Mamman et al. (2006) did not find significant differences across firms of different ownership (local and MNCs) for the implementation of HRM practices, the importance given to the HR function in organizational strategy, and HR managers' contribution to organizational strategy. Furthermore, the studies of Akuratiyagamage (2006), Mamman et al. (2006), and Wickramasinghe and Gamage (2011) provided evidence for the institutionalization of the HR function and the role of HR practitioners. Akuratiyagamage (2006) found that the majority of firms in the sample had specialized departments to manage human resources. Wickramasinghe and Gamage (2011) investigated a broad spectrum of manufacturing firms covering local, foreign, and joint ventures with ISO 9001 certification, and revealed that all the firms in the sample had the HR departments with about three to ten people performing the HRM tasks. This finding is important since there were only 1,402 industrial establishments operating in the country with 100 or more employees (Department of Census and Statistics, n.d.), and over 900 firms had ISO 9001 certification (*The Sunday Times*, 2008). Firms with less than 100 employees are considered to be SMEs and are discussed separately in the next section.

With regard to the practice of labor relations, state intervention has resulted in the enactment of a large number of labor statutes in Sri Lanka. In addition, Sri Lanka has ratified all eight core Conventions of the International Labour Organization (ILO), whereas many other countries in the region have not ratified them (Sarveswaran, 2010). An evaluation of the labor standards of Sri Lanka in the light of core Conventions of the ILO found that Sri Lankan labor standards are very much compatible with the principles embodied in the core Conventions of the ILO; local firms as well as MNCs have adopted the standards (Sarveswaran, 2010).

According to Mamman et al. (2006), the lack of significant differences between local private firms and MNCs in Sri Lanka imply that globalization is contributing to the diffusion and convergence of management practices. Accordingly, Mamman et al. concluded that "the drivers of globalisation such as non-governmental organizations, efficient communication systems, IT and international and professional institutions might have played some roles in the transfer of management practices and philosophies" (Mamman et al., 2006: 2017).

HRM in SMEs in Sri Lanka

When considering the management of SMEs, the larger the size of the establishment, the greater the chance that the establishment would be controlled by a male. Accordingly, females controlled 26 percent of the micro-enterprises, 8 percent of small-sized enterprises, 6 percent of the medium-sized enterprises, and 5 percent of the large-sized enterprises (Department of Census and Statistics, 2015). The leadership orientation of owner-managers were identified as either managerial, entrepreneurial, or a mixture of these two (Chandrakumara, De Zoysa, & Manawaduge, 2009). The entrepreneurial leadership orientation is more effective than managerial and mixed orientations on financial performance of SMEs. Further, the education background of owner-managers and their leadership orientation were positively correlated. Small- and medium-sized enterprises with more than seven years of business operation were actively engaged in business planning in Sri Lanka (Wijetunge, 2014).

SMEs face major HR issues due to staff shortage. This may have a correlation with the location of the enterprise, where 74 percent of micro-enterprises and 60 percent of small-sized enterprises were condensed in rural areas, whereas 50 percent of medium-sized enterprises and 61 percent of large-sized enterprises were in urban areas (Department of Census and Statistics, 2015). First, SMEs were lagging behind in the adoption of recruitment and selection practices (Priyanath, 2010). Although SMEs prefer to hire employees who could multi-task, they face difficulties in attracting employees. Employees were mainly recruited through personal contacts or existing employees, and were selected on personal favoritism. However, if owner-managers were better educated, appropriate selection and recruitment practices were adopted—conducting selection interviews, explaining the job role and responsibilities at the interview, and verifying the possession of skills to perform job tasks.

Second, the skill shortages of new hires were addressed through on-the-job training, delivered by existing employees prior to assigning job tasks due to poor person–job fit. However, once new hires' capabilities were enhanced to an acceptable level they leave for better prospects. Third, the provision of training is mainly on-the-job addressing operational and tactical skill needs to perform the job at hand. Enterprises have difficulties in releasing employees for training outside the workplace due to manpower and financial restrictions (Priyanath, 2010). Fourth, performance appraisal is not properly organized. Day-to-day monitoring of job tasks and guidance along re-work were the main monitoring and feedback mechanisms, and evaluation for potential is beyond the scope.

Small- and medium-sized enterprises adhere to government stipulated labor standards. Due to difficulties in retaining employees, SME owners pay salaries and wages without delay. Some well-managed SMEs provide food, accommodation, transport, and a New Year bonus and had implemented employee recognition schemes, such as Employee of the Month.

Overall, most SMEs lack proper organizational structure, job design, and the HR planning. As a result, SMEs faced the issues of effective utilization of human and physical resources. The level of adoption and effectiveness of HRM practices ultimately influence SMEs' access to finance, competitiveness, market relevance, and entrepreneurship.

HRM in the private sector: Bangladesh

Economic reforms and private sector led industrialization have helped Bangladesh to achieve desired economic growth and reach the status of a lower middle-income country. Mostly, SMEs and a few large family-owned conglomerates dominate the industrial sector of the country. However, HRM practices of these organizations are far from being the high performance oriented practices of the West (Mahmood & Absar, 2015). Common features of the main HRM practices in the Bangladeshi private sector are discussed under three subheadings, namely, recruitment and selection, HRD, and compensation and salary structures.

Recruitment and selection. The owners and managers of private sector consider the recruitment and selection of employees as a personal matter and utilize informal channels to hire desired employees. Private sector firms are not bound by any legal requirement to advertise jobs in the press, or adopt any formal recruitment and selection process. They recruit as and when required, and hire those whom they find as suitable (Mahmood & Absar, 2015). Most of the firms tend to hire the relatives of owners/managers to top positions, and this allows them to maintain power and gives them the ability to control the business. As a result, practices related to promotion, transfer, and remuneration are manipulated to suit personalized relationships (Mahmood & Absar, 2015). Firms use advertising to recruit personnel for jobs requiring higher levels of technical competencies only if they fail to find suitable personnel amongst their friends and relatives. On occasions, firms advertise in the press ostensibly to recruit managerial employees but in fact, these are more likely to be initiatives for publicity rather than initiatives for hiring. Therefore, social contacts and personalized relationships hamper the use of any formal approach for effective recruitment and selection of personnel.

Human resource development. The private sector is yet to perceive the importance of HRD for the betterment of both employees and organizations. Due to the labor surplus in Bangladesh, the HRD is considered as a cost rather than an investment. Therefore, it is hard to find any systematic practices for the HRD (Mahmood & Akhter, 2011). The indifferent attitudes of both management and trade unions coupled with large-scale ignorance about the need of developing employees pose a hindrance for the initiation and implementation of HRD programs.

The integration between industry and education and training institutions is limited. As a result, the influence of industry on the development of programs or other instructional processes of education and training institutions is limited. Therefore, the types of programs on offer are not relevant to the industry. Another important issue is the division between policy makers and civil society representatives on whether technical training or general education should be promoted as the HRD in the private sector.

Compensation and salary structures. Pay structures follow two main procedures, namely, minimum wage provisions where collective bargaining is absent due to the non-existence of effective trade unions and collective bargaining arrangements at the enterprise level in unionized organizations. However, it is rare to find formal or institutionalized pay structures in most local private sector organizations. Employees' pay is largely determined in an arbitrary manner based on personalized relationships (Mahmood & Absar, 2015).

The pay structures in large private sector organizations has some resemblance to that of public sector with two different pay structures for managerial and non-managerial employees. In the absence of any legal obligations and state regulations on pay for managerial employees, almost all local private sector organizations unilaterally design pay structures after taking into account job tasks to be performed in the respective departments/units of their organizations. Pay structures for non-managerial employees is determined through consultation and bargaining with the Collective Bargaining Agents (CBA). In general, such pay structure consists of eight to twelve pay grades depending on the organization's HR policy and CBA-management bargaining outcomes. Although managerial and non-managerial employees' pay grades are included in a unified pay structure, differences in employee categorization are explicit in pay structures across private sector.

Despite following either traditional HRM or well-designed HRM practices, private sector organizations in Bangladesh have achieved a steady growth and continuous success over the last twenty-five years. However, with the effects of globalization of business operations and intense competition of free market economy, the viability of such laissez-faire HRM practices is questionable. A slow and gradual move from traditional HRM to modern high-performance HRM is apparent in many medium- and large-sized private sector organizations in Bangladesh as discussed further in the next section.

HRM practices in MNCs in Bangladesh

The HRM practices in MNCs in Bangladesh are much better than those of the local public and private sector, and are considered as benchmarks in the local context. The better financial performance of MNCs is often attributed to their efficient and effective HRM practices. Multinationals, in general, use headquarters' prescribed job descriptions and job specifications in the recruitment process. In some cases, they modify the job specifications, adjusting educational qualifications to suit the country context. Multinationals use multiple evaluation mechanisms and selection committees to avoid nepotism and bias in the selection process (Mahmood, 2015). The use of multi-stage selection tests and the inclusion of expatriates in selection committees helps to neutralize undue pressure from government officials and political leaders.

With regard to the HRD, programs targeted at managerial employees are mostly delivered in foreign countries or corporate headquarters, and participants were selected with the recommendations from the headquarters. Programs targeted at non-managerial employees are designed and developed, as well as having the participants selected, by the HR managers in the Bangladeshi subsidiaries. In some cases, foreign experts are invited for the delivery of these programs.

Multinationals in Bangladesh use performance-related pay and promotion practices. They use key performance indicators to set annual goals and objectives at the individual level and perform annual performance reviews at the end of the financial year. The use of objective criteria for performance reviews ensures fairness and equity in pay and promotion decisions (Chowdhury & Mahmood, 2012).

Multinationals operating in Bangladesh comply with the labor law of the country. In a less institutionalized context of industrial relations (IR) in Bangladesh, multinationals seem to be one step ahead of domestic firms in complying with legally specified practices and regulations (Absar, Orazalin, & Mahmood, 2012). In contrast, most of the domestic private sector organizations show a reluctance to recognize trade unions and handle IR issues effectively, which has created a negative impact on labor management relations at the enterprise level. The reasons behind MNCs' adherence to legally specified IR practices may be due to the relatively weak position of trade unions in the labor legislation, the government's role in favoring multinationals, and/or the perceived impact of legally defined IR practices on MNCs' operations in Bangladesh.

Strategic approach to HRM and challenges faced by the HR function

This section reviews the available literature to describe the changes which have occurred in HRM practices, the strategic focus of practices, and the challenges faced by the HRM functions of the two countries in general—irrespective of the sector or ownership of the organization.

Recent changes in HRM in Bangladesh

Although HRM in Bangladesh still resembles traditional personnel management practices, some changes which have occurred in the recent past can be identified (Khan, 2013; Chowdhury & Mahmood, 2012). Many large organizations have established separate HRM departments and hired professional HR personnel with the relevant education and experience. A few organizations have even upgraded the status of HR managers and invited the head of HRM to the corporate board. The development of professionalism and the establishment of professional associations may have changed the attitudes of the business communities on the importance of HRM, which may have prompted this elevation of HRM roles. Shifts in the recruitment and selection practices are also visible in the country (Absar, 2011; Miah & Hossain, 2014). The private sector is beginning to emphasize competency-based approaches in recruitment and selection. Organizations are moving away from the traditional view of educational qualifications and experience to one which is focused more on individual achievements and work-related competencies (Mahmood & Absar, 2015). As the HR profession gaining momentum and HR managers are becoming better equipped, the use of competency models appears to be more widespread. The dissemination of competency-based practices in MNCs is quite evident across business sectors (Chowdhury & Mahmood, 2012; Mahmood, 2015). However, since competencies are assessed in a subjective manner, the manipulation of selection criteria can still be observed.

Globalization, the pace of industrialization, and the presence of MNCs have intensified the competition for talent. Attitudes toward employees are changing; instead of viewing them as a cost or a negligible resource, organizations are realizing the potential value of highly skilled employees. As a result, firms tend to invest in the HRD programs, and establish separate HRD departments. In some cases, newly created job positions of human capital manager and talent development manager indicate the increased presence of HRD in Bangladesh (Absar, Amran, & Nejati, 2014).

Multinationals and a few leading local organizations are trying to introduce performance-related pay practices (Absar, Nimalathasan, & Mahmood, 2013). However, the selection of performance criteria and the implementation of performance-related pay practices seem to still face the contentious issues discussed earlier. Further, the public sector is lagging behind in the adoption of performance-related pay practices. As a result, public sector organizations still consider seniority to be the main criteria for pay and promotion decisions.

Attitudes toward trade unions are also changing. Employers are taking initiatives to resolve industrial disputes by enabling unions and the management to cooperate at the plant or sector-level, thereby reducing government intervention. The bipartite dispute resolution mechanism in the garment and leather sectors seems to be a good example of an effective IR process. The Bangladesh Garments Manufacturers and Exporters Association (BGMEA) established a conciliation-cum-arbitration committee consisting of a chief arbitrator and eighteen members with equal representation from the BGMEA and labor organizations in the sector. In the leather sector, the Bangladesh Finished Leather, Leather Goods, and Footwear Exporters' Association, executive committees, and trade unions meet every two years to discuss employees' grievances. These institutes resolve many disputes through mutual consultation and understanding, which reflects amity between employees and the management. Other sectors are also in the process of adopting more congenial conflict resolution mechanisms, depicting positive signs for the future of IR in Bangladesh (Absar et al., 2013; Hossain, Sarker, & Afroze, 2012).

Strategic HRM in Sri Lanka

Research conducted since the early 2000s reports evidence for the institutionalization of HRM function and the strategic role of HR managers (Mamman et al., 2006; Wickramasinghe & Gamage, 2011). Firms have established specialized departments to perform the HRM activities. There is a high degree of strategic orientation of the HRM function, and the HR managers are gradually becoming a business partner. Firms introduced process improvement initiatives within the HRM function to fit into strategic priorities, such as the implementation of total quality management and lean production (Wickramasinghe and Gamage, 2011; Wickramasinghe & Wickramasinghe, 2016). Such initiatives made considerable changes by upgrading the role of HR function and the HR managers "steering" the initiatives and redesigning the HRM practices in line with business requirements. These changes imply a move toward a more strategic approach to the HRM.

However, line managers have been acquiring a more prominent place in the delivery of HRM practices during the recent past (Wickramasinghe, 2010a; Wickramasinghe & Wickramasinghe, 2016; Wickramasinghe & Fonseka, 2012). The role of line managers is very much higher in the situations of implementing new technologies (such as lean production) than that of HR managers (Wickramasinghe & Wickramasinghe, 2016). Further, finance departments, system analysts, and the IT departments have acquired a prominent role in reporting the HR information (Wickramasinghe & Fonseka, 2012). Although it is desirable to see the HR function driving the practice of reporting the HR information, one of the main factors that inhibited the HR managers' involvement was their lack of knowledge in this area. Furthermore, a considerable number of firms operating in the IT services do not have separate HR departments, and as a consequence, line managers and project managers hold the responsibility for the HRM activities. Still, these firms have implemented IT-based sophisticated HR systems, which allow line managers to deliver the services effectively. The main forces that drive organizations to seek IT-driven HRM solutions were identified as the need for cost reduction, higher quality services, and cultural change (Wickramasinghe, 2010a). The influence of IT on the delivery of HRM is persuasive and could be identified as a form of innovation in the HRM function in Sri Lanka.

For the HR managers to become an active strategic partner, their competency deficit as well as opportunity deficit have to be addressed adequately (Dharmasiri, 2004). Deficiencies in competency, education, and the experience of HR mangers operate as obstacles in the practice of strategic HRM (Dharmasiri, 2004; Sajeewanie & Opatha, 2007). The key competencies preferred for the HRM jobs were conceptual, technical, communication/language, handling IT/ICT, cultural, dealing with people, and leadership competencies (Arulrajah & Opatha, 2012; Dharmasiri, 2004). The lack of opportunities for HR mangers to get involved in the strategic decision-making was due to deficiencies in leadership qualities, the non-availability of supportive climate, and the non-existence of performance orientation in the HRM function (Dharmasiri, 2004). The hierarchical level to which the job position of HR manager is belonging has a positive effect in the practice of strategic HRM (Sajeewanie & Opatha, 2007). Overall, many HR managers felt that they are playing a symbolic role on the board. Still, Mamman et al. (2006) stated that their involvement at the board level at all is a significant improvement, especially in a developing country like Sri Lanka.

Challenges faced by the HR function in Bangladesh and Sri Lanka

Whether following traditional or well-designed high-performance HRM practices, the private sector in Bangladesh and Sri Lanka have achieved a steady growth and continuous success since the adoption of liberalized trade and investment policies. However, the survival and growth of business operations in the future will undoubtedly be influenced by the HRM practices adopted by the firms.

Specifically, first, although HRM capacity in Bangladesh is gradually improving, globalization brings pressures to improving the HRM practices in compliance with global standards of human rights, gender inequality, diversity, and ethical expectations (Mahmood & Absar, 2015). Therefore, HR managers often face the dilemma between global standards versus local needs, and the need to find avenues to integrate both international stakeholders' expectations and the country-specific HRM practices. Second, women's participation in the labor market has increased substantially in recent years, and therefore, Bangladesh needs to initiate changes in HRM policies such as working hours, work–life balance, maternity leave, and childcare benefits to accommodate gender specific needs and requirements.

Third, the generational gap between the millenniums and older employees poses challenges for the HR managers in Bangladesh. While earlier generations offered job commitment and loyalty in exchange for job security, the younger generation is demanding different dimensions of career growth in the non-traditional career era and other forms of rewards. Fourth, in relation to the above, the younger generation's expectations for work–life balance, flexi-hours, telecommuting, meaningful work, and performance-driven pay are adding new dimensions to HRM in Bangladesh. Fifth, although once considered as a labor abundant economy, competition for highly skilled personnel has intensified in recent years, and HR managers in Bangladesh are now required to implement talent management strategies to recruit and retain high-potential employees (Mahmood & Absar, 2015). However, it is expected that the emergence of the HR profession in Bangladesh will help deal with these challenges, and thereby help the country to achieve a higher level of economic growth and global integration.

In Sri Lanka, first, firms in new business sectors such as IT are likely to standardize jobs to facilitate rapid replacement by considering employees as "short-timers." Firms adopt various "poaching" strategies to recruit personnel, which increases the cost of recruitment and selection. This situation implies that firms are moving away from the internal labor market. Second, Sri Lanka has yet to learn how to reconcile work with family responsibilities. The Workers with Family Responsibilities Convention, Maternity Protection Convention, Part-Time Work Convention, and Home Work Convention of the ILO contribute to harmonizing work with family responsibilities (Sarveswaran, 2014). Sri Lanka is not a party to these Conventions, and does not have specific provisions, except the provision for maternity leave and nursing intervals to harmonize the two responsibilities. Further, although paternity leave is available in the public sector, it is not provided to employees by the private sector. This suggests that workplace flexibility strategies need to be a result of developments in institutional environment rather than firm-level rational decision-making. Consequently, an organization's people management strategies should be a product of evolving conceptions of the individual, and of individual rights institutionalized in labor legislation.

Third, due to the anti-union tactics propagated by the Sri Lankan governments, membership in the trade unions has declined steadily over time, and it was estimated that only about 15 percent of employees were members of a trade union in Sri Lanka (Ranaraja, 2013). This suggests the need for HR managers to take the lead in providing alternative mechanisms to maintain healthy employee relations. Overall, the HR function, irrespective of the business sector, needs to be equipped with resources to better respond to new developments in the employment landscape.

Conclusions

The economic growth of Bangladesh and Sri Lanka has been accompanied by policy level interventions, national campaigns, and programs under a comprehensive framework. Like other counterparts in the developing world, both countries face severe challenges in the sphere of industrialization. In order to survive and thrive in the increasingly competitive global economy, firms have realized the need to operate in a global market and the need to develop global strategies.

Both countries rely heavily on FDI while foreign investors are in a continuous search for locations that give them the best deal. As a consequence, Sri Lankan and Bangladeshi firms' preferred HRM practices may be conditioned by the global competitive environment. The new forms of work organization (such as project-based, together with virtual contexts) propagate temporary work structures and associated temporary work processes to deliver products and services. Successful transfer, implementation, and utilization of new processes and product technologies rely very much on the project-level human resource capabilities of the firms. Therefore, managing the workforce and the workplace is highly contested. The reaction of firms to these increasing economic pressures has been the replacement of traditional long-term employment with a new, short-term, transactional deal to employ personnel in the most efficient manner.

Competitive advantage is essentially internal to the organization and, if managed effectively, human resources could be the most expensive and valuable asset of an organization to gain sustainable competitive advantage. The state, as an employer in Bangladesh and Sri Lanka, has the responsibility to utilize its resources to the fullest. The state sector in countries with a higher level of responsibility for social development, like in Bangladesh and Sri Lanka, may face difficulties in achieving competitiveness. Nevertheless, the state sector needs to develop a coherent set of HRM practices. While HRM practices are considered as a source of competitive advantage, private sector organizations in both countries are yet to fully appreciate these developments. However, it was visible that the HRM practices adopted by MNCs act as benchmarks for domestic organizations, pressurizing them to adopt innovative HRM practices. Considering the size of the labor market and the level of unemployment of the two countries, business organizations could gain inimitable competitive advantage through the design and implementation of well-structured HRM practices. Therefore, a critical evaluation is needed to understand how far HRM practices could create a win–win situation for employers and employees, and the adjustments and adaptations required for the HR system to improve competitiveness at the firm and national level. Finally, the state should provide an appropriate and up-to-date trade and investment framework to balance the interests of employers, the workers, and the state. Such a system should be capable of protecting the interests of the investors for the benefit of the present and future workforce of the two countries.

References

Absar, N. (2011). Recruitment and selection practices in manufacturing firms in Bangladesh. *The Indian Journal of Industrial Relations, 47*(3), 434–449.

Absar, N., Amran, A., & Nejati, M. (2014). Human Capital reporting: Evidences from the banking sector of Bangladesh. *International Journal of Learning and Intellectual Capital, 11*(3), 244–258.

Absar, N., Nimalathasan, N., & Mahmood, M. (2013). HRM-market performance relationship: Evidence from Bangladeshi organizations. *South Asian Journal of Global Business Research, 1*(2), 238–255.

Absar, N., Orazalin, N., & Mahmood, M. (2012) Human capital reporting in emerging economies: A comparative study on the banking industry of Kazakhstan and Bangladesh. *Journal of Academy of Business and Economics, 12*(3), 28–36.

Akuratiyagamage, V. M. (2006). Management development practices: Empirical evidence from Sri Lanka. *The International Journal of Human Resource Management, 17*, 1605–1623.

Ali, M. A. M. H. & Opatha, H. H. D. N. P. (2008). Performance appraisal system and business performance: An empirical study in Sri Lankan apparel industry. *Sri Lankan Journal of Human Resource Management, 2*(1), 74–90.

Arulrajah, A. A. & Opatha, H. H. D. N. P. (2012). Skills required for key HRM jobs in Sri Lanka: An explorative study of news Paper advertisement. *Wayamba Journal of Management, 1*(1), 76–87.

Bhuiyan, S. (2008). Organizational change and learning in an institutionalized context: Case studies from Bangladesh. *Journal of Politics & Administration, 2*(1–2), 61–78.

Bhuiyan, S. (2011). Modernizing Bangladesh public administration through E-governance: Benefits and challenges. *Government Information Quarterly, 28*(1), 54–65.

Bhuiyan, S. (2012). Social capital and community development: An analysis of two cases from India and Bangladesh. *Journal of Asian and African Studies, 46*(6), 533–545.

Board of Investment of Sri Lanka (n.d.). Setting up in Sri Lanka. Retrieved from www.investsrilanka.com/setting_up_in/.

Budhwar, P. S. & Boyne, G. (2004). Human resource management in the Indian public and private sectors: An empirical comparison. *The International Journal of Human Resource Management, 15*(2), 346–370.

Budhwar, P. S. (2007). Guest editorial: People management in the Indian subcontinent. *Employee Relations, 29*(6), 545–553.

Central Bank of Sri Lanka (2014). *Sri Lanka socio-economic data 2014*. Retrieved from www.cbsl.gov.lk/pics_n_docs/10_pub/_docs/statistics/other/Socio_Econ_Data_2014_e.pdf.

Chandrakumara, A. & Sparrow, P. (2004). Work orientation as an element of national culture and its impact on HRM policy-practice design choices: Lessons from Sri Lanka. *International Journal of Manpower, 25*, 564–589.

Chandrakumara, A., De Zoysa, A., & Manawaduge, A. S. (2009). Leadership styles and company performance: The experience of owner-managers of SMEs. *4th international Asian Academy of Applied Business conference* (pp. 391–401). Makati City, The Philippines.

Chinniah, C. S. (1986). *History of administrative training in the public sector of Sri Lanka.* Colombo: SLIDA.

Chowdhury, S. & Mahmood, M. (2012). Societal institutions and HRM practices: An analysis of four multinational subsidiaries in Bangladesh. *The International Journal of Human Resource Management, 23*(9), 1808–1831.

CIA World Fact Book (2014). *South Asia: Sri Lanka.* Retrieved from www.cia.gov/library/publications/the-world-factbook/geos/ce.html.

Curran, L. & Nadvi, K. (2015). Shifting trade preferences and value chain impacts in the Bangladesh textiles and garment industry. *Cambridge Journal of Regions, Economy and Society, 8*(3), 459–474.

Department of Census and Statistics of Sri Lanka. (n.d.). *Census of industry—2003/2004.* Retrieved from www.statistics.gov.lk/industry/index.htm.

Department of Census and Statistics. (2015). *Non-agricultural economic activities in Sri Lanka—Economic census 2013/2014.* Colombo, Sri Lanka: Department of Census and Statistics. Retrieved from www.statistics.gov.lk/Economic/Non%20agri.pdf.

Dharmasiri, A. S. (2004). Enhancement of conceptual competencies of Sri Lankan managers for strategic decision making. *Sri Lankan Journal of Management, 5*(2), 195–227.

Freeman, M. A. (1996). Factorial structure of individualism/collectivism in Sri Lanka. *Psychological Reports, 78.* 907–914.

Gunasekera, T. (1994). *Hierarchy and egalitarianism: Caste, class, and power in Sinhalese peasant society.* Atlantic Highlands, NJ: Athlone Press.

Hoque, A. (2009). Does ideology matter?: Incentive, efficiency and management in the public sector. *International Journal of Public Administration, 32*(11), 929–950.

Hossain, C., Sarker, M., & Afroze, R. (2012). Recent unrest in the RMG sector of Bangladesh: Is this an outcome of poor labor practices? *International Journal of Business and Management, 7*(3), 206–218.

ILO. (2013). *Bangladesh: Seeking better employment condition for better socio-economic outcomes.* Studies on Growth with Equity Report. ILO Dhaka Office: Bangladesh.

Khan, S. (2013). *High performance work systems in the context of the banking sector in Bangladesh.* Unpublished PhD thesis, La Trobe University, Australia.

Mahmood, M. (2011) National culture vs. Corporate culture: Recruitment and selection practices of multinationals in a developing country context. *Journal of International Management Studies, 11*(1), 110–123.

Mahmood, M. (2015). Strategy, Structure and HRM policy orientations: Employee recruitment and selection practices in multinational subsidiaries. *Asia Pacific Journal of Human Resource, 53*(3), 331–350.

Mahmood, M. & Absar, N. (2015). Human resource management practices in Bangladesh: Current scenario and future challenges. *South Asian Journal of Human Resource Management, 2*(2), 171–188.

Mahmood, M. & Akhter, S. (2011). Training and development in Bangladesh. *International Journal of Training and Development, 15*(4), 306–321.

Mamman, A., Akuratiyagamage, V., & Rees, C. J. (2006). Managerial perceptions of the role of human resource function in Sri-Lanka: A comparative study of local, foreign-owned and joint-venture companies. *The International Journal of Human Resource Management, 17*, 2009–2020.

Mamun, M. A. (2009). Spending on human resource development: The scenario in the pharmaceutical industries. *Bangladesh Economic Chronicle, 1*(2), 1–3.

Miah, K. & Hossain, M. (2014). A comparative study of HRM practices between foreign and local garment companies in Bangladesh. *South Asian Journal of Human Resource Management, 1*(1), 67–89.

Nanayakkara, G. (1984). *Some behavioural orientations of Sri Lankan Managers.* Colombo: Sri Lankan Association for Advancement of Science.

Nanayakkara, G. (1992). *Culture and management in Sri Lanka.* Colombo: Postgraduate Institute of Management.

Niles, S. (1998). Achievement goals and means: A cultural comparison. *Journal of Cross-Cultural Psychology, 29*, 656–667.

Obaidullah, A. (1995). Reorganization of pay policy and structure in Bangladesh: Quest for living wage. *Journal of Asiatic Society of Bangladesh, 40*(1), 135–155.

Priyanath, H. M. S. (2010). Managerial deficiencies in the small and medium enterprises (SMEs) in Sri Lanka: An empirical evidence of SMEs in Ratnapura District. *Sabaragamuwa University Journal, 6*(1). DOI: 10.4038/suslj.v6i1.1692.

PSC (2013). *Annual Report of Bangladesh Public Service Commission-2013.* Dhaka: Author.

Ranaraja, S. (2013). *Emerging trends in employee participation in Sri Lanka.* Working Paper No. 46, Geneva: ILO.

Sajeewanie, T. L. & Opatha, H. H. D. N. P. (2007). Relationships between human resource manager-related factors and practice of strategic human resource management in Sri Lankan listed firms. *Sri Lankan Journal of Human Resource Management, 1*(1), 71–87.

Sarker, A. (2012) The political economy of privatization: The case of Bangladesh. *International Journal of Management, 28*(4), 595–611.

Sarveswaran, A. (2010). An evaluation of Sri Lankan labor standards in the light of the Core Conventions of the International Labour Organization. *Annual Research Symposium 2010.* Colombo: University of Colombo.

Sarveswaran, A. (2011). A critical evaluation of the termination of employment of workmen (Special Provisions) act in light of balancing the interests of employers, workmen and the State. *Annual Research Symposium 2011.* Colombo: University of Colombo.

Sarveswaran, A. (2014). An Assessment of the legal response to reconcile conflict between work and family responsibilities in Sri Lanka. *Faculty of Law Symposium—2014.* Colombo: University of Colombo.

Sri Lanka Tourism Development Authority (SLTDA) (n.d.). *History.* Retrieved from www.sltda.lk/history.

The Sunday Times (2008, September 7). Over 900 ISO 9001 certified companies in Sri Lanka. Financial Times section. Retrieved from www.sundaytimes.lk/080907/FinancialTimes/ft328.html.

Wickramasinghe, D. & Wickramasinghe, V. (2011). Differences in organizational factors by lean duration. *Operations Management Research, 4,* 111–126.

Wickramasinghe, V. (2007). Staffing practices in the private sector in Sri Lanka. *Career Development International, 12,* 108–128.

Wickramasinghe, V. (2009). Predictors of job satisfaction among IT graduates in offshore outsourced IT firms. *Personnel Review, 38*(4), 413–431.

Wickramasinghe, V. (2010a). Employee perceptions towards web-based human resource management systems in Sri Lanka. *The International Journal of Human Resource Management, 21*(10), 1617–1630.

Wickramasinghe, V. (2010b). Impact of time demands of work on job satisfaction and turnover intention: Software developers in offshore outsourced software development firms in Sri Lanka. *Strategic Outsourcing: An International Journal, 3*(3), 246–255.

Wickramasinghe, V. (2016a). Effects of reporting levels on team workers in new business sectors. *Performance Improvement Quarterly, 28*(4), 91–106.

Wickramasinghe, V. (2016b). Performance management in medium-sized enterprises. *Performance Improvement Quarterly, 29*(3), 1–25.

Wickramasinghe, V. M. (2006). Training objectives, transfer, validation and evaluation: A Sri Lankan study. *The International Journal of Training and Development, 10*(3), 227–247.

Wickramasinghe, V. & Chandrasekara, R. (2011). Differential effects of employment status on work-related outcomes: A pilot study of permanent and casual workers in Sri Lanka. *Employee Relations, 33*(5), 532–550.

Wickramasinghe, V. & Dabere, S. (2012). Effects of performance-based financial incentives on work performance: A study of technical-level employees in the private sector in Sri Lanka. *Performance Improvement Quarterly, 25*(3), 37–51.

Wickramasinghe, V. & De Silva, C. (2011). Use of shift work in globally distributed software development: Sri Lankan IT professionals' perspective. *Strategic Outsourcing: An International Journal, 4*(3), 228–247.

Wickramasinghe, V. & Fonseka, N. (2012). Human resource measurement and reporting in manufacturing and service sectors in Sri Lanka. *Journal of Human Resource Costing & Accounting, 16*(3), 235–252.

Wickramasinghe, V. & Gamage, A. (2011). High-involvement work practices, quality results, and the role of HR function: An exploratory study of manufacturing firms in Sri Lanka. *The TQM Journal, 23*(5), 516–530.

Wickramasinghe, V. & Garusinghe, S. (2010). An exploratory study of human resource aspects of international technology transfers to Sri Lankan private sector manufacturing firms. *International Journal of Operations & Production Management, 30*(6), 584–611.

Wickramasinghe, V. & Jayabandu, S. (2007). Towards workplace flexibility: Flexitime arrangements in Sri Lanka. *Employee Relations, 29*(6), 554–575.

Wickramasinghe, V. & Jayaweera, M. (2010). Impact of career plateau and supervisory support on career satisfaction: A study in offshore outsourced IT firms in Sri Lanka. *Career Development International, 15*(6), 544–561.

Wickramasinghe, V. & Karunaratne, C. (2009). People management in mergers and acquisitions in Sri Lanka: Employee perceptions. *The International Journal of Human Resource Management, 20*(3), 694–715.

Wickramasinghe, V. & Kumara, S. (2009). Differential effects of competency due to BPO and KPO industry differences in ITES sector in Sri Lanka. *Career Development International, 14*(2), 169–185.

Wickramasinghe, V. & Liyanage, S. (2013). Effects of high performance work practices on job performance in project-based organizations. *Project Management Journal, 44*(3), 64–77.

Wickramasinghe, V. & Nisaf, M. S. M. (2013). Organizational policy as a moderator between online social networking and job performance. *VINE, 43*(2), 161–184.

Wickramasinghe, V. & Perera, G. (2012). HRM practices during the global recession (2008–2010): Evidence from globally distributed software development firms in Sri Lanka. *Strategic Outsourcing: An International Journal, 5*, 188–212.

Wickramasinghe, V. & Samaratunga, M. (2016). HRM practices and post-promotion managerial performance—subordinates' perspective. *Evidence-based HRM: A Global Forum for Empirical Scholarship, 4*(2), 1–19.

Wickramasinghe, V. & Wickramanayake, N. (2013). Expectations and experience: IT jobs in offshore software development and commercial banks in Sri Lanka. *Information Technology & People, 26*(1), 50–76.

Wickramasinghe, V. & Wickramasinghe, D. (2016). Variable pay and job performance of shop-floor workers in lean production. *Journal of Manufacturing Technology Management, 27*(2), 287–311.

Wickramasinghe, V. & Widyaratne, R. (2012). Effects of interpersonal trust, team leader support, rewards, and knowledge sharing mechanisms on knowledge sharing in project teams. *VINE, 42*, 214–236.

Wijetunge, W. A. D. S. (2014). Strategic planning practices of manufacturing small and medium scale enterprises in Sri Lanka: An empirical study. *Global Journal of Commerce & Management Perspective, 3*(6), 102–109.

World Bank. (2010). Project appraisal document on a proposed credit in the amount of US$40 million to the Democratic Socialist Republic of Sri Lanka, Report No: 49190-LK, Washington, DC.

Yeung, A., Warner, M., & Rowley, C. (2008). Guest editors' introduction: Growth and globalization—Evolution of human resource management practices in Asia. *Human Resource Management, 47*, 1–13.

Conclusions

22

THE FUTURE OF HUMAN RESOURCE MANAGEMENT IN ASIA IN A WORLD OF CHANGE

Sunghoon Kim and Fang Lee Cooke

Introduction

Human resource management (HRM) is shaped not only by an organization's strategic intent but also by the institutional and cultural environments in which the firm is situated (Batt & Banerjee, 2012; Jackson & Schuler, 1995; Kim & Wright, 2011). Therefore, the HRM of Asian companies cannot be fully understood without properly contextualizing it into Asia-specific institutional and cultural arrangements. Every chapter in this Handbook provides current knowledge about how these Asia-specific environments have shaped different aspects of HRM and industrial relations (IR) in the region. In this conclusion chapter, we present an integrated summary of major insights presented in this Handbook. We also survey emerging challenges and opportunities for companies in Asia. We then propose several directions for managers and researchers interested in HRM in Asia. We wish to note at the outset that some overgeneralization is inevitable given the many different countries, large population, and institutional, economic, and socio-cultural diversity in Asia.

HRM in the context of Asia

Asian institutional and cultural environments are significantly different from those of Western countries. In an empirical study that compares thirteen Asian economies to five major Western countries, Witt and Redding (2013) suggest that Asian business environments have several distinctive characteristics. First, Asian economies tend to have relatively low levels of institutionalized trust, which causes economic actors to rely heavily on informal arrangements. Second, Asians' daily lives at the workplace are shaped by traditional hierarchical, collectivistic, and masculine cultures. Third, a significant amount of intra-national diversity is found in developing economies in Asia that emerged during the period of rapid industrialization and globalization, with some areas developing faster than others. In the following, we present an integrated summary of the Handbook by discussing how these special characteristics of Asian environments have shaped Asian HRM.

Low institutionalized trust and informality of employment relations

Asian economies are known to have relatively low levels of institutionalized trust, defined as confidence that a social system will force others to act honestly (Redding, 2005; Witt & Redding, 2013). Institutionalized trust is an important social mechanism that allows strangers to easily work together. When citizens cannot trust their legal, governmental, and cultural institutions to limit the opportunistic behaviors of fellow citizens, they find it difficult to work with people who are not friends or family. Asian countries have relatively low institutionalized trust, due in part to the ineffectiveness of their governments (Witt & Redding, 2013). In some countries, nation states even take a "predatory approach" toward their citizens, seriously undermining the public's trust in formal institutions (for a detailed discussion of Asian governments, see Chapter 2 in this volume).

The lack of trust in formal institutions leads Asian companies to heavily rely on informal arrangements with their employees (Witt & Redding, 2013). There are three distinctive phenomena related to these informal arrangements: (1) the prevalence of *informal employment*, in which workers are hired without proper labor contracts; (2) *incomplete law enforcement*, which generates a large gap between stipulated labor regulations and those that are implemented; and (3) *informal HR practices*, which are built on informal social relationships.

Informal employment. Working informally seems to be the norm rather than the exception in Asia (see Chapters 1, 5, 6, and 7). Although "informal employment" has somewhat different meanings across countries, it usually involves a lack of a formal written contract that provides workers with adequate legal protections and social security services. In India, over 90 percent of workers are estimated to be informally employed (see Chapter 7). In China, a large number of individuals, especially migrants from rural areas, work without being properly protected by labor regulations. Although informal employment is not officially recognized in the Chinese government's statistics, a recent estimate suggests that the number of informal workers now exceeds that of formally employed workers (Liang, Appleton, & Song, 2016). In Southeast Asia, informal employment dominates the labor market. For instance, 70 percent of workers in Indonesia are estimated to be under informal employment arrangements (see Chapter 18 for details). Even in relatively developed Asian economies such as Korea, informal and precarious employment is growing significantly.

The prevalence of informal employment in Asia has to do with underdeveloped formal institutions. When formal institutions are distrusted, economic actors do not feel obliged to expose themselves to government officials. La Porta and Shleifer (2014) found that many owners of informal businesses in developing countries do not see the benefit of registering their companies and believe that corrupted officials will abuse them regardless of their firms' legal status. If firms are registered, they have to pay much higher taxes and endure closer monitoring by government officials. Therefore, many firm owners believe that leaving their firms unregistered (and hiring employees informally) is beneficial for their business.

A major concern of informal employment is the potential exploitation of workers. Although not all forms of informal employment are exploitive in nature, workers without valid written contracts are essentially out of the reach of proper legal protection. As has been discussed in various chapters in this Handbook (see Chapters 5, 6, and 7), trade unions have offered very limited support to workers with informal employment. The informal sector tends to hire primarily socially disadvantaged workers, such as the uneducated, migrants with unstable legal status, and sexual minorities (see Chapter 14 for the case of sexual minorities), because they have limited access to decent regular jobs.

Incomplete law enforcement. A common phenomenon across Asia is the large gap between *de jure* and *de facto* regulations (see Chapters 5, 6, and 7). Although Asian states have developed labor laws that are designed to protect workers' interests, their enforcement has been often limited. For instance, China's labor regulations regarding overtime hours are actually more restrictive than those in some Western countries. However, a high proportion of Chinese companies violate this statutory regulation (Kim & Chung, 2016). Bangladesh has fairly strong labor regulations, and its government has signed many international conventions about labor rights. However, regulations in Bangladesh could not effectively protect workers' basic rights, as tragically evidenced by the collapse of a garment-factory building, Rana Plaza, which led to the loss of more than 1,100 lives and injured 2,500 in April 2013 (e.g., Berliner, Greenleaf, Lake, & Noveck, 2015).

The large gap between *de jure* and de facto regulations has much to do with Asian governments' prioritization of economic development over workers' well-being. In their pursuit of rapid economic growth in labor-intensive industries, Asian government labor authorities often turn a blind eye to employers who do not comply with labor laws and, at times, suppress workers' efforts to organize themselves. For instance, Korea's developmentalist government did not enforce many labor laws and suppressed trade unions. As a result, Korean trade unions have become some of the most militant labor organizations in the world (e.g., Lee & Lee, 2003). In Malaysia, political leaders publicly state that workers and trade unions are obliged not to undermine the nation's economic development and should be disciplined, loyal, and obedient (Crinis & Parasuraman, 2016).

Recently, Asian countries have introduced legal measures to better protect workers with precarious working conditions. Examples of these include: the Unorganized Workers Social Security Act (2008) in India, the Labor Contract Law (2008) in China, and the Protection of Fixed-Term and Part-Time Workers Act (2006) in Korea. Ironically, however, the introduction of more restrictive regulations has exacerbated employment precariousness and workers' vulnerability. In China, new labor regulations inspired many firms to reduce the number of direct hires and to significantly increase the use of agency employment and business outsourcing in order to avoid legal responsibilities (see Chapter 5). Similarly, in Korea, the introduction of a restrictive regulation that mandates companies to hire eligible temporary contractors as regular workers has encouraged many companies to further undermine the temporary workers' contracts so that they are not eligible for conversion to full-time positions (Cooke & Brown, 2015).

Governments' failure to effectively enforce laws is partially moderated by the efforts of nongovernmental organizations (NGOs), particularly at the international level. The "Better Work" initiative is a good example of this phenomenon. It began in Cambodia as a project of the International Labour Organization (ILO) and was expanded to neighboring countries, including Indonesia, Thailand, and Vietnam. Amengual and Chirot (2016) suggest that the Better Work project can effectively cause states to enforce regulations by allowing international regulators to collaborate with local labor mobilization activists. Although these initiatives help strengthen the regulatory systems in Asian countries, their impact remains limited, and securing compliance with labor laws is still a major challenge in many countries.

Informal HR practices. In order for human beings to cooperate, they must be able to trust each other (Rousseau, Sitkin, Burt, & Camerer, 1998). In countries in which the public has low confidence in formal institutions, the interpersonal trust embedded in informal social relationships enables stable economic transactions. This is reflected in the prevalence of HR practices in Asia that rely heavily on informal social relationships.

A useful example of such an HR practice is the relationship-based recruiting practice, which is ubiquitous across Asian countries. In this process, companies favor candidates with existing social relationships with current employees. In the Philippines, the notions of *"utang na loob"* (debt of gratitude) and *"pakikisama"* (getting along with others) play an important role in personalized transactions. A similar practice, *"compadre nepotism,"* prioritizes job applicants with existing personal connections to the company during recruitment (see Chapter 20). In Thailand, a process called *"Mee Sen"* systematically favors job applicants who have personal connections to the firm (see Chapter 18). In Middle Eastern countries, people who have *"wasta"* (personal connections to those in power) are significantly more likely to enjoy superior career outcomes compared to those who do not (see Chapter 14). In China, *"guanxi"* plays a significant role in most aspects of HRM, including recruitment and performance evaluations (see Chapter 16).

Particular emphasis is placed on personal relationships in family businesses. In Asia, family businesses are arguably the most common form of private enterprise; family ownership and control are key characteristics of Asian businesses (see Chapters 3 and 17). In family-owned firms, employees find it almost impossible to be promoted to top management positions unless they have a special personal relationship with the founding family. In Japan, an extreme case, competent managers are legally adopted into the founding family so that the company can remain family owned (see Chapter 3).

In some Asian economies, informal arrangements also occur in IR. For instance, in Singapore, there is no minimum wage. In addition, the national regulatory systems of Hong Kong, Macao, and Taiwan allow employers and employees to resolve labor issues in an informal way without significant legal intervention (see Chapter 17).

Hierarchical and collectivistic culture

Respect for hierarchy, collectivism, and masculinity are core cultural values that are common to most Asian countries. These cultural values have been developed and reinforced by various religious and philosophical traditions in the region. In India, for instance, Hinduism promoted the idea of a stratified social order, or caste. In East Asia, Confucianism significantly promoted respect for hierarchical order, prioritization of groups (particularly family) over individuals, and toleration of gender inequality (see Chapters 3 and 4). In countries in which Islam is the dominant religion (Malaysia, Indonesia, Turkey, and Middle Eastern countries), religious traditions justify distinctions between gender roles (Metcalfe, 2007).

Asian cultural values shape the way in which Asians understand their social world and influence how companies in the region organize their HR practices. For instance, respect for hierarchy is reflected in paternalistic employment relations, which are common throughout Asia (see Chapters 3, 8, and 10). In paternalistic organizational cultures, people in managerial positions feel obliged to provide fatherly care and protection to their subordinates and in return, they expect their subordinates to be personally loyal to them (Pellegrini & Scandura, 2008). The emphasis on collectivistic behavior in Asia is linked to the traditional popularity of collectivistic compensation systems. This pay system emphasizes internal equity (rather than external equity), seniority (rather than recent contributions to the firm), and the performance of the team/group (rather than that of the individual) (see Chapters 8 and 11). The masculine culture of Asia is expressed by the persisting gender inequality in the workplace (see Chapter 3).

Despite being influenced by traditional cultural values, some Asian companies experience positive outcomes by introducing HR practices that may appear counter-cultural. For instance, participative and empowering management policies were found to be effective in countries with hierarchical cultures, such as China, India, and Middle Eastern countries (see Chapter 10). Also, individualized pay systems have become popular in highly collectivistic Asian countries, including China and Korea (see Chapter 11). The growing attention to gender equality and work–life balance in highly masculine Asian nations is also noteworthy, considering the fact that these nations are dealing with skill shortages, work intensification, rising levels of labor disputes, labor retention problems, and firms' desire to improve their HR practices (see Chapter 14).

Institutional plurality

Another important feature of the Asian business environment is its plurality, that is, the coexistence of different characteristics within one country. In relation to HRM, three drivers of institutional plurality are noteworthy: (1) *marketization*, which deinstitutionalizes state-dominated economies; (2) *globalization*, which invites foreign firms to countries in which domestic firms have followed different HR practices; and (3) *migration*, which dramatically increases the number of foreign workers who are situated under different norms and regulations than locals.

Marketization and the growth of the private sector. The economic development of Asian countries largely coincided with their governments' effort to increase the role of the market in their national economies. This effort involves creating legal and cultural environments that support private entrepreneurs with significant degrees of autonomy and flexibility concerning the hiring and firing of employees. As a consequence, emerging economies in Asia have a significant number of vibrant private firms whose market-oriented HR practices differ from those of more traditional, slow-changing, state-owned firms (e.g., Khanna, 2007; Cooke & Saini, 2010).

This phenomenon is most visible in transitional economies, such as those of China and Vietnam (see Chapter 16). Before the marketization of these economies, the vast majority of Chinese and Vietnamese companies were state-owned and homogeneously regulated by socialist systems that required managements to provide employees with lifelong employment but no individualized incentives. This socialist employment arrangement was gradually deinstitutionalized as communist governments explicitly promoted economic liberalization. Although economic liberalization affected both state-owned and privately owned firms, its impact was felt strongly in the private sector because state-owned firms were still under the direct influence and protection of the government. The difference between state-owned and privately owned firms can now be readily observed in these economies. For instance, in China, state-owned firms are more likely to have active trade unions (which are controlled by the government) and provide stable employment than privately owned firms (see Chapter 16).

In developing Asian countries, the difference between state-owned and privately owned firms is often equated with a difference between companies of inefficient personnel management and companies with advanced HR practices. For instance in Vietnam, state-owned firms fail to provide their employees with reasonably competitive salaries due to the unreasonably bureaucratic government controls. Since employees in the public sector are paid less than the cost of living, they are essentially forced to find sources of supplementary income, which makes them vulnerable to corruption (see Chapter 16). Additionally, in Bangladesh and Sri Lanka, the HR practices of publicly owned firms tend to be more hierarchical, less competitive, and more bureaucratic compared to those in the private sector (see Chapter 21).

Globalization and the growth of the foreign sector. Since the 1990s, Asian countries have received significant amounts of foreign direct investment (FDI), which has led to a dramatic increase in the number of foreign multinational corporations (MNCs) (see Chapter 13). Foreign firms are, by nature, embedded in the institutional environment of their country of origin, which is, to varying degrees, different from that of the host country. When foreign firms come into a developing Asian country, they tend to carry their home-made HR practices, with limited local adaptation. Therefore, the growth of the foreign investment sector has increased the diversity of HR practices in the host Asian countries. It is common for researchers investigating Asian HRM to assume foreign ownership as an indicator of firms with different HR practices (see Chapter 18 for the case of Thailand).

The difference between the HR practices of foreign and domestic firms in developing Asian countries somewhat contradicts international business literature. International business scholars have argued that MNCs are under isomorphic pressure from the host country's local institutional arrangements (Björkman, Fey, & Park, 2007). In the case of developing Asian countries, however, this local isomorphic pressure seems to be limited, partly because developmentalist Asian governments offer distinctively favorable environments to MNCs in order to make their countries attractive to foreign investors. By locating themselves in special economic zones (SEZ) or export processing zones (EPZ), foreign firms could enjoy favorable taxation policies and significantly more relaxed labor regulations (see Chapter 7, for the case of Sri Lanka).

It should be noted that there has been some degree of convergence between domestic firms and foreign firms (i.e., the former has learned from the latter). The diffusion of Western HR practices into Asian firms is an important phenomenon, and it has been substantially discussed in many chapters of this Handbook (cf. Chapters 13 and 17). However, Asian HRM has not been completely Westernized. Although Western HR practices, or "global best practices," have been promoted in Asia through, for instance, MBA/EMBA and leadership programs, as shown in the chapters of this Handbook, these practices have not been widely diffused. In Korea, the adoption of global best practices became a fad and fashion after the 1997 Asian economic crisis. However, abandonment of the seniority-based HR system has occurred slowly (see Chapter 3). In Japan, the influx of FDI has begun to change the traditional lifelong employment system. However, the overall change in the HR system has been incremental rather than dramatic (see Chapter 5). In China, Western practices have, to some extent, changed the HRM landscape. However, many companies, especially those that are state-owned, still maintain elements of the traditional HR system (see Chapter 16). In Nepal, traditional HR systems still prevail (see Chapter 9). In Taiwan, Anglo-American HR practices have gained popularity but have been met with hidden resistance (see Chapter 17). In India and the Philippines, despite the growing popularity of strategic HRM, a large number of local firms still use traditional ways of managing people (see Chapter 20).

Migration and diversifying workforce. Over the last two decades, international and domestic labor migration has changed the structure of the labor market in many parts of the world, including Asia. According to a recent estimate, 75 million international migrants live in Asia (OECD, 2016). However, there is often no legal framework to ensure that migrants have equal opportunities in the workplace. In Middle Eastern countries, foreign workers are usually hired through an employer sponsorship system called "*kafala.*" This system requires foreign workers to be supported by a "*kafeel*" (sponsor), which could be an individual, a company, or an employment agency. Since the *kafala* system essentially prohibits migrant workers from changing employers, it seriously undermines the bargaining power of employees and makes unskilled foreign workers vulnerable to exploitative and abusive working conditions (see Chapter 19). In addition, several Asian governments introduced labor policies that explicitly favor local citizens, such as "Saudization," "Emiratization," and "Singaporean core." As for internal migrants, the Chinese *hukou* system undermines the rights of many workers who have migrated to an urban area without proper residential status (see Chapter 13; Zhang, 2010).

Another concern is the fact that the social climate of many Asian countries is discriminative toward outsiders, and thus the core organizational structures of many firms exclude foreigners. In ethnically homogenous countries such as Japan and Korea, foreign nationals are perceived as outsiders and find it difficult to adjust to the organizational hierarchy (e.g., Cooke & Brown, 2015). This phenomenon is observed in companies of all types and sizes. Although some large MNCs originating from Japan and Korea have been quite successful in the global market, it is difficult for foreign nationals to integrate into their organizational cultures (see Chapter 15). The discriminative social climate of Asian countries is further expressed by locals' sensitivity toward foreign workers' country of origin. As revealed in Chapter 14, in Middle Eastern countries, foreigners from Western countries are paid significantly more than immigrants from Asian countries. This could be attributed to the deeply rooted cultural assumption of White supremacy (see Chapter 14).

Emerging challenges and opportunities in HRM in the future

Moving forward, firms operating in Asia are likely to face many challenges and opportunities in HRM. In particular, challenges may arise from growing inequality within Asia and from emerging protectionist politics outside Asia. These pressures require governments and firms in Asia to respond at various levels and in different ways. At the same time, technological innovation, especially in information and communications technology (ICT), may provide different opportunities for firms to manage their human resources, albeit with implications for protecting workforce and employer data. Some of these issues are discussed in this section.

Challenges of inequality within Asia

Rising economic inequality is a worldwide issue. However, the rate of change in inequality has been notably faster in developing countries in Asia compared to those in other regions (Zhuang, Kanbur, & Rhee, 2014). Economic inequality in Asia is driven by various factors such as technological changes, globalization, and market-oriented reform (Zhuang et al., 2014). When Asian economies became globalized and marketized, advantages were enjoyed by skilled over unskilled workers, owners of capital over physical labor, employers over employees, and coastal cities over inland areas, causing a significant increase in economic disparity (Zhuang et al., 2014). While impressive economic growth significantly reduced the overall poverty level in Asia, it also produced much economic inequality.

Economic inequality at the macro level is closely related to HRM at the firm level. Through their HR practices, companies reproduce and perpetuate inequality in society. By hiring disadvantaged workers at low salaries, companies exploit the unequal structure of the labor market and thereby intensify social inequality (Stainback, Tomaskovic-Devey, & Skaggs, 2010). For instance, the Bangladeshi garment industry achieved impressive growth by taking advantage of lowly paid female workers who would not get a job elsewhere (Burke, 2015). Companies can also resist, delay, and undermine the government's effort to reduce social inequality (Kim & Chung, 2016). For example, in China, a significant number of companies, especially those with foreign investments, actively resisted a government-led unionization campaign (Kim, Han, & Zhao, 2014).

The rising inequality in Asia has produced serious challenges for firms' HRM and IR. When economic inequality is pervasive in society, chances are high for various stakeholders (i.e., governments, NGOs, and trade unions) to pressure employers to significantly improve the working conditions of their employees (Kerrissey, 2015; Song, 2014). This pressure on employers could be intensified by disgruntled workers who are willing to participate in collective actions. For example, growing economic inequality led to Chinese workers to engage in strikes, mostly in a self-organizing manner (Elfstrom & Kuruvilla, 2014). The threat of labor unrest is particularly challenging for large MNCs that need to maintain a positive public image (Musteen, Rhyne, & Zheng, 2013). This pressure is also a difficult challenge for small- and medium-sized Asian companies, because it may require substantial adjustments in established business models that exploit economically disadvantaged workers.

Implications of global politics outside Asia

The political economy and public policy play an important role in shaping the regulatory and business environment that impact the work experience and well-being of the workforce. The deepening level of economic globalization that has led to the encroachment of government/institutional power in nation states, particularly in liberal market economies (Hall & Soskice, 2001), as well as many significant events that occurred in world politics in 2016, such as Brexit and Donald Trump's successful presidential election, suggest that the grassroots of society have become discontent with their losses due to globalization and that they are ready to mobilize their political power collectively to fight back. Although it would be short-sighted and narrow-minded to treat both victories of the grassroots as simply outcomes of politico-economic battles between the working class and the elites whose growing power has led to the widening disparity between the rich and the poor, globalization has demonstrably had a negative impact on the grass-roots working class in developed economies (Kalleberg, 2009).

Such grass-roots movements may exert pressure on Western countries to introduce or reinstate policies to address the imbalance, including bringing back employment opportunities. Indeed, Trump won the US presidential election by promising protectionism in international trade and aggressively strict immigration policies. Rising protectionism in global trade is likely to affect job opportunities in developing Asian countries that have been relying on manufacturing export or offshore business process outsourcing (BPO) (Morales & Lema, 2016). Changes in immigration policies in high-income countries may affect migration patterns from Asian economies. The emerging new dynamics of global politics will also affect developed Asian economies such as Singapore and Hong Kong whose economies are inherently sensitive to global economic changes.

Impact of technological innovation

Technological innovation is impacting HRM in Asia in many ways. These include, for example, employment opportunities, skill requirements, and the way in which personal information may be used to manage the workforce.

First, technological change may lead to the displacement of workers and deskilling of the workforce. The impact of technological change on employment opportunities has long been a topic of debate in the fields of labor market studies, industrial relations, human resource management, and critical management studies (e.g., Braverman, 1974; Scarbrough & Corbett, 1992; Sturdy, Knights, & Willmott, 1992). Many studies have examined the potential impacts of technology on the workforce in industrialized economies in the 1970s to the 1990s. Since the late 1990s, economic globalization has attracted research attention to assess how less-developed countries, particularly those in Asia, have benefited from the offshoring of production and service activities from Western countries, especially Anglo-Saxon countries, resulting from significant job losses and the decline in the job quality of the latter (e.g., Kalleberg, 2009). However, developing Asian countries like China are now entering a new stage in which economic growth is being achieved without significant employment growth, and this phenomenon is closely linked to technological changes.

This has occurred on multiple fronts. One is robotic automation technology that can replace low-skilled labor in the manufacturing sector. It is estimated that more than 60 percent and 73 percent of manufacturing workers in Indonesia and Thailand, respectively, are at risk of losing their salaried jobs owing to robotic automation (Chang, Rynhart, & Huynh, 2016). In China alone, several million manufacturing jobs are expected to disappear in the next decade or so. For example, Foxconn, which employs around 1 million workers in China, has already installed 40,000 robots (called Foxbots) in its factories in China and laid-off some 60,000 employees in its Kunshan factory (near Shanghai) (Tencent, 2016). The garment industry is also heavily affected by technological change. The growing use of automation technology such as sewing robots is estimated to affect 86 percent and 88 percent of salaried textile workers in Vietnam and Cambodia, respectively (Chang et al., 2016).

Internet-based software technology also transforms the shape of labor markets in Asia. The growth of e-commerce significantly changes the pattern of economic transactions and thereby impacts the mode of employment in the retail sector. Chang et al. (2016) noted that 85 percent and 88 percent of retail sector workers in Indonesia and Philippines, respectively, are estimated to be at risk of losing their salaried jobs owing to automation and information technology. In this sector, the traditional mode of employment has shrunk, and non-standard employment has increased significantly, particularly in the form of self-employment, as seen in China (e.g., Wang, Cooke, & Lin, 2016). Software technology also seriously affects the BPO industry, where cloud computing and automation software undermine the viability of traditional business models. Chang et al. (2016) estimated that 89 percent of salaried workers in Philippines' BPO sector are exposed to the impact of this technological change.

Second, technological change is reshaping the pattern of skill requirements in the workforce. The shift from traditional modes of production and a low-skill-based economic structure toward a high-tech and knowledge-based economy means that the new jobs created are those that require new skills, knowledge, and competences. Because the skills required for knowledge-based jobs are fundamentally different from those required for traditional unskilled jobs, these emerging new jobs are most likely to be filled by the educated younger generation rather than by those displaced from production lines and low-end service jobs. This could be a serious problem for some developing Asian economies, where the education system does not provide enough numbers of high-skilled workers.

Third, technological changes open a new door for digitally informed HR practices. We have now entered an era of ICT-enabled big data management in which personal data may be collected, often via third parties, with or without the implied consent of those concerned, and aggregated through sophisticated data analytic techniques to identify patterns and trends to inform management solutions. For example, Walmart stores in China use customer flow information to determine their required staffing level by asking employees to work overtime at short notice or using part-time employees to cover peak periods. This means that workers have very little slack time during their shift period, and work is intensified (Xie & Cooke, 2016). Samsung, a Korean conglomerate, evaluates job applicants using big data technology. In this process, a computer software estimates applicants' future performances by analyzing their information in the light of large historical data accumulated from thousands of employees who have worked for the company over the last twenty years (Lee & Won, 2015).

As another example, Huawei (a leading Chinese IT company with a strong global footprint) prides itself on providing fresh and delicious meals for its staff to keep them happy and motivated to work. It uses mobile technology to enable its employees to select their meals from a wide variety of choices in advance and sends this information to the canteen so that it knows the level of demand for specific dishes. Huawei also informs its staff of peak times at the canteen so that they can adjust their meal times to avoid wasting their time in a queue. This is considered a win–win solution for both the company and the staff, as both are making the best use of the employees' time to increase productivity or maximize rest times.

Still another example is that the taxi companies that use taxi-calling software (similar to that of Uber) in manufacturing zones or business/industrial parks in developed cities such as Shenzhen, Dongguang, Foshan, and Zhuhai in Guangdong province in China can provide aggregate information of which taxi-calling software workers from particular companies like to use, when they finish work, how many hours of overtime they work, where they like to go for their social life/entertainment, how far they travel for their social life, and the average amount they spend on taxis per week (Luo, 2016).

In countries like China where ICT is developing fast but data protection regulation, including for employee privacy, is lagging, it is unclear what direction it may take in terms of data mining and analytics that may be used for HRM and what impact this may have on employees. However, it is clear that information can be generated, collected, and analyzed by and beyond the employing company and can be used to understand business activities and inform HRM decisions, including benchmarking against competitor firms.

Implications for firms operating in Asia

Firms in Asia face a different set of HR and IR issues from those in the rest of the world, although some concerns are shared and lessons may be learned from others. The continuing institutional and cultural traditions and emerging changes experienced in Asia have many related implications for firms operating in this continent, particularly foreign MNCs. One shared perception of senior executives of Western MNCs with subsidiaries in Asia, as emerged from the interviews with them by one of the authors of this chapter (Cooke) in 2013, is that local managers have skills for and attention to the safe operation of the business, but little HRM and IR competence or interest. This perception was supported by findings from interviews and informal conversations by Cooke with local managers and professional staff in her ongoing research of HRM and IR in China and India (e.g., Nankervis, Cooke, Chatterjee, & Warner, 2013). In Indonesia, the IR capacity is very immature at both institutional and workplace levels (e.g., Rupidara & McGraw, 2010). Accordingly, we explore some of the implications for firms operating in Asia.

Developing HRM and IR capacity to effectively handle institutional immaturity

As discussed earlier, a defining feature of Asian institutional environments is its institutional immaturity characterized by relatively low institutionalized trust. In practice, this is represented in incomplete law enforcement and heavy reliance on informal employment arrangements. On the one hand, institutional immaturity provides opportunities for firms to enjoy a significant degree of managerial discretion and even chances to influence their institutional actors such as governments and labor authorities (e.g., Child & Tsai, 2005). On the other hand, immature institutional environments increase the risks and uncertainties of handling labor issues, in turn increasing the chance of Asian companies suffering from a "corporate social responsibility crisis" (Zhao, Tan, & Park, 2014). Because the formal rules of the game do not provide straightforward guidelines for action, organizations, especially those of foreign origin, may struggle to find proper solutions to their labor-related problems.

Institutional immaturity and ambiguity suggest that companies operating in Asia need to develop HRM and IR capacities in such a way that they can effectively and responsibly engage with their institutional actors. For MNCs, this may involve assessing the role of corporate HR/IR teams in IR capacity building and their broader impact on the IR institutional environment of the host country. For example, the corporate HR/IR teams of MNCs may lobby directly with host country authorities to influence labor legislation and enforcement levels. The dynamic process of cross-border learning and outcomes of interactions between the corporate local HR/IR teams and the other key stakeholders in local and national IR institutions will reveal the extent to which foreign MNCs may help shape local IR systems and practices on the ground as well as at the policy level and how local actors may respond.

Developing HRM and IR capacities to effectively handle Asia-specific cultures

Although firms worldwide face the universal challenges of how to recruit, motivate, and retain the best staff to remain competitive, what kinds of HR practices prove to be most effective and in what circumstances is a context-specific question. Developing the capacity to handle the uniqueness of Asia-specific cultures and their related HR/IR phenomena will enable firms to design better HR solutions.

For instance, despite the hype of intrinsic value in enhancing employee satisfaction and engagement in high-performance HR practice literature, material incentives may prove far more effective in motivating employees in Asian societies (Chen, 1995). Similarly, Asian people may have different work ethics than their counterparts in other parts of the world, and the notion of work–life balance/conflict may take on significantly different meanings and invoke different management attitudes and practices than those found in the West (e.g., Cooke & Saini, 2012). Firms may therefore look for local solutions, instead of ones imported from the West, for effective people management. This requires firms to develop a better appreciation of Asian cultures and build cultural expectation into their HR policies and practices, so that employees feel more "at home" at their workplaces.

Developing HRM and IR capacities to cope with changing environments

There is a pressing need for building HRM and IR capacities in developing Asian countries so that companies can effectively cope with changing environments. From much of the discussion in this Handbook, the HRM and IR institutional environment in Asia has clearly undergone fundamental changes. Rapid economic development, transitions from a planned economy, globalization, and changes in workforce demographics have pressured Asian companies to explore new ways of running their HRM and IR practices. As mentioned above, the emerging challenges of rising social inequality, protectionism in global politics, and technological changes are likely to bring additional pressures on organizations operating in Asia.

Therefore, it is crucial for local companies and MNCs in Asia to enhance their HRM and IR capabilities to effectively manage change initiatives. Companies that have strong and effective HRM can effectively respond to environmental changes. For instance, Ryu and Kim (2013) showed in their study of Korean companies that institutional changes may undermine the efficacy of HRM; however, this can be overcome by having a proactively functioning HR department. In a study on the effect of the Emiratization policy in UAE, Rees, Mamman, and Braik (2007) found that a company with capable HRM can use institutional change as an opportunity to initiate strategic reformation at the firm.

Future research agenda

Asia offers fertile ground for innovative HRM research that could make important scholarly as well as practical contributions. For future research on Asian HRM to fully realize its potential, researchers might take into account the following.

First, Asian HRM researchers need to be aware of the hidden assumptions of existing HRM theories. Western HRM philosophy and theories are premised on political systems, ideological beliefs, and cultural values that are fundamentally different from those that prevail in Asia. For example, the Western approach to HRM tends to assume that employees live in a democratic society where employees are sensitive to the issues of fairness and equity. Such an assumption may not be relevant in developing Asian economies that are undergoing a rapid growth period against a context of political inequality (despite the espoused political equality in many Asian countries) and economic inequality; even for India, as the largest democratic country in the world, political and economic inequality has been a key feature. In addition, the Western HRM literature tends to assume that the government and private enterprises are separate entities who have their own unique domains of activities. This premise may not be relevant in developing Asian countries in which economic growth is driven by heavy governmental involvement (see Chapter 2). This involvement extends to HRM and IR at various levels (e.g., Cooke, 2011) where institutional arrangements may be inadequate.

Recognition of the Western-biased nature of existing HRM theories suggests that Asian HRM researchers should be cautious when applying Western-developed theories to explain Asia-specific HRM and IR phenomena. This also suggests that Asia can provide HRM researchers with opportunities to challenge the established conceptual assumptions in the HRM literature that have been built primarily on Western experiences.

Second, Asian HRM researchers need to develop an in-depth understanding and appreciation of the context they are studying. To date, many Asian HRM studies have focused on issues that are important for a Western audience. Although some of these issues are also important for the Asian audience, many of them are not necessarily relevant as concerns of Asian organizations. In this process, the issues and problems that are most critical for the Asian audience have often been ignored or marginalized. Even when studies examined issues that are shared across economies, they tend to underplay Asia-specific causes and practical solutions. This has led to the situation where important Asian phenomena have been seriously under-studied.

The lack of deeply contextualized Asian HRM research is partly due to the methodological trend in HRM scholarship. In the last two decades, HRM research has been heavily influenced by the positivist approach that aims at identifying and confirming the relationships between specific types of HR practice and performance. These studies are characterized by increasingly sophisticated research instruments and analytical tools, but contribute little to understanding the complexity of organizational life or to informing management practices (e.g., Alvesson, 2009; Jackson, Schuler, & Jiang, 2014; Kaufman, 2015). Asia-based HRM research is no exception to this trend. Many Asian studies have focused on replicating Western-based empirical findings in the Asian context, thus making limited contributions to the literature.

To develop a deeper understanding of the workings of HRM in Asia, it will be essential to adopt a qualitative approach to explore the societal norms and values, cultural traditions, and economic and moral standards of Asian societies. This requires that Asian scholars avoid uncritically adopting Western-centric approaches when framing their research questions. Asia should be more than simply an empirical testing site for Western management philosophies and theories. Instead of setting the goal to that of simply confirming or incrementally extending Western theories with de-contextualized data from Asia, Asian HRM research needs to start by focusing on the practical problems in Asia, and then formulating original theories that can better explain the empirical findings in Asia and beyond. Studies that superficially project Asia from a Western angle have limited practical relevance and utility. Here, we are not imposing a West versus Asia divide. Rather, our intention is to point out the continuing dominance of Western thinking in HRM research and to call for a more balanced and Asia-oriented approach by echoing influential scholars on Asian management research (e.g., Tsui, 2004; Meyer, 2006).

Promising areas of research

Asia presents rich empirical contexts for practical insights that are essential to building innovative theories. In the following, we outline several promising research areas as indicative examples.

Interaction between HRM and social environments. The inefficacy of the formal regulatory system in governing labor-management/capital relationships has been well noted in this Handbook. We have also learned about the role of religiosity in influencing HRM and workplace relationships. More in-depth studies to explore the interaction between HRM and social environments will therefore be fruitful in terms of gaining an understanding of the role of informal and social regulations in shaping workplace relationships and HRM practices. For example, what types of soft regulation are mobilized and how are they mobilized in governing employment, the labor market, and workplace relationships? Is religion an oppressor as well as a liberator of equality in the workplace? How do work ethics informed by societal values and religiosity impact the perception of the work–life balance?

Grievance and dispute management. Few studies exist that examine grievance management in workplaces in Asia (e.g., Cooke, Xie, & Duan, 2016). Given the rising number of labor disputes in many Asian countries, the effective detection and management of employee grievances may be able to prevent more confrontational disputes that may occur at a later stage. More research on this issue in the Asian context will be helpful for us to understand sources of workforce grievance, forms of expression, the types of institutional and organizational mechanisms— if they exist—for grievance management, and their effectiveness. Here, greater integration of the HRM and IR fields will be fruitful for examining how firms may be using HRM interventions innovatively to produce better IR outcomes. For example, in Asian countries and sectors where formal procedures are absent in grievance management, what role do traditional and emerging IR institutional actors play in grievance redressal? How might employee voice systems and practices be deployed to detect and resolve workplace grievances? What space is available for alternative organizing bodies and voice mechanisms? Research on these topics should also take into account the diversity of the workforce and mobilize different theories to reflect the interests, powerbases, and concerns of different groups of workers.

As in all societies, labor conflicts, in both subtle and overt forms, exist in Asian countries. While the confrontational expression of labor discontent may be suppressed in autocratic regimes, there are now increased political opportunities for workers to voice their discontent about their employment terms and conditions, despite the lack of institutionalized workers' rights protection in some countries (Cooke, 2014). However, the bulk of the research on labor disputes in developing Asian countries has focused on the distinct absence of employee power on the one hand and the highly publicized radical conflict clashes on the other. It would be enlightening to examine the subtler forms of labor resistance or of informal collective bargaining that may be expressed in line with cultural traditions, which may prove to be effective in achieving what the workers want without directly challenging the employer's authority and upsetting the hierarchical relationship. Such an approach may be more productive in maintaining the employment relationship.

Role of technology. As noted earlier, the rapid development of ICT offers promising opportunities as well as challenges to HRM in Asia. More research should be conducted on the role of ICT in the delivery of the HR function and its impact, both positive and negative, on the workforce. Research could also be conducted to understand the relationship between HRM, innovation, and productivity, and the responsibility of individuals, firms, and the state in meeting the present and emerging skills' needs for technology-driven high-growth economies in the Asian context.

Unexamined emerging Asian countries. As contributors to this Handbook have observed, high quality research on HRM and IR in Asia has been focused on a limited number of developed countries such as Japan or on large emerging economies such as China and India. Relatively small Asian countries and countries with a short history of economic development have received limited scholarly attention to date. As globalization continues and as these countries are catching up at an accelerating pace, there is a compelling need to engage with the research on, and with the business communities of, "smaller" Asian countries, and develop more knowledge on these countries.

Conclusions

Countries around the world, developed and less developed alike, are facing substantively different challenges to, as well as opportunities for, their people management as they transition from one political regime to another, from one popular ideology to another, and from one type of economic structure to another. However, many of them share one fundamental challenge: how to achieve efficiency, quality, and high performance through workforce fairness, equity, well-being, and social justice in a globalized world of work? For Asian countries, how will globalization unfold in the foreseeable future? How will this affect their public policies, labor regulations, labor markets, employers' strategies, and organizational practices? How will notions such as the Green economy, just transitions, decent work, and the moral economy impact these countries at various levels and be translated into workforce-oriented HRM practices? And how will researchers capture these dynamics and influence policy decision-making and management practices?

References

Alvesson, M. (2009). Critical perspectives on HRM. In J. Storey, P. Wright, & D. Ulrich (Eds.), *The Routledge companion to strategic human resource management* (pp. 2–68). London: Routledge.

Amengual, M. & Chirot, L. (2016). Reinforcing the state transnational and state labor regulation in Indonesia. *Industrial and Labor Relations Review, 69*(5), 1056–1080.

Batt, R. & Banerjee, M. (2012). The scope and trajectory of strategic HR research: Evidence from American and British journals. *The International Journal of Human Resource Management, 23*(9), 1739–1762.

Berliner, D., Greenleaf, A., Lake, M., & Noveck, J. (2015). Building capacity, building rights?: State capacity and labor rights in developing countries. *World Development, 72*, 127–139.

Björkman, I., Fey, C. F., & Park, H. J. (2007). Institutional theory and MNC subsidiary HRM practices: Evidence from a three-country study. *Journal of International Business Studies, 38*(3), 430–446.

Braverman, H. (1974). *Labor and monopoly capital.* New York: Monthly Review Press.

Burke, J. (2015, April 22). Bangladesh garment workers suffer poor conditions two years after reform vows, *Guardian.* Retrieved from www.theguardian.com/world/2015/apr/22/garment-workers-in-bangladesh-still-suffering-two-years-after-factory-collapse.

Chang, J. H., Rynhart, G., & Huynh, P. (2016). *ASEAN in transformation: How technology is changing jobs and enterprises* (No. 994909343402676). International Labour Organization.

Chen, C. C. (1995). New trends in rewards allocation preferences: A Sino-US comparison. *Academy of Management Journal, 38*(2), 408–428.

Child, J. & Tsai, T. (2005). The dynamic between firms' environmental strategies and institutional constraints in emerging economies: Evidence from China and Taiwan. *Journal of Management Studies, 42*(1), 95–125.

Cooke, F. L. (2011). The role of the state and human resource management in China. *The International Journal of Human Resource Management, 22*(18), 3830–3848.

Cooke, F. L. (2014). Chinese industrial relations research: In search of a broader analytical framework and representation. *Asia Pacific Journal of Management, 31*(3), 875–898.

Cooke, F. L. & Brown, R. (2015). *The regulation of non-standard forms of employment in China, Japan and the Republic of Korea.* Working paper No. 64. Geneva: International Labour Organization.

Cooke, F. L. & Saini, D. S. (2010). (How) does the HR strategy support an innovation-oriented business strategy?: An investigation of institutional context and organizational practices in Indian firm. *Human Resource Management, 49*(3), 377–400.

Cooke, F. L. & Saini, D. (2012). Managing diversity in Chinese and Indian firms: A qualitative study. *Journal of Chinese Human Resource Management, 3*(1), 16–32.

Cooke, F. L., Xie, Y. H. & Duan, W. M. (2016). Workers' grievances and resolution mechanisms in Chinese manufacturing firms: Key characteristics and the influence of contextual factors. *The International Journal of Human Resource Management, 27*(18), 2119–2141.

Crinis, V. & Parasuraman, B. (2016). Employment relations and the state in Malaysia. *Journal of Industrial Relations, 58*(2), 215–228.

Elfstrom, M. & Kuruvilla, S. (2014). The changing nature of labor unrest in China. *Industrial and Labor Relations Review, 67*(2), 453–480.

Hall, P. A. & Soskice, D. (2001). *Varieties of capitalism: The institutional foundations of comparative advantage.* Oxford: Oxford University Press.

Jackson, S. E. & Schuler, R. S. (1995). Understanding human resource management in the context of organizations and their environments. *Human Resource Management: Critical Perspectives on Business and Management, 2*, 45–74.

Jackson, S., Schuler, R., & Jiang, K. (2014). An aspirational framework for strategic human resource management. *Academy of Management Annals, 8*(1), 1–56.

Kalleberg, A. (2009). Precarious work, insecure workers: Employment relations in transition. *American Sociological Review, 74*(1), 1–22.

Kanbur, R., Rhee, C., & Zhuang, J. (2014). *Inequality in Asia and the Pacific: Trends, drivers, and policy implications.* London: Routledge.

Kaufman, B. (2015). Evolution of strategic HRM as seen through two founding books: A 30th anniversary perspective on development of the field. *Human Resource Management, 54*(3), 389–407.

Kerrissey, J. (2015). Collective labor rights and income inequality. *American Sociological Review, 80*(3), 626–653.

Khanna, T. (2007). *Billions of entrepreneurs: How China and India are reshaping their futures and yours.* Boston, MA: Harvard Business School Press.

Kim, S. & Chung, S. (2016). Explaining organizational responsiveness to emerging regulatory pressure: The case of illegal overtime in China. *The International Journal of Human Resource Management, 27*(18), 1–22.

Kim, S., Han, J., & Zhao, L. (2014). Union recognition by multinational companies in China: A dual institutional pressure perspective. *Industrial & Labor Relations Review, 67*(1), 34–59.

Kim, S. & Wright, P. M. (2011). Putting strategic human resource management in context: A contextualized model of high commitment work systems and its implications in China. *Management and Organization Review, 7*(1), 153–174.

La Porta, R. & Shleifer, A. (2014). Informality and development. *The Journal of Economic Perspectives, 28*(3), 109–126.

Lee, W. & Lee, B. (2003). Korean industrial relations in the era of globalization. *Journal of Industrial Relations, 45*, 505–520.

Lee, D. & Won, H. (2015, December 29). Samsung used big data in selecting new employees. *Maeil Business News Korea.* Retrieved from http://news.mk.co.kr/newsRead.php?year=2015&no=1224326.

Liang, Z., Appleton, S., & Song, L. (2016). *Informal employment in China: Trends, patterns and determinants of entry.* IZA Discussion Papers, No. 10139.

Luo, S. S. (2016, September 6). What time does Foxconn's staff finish work? DD (taxi-calling platform) says it knows. Retrieved from http://m.jiemian.com/article/839269.html?from=timeline&isapp installed=0.

Metcalfe, B. D. (2007). Gender and human resource management in the Middle East. *The International Journal of Human Resource Management, 18*(1), 54–74.

Meyer, K. E. (2006). Asian management research needs more self-confidence. *Asia Pacific Journal of Management, 23*(2), 119–137.

Morales, N. J. & Lema, K. (2016, December 8). Philippines outsourcing firms hit by Trump and "Trump East." *Reuters*. Retrieved from www.reuters.com/article/us-usa-trump-philippines-idUSKBN13X2Q6.

Musteen, M., Rhyne, L., & Zheng, C. (2013). Asset or constraint: Corporate reputation and MNCs' involvement in the least developed countries. *Journal of World Business, 48*(3), 321–328.

Nankervis, A., Cooke, F. L., Chatterjee, S., & Warner, M. (2013). *New models of human resource management in China and India*. London: Routledge.

OECD. (2016). *Labor migration in Asia Building effective institutions: Building effective institutions*. OECD Publishing. Retrieved from www.oecd.org/migration/labor-migration-in-asia-building-effective-institutions.pdf.

Pellegrini, E. K. & Scandura, T. A. (2008). Paternalistic leadership: A review and agenda for future research. *Journal of Management, 34*(3), 566–593.

Redding, G. (2005). The thick description and comparison of societal systems of capitalism. *Journal of International Business Studies, 36*(2), 123–155.

Rees, C. J., Mamman, A., & Braik, A. B. (2007). Emiratization as a strategic HRM change initiative: Case study evidence from a UAE petroleum company. *The International Journal of Human Resource Management, 18*(1), 33–53.

Rupidara, N. S. & McGraw, P. (2010). Actors, institutional change and stability in the Indonesian industrial relations system. *Journal of Industrial Relations, 52*(5), 613–630.

Rousseau, D. M., Sitkin, S. B., Burt, R. S., & Camerer, C. (1998). Not so different after all: A cross-discipline view of trust. *Academy of Management Review, 23*(3), 393–404.

Ryu, S. & Kim, S. (2013). First-Line managers' HR involvement and HR effectiveness: The case of South Korea. *Human Resource Management, 52*(6), 947–966.

Scarbrough, H. & Corbett, J. (1992). *Technology and organization: Power, meaning and design*. London: Routledge.

Song, J. (2014). *Inequality in the workplace: Labor market reform in Japan and Korea*. Ithaca, NY: Cornell University Press.

Stainback, K., Tomaskovic-Devey, D., & Skaggs, S. (2010). Organizational approaches to inequality: Inertia, relative power, and environments. *Sociology, 36*(1), 225–247.

Sturdy, A., Knights, D., & Willmott, H. (Eds.) (1992), *Skill and consent: Contemporary Studies in the labour process*. London: Routledge.

Tencent (2016, October 16), Production workers are going to cry: Foxconn newly installed 40,000 robots in China. *Tencent*. Retrieved from http://tech.qq.com/a/20161006/009459.htm.

Tsui, A. S. (2004). Contributing to global management knowledge: A case for high quality indigenous research. *Asia Pacific Journal of Management, 2*(4), 491–513.

Wang, J., Cooke, F. L., & Lin, Z. H. (2016). Informal employment in China: Recent development and human resource implications, *Asia Pacific Journal of Human Resources, 54*(3), 292–311.

Witt, M. A. & Redding, G. (2013). Asian business systems: Institutional comparison, clusters and implications for varieties of capitalism and business systems theory. *Socio-Economic Review, 11*(2), 265–300.

Xie, Y. H. & Cooke, F. L. (2016). From quality to cost? The evolution of Walmart's business strategy and human resource practices in China and their impact on industrial relations (1996–2016), paper presented at the conference of HRM of multinationals in and outside of China, Rutgers University, USA.

Zhang, H. (2010). The Hukou system's constraints on migrant workers' job mobility in Chinese cities. *China Economic Review, 21*(1), 51–64.

Zhao, M., Tan, J., & Park, S. H. (2014). From voids to sophistication: Institutional environment and MNC CSR crisis in emerging markets. *Journal of Business Ethics, 122*(4), 655–674.

Zhuang, J., Kanbur, R., & Rhee, C. (2014). *Rising inequality in Asia and policy implications*. ADBI Working Paper 463. Tokyo: Asian Development Bank Institute. Retrieved from www.adbi.org/working-paper/2014/02/21/6172.rising.inequality.asia.policy.implications/.

INDEX

Page numbers in *italics* denote tables, those in **bold** denote figures.

360-degree feedback 161, 193

absorptive capacity 170
Academy of Human Resource Development (AHRD), India 375
Accord on Fire and Building Safety in Bangladesh 140
Act on Protection of Fixed-Term and Part-Time Workers, South Korea 97
adjustment model 234
adult adoption, Japan 52, 418
Africa 34, 248
agency employment: China 95; Japan 90–1, *91*, 96; South Asia 132, 133–5, 141; South Korea 96, 97
aging populations 25, 40, 171, 222, 232, 282, 368
All-China Federation of Trade Unions (ACFTU) 95, 97–8
Allen, J. 7
Amengual, M. 417
ancestor worship 57
appraisals *see* performance management systems (PMS)
Asia Pacific Journal of Human Resources 226
Asian economic crisis (1997) 27, 53, 88, 91–2, 111, 113, 162, 285
assertiveness skills training 160
Association of Southeast Asian Nations (ASEAN) 109, 111, 112, 115–16, 333
Australia 158, 205
authentic leadership 190
authoritarian leadership 184–5
automation technology 423

Bahrain 39, 257, 357

Bangladesh 392–409; compensation practices 397, 404, 405, 406; cultural context 394–5; economy 130–2, 393; external dependence *31*; foreign direct investment (FDI) *31*; gender inequality 258; industrial relations 128–30, 132, 136, 137–40, 141–2, 397, 404, 405, 406; labor market 130–2, 393–4, *393*; labor regulation 128–30, *134–5*, 136, 417; multinational companies 404–5, 406; new trends in HRM 405–6; performance management 405; recruitment and selection 403–4; religion and religiosity 394–5; remittances 38; socio-economic context 392–4, *393*; state influence on HRM *33*; state model *25*, 38; state sector 395, 397; trade unions 130, 136, 138, 140, 397, 404, 405, 406; training and development 397, 404
Bangladesh Finished Leather, Leather Goods, and Footwear Exporters' Association 406
Bangladesh Garments Manufacturers and Exporters Association (BGMEA) 406
Bank of China 95
bargaining *see* collective bargaining
behavior-based performance measures 212–13
benevolent leadership 184–5
Better Work Programme 123, 417
Bharatiya Janata Party (BJP), India 135
Board of Investment (BOI), Sri Lanka 137, 142
bonuses 100, 280, 302, 323, 344, 346, 376; seasonal 53–4
BPO *see* business process outsourcing (BPO)
brain drain 222, 224, 231, 282, 304
broaden-and-build theory 170
Brunei 72, 115
Buddhism 4, 47, 67, 70–1, 74–5, 77, 78, 79, 122, 339

business process outsourcing (BPO) 167, 232, 376–7, 386, 398, 422, 423

call centers 244
Cambodia: automation technology 423; compensation practices 117, **117**; external dependence *31*; foreign direct investment (FDI) *31*; labor regulation 112, 123, 417; state influence on HRM *33*
capitalism, and religion 73, 78–80
caste/tribal inequalities, India 259
casual employment *see* non-standard employment
Catholicism 72
ceremonies, company 57–8
chaebols 159, 275
chambers of commerce 121
Chiang Kai-shek 48
China 295–309; aging populations 232; automation technology 423; capitalism 78–9; Christianity 72; company ceremonies and rituals 57, 58; compensation practices 53, 54, 100, *101*, 207, 208, 301–2, *308*; Confucianism 47, 59–60, 78–9; economy 87–9, 296–7; employee retention 55, 56; expatriate employees 235; external dependence *31*; family businesses 51; fertility rates 88; filial piety allowances 56; foreign direct investment (FDI) *31*, 34, 223, 240; gender inequality/discrimination 56, 265–7; and global financial interests 27; *guanxi* 5, 49, 74, 159, 193, 301, 418; *hukou* (internal passport) system 245, 420; imperial examinations 50; industrial relations 8, 39, 58, 59, 95, 97–8; innovation 166, 170–1; international assignments 59; "iron rice bowl" system 55, 88, 296, 300; Islam 71; labor market 87–9; labor regulation 93, *94*, 95, 299–300, 417; marketization 97, 100, 419; multinational companies 4, 240, 241, 243, 244, 245, 247, 248; non-standard employment 6–7, 89, 95, 416; one child policy 88; performance management 301, *308*; power distance 157; protections against dismissal 158; recruitment and selection 50, 51, 300, *308*; religion and religiosity 47, 59–60, 71, 72, 78–9; retirement 56; rural to urban migration 8, 35, 89, 420; seasonal bonuses 53, 54; state influence on HRM *33*, 35, 39; state model *25*, 34; state sector reform 88–9, 241; talent management 222, 224, 231, 232; trade unions 95, 97–8; training and development 55, 300–1, *308*; trust 73–4
Chinese Communist Party 47, 53, 58, 88, 98, 296–7, 301
Christianity 4, 67, 72–3
Citibank Asia 193
coaching 192, 194–5
collective bargaining 9, 98, 364; South Asia 132,

133, 135, 136, 139, 141, 397, 404; Southeast Asia 121–2
Collective Bargaining Agents (CBA), Bangladesh 404
collective performance-based pay 52–3, 203, 206, 214–16
collectivism 155–6, 160, 277, 418–19; and compensation practices 52–3, 203, *205*, 206, 208, 215; and leadership styles 184
Communist Parties 38, 39; China 47, 53, 58, 88, 98, 296–7, 301; Vietnam 38, 53, 115, 118, 298
compadre nepotism, Philippines 377, 378, 383, 418
company ceremonies and rituals 57–8
company dinners 58
company entrance exams 50–1
comparative institutional advantage 158–9
compensation practices 201–17; Bangladesh 397, 404, 405, 406; bonuses 53–4, 100, 280, 302, 323, 344, 346, 376; China 53, 54, 100, *101*, 207, 208, 301–2, *308*; and Confucianism 52–4; cultural psychology perspective 210–17; degree of pay differential 212–13; empirical studies 204–10; gender pay gap 32, *33*, 56, 260, 266; Hong Kong 206–7, 320; India 140–1, 207, 208, 209; Indonesia 116–17, **117**, 205, 207, 208, 342–3; and innovation 169; Japan 53, 101–2, **103**, *276*, 280, 281; Macau 320; Malaysia 116–17, **117**, 205, 344; and malleability of self versus world 214; and national culture 52–3, 201, 202–10, *205*; and performance management 151, 154–5; Philippines 116–17, **117**, 379; and religion and religiosity 52–4, 76; seasonal bonuses 53–4; seniority-based pay 53, 89–90, 101–2, **103**, **104**, 201, 203, *205*, 206, 280; Singapore 208; and social loafing 214–16; sorting effects 213–14; South Korea 53, 102, **104**, 201, *276*, 280–1; Sri Lanka 401; Taiwan 53, 320, 322–3; Thailand 116–17, **117**, 342, 346; Vietnam 53, 116–17, **117**, 306–7, *308*
competence rank system, Japan 89–90, 101–2
conformity pressures 215–16
Confucianism 4, 5, 46–61, 67, 69–70, 418; and capitalism 73, 78–80; company ceremonies and rituals 57–8; and compensation practices 52–4; and employee retention 55–6; and gender discrimination 56–7, 266; and industrial relations 58–9, 76–7; and international assignments 59; and leadership styles 184; as managerial strategy 59–60; and managerial succession 51–2; and recruitment and selection 49–51, 349; and training and development 54–5, 75; virtues and ethics of 48–9
contingency theories of leadership 187–8, 190–1
contract employment *see* agency employment
Contract Labour (Regulation and Abolition) Act, India 133

coordinated market economies, and performance management 158
corporate social responsibility 349, 424
country-of-origin effects 247–9
cultural psychology perspective of compensation practices 210–17
culture *see* national culture; organizational culture

Daoism 47, 67, 69, 70, 78, 185, 194
data protection 424
Deng Xiaoping 296
development *see* training and development
developmental states 24, 25, *25*, 28, 32–5
discrimination 74, 76; caste/tribal 259; ethnic 259, 260; non-standard workers 97; religious 259; sexual orientation 261–3; Singapore 365; *see also* gender inequality/discrimination; inequality
dismissal, legal restrictions on 89, 158–9
dispatched employment: China 95; Japan 90–1, *91*, 96; South Asia 132, 133–5, 141; South Korea 96, 97
Dispatched Labor Act, South Korea 96
dispute management 427; *see also* industrial relations
distributed leadership 189
diversity *see* workforce diversity
Doi Moi period, Vietnam 115, 118, 298, 306
dormitory labor regimes 245
dual labor markets 38
dual-career couples 235
Dubai 355–60, *359*, 366–9

e-commerce 423
economic liberalization 419; South Asia 131, 135, 374–5; South Korea 285
Economically Active Population Survey, South Korea 92
economies, national *see* national economies
education: and Confucianism 54–5, 56, 75; gender discrimination 56, 258; and religion and religiosity 74–6; repetitive learning 75–6; *see also* learning; training and development
education-based pay 205
effect sizes 210
electronic HRM (eHRM) 348, 349
Emirates Airlines 355, 367
Emiratization policy, UAE 39, 356, 357, 360, 368, 420, 425
employee relations *see* industrial relations
employee retention 89–90; and Confucianism 55–6; Japan 55, 89, *276*, 278, 279; South Korea 55–6, *276*, 278–9
employee stock ownership plans (ESOPs) 206
employer associations 121, 139
Employment Act, Singapore 364
employment dualism 244–5
Employment Protection Database 158, 162

employment protection legislation 152, 158, 162
employment regulation *see* labor regulation
employment relations *see* industrial relations
Employment Security Law, Japan 90, 93
empowering leadership 187, 189, 194
enabling states 25, 28–9, 34, 35–6
enterprise unions: Japan 98; South Korea 98–9
EOI *see* export-oriented industrialization (EOI)
EPZs *see* export processing zones (EPZs)
equal opportunity 256–68; China 265–7; East Asia 259–60; gender 257–60, 265–7; Middle East 257–8; Saudi Arabia 263–5, *264*; sexual orientation 261–3; South Asia 258–9
errors, honoring 174
ethical behavior 67–9
ethical leadership 190, 194
ethnocentric management practices 281–8
European Union 26, 111
evidence-backed performance management 154
examinations: formal selection 50–1; imperial 50–1, 56
Executive Opinion Survey 32, *33*
expatriate employees 38, 234–5, 420–1; China 235; Japan 235, 282–4; Saudi Arabia 263–5, *264*; Singapore 356, 362, 363–4, *363*, 366; South Korea 282, 285–8; Southeast Asia 34; United Arab Emirates 356, 357, 358, 366–7; *see also* international assignments
exploiting states 25, 28, 29, 37–8
export processing zones (EPZs) 137, 138, 141, 240, 249, 420
export-oriented industrialization (EOI) 32, 109, 110, 338, 339, 393, 402
external dependence 25, 30, *31*
external internationalization 289–90

Fair Consideration Framework, Singapore 365
familism 73, 77, 345
family allowances 54
family businesses 51–2, 73, 418
favoritism *see* nepotism and favoritism
FDI *see* foreign direct investment (FDI)
Federation of Korean Trade Unions (FKTU) 98–9
feedback: 360-degree 161, 193; peer 161; in performance management 150, 151, 153, 155, 157, 161, 301, 305
feminine cultures 156, 204, *205*
fertility rates 88, 282, 362, 365
filial piety allowances 56
filial piety, in Confucianism 48
financial crises 88; Asian (1997) 27, 53, 88, 91–2, 111, 113, 162, 285; global (2008) 6, 88, 223
fixed-term employment: China 88; South Korea 97
flexible working hours 169, 398–9
foreign direct investment (FDI) 30, *31*, 34, 35, 111, 166, 223, 240, 317, 419–20

foreign employees *see* expatriate employees
foreign-owned enterprises 30, *31*
formal selection examinations 50–1
FOTILE 59–60
Foxconn 244, 248, 423
Free Trade Zones and General Services Employees
  Union, Sri Lanka 141
Freedom House 34
Freedom in the World survey 32, *33*, 36
Freezones, UAE 356, 357
future research agenda 426–8

Gandhi, Indira 130
GCC *see* Gulf Cooperation Council (GCC)
GCI *see* Global Competitive Index (GCI)
gender inequality/discrimination: China 56,
  265–7; and Confucianism 56–7, 266; East Asia
  259–60; education 56, 258; gender pay gap 32,
  33, 56, 260, 266; Middle East 257–8; South
  Asia 258–9
General Survey on Working Conditions, Japan
  101, 102
Generation Y employees 233
generational differences 233–4
Gini coefficient 32, *33*, 35
Global Competitive Index (GCI) 30, 31–2, *31*, *33*
global financial crisis (2008) 6, 88, 223
global financial interests 27
Global Gender Gap Index 32, *33*
global HR integration 281–8
Global Leadership and Organizational Behavior
  Effectiveness (GLOBE) Research Program
  185–6, 187, 192
Global Talent Competitiveness Index 224, *224*
global talent management 247
global value chains 26–7
globalization 3, 4, 7, 162, 281–8, 289, 322–3, 385,
  386, 406, 407, 419–20, 422
goal-setting theory 150–1
grass-roots movements 8–9, 98, 120, 422
green HRM systems 348, 349
grievance management 427; *see also* industrial
  relations
group meals 58
group performance-based pay 52–3, 203, 206,
  214–16
guanxi 5, 49, 74, 159, 193, 301, 418
Gulf Cooperation Council (GCC) 39, 357; *see also*
  Saudi Arabia; United Arab Emirates (UAE)

Habibie, Bacharuddin Jusuf 335
Hay job evaluation system 346
health and safety, Singapore 364, 365
higher and further education, China 89
Hinduism 67, 70, 73, 418
Hofstede, G. 155, 156, 184, 187, 201, 203, 337–8
holidays 277–8

homosexuality 261–3
Honeycutt, E. D., Jr 344
Hong Kong 314–26; company ceremonies and
  rituals 58; compensation practices 206–7, 320;
  economic and industrial structure 316–17, **316**;
  family businesses 51; foreign direct investment
  (FDI) 223, 317; multinational companies 321;
  new trends in HRM 323–4; performance
  management 319–20; recruitment and selection
  318; state model 25, *25*; strategic HRM 320;
  training and development 319
Hope Solidarity Union, South Korea 99
household contract responsibility system, China
  296–7
HRM style, and state influence *25*, 29–30, 31–2,
  33, 34, 36, 38–9
Huawei 423–4
hukou (internal passport) system, China 245, 420
human capital flows *see* talent management
human resource development *see* training and
  development
Human Resource Development Act, Malaysia 343
Human Rights Watch 366, 369

ILO *see* International Labour Organization (ILO)
IMF *see* International Monetary Fund (IMF)
imperial examinations 50–1, 56
import substitution industrialization (ISI) 130, 137,
  339
income inequality 34, 111
independent self-construal 211, 212–13, 216
India 373–87; call centers 244; caste/tribal
  inequalities 259; compensation practices 140–1,
  207, 208, 209; cultural change 157; economy
  130–2, 374–5, *374*; external dependence *31*;
  foreign direct investment (FDI) *31*, 240; gender
  inequality 258, 259; and global financial
  interests 27; industrial relations 8, 128–30, 132,
  133, 137–41, 374; innovation 166, 167, 170,
  172–5; institutional context 374–5; labor
  market 130–2; labor regulation 128–30, 133–5,
  134; multinational companies 4, 240, 243, 248;
  performance management 153, 159, 378–80,
  382, 383–4; power distance 157; protections
  against dismissal 158; recruitment and selection
  376–8, 382–3, *382*; remittances 38; state
  influence on HRM *33*; state model 37, 38;
  strategic HRM 384–7; talent management 226,
  231; trade unions 129, 130, 132, 133, 138–9,
  141, 374; training and development 380–2,
  382, 384
indigenous practices 5, 373, 378, 417–18; *see also*
  guanxi
individual performance-based pay 53, 203, 206,
  212–14
individualism 155–6; and compensation practices
  52–3, 203, *205*, 206, 208, 215

Indonesia 333–50; automation technology 423; compensation practices 116–17, **117**, 205, 207, 208, 342–3; economy 110–11, *334*, 335; external dependence *31*; family businesses 51; foreign direct investment (FDI) *31*; gender inequality 260; industrial relations 109–10, 112–16, 117–22, *120*, 337–8; labor market 111–12; labor regulation 109–10, 112–17, *114*, **117**, 122–3; minimum wages 116–17, 342; non-standard employment 116, 416; population *334*, 335; protections against dismissal 158; recruitment and selection 341–2; religion and religiosity 72; role of HR function 346–7; state influence on HRM *33*; state model *25*; strategic HRM 348; talent management *225*, 348; trade unions 112–13, 116, 117–20, *120*, 337; training and development 342; workforce diversity 348
Indonesia-Malaysia-Thailand Growth Triangle (IMT-GT) 333
Industrial Arbitration Court, Singapore 364, 365
Industrial Disputes Act, India 129, 133, 374
Industrial Disputes Ordinance, Pakistan 135, 136
industrial organization, and performance management 159
Industrial Peace Act, Philippines 113
industrial relations 8–9, 37, 39, 427; Bangladesh 128–30, 132, 136, 137–40, 141–2, 397, 404, 405, 406; China 8, 39, 58, 59, 95, 97–8; and Confucianism 58–9, 76–7; India 8, 128–30, 132, 133, 137–41, 374; Indonesia 109–10, 112–16, 117–22, *120*, 337–8; Japan 8, 59, 98; Malaysia 109–10, 112–16, 117–22, *120*, 338; Pakistan 128–30, 132, 135–6, 137–40, 141; Philippines 109–10, 112–16, 117–22, *120*; and religion and religiosity 58–9, 76–8, 122; Singapore 364–5, 368; South Korea 8, 58, 59, 96, 98–9; Sri Lanka 128–30, 132, 137–40, 142, 396, 408; Taiwan 58, 59; Thailand 109–10, 112–16, 117–22, *120*, 339; United Arab Emirates 39, 360, 368; Vietnam 8, 39, 109–10, 112–16, 117–22, *120*
Industrial Relations Act, Pakistan 136
inequality 74, 76, 256–68, 421–2; East Asia 259–60; income 34, 111; Middle East 257–8; nationality and tribalism in Saudi Arabia 263–5, *264*; sexual orientation 261–3; South Asia 258–9; and state influence on HRM *25*, 30, 32, *33*, 34, 37, 39; *see also* gender inequality/discrimination
influencing states *25*, 28, 29, 32–4, 38
informal HR practices 417–18
informalization of employment 6–7; *see also* non-standard employment
information technology 422–4, 428
in-groups and out-groups 154, 277
InMobi 175

innovation 166–76, *168*; China 166, 170–1; India 166, 167, 170, 172–5; Japan 171; reverse 170; technological 422–4, 428
inpatriation 285–6
institutional immaturity 424–5
institutional permissiveness 323–4
institutional plurality 419–21
institutionalized trust 416
institutions, and performance management 152, 158–9
interdependent self-construal 211, 212–13, 216
internal internationalization 289–90
internal migration 8; China 8, 35, 89, 420; Southeast Asia 112
internal passport (*hukou*) system, China 245, 420
internal retirement 299
international assignments 285, 289–90; and Confucianism 59; and leadership development 191–2; *see also* expatriate employees
international framework agreements 26
International Journal of Human Resource Management, The 226
International Labour Organization (ILO) 26, 34, 95, 115, 123, 139, 295, 364, 368, 402, 408, 417
International Monetary Fund (IMF) 26, 115, 263, 285
internet-based software technology 423
intrinsic motivation theory 170
Iran *31*, *33*, 257
Ireland 208
"iron rice bowl" system, China 55, 88, 296, 300
Islam 4, 67, 71–2, 74, 75, 76, 77–8, 257, 258, 418
Islamic jurisprudence 257

Japan 275–90; adult adoption 52, 418; aging populations 25, 40, 171, 232; capitalism 78, 79; company ceremonies and rituals 57, 58; compensation practices 53, 101–2, **103**, *276*, 280, 281; competence rank system 89–90, 101–2; Confucianism 47–8; economy 87–8, 89–91; employee retention 55, 89, *276*, 278, 279; expatriate employees 235, 282–4; external dependence *31*; family allowances 54; family businesses 52, 73, 418; fertility rates 88, 282; foreign direct investment (FDI) *31*, 223; gender inequality 260; global HR challenges 281–4, 288; imperial examinations 50; industrial relations 8, 59, 98; innovation 171; *keiretsu* 159, 275; labor market 87–8, 89–91, *91*; labor regulation 93, *94*, 95, 96; management practices 6, 171, 241, 276; multinational companies 4, 240, 242, 246, 247, 275; non-standard employment 90–1, *91*, 96, 98; organizational culture *276*, 277, 278; performance management 152; protections against dismissal 89, 158; recruitment and selection *276*, 278, 279; seasonal bonuses 53, 54;

Japan *continued*
  and state influence on HRM 36; state influence
    on HRM *33*; state model 25, *25*, 35–6; talent
    management 231, 282–4; trade unions 98;
    training and development *276*, 279, 280
Japan Exchange Group 90
Japan Productivity Centre 90, 101
job rotation 160
job security 55–6
Joint Foreign Chambers of the Philippines 383
Jordan *31*, *33*
Journal of World Business 226
Juniper Networks 174

kafala system 39, 420
kaizen (continuous improvement) 277
keiretsu 159, 275
Knowledge and Human Development Authority,
  UAE 358
Korea: Confucianism 47; imperial examinations
  50; *see also* South Korea
Korea Labor Institute 96
Korea Metal Workers' Union (KMWU) 99
Korean Confederation of Trade Unions (KCTU)
  99
Korean Finance Industry Union (KFIU) 99
Korean Health and Medical Workers' Union
  (KHMWU) 99
Korean Labor Union Confederation (KLUC) 99
Kuwait 39, 189, 357

Labor Code on National Manpower Development
  Program, Philippines 384
Labor Contract Law, China 95, 98, 417
Labor Contract Law, Japan 89
labor contracts: China 88, 299, 302; Vietnam 307
labor disputes 8–9; *see also* industrial relations;
  strike action
Labor Law, China 299–300
labor laws *see* labor regulation
labor market, Bangladesh 130–2, 393–4, *393*
labor markets: China 87–9; dual 38; Japan 87–8,
  89–91, *91*; segmented 248–9; Singapore 362–4,
  363; South Korea 87–8,
  91–3, **92**, **93**; Southeast Asia 111–12; Sri Lanka
  130–2, 393–4, *393*, 398; United Arab Emirates
  358–60, *359*
Labor Protection Act, Thailand 34
labor regulation: Bangladesh 128–30, *134–5*, 136,
  417; Cambodia 112, 123, 417; China 93, *94*,
  95, 299–300, 417; incomplete law enforcement
  416–17; India 128–30, 133–5, *134*; influence of
  multinational companies 123; Japan 93, *94*, 95,
  96; Pakistan 128–30, *134*, 135–6; Singapore
  364, 368; South Korea 93, *94–5*, 96–7, 417;
  Southeast Asia 109–10, 112–17, *114*, **117**,
  122–3; Sri Lanka 128–30, *135*, 137; and

supranational institutional pressure 26, 115;
  United Arab Emirates 357–8, 360, 368;
  Vietnam 109–10, 112–17, *114*, **117**, 122–3
labor relations *see* industrial relations
Labor Standards Act, South Korea 96
Labour Act, Bangladesh 136
Laos *25*, 37, 112, 117
latecomer theory 247–8
leader–member exchange theory 154
leadership 183–91, 194–5; Asian styles of 184–5;
  authentic 190; authoritarian 184–5; benevolent
  184–5; contingency theories of 187–8, 190–1;
  definitions of 183–4; ethical 190, 194;
  participative 187, 189, 194; paternalistic 184–5,
  194; preferences of Asian employees 185–6,
  191; self-protective 187; servant 190, 194;
  shared 189; transactional 186; transformational
  186, 188–9, 190, 194; value-based theories of
  185, 187; Western models in Asia 186–91;
  women 193
leadership development 191–5
lean management 160
learning: and innovation 170; repetitive 75–6; *see
  also* education; training and development
learning organizations 170
Lebanon *31*, *33*, 257–8
Lee Kuan Yew 361
legal environment, and performance management
  158–9
Lesbian, Gay, Bisexual, and Transgender (LGBT)
  minorities 261–3
liberal market economies, and performance
  management 158
liberal states *25*, 28, 29, 35
life expectancy 282
lifetime employment: China 296, 299, 419; and
  Confucianism 55–6; Japan 89–90, 260; and
  performance management 158; South Korea
  102
livelihood support 54
localization policies 39, 263, 356, 357, 360, 368,
  420, 425
long-term employment *see* lifetime employment
long-term orientation 156
"Look East" policy, Malaysia 336, 338
loyalty, in Confucianism 48, 49, 53
Luong, Brian 304

Macau 314–26; compensation practices 320;
  economic and industrial structure 316–17, **316**;
  multinational companies 321–2; new trends in
  HRM 323, 324; recruitment and selection 318;
  strategic HRM 320–1; training and
  development 319
Malaysia 333–50; compensation practices 116–17,
  117, 205, 344; cultural change 157; economy
  110–11, *334*, 336; external dependence *31*;

family businesses 51; foreign direct investment (FDI) *31*; gender inequality 260; industrial relations 109–10, 112–16, 117–22, *120*, 338; innovation 172; labor market 111–12; labor regulation 109–10, 112–17, *114*, **117**, 122–3; migration 34, 112; minimum wages 116–17, 344; population *334*, 335–6; protections against dismissal 158; recruitment and selection 343; religion and religiosity 72; role of HR function 347; state influence on HRM *33*, 34, 35, 39; state model *25*, 32–4, 38; strategic HRM 348–9; talent management 224, *225*, 232, 348; trade unions 112, 117–20, *120*, 338; training and development 343–4; workforce diversity 348–9
Malaysian Investment Development Authority (MIDA) 32
malleability of self versus world 214
management practices: Confucianism as strategy 59–60; country-of-origin effects 247–9; diffusion of 242–4; ethnocentric 281–8; Japanese model 6, 171, 241, 276; multinational companies 240–50; *see also* performance management systems (PMS); talent management
management-by-objectives (MBO) 379
managerial succession, and Confucianism 51–2
Mao Tse-Tung 296
marketization 3, 419; China 97, 100, 419
masculine cultures 156, 204, *205*
maternity leave 204, 365, 408
mentoring 188, 192, 193, 194–5
Mercer 192
mergers, acquisitions, and divesture, Japan 90
merit-based pay *see* performance-based pay
Middle East: employment relations 39; equal opportunity 257–8; leadership styles 188; migration 39, 357, 358, 420; state influence on HRM 39; state models 37; unemployment 39; workforce diversity 257–8
migrant workers *see* expatriate employees
migration 8, 420–1; *kafala* system 39, 420; Middle East 39, 357, 358, 420; Southeast Asia 34, 112; *see also* rural to urban migration
minimum wages: Bangladesh 404; Indonesia 116–17, 342; Malaysia 116–17, 344; Pakistan 132; Philippines 116–17; Sri Lanka 401; Thailand 116–17, 342, 346; Vietnam 116–17
MNCs *see* multinational companies (MNCs)
Mohammed Bin Rashid Al Maktoum Foundation, UAE 358
moral character, and recruitment 51
multinational companies (MNCs) 4, 275, 424–5; Asia as host of 242–6; Asia as origin of 246–9; Bangladesh 404–5, 406; China 4, 240, 241, 243, 244, 245, 247, 248; country-of-origin effects 247–9; employment dualism 244–5; Hong Kong 321; India 4, 240, 243, 248; influence on labor regulation 123; Japan 4, 240, 242, 246, 247, 275; Macau 321–2; Singapore 362; South Korea 4, 246, 247, 275; Sri Lanka 401–2; subsidiary management 240–50; Taiwan 248, 322; and talent management 222, *227–30*, 230, 231, 233–4, 247; Thailand 341, 344–5, 346; United Arab Emirates 240, 358, 360; Vietnam 303–6, 306
multi-skilling 340, 344, 400, 403
mutual monitoring behaviors 215–16
Myanmar *25*

national culture: and compensation practices 52–3, 201, 202–10, *205*; and performance management 152, 155–7; and talent management 231
national economies: Bangladesh 130–2, 393; China 87–9, 296–7; Hong Kong 316–17, **316**; India 130–2, 374–5, *374*; Indonesia 110–11, *334*, 335; Japan 87–8, 89–91; Macau 316–17, **316**; Malaysia 110–11, *334*, 336; Pakistan 130–2; Philippines 110–11, 374, *374*; Singapore 361; South Korea 87–8, 91–3; Sri Lanka 130–2, 393; Taiwan 316–18, **316**; Thailand 110–11, *334*, 337; United Arab Emirates 357; Vietnam 110–11, 297–8
National Human Resource Development Network (NHRDN), India 375
National Industrial Relations Commission, Pakistan 136
National Pay Commission (NPC), Bangladesh 397
National Trade Union Congress (NTUC), Singapore 364
National Wage Advisory Council, Malaysia 344
Nepal *31*, *33*, 172
nepotism and favoritism 49–50, 74, 417–18; Philippines 377, 378, 383, 418; Saudi Arabia 264–5; Thailand 345, 418; Vietnam 303–4; *see also guanxi*
network-based recruiting 49–50, 74
New Economic Policy (NEP), Malaysia 336
New Order regime, Indonesia 112–13, *120*, 335
New Zealand 158
non-government organizations (NGOs), and labor relations 116, 119–20, 140, 417
non-standard employment 6–7, 8, 416; China 6–7, 89, 95, 416; Japan 90–1, *91*, 96, 98; South Asia 131–2, 398; South Korea 37, 91–3, **92**, **93**, 96–7, 99; Southeast Asia 112, 116, 416; and trade unions 98, 99

objective performance measures 212
OECD 97, 158, 162
Oman *31*, *33*, 39, 257, 357
one child policy, China 88
on-the-job training 279, 300, 304, 344, 345, 400, 403

organizational culture: Japan *276*, 277, 278; and performance management 152–3; South Korea *276*, 277–8
organizational prestige 56
Overseas Citizen of India (OCI) Card 231
ownership structures, Japan 90

PageUp People 348
Pakistan: economy 130–2; external dependence *31*; foreign direct investment (FDI) *31*; gender inequality 258; industrial relations 128–30, 132, 135–6, 137–40, 141; labor market 130–2; labor regulation 128–30, *134*, 135–6; state influence on HRM *33*; state model *25*; state-owned enterprises 37–8; trade unions 129, 132, 135–6, 138
participative leadership 187, 189, 194
Part-Time Work Law, Japan 96
paternalistic leadership 184–5, 194
paternity leave 365, 408
patrimonial oligarchy 37
pay 201–17; Bangladesh 397, 404, 405, 406; bonuses 53–4, 100, 280, 302, 323, 344, 346, 376; China 53, 54, 100, *101*, 207, 208, 301–2, *308*; and Confucianism 52–4; cultural psychology perspective 210–17; degree of differential 212–13; empirical studies 204–10; gender inequality 32, *33*, 56, 260, 266; Hong Kong 206–7, 320; India 140–1, 207, 208, 209; Indonesia 116–17, **117**, 205, 207, 208, 342–3; and innovation 169; Japan 53, 101–2, **103**, *276*, 280, 281; Macau 320; Malaysia 116–17, **117**, 205, 344; and malleability of self versus world 214; and national culture 52–3, 201, 202–10, *205*; and performance management 151, 154–5; Philippines 116–17, **117**, 379; and religion and religiosity 52–4, 76; seasonal bonuses 53–4; seniority-based 53, 89–90, 101–2, **103**, **104**, 201, 203, 205, 206, 280; Singapore 208; and social loafing 214–16; sorting effects 213–14; South Korea 53, 102, **104**, 201, *276*, 280–1; Sri Lanka 401; Taiwan 53, 320, 322–3; Thailand 116–17, **117**, 342, 346; Vietnam 53, 116–17, **117**, 306–7, *308*; *see also* performance-based pay
peer feedback 161
performance management systems (PMS) 76, 149–62, 234; Bangladesh 405; China 301, *308*; convergence towards global standards 162; customization of practices in Asia 159–61; decentralization of 152, 161; distal factors 151, 152; distortion factors 151, 154–5; effects of culture on 152, 155–7; Hong Kong 319–20; impact of institutions on 152, 158–9; India 153, 159, 378–80, *382*, 383–4; intervening factors 151, 154; Japan 152; judgment factors 151, 153–4; key components 150–1; Philippines 378–80, *382*, 383–4; proximal factors 151,

152–3; Saudi Arabia 153; Sri Lanka 399, 403; and strategy 161; Vietnam 305–6, *308*
performance standards 153–4
performance-based pay 151, 201–2; Bangladesh 405, 406; behavior-based 212–13; China 100, 301–2; cultural psychology perspective 210–17; degree of pay differential 212–13; empirical studies 204–10; group 52–3, 203, 206, 214–16; India 141; individual 53, 203, 206, 212–14; and innovation 169; Japan 101–2; and malleability of self versus world 214; and national culture 52–3, 201, 202–10, *205*; Philippines 379; results-based 213; and social loafing 214–16; sorting effects 213–14; South Korea 280–1; Sri Lanka 401; Taiwan 323
Person of Indian Origin (PIO) 231
Personnel Management Association of the Philippines (PMAP) 375, 379, 383
Pew Research Centre 261
Philippine Labor Flexibility Survey (PLFS) 380
Philippines 373–87; automation technology 423; compensation practices 116–17, **117**, 379; economy 110–11, 374, *374*; external dependence *31*; family businesses 51; foreign direct investment (FDI) *31*; industrial relations 109–10, 112–16, 117–22, *120*; institutional context 375–6; labor market 111–12; labor regulation 109–10, 112–17, *114*, **117**, 122–3; minimum wages 116–17; nepotism and favoritism 377, 378, 383, 418; non-standard employment 116; performance management 378–80, *382*, 383–4; recruitment and selection 376–8, 382–3, *382*, 417–18; remittances 38, 39; state influence on HRM *33*, 38, 39; state model *25*, 37, 38; strategic HRM 384–7; talent management 224, *225*; trade unions 113, 117–20, *120*; training and development 380–2, *382*, 384
piece-rate pay 151
PMAP *see* Personnel Management Association of the Philippines (PMAP)
PMS *see* performance management systems (PMS)
Poland 234
policy-capturing studies of compensation practices 206–8
political economy, and performance management 158
political systems 4
power distance 156, 157, 160, 277, 395; and compensation practices 203, *205*, 206, 208; and leadership styles 184, 186, 189, 190–1
predatory states 24–5, *25*, 28, 37–9
PricewaterhouseCoopers (PwC) 192, 223, 360
Private Employment Agencies Convention 95
profit-sharing schemes 281, 320, 401
promotion: China 301; gender discrimination 56; seniority-based 53

Protection of Fixed-Term and Part-Time Workers Act, South Korea 97, 417

protectionism 247, 422

Protestantism 72–3

Public Administration Training Centre (PATC), Bangladesh 397

Public Service Commission, Bangladesh 397

Public Services Commission, Sri Lanka 396

"putting-out" system, Thailand 339

Qatar 25, *31*, *33*, 38, 39, 189, 357

Rana Plaza garment factory, Bangladesh 140

Reading Management, South Korea 55

recruitment and selection: Bangladesh 403–4; China 50, 51, 300, *308*; and Confucianism 49–51, 349; gender discrimination 56; Hong Kong 318; India 376–8, 382–3, *382*; Indonesia 341–2; Japan *276*, 278, 279; Macau 318; Malaysia 343; Philippines 376–8, 382–3, *382*, 417–18; and religion and religiosity 49–51, 73–4, 349; Singapore 51; South Korea 50, 51, *276*, 278–9; Sri Lanka 398–9, 403, 408; Taiwan 51, 318–19; Thailand 344–5, 349, 418; Vietnam 303–4, *308*; *see also* relationship-based recruiting

regulatory states 23–4, 25, *25*, 35–7

relationship-based recruiting 49–50, 74, 158, 159, 417–18; Philippines 377, 378, 383, 418; Saudi Arabia 264–5; Thailand 345, 418; Vietnam 303–4; *see also* guanxi

religion and religiosity 4, 5, 66–80, 418; Bangladesh 394–5; Buddhism 4, 47, 67, 70–1, 74–5, 77, 78, 79, 122, 339; and capitalism 73, 78–80; Christianity 4, 67, 72–3; and compensation practices 52–4, 76; definitions of 67, 68; ethical behavior 67–9; and gender inequality/discrimination 56–7, 257; Hinduism 67, 70, 73, 418; and industrial relations 58–9, 76–8, 122; Islam 4, 67, 71–2, 74, 75, 76, 77–8, 257, 258, 418; and recruitment and selection 49–51, 73–4, 349; role in East Asian societies 69–73; Taoism 47, 67, 69, 70, 78, 185, 194; and training and development 54–5, 74–6; *see also* Confucianism

religious discrimination 259

remittances 38, 39

remuneration *see* compensation practices

RENGO (Japan Trade Union Confederation) 98

repetitive learning 75–6

Republic of Korea *see* South Korea

research and development expenditure 166

results-based performance measures 212

retention *see* employee retention

retirement: company ceremonies 57; gender discrimination 56; internal 299; mandatory age-related 53, 57; raising age of 36

reverse innovation 170

reward *see* compensation practices

rituals, company 57–8

robotic automation 423

rural to urban migration 8; China 8, 35, 89, 420; Southeast Asia 112

Russia 207–8

Samsung 50, 52, 57, 278, 287–8, 289, 423

Saudi Arabia: expatriate employees 263–5, *264*; external dependence *31*; foreign direct investment (FDI) *31*; gender inequality 257; performance management 153; Saudization policy 263, 420; state influence on HRM *33*; tribalism 263, 264–5; *wasta* 263, 264–5

Saudization policy 263, 420

saving face 160

scientific management 160

seasonal bonuses 53–4

segmented labor markets 248–9

selection *see* recruitment and selection

self-protective leadership 187

Selmer, J. 235, 378

seniority-based pay 53, 89–90, 101–2, **103**, **104**, 201, 203, 205, 206, 280

seniority-based promotion 53

servant leadership 190, 194

service sector, Southeast Asia 111

Seventh Central Pay Commission, India 140–1

sexual harassment 258

sexual orientation 261–3

SEZs *see* special economic zones (SEZs)

shared leadership 189

Sharia 257

Shibusawa Eiichi 48, 59

shift work 399

short-term orientation 156

Singapore 355–6, 360–9; aging populations 222, 232; capitalism 78, 79–80; compensation practices 208; Confucianism 48, 79–80; economy 361; employee retention 56; expatriate employees 356, 362, 363–4, *363*, 366; external dependence *31*; fertility rates 362, 365; foreign direct investment (FDI) *31*, 223; gender discrimination 56; industrial relations 364–5, 368; innovation 172; labor market 362–4, *363*; labor regulation 364, 368; multinational companies 362; recruitment and selection 51; state influence on HRM *33*; state model 25, *25*; talent management 222, 224, *225*, 231, 232; trade unions 364–5, 368; training and development 365–6

Singapore Airlines 355, 362, 367

Skill Development Promotion Act, Thailand 34

skill-based pay 206

Skills Future, Singapore 365–6

skills shortages *see* talent management

Skytrax 367

small and medium enterprises (SMEs) 176, 275, 317, 322; Sri Lanka 402–3; Vietnam 303, 304, 305

SMART goals 151, 155

social comparison 212, 213

social loafing 214–16

social upgrading 245

SOEs *see* state-owned enterprises (SOEs)

software technology 423

South Korea 275–90; capitalism 78, 79; *chaebols* 159, 275; company ceremonies and rituals 57–8; compensation practices 53, 102, **104**, 201, *276*, 280–1; cultural change 157; economy 87–8, 91–3; employee retention 55–6, *276*, 278–9; expatriate employees 282, 285–8; external dependence *31*; family allowances 54; family businesses 52; fertility rates 88, 282; filial piety allowances 56; foreign direct investment (FDI) *31*, 35, 223; gender inequality/ discrimination 57, 260; and global financial interests 27; global HR challenges 281–2, 285–8; industrial relations 8, 58, 59, 96, 98–9; innovation 172; international assignments 59; labor market 87–8, 91–3, **92**, **93**; labor regulation 93, *94–5*, 96–7, 417; multinational companies 4, 246, 247, 275; non-standard employment 37, 91–3, **92**, **93**, 96–7, 99; organizational culture *276*, 277–8; protections against dismissal 158; recruitment and selection 50, 51, *276*, 278–9; seasonal bonuses 53, 54; state influence on HRM *33*, 36, 37; state model 25, *25*, 35; talent management 282, 285–8; trade unions 96, 98–9; training and development 55, *276*, 279–80

special economic zones (SEZs) 137, 138, 141, 240, 249, 420

spirituality *see* religion and religiosity

Sri Lanka 392–409; compensation practices 401; cultural context 394; economy 130–2, 393; external dependence *31*; foreign direct investment (FDI) *31*; industrial relations 128–30, 132, 137–40, 142, 396, 408; labor market 130–2, 393–4, *393*, 398; labor regulation 128–30, *135*, 137; multinational companies 401–2; non-standard employment 398; performance management 399, 403; recruitment and selection 398–9, 403, 408; remittances 38, 39; small and medium enterprises 402–3; socio-economic context 392–4, *393*; state influence on HRM *33*, 39; state model 25, 38; state sector 395, 396; strategic HRM 406–7; trade unions 130, 137, 138, 141, 396, 408; training and development 396, 399–401, 403

state influence on HRM 23–40; developmental states 24, 25, *25*, 28, 32–5; enabling states *25*, 28–9, 34, 35–6; exploiting states *25*, 28, 29,

37–8; external dependence 25, 30, *31*; and global financial interests 27; and global value chain pressures 26–7; and HRM style *25*, 29–30, 31–2, *33*, 34, 36, 38–9; and inequality *25*, 30, 32, *33*, 34, 37, 39; influencing states *25*, 28, 29, 32–4, 38; liberal states *25*, 28, 29, 35; measurements of 30–2, *31*, *33*; outcomes of *25*, 29–30, 31–2, *33*, 34–5, 36–7, 38–9; predatory states 24–5, *25*, 28, 37–9; regulatory states 23–4, 25, *25*, 35–7; state models 23–5, **24**, *25*, 30; and supranational institutional pressure 26; typologies of 27–9, **28**; and voice *25*, 30, 32, *33*, 34, 36–7, 39; welfare states 23, 24, 25, *25*

state-owned enterprises (SOEs) 37–8; China 88–9, 249, 419; Pakistan 37–8; Vietnam 37, 38, 115, 298, 303, 304, 305, 306, 419

strategic balance theory 167

strategic HRM: Hong Kong 320; India 384–7; Indonesia 348; Macau 320–1; Malaysia 348–9; Philippines 384–7; Sri Lanka 406–7; Taiwan 321; Thailand 349

strategy, Confucianism as 59–60

strike action 34, 39; China 8, 35, 39, 98; South Korea 99; Sri Lanka 141; Vietnam 39

subcontracting 132

Suharto 112–13, 120, 335

supranational institutional pressure 26, 115

Taiwan 314–26; compensation practices 53, 320, 322–3; Confucianism 48; economic and industrial structure 316–18, **316**; external dependence *31*; family businesses 51, 52; foreign direct investment (FDI) *31*, 35; gender discrimination 56; industrial relations 58, 59; innovation 172; multinational companies 248, 322; new trends in HRM 322–3, 324; recruitment and selection 51, 318–19; state influence on HRM *33*; state model 25, 35; strategic HRM 321; training and development 319

talent management 7–8, 222–36, 318; challenges for foreign talent in Asia 234–5; China 222, 224, 231, 232; concept of 223, 225–6; factors influencing talent flow 230–1; and gender equality 260; global 247; India 226, 231; Indonesia *225*, 348; Japan 231, 282–4; literature review 226–30, *227–30*; Malaysia 224, *225*, 232, 348; Singapore 222, 224, *225*, 231, 232; South Korea 282, 285–8; talent supply challenges 223–4, *224*, *225*, 231–4; Thailand *225*, 232, 349; *see also* expatriate employees

Taoism 47, 67, 69, 70, 78, 185, 194

Tatli, A. 266

taxi-calling software 424

team-based management 160

Technical Education and Skills Development Authority (TESDA), Philippines 380–1

Technical Intern and Trainee Program (TITP), Japan 36
technical-vocational education and training (TVET) system, Philippines 380–1
technological innovation 422–4, 428
technology transfer 30, *31*
temporary staffing agencies, Japan 90–1, *91*
tenure-based promotion 53
Thailand 333–50; automation technology 423; compensation practices 116–17, **117**, 342, 346; economy 110–11, *334*, 337; employer associations 121; external dependence *31*; family businesses 51; foreign direct investment (FDI) *31*; gender inequality 259; industrial relations 109–10, 112–16, 117–22, *120*, 339; labor market 111–12; labor regulation 109–10, 112–17, *114*, **117**, 122–3; migration 34, 112; minimum wages 116–17, 342, 346; multinational companies 341, 344–5, 346; non-standard employment 116; population *334*, 336; protections against dismissal 158; recruitment and selection 344–5, 349, 418; role of HR function 347; state influence on HRM *33*, 34, 39; state model *25*, 32–4, 38; strategic HRM 349; talent management *225*, 232, 349; trade unions 113, 117–20, *120*, 339; training and development 345
Theravada Buddhism 122, 339
thirteenth month salary 53, 342–3
township village-owned enterprises (TVEs), China 296–7, 300, 301, 302
trade agreements 26, 115, 118
Trade Union Act, Malaysia 119
Trade Union and Labor Relations Act (TULRA), South Korea 37
Trade Union and Labor Relations Adjustment Act, South Korea 96, 99
Trade Union Law, Indonesia 119
trade unions 9, 26, 37, 39, 77, 78; Bangladesh 130, 136, 138, 140, 397, 404, 405, 406; China 95, 97–8; and Confucianism 58–9; India 129, 130, 132, 133, 138–9, 141, 374; Indonesia 112–13, 116, 117–20, *120*, 337; Malaysia 112, 117–20, *120*, 338; Pakistan 129, 132, 135–6, 138; Philippines 113, 117–20, *120*; Singapore 364–5, 368; South Korea 96, 98–9; Sri Lanka 130, 137, 138, 141, 396, 408; Thailand 113, 117–20, *120*, 339; trade unions 98; United Arab Emirates 360; Vietnam 117–20, *120*
Trade Unions Act, India 129, 133
Trade Unions Act, Singapore 364
Trade Unions (Amendment) Act, India 133
training and development: Bangladesh 397, 404; China 55, 300–1, *308*; and Confucianism 54–5, 75; Hong Kong 319; India 380–2, *382*, 384; Indonesia 342; and innovation 169; Japan *276*, 279, 280; Macau 319; Malaysia 343–4;

Philippines 380–2, *382*, 384; and religion and religiosity 54–5, 74–6; Singapore 365–6; South Korea 55, *276*, 279–80; Sri Lanka 396, 399–401, 403; Taiwan 319; and talent management 232; Thailand 345; Vietnam 304–5, *308*
transactional leadership 186
transformational leadership 186, 188–9, 190, 194
transgender identity 261
Trans-Pacific Partnership (TPP) 115
tribalism, Saudi Arabia 263, 264–5
Tripartite Alliance for Fair and Progressive Employment Practices (TAFEP), Singapore 365
tripartite bodies 117, 129, 137, 139, 333, 364
trust 73–4, 416
Turkey 189, 257; innovation 172; sexual orientation 261–3
Turner Broadcasting International 191

UAE *see* United Arab Emirates (UAE)
uncertainty avoidance 156, 203, *205*, 206
unemployment: China 89; Middle East 39; Saudi Arabia 263; Southeast Asia 111
unionism *see* trade unions
United Arab Emirates, trade unions 360
United Arab Emirates (UAE): Dubai 355–60, *359*, 366–9; economy 357; Emiratization policy 39, 356, 357, 360, 368, 420, 425; expatriate employees 356, 357, 358, 366–7; external dependence *31*; foreign direct investment (FDI) *31*; gender inequality 257; industrial relations 39, 360, 368; labor market 358–60, *359*; labor regulation 357–8, 360, 368; multinational companies 240, 358, 360; state influence on HRM *33*, 39; state model *25*, 38
United National Party (UNP), Sri Lanka 130, 137
United States: compensation practices 206–7, 208, 209; performance management 152; psychometric tests 50; trade agreements 115, 118
university graduates, China 7, 89
Unorganised Workers' Social Security Act, India 132, 417

value-based theories of leadership 185, 187
Vietnam 295–6; automation technology 423; compensation practices 53, 116–17, **117**, 306–7, *308*; Confucianism 48; economy 110–11, 297–8; employer associations 121; external dependence *31*; family businesses 52; foreign direct investment (FDI) *31*; imperial examinations 50; industrial relations 8, 39, 109–10, 112–16, 117–22, *120*; labor market 111–12; labor regulation 109–10, 112–17, *114*, **117**, 122–3; marketization 419; minimum wages 116–17; multinational companies 303–6, 306; non-standard employment 116;

value-based theories of leadership *continued*
  performance management 305–6, *308*;
  recruitment and selection 303–4, *308*; small and
  medium enterprises 303, 304, 305; state
  influence on HRM *33*, 38, 39; state model *25*,
  37, 38; state-owned enterprises 37, 38, 115, 298,
  303, 304, 305, 306, 419; trade unions 117–20,
  120; training and development 304–5, *308*
Vietnam General Confederation of Labour
  (VGCL) 118
Vietnamese Communist Party 38, 53, 115, 118,
  298
Vision 2020, Malaysia 336
voice, and state influence on HRM *25*, 30, 32,
  33, 34, 36–7, 39

Wage Protection System, Dubai 368
wages *see* pay
wasta 263, 264–5, 418
Weber, Max 73, 78
WEF *see* World Economic Forum (WEF)
welcome ceremonies 57

welfare corporatism 246
welfare states 23, 24, 25, *25*
women: leadership 193; retirement 56; *see also*
  gender inequality/discrimination
worker councils, Sri Lanka 142
Worker Dispatching Law, Japan 90–1, 96
workforce diversity 256–68, 420–1; China 265–7;
  East Asia 259–60; gender 257–60, 265–7;
  Indonesia 348; and innovation 169–70, 171;
  Malaysia 348–9; Middle East 257–8; Saudi
  Arabia 263–5, *264*; sexual orientation 261–3;
  South Asia 258–9
working hours: flexible 169, 398–9; long 277,
  286; shift work 399
Workplace Safety and Health Act, Singapore 364,
  365
workplace-based employee benefits 5
World Bank 26, 115, 131, 344, 393
World Economic Forum (WEF) 224
World Economic Forum (WEF) 30, 31–2, *31*, *33*
youth unemployment: Saudi Arabia 263; Southeast
  Asia 111

For Product Safety Concerns and Information please contact our EU
representative GPSR@taylorandfrancis.com
Taylor & Francis Verlag GmbH, Kaufingerstraße 24, 80331 München, Germany

www.ingramcontent.com/pod-product-compliance
Ingram Content Group UK Ltd.
Pitfield, Milton Keynes, MK11 3LW, UK
UKHW011455240425
457818UK00021B/830